I0605389

THE MAKING OF MODERN LOS ANGELES

ORO
EDITIONS

THE MAKING OF MODERN LOS ANGELES
A CHRONICLE

NICK PATSAOURAS

THE BOY FROM ATHENS

with Jim Birakos

I dedicate this book to my mother, Evangelia, who deserves all the credit and my deepest gratitude for guiding, nurturing, and shaping who I am.

And to my family — Sylvia, Tanya and Alexi — for their endurance and support for the person I have become.

CONTENTS

Angels Walk

FOREWORD

Public buses in Los Angeles, as they head to the center of the city, bear the name "Patsaouras Transit Plaza" above their windshields.

Who is Patsaouras? What has he done to merit the honor?

The buses' destination is not "Union Station," "Civic Center," nor "Downtown," but rather the legacy of Nikolas Patsaouras—who journeyed from Athens, Greece, as a young man—an engineer, civic visionary, and resolute aspirant for the public good.

This is Nick's story. But it is more than that. In addition to his unvarnished recollections as a formidable force in the evolution of Los Angeles, Nick has interviewed many contemporary civic leaders. It is their combined stories, in their own, often unedited, unembellished words, that, together, chronicle the legacy of Nick Patsaouras. It is a story that every Angeleno should know.

Nick is rational. In the long Greek tradition, Nick applies an engineer's methodical logic to the complex challenges of a major city.

Nick is blunt. The candor in this narrative is unusual in memoirs; no punches are pulled. Nick is nothing if not opinionated—once, now, and always.

Nick was there. In the transformation of Los Angeles from a sleepy agglomeration of suburbs into one of the world's greatest cities, Nick Patsaouras was at the center, often behind the scenes but never quietly, in politics (a Greek word if ever there was one), land use planning, transportation, the 1984 Olympics, the downtown renaissance, arts and music, culinary primacy, and more, at each step of the way. Especially in a city that prides itself on mobility—upward social mobility, fast-moving freeways, open-ended opportunities—the man at the hub of the transit system saw it all.

With the precision of Pythagoras, the persistence of Demosthenes, and the declamation of Pericles, this is Nick's story.

So, απολαύστε το ταξίδι! Enjoy the journey!

—Dan Rosenfeld

PROLOGUE

I wrote this book because I have useful insights and observations to present that I hope will benefit the city I love. I am not a historian and this book is not a history.

It is a book that chronicles the fifty-year political and civic odyssey of modern Los Angeles from the viewpoints of major political, cultural, academic, and business leaders as well as my own. I personally gathered valuable information regarding the making of modern Los Angeles that I want to share with present and future leaders.

As I wrote the book, I knew how blessed I have been throughout my life. I came to Los Angeles at age seventeen, dedicated to schooling, and who then achieved a successful career in electrical engineering. The American dream never entered my mind. The American promise had occupied that space, the notion that hard work and worthy pursuits yielded fitting results. In turn, I promised America repayment through robust public service.

Public service was inculcated in my mind since my high school days when we were taught philosophy and political theory. We learned that in ancient Greece a person who did not get involved in civic affairs was defined as private (*idiotis*). The Greek historian Thucydides wrote, "We are the only ones who, whoever does not participate in political 'commons,' we do not consider to be idle, peaceful, but useless citizens." With the passage of time, the word *idiot* came to be synonymous with the word *dumb*.

"It can be argued," historian Kevin Starr wrote in 2003, "that few cities in the history of the human race have embarked upon a comparably ambitious program of public and private works. The building of the Acropolis in Athens, the redesign and reconstruction of Rome, the rebuilding of London after the fire of 1666, the high-rises and subways system of Manhattan as they emerged in the first three decades of the twentieth century—all these projects are in the league in which Los Angeles now finds itself." I was blessed to be involved directly or indirectly in this "ambitious program."

By plunging into the enigmatic political, civic, and cultural life of my adopted metropolitan area, I directly influenced a number of events, such as helping secure funding for the Los Angeles Metro Rail, thus catapulting the city into world prominence.

For half a century I was fortunate to befriend mayors, governors, presidential candidates, and presidents, and I helped deliver benefits to the public as a member of the transportation and water and power agencies. En route, I gathered captivating and intriguing details of crucial decisions often made for the benefit of private interests and not for public service.

Fifteen years ago, I decided to write a book on my experiences. I interviewed more than two hundred key individuals from the political, business, academic, and cultural fields who shaped the city, and with whom I had genuine relationships. The conversations were candid, informative, and insightful.

I witnessed and participated in the development of Los Angeles as a world-class city. The picture-perfect city skyline did not mushroom without flawed backroom deals, and I describe some of them.

In this book I cover political intrigue, the Northridge earthquake, the renaissance of the rail system led by Mayors Tom Bradley, Antonio Villaraigosa, and Eric Garcetti, each with his own plan.

I describe in detail how the courageous stands of certain individuals preserved the city's heritage, the battles waged by the Los Angeles Conservancy, the creativity of architect Brenda Levin, the persistence and perseverance of preservationist John Welborne, the ingenuity of developer and civic leader Nelson Rising, and the leadership of ARCO Chairman Lodwrick Cook.

I chronicle the vision and the efforts of Lewis MacAdams, my friend and founder of Friends of Los Angeles River, and of Melanie Winter and Dan Rosenfeld to revitalize the Los Angeles River.

Insights from cultural leaders on the arts in Los Angeles are detailed.

The smog saga and related conspiracy of the auto industry is explained.

I point out how shortsightedness and political selfishness squandered an opportunity to create a public space in Los Angeles like Trafalgar Square in London, Red Square in Moscow, Tiananmen Square in Beijing, Union Square in San Francisco, or the Pnyx in ancient Athens.

I describe the controversies and the personal blame-game that took place in the initial planning and designing of a dazzling landmark, the Walt Disney Concert Hall.

I explain how I watched homelessness become an existential crisis because our city and county leaders ignored it over the last thirty years and are now spending billions of dollars with very little tangible results, and I describe how we evolved into "The Homeless Industrial Complex."

I delve into the legendary Gloria Molina's battles as the first Latina to rise to the pinnacle of local politics, her crusade to build the Los Angeles County and University of Southern California Medical Center (LAC + USC Medical Center), her leadership to scuttle Governor George Deukmejian's efforts to build a prison in slighted East Los Angeles, how she tried unsuccessfully amid political infighting and corruption to prevent the demise of the Eastside subway, her vision in establishing La Plaza de Cultura y Artes, and her determination to make the Gloria Molina Grand Park a reality.

I cover from my own personal experience a serious public betrayal that was staged by a governmental agency and a media conglomerate.

In addition, little-known facts are explained, such as the controversy over the Olympic flame. My personal participation helped diffuse the dispute between the 1984 Los Angeles Olympics Committee and the citizens of Olympia, Greece.

Also depicted is my over forty-year support of minorities and women's rights in private and public arenas and in government. How I vigorously worked to expand greenspace and promote the arts and led the efforts early on for cleaner energy in Los Angeles. I also define how my demand for accountability to taxpayers during my presidency of the Los Angeles Department of Water and Power board and through my authoring of "Ratepayer Advocate" yielded positive results.

I wrote this book to inspire, inform, and challenge the reader to get involved in public service. I sincerely hope I will succeed.

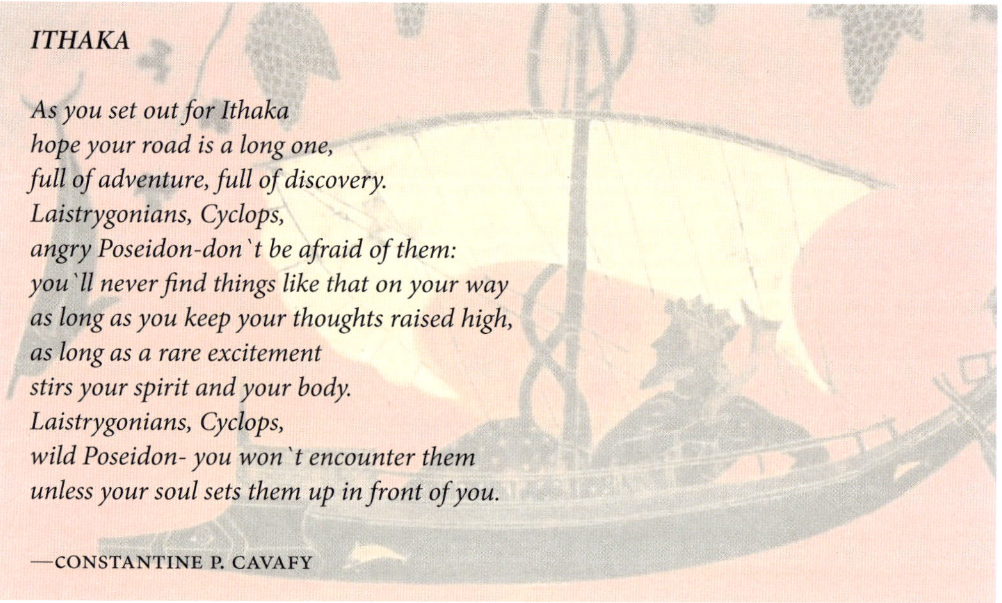

ITHAKA

As you set out for Ithaka
hope your road is a long one,
full of adventure, full of discovery.
Laistrygonians, Cyclops,
angry Poseidon-don`t be afraid of them:
you`ll never find things like that on your way
as long as you keep your thoughts raised high,
as long as a rare excitement
stirs your spirit and your body.
Laistrygonians, Cyclops,
wild Poseidon- you won`t encounter them
unless your soul sets them up in front of you.

—CONSTANTINE P. CAVAFY

The renowned Greek poet Constantine Cavafy encourages us to enjoy the journey to our Ithaka rather than rush toward the end. The journey is more important, exciting and pleasant than any arrival at a final destination.

The poem *Ithaka* seems to speak to Odysseus, the hero of Homer`s epic poem, the Odyssey, during the return to his homeland, the legendary Greek island, but Cavafy speaks to us, too. We have the responsibility to travel to Ithaka in our own lives, for self -discovery, exploration and growth.

Consumed in our daily lives by easy and quick gratifications, we tend to forget that the journey is not only a path where we can gain knowledge, wisdom, and abundant new experiences, but it is also pleasurable and fulfilling.

Cavafy reminds us that the reward lies not in reaching our goals but in becoming who we are. Throughout my life's journey, I had to fight my own Laistrygonians, Cyclops, and angry Poseidons, and, as a result, I believe I came through it all a stronger and wiser person.

CHAPTER ONE

THE BOY FROM ATHENS

The Nazis patrolled the street of Athens when I was born on December 4, 1943. Italians invaded Greece on October 28, 1940, but the Greeks pushed the Italians back into Albania. Germans then occupied Greece in 1941. During the occupation by the Axis powers from 1941–1944, an estimated 300,000 people died of starvation in Greece, at that time a country of about 7 million. Greece had a solid resistance movement. The Allies began to liberate France and other parts of Europe, including Greece, in 1944. While World War II was over by 1945, the conflicts between Communists and the West that marked the beginning of the Cold War began to play out in the Greek Civil War, with confrontations that began in 1944 and then infighting from 1946–1949, which left Greece in more ruin than during World War II. The nation's food supply had quickly collapsed, and tangible misery affected everyone. Each day was a challenge for poor families like mine.

The house where I was born was a single room that served as kitchen, study, and sleeping quarters. My living room was the unpaved street where I spent most of the time when not in school. We had neither electricity nor running water. Every morning we fetched water from a cold-water faucet in a common yard that also served three other families. Our morning cleansing was a quick splash on our faces.

The song ***Words of Grievance ("Paraponemena logia")*** sung by George Dalaras, describes the surroundings of my childhood (*"At the desks of need and in the school of poverty we learned the society...")* It is a song that I love to do the zeibekiko dance whenever I have a chance.

Christmas gifts were clothes, shoes, and books. It was rare when I could afford to rent a bicycle for ten minutes.

My neighborhood, Votanikos, was named for a large botanical garden nearby, less than a fifteen-minute drive from the Old Royal Palace and seat of the Hellenic Parliament in Athens' City Center. But we were worlds apart. Truly, like they say, we lived on "the wrong side of the tracks," in poverty's deep pocket. Still, our toughness became legendary. Our neighborhood's *mangas*—a Greek word that characterizes a tough but honest guy from a poor family, loved by women and idolized by friends—was celebrated in songs. Some phrases and tunes constantly resonate in my mind: "*A mangas at Votanikos. He tells what he wants without fear...*"

I am the oldest of three children, with a sister, Sevi, two years younger, now a retired banker, and a brother George, four years younger, now deceased. In his teen years, George

Me as a boy.

had taken the wrong fork on the road until he met a Pentecostal pastor. At seventeen, Jesus came into his life, and he felt reborn. He received a law degree from the University of Athens graduating at the top of his class with honors. A successful attorney with a life dedicated to Christ, he also became a pastor and built the country's largest Foursquare Church, which provided charities and youth programs throughout Greece and Eastern European countries. Historically, the predominant religion of Greece is Greek Orthodox, practiced by more than 90 percent of the population. Other faiths have never gained wide acceptance.

At that time four Air Force officers were accused and prosecuted for proselytism and sentenced in the Lower Court, the Court of Appeals, and the Supreme Court. My attorney brother escalated the case to the European Court where the officers were acquitted. Happily, he said, "We not only won the case, but also the freedom of speech for our faith."

In another case that lasted from 1981 to 1984, Don Stephens and Allan Williams, two Americans and leaders of the organization Youth with a Mission, along with a Greek missionary Kostas Makris, were sentenced to three and a half years in prison in Lower Court because they gave a New Testament pamphlet to a boy. They became known worldwide as "the Athens Three." Some 500,000 letters poured into the Greek President's office from around the world, including those of Presidents Carter and Reagan. My brother took the case to the Appeals Court and again was victorious.

My parents had met in Athens. My mother, Evangelia, was born on the island of Amorgos, one of the smaller islands in the Cyclades, an archipelago that includes Mykonos, Santorini, and Milos, and that encircles the ancient sacred island of Delos. My father, Vasilis, was born on the west coast of Greece, in Nafpaktos, an ancient Athenian naval base. He was orphaned as a boy, as was my mother who lost her father early in life. She was sent to live with her aunt where she kept house, cooked, and cleaned. I remember her to always being a neat and tireless housekeeper, strong and dedicated to her family. So spotless was our one-room house, neighbors rightfully joked that "you could eat off the floor."

Our furnishings were meager. In an icebox we stored whatever food we could. We had a small table for a gas stove, and a larger one in the center that served as a dining table. When a window would break or the front doorsill would leak, my mother would stuff clothes in the gaps to stop the rain from pouring into the house.

My mother was hardworking, honest, loving, and goodhearted. She held two jobs to help support us. My father was periodically unemployed, but eventually landed a permanent job as a security guard for the telephone company. During the day, my mother worked in a factory pressing clothes with a hot-coals iron—there was no reliable electricity then—and at

My birthplace, it all began here.

My parents, Evangelia and Vasilis.

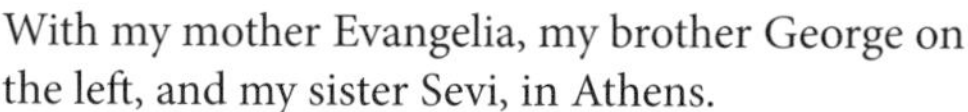

With my mother Evangelia, my brother George on the left, and my sister Sevi, in Athens.

Reviewing my high school diploma.

night she would repair nylon stockings. In the 1940s and '50s, if a stocking had a run, women would not discard them, but mend them, and my mother did.

When I was six, I would take my brother and sister to the public nursery. Our route required passage through an alley where some bullies bunched and extracted a toll. I will never forget one eventful day. Usually, I would use marbles to bribe our way through, but there were none left. Small as I was, I put up my fists and stood my ground. Challenged, the bully ran off. Thereafter, I learned how to deal with bullies.

As mentioned, my mother was disciplined and industrious and my father was elegant and attractive, standing six feet two inches tall, a generous man, unable to hold on to money. On Sundays he would have a glass of wine from a bottle that I would fetch for him from a nearby taverna.

He probably was not a good provider, but he was a good father. Because of him, all three children succeeded. We knew that when he came home it was best that he find us inside studying. Unlike our teachers, he never struck us, but his stern look was enough to discipline us. He knew that only through education our lives would improve, and we would thrive and be able to move out and up. It was my father who introduced me to the symphony. When possible, he would take me to concerts or to the opera, but unable to afford two tickets he would buy one for me, leave me alone at age ten or eleven, and pick me up when the performance was over. My appreciation of the arts was born then. My life's regret is that I never learned to play the piano.

My brother George.

With my sister Sevi.

Whenever he got paid a joyful trip to the market ensued. Men at that time shopped for food and essentials, and he selected the best meat, fruits, and cheeses. Being more expensive, the portions were small and lasted only a truly fleeting time. Often, we would wake up in the morning and ask, "What are we going to eat today?" Thankfully, mother was an inventive cook, and she would whip up an omelet, fried potatoes, or rice.

Of course, we did not have our own telephone. Our phone access was through our baker who was a few feet across the railroad tracks. Since we also did not have an oven to cook moussaka, baklava, pastitsio, or oven potatoes, we would take the baking pots or sheets to the baker's oven. At times, my mother would get upset with the baker and send us to another baker farther down. But he knew how to get my mother to return. "Mrs. Evangelia," he would call out, "telephone call from your sister." An excuse to talk her out of her discontent.

Core values are built in your youth. But so are habits. To this day, I dislike the telephone; my conversations are succinct, to the point and without small talk. Having lived with five people in one room, learning to control noise or to silently close the door was a requisite, another habit I have carried with me all my life. I loathe slamming doors or cupboards.

It is strange how vivid and powerful tiny fragments of experiences remain embedded in your memory after so many decades. When I was ten or eleven, Maritsa Vakirtzoglou—a young lady who lived nearby—would take me on Sundays to the Athens Cathedral, the central Greek Orthodox Church, where I served as an altar boy. Fascinated by the presence of royalty and top government officials and military chiefs who attended on major holidays, and the elaborate vestments of priests and bishops and intricate ceremonies, thoughts of becoming a priest crossed my mind. By the time I reached my teenage years that inclination had dissipated. After church service Maritsa would take me to the National Gardens, located between Parliament and the Palace, creating a multitude of fond memories. There were lakes with ducks, numerous sites that housed animals, and diverse street vendors—all delivering a special Sunday afternoon. During my travels to Athens in recent years, I would, for nostalgic reasons, revisit the Royal Gardens only to find them woefully abandoned. Was it my sentimental longing that was disturbed?

When I was growing up Greece had no television networks and families were more inclined to get out of their homes for social activities. Television can imprison us in our homes. During those days cars were few. Rare indeed was the family who could afford one. Today most families easily drive to the beaches or to the mountains. Greece is famous for its beautiful beaches. However, in those years, we had to take three buses to get to a beach and so we seldom swam in the crystal-clear waters.

When I was fighting for federal funding of Metro Rail, one of my arguments was that rail would make it possible for a family from South or East Los Angeles to go to the beach in Santa Monica. My vision was fulfilled when the Expo Line was built. A few years later the Regional Connector made it that much more convenient.

But it is still very disheartening for me as I realize that those lively and carefree scenes are fading away forever. The proud declaration of a cousin still vibrates in my ears: "Now we have a car, we can go and find a very secluded beach." That was a disturbing proclamation, in a sense, considering how societies are bound together by neighborhoods, schools, and family gatherings to share common public spaces. Too many people today are isolated, cut off from community life. If you visit Athens in the summer, you will see people on their balconies, not engaged in outside activities, not strolling the sidewalks anymore, but sitting with their backs to the outside world, facing their televisions inside.

In my childhood days, life was in the street. During the summer, families would set up chairs by their front doors, snack on sunflowers or pumpkin seeds, converse, and share jokes. The unpaved street was a safe and hospitable playground for kids. We played soccer with a ball made from clothes wrapped with strings. Two stones were our posts. Our knees and legs were perpetually scratched up. Boys did not wear trousers until their early teen years.

Having experienced it firsthand, let me offer a word about poverty. People tend to stigmatize poverty by often blaming the impoverished themselves. I beg to differ. We grew up poor, but we maintained dignity, and self-respect. We were clean, well behaved, thoughtful, and gentle. Stereotyping people who have no material possessions is very disturbing to me. Colombian writer Juan Gabriel Vasquez wrote: "*Experience or what we call experience, is not the inventory of our pains but rather the learned sympathy towards the pain of others.*"

I developed love and appreciation for America in my early years. President Harry Truman decided that Europe needed assistance after World War II. The Marshall Plan, also known as the European Recovery Program, was enacted in 1948 and provided more than $13 billion to help finance rebuilding efforts on the continent. US support to Greece amounted to $2 billion (which would be worth more than $21 billion today). It helped rebuild Greece's infrastructure and aided the populace with other programs. I remember waiting anxiously for the "boxes from America" full of rice, chocolate bars, and powdered milk, a feast at that time for the whole family. These memories are indelible in my mind and heart.

When I came to the United States, phones in Greece were not as easily accessible or available, and international calls were relatively expensive. So, for the first eight or nine years, I communicated with my family through the mail. Now I can understand the worry of my parents, but mainly my mother, when I left home at the age of seventeen for the other side of the world, communicating only with an occasional letter. More than sixty years later that memory still causes sadness.

My mother had three sisters in Athens, two of whom lived in the suburbs (Evanthia and Tasia) and periodically we would visit them on a Sunday. That entailed taking two buses, which I remember intensely because transferring from one bus to the other required walking in front of the Grande Bretagne, the luxury hotel in Athens where all the diplomatic affairs, formal government and business undertakings would take place. It was the hotel for the rich tourists. One day, I promised myself, I am going to be able to afford to stay there.

Intuitively, I believed in a quote often used by Robert Kennedy, "Some men see things as they are and say why? I dream things that never were and say why not?"

Many years later, in 1984, when I led, along with Los Angeles mayor Tom Bradley, a delegation to Athens to establish the Los Angeles–Athens Sister City Affiliation, we stayed at the Hotel Grande Bretagne. Since then, every time I visit Athens, I stay in the Hotel Grande Bretagne.

I also fondly remember two other aunts, my Aunt Irene, my mother's sister, and my Aunt Yiannoula, my father's sister. Whenever my Aunt Irene visited us, she would bring us a box of pastries, such as Napoleons, cannoli, and tiramisu. In Greece, in those years, we did not celebrate birthdays, but mainly name days. My Aunt Irene would always remember December 6th, my name day, and Sevi, George, and I would look forward to that date. As for my Aunt Yiannoula, she would cook for me a special eggplant dish when I visited, and to this day I think it is the best ever, because it was cooked with love.

I walked to my high school—which was later torn down and turned it into a parking lot—in Plaza Koumoundourou, a dilapidated working-class area that today includes the headquarters of Syriza, the former ruling party in Greece. My high school sat at the foothills of the Acropolis and the Parthenon was the first thing I saw when I woke up in the morning, and the last thing I saw before I fell asleep at night. Whether in school or on a stroll, the Parthenon always loomed over me. As school kids, we would visit the Acropolis and Parthenon to learn the history, art, and archeology of the ancient site. While there we wondered why tourists, mainly Americans, would make the climb up this hill. Seeing it every day, we were taking this extraordinary site for granted. Long after I had settled in the United States and started a family, I returned to Athens with my wife, Sylvia, and our nine-month-old daughter, Tanya. And as we climbed up the hill to the Acropolis, and I saw the view of the Parthenon unfolding before me, tears appeared in my eyes because, for the first time, I was able to appreciate the magnificence, the beauty, the symmetry, and the elegance of that temple. There and then I realized why millions of visitors over the years come here.

My high school, an all-boys school near the base of the hill where the Acropolis stands, had eight rooms that had to be shared by senior students in the morning and the lower classes in the afternoon. We received a good education. We were taught classical Greek, French, and Latin. I was able to read Homer in classical Greek and Cicero in Latin. We were advanced in science courses, which helped me a lot when I attended Los Angeles Valley College in the San Fernando Valley.

Discipline in high school was stricter than the army. I refer to it as "character formation." We would line up every morning in rows of three. When the teacher entered the room, the students would stand up to show respect. Our strict headmaster would check our nails for cleanliness, and haircuts for adherence to military style. Talking was absolutely forbidden. A classmate was caught with a cigarette and dragged by the headmaster, no more than five feet seven inches tall, into his office to be beaten badly with a ruler. Corporal punishment was prevalent and customary. Of course, we did not dare tell our parents, fearful of getting a second round of punishment for causing trouble in the first place.

At that time, my high school had neither cooling nor heating systems. Greece is known for its four distinct seasons, so it gets very cold and very hot. Nowadays, I do not get cold, I do not get hot, I do not get hungry, I do not get thirsty. The classroom environment was as unforgiving as the weather. Professors were very demanding, repeatedly calling us before the class to present material or solve a problem—whether it was geometry, algebra, chemistry, physics, to narrate history, or recite classical Greek—with no warning. So, every day, we had to be prepared. My high school classmates came from a mix of backgrounds. Some had parents who were professionals, and some who were working poor. Yet most of my classmates went on to become doctors, attorneys, engineers, architects, and accountants.

I excelled in classical Greek and literature, but I also did very well in mathematics, calculus, and chemistry. In the last year of high school, when everybody was expecting me to go to university and become a university professor, I decided I wanted to become an engineer. In those years, Greece had only three universities: the University of Athens, Aristotle University of Thessaloniki, and Athens Polytechnic, a prestigious school for architects and engineers. At the Polytechnic where I would have gone, the rate of successfully passing the entrance exams was only five percent. Geniuses, and the children of politicians and generals would be admitted. And, since I did not belong to any of those categories, I inquired about pursuing my studies in the United States. My family knew a lady whose brother was living in Los Angeles. He was an electrical engineer, and he was willing to sponsor me to attend Los Angeles Valley College.

College fall quarter classes were beginning on September 13, 1961, but as the deadline to start school was growing short, my father still did not have the $500 for the airfare. I have always believed that God appears in challenging times. One day my father and I were walking on one of the boulevards in Athens when he bumped into an old acquaintance he had not seen in many years from his hometown of Nafpaktos. My father asked him what he was doing, and he replied, "I'm a travel agent." So, my father said, "I would like to come and see you tomorrow." After that visit, the man agreed to advance my plane ticket. It took my father a year or two to repay the airfare. But it was another example of how devoted he was to his family, despite his limited means.

I remember the night before I left Athens to come to the United States. I was only seventeen years old, right out of high school, feeling free and excited to be my own man. That lasted until the airplane took off. Then, three or four minutes into the flight, I suddenly thought, "Where am I going?!" I felt desperate, helpless, and I realized that we are all tough until we really find ourselves in a dire situation. When I landed in New York and was going through customs, I heard officers asking questions. Not understanding English, I became terrified with thoughts of being rejected. Fortunately, I was not confronted with that situation. Today, I look back on that day with amusement, but for a seventeen-year-old émigré it was very intimidating. Meanwhile, I had assumed the air ticket covered the cost of a taxi from one terminal to the other, but I was wrong. The taxi driver shook his head and pointed to the bus. I got on board, and, by God's miracle, I got off at the right terminal for my connecting flight to Los Angeles. Once I checked my suitcase, I went to a nearby snack counter for an orange juice. "Origin," I bashfully said. People there started to laugh so loudly I turned and left without getting my orange juice.

I finally arrived and got settled here, but I was a few days late for classes at Valley College. My first day, the foreign student advisor, Dr. Pagliaro, a nice man and kind human being, took me around the campus. Pointing out the temporary classrooms, he said, "These are bungalows." Realizing I had no idea what a bungalow was, he reassured me, "Don't worry, don't worry. Eventually you'll learn." What little English I knew, I had learned in a crash course over three months after I decided to come to the United States. A high-school classmate of mine, Michael Mantas—also from a poor family, but who eventually became a successful ophthalmologist—generously taught me a few basics after school, but it was inadequate.

I was fortunate that in my high school in Greece, we were advanced in calculus, physics, and chemistry, so the first classes that I took in junior college were science requirements that I easily passed. Although my science classes were no problem, I had to take the same English class that American students did and, of course, I failed with a D and had to repeat the course. Slowly, my English improved, and I was finally able to move on. Learning English came mostly from listening and reading, resulting in a strong accent to this today, nearly sixty years later.

During my first semester at junior college, my physics professor asked what my major was. When I told him electrical engineering, he laughed, stating, "You will never be an engineer. You should consider studying an easier subject." Frightened, demoralized, and unable to sleep, I was truly devastated by the professor's comment. My inner compass, however, and not fear, directed me to make the right decision and follow my goal, and that was to graduate with an electrical engineering degree. I believe we should listen to other voices, adjust our direction if necessary, but never be swayed in our decisions by naysayers, contrarians, doubters, or timid souls, and definitely not by fear.

Against the odds, I graduated from California State University, Northridge, at the top of my class and became a successful electrical engineer. A few years later I gave the commencement speech at the CSUN engineering graduation ceremony. I was also honored by CSUN with the "Entrepreneur of the Year" and "CSUN's School of Engineering and Computer Sciences Outstanding Alumnus" awards. I was the youngest, by fifteen years, practicing

CSUN Outstanding Alumnus Award, in 1980, with Sylvia.

professional electrical engineer in Southern California and the youngest to serve as president of the Association of Consulting Electrical Engineers in Southern California. The lesson here is that an individual, often a teacher, can set the course of a life, just as former Los Angeles Mayor Antonio Villaraigosa remembers how his high school teacher, Herman Katz, changed his life.

In those early days I remember nights I would cry when I considered how long four years of schooling were, before graduation and my return to Greece. Even now, when I hear the song, ***"I wander like an exile" (San apokliros gyrizo)*** sung by Sotiria Bellou, one of most famous Greek singers of *rebetika* (Greek blues), tears swell up in my eyes. It is, if not the most, one of the most popular songs with Greeks who left the motherland.

I wander like an exile,
in this hostile foreign land—
strolling, miserable,
far from my mother's embrace.
...
And I cry too, my dear mother, for you,
for I haven't seen you in years.

I can only imagine my mother's pain for not hearing my voice or seeing me for ten years.

I really had no social life growing up in Greece. I left in 1961, and television did not arrive until 1966. We could not afford to go to the movies. But there was one outdoor movie screen, *Lais*, on a second floor in the neighborhood, and we would look up from the ground floor to see pictures move but we did not know what the story was about. By the time I finished college I had seen very few movies. Looking back, I believe I was emotionally challenged to deal with so many accumulated obstacles: away from family, no language, speaking little English, having no friends and coping with a demanding program. My days in college were not happy. An exhaustive schedule prevented me from spending time in the library or the cafeteria to socialize. I would work full-time, initially as a draftsman and two years later as an electrical designer, while being a full-time student. By law, as a foreign student I had to take twelve and a half units. At night after work, I studied with my dictionary.

My daily routine had me take the bus early in the morning for my 8:00 a.m. class. After three consecutive courses, I caught the 10:50 a.m. bus to work. At 5:00 p.m., I was back on the bus returning to the university until 9:00 p.m. The bus then took me home where I studied for two or three hours, grabbed three to four hours of sleep, then got up again at 5:00 a.m. to continue my studies before catching the bus back to school for my morning class. I worked five days a week from noon to 5:00 p.m., and all-day Saturday. Sundays were set aside to catch up with my reading and my laboratory work. In college, I befriended another foreign student, an Israeli named Ernest Amster, who owned a car. When he could, he would drive me to the office, he was kind of my older brother. We would study together on Sundays.

I did not learn to drive until I bought a used car during my last year at San Fernando Valley State College, now California State University, Northridge, where I received my Bachelor of Science degree. Sometimes, I assess life's paradoxes and smile. As a student I depended solely on the bus for school and work. A few years later I was the president of the Southern California Rapid Transit District board of directors, the governing body of the public transportation agency.

Here a note of personal gratitude is in order. I want to express my appreciation to the people of California, because my education at that time was almost free. Tuition at junior college was about $6, and the cost of books was only $15 a semester. At Valley State College, the tuition was $60 a semester, and the cost of books was only $50 or $60. Without these very low costs, I would not have been able to finish my education. I could not wait until I graduated. During the last year, I counted the days and eventually the hours when I would finally earn my Bachelor of Science degree.

While I was in college, I was working in a small engineering firm, J. C. Athans, the electrical engineer who sponsored me to come to Los Angeles. Although I came here when I was seventeen, by the age of nineteen, through practical experience, I had become a good designer. I designed electrical systems for the courthouses at Norwalk and Pomona, Los Angeles County's MacLaren Children's Center for foster children, and the Traffic Courts in downtown Los Angeles.

I knew that eventually I would want to have my own business, which meant that I had to pass two state exams. The first is the engineer-in-training exam, on which one is tested on science subjects such as physics, chemistry, and calculus. After you pass, you can apply to take the Professional Engineer (PE) exam to be tested in your specific field, whether mechanical, electrical, structural, or civil engineering. When I took the engineer-in-training test in my last semester of college, I had not yet studied fluid dynamics, a subject in the tests, but I still passed.

Upon graduation, on paper I qualified to take the State of California Professional Engineers exam, which required a Bachelor of Science degree, the engineer-in-training certificate, and four years of practical experience, which I had. At age twenty-four, the State Board of Registration for Civil and Professional Engineers did not allow me to take the PE exam because "they considered me too young," as I was told years later by a colleague who happened to be on the board when I applied. I did not give up, and several months later, in August 1969, I finally took the P.E. exam. I knew that same day that I had passed, so I went to my employer John E. Silver and said, "John, I think I passed the P.E. exam, so please start to find my replacement. I'll wait as long as you need." I felt a personal responsibility to give ample notice and did not consider a two-week notice proper.

Several months later, on Christmas Eve, 1969, I received the letter from the State notifying me that I had passed the exam. My employer was unable to replace me until June 1970, and I remained on the job, something he appreciated. After I left, any small work he did not want he referred to me. I was especially grateful for his nominating me to become president of the Association of Consulting Electrical Engineers in Southern California. It is said that if you do a good deed, it will come back to you sooner or later.

In 1970, I formed a consulting electrical engineering company, Nikolas Patsaouras & Associates, Inc. Over forty years, I designed systems for all types of buildings, including Sheraton Hotels in Tyler, Texas, and Baton Rouge, Louisiana; Big Sky resort in Montana; industrial plants for Martin Marietta, Magnavox, Pitney Bowes, the *Los Angeles Times*, and *Los Angeles Daily News*; Los Angeles city and county fire stations, courthouses, US post offices, public libraries and schools; medical facilities, such as Martin Luther King/Drew Trauma Center, Kaiser Permanente's surgical center in Woodland Hills, and Good Samaritan Hospital in Anaheim; the Luckman Fine Arts Complex at California State University, LA, and the Engineering and Computer Science building at California State University Long Beach; shopping centers from Calexico to Santa Rosa; department stores and shopping malls in Iowa and Missouri; supermarkets such as Ralphs, Vons, Pavilions and Gelson's throughout Southern California; St. Anthony's Greek Orthodox Church in Pasadena and Eagle Rock Baptist Church; and synagogues including Stephen S. Wise, Temple Isaiah, Valley

Beth Shalom, Ahavot Shalom, and Aliyah. I also performed electrical engineering for many high-rise condominiums along Wilshire Boulevard in Los Angeles and for downtown office buildings.

Two incidents stand out from those early days while getting my business on its feet. The first involved the Society of Professional Engineers, which met once a month for dinner at the Biltmore Hotel in downtown Los Angeles. Often, I would be in the elevator or in the monthly meeting, and I would be asked whom I worked for. Since I was only twenty-six, averse to answer, it took me a few seconds to say, "Well, I have my own company." The other incident, again at the Biltmore, occurred a few months later. There was an electrical engineer with a Greek last name. Excitedly, I went up and introduced myself and asked, "Are you Greek?" He just walked away, brusquely replying, "No, my father was." A foolhardy response, I considered, and was disappointed.

When I started my business, my wife, Sylvia, would come to my office at Third Street near La Cienega Boulevard to help with secretarial work and bookkeeping. Sylvia became a fulltime mother when our first child, Tanya, was born, followed by our son Alexi. She later earned a degree in urban planning and political science at CSUN and a master's degree in urban planning from the University of California at Los Angeles, and she went on to serve on city, county, and state commissions, including the Board of Commissioners for the Los Angeles World Airports; the Los Angeles Homeless Services Authority; the State of California Commission on Regions; and the City of Los Angeles Board of Recreation and Park Commissioners, nine years as president.

Tanya received an undergraduate degree in political economy of industrial societies and a Master's degree in landscape architecture from the University of California, Berkeley. She interned with Tree People and served as a volunteer in the Peace Corps in Botswana, Africa. Alexi received an undergraduate degree in history and political science from Stanford University and a law degree from Yale. He later practiced law in London and studied philosophy at Oxford, England, and UCLA.

In 1984, I formed the Marathon National Bank with a few Greek American friends. The bank's business dealings with the Greek American community, as it turned out, were negligible. But the bank was highly successful. It became profitable within only a few months, when usually banks would take at least a year or two after their inception to start turning a profit. The reason, I believe, is that the board paid attention. As chairman, I had formed an executive committee that met every Monday to review the loans and ensure that we had proper oversight of the bank and its management.

I obtained my United States Citizenship on May 31, 1974. It is a seminal date in my life. I am very proud to be an American, what it means and symbolizes. At the same time, I have not forgotten my Greek heritage. *Los Angeles Magazine* noted, "Patsaouras, an immigrant flies his Greek origins like a spinnaker in a stiff breeze."

Politics was imbued in me at an early age. My father always brought home a newspaper or two, which I read avidly. National and international affairs always held my interest. As a teenager, I used to walk every day to my high school by the Kerameikos cemetery, where, according to Thucydides, Pericles said of his fellow Athenians, "*We alone regard a man who*

With my family: Alexi, Sylvia, and Tanya.

With Alexi and Sylvia at Alexi's Stanford graduation.

With Tanya and Sylvia at Tanya's UC Berkeley graduation.

takes no interest in public affairs, not as a harmless, but as a useless character, and if few of us are originators, we are all sound judges of policy." That public service ethos was inculcated in my mind not only by my teachers, but also by my daily Kerameikos walk. Kerameikos was the potters' quarter of the ancient city, from which the English word "ceramic" is derived. Notable warriors and statesmen were buried there, including Pericles. It is an archeological site that contains a series of famous monuments. Consequently, I have served on county and city commissions that oversaw the construction of a number of public works projects over the last forty years.

Along with my keen and mounting interest in politics I developed a passion for supporting and promoting the arts, inspired by my father's encouragement as I was growing up. I served on the board of directors of the Los Angeles Ballet. I joined the Guild of the Opera Associates, San Fernando Valley Cultural Foundation and the Fraternity of Friends of the Music Center, whose membership eventually led me to be a Founder of the Music Center to the present day.

I have no hobbies. I just have two passions: gardening and birds. I am attached to plants and trees I have planted over the last fifty years. My dozen fruit trees give me great pleasure with their fruits and beautiful flowers, especially the apple tree flowers with their sweet aroma.

I have half a dozen bird feeders scattered around the yard, enticing beautiful birds such as blue jays, spotted towhees, nuthatches, chickadees, finches, robins, hummingbirds, woodpeckers, and many others, whose early morning singing brings joy to the ears and serenity to the mind. The morning singing of my canary "*Exipnos*" (smart in Greek) sets me in a happy mood as I start my day.

I immensely enjoy dancing the Greek dance zeibekiko to different tunes, bringing back childhood memories, not all pleasant, but always sweet. It has been said, "Dance is the hidden language of the soul."

I always keep in mind, "Find magic in the little things, and big things you always expected will start to show up."

My parents left us no material inheritance, but they bequeathed us something far more valuable: abundant love, affection, and respect for the principles of hard work, honesty, integrity, discipline, and a sense of optimism and direction. These pearls, beyond precious gifts—particularly from my mother—provided a crucial component in shaping my character.

Vine Lilac-Hardenbergia Violacea. Planted by my son Alexi 30 years ago.

CHAPTER TWO

LOS ANGELES' MODERN POLITICAL AND CIVIC ODYSSEY

The price good men pay for indifference to public affairs
is to be ruled by evil men.
—PLATO

For many years Los Angeles was described as an urban configuration sprawling over five hundred square miles and consisting of myriad suburbs seeking a center. It was an enormous area distinguished by its dazzling sun and Hollywood allure. But was it viewed as a respected, dynamic city? East Coast detractors claimed it lacked cultural works and vitality, all essential parts of a great city. Further, it was a place fashioned for vehicles, not people. Horizontal Los Angeles managed to overcome all of this, despite itself. Slowly, the skyline changed, and the city steadily became more cosmopolitan and less provincial. Founded on September 4, 1781, almost seventy years before California was admitted to the Union, it catapulted into national and international significance during the last half century mostly because of the perception of far-sighted politicians and power players and the conviction and vision of a five-term mayor.

True, shifting demographics compelled adjustments to the existing power centers, leading to the establishment of energetic political alliances. Latino and African American groups organized and mobilized, becoming more politically skilled, gradually attracting donors, and disrupting the insular power blocs of corporate Downtown, Chamber of Commerce, labor and union groups, industry, the Westside might, and the San Fernando Valley ascendancy. A more diverse and less isolated city sluggishly materialized. A city seeking a new vision.

Contemporary Los Angeles had a complicated birth. The area grew faster than any other United States metropolitan area as a World War II wartime industrial city, producing ships, aircraft, and war supplies. Almost a quarter million African Americans migrated from southern states for defense-related jobs. Many returning servicemen from the Pacific War found better job opportunities in the Los Angeles area and did not go back to their hometowns in the Midwest and South. At the same time, prevalent discrimination against Mexican Americans forced many into urban barrios in poor areas.

In the most recent years Los Angeles had six mayors: Thomas Bradley (1973–93); Richard Riordan (1993–2001); James Hahn (2001–05); Antonio Villaraigosa (2005–13); Eric Garcetti (2013–22); and Karen Ruth Bass (December 2022–present). The mayor is the chief executive of the city and has responsibility for its general welfare, but he/she is branded by the vision of Los Angeles and whether measures advocated yielded quantifiable results.

Dodger Stadium.
Photo: Jake N.

The city's transformation into a diverse and renowned world city with a striking skyline and invigorated financial and business districts, with a rail system, museums, artistic verve, and exceptional cuisines were all successful facets of Bradley's vision. Commissions were finally opened to women and minorities. And City Hall was accessible to all.

In Los Angeles County the network of interconnected freeways today serves close to ten million people. Construction began in the 1950s and some routes went through communities of color and ethnically mixed neighborhoods. Some routes were said to have been planned as slum-clearance projects. Absent political clout, impacted communities became casualties of transportation planners and their political mentors.

Roz Wyman, the youngest person ever elected to the Los Angeles City Council at twenty-two, figured that a great American city needed the arts, and it needed baseball. In an interview she explained that whenever she promoted the city to investors and major companies, she was asked what it offered in sports. Aware of Walter O'Malley's frustration in Brooklyn to secure a new stadium, she signed a letter from the City Council stating Los Angeles's interest in obtaining a major league team. Two years of discussions and evaluations ensued, and the Dodgers agreed. On April 18, 1958, a parade wound through city streets leading the baseball players to the Coliseum where 78,672 fans saw the Dodgers play in their new home. Initially, major league baseball did not want O'Malley to move since no team was west of St. Louis and the added travel costs would burden the franchises. When Wyman heard that Horace Stoneham of the Giants was not making money in New York, she contacted people in San Francisco to help generate momentum for the team. Meanwhile, O'Malley suggested to Stoneham to talk to San Francisco mayor George Christopher, the Greek-born who lost California's governorship to Ronald Reagan in 1966, and explore relocating the team, thus preserving the celebrated rivalry.

O'Malley would say that Dodger Stadium was the house Wyman built. But Wyman also wanted to help construct a City Council that had African American and Latino representation. "People are not being treated right," she had told Police Chief William Parker before the 1965 riots. "You don't listen to them." She had no fear of Parker and told him so. She said that the Chief had a file on every City Council person, but not one on her.

MINORITY GROUPS ENTER THE POLITICAL SCENE

In the modern-day Los Angeles City Council, the first successful thrust into political prominence by an African American was charismatic Gilbert Lindsay. He had worked up from city janitor to City Council member representing the meandering 9th District that included new skyscrapers in downtown's financial district to the neighborhoods of underprivileged South Central Los Angeles.

When the first Mexican American City Council member Ed Roybal won election to Congress, Lindsay received the strong backing of prominent local political brothers Gordon and Kenneth Hahn and was appointed to the vacant seat in January 1963. Later that year, and for eight successive terms, he won reelection. Darlene Kuba was a staff member to Lindsay for seventeen years, hired by the councilman when she was sixteen years old right after graduating from high school. She remembers listening to stories of his years as janitor with the Department of Water and Power. "He had to work in the sub-basement levels cleaning toilets, and it would be during the graveyard shift at night because they didn't allow anybody of color to work during the day on the main levels." Ms. Kuba said her boss was an excellent mentor. "I want you to continue to go to school," he told her, and she did, receiving her bachelor's in criminal justice while working full time. Then she obtained another bachelor's in Sociology. Lindsay continued to encourage her. "Now, get your master's," and she did, in Public Administration. Like an unwavering father, Lindsay pushed further. "I want you to get your doctorate because politics is very uncertain. You could always fall back on your degrees because nobody can take that away from you."

During the same year Billy G. Mills was elected to the City Council's District 8. Critical of both then mayor Sam Yorty and Police Chief Parker, the new councilman held that he had been stopped by the police seventeen times because he was seen driving a city vehicle at night. In 1972, he ran unsuccessfully for Congress, losing to Yvonne Brathwaite Burke, an attorney and member of the California State Assembly who became the first African American woman to represent the West Coast in Congress. Mills was appointed to the Superior Court bench by Governor Reagan in 1974 and served until his retirement in 1990.

Most significantly, in 1963, a retired LAPD lieutenant and attorney, the grandson of a slave, won two elections, one for the unexpired City Council term left by Charles Navarro when he was elected city controller, and another for the full term. On April 15, 1963, City Council Member Tom Bradley was sworn in. Ten years later, in 1973, Bradley defeated Yorty and became the first African American mayor of a predominantly white American city. Bradley changed Los Angeles forever. The city's renaissance had commenced.

In 1963, Mervyn Dymally, an inspired and resourceful thirty-seven-year-old from Trinidad and Tobago, of African and Indian ancestry, who had become a US citizen six years earlier, won election to the California Assembly 53rd district, the first of a series of public offices he would hold spanning forty-five years of successful campaigns for the State Assembly, the State Senate, and the US Congress. In 1974, he became California's first elected Black lieutenant governor of California. Dymally was reported stating that he was motivated by the life of the 19th-century African American educator Booker T. Washington and went on

With mayor of Los Angeles Tom Bradley and Sylvia.

to earn his Bachelor's, Masters', and Doctorate degrees, and worked determinedly to improve education and access to healthcare throughout his productive career. He confided to me that the causes of the 1965 riot was lack of adequate health care and transportation. "Out of the McCone Commission, the Southern California Rapid Transit System resulted, and out of that the MTA," he said. "A little anecdote based on your expertise in transportation," he added. Supervisor Kenneth Hahn moved quickly to build the Martin Luther King, Jr. Hospital, which opened in 1971. I was the electrical engineer for the King-Drew Trauma Center. While many experts thought they knew the cause of the riot he did not share that view. "It just happened, and it happened with an isolated incident…just exploded." But it took thirty-four lives, he lamented.

The chronicle of expanded African American political representation, Dymally said, really began at the start of the '60s. John F. Kennedy had appointed Assemblyman Gus Hawkins as chair of Community Groups for Kennedy, and Congressman Ed Roybal to head up the *Viva Kennedy* movement. He also told me that civil rights efforts were inspired by the National Association for the Advancement of Colored People (NAACP) and the presence of Martin Luther King, Jr., and the Congress of Racial Equality and the United Civil Rights Committee. Impressed with Bradley's career, Dymally said: "This police officer was involved in Democratic party politics, and the Crenshaw Democratic Club that represented the area in which he lived in the Crenshaw district, and he was very active in Kappa Alpha Psi." This is the oldest, predominantly African American, Greek-letter society, and Bradley became its grand polemarch in 1964–67, the fraternity's national president and chairman of the Grand Board of Directors. Dymally closely followed the development of African American political trailblazers, remembering Lindsay's initial appointment to the City Council that was aided by the support of Roz Wyman and Kenneth Hahn, and the conditions that led to "an explosion of interest in politics coming from the civil rights movement.

There was a sense of consciousness about getting into politics to change the system." He referenced the Supreme Court's rulings of the 1960s—"one man one vote." With that decision, Los Angeles County was redistricted and changed from one senator to thirteen. He became the first Black man to serve in the California Senate in 1966. Prior to the ruling, "thirty-nine senators came from cow counties," he said. The federal law states that districts must have nearly equal populations and not be drawn up to discriminate based on race or ethnicity. Chief Justice Earl Warren, a former California governor, had said that people should be counted, not trees. A redrawing of district lines to influence elections in favor of a political party, candidate, or ethnic group, known as "gerrymandering," would not be allowed under federal law. Dymally became California's 41st Lieutenant Governor and moved on in 1980 to the US Congress for twelve years, following a return to the California Assembly for six years before retiring. Years ago, he realized, he said, that the state was changing, and a Black program alone would not suffice, it must be integrated. That's when he began to work with Richard Alatorre.

ALATORRE INFLUENCES LATINO POLITICIANS

The Latino immersion into Los Angeles politics was also the consequence of racial and anti-immigration sentiments and subterfuges. Mexican American activists were driven onto the operative political landscape in search of equality. They fought the existing public sentiment that upheld ploys and that criminalized their ethnic group with anti-immigrant rhetoric and numerous legislative initiatives targeting immigrants—their parents.

Alatorre, acknowledged as one of the most influential Latino politicians in the state, had prepared himself well for the struggle for fairness. Brought up in East Los Angeles, he was a student body officer every year since junior high school, culminating his youngest political run as student body president at Garfield High School. With a bachelor's degree in sociology from California State University in Los Angeles and a master's degree in public administration from the University of Southern California, Alatorre began teaching at California State University in Long Beach and the University of California at Irvine. But the challenges he sought were not found in just teaching. Moreover, he had a theory: "Whatever you're going to do, if you can't do it in a year, you're never going to do it." He told me that teaching was the only job in which he stayed longer than a year. He did not count his elected political tenure of over a quarter century as a job but as an opportunity.

Seven days before the 1960 presidential election, he heard John F. Kennedy speak at the East Los Angeles College football stadium and was excited and volunteered to help. Eight years later he worked on Sen. Robert Kennedy's presidential campaign in California. An effective promoter of minority civil liberties, Alatorre had gained access to key people everywhere and had also worked with the Association of Mexican American Educators and its president Phil Montez. The weekend before the 1968 primary the "Chicano 13" group, including Sal Castro, an educator and activist, and others, were indicted for a conspiracy to disrupt the schools by staging high school walkouts protesting unequal conditions in the Los Angeles Unified School District schools. A decision had to be made. Do they bail them out? Sen. Eugene McCarthy, who briefly entered the race for president in 1968, called Alatorre. Saying he felt strongly about this movement, he volunteered to contribute $100,000. His caveat, a press conference the day before the California primary. "Kennedy was going to kill him anyway," Alatorre believed, but he did not like the idea of the press conference because of his allegiance to Kennedy. Nonetheless, a major lesson in clever political stratagems was attained. Alatorre called Frank Mankiewicz, Kennedy's press secretary. "You gotta match the $100,000, or people will see him really caring for our community." Later he received the reply: "You got it." It was arranged that a check would be picked up in the morning. Philip Montez, western regional director for the US Commission on Civil Rights, cautioned Alatorre to immediately cash the check because political money disappears quickly from accounts. When he arrived at the bank at the earliest possible hour, there was no money in the account. Another call to Mankiewicz followed: "Who the fuck you think you are dealing with? We are going to denounce." Quickly that morning someone came to the bank with the money in hand and it was put into the "Chicano 13" defense fund. On election Tuesday Kennedy received 90 percent of the Chicano vote, Alatorre recalled.

With Councilman Richard Alatorre.

A man known for his forthrightness and graciousness, for being a blunt and hard deal maker, his first sojourn into the election process confirmed for him what he had to overcome to succeed. He had contacted Assemblyman Wally Karabian, who held a leadership position with California Democrats and later served as Assembly majority leader and asked for a job in Sacramento. David Roberti, Assemblyman from the 48th District, had decided to run for the Senate. Karabian told Alatorre he would lend him to the Roberti campaign, to do a good job there, and then he would support him for that Assembly post. "I always dreamt of running for political office," he said, and worked on the Roberti campaign for six months. "I was like an appendage to Roberti and worked the El Sereno, Lincoln Heights and every neighborhood where Chicanos were." Roberti was elected to the Senate's 27th District.

Bob Moretti, Speaker of the Assembly and a protégé of powerful Jesse Unruh, was thinking about running for governor, and he also desired to develop a relationship with Roybal, who wanted to play a role in California politics. Moretti had no reason to dislike Alatorre, but he called him into his office and said, "I like you but get the hell out of the race." Alatorre asked him to reconsider and explained his program. Moretti's response was direct, "You don't understand." Alatorre stayed.

Political times were edgy in the State in 1971. A reapportionment bill had passed both Houses controlled by Democrats only to be vetoed by Gov. Ronald Reagan. The Committee to Elect the President, Richard Nixon, was operating aggressively and hired a political operative named Don Segretti, the dirty tricks functionary, who Alatorre said, used his first election as "a little training ground." Alatorre's opponents, Republican Bill Brophy, and a liberal Latino, Raul Ruiz of the La Raza Unida Party, were seen as devious artifices to prevent him from being elected. The heavily Democratic district would have gone to Alatorre, absent two events: the emergency of La Raza Unida, created in 1970 to combat the Democratic Party, and the recipient of $200,000 (according to an Alatorre cofounder and former Segretti employee); and a drive-by shooting of Brophy's house two days before the election.

Alatorre told me that Brophy had lots of money and appeared to have hired some "dope friend" to shoot through the window of his own house to get publicity. The day before the election this became an incessant item on the news. It was done so that people would think, *Mexicans were violent and lowlifes, and here's this nice white boy. Who could have done this, but a Mexican?* Alatorre thought. The election results validated Alatorre's thinking: Brophy won by 1,570 votes with Ruiz gaining 8 percent of the votes. Brophy's name later came up during a congressional inquiry into Panamanian drug trafficking, in which he was alleged to have attempted to help with the sale of cocaine in California.

In the meantime, political aspirations for an upward movement generated friction and quarrels, with Moretti manipulating friends and raising funds in preparation of a governorship run. He had already emerged as a staunch opponent to Reagan. His hopes were dashed when Jerry Brown, California's Secretary of State, and the son of the former governor, decided to enter the race. Allies of Moretti sought independence from him, such as Karabian, who had decided to run for Secretary of State.

"I SAID I WOULD DO IT"

Yvonne Brathwaite Burke was practicing law and was also a hearing officer for the Police Commission in 1965 when the riots erupted. She lived in the embattled zone that was barricaded off by the National Guard. "The only time I had hives was walking through there" she said. To get to her office she was stopped and painstakingly questioned. In turn, she organized a legal defense for some of the people arrested. Later, as an attorney for the McCone

Commission, she collaborated closely with Warren Christopher, a partner with O'Melveny & Myers and later the chair of the Christopher Commission that investigated the LAPD in the aftermath of the Rodney King beating. Under Clinton, Christopher served as Secretary of State.

I had also met Christopher during the Dukakis campaign when he gave me suggestions and advice to convey to the presidential candidate. She recalls that while doing analyses for the final McCone report, and prohibited from going into the riot zone, somebody concluded that some of us should get involved in politics. "I said I will do it and had no clue. I wasn't involved in politics." But she was involved in the civil rights movement. The incumbent of the 63rd Assembly District, Don Allen, was retiring. A campaign was quickly organized. She was thirty-one years old. Without real funds, and in a predominantly white district, she won and became the first African American woman elected in Sacramento.

After serving there for six years she ran for Congress, serving from 1973–79. In the 1972 Democratic National Convention she became vice chairperson, the first woman of color to hold that position. After leaving Congress, Gov. Brown appointed her to fill a vacancy in District 4 of the Los Angeles County Board of Supervisors, the first female and first African American on the powerful board. In 1980 she was defeated while seeking a full term as supervisor, only to return ten years later narrowly defeating State Senator Diane Watson for a seat on the board.

LOS ANGELES WINS GOLD MEDAL

The legendary Los Angeles Olympic Games of 1984—the first Games organized without public funding—were officially awarded to the city on October 20, 1978, by International Olympic Committee President Lord Killanin and Los Angeles Mayor Bradley at the White House in Washington, DC. Athletes from 140 countries participated, although Russia had decided to boycott. A celebratory atmosphere was sustained throughout the sixteen-day period, and long before and after the Games. Los Angeles was closely followed and hailed internationally. Bradley's cherished dream became a historic reality. Los Angeles won a gold medal. Peter Ueberroth was appointed president of the LA Olympic Organizing Committee on March 26, 1979, on a vote nine to eight. Yvonne Brathwaite Burke was the deciding vote, according to her husband, Bill Burke.

Ueberroth in turn chose sixteen executives to serve as "commissioners" for each of the sports. Burke was surprised when Ueberroth asked him to be the Commissioner of Tennis. Burke was in the mining business in West Africa, had played collegiate tennis for Miami, but had never organized a tournament. He told me that when Ueberroth first called him, he was cautious and put on an old suit "because I knew he was going to ask me for some money, and I didn't want to look too good."

For eight months Burke traveled to tennis tournaments all over the world to see how they were organized, how security was employed, how crowd control was handled, how many tee shirts were sold, how umpires were selected. Tennis, he said, was removed from the Games

Los Angeles Marathon Race. Photo: Kcyer

in 1924 for advocating professionalism. Now it was coming back. So, he sought help from his boyhood idol, Jack Kramer, the world's best tennis player in 1946–53 and the leading promoter of professional tennis tours in the 1950s and 1960s. "No," he was told. After numerous breakfasts and lunches, Kramer agreed. "I'm going to weigh four hundred pounds if I don't say 'yes.'" Burke said the whole Kramer family jumped in; the tennis Olympic tournament was very successful. He recollected that Kramer was the first promoter to have a black player, Bobby Ryland from Cleveland, play in professional ranks.

When Burke attended a "Big Brothers" dinner at the Beverly Wilshire, someone he knew from the Olympic Games stopped to say hello and informed him that LA was considering hosting a marathon. From the hotel's pay phone Burke called Bradley at home, to express interest. "We'll probably have to put it out to a Request for Proposal (RFP)," was the reply. It took two years to get it done. Staff at City Hall was opposed to his getting the agreement and scored other applicants ahead of him. He remembered Gil Lindsay on the floor of the City Council saying: "Bill Burke has never organized a marathon. Well, to my recollection, Ueberroth had never organized an Olympics before and look at the job he did." With Councilman David Cunningham, Jr's, support, Burke got approved.

The result: Los Angeles held the largest first-time marathon in the history of the world, and it held that record for seventeen or eighteen years. The marathon was a big success, Burke told me, and everyone thought it was easy. But the first marathon lost money. Appreciatively, he reminisced, "You arranged for us to get some bus cards to thank all the runners and volunteers. Some guy came up to me to say this showed class, after the event lost money. I said, 'thank Nick Patsaouras, that's why it was done.'"

Burke also recalled that Bradley always carried a #10 envelope in his coat pocket, and when he wrote something on it, it was done. If he listened and shook his head, it meant he was listening to you, but unless it was noted on the envelope, he did not concur. Burke was also very close to Muhammad Ali and remembered Ali's letter to the Coastal Commission supporting his appointment.

Willie Brown, another close ally, was asked by Burke to appoint him to a vacant seat on the governing board of the South Coast Air Quality Management District, and Brown immediately agreed. Burke became chairman of the smog board in 1997 and served until his retirement in 2021. The agency's Environmental Justice Community Partnership, which builds stronger ties with environmental justice groups and local communities, is a Burke creation, enabling projects to address environmental inequities in communities of color.

TORRISTAS AND MOLINISTAS

Gloria Molina was twenty years old when she determined that the political system needed changing—that Latinos had to be elected. The year was 1973. A legal secretary during the day, she was a volunteer typist for various community organizations, as well as for the Western Center on Law and Poverty. Alatorre was once married to Stella, her coworker, and he came in search of her. "You didn't see young Mexicans in a suit at that time. He was cool." She had seen Alatorre once before, and she kept bumping into him thereafter. "While there was discrimination in our community and we weren't moving up," she said. "We started what was called *Comision Femenil Mexicana Nacional* (Mexican National Women's Commission) and decided to appear before the California Commission on the Status of Women holding hearings in Los Angeles."

As president of the group, she told the commission, "We are all here, and you are all white women. You can't represent who we are." Alatorre, now a member of the Assembly, set up a meeting with Gov. Reagan in Sacramento. With difficulty they raised the $34 round-trip tickets and the meeting lasted less than forty seconds. As a favor to Alatorre, the governor said, "Yeah, yeah, I'll do it." Reagan did appoint a Latina, a Republican. "That emboldened us," she reminisces. "It was a teeny step, but a very significant step."

Alatorre's chief of staff, Lou Moret, was impressed with Molina's astuteness and ability to organize and execute programs and asked her to work on Art Torres' run for the Assembly. She found Torres to be focused and immersed herself fully in his campaign. He won, and in turn wanted her to be his chief of staff.

Molina craved an opportunity to work on Carter's 1976 presidential drive in California and not only did Torres give her the time, but also got her a job on the campaign to organize Latinos up and down the state. Although Carter lost the state by less than 2 percent, he did beat Gerald Ford by a narrow margin for the presidency and she found employment in the White House for two years. It was a revelation. "I didn't realize we were so nonexistent. I mean nonexistent. People didn't know who we were." She worked on boards and commissions—not high-end commissions—and always put Latinos on them, only to have her boss cross them off, "like if they didn't have political palanca that other people did," she said, referring to the Spanish word meaning "a lever" that enables successes. She returned to California, became director of Intergovernmental and Congressional Affairs in the Department of Health and Human Services, Region IX office, in San Francisco, and eventually ended up working for Willie Brown.

Successful, fervent movements for political equality result in undertakings that engage the beleaguered. Common people lead the struggle, not the leaders. Thus, the name, "grassroots." From the bottom up. Frequently, as objectives are being achieved and representation gained, political quarreling between members of the same group develops. Achieving and holding power for some becomes the newer objective.

After much hesitation, and aware of her individuality and "big mouth" as she confessed, Molina determined to seek public office, becoming the first Latina in history to be elected to the California State Legislature in 1982, the Los Angeles City Council in 1991, and the Los Angeles County Board of Supervisors for 23 years. The 1991 campaign against then Senator Torres for Supervisor was the most bitter, beating her former boss and early supporter, 55.4 percent to 44.6 percent. According to the *Los Angeles Times*, it was a nationally watched campaign and one of the costliest in county history as Molina and Torres together spent more than $1.7 million. The political conflict gave birth to a new Eastside terminology, "Torristas and Molinistas," likened to the Hatfields and McCoys. When Torres conceded defeat on election eve, according to the *Los Angeles Times*, he said: "Gloria Molina, I gave you your first job. Gloria Molina, I supported you for the Legislature. Gloria Molina, you are the winner, and I congratulate you."

Jaime Regalado, emeritus professor of political science at California State University, Los Angeles, wrote that Molina came to be widely perceived as having a pointed, harsh, and frequently unfriendly governing style. The nature of her victory, he said, shaped her reputation as a giant killer, machine buster, and vibrant voice for women. Regalado also remembers a Los Angeles when the City Council, dominated for years by Republican white males, "changed complexion," a bit slowly at first with the election of several Jewish members, then with the coalescing between the Westside and the Southside where the Jewish council members were supportive of African American candidates. He also recalled Bradley's first run for mayor where then mayor Yorty "used fear a lot, and fear of the Watts riots which were not too distant at that time."

It was then that Regalado decided to major in political science. He explained to me that he grew up in a society that was becoming divided, but at the same time had strong elements of a more progressive push from the grassroots, of many different movements, including the Latino community. "The forerunner to that, of course, was the civil rights movement which was largely African American." We were watching, he added, and studying and demonstrating. He is no longer in the streets, but when his son goes to protest, he asks him to relate his experience when he returns. Regarding Los Angeles City Council, Regalado said there is no camaraderie today like the days of John Ferraro when coalitions existed. The reforms in the Charter are probably good for the most part, "but I am not sure we are a better-governed city because of these. There still exists fifteen chiefs and an administrative person we call mayor." He reminisced about Bradley and expressed esteem for his coalition of labor and business, which unfortunately is now gone.

A POLITICAL QUARTERBACK

A quarterback in politics runs an electoral district and converges with people to grasp their needs—and acts on them to reap a benefit for his boss. His ear is planted to the ground and his eyes relentlessly scan the political chessboard. He ceaselessly prepares for fundraisers, scrutinizes potential candidates for unfilled positions, and coordinates and unifies. Lou Moret was a political quarterback. Following graduation from UCLA he went to work for Assemblyman Karabian in 1969, who represented the 45th District, to run a voter registration drive. "We had never met," he told me. He was told to see Joe Cerrell, the pioneering political consultant and organizer, who gave him a list of people to meet. Amongst them was Congressman Lionel Van Deerlin of San Diego who won as a Democrat where Democrats didn't win, because he registered people to vote, mainly minorities. Moret was a fast learner. He had to be deputized so that he in turn could deputize volunteers to man registration tables in front of markets. In a three-month period, he had registered over 10,000 voters in East LA. While Karabian's first victory in 1966 was marginal, in 1970 he won by a huge margin (65 percent) and was later appointed assembly majority leader.

Under him were the majority of consultants. Karabian called Alatorre and offered him a consultancy. He had surmised that then state Senator George Danielson would be elected to Congress and that David Roberti would win his vacated senate seat in a special election. Alatorre could then run for Roberti's Assembly seat, which he won the second time around. Friends since boyhood, Moret became Alatorre's chief of staff. The task of organizing Latino politicians and influence-makers began. Moret coordinated the group but didn't cut the deals. "I set the parameters, then Alatorre and Torres made the decision," he said. "I go back and renegotiate. I am the dirty one, the one that's gotta be the hammer, I've gotta be the deliverer of bad news, the one that makes the enemies." He wanted his political leaders loved. "They were never mean to anyone." In time his group would grow, and it would select and support candidates for various offices. When he went to Washington, DC, in 1977, "the team started to get a little disarrayed. Nobody wanted to fill that vacuum."

In a news article by Tony Castro on March 17, 2014, Gloria Molina said she remembers when she decided to run for a legislative seat in 1982, "she approached Moret, her longtime friend and mentor, then an aide to Alatorre, fondly known as the godfather of the state's Latino political leadership." Moret told her, "You can't run. You can't win. What are you talking about? You can't raise money. You can't get endorsements." She responded, "I think I can do it,' and she did.

Cesar Chavez, the renowned American labor leader (United Farm Workers) and civil rights activist, had cultivated individual relationships with numerous Latino politicians in California, including Alatorre and especially Torres. Regularly, the politicians would go to see him. In the 1980 Assembly Speakership election campaign, Chavez endorsed Howard Berman over Leo McCarthy. Torres had been close to Chavez and once marched with him. Further, the UFW had become one of the state's largest political donors and had given the Berman campaign support to unseat McCarthy.

The Berman-McCarthy battle was like the mafia wars, Jim McDermott told me. "There was a real visceral hatred toward Berman by a lot of the McCarthy people because he was doing deals in the back." On the way to the Sacramento airport, said McDermott, Berman made the mistake of using the car phone saying how they were going to get Leo, that they had the votes. "The Sergeant at Arms went to Speaker McCarthy and said: 'I just heard these guys are ready to bump you off.' ...Willie Brown now enters the race," Moret told me, after Karabian met with Alatorre and Torres. Alatorre would get reapportionment with a Brown victory.

When Chavez found out that Torres had turned, "he goes ballistic. They never had the relationship they had from there on. Chavez refused to talk to him." Eventually, in the Assembly vote, the Republicans considered Berman as an ideologue liberal and Brown as a practical politician who used to say, "Hey, we want a piece of the piece, and we've gotta have a pie to have a piece of it." Brown won and became the longest serving Speaker in California history.

A CITY UNLIKE OTHERS

As minority groups organized, created coalitions, and raised funds to squeeze through Los Angeles's narrow political doorways, other activists merged in to reevaluate the city and its future. "I've always been very curious and involved in different ethnic communities," Donna Bojarsky related to me, "and this was an asset in a city like this, not a liability." She said, "Los Angeles is spread out, unlike New York where people must live on top of one another. There, you must see other people. Here you can live without that." She added, "We're incurious, people are happy in their own little enclaves." Bojarsky founded the "Future of Cities: Los Angeles" in 2015, whose purpose was to bolster the city's identity through the participation of leaders from all areas to converse and contribute decisions that influence the city's future. She was also co-founder of the New Leaders Project to build bridges across the city between the civic and Jewish communities. Additionally, she served as the Jewish rep for Mayor Bradley, whom she said: "was a uniting, towering figure who managed to engage different ethnicities and divisions in the city."

She recalled the first Martin Luther King, Jr., holiday in 1986 when the Jewish Federation had decided not to close for the day but have an assembly at lunch time. Mark Ridley-Thomas, then head of the Southern California Organizing Committee, threatened to picket the organization if it did not close, and it ended up closing. "Somebody somewhere should have caught that," she said, that is why she started the new leaders program. She also remembers Muslim leader Louis Farrakhan's speech at the Forum, which she attended, where he called Israel a "wicked hypocrisy," according to the *Los Angeles Times*. Farrakhan said he was not anti-Semitic, and the US should have prevented the holocaust, but added, "Don't push your six million down our throats when we lost 100 million (to slavery). We weep for Jews but who weeps for us?"

"This taught me that my generation, particularly the Jews, had no understanding of the needs and perspective of other communities," she said, adding that the crisis over Farrakhan was very much about people not able to stretch themselves to see the other person's point of view, and criticized the existing discontent of Jewish leaders with Bradley. They wanted the mayor to condemn Farrakhan before he spoke. Bradley became the focus of a tug of war between the Black and Jewish groups but stayed with his earlier decision not to make a statement before the speech. True to his word, he did comment after the speech, saying that his private attempts to stop the minister from making inflammatory remarks had a partial success. He told a press conference, "The sad truth is that there were passages that contained undercurrents of anti-Semitism. I repudiate racism, hatred, violence, and bigotry, wherever it occurs. I make no exception. This includes Minister Farrakhan."

POLITICS FROM THE WESTSIDE

Edmund D. Edelman, a UCLA graduate in political science, as well as a Bachelor of Laws degree, grew up in a traditional Jewish family. He became an arbitrator with the Federal Mediation and Conciliation Service, then a deputy legislative counsel in Sacramento, a counselor to the Subcommittee on Education of the House, and a special assistant to the general counsel of the National Labor Relations Board. Then, in 1965, he decided to challenge prominent city Councilwoman Roz Wyman for Los Angeles's 5th District, based on the recommendation of Marvin Holen, later the Chairman of the Board of United Pacific Bank, member of the board of directors of the Southern California Rapid Transit District and a friend of mine.

The Edelman-Wyman campaign was harsh and tangled in court issues and lawsuits. Claiming that Wyman had grown apart from her district, he won and served for nine years before becoming a Los Angeles County Supervisor, 2nd District, 1975–94. The formidable five-member county board held a conservative majority with Pete Schabarum, Jim Hayes, and Michael Antonovich, while Edelman and Kenny Hahn were the liberal minority.

When Deane Dana defeated Yvonne Brathwaite Burke in 1980 for the fourth district seat, Edelman said, "he won by a fluke. He beat Yvonne because it was the wrong district." Dana was always scared," he told me, "When we voted I took the third vote—the critical one—he would follow, scared of being alone, never comfortable as a supervisor." Hahn, he fondly remembered, "was a masterful politician, he picked issues that resonated with the voters."

With Governor Jerry Brown and Sylvia.

Smiling, Edelman recalled Schabarum's reaction to a news article, which reported that although Edelman lost to him in the board room, he beat him on the tennis courts. Schabarum, a former pro football player, angrily sent him a nasty letter saying, "How can you say that in public?"

Edelman remembered going to Gov. Jerry Brown in Sacramento because people "were haranguing us" for tax increases. Proposition 13 had been introduced to protect homeowners at a time of rapidly increasing housing values. "We put forward Proposition 8," he told me, aiming to give temporary relief to those who saw their home values reduced in a declining market. "Both won, but Prop. 13 had more votes." He admits it was too little, too late. His vacated council seat drew three prominent candidates: Zev Yaroslavsky, once the executive director of the Southern California Council on Soviet Jewry; Fran Savitch, a top aide to Mayor Bradley; and Roz Wyman, who wanted to retake the seat she once held. Savitch won the primary, but third-place Wyman endorsed Yaroslavsky who won 54.5 percent to 45.5 percent.

Yaroslavsky told me, "I'm a civil libertarian and a passionate believer in the Constitution, the right to free speech," that's why he fought the Soviet Union, it did not allow freedom of speech and punished those who spoke out against the government. When he became a councilman, he discovered that the police department kept dossiers on prominent people in Los Angeles, elected officials, community activists, reporters. Through an American Civil Liberties Union lawsuit, he discovered his organization was one of the targets. Police Chief Ed Davis "liked my spunk," he recalls, "and liked the fact I didn't take his guff," and later endorsed him when he ran for supervisor.

Then in 1978 Daryl Gates came in who was a much more corporate kind of a guy with everyone reporting up the chain of command—so he depended on his top brass. "Over the years he had some excellent brass, and he had some not so excellent people and some of the people at the top were obsessed and paranoid about me, about people like me, about the ACLU." He said that rogue people in the department sought to expand the Public Disorder Intelligence Division (PDID) squad. "To what extent Gates himself was aware of this, I don't know," he added, "I think he had to be aware of some of it." To find a way for any citizen to apply for a copy of his file, if the file was not sensitive, Yaroslavsky introduced a Freedom of Information Ordinance for the City of Los Angeles. The number two to Gates, Assistant Chief Robert Vernon, testified before the council that the approval of Yaroslavsky's proposal was the most reckless thing the council could do. A much-weakened ordinance was passed, eight to seven, with the people "who were totally in the pocket of the LAPD voting against it." He decided it was better than nothing, and accepted the weakened one, but in the end it was meaningless. "They denied they ever had files, but with the lawsuit things started to dribble out. They did have a file on me." Nothing sexy in these files, he explained, but newspaper clipping and leaflets. However, to him it was offensive because taxpayer money was being spent to keep files on newspaper clippings. They were not a news clipping service. Yet, there were members who agreed with the police, including his closest colleague and friend, Councilman Marvin Braude. "I've never trusted authority, and never taken authority's word on anything," he told me. "My overall feeling on authority and my overall feeling about infringement on peoples' personal privacy was what drove me and drives me to this day." For a law enforcement agency to use public resources to compile information, there needs to be a law enforcement purpose for it, he insisted.

When Joel Wachs became City Council President in 1981 (having said he would support Pat Russell for the presidency but abruptly voted for himself), winning eight to seven, Yaroslavsky was appointed chairman of the Police Committee. The PDID was eliminated and a new unit, the Anti-Terrorism Division initiated. He conducted hearings on the carotid artery choke hold the LAPD was using, which had caused numerous deaths. However, Chief Gates, interviewed by the *Los Angeles Times*, said, "We may be finding that in some blacks when it is applied the veins and arteries do not open as fast as they do in normal people." He refused to apologize, telling the *Los Angeles Times*, "You don't apologize for something where you don't believe you offended anyone. If anyone has been offended, I am sorry for that. I never said blacks were different from whites." His explanation did not appease critics. At the direction of Bradley, who said that Gates's four-years on the job were four years of disparaging remarks about blacks, Latinos, and Jews, the Los Angeles Police Commission opened an unprecedented disciplinary investigation over this matter. Subsequently, the Commission severely restricted use of the choke hold.

According to Yaroslavsky, he and Wachs became rivals as potential mayoral candidates, and he was pulled off the Police Committee and made chairman of the personnel committee. "I had no one to fear," he said, "I feared keeping my mouth shut. I would not be true to myself." He related a "slave auction" event in the late 1970s of the gay community, whereby someone puts himself up for auction and those in the audience make bids, the winner taking him home. It was consensual, but the LAPD had a problem with it and busted one auction just outside his district. "They brought in dozens of police officers, helicopters, the whole nine yards. Everybody there was arrested and booked on 'indentured servitude' charges. It became an outrage. It was on every television station in town."

It also became a cause célèbre in the gay community. A week following the police bust, a mock slave auction was scheduled for Troupers Hall on La Brea Avenue near Hollywood Blvd. "Everybody was invited, it was basically to protest the LAPD raid," he remembered. "No politician in his right mind in those days would have been seen dead or alive there, and no one was there." He approached his wife, Barbara, and said: "You gotta come with me. God forbid anybody should think I'm gay." His presence was announced, and fifteen television cameras focused on him. "It taught me a lesson that I've carried with me ever since: *Don't hide!* If you're going to support somebody, be upfront about it." Nevertheless, he said, "I became the darling, if you will, of the gay and lesbian community, not only on that issue but "on a host of other issues."

In 1978, there was an initiative on the State ballot, Proposition 6, also known as the Briggs Initiative named after Republican Sen. John Briggs who represented parts of Northern Orange County and San Bernardino. It would have prohibited gay teachers from working in the state's public school system. Yaroslavsky remembers that polls showed it winning by an overwhelming margin. "Nobody wanted to touch it with a ten-foot pole," he said. Former LA mayor Sam Yorty had a television program on Channel 13 every Friday night, and he was asked to appear to debate Briggs. When the program started Yorty began supporting the proposition's intent "that was his political predisposition," Yaroslavsky added. Briggs tried to argue the Bible, not knowing that Yaroslavsky used to teach Bible in Jewish synagogues, as well as confirmation classes. Further, he had researched the proposition language and said on the air that not only gay teachers would be banned from teaching, but anybody who knew a gay teacher or had knowledge of a gay teacher and did not report it. "Yorty started going after Briggs. I did not have to say another word." Later, Ronald Reagan, now preparing for his presidential run, came out against it, and strong opposition followed. For Yaroslavsky, it was a transparent violation of the Constitution. The measure was defeated 58.4 percent to 41.6 percent.

Yaroslavsky often described his 5th City Council district as a donut, with Beverly Hills being the donut hole. "Every part was Beverly Hills adjacent," he said, "the most desirable real estate in the city, both commercially and residentially." His friend, Braude, represented the 11th district, to his left, and between them they had the entire west side. Before the recession of the early 1980s there was an upsurge of high rises, double or so those built on the Wilshire corridor. While developers met the requirements of the master plan, a political storm was fermenting over the rapid high-rise expansion. "I did everything I could to slow it down," he said, including the passage of new zoning ordinance with height limits, floor area ratios or density limits. The Beverly Center, an eight-story mall opened in 1982 with its curious shape and lack of street frontage due to angled streets, met all the zoning requirements, but was considered too big for that site. Same was true of the Westside Pavilion, once a shopping mall in the area and future UCLA Research Park. "Under today's rules they would never have been built." He also commented on the Fujita Building in Encino which he said was like the Great Wall of China, a big five-six story structure a block long, which cast a perpetual shadow on single family homes behind it. "We were getting killed by these projects that were being developed while meeting all ordinances." To cut densities in any meaningful way through action by the City Council was not possible since it was "controlled and dominated by pro-development forces."

So, he suggested to Braude, since nothing could be done the conventional legislative way, they should use initiative power through a vote of the people. They would write their own ordinance, raise the money, circulate petitions, get the requisite number of signatures to get it on the ballot, and campaign for it. Proposition U was the result of these efforts and became a ballot initiative in November 1986. Its purpose was to slow the development of high rises in the city (the downtown business core was exempt) by establishing density levels. It also specifically reduced the allowable size of new buildings on 70–85 percent of the commercial and industrial areas of Los Angeles by one-half. In an editorial, on October 29, 1986, the *Los Angeles Times* said it agreed "with the general goals of Los Angeles City

Proposition U. It would wipe the planning slate as clean as it can get in a city of three million people and give Los Angeles a fighting chance of mixing business with the pleasures of neighborhood living in ways that will allow it to grow gracefully. But we are troubled by the concept of broad-brush planning through the initiative process...Those uncertainties warrant a no vote on Proposition U." The proposition was approved by the voters in Los Angeles by more than 65 percent.

"City councils and successive mayors have looked for ways to circumvent Prop. U, and they have done so in a lot of cases," Yaroslavsky decried. The value of land is determined by what a developer thinks he can get the zoning to be. "People buy property at very low prices with the expectation that maybe they'll get the City Council and mayor to rezone it, double the density, and double the value." Slowing down such approaches is an issue that hasn't died. It's a work in progress, he cautioned.

PLANNING FOR A MEGA CITY

While ignored ethnic groups slowly gained visibility and representation in various local and state offices, and while those newly elected strategically measured their upward prospects, activists in numerous planning disciplines focused on Los Angeles and what it needed to become a mega city, with all the amenities and obligations.

Mark Pisano began his career with the Southern California Association of Governments (SCAG) in 1976, a group of local governments from six southern California counties that together make up the nation's largest regional planning agency. He was immediately told the region was too large, too complex, and unmanageable. Break it up, he was advised. Not so, he felt the issues facing the area could not be solved by its parts. It needed an economic base—jobs. "This was an issue that I brought forward to the early leadership of my organization, namely Mayor Bradley and Councilwoman Pat Russell," he explained to me. A blueprint for the region was created, on how it could grow and develop, and both Bradley and Russell supported initiatives that were launched. But in the later years he said, "the greatest disappointments that I've seen is the succession of three mayors who didn't do a thing about it." He emphasized that the city in 2015 had fewer employees than it had in 1980. "I think it's an inherently underlying fatal flaw of the city that it has not had mayors who have made job creation their number one priority, and that included a mayor who was a business leader during that time."

Pisano, called visionary and thinker by colleagues, said that his organization needed to do a comprehensive regional plan for this region, which became a divisive issue. Critics said he must focus on transportation and stop trying to work on the economy. He praised urban planner Sylvia Patsaouras who joined SCAG to head the development of the centerpiece, the driver, for the comprehensive plan. However, it unraveled when Russell lost her election. "We could not get the business leaders to pick up and move the economic strategies." He explained that the socioeconomic variables of the region have not been favorable. "We are a gateway for immigrants, which is good," he said, but on the other hand we got overwhelmed, and it pushed back our public amenities. We couldn't keep up with it." To do so, you need an economic base so you can spread those costs, and we didn't have it here. Pisano said that the region never developed the solidarity of business, labor, and government to coalesce resources coming here. The single most important issue in Southern California is our institutional design, meaning how we work together as an organization.

"We did not do the job," he admitted to me and spoke of legislation that took two years to pass on how to economically develop and fund infrastructure and amenities. It was called *Enhanced Infrastructure Financing Districts* (EIFDs), which were financed through tax increments generated from the growth in property taxes collected from the affected area and designed to provide financing for a broad range of infrastructure work, including traditional public works. Although he took this matter up with the leadership, "the City of LA couldn't get anywhere with it. ...The political leadership is the ingredient that is most missing," he said, something he had not seen since Bradley and Russell. Other cities within Los Angeles County have successfully used EIFDs.

Ever since his start at SCAG, the homeless issue has been on his watch. "It does not take rocket science to figure out the causes," Pisano said, pointing to an employment machine that is not generating the kind of employment opportunities needed, and coupled with the high cost of housing, and the many immigrants in the socioeconomic base that we have, these are the predictable results. "It's a misguided strategy to think that we're going to solve the homeless problem by providing some services to people and getting them moved into shelters." The long-term solution is to deal with our cost structure issue, including the way we finance things, and deal with the issue systemically. To deal with the time that it will take, he said, we must humanely deal with the needs of individuals as we implement our strategy. Since leaving SCAG, Pisano joined the University of Southern California's Price School of Public Policy as a senior fellow, researching how the state's changing demographics will influence the state's economic growth.

"In the Bradley era we had leadership in multiple organizations," he reminisced, "and people with different political persuasions vied and competed and beat the hell out of one another. Yet that leadership moved the region, moved the city, and it was done. One sector could not dominate, labor was at the table along with business and community groups and the region progressed on a positive trajectory." Since then, "we just haven't had that." Pisano continued, "If you believe in the spirit of LA then you believe that innovation and ingenuity will arise out of new ideas. The question is, will they be allowed to be demonstrated?" After all, LA did things for itself—the notion of dependency was not there. It paid out of its taxes for its water system, the Colorado River Aqueduct and the California State Water Project, which extends two-thirds the length of the state.

Furthermore, entertainment did not exist before the sense of film. High-tech ingenuity came out of the science of this region: Caltech invented the chip and the aerospace industry was developed in the LA area. The leaders of tomorrow, according to Pisano—those leaders with an overarching vision—are going to be people who allow LA to transform itself. There is a difference in leadership. However, he cautioned, "the economy of the city of LA is becoming a third world economy with over one million more people than 1980, three quarters of whom live in poverty. It's a city that doesn't understand, and a civic structure that doesn't understand that it must rebuild an economic base, and a region that's struggling." When asked about programs like Rebuild LA and the loss of jobs coming because of riots and the shutdown of GM's Van Nuys plant in 1992, Pisano said that "government doesn't build and now the market is not allowed to operate. We haven't figured out the politics of redistribution and the politics of protection have kept the market at bay. ...Both the county and the city do not have revenues," he added. Efforts to create fiscal sustainability have failed. Enterprise financing and funding may provide an answer.

Hasan Ikhrata, executive director of SCAG following Pisano, said that people are getting older in the Los Angeles area and by 2027 one in five will be over sixty-five years of age. He told me that a different transportation system will be demanded, a different health care system and housing, as well. "People will want urban living, and the ability to walk to the theater. Young people want to be mobile and change jobs." He was uncertain about California continuing to be "the place to be," because "business is leaving due to regulations." But people have expressed in surveys what they want. "They want parks, safe walks, bicycle amenities, and more interconnected transit systems." While SCAG makes plans, these plans mean little if they are not implemented. Ikhrata expressed the need for his agency to work closely with the cities and counties to execute the planning of experts.

Problems and opportunities facing Los Angeles were Bradley's foremost concern. He sought to chart a comprehensive plan to address both current issues and those of the next century, so he gathered a blue-ribbon panel of individuals drawn from the city's elites to fashion the future of Los Angeles. The results, published in 1988, were to be viewed "not as an end but as the beginning of a dialogue about the future of Los Angeles." In March 1986, the Los Angeles 2000 Committee's planning process commenced with the help of strategic planners at RAND. Early in the process the blue-ribbon panel had agreed on five goals for Los Angeles, each of which contributed to the area's quality of life. And it said the goals can only be achieved by addressing many issues simultaneously.

By the year 2000 it wanted a Los Angeles to be a city of livable communities with a healthful physical environment, a place where all individuals can grow and learn and be fulfilled and to be a great crossroads city where the diversity of its people enriches its urban fabric. In its survey for the panel, RAND found that despite broad consensus on major issues, various groups differed on other points. Whites and upper-income people were more inclined to rate the weather and the geographic diversity of Los Angeles as its best features, while minorities were more inclined to emphasize the economic opportunities and, unlike whites, a substantial fraction of them favored continued growth.

Jane Pisano, PhD, president of the Los Angeles 2000 Committee and former president of the Natural History Museum of Los Angeles County (who is credited with making the museum brighter and more high-tech and interactive with the help of $135 million reinvention), told me that "Bradley had a gravitas and a dignity about him," and he was the perfect person for that moment in creating an overarching vision. "If he ran now, he'd be eaten up, I think."

"He had this big, bold investing in infrastructure vision, and he didn't get all of it. He got some of it, and he was very much in the mode of city fathers who had big dreams, who had big visions, and it's not an accident that they were growing their companies while they were growing their city, while they were growing a region." She said that what was good for their companies was good for the city, and what was good for the city was good for their companies. "That's an alignment of interest and power and influence that sort of propelled us in that direction, to invest in infrastructure."

Critics of the *LA 2000* report claim that relevant recommendations did not include funding mechanisms, allowing City Hall to foot-drag, and that it overlooked major issues like climate change, homelessness, and a crumbling infrastructure. Jane Pisano said when she was actively engaged in the life of the city, people took for granted a kind of civic arc that really reached its peak in the Olympics. "That was extraordinary, but I can't remember any public act since then that rose even partly to that equation." Years earlier, in a 2002 interview with *The Planning Report,* Pisano said that leadership and vision are everything. The cities that are "achieving their destiny are ones that have experienced and benefited from extraordinary leadership, which implies the vision and will to realize that vision."

I questioned Jane Pisano on polarization, like the anger that persisted on the issue of secession. "Unfortunately," she replied, "the anger has not been channeled to anything constructive. In large part it's all based on values and a belief that people want small government, that their government is listening to them, responding to them, and spending their money well. The truth is that all these people who are angry at the government are getting their fair share of Social Security dollars, Medicare dollars, Medicaid dollars—and Medicaid's what shot through the roof—and unemployment insurance. A lot of people are just ticked off because their standard of living has gone down, or they can't get a good paying job."

PARTICIPATORY POLICY MAKING

In the City of Angels there are people genuinely afraid of growth—of change. Therefore, they want the government to block change from taking place. Yet others believe that it is the duty of government to prepare for change. This collision of political will became very apparent to Dan Garcia when he was appointed to the Los Angeles Planning Commission in 1976. He had been practicing law for a few years and although he had been a hearing officer for the Fire Commissioner, he was apprehensive since he didn't know anything about planning. He expressed this concern to Councilman Zev Yaroslavsky. "Well," Yaroslavsky said, "as near as I can tell nobody else does either."

Garcia learned quickly. He ardently advocated uniformity between zoning and the general plan at a time the system of planning and zoning for the city was completely off kilter. He told me he got a lot of push back from developers "because they thought I was being overly severe and strict because I thought, God forbid, the zoning and the general plan ought to be consistent." A few months following his appointment to the Commission he was made vice president, and then president in 1978, where he served for ten consecutive years. Los Angeles adopted the nation's first land use ordinance in 1908, establishing residence-only zones. The city was zoned comprehensively for the first time in 1946. The initial eighty-four-page document defining the baseline had grown to more than 600 pages of complex and unbending rules with height districts, floor air ratios, and bizarre zoning patterns. It was all patchwork. Garcia, with Cal Hamilton, the visionary but controversial Los Angeles city planning director, and other specialists using new technologies and massive hearings, rezoned the entire city. As Garcia told me, this had never happened before in any modern city, at least nationally. "We downzoned in an extraordinary way the overall capacity of the city to reflect what the community plans showed when you put them all together."

Zoning is the primary legislative tool through which land use is locally governed in the United States. "I was consistent over the years because I thought the core of the center's concept was good. There had to be urbanized centers that produce economic-generating activity on one hand, but we also had to protect the single-family neighborhoods on the other." He emphasized that the real combat was over transitional areas where more design controls with special planning was needed.

Hamilton's *pedways* project, elevated pedestrian walkways to remove walkers from the menace of street traffic, was first introduced in the *1970 Concept Los Angeles: The Concept for the Los Angeles General Plan*. They were the first phase of what would become, but never did, mechanized people movers. Edward Helfeld, the then administrator of the Community Redevelopment Agency, did not like Hamilton's concept. Garcia visited a couple of high rises that would be connected by the *pedways*, and called the plan, "ridiculous. It's not going to happen. It assumes a rate of growth that hasn't materialized so far," he said. Hamilton never quite forgave him, he added. "I thought it was nuts," he continued. "I mean, the spatial relations, you'd have to have mile-long walkways. There's no way in the world." After that, professional interactions degenerated into tribal war between them about specific plans, an irritated Garcia admitted. He protested. "The planning department represents the whole city. We are spending 90 percent of our money on three districts. This is dumb. We need to do some stuff to clean up the industrial zoning in East LA."

He restated his role in the realignment of the Metro Rail, which came through his Commission. "I tried to help you guys," he said. "I'll never forget this, the Crenshaw stop (Crenshaw and Wilshire) and the people who, for years, appeared before me whining about heavy development and traffic."

On October 29, 1990, Garcia was pitched into the center of the storm—the power struggle between Bradley and Police Chief Gates. Bradley appointed him to the five-member Police Commission that monitors the Los Angeles Police Department. His job: reassert the commission's role as the overseer of the department. Interestingly, on that date I was Gates's guest of honor at the Police Academy Graduation. A few weeks before Garcia's appointment, the mayor and the police chief had a rare public exchange of criticisms over police conduct in handling of an investigation. Anxieties swelled further for Garcia as he assumed the commission presidency, just three days before the first hearing in the Rodney King case. "I conducted the hearings in South Central Los Angeles," he related to me. "There were a thousand angry people in the auditorium and twenty cops on stage to keep peace." Before the meeting began, he was told the cops would leave because they'd be a source of anger. "By God, I slogged it out. I got a bunch of death threats, but then I suspected Daryl."

"You suspected Daryl?" I asked. Garcia explained that he was leaning toward a suspension for the police chief, and it was supported by the police manual whenever there's an accusation of misfeasance or malfeasance. John Ferraro, president of the City Council and once Garcia's friend, called him. "I'm going to destroy you if you do this." Since the mayor was on a plane to Sacramento, Ferraro claimed he was the acting mayor. It became bitter. Garcia explained. "I can be removed but I cannot be told what I can or cannot do." As the hearing continued, some lawyers approached Garcia. "There's a criminal investigation about you. You have a conflict," he was told. "Finally, I got them to say what it was. Three or four years before some commissioners raised funds for the mayor. Nothing came of it."

Responding to another of my questions, Garcia said he was afraid. "I got to the point where I was going to read the order to Daryl and said: "Look, I'm not doing this because I enjoy it, or because I want to punish you, it is a procedure." Daryl looked at him, he said, and "I swear to God there was fear in his eyes." Gates reminded Garcia that he had friends on the City Council. The next day the council called him in. "For four hours they all trashed me, except for Mike Woo who thought I was right." Since the meeting was not posted, a city attorney said it was a violation of the Brown Act. "They reinstated him before the lawsuit had been filed."

So, Garcia sued the City Council. The suit was based on a constitutional question of whether they had the authority to do it. "The judge was very unkind to us," he added. Although big law firms had offered to help, "Daryl got to them," and nobody represented him. The case was lost. Less than seven months after his appointment, Garcia resigned, saying that the integrity of the civilian panel had been "severely damaged" by an ongoing dispute with the City Council. According to the *Los Angeles Times*. Garcia attacked the council for "interjecting" itself in Police Commission business by effectively reinstating Gates after the commission placed him on leave. He also criticized the council for withholding funds for a commission investigation of Los Angeles Police Department management in the aftermath of the police beating of Rodney G. King.

REBUILDING LA

Los Angeles was a fractured city and became even more so in 1992 when a jury acquitted four police officers in the beating of black motorist Rodney King. An attorney for O'Melveny & Myers, Rocky Delgadillo, was sitting in his Century City office watching the smoke plumes "come up from my city. I was crying inside. I decided I must do something about this."

As Delgadillo related to me, about one week after the riots there was a lawyers' task force meeting in downtown LA and hundreds of attorneys showed up. Peter Ueberroth, the celebrated chairman of the Los Angeles Olympic Organizing Committee for the Summer 1984 Games, approached him and asked him to work on his new nonprofit Rebuild LA. Warren Christopher, a partner at his law firm, thought it would be a good idea and he was loaned to the nonprofit for eighteen months.

His earlier job was to negotiate theatrical motion picture deals as an entertainment attorney. His new assignment was to oversee economic development. He was directed to "go create jobs in the inner cities." Literally spoon-fed by experts who had traveled the country to review the job-creation efforts of other municipalities, he had to learn from the seat of his pants. Ueberroth resigned from Rebuild LA about a year after being appointed amid growing criticism that the program was wavering. When it began, it had been estimated that $5 billion was needed to develop 75,000 jobs along with viable housing and retail in the riot area.

Delgadillo told the *Christian Science Monitor* on April 29, 1993, the public was asking too much, too soon. "The way we get kicked around, you'd think we were supposed to solve decades of inner-city neglect overnight." Moreover, annoyed by what was seen as inaction, grassroots groups began to compete with Ueberroth's organization and sought to coalesce a sense of community by empowering inner-city blacks. Yet, the Rev. Cecil Murray, pastor of the First AME Church in South Central Los Angeles, expressed skepticism of these groups, noting that "grassroots does not have enough empowerment, government does not have enough will, and Rebuild LA does not have the mandate" to solve this city's widespread social ills.

With four more months left on Delgadillo's agreement to work on the project, Linda Griego, a prominent entrepreneur, philanthropist, president, and chief executive officer of the Los Angeles Community Development Bank, and deputy mayor in the Bradley administration, came on board as president and CEO of Rebuild LA. Nonetheless, in 1993 with the election of Mayor Riordan, Delgadillo was asked to spend two weeks updating him regarding the inner city. "Those two weeks turned into eight years," he told me, becoming first an assistant deputy mayor and then a deputy mayor putting into play all the private sector principles he had learned from Ueberroth. It was like open field running on economic development, without design. Riordan told him, "Go make mistakes so long as you're doing it for the right reason. Don't be lazy, have integrity, tell the truth." He put an LA business team together, cold-called CEOs, and developed projects. Keeping companies from leaving was considered a victory.

He recalls being the go-between Riordan and Councilwoman Jackie Goldberg of the 13th District, the first out lesbian woman to hold seat on the Los Angeles City Council. She was instrumental in shaping the Hollywood Property Owners Alliance, which in October 1992, acknowledged that while "Hollywood Boulevard is the place where people come to experience excitement and glamor, relive Hollywood's past glory, and enter its world of myths and imagination…they find a problem area in a state of disrepair. Much needs to be done to enhance that excitement and make the glamor a reality."

Consequently, the Kodak Theatre (now known as the Dolby Theatre) was built in the Ovation Hollywood shopping center and entertainment complex, on Hollywood Boulevard and Highland Avenue. For more than twenty years it has been the venue of the annual Academy Awards ceremony. Considered to be a key project in the revitalization of Hollywood, the Eastman Kodak Company paid $75 million for naming rights until it went bankrupt, and Dolby Laboratories signed a twenty-year naming agreement in 2012. "I think if you asked Goldberg today, she'd probably say that she didn't do the project right, but it got done," he admitted.

According to Delgadillo, Magic Johnson wanted to open movie theaters in the inner city and approached Riordan. "You don't know how to run movie theaters, how are you going to make money?" he was asked. "Well, I'm Magic Johnson," was his reply. Riordan agreed and called the head of Mann Theaters to see if he wanted to partner with Magic for an inner-city project? "No!" was the response. Biggest mistake he ever made, said Delgadillo. Loews stepped up, Magic partnered with Ken Lombard and Magic Johnson Theaters were built patterned after the Loews Cineplex Entertainment model. They were first-rate high-quality multiplexes in urban neighborhoods with the newest technologies, the same as if built in Beverly Hills. Local economic growth was encouraged, and job development was promoted. Movies of particular interest to African Americans were screened, some becoming communal events. It was reported that the theater complex drew more than one million visitors a year.

One thing he learned from economic development, Delgadillo said, was to talk to people on the ground, otherwise it won't be done right. "Government tends to sit in ivory towers, it's easy, it's beautiful." So, he created the Neighborhood Prosecutor Program. Problems were identified and addressed. No one cared, he told me, drugs, gangs, prostitution, all of that. LAPD wouldn't drive down some streets; they were too dangerous. "When we started there were six gangs under injunction. When I left, there were seventeen."

In 2001, Delgadillo ran for Los Angeles City Attorney against Councilman Mike Feuer and won, 52.4 percent to 47.6 percent. Riordan had remained neutral until finally endorsing him, spending more than $265,000 during the runoff, according to the *Los Angeles Times,* and the outdoor advertising industry over $425,000 on scores of billboards promoting him. In 2005 he ran again, this time unopposed. The next year he challenged Jerry Brown, then mayor of Oakland, for Attorney General and lost, 63.3 percent to 36.7 percent. He tried again in 2010 and came in fifth (with 10.1 percent) in a field of eight in the primary, with Kamala Harris winning.

* * *

Following the riots, people from various sectors—political, business, and the community—sought a central entity to focus on rebuilding the community. Ueberroth, highly respected for his Olympics leadership, became the prominent co-chair of the Rebuild LA consortium. As consequent skepticism surfaced, Tony Salazar, a Latino community development specialist, was also named co-chair to be more reflective of the community. He joined co-chairs Barry A. Sanders, a corporate lawyer, Bernard W. Kinsey, a former Xerox executive, and, later, Linda Wong, executive director at the Center for Urban Education at USC. The leadership now consisted of two white men, one Latino, one African American, and an Asian woman.

Salazar confessed to me that his ascension to co-chair was a formality, equated by him, to a "sacrificial lamb." Ueberroth had discussed with him the mechanics of how to rebuild in urban areas. "I need people here that understand how to rebuild and how to work in distressed neighborhoods," he was told, and was invited to be on the board. But the Latino leaders demanded a Latino co-chair, yet nobody really wanted to step up, according to Salazar. "I was the new guy, and everyone said for me to go, and I didn't know any better, so I went." The direction was uncertain, it was a political minefield, he added, and no one wanted to take the risk. Rebuild LA slipped to the status of a miniature city government, according to Salazar. "People came to seek higher minimum wages, to reform the school district, every city problem got dumped on this organization, every single one. It became an entity viewed from the outside as the problem solver, but not just for rebuilding.

So, the weight of all prevented the organization from really doing its job. Social issues took precedent. They marched on the organization. They came and fought for basically good things; but they were just fighting in the wrong place." When Riordan became mayor, he stood on the periphery, according to Salazar. "He did not dive in. Didn't want to get too tainted with what was happening. It just kept going down from that point. Ueberroth finally left."

Salazar explained that when Linda Griego came on board, the co-chairs all got out of the way. She was the person now running it all, overseeing it all; she was in charge. She stayed there until it disappeared. Ueberroth's Rebuild LA had a grand initial entrance, and a grander promise. Slowly, however, uncertainty and even resentment from many community groups emerged and his role as rescuer of the inner city was questioned. He did not exemplify the ethnic makeup of the areas he was to rejuvenate. On May 22, 1993, he told Calvin Sims of the *New York Times*, "I don't know why the focus was on me. Maybe it was because I was the only appointment of the mayor. Maybe it had some racial overtones because I'm white. I don't know."

COMMUNITY INVOLVEMENT DURING RIOTS

"It was too large to be effective and as functional as it could be," said the Rev. Dr. Cecil "Chip" Murray, who served for twenty-seven years as pastor of the historic First African Methodist Episcopal Church (FAME), located at the Jefferson Park neighborhood of the West Adams district. During his tenure, Rev. Murray transformed a 250-member house of worship into an 18,000-person megachurch. His work yielded multi-million-dollar community and economic development programs that brought jobs and housing to many neighborhoods.

The reverend explained to me the riots had caused the greatest damage to the most impoverished areas of the community. "I guess I can understand the anger, I can understand the anguish, the anxiety, but I cannot understand the reaction or justify it, but it was a reality, so we have to go into the reality mode of damage control, of repair and rebuilding." He recounted the preparations made while awaiting the Rodney King verdict on April 29, 1992. "Our challenge was to find a way to keep the city cool in the event the decision was antithetical to what people thought it should be. The vast majority felt the policemen were in error, but that was the stage of the Daryl Gates mentality, a mentee of Parker—the police did not have the most positive image." The plan, he continued, was to go to ten different areas in south Los Angeles, ten men at ten different areas. If the verdict was not guilty, the temperament of the community would be negative. They were to meet at the church and keep their commitment toward civility and peace and order. Expecting an overflow crowd, megaphones were placed on the roof of the church. Mayor Bradley addressed the group, and his message of peace and order was well received.

After seven days of deliberations, the jury acquitted the four officers on almost all charges. Two ushers reported to Rev. Murray that there were immediate fires on the western horizon. He looked south and saw fires there as well. In the immediate vicinity isolated flames were noticeable. Rather than dispatching his groups of ten to different locations, they were sent to areas with fires. The local fire station was notified, but the reverend was told gangs were throwing rocks at fire trucks. "If you come, we guarantee you that you will be protected," he told the firemen. His group of volunteers immediately formed a line between the gangs and the firemen who were putting out the flames. "We admonished the gangs. They demonstrated, lots of rhetoric and street talk, but they disappeared."

Calling Los Angeles the most multinational city in America, most multilingual, which came of age with the Summer 1984 Olympics, the challenge that remains is "how we could become not one people, but one agenda, one philosophy of civility, and in the age of the civil rights movement, how we could be different people without allowing our differences to make a difference." He told me, "You were there as one of the founding fathers of the transportation system, the birth of the Metro Rail, the birth of rail transportation that was a salvation to our city because as we become a conglomerate, we have to be accessible."

One of my initiatives following the civil disturbance of 1992, called "Operation Food Basket," was for LACTC to provide transportation in areas where markets had been burned with free taxi rides to doctors' offices, food banks, battered women's shelters, and other locations. Social service agencies for the homeless, the poor, and other groups distributed the taxi vouchers. Along with LA Taxi, the First AME Church was used as the program broker to ensure integrity. According to a report in the *Los Angeles Times*, during the first six months of the program some 60,000 taxi coupons worth $7 apiece had been distributed to social service agencies, primarily in South-Central Los Angeles and Hollywood.

Joel Kotkin, widely known for his work in demographic, social, and economic trends nationally and internationally, cited my experience as an example when explaining preparatory Los Angeles, noting that it is the place where you could go, and no matter who you were, no matter what your background, whether you had an accent, you could move forward and build a business. This is really what a city is for. "When I hear people talk about a football team, or an art museum, that's not what makes a city," he said. "What makes a city is its transformative experience. Will LA be successful? This idea that LA as an incubator of new and successful businesses that are creating jobs, is an option that exists. ...People come to Los Angeles and do something they couldn't do somewhere else, that's what a city is about," he continued. However, after studying surveys and evaluating analyses, Kotkin surmised that the city has declined in every sector, more rapidly than competitive regions in the finance and business sectors.

Only in entertainment does Los Angeles remain strong. "For virtually everything else, we're in trouble." The numbers show that Los Angeles is in terrible shape for jobs. "We have a media and a political leadership which thinks that building a bunch of condos downtown and taking it out of the public purse is a great idea. That putting in a football stadium will turn things around." He said that football stadiums do nothing. Eight times a year when a bunch of rich people go to a game doesn't change anything, he decried. "I'm amazed at the lack of reflection, of looking at numbers and thinking, not only what are we doing, but how are we doing compared to other people. Los Angeles has great assets," he concluded. Kotkin, a fellow in urban studies at Chapman University, said he worked with Linda Griego on Rebuild LA where there was a focus on job creation, and that was totally lost. "What we really need to do is start focusing our investments on things like infrastructure and growth."

REFORMING A SEVENTY-THREE-YEAR-OLD CHARTER

The City Charter identifies Los Angeles as a mayor-council-commission form of government. It was initially adopted by the voters effective July 1, 1925. A mayor, city controller, and city attorney are elected by city residents every four years, as well as fifteen City Council members representing fifteen districts. Today, these elected officials may serve two terms, except for council members who can serve three terms, the result of adopted term limits provisions. To manage Los Angeles, a coordinated resolve between a strong mayor and a powerful City Council is essential. But the relentless power struggle between the two entities consistently thwarts city governance. A mayor, like Riordan, wanted to be a boss-mayor, like New York or Chicago. However, council members reason they are the peoples' representatives and clutch on to more power than other City Councils, with formidable influences over land use and planning.

In response to intense calls for charter reform, the City Council chose an Appointed Charter Reform Commission to revise the seventy-three-year-old document. Riordan, a venture capitalist, deemed it proper that the boss should manage the company and concluded more power should be in the hands of the mayor. He made charter reform a priority in his second term. According to Erwin Chemerinsky, often referred to as the most frequently cited American legal scholar, the mayor was provoked by the council's action and put up his own money to get an initiative on the ballot to gain an Elected Charter Reform Commission. He then raised $2 million from business for his slate of candidates to be elected. As a result, two competing commissions were created. The lingering question was: could they surmount the political enmity existing at City Hall and find common ground? Each commission began to meet separately.

"I have no doubt that the appointed commission didn't want us to be there," said Chemerinsky, becoming the chair of the Elected Charter Reform Commission. According to George Kieffer, a partner at Manatt, Phelps & Phillips and former chair of the Board of Regents of the University of California, and the chair of the appointed commission, the first elected commission chair, former state Senator Gloria Romero, "was discarded because she wasn't getting along with people." The two commissions pursued largely parallel paths for the first year and several months, Chemerinsky told me. "Occasionally we'd get a conference committee to work out our differences, but the reality is we disagreed about everything." The appointed committee, he recalls, was taking the existing charter and making changes. We saw ourselves as writing on a blank piece of paper. "They perceived us as reckless and not having sufficient knowledge. We perceived them as just tinkering, and too beholden to the existing interest groups." Furthermore, he said they were staff-driven while his group were people who largely saw this as a steppingstone to political office. But the deadline was set. The proposal had to go on the ballot in the spring of 1999.

Although described as the "puppets of the City Council," Kieffer said a budget was provided for his commission and work began immediately. Through a structured, deliberate process a national search for an executive officer was conducted and a staff developed. In the meantime, Riordan got his commission underway with a negative first step; in the election for commission members, he loses most of his endorsed people. Labor wins. "Now we have a problem," Kieffer told me. Riordan approached Miguel Contreras, a member of the appointed group and political director of the Los Angeles County Federation of Labor, credited for resurrecting the labor movement, became satisfied with the promise that nothing would be done with Civil Service. The people endorsed by labor on the elected commission knew labor, but they were kind of "mishmash" about what should be done with the charter, Kieffer added. The other people on Riordan's commission, probably two-thirds of them, wanted to run for office.

Riordan hard-pressed his commission members with Bill Wardlaw, the mastermind of the mayor's 1993 campaign and trusted friend, because "he has to swing them," Kieffer added. Riordan's assessment of a new charter was widely proclaimed: "It won't cost the city any money. This is going to be privately financed." That didn't happen. When he sought money from the City Council for his commission he was turned down. For months the mayor's group struggled without funds. Finally, in response to outside pressure, the council provide the same budget given to the appointed commission. Despite that, the mayor's group did not know how to run the commission, they had not been involved in government, or led things, said Kieffer. "They hired an executive officer from New York because Riordan wanted more New York-like power. You can't put one system on top of another, so it was very confusing."

As the chair, Chemerinsky organized as best he could, and they got a lot of attention. A public disaster loomed in Kieffer's mind. "Two commissions to do one charter? Only in LA." He spent time with groups like the Urban League, the *Los Angeles Times*, media people, and other opinion leaders to try to solidify his commission's credibility. "We thought they might disband us, throw us out. …I knew we had the advantage if we could get the two commissions together," he recounted to me. Even though he had decided at the start to keep everyone abreast of their progress, including the mayor's office, "they made a big mistake, they underestimated me and underestimated what we would do." The elected commission had the ability to go to the voters while his commission would go to the City Council. "They thought we were irrelevant, and they didn't read anything we sent them."

In the meantime, the elected commission was doing unusual things, they wanted a Bill of Rights, adding abortion rights in the charter, and it all became public. Chemerinsky's leadership held them together. In the end he became convinced the drafts of the appointed commission would be used in a coordinated discussion, whereby a Unified Charter could be produced. This approach received nasty repercussions. "In the end they tried to get him fired," noted Kieffer. "They threatened him. He barely had the votes to hang on to the chairmanship." Chemerinsky remembers the fall of 1998 when Kieffer called him. "If both commission proposals go on the ballot," Kieffer had said, "they will both lose. Your supporters will be our opponents, our supporters will be your opponents." All the time spent will have been wasted. "We've got to get one proposal and if it's going to happen it's going to be the two of us, or it's not going to happen." They got together and identified twenty-five issues they disagreed on—and started with five, slowly working out a compromise. Acceptable positions on specific issues from each commission were quickly processed, and where there was disagreement, a middle position was carved out. A package of five issues were then taken to a conference committee. Then another five issues were scrutinized and when agreement was reached, they also went to another conference committee.

Some issues, like the power of the mayor, almost caused everything to break down. The elected commission had written it as the mayor wanted, the appointed commission had not. Riordan came out very strongly against the appointed commission, said Chemerinsky. "There was a lot of drama. The mayor lost that fight." In his book, *The Mayor,* published in 2014, Riordan said, "it was maddening to watch Chemerinsky, a liberal ideologue and darling of the *Los Angeles Times*, go out of his way to make compromises with the council's commission, trying to please the political establishment. In doing so, Chemerinsky was undercutting the entire purpose of an elected commission, which was to give citizens a strong hand in reforming city government. Whenever I saw that the commission was straying from its mission, I hammered the law professor, who sometimes told me one thing and then did something completely different."

When I asked Chemerinsky how Riordan lost his own proposal, he responded, "Can't really talk about what happened, but Riordan pushed extremely hard that the elected commission have one proposal, a separate proposal that he would financially back and make sure it won. The elected commission abandoned him and approved the single proposal." The city charter, approved by the voters 60–40 percent on June 8, 1999, replaced the 1925 document that had been amended over 400 times, Chemerinsky concluded that it provided a more coherent document, somewhat increasing the power of the mayor by giving him more authority when it comes to hiring and firing personnel. It also established the Neighborhood Council System and the Department of Neighborhood Empowerment, thus promoting more citizen participation and makes government more responsive to local demands.

Raphe Sonenshein, executive director of the Pat Brown Institute at Cal State LA, and executive director of the appointed commission, wrote in 2010 about the intricate policy and political questions that were ultimately resolved in charter reform. The realistic threat of secession by the San Fernando Valley produced intense pressure to reform the existing and bulky document that "made governance complicated and hemmed in the authority of the mayor," he wrote. Described in a *Los Angeles Times* article by Jim Newton on June 9, 2006, as a "civically engaged intellectual…honestly dispassionate yet utterly committed," Sonenshein said Riordan created his commission to destroy the City Council's commission.

He told me that "you would get one Riordan on Monday, another one on Friday. He could be goofy, serious, hard-working, lazy, very smart, and very inattentive." Sonenshein got to see the whole range of Riordan and ended up "liking him quite a bit," despite his "pretty nutty ideas and not much interest in learning the way of politics and government which often caused him no end of grief" because of weak follow-through.

Bradley, he said, was the same Bradley all the time. He had dealings with him. Sonenshein called him a great man, who was different than your normal politician, and did many things that no normal politician would do. And, he added, "Bradley is the most important mayor that LA as a city ever had, so he's in a class by himself." Los Angeles mayors are always in trouble for being too political. Sonenshein pointed out they are accused of interfering in commissions and in departments. Before his work on the charter, the City Council did not see itself as a legislative body but as co-administrator—and that was the problem in city government. Now, he noted, mayors need to have eight votes in the City Council. "I think it is a dramatic change."

Charters can be revitalized, and lethargic visions awakened, but it takes determined action to make perceptible and lasting progress, especially in inimitable Los Angeles. "Bradley was the key," according to Sue Laris, former editor and publisher of the weekly *Downtown News*. "Here's the vision for downtown," Bradley had said, "This is going to be where the workforce is, adjacent to where people are living," thinking about the African American community. Immediately he directed his thoughts to the Community Redevelopment Agency (CRA/LA) that was created to attract private investment into economically depressed regions.

A savvy James M. "Jim" Wood was the chair of CRA/LA. He loved Bradley's vision and moved quickly to help regenerate depressed sectors, eliminate slums, and preserve historic areas. Furthermore, he encouraged and advanced economic development and established and maintained employment prospects. Wood did a great deal more. Later, as the head of the LA County Federation of Labor, he established understandings between developers, public officials, and labor unions, making construction of today's downtown a reality—another Bradley vision. Frequently the mayor would drive to Bunker Hill and view, with a perceptible grin, the Los Angeles skyline he loved.

* * *

Oprah Winfrey was determined to do a big show after the 1992 riots in Los Angeles. She had asked her executive producer to organize a Korean panel and a black panel to discuss the absence of aid to Korean grocers by the LAPD during the looting. Tina Choi, a friend of the producer, was hired by Harpo Productions to help create the panels, and she immediately began making contacts, first with First AME Church, the Police union, and Korean leaders. A revelation made by Bill Violante, president of the Los Angeles Police Protective League, startled her. "We wanted to come to their aid, but we were told we needed to stand down and wait." The show was taped and aired.

When she finished her degree at Berkeley, Choi received another call from Violante, now the new deputy mayor for Riordan, who wanted her to interview for a deputy job with the mayor. The first question of an exhaustive interview was: "Do you play chess?" The answer came quickly. "I'm an Asian-Korean immigrant, I play golf, piano, and chess." She was hired within the hour. Choi told me that at school she majored in political science, political economics, and had a theoretical appreciation and understanding of politics. However, when she began working for Riordan "everything flew out the window." Nothing she had studied prepared her for Riordan. "He was a hybrid, a kind of Rockefeller marries the Kennedys, the best of both worlds." Riordan was very impatient, remembers Choi. "We went through many staff, I can't even tell you how many press secretaries, how many chiefs of staff, because he had a very high sense of performance and expectation. He wanted immediate results. The City Council was very critical," she said. "Alatorre and Ferraro were good allies from Riordan's view because they were honest with him, and he respected that."

Reflecting on the riots and the earthquake, Choi said it was a time when a "cut-throat business leader and a partisan were needed to lead the city. "That's what Dick does." She suggested that resentment of Riordan by other politicians stemmed from his ability to move forward without their help. "Dick's magic was his desire to move things forward. It doesn't always mean you get where you want to go, but I think his goal was to keep the conversation and the vision moving."

* * *

Having dealt with most of the mayors, Sonenshein told me he scored Bradley very high and considered him an extraordinary character. He considers Riordan a "moderately successful mayor," and likely the last Republican in an increasingly Democratic city. Regarding Hahn, he called him "an odd duck" but very smart, "maybe one of the smartest people in that office." Very laconic, Hahn would sit in a room, put his long legs out, sit back, and some days it would seem he didn't care at all. "But when he focused, he was very sharp and really very smart." In Sonenshein's view Hahn was "a classic example of a one-time mayor who did some very good things and was a good guy." However, he added, he made two courageous decisions that cost him his job: he fired then Police Chief Bernard Parks, and strongly opposed secession of the San Fernando Valley. Getting Parks out was politically unpopular, and Hahn didn't lay the proper groundwork. Also, the approach taken to raise money to fight the breakaway factions and the way he dealt with City Controller Laura Chick "was fatal to his being re-elected." Hahn had cited a higher crime rate and low police morale, including an exodus of officers from the department, and called the police chief a failure in news reports. In the anti-secession drive, Hahn had raised $5.5 million—nearly four times the combined amount of the San Fernando Valley and Hollywood cityhood committees.

Meanwhile, Chick had released an audit critical of Hahn's administration three weeks before the mayoral runoff—having endorsed Hahn's opponent Councilman Villaraigosa for mayor the month before. In October 2002, Hahn selected William J. Bratton, the former boss of the New York City Police Department, to head up the LAPD. Called the nation's top cop, Bratton's enigmatic relationship with then Mayor Rudolph W. Giuliani often caused tension and sometimes turned into an open rift. Sonenshein said that Bratton was "a big loudmouth and Giuliani wouldn't accept him." In Los Angeles, he said, "if you don't screw up you can be as big a loudmouth as you want. But the minute you screw up, you're out on your ear."

Villaraigosa was the first example of someone coming in having held a top spot in Sacramento and treating the City Council a bit more like the legislature. From the start of his mayoral career, he depended on his Inner Circle, all of whom were close friends and advisers and included, besides me, an electrical engineer, Jimmy Blackman, his chief of staff; Maria Elena Durazo, president of Unite/Hero Local 11; Martin Ludlow, councilman; Gloria Molina, supervisor; Fabian Nunez, speaker of the Assembly; Jesus Quinones, attorney with Geffner & Bush; and Cynthia Ruiz, a campaign volunteer. "Villaraigosa was a much better mayor than people think," said Sonenshein. He considers him the most politically skilled of the mayors, in some ways maybe more politically skilled than Bradley, because Bradley's skill was being Bradley. A gifted speaker with remarkable early success with the City Council, he got a hike in the trash collection fee to make good on his promise for 10,000 officers.

SUPPORT FOR MINORITY GROUPS

"The Olympics of 1984 was a culminating event for Los Angeles in terms of who we are," Bob Hertzberg recounted to me. The former speaker of the State Assembly and Majority Leader of the California Senate had described the city as unique, glued together almost like London with numerous communities coming together. But it was a package formed by natural beauty and Hollywood, an incredible place.

An attorney, and law partner with his father in Hertzberg & Hertzberg, he came from the San Fernando Valley where the secession movement was robust. And although he helped write the laws to allow the vote for secession, he never supported it. "It wasn't right," he said, "but the system was unfair. I did not support it because I did not think it got to the objective of making government better." At that time, the San Gabriel Valley had 131 elected officials while the San Fernando Valley had seven, he said. Services were 25 percent more. "There was historically a big issue about racism and segregation and stuff, and okay, this community says we're only going to be Jews, and this community says we're going to be Greeks, or whatever the case may be; but what's happened the last thirty or forty years has been a real evolution of law. You cannot do that stuff anymore."

I asked him to evaluate the mayors and appraise their roles in shaping the city. "Bradley," he said, "was the first time the city came together. The liberal Jews on the West side came together to support an African American candidate. Big city mayors got to love and breathe the city every day, and you got to embody that love to everyone, and they got to see it and feel it. Bradley did that. His early vision, although it was a little different for Bunker Hill, was a big deal." Bradley's vision was to turn Los Angeles into a world-class city and give it a skyline. The old law that prohibited buildings from being higher than City Hall was replaced with strong measures requiring buildings to be capable of surviving huge earthquakes. His vision became a reality. "The 1984 Olympics was a staggeringly big day for Los Angeles," Hertzberg continued. "It was on the globe; we were a shining moment. He was extremely important, a very big visionary who really helped put us on the map."

"Riordan was tough enough to turn LA around because he demonstrated sincerity in a very palpable way," he told me. "In his quirky way he really showed a deep concern and a deep commitment." The Richard and Jill Riordan Foundation bought a two-acre property for the Puente Learning Center for $2.1 million. The center, in Boyle Heights, offers a tutoring program for elementary school children as well as English as a Second Language classes for adults. "He also gave the Valley some comfort having felt disrespected by the Bradley administration," said Hertzberg.

"Hahn was a reluctant mayor," Hertzberg continued. "I never thought he was corrupt, or a bad guy, I think he cared, I think he was smarter than most people thought." His father (Supervisor Kenny Hahn) was a great public servant, he noted. It is almost like being in royalty when you're stuck with the king. It became problematic at a time where the world was growing and the challenges were greater, and Hahn was not thinking strategically or looking at the big picture. That is what motivated Hertzberg to run for mayor. Run he did, and came in third, narrowly missing the cutoff with Villaraigosa first and Hahn second, just 5,800 votes ahead of Hertzberg.

"I know Antonio Villaraigosa extremely well," he confided. "I give great credit to him for his energy and his willingness to do all that's necessary." But, he said, you cannot delegate to Austin Beutner. "Leadership is deeply personal as mayor. I do not buy this economic downturn stuff. We knew it was coming."

Beutner, recommended to Villaraigosa by Riordan and Eli Broad, one of the world's wealthiest people, was appointed in 2010 to be LA's first deputy mayor with oversight of twelve city agencies, including the Port of Los Angeles, Department of Water and Power, and the Housing Authority, with over 17,000 employees. He also served as general manager of DWP. A former investment banker, Beutner was once the publisher and chief executive of the *Los Angeles Times* but was dismissed in 2015 after only a year in that position. It was not a voluntary dismissal, he wrote on Facebook: "I am not departing by choice, nor is this some 'mutual agreement.'" Quick exits from top positions continued to afflict Beutner who also stepped down in April 2021, from superintendent for the Los Angeles Unified School District after three years on the job.

Earlier, in 2013, with Villaraigosa's term ending, Beutner unveiled a push to run for Los Angeles mayor but, a year later, he suspended his efforts and dropped from the race after polls showed him attracting a depressing 2 percent of likely voters. Said to be a quick study, gifted listener, and a skilled negotiator, Beutner did not escape internal criticism when he promoted himself as a City Hall outsider despite his overseeing of twelve city departments and was Villaraigosa's frontrunner on job creation. The *New York Times*' Adam Nagourney wrote on February 21, 2012, that Beutner "has been sharply critical of 'the barnyard called City Hall,' as he describes his former place of work." I personally overheard Beutner's dissing comments regarding Villaraigosa, dubbing the mayor "incompetent" and City Hall "in chaos" when Beutner was having breakfast with a lobbyist at the Pacific Dining Car. After only one year on the job at City Hall, he decided to run for mayor. I strongly believe from my own experience that you cannot change the system unless you know the system.

NEVER ON SATURDAY OR SUNDAY

Ira Reiner, former Los Angeles City Attorney and Los Angeles County District Attorney, decreed early in his career not to go politicking more than one night a week, and never on Saturday or Sunday. If absolutely compelled by fundraising obligations to go out twice in one week, he wouldn't go out at all the week following. Mayor Bradley, on the other hand, never spent an evening at home, unless it was for an event there. In fact, his schedule was filled out by his staff. Only his wife's birthday and their anniversary were off limits. It was known that Supervisor Ed Edelman never went out in the evenings or weekends. Reiner would not allow politics to become a prison for him, without a moment or a day with time off. But then again, Reiner did not get into politics by accident. Nor did he get into politics by intent. He was a bit of an activist trying to stop the planned Malibu freeway from going down the beach. It was suggested to him to run for City Attorney in 1973. "Sure, I'll run," he had said, and since he had no idea what he was doing got 3 percent of the vote, "what is about what I deserved," he acknowledged to me. However, his exposure got him an appointment to the Fire Commission. Then he was elected to the Los Angeles College Board of Trustees and won the 1977 election for city controller.

While city controller, he took a warrant, blew it up to the size of a tabletop, stamped it "Cancel," and told the City Council he would not sign this warrant that was to cover expenses for "first-cabin trips to Europe and Asia" taken by the Harbor Commission and council members. The more furor it caused the happier and more popular Reiner emerged. Four years later, with 60 percent of the votes, he became city attorney.

During breakfast with Reiner at the Pacific Dining Car in 1983, I shared a political county-wide poll showing him running strongly throughout the entire area. Although a county mayor position did not exist, if it did, I told him he could win. Reiner was exploring running for Supervisor—despite the fact he disliked the likely possibility of having to move. The poll influenced his decision. Although he placed ahead of everyone in their own supervisorial districts, except for Schabarum, running for District Attorney appeared an easier undertaking, like picking low-hanging fruit. He filed a few days before the deadline in 1983, beat incumbent Robert Philibosian and served in that post for eight years. In 1992, he withdrew from the race for his reelection against his chief deputy, Gil Garcetti, saying it would necessitate a negative campaign to win and he did not have the stomach for it. Once considered the silver-haired star of local politics with even a possible shot at governorship, his withdrawal from the race brought an end to Reiner's career.

SHRIVER AND THE KENNEDY MAGIC

Eunice Mary Kennedy Shriver's sister, Rosemary, was born with intellectual disabilities. An article written by Eunice in the *Saturday Evening Post* in 1962 is considered a seminal moment in changing public attitude toward people with intellectual disabilities. Their brother, President John F. Kennedy, often spoke openly about Rosemary's condition. Her disability was an inspiration for Eunice, who founded the Special Olympics, the world's largest sports organization for children and adults with intellectual disabilities and physical disabilities. Today, there is year-round training and sports activities for 5 million participants in 172 countries. The first Special Olympics Games were held in Chicago in 1968. Eunice's children held tightly to their mother's zeal for philanthropy and public service. Bobby Shriver, the eldest son, became an activist, attorney, and journalist. He served as a member of the Santa Monica City Council from 2004 to 2012, and was its mayor pro tem in 2006, and mayor during part of 2010.

In 2004, he visited the Veteran's Administration facility to find three completely empty buildings with asbestos in the ceiling and toilets upside down on the floor. A vet was sleeping outside in a dumpster. "I can fix this," Shriver said. "This is the biggest VA complex in America, 387 acres. Why weren't there any housing units built? There's not one housing unit for a woman vet." He started trying to solve the problem only to get increasingly frustrated. He said that despite his numerous tries he couldn't get a meeting with Congressman Henry Waxman. "He felt I was criticizing him. This was his district, and he was in Congress a long time. He was a powerful guy. The facts were, he hadn't built housing."

We resorted to filing a lawsuit to get the action moving. "This was the responsibility of our elected officials," he said, number one being Waxman, and then Senators Diane Feinstein and Barbara Boxer. "I don't know the reason, they wouldn't say." When Robert McDonald became the eighth United States Secretary of Veterans Affairs, the retired chairman and president of Procter & Gamble, Shriver flew to Washington to meet with him. He was a marketing expert and would understand what was being sought, to provide a service to people who are in dumpsters. "In three hours, we made a deal," he said. The terms of the deal were the first ever land use plan which included an entity to coordinate the therapeutic and health plans, and an entity to coordinate those activities which we were to form and finance, he added.

But to frustrate the issue, Zev Yaroslavsky said the deal was technically called "enhanced -use leases" and it appeared to be a move by President George W. Bush to privatize the land though this device. Shriver, who knew his way around the Bush White House, spoke to Bush and Josh Bolten, chief of staff, and Carl Rove, the deputy chief of staff, and he was told that was not the case, at all. "By getting everybody excited and saying, 'Bush is threatening us,' they got legislation which had the effect of preventing any housing from being built.

More specifically, legislation by Waxman and Feinstein prohibited an enhanced-use lease covering any land or improvement of the Veteran's Benefits and Services Act of 1988, or the Military Construction and Veterans Affairs Act of 2008, unless specifically authorized by law. Research I conducted revealed that, while the VA has hundreds, if not thousands, of housing projects, the Waxman-backed law affected only one project, the West LA campus. Much later, Senator Feinstein saw she was wrong and got the legislation repealed, said Shriver. Regarding Waxman, Shriver told me, "He's running for cover. He doesn't have the courage to come in and say, 'you know what, I'm sorry about that. You were right, I was wrong, and good for you that you persisted.'"

Congressmen Ted W. Lieu and Jeff Miller co-authored legislation H.R. 5936, the Los Angeles Homeless Veterans Leasing Act of 2016 that authorizes the VA Secretary to enter into leases at the West Los Angeles VA to provide for permanent supportive housing for veterans. Congressman Lieu had started working on this issue in April 2007.

GEORGE TAKEI—ACTIVIST AND CRITICAL PLAYER

George Takei, the admired "Mr. Sulu" in the original *Star Trek* series, and political activist, was appointed by Mayor Bradley to the board of directors of the Southern California Rapid Transit District. He served from 1973–1984 and became a critical figure on my team to initiate and plan the Los Angeles subway system. In 1978, he was called away from the set of *Star Trek: The Motion Picture*. to deliver the tie-breaking vote for the creation of the subway system in Los Angeles. When offered an opportunity to appear in a *Simpsons* episode titled, "Marge vs the Monorail," Takei turned it down because he was a strong supporter of public transportation. The role was instead offered to Leonard Nimoy, who accepted it. Takei related to me that during his RTD years he was closeted.

When Gov. Arnold Schwarzenegger vetoed the Marriage Equality Bill, Takei concluded that he had lived his entire adult life with his guard up, not only as an actor but in public service. "It's very uncomfortable, sometimes they are making gay jokes and you had to bite your tongue in an environment like this." He was sixty-eight then. So, he spoke to the press and lambasted the governor. Earlier, Schwarzenegger had asked him in the elevator what contributed to the renaissance of his career. Takei said, "It was coming out. I got cast in more guest shots on TV."

He spoke often of the regrettable internment of Japanese Americans. Takei's father would tell him that democracy is dependent on people who cherish ideals because great men are also fallible human beings and they can make mistakes, so everyone must be engaged in the process to keep that sort of thing from reoccurring. "I hear echoes of it today," he sighed.

Takei referenced what occurred on February 19, 1942—almost two and one-half months after Pearl Harbor. President Franklin D. Roosevelt signed Executive Order 9066, clearing the way for the incarceration of nearly 120,000 Japanese Americans during the war. By March, the first wave of evacuees arrived at the Manzanar War Relocation Center in the California desert and moved into tarpaper barracks for the next three years. Today, that order lives in infamy. It wasn't until 1988 that the Congress passed the Civil Liberties Act which stated that a "grave injustice" had been done to Japanese American citizens and resident aliens during the war and established a fund that paid some $1.6 billion in reparations to formerly interned Japanese Americans or their heirs.

AN ETHICS ROADMAP

The Greek philosopher Aristotle said it a long time ago: "All persons ought to endeavor to follow what is right, and not what is established."

Observing the uplifted Los Angeles skyline and cherishing its globally established icon, Bradley yearned for excellence within—he envisioned a guide outlining the standards of ethics and integrity for his beloved city. To accomplish this, he appointed Geoffrey Cowan in 1989 to chair a seven-member ethics commission. Cowan was notably suited for the assignment. The son of the former president of the CBS television network and professor at the Columbia School of Journalism, after graduating from law school he moved to Washington, DC, where he co-founded the first public interest law firm in the United States, the Center for Law and Social Policy. The Cowan Commission was a select, independent group that included Rabbi Allen I. Freehling, senior rabbi at the University Synagogue; Antonia Hernandez, president and general counsel of the Mexican American Legal Defense and Education Fund; Archbishop Roger Mahony of Los Angeles; Margaret M. Morrow, past president of the Los Angeles Bar Association; Gilbert T. Ray, a prominent lawyer; and Delbert E. Wong, a retired Superior Court judge. Together they set out to establish a new age of decorum for local government. "We decided not to take any city money," Cowan told me. "And we decided we would be independent of Tom Bradley. We would write our own charter."

After establishing a set of principles, the panel held hearings throughout the city. "Ultimately, the commission wrote a lot of the new finance law as well as an ethics law that wasn't just a code. It was something forceful," Cowan added. When a final draft was adopted, the *Los Angeles Times* immediately hailed it. In an editorial on November 27, 1989, it said: "The council now should set aside the dithering of its own ad hoc ethics committee and enact this package as the commission has recommended. If the council fails to do so or attempts to weaken these proposals, the *Times* will vigorously support a campaign to write them into law through the initiative process." Cowan clarified that his commission had two proposals, one for ethics and campaign finance law, very strong, and a separate proposition stating that City Council people should be paid better, that their job was full-time, and they shouldn't be able to have a second job. "We felt the pay raise concept should require a separate vote," however, he added, they had to tie the ethics code to the pay raise proposal for the City Council to place it on the ballot. In June 1990, the Cowan commission's proposals were adopted through a public referendum, giving Los Angeles the most comprehensive ethics package of any city in the nation.

Among other things, the code required all elected officials, high-ranking civil servants, including candidates for office, to disclose investments, as well as their homes, and list the names of their stockbrokers. Outside earned income and honorariums were banned, and tough controls were placed on lobbying by former government employees. For this effort Cowan was named "Man of the Year" in 1989 by the Council of Government Ethics Leaders. Later, President Clinton appointed Cowan to serve the nation as the director of Voice of America, the international broadcasting service of the US Information Agency. He served as its 22nd director. His father, Louis Cowan, had been the 2nd director of VOA from 1943 to 1945. Cowan has served as a professor at the University of Southern California, where he holds the Annenberg Family Chair in Communication Leadership and directs the Annenberg School's Center on Communication Leadership & Policy.

Nate Holden swirled around the political circuit a few times. He had been working as a deputy for Supervisor Kenny Hahn when the 30th District Senate seat opened in 1974. The Black Caucus, he told me, "came out against me." He played dumb. "My mother said, 'you stop talking so much about you're gonna win,' so I kept my mouth shut." Everyone ganged up against me. "Oh, Nate, he just runs, runs, runs. He's never gonna win." But he did, only to give up his office after four years to campaign for a Congressional seat ultimately won by Julian C. Dixon. Holden ran for office many times: in 1987 he was elected to the 10th district seat on the City Council. Two years later, in 1989, he unsuccessfully challenged Bradley for mayor, but remained on the City Council until 2002. When he left the senate in 1978, Holden went back to his deputy position with Hahn, who later appointed him to the board of the Southern California Rapid Transit District where he served from 1983 to 1987. It was a period of concentrated endeavors to obtain federal funding for a metro rail system in Los Angeles. Holden repeatedly reasoned that "the federal government was not putting any money anywhere to dig a hole unless the local government imposed a tax on themselves."

He used as an example the San Francisco Bay Area Rapid Transit District, which connects the San Francisco Peninsula with communities in the east and south bay. It was formed in 1957 and opened for service in 1972. He said funding for it was a 90/10 scheme, with 90 percent coming from the feds and the 10 percent from a locally imposed property tax.

Having worked closely with Holden when I was president of the Southern California Rapid Transit District, Holden reiterated his work in various capacities. He told of a meeting between Hahn and Bradley discussing a possible system through Burbank-Glendale and digging of a tunnel going to the Valley. They aren't going to build anything," he thought. Except for study funds, the feds did not give money for the plans; they wanted local financial commitments. Over time, I observed another side of Holden. He would switch votes in a second without prior warning.

Holden worked for the passage of Proposition A, which subsidized a fifty-cent bus fare in the 1980s, thus creating the county's first sales tax to assist in transportation projects. Although the vote was close, a two-thirds majority was not attained, and the issue ended up in court. The ruling validated the proposition, stating that two-thirds is only required for property taxes and not a sales tax. Described as being gruff and rough with a big heart by former council president John Ferraro, his standing with Mayor Bradley was constantly fading and in 1990 he was removed from the Los Angeles County Transportation Commission because of a poor attendance record and a contentious style. Richard Alatorre replaced him.

THE ART OF POLITICS

"Politics is never a science, it's always an art." That's what Stuart Spencer told me at his home in Indian Wells, California. More so, it's a modern art of campaigning that he formed and used in both Ronald Reagan's gubernatorial campaigns, and presidential runs. Spencer was rightfully called "Reagan's political guru." During the campaign in the early 1980s to secure federal funding for Los Angeles's Metro Rail, I worked closely with Spencer and Mickey Kantor, later the US Secretary of Commerce, who were lobbying Republican and Democrat legislators in Washington, DC. When the funding issue stalled, Spencer arranged meetings for some Los Angeles officials and me with Reagan's most prominent staff: David Stockman, director of the office of management and budget, and Edwin Meese, counselor to the president and later US Attorney General. Meese, along with James Baker, later the Secretary of State, and top aide Michael Deaver, became Reagan's core leaders in the White House, and came to be known as the "Troika Meese." Spencer's start in politics—conducting an outreach program—was in the barrio, which he described as "eight square miles and called East Los Angeles." Then, he added, the people there were all Mexican Americans. "Today there are many Guatemalans and Hondurans, and so forth. Still, 90 percent are of Mexican extraction."

Raised in Alhambra, he joined the navy at eighteen in 1945 and afterwards graduated from East Los Angeles Junior College with an AA, and from California State University, Los Angeles, with a BA degree in Sociology in 1951. Ten years later, with his friend Bill Roberts, they established Spencer-Roberts & Associates, Inc., being among the first professional campaign managers in the state. A year later, he managed Sen. Tom Kuchel's campaign for United States Senate, and then he managed Nelson Rockefeller's presidential campaign in 1964.

It was the Nixon-Kennedy debate that opened his eyes to the power of television in political campaigns. He listened to the debate on radio and thought Nixon had won. But those who saw it on television considered Kennedy the winner. Body language and looks were the determining factor. He called Reagan "natural" because of his actor's experience, and far superior as a candidate in terms of his ability to communicate.

Spencer believed that California would have a Mexican American governor "in the next twenty years," and "will be run by Mexican Americans over the next decade. It is their state." While it is a plus for the Democratic Party, it will become a problem, he added, because they will be taken for granted. "If the Republican Party ever gets any smarts there will be a lot of openings for the two-party system to get into the community, and it will, it will." Since Spencer was very close to Reagan, I asked him if the president loved Los Angeles. "Yeah, I'd say, better to say he had love for Southern California. He was from California. He liked the horses, he liked riding, liked the rancho style, the weather. He was sort of a macho guy."

CONTROLLING THE AGENDA

Panic swept over Los Angeles and local governments throughout the state with voter approval of Proposition 13 in 1978. A limit was placed on the tax rate for properties, and they would no longer receive their share of property tax money. Alarmed by this economic restrain local lawmakers scrambled to Sacramento in search of assistance, and the state responded by furnishing bailout money. Los Angeles scored well. Fourteen years later, with California facing a huge budget deficit, Willie Brown, then Speaker of the Assembly, backed a proposal to limit the bailout. His tone was bleak. The bailout should never have existed, he said, local government became addicted to it. “They became like heroin addicts. You have to keep feeding them,” he told the *Los Angeles Times*.

Marcus Allen, who served in critical public policy and management roles over the last thirty years, including as deputy chief of staff in charge of operations and finance for Mayor Villaraigosa, related to me that about one-third of the city’s tax rate during that period was at risk of being raided by the state. Immediately, a political task force was organized and led by Ron Deaton, the city’s chief legislative analyst and once head of the Department of Water and Power. Assemblyman Richard Katz, Senator David Roberti, and then City Councilman Zev Yaroslavsky were all present and became engaged in two years of intricate deliberations. To his great advantage, Deaton knew computers, spreadsheets, and analyses to drive deals, recalled Allen, then a young analyst. Allen was dispatched by Deaton to the state Franchise Tax Board to collect all the property tax data of California cities. “He flew me up to Sacramento and I got all the tax data, which I put on a spreadsheet and on a laptop. We were the only ones with data on every city.” Whenever the governor’s office or Speaker would discuss possible formulas, Deaton and he would run the numbers and print a spreadsheet.

At one point Willie Brown turned to Allen and asked him what he was working from. When told, the Speaker wanted a copy, then expressed doubt over the accuracy of the information, suggesting that the data was skewed. He placed his top analyst and Allen in a room to compare data and notes. When his analyst concluded the data was correct, “we controlled the discussion,” a gratified Allen realized. According to Allen, Deaton always devised opportunities to drive points home. Trying to get better numbers and avoid large cuts, he would call Yaroslavsky to Sacramento and have him walk the Assembly and Senate floors, then hold a press conference to push opponents into corners. Political savvy on deal making in Sacramento is essential if one wants to survive thorny negotiations. Deaton figured the deal was going to be made at one or two in the morning and at last-minute agreements in the hallways. At one point Los Angeles was facing losing $300 million with the shifting of property taxes. The counties lobbied Sacramento, thought the deal was cut, and went home. “We stayed,” said Allen, “and two days later the deal was made.” He explained that while they got their property taxes shifted, Deaton got a rider, a bill that allowed Los Angeles to take money off the port, thus receiving $57 million in lieu of getting property taxes. The counties lost; the city won. “Technology and lobbying skills won the day,” Allen concluded.

A few years later, Allen became a budget analyst for Yaroslavsky, former county supervisor. “For his first county budget,” Allen said, “Zev was not really engaged. Barbara, his wife, was running for his former City Council seat and Zev was learning the county operations.” So, Allen was driving the budget, meeting with county bureaucrats and handling issues of budgetary interest. Then the LA County and USC medical center turned into a hostile swordspoint struggle between Zev and Gloria Molina. The real issue: how many beds were being placed at the medical center. Gloria’s number, according to Zev, would bankrupt the county.

At three consecutive press conferences, Yaroslavsky kept repeating the same phrase, that a hospital this size will potentially make the county insolvent. Later he told me, “I’m not just pitching details, I’m trying to write headlines.” True enough, that was the next day’s headline. Kevin Acebo, veteran campaign manager for Yaroslavsky, pulled Allen aside at the

Hall of Administration and said: “Look, we’re going to run this place. We’re going to own it. Remember, it’s a five-member board and it takes three votes to do anything, and four votes for big issues.” The plan was to pick up Yvonne Braithwaite Burke’s vote by going through her people, for social issues. For fiscal matters, they would work with Deane Dana’s chief of staff Don Knabe, to get a vote. On the hospital issue, it was all upside down, no one knew where people stood.

When Villaraigosa became mayor on July 1, 2005, he tapped a group of City Hall veterans to build a better Los Angeles, including Allen to tackle a difficult budget forecast. I asked Allen about the mayor’s legacy. “Public safety,” Allen responded. I suggested that his legacy will also be the half-cent sales tax increase passed in 2008 (Measure R) to fund critical transportation projects over the next thirty years.

NARROW INTERESTS TO BROADER INTERESTS

Having known Mickey Kantor, I was interested in his perspective.

Kantor reminisced with me how Bradley transformed power, shifting it away from a few powerful downtown individuals with narrow interests to all city factions with broader interests. “It was a terrific change from where LA used to be,” he said. Although the weak-mayor concept was preset, Bradley exercised power just by assuming it. “Instead of having the City Council run the mayor, he led the council.” Kantor added, “the council needed to be directed just like any other legislative body.” Kantor, whose focus has been on corporate and financial international transactions and has served as US Commerce Secretary, also worked closely with me and other Los Angeles leaders over many years on building a subway system.

It was an explosion in the Ross Dress for Less department store in the Fairfax District that alarmed residents on March 24, 1985, and unsettled Congressman Henry Waxman, as did the pressure he received from residents who confessed fear the system might transport unwanted minorities into their area. A pocket of high pressure and highly concentrated methane gas below the surface forced its way into the department store, resulting in the blast. The congressman intensified his vocal criticism of the 18.6-mile rapid transit system and persuaded House colleagues to back a construction ban until local transit officials could prove that it would not trigger underground gas explosions. “Waxman was adamant about stopping the subway. It was a tragedy because day after day, week after week traffic got worse, business was adversely affected, as were people’s lives,” Kantor stated. Despite numerous engineering studies proving that no danger existed, and that the situation could be safely controlled just as it was done in many other cities around the globe, Waxman remained obstinate. In 2005, he finally reversed course and authored legislation to repeal the ban,

Kantor believed Los Angeles is not a failing city, but a growing city, the tax base is not decreasing but increasing and the desire for people to settle here continues to ascend. Having been a member of the Christopher Commission, which was formed in April 1991, four months after the Rodney King beating, he judged then Los Angeles Police Chief Charlie Beck (2009–2018) to be impressive, having established a quality connection between his department and the police. Discussing the school district, Kantor said he considers the school district to be "unbalanced in the sense that teachers' unions have too much power—and I'm a supporter of unions." The kids must come first, he continued, and teacher evaluations should be taken seriously, disliking the concept of "last hired, first fired."

"Los Angeles is a mature city, we're not hemmed in by land or by vision and its potential is unlimited, it is still the great meritocracy that Bradley focused on." He continued, "Nick, take yourself as an example of meritocracy. You came here young, knew no one, were not pushed aside but allowed to participate, and got successful and involved deeply in civic life." Kantor said, "President Clinton loves LA and used to come here all the time, loved the idea how open the city was and the idea of possibilities it presented. It wasn't the same in Arkansas, you didn't have the same resources or people, or openness." It was Clinton who appointed Kantor to be the US Trade Representative.

On December 15, 1993, in Geneva, Switzerland, he spearheaded negotiations that created the World Trade Organization, the Uruguay Round, and North American Free Trade Agreement (NAFTA). Called the most comprehensive trade agreement in history, the Uruguay Round was adopted by negotiators from 117 countries prescribing, among other things, that tariffs on industrial products be reduced by an average of more than one-third and that trade in agricultural goods be progressively liberalized.

"The core of Los Angeles is downtown, it's where you go to from all sides." Bruce Karatz, businessman and philanthropist stressed when he spoke with me—years before the greater extension of the Los Angeles Metro Rail to its current two subway lines and five light rails. Karatz moved from house counsel to chairman and chief executive officer of KB Home and became known for his efforts to rebuild Los Angeles after the 1992 riots, as well as New Orleans after the devastation of Hurricane Katrina. "You had tremendous influence on transportation," he told me, "which is the key element to making LA a more livable and prosperous city." He explained that he spent most of his life on the Westside and didn't go downtown. When he lived in France the Train à Grande Vitesse (TGV) high-speed train was constructed, and it resulted in high industrial development giving life to communities that were dormant. On his return from France, at dinner with then Councilman Yaroslavsky, he asked, "Why don't we make a tunnel underneath Westwood so through traffic can miss Westwood and avoid creating traffic jams?" It was only half a mile. "Don't have the money," was Yaroslavsky response. "What do you mean?" he insisted. "How did they get the money in France? There are ways. Transportation requires investment, and we get it back multiple."

He believes that Los Angeles has become a better place, more diverse. He likes the ethnic neighborhoods and people have gotten used to them. "You can live in Bel Air and drive to Monterey Park for dim sum, or go from Pasadena to Chinatown, or for Korean barbecue on Olympic and Western. In New York you go to Little Italy for Italian food, or you go to Astoria for Greek food. LA people didn't like that, now we talk like that." Restaurants and stores give the city vitality, making it a more exciting place, he added. Working with Mayor Riordan in the early 1990s, Karatz cochaired the Mayor's Alliance for a Safer Los Angeles, raising over $16 million to pay for 1,700 computer workstations and other related technology at police precincts.

RIORDAN'S FRIEND AND STRATEGIST

Bill Wardlaw, influential political insider and often referred to as "Mayor Riordan's best friend," told me that Riordan got interested in the city because of Tom Bradley. "He put him on the Recreation and Parks Commission, in so many ways tutored him, and gave him civic lessons in Los Angeles." Wardlaw, a wealthy corporate lawyer and shrewd political campaigner, had initially convinced Riordan to run for mayor, then guided him to victory.

Riordan's fundamental commitment was to make the city a better place, Wardlaw said. "Some people did not agree with Riordan's vision, but he really did it for the right reasons. He wasn't a career politician." When I asked Wardlaw to compare the style and personality of LA mayors, he said, "Bradley was extraordinarily important for this town and in the first several terms of his administration great change took place." Wardlaw referred to a coalition organized by Bradley which effectively moved the city forward and made progress in transportation, building downtown, and improving life in the area.

"Near the last part of his administration times changed, the economic conditions turned on him," Wardlaw said. Problems between the mayor's office and the police department, the riots, all set the stage for a different mayor. That's where Riordan, an outsider, strode in. "People didn't think a Republican businessman could ever be mayor of this town, but the atmospherics of that time, the pressures, made it possible," he said. "What he wanted to do was make the community better, it was his fundamental commitment and orientation." After twenty years of the same administration Riordan brought a different group of people into play, thereby creating a renewal of energy, explained Wardlaw. "They might have been disproportionately business oriented but that pushed City Hall to change for the better."

Hahn, who followed Riordan's mayoralty, was called "a transitional figure" by Wardlaw. He voiced respect for some Hahn choices, such as his "courageous decision on the police chief" that cost him politically—when Chief Bernard Parks' second term was not renewed, and former New York Police Commissioner Bill Bratton was brought in. Wardlaw told me that Hahn surrounded himself with a very mediocre staff that was not very effective, leading to decisions that were politically hurtful.

For his 2001 election, Hahn had accumulated more resources than his opponents, leading Wardlaw—now Hahn's campaign chairman—to state that no one will be able to catch the then city attorney. "No one will have the resources that we have." Wardlaw's move to Hahn fueled the long-standing feud with another mayoral candidate, Steve Soboroff, and a break with Riordan. A real estate executive and chairman of the Harbor Commission, Soboroff had spearheaded the Alameda Corridor project for Riordan and had received his endorsement. In the primary election he placed third behind Hahn and Villaraigosa.

Regarding Villaraigosa, who defeated Hahn four years later, Wardlaw said he was symbolically an extraordinarily important mayor, Latino, very articulate, handsome, who brought hope. "Over time the economy turned against him, making it difficult to accomplish what he wanted. He wasn't equipped to deal with the downside. Like Hahn," Wardlaw added, "his staff may not have been as effective in some places, but he brought new people into the process with energy, for a while. He attracted volunteers and tapped great talent that made his administration go forward. I recalled being on the Villaraigosa transition team and the excitement of that period, a myriad of people expressing strong interest to be a part of the administration."

Wardlaw said that people who knew Riordan thought he could never be mayor because he lacked discipline and had a short attention span. He was unusually smart and a multitasker—something that drove people crazy. He thought he could handle two things simultaneously. "Engaged in a conversation, he'd be fiddling with a piece of paper all the time and you'd be sitting there wanting to strangle him."If Riordan had a weakness, it was his frustration with the political process which required excessive time to resolve simple things. "If it was the right thing, everyone should get on board. How could anybody think differently? Possibly he deemed his position analogous to chairman in the private sector. There he would say: 'do it this way,' and it was done. As mayor he would get very frustrated and show it with what some perceived to be disdain," Wardlaw noted. "If it was so simple and you didn't get it, there's only one explanation, you're a fool," He may not have said it in those words, but it was very clear what the meaning was.

ANOTHER VOICE FOR LATINOS

City Councilman Mike Hernandez, when he joined the Council, told Mayor Bradley that he was frustrated trying to understand the Community Redevelopment Agency budget. "Well, let's look at it," Bradley responded. They did and agreed that five years of income was being spent in two years—they were overspending. Hernandez said it became apparent to him not to rubber-stamp budgets but to question them until he gained full comprehension. "I saw Bradley as someone who was willing to do work. I couldn't do that with Riordan," he said. But he did have a good relationship with Riordan on economic development projects like the Staples Center. "They needed me to be the lead."

Hernandez explained to me the first thing he learned as councilman was that real power at City Hall does not rest with the council, nor the mayor, but with the Chief Legislative Analyst (CLA). "When I wanted to get a message across, and people weren't paying attention to me, I would ask the CLA to draft a motion knowing that Council President Ferraro and members would study it." As a paradigm, he articulated councilmember Jan Perry's aggravation in 2001 when she needed money for a project. Hernandez advised her to take a certain percentage of the parking meter money from downtown. Ron Deaton, then CLA, wouldn't allow that, she countered. Hernandez's solution was clever. "Yes, you're going to find out that Ron will not let you do what you want to do, but he's going to find you your money." Hernandez's ten-year period of service, 1991–2001, was notable for its explosive start. A five-month hiatus existed between Molina's election to Supervisor and his election to her City Council seat, during which time the Los Angeles County Transportation Commission chose to put a maintenance facility for Metrolink at Taylor Yard. It had become a rail yard in the 1920s and was being prepared for similar work by the county. "The community did not want it to basically continue to be a railroad maintenance yard, and we started to question what was going on," Hernandez said. With Hahn the city attorney, they threatened to sue the County Transportation Commission since no Environmental Impact Report (EIR) was prepared. After protracted dialogues, a settlement was reached that included the future construction of a pedestrian and bicycle bridge, and a Transportation Opportunity Grant Program at Franklin High School to train students in the field of transportation. Hernandez said the stakeholders were also brought together and agreed to fund a feasibility study on the Taylor Yard.

It was then that he met Phil Anschutz, a very rich man and active philanthropist, who along with billionaire Ed Roski Jr., was looking for land to build a basketball stadium. Both had financial interests in sports—Anschutz had just bought the LA Kings. While many sites were evaluated, Steve Soboroff concluded that a stadium by the Convention Center would be best. Hernandez was appointed by council president Ferraro to chair the ad hoc committee on the Staples Center. Alatorre, Hal Bernson, Ferraro, and Rita Walters, a Staples opponent, were on the committee. "Rita lost all votes four to one," Hernandez remembered. The project was finally supported by the full City Council in October 1997. Jerry Buss, owner of the Lakers, agreed to bring his team downtown. Soboroff also persuaded the Los Angeles Clippers to come to Staples.

Hernandez recounted the riots following the Rodney King verdict on April 29, 1992. "I came out to defend the Latino community," he told me. "I'm at City Hall and the reporters are covering the looters. A kid comes out of an appliance store carrying a television. The reporter says, 'Look at the looters, they look like immigrants.' I freaked out. ...It doesn't matter what this guy's status is in this country, he's a looter." Saying that, Hernandez appeared on every station denouncing the media and explaining that riots are the result of social injustice that the division existed, and the city wasn't recognizing it. "Meanwhile," he added, "the Council was saying, 'what makes you think that's going to stop these riots? This is going to go on for months, forever.'" His response was intentional. "What makes you think we're going to have a city at the end of the month?"

FIRST ASIAN AMERICAN AT CITY HALL

There are over one half million people of Chinese extraction in the greater Los Angeles area today, representing about 4 percent of the population. Arrival in the city began in 1850. The community grew and prospered and like all minority groups sought political representation. In 1981, Michael Woo, the thirty-year-old staffer to Sen. Roberti, decided the time was now and energetically jumped into a race for the Los Angeles City Council. His opponent was Greek-American Peggy Stevenson, who held the seat from 1975 following her husband's death, Councilman Robert Stevenson (1969–1975). She won reelection following an aggressive and demanding struggle. However, in 1985 a notoriously expensive campaign followed and Woo unseated Stevenson.

The *Los Angeles Times* wrote, the day after the election: "Elected in a near landslide Tuesday, Michael Woo, the grandson of a Chinese laundryman, became the first Asian member of the Los Angeles City Council by tapping several traditional sources of political power:

family wealth, ethnic pride, younger voters, and a festering discontent with an incumbent officeholder."

Woo's father, Wilbur, left the family's ancestral village of Kaiping, China, in 1940 to study at UCLA, and was forced to stay in the United States during World War II, while his wife Beth remained in China under Japanese occupation. A retired banker and merchant, Wilbur had contributed almost one-half million dollars to his son's campaign.

After eight years in office, Woo left his council seat in 1993 to run for mayor against Richard Riordan and lost 54 to 46 percent. When I asked him what he would have done differently in the race for mayor, he said: "I would not have run against a multimillionaire, if I did not have a candidate with unlimited funding, I think I would have won." He pondered that it would have been very hard for a non-white candidate to run the year after the 1992 riots, although he did amazingly well with black voters and fairly well with Latino voters. "Surprisingly, I did less well with Asian voters," he said, and his Achilles heel was he did not receive much support from white voters. "A lot of Bradley supporters were backing me, but I think a lot of voters, especially white voters, wanted change. It was hard for me on one hand to appear to be a kind of unofficial heir to the Bradley coalition when many white voters were wary about the role of minorities in the city," he added. "So, even though I wasn't Black or Latino, I was widely perceived as being identified with them and it was hard to win a majority of white votes in that situation. There weren't enough minority votes to pull it off." Bradley had not endorsed him in that campaign. The perception of Woo's strategists was the mayor's reputation had been damaged at that time and an endorsement would have hurt him. However, Woo spoke to me highly of Bradley's influence on Los Angeles, on internationalizing the local economy, taking on of major projects such as the 1984 Olympics, starting rail transportation, building downtown, and positively impacting race relations after the Watts riots. Bradley transformed the city and mayors who followed had the benefit of working with the base he established, he said. But they didn't have the same impact.

When he was preparing his run for mayor, Woo identified the nation's best city fathers, and why they were successful. He concluded it came down to how the mayor made choices, how priorities were identified, where time was spent, and what important things had to be done. Sometimes mayors become obsessed with long-term projects rather than low-cost temporary projects that can be made permanent if they work. "Given the institutional limits on the mayor, there are ways in which he can transcend them partially by force of personality, partially just by being strategic by where to speak out, when to speak out, and by a choice of issues," he said. As an example, he again pointed to Bradley.

"I think the mayor who pursues a strategy of costly big ideas and short-term temporary projects would make a difference." His example of a big idea was to have a World's Fair, or World Expo, out in Palmdale or Lancaster, and taking it to the development of an international airport with a rail connection to the rest of the city. "I never talked about it," he said, "he was persuaded by his staff not to, for fear it would terrify the voters." When I asked him to look ahead for Los Angeles, a decade or two, he replied: "The combination of the historic role of a city as a source of new ideas, and its historic role as a marketplace, can be a real strength and can have implications for the arts, for architecture and the economy." With the likelihood that people with money from China are looking for places to invest, he said that Southern California and Los Angeles could be a big beneficiary of all of that.

KOREATOWN

The Korean community in Los Angeles was also enlarged with the elimination of Asian immigration exclusion laws in 1965. A decade later an ethnic neighborhood grew and matured in the vicinity of Olympic Boulevard and 8th Street, with most businesses coming under Korean ownership. The economic decline of that period in the trendy mid-Wilshire area resulted in vacant office spaces and inexpensive housing. Once the hub of Hollywood's renaissance with the Coconut Grove, Brown Derby, and the Ambassador Hotel, it was transformed into an energetic Koreatown with an abundant cultural mixture.

Korea-born Chris Pak, an architect with a degree from Cal Poly Pomona, has lived in Los Angeles with his parents since 1970. Seeking to nurture relationships, meet people, and move up professionally, he became active in the Korean American Coalition in 1983. A topic before the coalition was the proposed downsizing of the Koreatown area. Pak became aware of how city planners used floor area ratios (FAR) to impose growth limits in a community. With the Santa Monica Freeway (I-10) already jammed, people were using Olympic Boulevard to travel west. Planners deemed that by controlling growth, traffic flow could also be controlled. By controlling growth in Koreatown, the local community would suffer to benefit another community.

Following copious conferences and discussions, the plan—known as the Wilshire Community Plan—was to be reorganized to accurately synthesize the prevailing visions and objectives of the area's residents and property owners. As Pak related to me, Korean immigrants came to America because they didn't like politics in Korea. "Upward mobility was based on who you knew and who your contacts were, not about your ability." That stigma remained among many who arrived, and they generally avoided politics. But Pak's parents encouraged him to get involved, and he began by getting Korean Americans registered to vote.

He also met Councilman Nate Holden and attended a fund-raising event. "Nate sometimes didn't talk about issues at all. He would say, 'if you're my friend, you're my friend. I'm going to help you, no questions asked.'" Later, Holden said to him that instead of attending fund-raisers he should hold one. "So that's how I got my start," he said. He recalled it was 1993 and mayoral elections were approaching. He named some of the candidates: Patsaouras, Richard Riordan, Joel Wachs, Michael Woo, Nate Holden, Tom Houston, Julian Nava, and Richard Katz. "Being Asian American, I helped Michael Woo," he said.

Riordan won the election. By coincidence, current Congresswoman Michelle Steel Park's husband, Shawn Steel, a staunch Republican and supporter of Riordan, asked for Pak's resume to submit to Riordan's office, since he had expressed an interest in creating diversity in city commissions. Surprisingly, he got a call informing him of his appointment to the Metropolitan Water District to be one of fifty-one commissioners—the first ever Asian American.

"There were people on the board longer than I was alive, so when you talk about water-buffalo, that was the agency," he said. But the experience taught him to meld politics into his network. "It isn't because you sit on commissions that you get jobs," he said, "it's because of people you meet in those positions, and people you nurture. It's never about a one-time deal, it's about longevity, consistency, and reputation."

In 1992, he was appointed to the Board of Zoning Appeals—to the seat I had vacated. After Charter reform, Riordan appointed him to the commission of the Department of Neighborhood Empowerment. After a year he served on the Airport Commission. From there, with Hahn being mayor, he ended up at the Recreation and Parks Commission. "I served on five different commissions in the City of LA from the first time I started getting involved in politics and civic service," he proudly told me. He looked at those commission positions as a representative of the Korean American community. "A lot of people got to know the Korean community through what I do and what I say and my actions," he added.

Pak was bullish on Korean entrepreneurs, like Dr. David Lee who bought buildings vacated by insurance companies and law firms moving to Century City. "I think he is now the largest commercial office building landlord in Southern California." In addition, according to Pak, he would allow Korean American professionals to get into space on Wilshire Boulevard, at a relatively good price. Wilshire was quickly dominated by Korean American businesses. The week-long riots of 1992 were a rude awakening for Korean business owners who sustained about one-half billion dollars in damages, the result of long-festering cultural quarrels with African American customers. "The diversity of Los Angeles is also some of its weakness," Pak said, "because in some ways it is too segregated. We have different communities in different pockets." Koreatown became a concentrated area allowing living, working, and playing—maybe the only area in Los Angeles with that density zoned for residential, business, commercial, and retail functions. Its prized location is fifteen minutes from downtown, fifteen minutes from Hollywood, and fifteen minutes from Beverly Hills. Furthermore, the new generation that moved out of the area to the suburbs with their affluent parents are returning, thereby reenergizing the community.

ARMENIAN COMMUNITY IN LOS ANGELES

Los Angeles today has the biggest Armenian population outside of Armenia. It was no easy feat. American xenophobia was politically expressed through the 1924 Immigration Act adopted by the House of Representatives, limiting immigration through a national origins quota system. Using the 1890 national census as a base, it provided immigration visas to 2 percent from each nationality—thereby limiting entrance to people from eastern and southern Europe. But Armenians were compelled to resettle for one appalling reason—they were victims of ethnic cleansing by the Ottomans. Through systematic extermination more than 1.5 million Armenians were killed beginning in 1915. Those who could escape Turkey rushed to Egypt, Syria, Lebanon, Iran, and the Soviet Union—only to embark on another journey, this time to America. President Joseph Biden, on April 24, 2021, formally recognized those

Armenian Genocide Martyrs Monument, Montebello,California. Photo: Benoit Prieur

killings in Turkey as being acts of genocide.

Jack Messerlian, former mayor pro tem of Torrance and former Armenian National Committee chairmen, reminisced with me that his uncles arrived in 1922, just before immigration was stopped with the 1924 law. The next major wave took place in the 1970s by students who later married and were joined by their families. The 1975 civil war in Lebanon and the fall of the Shah in Iran created a newer surge, swelling the Armenian community in Los Angeles to over 300,000. The numbers grew even more with the collapse of the Soviet Union. "Unlike the early immigrants," said Messerlian, the newcomers arrived with education and money." Armenians may have left Turkey behind, but the horrors of the atrocities they suffered could not be forgotten. "Every Armenian American living today is touched by the genocide," said Messerlian. "If it was not your parents, it was your grandparents, or great-grandparents. To the credit of the community this has been kept alive because a crime has been committed and has gone unpunished." There is a responsibility not to forgive and forget, he maintained. "Eventually, someday, if Turkey comes to terms with its past, maybe some of us will forgive, but to forget, it's difficult." He likened the genocide to the Jewish holocaust.

I mentioned the Republic of Cyprus, divided since Turkey's shameful invasion in 1974, and noted that when I was Southern California finance chair for Vice President Walter Mondale in 1984, I questioned the presidential candidate on the Cyprus issue, only to be told to my surprise that "foreign policy is handled by the State Department." Messerlian was proud of the work performed by the Armenian National Committee of America (ANCA) the largest and most influential political organization working throughout the nation representing the concerns of the Armenian American community on a broad range of issues. Additionally, he was inspired by the Armenian Genocide Martyrs Monument in Montebello, unveiled in April 1968, to honor the martyrs of the Armenian genocide perpetrated by the Turkish government, as well as to honor all victims of crimes against humanity. Building of the monument was a major achievement following three years of negotiations and debates—and fund raising—to erect a monument in a public park.

Through the years, I have come to know several Armenian Americans in the former and current political life of California and Los Angeles: Gov. George Deukmejian of California; Robert Philibosian, LA County District Attorney; Bob Moretti, Speaker of the California State Assembly; Walter Karabian, Assembly Majority Leader; Assemblymember Adrin Nazarian, 48th Assembly district; Paul Krekorian, the first Armenian American to be elected to the LA City Council; Rep. Karen Lorraine Jacqueline Speier, 14th Congressional District; and Rep. Anna A. Georges Eshoo, 18th Congressional District.

VALLEY SECESSION

While Los Angeles flourished and its image swelled globally, a crack appeared in its northern appendage. Some San Fernando Valley business leaders, politicians, and residents argued they were not being properly represented; they were short-changed in services received. A movement commenced seeking to split Los Angeles and transform the Valley with its 1.5 million residents into the sixth largest city in the nation. If successful, the contemplated secession would signify a stunning, massive exodus from the urban core. But behind what was asserted—anxieties over "fair share," decentralization of city government, and control over land-use policies—lurked another, darker issue: social separation. For some, secession was reasoned to be white flight from the basin to the valley.

Valley separation was an old idea that still percolated. Following four decades of hindered efforts, the movement was reenergized in 1998 after a survey financed by Valley business leaders David Fleming and Herbert Boeckmann found that 58 percent of 1,205 likely Valley voters favored an independent city. Under the guidance of the Valley Voters Organized Toward Empowerment (VOTE) group, chaired by Richard Close, a diverse coalition of residents, activists, and business leaders, some 4,000 volunteers began to circulate a petition calling for a study on secession. They successfully gathered signatures of 25 percent of the area's registered voters that were required to trigger the Local Agency Formation Commission (LAFCO) to conduct a comprehensive fiscal analysis of secession. LAFCO, in 2002, decided to put the issue of Valley secession on the November ballot.

Fleming was a leader for Riordan in the charter reform movement for Los Angeles. He co-chaired a voter initiative in 1997 to reform city government, but believed, as did Riordan, that charter reform must be kept away from the City Council members. His solution was to place a measure on the ballot approving the creation of an elected commission to revise the charter. The measure passed; however, the City Council had already created an appointed commission. As a result, two opposing commissions undertook charter reform. Before he joined Riordan on charter reform, he remembers a press conference he held in 1966 where he held up a copy of the chunky 800-page LA charter in one hand and the eight-page US Constitution in the other. "There's something wrong with this picture," he had said. He also spoke at length with Robert Hertzberg on what the charter should provide.

Comparing differences between the Constitution and the charter, he said that the Founding Fathers had the parts and had to create the whole. "Here, we have the whole and are trying to create parts." Fleming, later named to the board of the Southern California Metropolitan Water District and the Los Angeles City Ethics Commission, told me that Los Angeles is the only major city in the world bisected by a mountain range. "While it's a geological barrier, it's also a political barrier," he said, and there's relatively small interplay between those who live in the basin and the valley. "Basically, you have two cities from a geologic standpoint," he continued. The feeling in the Valley was that Los Angeles City Hall thought life stopped at Mulholland Drive, an arterial road carelessly tracking the ridgeline of the eastern Santa Monica Mountains and the Hollywood Hills, tendering striking sights of the basin and the valley. In addition, fewer Valley council members were on the City Council than those representing the rest of Los Angeles. "We always felt we pay more in taxes and get less back in services than anybody else," Fleming noted. The secession movement came to a head with Assemblywoman Paula Boland, Granada Hills, whose bill in 1996 would have removed the veto power of the LA City Council over applications to leave the city. It was argued that no City Council should have absolute right to deny residents the right to determine their own governmental organization. The bill failed in Sacramento by a nineteen to eighteen votes, shy of the twenty-one needed for passage.

Former Assemblyman Richard Katz, an unsuccessful candidate for Los Angeles mayor in 1993, became a major proponent of the secession movement, co-chairing the initiative effort known as Measure F on the 2002 ballot. Five years earlier he worked fervently to block a bill giving the Valley a vote to secede. Katz's move was seen as an attempt to make himself a vanguard candidate for Valley mayor, if secession succeeded. Mayor Hahn spoke out against the "terrible idea of breaking up this great city of Los Angeles," He formed LA United, the political action committee to oppose the ballot initiative, and raised $5.5 million—nearly four times the combined amount collected by the Valley and Hollywood cityhood groups. The election results backed Hahn's view by an 80.5 to 19.5 percent vote, although in the Valley 50.7 percent approved it.

A companion measure that would have allowed Hollywood to secede also failed. Fleming said they were heavily outspent in the Valley separation movement; he was the largest single contributor putting in about $350,000 and Boeckmann added another couple of hundred thousand, "but basically we didn't have much, and we didn't do much as far as the campaign was concerned." When people now ask him about secession he says, "You know, we lost the battle, but we won the war. We brought this to the attention of City Hall that it better take care of the Valley. The Valley had streets repaired, got new parks, and stuff that formerly never would have happened were it not for secession." He confided to me that if Riordan had not won the Valley he wouldn't be elected, and Woo would be mayor. Reminiscing, Fleming said when he first moved to the Valley in 1956 it resembled Iowa. "Most people were upwardly mobile, they were white, and there were very few minorities. Today, as far as ethnic makeup is concerned it is completely different. It's more like New York."

Another reason for the Valley's failure to separate was the "politicization of the Department of Water and Power," according to Brendan Huffman, former president of Valley Industry & Commerce Association (VICA). He told me that DWP was used as a public information arm to defeat secession. At the height of the Valley debate, legal advisors expressed a belief that bond agreements would make it difficult to split the city Department of Water and Power between new and old municipalities. State law and bond agreements prohibit dismantling the agency if that would jeopardize the value of the bonds.

These prohibitions would force the new Valley entity to contract DWP services until other arrangements are made. When Hahn first won his mayor's race in 2001 many believed that a newer political dynasty was launched. His father, the venerated supervisor, had provided a magic name and years of distinguished public service. Instead, he became the first one-time mayor of the city since the Great Depression. Hahn's political future was heroically forfeited by his alienation of vital voters in his battle against Valley secession.

Fleming offered to me his views of Bradley, lauding him for building downtown and for constructing bridges between various groups, but said that 20 years was too long to be mayor. Riordan, whom he knew for years as a lawyer and a businessman, was surprised when he heard from Sherman Block, former Los Angeles County Sheriff that he was running for mayor. "Come on, you've got to be kidding. Why would you want to buy what you already own?" Regarding Hahn, he called him a prince who didn't want to be king, "a nice guy who never wanted to be mayor." As for Villaraigosa, he said his power was organized labor and public employees' unions.

A COLUMNIST'S OPINION

When Riordan began his run for mayor of Los Angeles in 1993, Bill Wardlaw, the wealthy attorney who convinced him to run—and made it happen—set up a meeting with Harold Meyerson, then the executive editor of *LA Weekly*, the nation's largest metropolitan weekly. The location for the encounter was a deli at the southernmost end of the Santa Monica Plaza. "I'm a little early," he recounted to me, "but Riordan is even earlier." He was already sitting down. Meyerson walked over and introduced himself. "Hello, Mr. Riordan. You've got a smudge on your forehead." "Well, yeah," was Riordan's response. "It's Ash Wednesday."

Meyerson recalls a Los Angeles of the early 1990s that survived "one catastrophe after another." Interviewed after the 1992 riots by Anna Deavere Smith, the actress known for her roles as National Security Advisor Dr. Nancy McNally in *The West Wing*, he was asked what he thought of the crisis, "Which one?" he replied, because "you not only had the riots, but you also had the collapse of the middle part of the economy, you had all kinds of stuff." It was a line he had used to describe Los Angeles' economy and later to define the American economy as a whole: the bottom hadn't fallen out, the middle had. Specifically, he was referring to the post-cold war collapse of aerospace that was the largest private sector employer of the Southern California area. Aerospace employment was around forever, and suddenly it wasn't, as he told me.

He also alluded to what he called the "two waves of deindustrialization in LA" the first being local auto manufacturing that collapsed after the industry consolidated and Japanese competition intensified in the 1970s and 1980s. "That work force was a lot of blacks as well as whites," he said. On the other hand, aerospace "was mainly whites." A major out-migration of the aerospace folks took place, he continued, and many moved to Arizona, Nevada, and the Pacific Northwest. "If they couldn't find comparable employment here, they might as well go to a place where the living expenses are lower." Meyerson said this was also the peak of immigration. The city was losing middle-class jobs and creating low-quality jobs. Essentially, with the loss of industry there was nothing left. "The economy became bipolar."

He remembered as a kid there were "tons of really major businesses headquartered in LA like banks, oil companies, and department stores. The studios were owned somewhere else. Only Disney is the major company headquartered here."LA became the home for absentee landlords. ARCO was once huge in the area, as was Percy G. Winnett, the chairman of Bullocks, Ed Carter from The Broadway. "I'm a guy who sides with labor," Meyerson said, "but I suddenly realized without a business elite who's going to push for civic development? We can fight over what kind it should be, but someone's gotta push for it in the first place."His fear for Los Angeles is that a two-tier city scheme increases with a consistently marginalized middle class. "Let's see where the minimum wage takes us, if there can be a political movement for paid family leave, if there are changes in middle-income jobs which are currently in the public sector," he pointed out.

He alluded to the decaying infrastructure and noted that could be a source of middle-income jobs. It was obvious to him that Los Angeles would no longer be shaped solely by the historic civic and business elite, but also by the various liberal factions located throughout the city. Meyerson praised the work of the late Miguel Contreras, under whose political leadership the County Federation of Labor became a vehicle for socialization, education, and voter registration and mobilization. Contreras was supported by the renowned labor organizer James Wood whose work transformed the city through the powerful Los Angeles Community Redevelopment Agency.

When he was in Washington, DC, a few years ago he participated in a panel sponsored by the Congressional Black Caucus at a time when a documentary film on Mayor Bradley was released. He recalled the time when he was twenty-three and just back in Los Angeles from college in the east when the mayor was first elected. "The black population of the city was 19 percent, and they had a huge turnout, which means he was elected by blacks, but also the west side Jews and a bunch of liberals around town," he told me. "Honestly, there weren't that many Latinos in LA. Part of what Bradley did was the demographic diversification of City Hall and the city work force," he continued.

"In a sense his campaign was the municipal version of the civil rights movement," he said, "the Blacks and the Jews, etc., coming out of the 1960s." He called Bradley's ability to mobilize elites, the presence of high rises downtown, and the Olympics to be remarkable feats. "By the end of his term it was kind of the last gasp of the old coalition. His final term was nothing to write home about."

Meyerson referred to Riordan as an intermission between the dominant African American-Jewish coalition and the multiracial coalition that he thought was certain to follow Riordan into office. "I never thought Riordan would have won had it not been for the 1992 riots," he said, adding that turning Los Angeles around was very tough, and that was his slogan. In his 1993 campaign, Riordan vowed he would add 3,000 officers to the 7,600-officer force in his first term and would not run again if he failed to meet that promise. Riordan did not keep that promise, and he did run again. At the time, then Police Chief Williams advised the addition of so many officers, so quickly, was not a reachable target.

Regarding term limits, supported by Riordan, Meyerson bluntly asserted the movement was the outcome of "a bunch of right wingers in the Valley." To the dismay of backers, it backfired. Its effect was to elect Latino Democrats because all the incumbents got term limited out and the districts steadily became more Latino. He ironically referred to the law of unintended consequences.

He also said Hahn beat Villaraigosa in 2001 for mayor because of the Black vote, as well as the vote in the Valley, which he lost in his reelection bid. "Antonio did better with the Jewish and Latino vote." To Meyerson it was unimaginable if his father hadn't been Kenny, Hahn would ever have gotten into politics at all.

Recalling the 1993 KCET mayoral debate with eight candidates, including me, he drew the straw marked Riordan and asked tough questions. "The mayor snarled at me for several years," he said.

Meyerson first got to know Villaraigosa in the late 1980s. "He was on the American Civil Liberties Union board, obviously a comer, and we backed him when he ran the first time for the Assembly. Very impressive, very energetic, a down-the-line progressive which is sort of the *LA Weekly*'s politics," he said. Changes that swept over the Los Angeles area will likely sweep over California and the nation, according to Meyerson, and that will create a new political landscape. He had no misgivings that emerging Latinos will be Democrats and not Republicans due to their miserable handling of the Latino population, and due to the labor movement's heavy mobilization in this area.

A MAN FOR ALL SEASONS

It was almost five Wednesday morning when Tom Bradley called Nelson Rising. Exit polls showed on election night in 1982 the mayor winning California's governorship in a tight race against Republican George Deukmejian. "Yes, you were right," Bradley said. "I take no satisfaction in knowing I was right," Rising said in one of our conversations. As chairman of Bradley's gubernatorial campaign, he had advised the mayor against taking a position on Proposition 15, a ballot initiative requiring owners to register their handguns and setting procedures for transfer of ownership.

With Nelson Rising, left and Ira Yellin

"Tom, if you support the gun control initiative, you will not win," Rising had cautioned. He felt that a lot of people who otherwise wouldn't vote would come out to do so. But Bradley, as a police officer, had witnessed the destruction wrought by Saturday Night Specials and was convinced the initiative must be supported.

Regrettably for the mayor, a huge voter backlash resulted in inland conservative precincts and Deukmejian won by less than one percent. Later, the *Los Angeles Times* reported, that an analysis of the vote after the election indicated that a high percentage of "crossover" Democrats and independents who voted for Deukmejian might not have voted at all had it not been for the gun control issue. Bradley's support for the Raiders football team produced another unhappy result. While Angelenos loved Bradley for luring them to the city, Oakland fans did not, and the Alameda County results proved it.

I recall being at the Biltmore Hotel election night and noticing Rising's gloomy disposition early in the evening. It was the absentee ballots that caused him concern. The Republicans had "an extraordinarily sophisticated absentee ballot program," he said, and he was getting information from campaign consultant David Garth in New York who told him, "Nelson, we're getting some things we don't like in some of our numbers." Rising's close camaraderie with Bradley was established over many campaigns.

A real estate developer, he chaired Bradley's 1973 successful run for mayor against Sam Yorty, which made Bradley the first African American mayor of a major American city with a predominantly white population. After attending UCLA on a football scholarship, Rising earned a degree from its law school and became an associate at the Los Angeles-based law firm of O'Melveny & Myers in 1967. His love for political dealings began when he managed a campaign chaired by Warren Christopher that put John Tunney in the Senate in 1971.

He told me that Tunney and Cesar Chavez were not friends. "He was very much in favor of the United Farm Workers." But the UFW created a secondary boycott against grape growers and Tunney's 38th congressional district had grape growers in Riverside and San Bernardino. "After John won the senate primary I went to Delano, where the UFW was located to make peace. There was hostility because Tunney didn't believe a secondary boycott was right." Rising's career has a storybook ambiance. Aside from being a top political strategist, his four decades in the real estate industry included leading two large publicly traded real estate companies and chairing the Federal Reserve Bank of San Francisco. He also built some iconic buildings and communities in California.

He was a political mentor to me, and in one conversation Rising spoke of how Bradley was determined to make transportation in Los Angeles his first and foremost program. "We had committed in the course of the 1973 campaign that we would have a mass transit system." A year later a ballot initiative chaired by Rising and Thornton Bradshaw, president of ARCO passed the two-thirds threshold in the city but lost in the county.

"It's just amazing how these twists foiled our achieving important goals." he said. Although he didn't have the data, he was confident the reason the initiative lost was due to funding from those who didn't want transit. The auto industry people were in favor of Los Angeles being a single-passenger automobile-dependent city. "You know this better than anybody," he told me, "You worked hard to get transit, all things you did to make this happen, it's going to be the bones of how this whole region is going to be able to sustain its population." Bradley never gave up, he continued. "He sought an alternative route which was federal funding." However, his efforts to have a Wilshire line were initially futile because of Congressman Henry Waxman, added Rising. "He did not want that line to go through his neighborhood, his district, as if someone was going to get on a train, get off and steal somebody's TV set and get back on the train."

Rising greatly respected Bradley, called him a tireless worker seven days a week, a man who possessed great energy and a genuine love for people. "He was color-blind," he said, "and accepted people for who they were. He embraced the diversity of our city." The powerful coalition he built was based on personal magnetism.

When I asked about his involvement in the imposing Library Tower, which was completed in 1989 and is a 1,018-foot skyscraper—the third tallest building in California—and symbolizes Los Angeles's skyward climb to global city status, Rising said he was brought in as a partner in charge of the project. His understanding of density transfer provisions played a key role. Downtown is zoned at a 6 to 1 FAR, the floor area ratio that is the proportion of a building's entire useable floor area to the total area of the site on which it is situated. "But we had the ability to transfer air rights from one site to the other. The concept was to transfer density from the central library by forever limiting what can be built there." Although known locally as the Library Tower, it was formerly the First Interstate Bank World Center and now the US Bank Tower, and located at 633 W. 5th St., downtown.

Rising was also partner-in-charge of Playa Vista, a 1,087-acre planned community located near Playa del Rey, property once owned by billionaire Howard Hughes. It took more than four years for the Los Angeles City Council to give the project its blessing. Playa Vista is a planned community with residential, commercial, and retail components, constructed under green development guidelines with an energy savings system and design techniques that promote conservation and protect the environment. The Playa Vista project is one of Rising's greatest accomplishments because it took the competence of a developer and the proficiencies of an adept political authority to achieve it. Ruth Galanter, the City Councilwoman who represented the area, initially won election in 1987 after opposing Summa Corp.'s earlier plans to develop the property at the base of the Westchester bluffs. She subsequently became a key supporter for what was called the largest real estate developments ever contemplated for Los Angeles. Rising said that Galanter had made it very clear that community support for the project was a necessity, thus triggering hundreds of local meetings to be held. "We were developing our plans and listened to people," he said. The issue of the wetlands had to be resolved, and it was, making the Friends of Ballona Wetlands happy.

Reflecting on his political beginning, he explained how he got immersed in the Bobby Kennedy primary in California. He was placed in charge of a downtown motorcade to be organized upon Kennedy's arrival from Oregon. "It was going to be an absolute smash," he said, but after Kennedy lost Oregon concerns surfaced over a possible Los Angeles failure. Jerry Bruno, the head advance man for President Kennedy and then Bobby, received a telephone call at the Ambassador Hotel. "Who's advancing the motorcade?" he was asked. When told that it was Nelson Rising, the response was: "Who in the hell is he?" "It turned out the motorcade was spectacular," Rising said, and he remembered Roger Mudd on the evening news saying that Kennedy may have lost in Oregon, but they love him in California. "A week later Kennedy wins California," said Rising and he and his wife, Sharon, were at the Ambassador when they heard the shots. "It was a pretty tragic and terrible evening."

Rising introduced me to Ted Kennedy, who won California's presidential primary in 1980 against Jimmy Carter. Rising spoke about how Ted Kennedy lit up a room when he walked in, a man with a great sense of humor and an unbelievable passion. He recalled Kennedy's speech focusing on those who had not reached the American dream. One powerful line still resonated: "What do we say to the faces pressed against the windows of our affluence?"

SENATOR TED KENNEDY

Bill Carrick, who was my campaign consultant when I ran for political office, is an established media and political consultant hired mostly by Democratic candidates. He packaged messages, spinned reporters, and won elections. Sen. Edward Kennedy said he "has that sort of down-home appearance and accent, but behind that kind of innocent-looking face is a bear-trap mind and a will of steel." Carrick served as political director for the senator in the 1980 Democratic Party presidential primaries. He was also a senior advisor to President Bill Clinton's reelection campaign in California and ran Jim Hahn's successful mayoral election in 2001.

It was Kennedy and transportation that Carrick and I discussed over lunch in Los Angeles.

Whenever Kennedy came to Los Angeles, he spoke of it as a great town that was being ruined because it lacked transit. "We got to fix this," he would say. Carrick told me, "It is something he really believed; it was like a fixation with him. So, you were of particular interest to him because you were doing something about it." "Kennedy liked the details involved in mass transit, and you knew all of them." In fact, Carrick recalled a time when Kennedy was in a committee session in Washington and asked his staff to pull him out of committee when I arrived. As Kennedy approached his office, I heard his booming voice, "My good friend Patsaouras is here." One of the women doing the scheduling went to Carrick and asked, "Who the hell is this Patsaouras?" Carrick's response was swift. "You know, the senator likes him a lot and he is involved in transportation in LA."

Kennedy knew a lot of people in Los Angeles, especially in entertainment, since his dad was in the movie business. However, he felt that becoming a truly great world-class city could be problematic, absent mass transit. Without that, Los Angeles would remain a big, sprawling suburb. Kennedy also regularly discussed the transit issue with Mayor Bradley and shared his experience with the mass transit systems of Boston, New York, and Washington, DC, having lived through most of their development. Carrick recalled Kennedy's work with Tip O'Neil on the "Big Dig" megaproject in Boston that rerouted the chief highways of the city into a one-and-a-half-mile tunnel; constructed another tunnel leading to Logan International Airport; and built a bridge over the Charles River along with green space vacated by elevating a roadway. Despite the cost overruns and the construction disputes, Boston became an improved city as a result. Before, the airport was separated from the city and everything clogged up in Boston, Carrick added. "Kennedy was a visionary when it came to transit systems."

A native of South Carolina, Carrick said politics were easier there compared to Los Angeles. While we had African American and white candidates, there was no ethnic complexity like Los Angeles. "The diversity here is deep and coalition-building more complicated," he shared with me. Carrick advised Richard Riordan on his 1993 election but did not consider him a conservative Republican. He received Republican support because they wanted to be relevant in city politics. "The perception of Riordan is that he was self-funded and essentially bought the mayor's office, but he was a better candidate than that, and was a big philanthropist" Carrick said. As a devout Catholic, for Riordan the social gospel was part of his philosophical value base.

The *Los Angeles Times* essentially focused on a Riordan-Michael Woo race. "I think they thought that Woo would win the run-off. There were also countless community forums and debates and quasi-debates which were hard to cover," added Carrick. "However, as I remember, Riordan would walk into a debate auditorium surrounded by eight to nine staffers, creating an image of a winner. Almost everyone else walked in by themselves. Riordan was not an experienced candidate in terms of speaking skills," reported Carrick who attended debates to see who would support him in an eventual run-off. "Woo was a candidate every other candidate wanted to hate. His negative attacks on Riordan were highly personalized. Woo's campaign was engineered to get him to the run-off. Once there, however, he wasn't well-suited," Carrick said. I recall when Woo called me and said, "Hey, Nick, how about endorsing me?" On the other hand, I met with Riordan and Bill Wardlaw at least three to four times before issuing my endorsement.

AS THE HARBOR BLOSSOMS, SO DOES AIR POLLUTION

It's a given. Port people always fix their eyes on the sea and their backs to the land, and for good reason. The seaport was the hub of a nation's commerce for millennia. Los Angeles political and harbor guardians correctly viewed the sea as a benevolent highway. Devoted efforts over many years established a mercantile and industrial community at the harbor to handle and process goods from distant lands. The port made the city wealthier, bigger, and more powerful.

Today it is the busiest container port in North America, and has been so for decades—a leading economic driver at the local, regional, and national levels, and a vital generator of jobs, business, and tourism. To achieve this, coastlines were redesigned, waterfronts reshaped, and political and cultural factors remodeled to enhance port activity and to increase enterprise. Widely promoted as "America's Port," it adjoins the separate Long Beach container port. Together they employee over 850,000 people. But while port people kept their eyes on the sea, a disturbing storm appeared on their environmentally sensitive back.

A *Los Angeles Times* opinion article in August 2021 was straightforward: "With smoke-belching container ships, diesel cargo-moving equipment, and thousands of polluting trucks, the ports of Los Angeles and Long Beach are the single largest source of pollution in the nation's smoggiest area." What happened? Geraldine Knatz recounted to me the causes of the port's quandaries, especially the complications of transportation, a vital harbor prerequisite. Knatz was the Los Angeles Port's executive director for eight years. Interestingly, prior

Los Angeles Harbor. Photo: Zyzx

to that she was managing director of the Port of Long Beach. "Back in the 1970–1980s the thirty-acre terminals and marginal piers that had big sheds on them were no longer fitted for containers," she said. "So, we had to rebuild the port." Major projects ensued at both harbors, including dredging and landfilling. The environmental focus was on habitats. The public outcry was loud: at the cost of modernization, habitats were being destroyed. "Our conservation emphasis was on creating habitats and on dredging," she continued. "We were not thinking about air quality." Quickly, the harbor fashioned larger container terminals. Since lots of cargo was headed back east, the rail facilities had to be advanced and on-dock rail terminals created. "We were sued by the Class I railroads because they didn't like the idea; they thought everything should be trucked to them," she related to me.

Changes in rail services to the harbor had to be made, so both Los Angeles and Long Beach came together and created the Pacific Harbor Line, a short-line railroad. However, as soon as the trains shipped out, neighborhood protests arose. Countless complaints were registered: people were stuck at grade crossings; homes were now situated alongside rail corridors; the noise was aggravating; major arterials were all congested. "*The Alameda Corridor* project was conceived as the solution to traffic congestion, and to allow the ports to grow and create bigger terminals. In essence, the Corridor was a freight rail 'expressway' from the ports to the transcontinental mainlines of the BNSF Railway and the Union Pacific Railroad that terminate near downtown. 'Everything that we did used diesel,'" Knatz admitted. However, based on its potential to cause cancer, diesel exhaust had been classified as a toxic air contaminant.

Diesel engines emit a complex mixture of contaminants, including soot, and forty cancer-causing substances most of which are absorbed into the soot particles. These toxic gases and small particles—one-fifth the thickness of a human hair—are drawn into the lungs as people breathe and contribute to a range of health problems. Knatz explained the involvement of the South Coast Air Quality Management District and how "all of a sudden our world changed." The district performed a study on the impacts of transportation on health in the LA Basin and presented it to the LA Port Board. A map was held up "with a big red blob," according to Knatz, who explained that this was the area where the greatest health issues associated with transportation were found. "It covered the major transportation corridors down to the port and the entire port area."

At that time some 40,000 truck trips per day were coming in and out of the two harbors. "Our forecast of growth showed that by 2020 that number would increase to 90,000 truck trips per day." Later, when the China Shipping Terminal sought expansion of its container terminal, litigation by the community followed. The settlement involved looking into ways to reduce emissions and deal with public health. Los Angeles was the first port to investigate plugging a ship into electric power, avoiding its engine operations while docked. She called this a "watershed event for both harbors." Health, therefore, was to be a major component of Environmental Impact Reports (EIR). But the LA City Attorney's office did not want the port to look at health issues because they might result in litigation. Further, Knatz confessed, planned projects required inclusion of health impacts in the EIR and her board "would not want to approve additional cancer exposure when they adopted a project. We went through a period of seven years with no EIRs approved at either port." Finally, for the port to be below the air pollution threshold of significance it would require mitigation measures to be adopted. "We reached out to Long Beach," Knatz recalled, "to join the effort to meet the health risk threshold together and the first-ever plan was adopted jointly by the ports.

This was the first time since 1929 that members of both boards had met." Consequently, among other things, low sulfur fuel was required by ships entering the ports, newer and more efficient trucks were only allowed in the harbor areas (trucks are responsible for 25 percent of port emissions), controls on dredging were adopted, ships while docked were plugged into shore power or had their exhaust scrubbed by hooking up to machines known as bonnets or "socks on a stack," and electrification for cargo handling equipment was required. "We were moving forward," she said, "toward a zero-emission port." In fact, Los Angeles Mayor Eric Garcetti and Long Beach Mayor Robert Garcia have pledged to meet the zero-emissions goal by 2035. To hclp truckers buy zero or near-zero emission models, a fee was imposed on shipping containers in both ports. Electrification strategies were first initiated by David Freeman, president of the LA Harbor Board of Commissioners and me, when I was president of the LA Board of Water and Power Commissioners.

Asia was the source for most port business. And more business meant more air pollution. Beginning with Tom Bradley in 1988, all mayors have traveled to Asia in search of port commerce and environmental improvements. Bradley visited Beijing, Shanghai, Tokyo, Taipei, Hong Kong, China, and Manila during a two-week trip that yielded increased port activity, beginning with shipments of hundreds of tons of wastepaper to Shanghai. The mayor maintained that all users of the port can exist and prosper and supported recreational facilities including the new $45 million marina. Ten years later, Mayor Riordan headed to Asia to lobby for port activity with a large group of entrepreneurs seeking expanded ties with local counterparts. His trip climaxed with the signing of a deal that was expected to generate jobs and grow the port by more than $1 billion. He was successful in keeping the port's largest customer, Evergreen Marine Corp., despite efforts to lure it to Long Beach and Seattle.

In May 2002, Mayor Hahn took a delegation of fifteen business officials to Asia seeking ways to benefit from increased trade and tourism. He discussed plans with six major shipping companies to reduce pollution by plugging into the port's power system and turning off diesel fuel engines. In a first "state of the harbor" address he touted proposals to bridge the divide between the port and surrounding communities burdened by truck traffic, diesel emissions, and expansion projects.

In 2013, Mayor Villaraigosa signed a memorandum in Beijing to expand and modernize the port's Yang Ming terminal facility, including the construction of a new 1,260 linear feet dwarf, allowing the largest and most modern ships to call. He called the port the economic driver for the region. His earlier two trips to Asia in 2006 and 2011 had created strong ties and he followed up to ensure these relationships remained vibrant. He had also launched the ambitious *Clean Truck Program* that banned over 10 percent of the port's dirty diesel trucks to help curb emissions.

In 2014, Mayor Garcetti led a delegation of business leaders and city officials, including the Port of Los Angeles, on a trade mission to China, South Korea, and Japan, claiming that as Los Angeles emerges from the recession it is important for the city to aggressively promote international trade and tourism. The trade mission was an investment in the economic growth of the port. A few years later he entered a pilot program with the Port of Jakarta to help increase the flow of goods between the two ports, collaborating on digital supply chain strategies as well as trade competitiveness, infrastructure development, and suitable operations. He pushed for efforts to create a greener future for the region by establishing the formation of a freight advisory committee comprised of environmentalists, shippers, and community members focused on reducing emissions.

While port business has increased through the efforts of mayors and port officials, it is a fact that smog and other toxic contaminants are creeping up and the cleanup program demands escalation. A review of data proves that on the Los Angeles side, compared to 2020 levels, the port area cancer-causing diesel particulate matter rose 56 percent, smog-forming nitrogen oxides jumped 54 percent, and greenhouse gas emissions increased 39 percent, while the Long Beach side saw diesel particulate matter increase by 42 percent, nitrogen oxide emissions going up 35 percent, and greenhouse gases rising by 35 percent. New congestion-reduction measures and a new ship queuing system will help reduce emissions from ships anchored, but it becomes imperative that long-delayed regulations from the air district be quickly adopted, and for the state agency to hasten its pursuit of zero-emission trucks.

CHAPTER THREE

TRANSPORTATION

Transportation should not simply be the random movement of people. At its best, it can bring people together spiritually as well as physically, as it speeds them towards their destinations. A great transit center should, therefore, teach people about where they come from, celebrate the place where they have arrived, and inspire them as they continue on their journey.

—NICK PATSAOURAS
Caption on Bust of Nick Patsaouras
at Patsaouras Transit Plaza, Union Station

FUNDING OF THE METRO RAIL

The Impossible Dream | Almost a century ago a historic groundbreaking ceremony took place for Los Angeles's first subway—a tunnel less than one mile long from Glendale and Beverly Boulevard to 4th and Hill Streets Downtown. Following the edicts of Prohibition, a bottle of ginger-ale was used to christen opening day in November 1925. It was estimated that 1,000 daily car movements would be eliminated from congested Downtown at a cost of $3.5 million.

This was the first act of an indispensable program for emerging Los Angeles—and it was promising. However, the second act took more than a half century to play out. During the intervening phase, the city surrendered its soul to the automobile and the first auto-dependent metropolis was conceived.

It doesn't take rummaging the dusty annals of Los Angeles's history to understand that a region's transportation system is analogous to the circulatory system of the body. Without a healthy transportation anatomy, the region perishes. Further, social dissatisfaction over inadequate public transportation has caused urban upheavals in many corners of the world. Even the McCone Commission's investigation of the 1965 Watts riots called for a more efficient public transportation system.

Subways revolutionize the way people live and travel—communities are connected; new economic opportunities are created; traffic congestion is reduced; air quality is improved; travel time is decreased; and better job opportunities become accessible. Aware of that, many cities acted early. Boston opened its subway system in 1897, and New York in 1904. The underground or tube in London, the oldest transport system of its kind in the world, opened in 1863, followed by Paris' Métro in 1900.

With his election in 1973, Mayor Tom Bradley became intensely committed to a modern, comprehensive, world-class transportation system for Los Angeles and led the challenging campaign for one, persistently rebuking irrelevant attitudes and detrimental political naysayers. Bradley made building a subway in LA his top priority. He was its leader and advocate through battles and eventual victories in securing federal funding.

Los Angeles was fortunate to have Bradley as mayor during that critical period and not Richard Riordan, who was quoted in the *New York Times* on June 12, 1999, saying, "We should get out of the subway business. We never should have started in the first place." Further, in the *Washington Post* in June 2000 Riordan said he never would have undertaken the project and believed that no more subway lines should be built.

I was a relentless point man and chief advocate for the Los Angeles Metro Rail system, which today consists of seven lines—including five light rail lines and two subway lines—and connects with the El Monte Busway and Orange Line busway, the Metrolink commuter rail system, and several Amtrak lines. Bradley called me "the absolute champion of this project." Envisioning and creating the system for Los Angeles took years and millions of dollars. It was so death-prone, some claimed it had nine lives. Each step was a series episode, and each funding element was replete with dramatic climaxes, with good guys and bad guys.

HOW IT ALL BEGAN

The planning phase for the first Metro Rail Segment started in March 1975. The search for project funds began and, in December 1976, some 21 months later, the US Department of Transportation (DOT) approved funding for $2.5 million for preliminary engineering and environmental study identifying major alternate routes within Los Angeles County. A preferred alternative route (18.6 miles) started at Union Station, went through Downtown and out to Wilshire Boulevard, up Fairfax and back toward Hollywood before heading out to the San Fernando Valley. Funding for $15.6 million was approved for Phase I preliminary engineering in June 1980. To advance the project required federal funding, and lots of it. However, the Feds insisted that local funding must be first committed before any federal financing became available.

I liken legendary Los Angeles County Supervisor Kenneth Hahn to Archimedes, the ancient Greek mathematician who said, *Give me a place to stand, and a lever and a fulcrum on which to place it, and I will move the whole world.* The fulcrum Hahn used was Proposition A, that he initiated and eventually placed on the ballot, and which was used as a lever to secure federal funding for the LA subway system. Hahn's plan would dedicate funding for both bus and rail with 25 percent to be returned to local governments, 40 percent to lower bus fares and to improve the bus system, and 35 percent for rail. In November 1980 voters passed the proposition by a 54–46 margin, imposing a one-half cent sales tax. As a result, this made it possible to fund the construction of the rail transit system and multi-modal local transit

With Supervisor Kenneth Hahn. Photo: courtesy of Metro

projects in the County. The Wilshire subway would be the project's backbone. Supervisor Hahn used the Los Angeles County Transportation Commission (LACTC) that California Assemblyman Walter Ingalls, then Chairman of the Assembly Transportation Committee had established in 1976, to place Proposition A on the ballot.

In July 1981, the Southern California Rapid Transit District (RTD) awarded $6 million worth of contracts for engineering of the first segment of the Metro Rail starter line. The following year an additional $42 million was approved for continued engineering.

With the adoption of route and station locations by the RTD in 1982, strong opposition was voiced by numerous groups, chief among them the Hancock Park Homeowners Association. They were alarmed about prompting gentrification where land values increased and long-time residents priced out. More realistically, they feared an influx of new residents that could change the character of their community, and they feared the potential for crime by subway riders. The Westside Civic Federation, an alliance of homeowner and community groups, said it opposed both elevated and subway routes on Wilshire through the Fairfax area.

Behind the expressed opposition lurked racial motives and the fear that minorities would ride the trains "to come and steal televisions." Renowned actor George Takei, an RTD board member and Hancock Park resident, said "low-income people" were unwelcome by the residents, and they "didn't want those people." Even Senator David Roberti acknowledged that area residents "didn't want working people stopping here." When asked if this referred to blacks, he replied, "I think so." The Hancock Park homeowners and the Wilshire Homeowners Alliance, collectively known as "Rapid Transit Advocates" (RTA), filed a lawsuit against RTD on January 18, 1985, on the narrow issue of whether Appellants RTA had a standing to argue that RTD had violated the Urban Mass Transportation Act. The Federal 9th Circuit Court of Appeals found that RTA did not have standing and the case was dismissed.

On September 23, 1986, on an appeal brought by RTA, the California Appellate Court held that there was no requirement that the RTD's proposed rail project be consistent with the general development plans of counties and cities. The South Brookside Homeowners Association, another opponent of the subway, noted it was unable "to accept what appears to be an unwarranted assault on our neighborhood." Likewise, the Boulevard Heights Homeowners Association claimed that a subway station at Crenshaw "would destroy the surrounding neighborhoods." Curiously, the City of Beverly Hills opposed the subway because it would result in an "alien invasion."

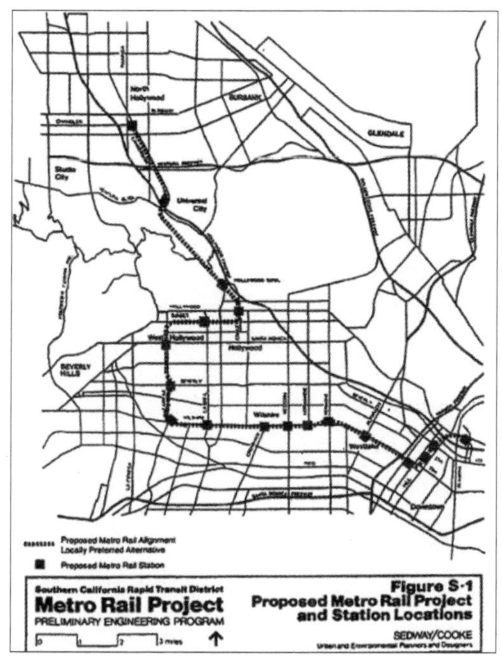

Original Red Line route with a Hollywood Bowl Station. Courtesy of Metro

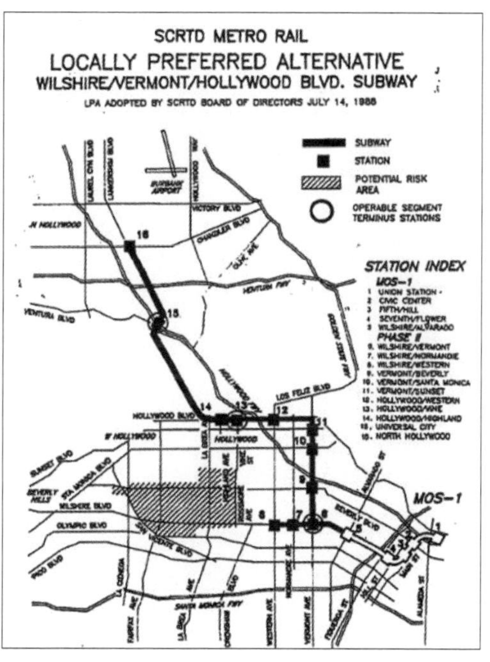

Built Red Line without Hollywood Bowl Station. Courtesy Metro

Arch project opponent, influential Congressman Henry Waxman from the Westside, had said the key first phase of the proposed Los Angeles Metro Rail system is too risky to construct as a subway and had called on the Los Angeles City Council and the RTD to abandon that part of the project. Reporter Ryan Reft, writing about the Los Angeles Subway in *Topics of Meta*, on January 28, 2015, said the Fairfax situation differed from Hancock Park. "Home to a long-standing Jewish population dating back to just after World War II, residents worried about rising property values and rents negatively afflicting the neighborhood's aging residents." He quoted then subway opponent Los Angeles City Council Member Zev Yaroslavsky, an ally of Congressman Waxman: "Henry and I were both elected seven years apart…and we were elected by the same constituency of old Jewish mothers who are important to us both culturally and politically." Roberti concurred, "It would pretty much destroy an ethnic community that was long established in Los Angeles. If your constituents don't want thousands of commuters coming in, there's not a politician in the world who is not going to respond to that, okay?"

Following a protracted period of bickering among community groups, business heads, and elected officials, the RTD proposed to replace the subway in Hollywood with an aboveground line. The trains would run on Sunset Boulevard through the heart of Hollywood and on Wilshire Boulevard into the Fairfax District but deferred until December 1988 a decision on whether to build below or above ground on Wilshire Boulevard. Despite its attempt to balance the interests of all parties, the RTD came under vigorous attack by homeowners and businesses closest to the proposed elevated routes over fears of possible noise, vibrations, and the likely graffiti on trains. Similarly, a line 20–30 feet above ground—from Universal City to Chandler Boulevard in North Hollywood—in the middle of the redevelopment area, also encountered stiff opposition.

NOW YOU HAVE IT, NOW YOU DON'T

In August 1983 President Reagan signed a Department of Transportation funding bill for fiscal year 1984 providing $117.2 million for the start of construction of the Metro Rail. Consequently, in September 1983, $32.6 million was approved for the acquisition of the Santa Fe Rail Yard, and another $14.8 million for advanced land acquisition.

In the meantime, in June 1984, the Urban Mass Transportation Administration (UMTA) ranked the RTD Metro Rail project the nation's No. 1 cost-effective new rail project. But funding for Metro Rail stalled in 1984 and hopes for Los Angeles' entry into world-class status with a world-class transportation system began to diminish.

I turned to Stu Spencer, the celebrated political consultant who ran Reagan's campaigns for governor and president. Spencer set up a meeting with David Stockman, the President's budget director, in the West Wing of the White House. In addition to Stockman and me as RTD president, present at the meeting were Ed Meese III, counselor to the president and later US Attorney General; Craig Fuller, chief of staff for Vice President George Bush; Mike Lewis, RTD board member; John Dyer, general manager of RTD; Ray Remy, president of the Los Angeles Chamber of Commerce and former chief of staff for Mayor Bradley; Rodney Rood, assistant to the chairman of ARCO; and Spencer. (Rood was a central figure of the 1984 Olympics in Los Angeles. He and insurance executive George Gibbs, Jr., were co-chairs of a Downtown business group forcefully seeking political support for the Metro Rail system.)

Stockman walked in when everyone was present. He shared friendly chats with Meese, Fuller, and Spencer. Then he asked: "What do you need?" "We need a Letter of Intent (LOI) for the Los Angeles Subway," I instantly responded. "Oh, is that it?" was Stockman's response. "Well, yeah, I signed off on that."

A Letter of Intent was confirmation that the Federal Government would fund the project.

Overjoyed by the unexpected response, I was especially fortified by the knowledge that almost $650 million was secured for the subway in less than 20 minutes. And assured with the blessings of the White House, at that.

After immeasurable red-eye trips to Washington, DC and many other parts of the country to meet with Urban Mass Transportation Administration (UMTA) officials on the Metro program and with key political leaders, I called my wife, Sylvia, before the flight home. "We finally got it," I said, and assured her that days away from home would now be minimized.

But the promise was short-lived. The very next day in Los Angeles my phone rang. It was Penelope Simison from the *Los Angeles Daily News* who asked, "How did it go yesterday?" "Terrific," was my cheerful response. "We got the Letter of Intent, and we are ready to roll." "That's not what I was told," was her response. "Stockman's press secretary, Ed Dale, acknowledged the budget director did say he would approve the Letter of Intent. But he misspoke. That's what he told UMTA." I was stunned. "Misspoke?" I asked. "Yeah, the press secretary said that Stockman did not understand the meaning of a Letter of Intent."

I could not believe that the nation's most prominent budget director was unaware of Letters of Intent, the typical document by which two parties outline details of an intended action. It was obvious to Rood, who was present at the meeting, that both Stockman and Meese had concurred on a commitment for the first 4.4 miles and showed no ambivalence over the document being sought. I immediately called Mayor Bradley who listened carefully to the bad news and spoke persuasively. "Nick, we'll march on. We'll keep going, and we'll get the subway."

For me, it was a lesson never to be forgotten. When Stockman agreed on the Letter of Intent, I should have marched to the lawn of the White House with him and Meese and proclaimed victory. It would have made a "misspoke" excuse difficult to issue later.

AN EXPLOSION AND AN OUTBURST

On March 24, 1985, an explosion rocked the Ross, Dress for Less department store located in the Fairfax District. It was Sunday afternoon, and the store was filled with employees and bargain shoppers. After a rigorous investigation it was determined that a pocket of high pressure and high concentration methane gas existed below the surface. A plume forced its way into the building, resulting in the explosion. After four days, the store reopened for business.

But the explosion rocked more than the store. Critics of the Beverly Hills, Hancock Park and Fairfax subway found a new battle cry: methane gas. For Congressman Waxman, the most vocal opponent, it was a gift, an opportunity to cover his strident opposition. Numerous observers suspected that veiled racism hid behind the incessant protesting. The predominantly white neighborhoods feared invasion by minorities riding the train.

To allay the fear of methane explosions, I pointed out to Waxman that the Los Angeles County Department of Public Works was constructing a storm drain within feet of the proposed subway tunnel at that time. "I have no control over the city," Waxman responded.

The Los Angeles Department of Building and Safety was quickly on the job and had tested waterproofing membranes for use as methane barriers. The Department also oversees the development of methane mitigation systems in all new construction projects within the city and has proven the preventive measures it utilized to eliminate the risk of methane intrusion inside structures.

Two months later, on May 1, 1985, Mayor Bradley, Bill Robertson, LA County AFL-CIO chief, and I headed to Washington, DC, to testify before House and Senate subcommittees in companion hearings. The main objective was to seek $150 million to build the first four miles of the Metro Rail from Union Station into the Wilshire Corridor, and to free up $129 million previously approved but held up due to Reagan's announced plan to abolish funding for new rail starts, a Stockman tactic. "Los Angeles's ability to play its vital role in America's economic future is inextricably tied to Metro Rail," the mayor testified. Following a series of private meetings with key legislators, Mayor Bradley felt optimistic about Los Angeles's chances of receiving the money.

Virulent opponent of the project, California Congressional Representative Bobbi Fiedler (R-Northridge), had called the $3.3-billion project a "turkey" that will "rob some of the poorest in my community." The mayor had called Fiedler's charges "a fraud." The *Los Angeles Times* reported Bradley saying, "She has not given us a straight story from the first time she ever opened her mouth on this issue of Metro Rail." Fiedler sought to scuttle the program in strong support of the Reagan Administration's efforts to trim the federal budget deficit. But she stood alone among California's 45 House members.

Both Senators Pete Wilson and Alan Cranston actively backed the City's request for funds. Cranston said the planned system was critical, especially since "California is America's gateway to the Far East." Wilson, in turn, acknowledged that the "project has the most widespread possible political and community support." Fiedler's discordant testimony was questioned in the hallway where heated arguments broke out between her and Los Angeles officials who accused her of lying to the Senate subcommittee. She had testified that, "last month the voters of Los Angeles, in their first opportunity to vote directly on the issue of the subway, rejected a proposal to tax homeowners for the project, by a margin of 73 percent."

Los Angeles deputy mayor Tom Houston angrily called Fiedler "a liar" and officials accused her of grandstanding before the Senate Appropriations Subcommittee on Transportation. "That statement is an out-and-out lie," Houston said, adding that the "non-controversial" ballot proposition "called for exempting residential property owners from paying Metro Rail. Everyone favored it." Houston was right. The proposition barred City officials from imposing special taxes on homeowners who live near the subway stations.

During the hearing Fiedler also held up a newspaper with the headline: "Deukmejian Dumps Metro Rail." Congressman Julian Dixon from California and chair of the House Ethics Committee would have none of that. Probably unknown to Fiedler, Dixon supported the project and was actively involved in securing federal, state, and local funds. He countered, "When you read the article the Governor clearly says he would stand by his commitment to provide $400 million in state funds, if the federal funding continued. Is that not true?" he asked Fiedler. "It was," she admitted.

Still, Fiedler insisted that estimated subway costs had soared to $250 million a mile from an original $100 million, but I said the $250 million was the front-end cost for the first phase construction that included the maintenance yards. "The long-term average, I pointed out, "would be $180 million, very much in line with other cities' rail lines." While still in the hallway, Fiedler turned to me and yelled, "If you guys spent more time administering the bus system the community would be better off." Like Waxman, she charged that methane posed an unacceptable danger to the subway, only to be told by transit officials that developed techniques of safe construction and tunnel sheathing sufficiently reduced hazards.

Fiedler, a Republican, had won election to Congress by 750 votes over incumbent James Corman who represented California's 21st Congressional District for 20 years. Although the district was 62 percent Democratic, Jimmy Carter's conceding the election to Reagan in 1980 while the polls were open in California kept Democrats from going to vote, according to analysts.

Although representing Northridge, she became actively involved with the powerful Westside Waxman-Berman-Levine political machine to stop the subway. During her campaign against the subway, Fiedler sought exposure in preparation for her ambitious challenge against Cranston for the United States Senate in 1986. However, in the Republican primary she came in fourth with 7.2 percent of the vote. Cranston won reelection against Republican Ed Zschau. Fiedler also killed the Downtown People Mover. A grant Los Angeles had sought to build the system was diverted to the Miami-Dade County Department of Transportation and Public Works, which built its Metromover, a fare-free elevated downtown people mover.

Intriguingly, on August 29, 1985, the *Los Angeles Times* speculated that Rep. Berman, Waxman's close ally and associate in the influential Berman-Waxman political organization had carried out an 11th-hour fight over Metro Rail funding in order to undercut Mayor Bradley, the transportation system's protagonist, in his possible second gubernatorial bid.

A TRIUMPHANT OUTCOME

In July 1985, two months after the Washington, DC, hearings, the House Appropriations Subcommittee on Transportation sounded the victory bell: it approved $130 million in new start-up funds and provided an unprecedented directive obligating the Administration to provide $427 million for the initial 4.4-mile segment. Importantly, the Subcommittee directed the Urban Mass Transportation Administration to issue a "letter of intent" and "full-funding contract" guaranteeing that Los Angeles would get $129 million that the transportation administration had withheld over the last two years, the $130 million just approved plus an additional $168 million yet to be appropriated. Together with funds already received, a total of $603 million would be provided in federal gas tax money, the amount Los Angeles needed to build a 4.4-mile starter line from Union Station to Alvarado Street and Wilshire Boulevard. "That's as strong a direction as one could ask for from the Congress of the United States," Bradley said in Los Angeles. Along with me and City Council President Pat Russell, he called a press conference to applaud the action. "This is a major step," he said. "It shows that if you are tenacious and won't give up, you'll succeed. We feel great."

"I'm so happy I could dance," I said at the press conference. "This marks the first time since we began the project eight years ago that a Congressional committee has specifically required the Administration to approve the construction of the Metro Rail." "It's that simple," echoed County Supervisor Ed Edelman. "We must get this four-mile backbone system now or we won't have a regional transit system."

Ernani Bernardi, the anti-Metro Rail City Councilman who had said he was unhappy when he casted "Yes" votes, longed for program derailment even after the crucial House subcommittee vote. "There still is a long way to go, isn't there?" he hinted.

In August 1985, the RTD formed an Independent Review Board of outside experts to review the design, construction, and operation of Metro Rail in gaseous areas. After two months of painstaking analyses the board stated that "because detailed planning and design has gone into the project, there is no doubt that this project will be the model that other projects in gassy ground will emulate." The final report was issued in January 1986, with a definite project conclusion: "feasible to construct and operate." Many efforts to convince Waxman that tunneling through the Fairfax area would be safe failed. Things began to unravel quickly. In September 1985, lobbyist Mickey Kantor, later the United States Secretary of Commerce, along with Dyer and me, flew to Washington in a last-ditch attempt to convince Waxman to drop his opposition to the project. Mayor Bradley joined to add the prestige of his office to the effort.

Waxman, who chaired a powerful subcommittee that investigated health and environmental safety issues for the House, insisted that problems remained unresolved as the transportation bill made its way to the House floor.

Waxman had formed an "unholy alliance" with Fiedler, according to those involved in the effort to sway him. They worried the representational power of a liberal Democrat and a right-wing Republican could render Metro Rail a final blow. Congressman Dixon was asked to become the intermediary since he was trusted by both sides, and his office was used as the situation room. Waxman, however, was adamant, rejecting one proposal after another. During the enduring discussions, Dyer approached me. "Waxman will drop his opposition if he has veto power over all consultants and contracts." "John, that's crazy," I responded. "I cannot support that, and neither will my board. I am certain of that."

Time elapsed without any resolution. At 1:00 pm the floor debate in the House was in progress and the RTD delegation was carefully observing it through closed-circuit television in Dixon's office. Mayor Bradley had to return to Los Angeles. I had to move quickly. I unpacked sketches of graphs, topography, and plots displaying the methane gas zones and contemplated an escape route. When I believed a viable solution existed, I huddled with Dyer. If the route bypassed the Fairfax area and went south to Pico/San Vicente, methane ceases to be problematic. A quick proposal was drawn up and presented to Waxman. He accepted it. The clock was now challenging everyone's resolve. It now read 1:15 pm.

The debate continued on the House floor despite the absence of many members who generally show up when the chair calls for a vote. It is customary. They have already determined how they will vote. Since only House members and staff are allowed on the floor, an effort had to be launched to apprise Representatives of a critical change: Waxman was no longer co-sponsor of the legislation. He had changed his mind. Lobbyists and RTD staff were dispatched to the different floor entrances to inform members of Waxman's new decision. In the meantime, I, with the RTD contingent, were following events from the gallery. Down below, Fiedler was approached by Waxman who whispered into her ear, and she turned white. Her once-ally had abandoned her, she later commented. She felt betrayed. But she was not through. When the chair called for a vote, Fiedler immediately raised a point of order: "Since the bill was on the printed Congressional Register, can the vote proceed on a last-minute amendment?" A ten-minute recess was provided for the parliamentarian to research and decide.

I remember those ten minutes lasting an eternity. The decision came quickly; the vote could proceed. Waxman had pulled the provision that would delay funds until the entire route could be examined and considered safe from potential gas explosions. If left in, he admitted later, that provision would have threatened the entire project. Dixon and Waxman offered a compromise amendment requiring the subway to be re-routed to Pico/San Vicente, avoiding the Fairfax district.

The full House, on a 242-172 vote, authorized $117.2 million for construction of the mass transit system. But there was one caveat. No tunneling would be permitted in the Fairfax district. According to the *Los Angeles Times*, Waxman said, "I think I've gotten everything I wanted." He was determined to kill the entire project if Metro Rail's backers did not reexamine the hazards of tunneling through gas pockets.

"We have a historic vote," Bradley declared. "Metro Rail is like a cat with nine lives," he said at a news conference. "People in the media and others have proclaimed it dead at least nine times, and yet today, we have a historic vote in the House of Representatives." *Los Angeles Times* investigative reporter Rich Connell described me as "slightly haggard" after spending three days scurrying around Capitol Hill to shore up support for the beleaguered project. But, as I was quoted at the time, the end result was "a cause for celebration."

Never-built Hollywood Bowl Station, designed by Frank Gehry. Photo: Courtesy of Metro

However, despite the distinctive victory, diverting the subway route meant wasting $125 million in design and years of delay. Additionally, the Hollywood Bowl Station was deleted as the result of a new route that moved up Vermont through Hollywood and to the Valley. The Hollywood Bowl station had been designed by celebrated architect Frank O. Gehry in the shape of a horn. Eventually the Pico/San Vicente route had to be disregarded because of the presence of underground hydrogen sulfide.

Environmentalist Dorothy Green, founding president of Heal the Bay, and developer James McCormick went to court to prevent further planning or construction of the mid-city extension.

The "Hail Mary" pass, in football vernacular—a desperate long offensive toss with a prayer—best describes the compromise I offered with the Pico/San Vicente concession to save the Metro Rail. It worked. Today (after voter approval of Measure R in 2008) the subway goes through the Fairfax area, and it was constructed without incidents or methane explosions.

The House and Senate subcommittees companion hearings in May yielded firm results on December 12, 1985, when a House-Senate conference committee approved a bill ordering release of $129 million appropriated by Congress in previous years for subway construction but held back by the Administration. Further, it appropriated an additional $101 million, a split between the $117 million approved by the House and $85 million by the Senate. In a separate document it was noted that as part of the full funding contract, the federal government would pay its share of the Minimum Operable Segment-1 (MOS-l), calculated to be $429 million. The compromise pleased me. Included was an order for the Administration to negotiate with the RTD on a full funding contract for MOS-1.

A week later President Reagan signed a federal spending bill containing money for the MOS-1. It was always understood that the Metro Rail system would be built in stages. As I explained, the initial system represented by MOS-1 comprised a 4.4-mile segment to be constructed with five stations and yard and shop facilities.

DESERVED ACKNOWLEDGMENTS

Mayor Bradley praised me for my unequivocal resolve in leading this project, calling me the "absolute champion in this effort." Once a promise when he was elected, it was now becoming a tangible transportation system. "It's been a long haul, but at long last it appears construction will begin." With an evident minimal grin and a subtle barb, he added, "If we had a dollar for every time somebody said Metro Rail was dead, we could have built this system."

Not only was I pleased, I asked the President to instruct Elizabeth Dole, Secretary of Transportation, to proceed quickly so that "your fellow Angelenos can ride Metro Rail at the earliest possible time." And I expressed gratitude. "Thank you, Mr. President," I said and added a favorite movie quote: "You have made our day."

I also thanked Barry Engelberg, RTD Director of Government Affairs, and Roger Slagle, RTD's Legislative Analyst, both of whom had persistently toiled for a successful outcome.

Announcing approval of the Metro Red Line Full Funding Grant Agreement. With, from left: Supervisor Kenneth Hahn, Councilman Nate Holden, Supervisor Deane Dana, and Mayor Tom Bradley. Photo: courtesy of Metro

But thanking the President was not enough to keep Reagan from making one final attempt to scuttle the program. In a puzzling statement issued in February 1986—less than two months after he signed a spending bill that contained money for the initial construction of Metro Rail—he denounced financial support for it and held it up as an example of "a ton of fat in this trillion-dollar government." While delivering his weekly radio chat from the Oval Office, Reagan's comments marked the first time he personally publicly opposed the project, although his Administration had long been unfavorable. He had asked for funding appropriated by Congress in 1984, 1985, and 1986 to be rescinded.

Bradley found the President's action "puzzling." He said it was "pretty quick to have that kind of change of heart." He continued his firm push for the system. At the Democratic Party State Convention, he told reporters, "We're still very positive about groundbreaking," and even suggested that it was possible to break ground on the first 4.4-mile section of the system during the year.

I told the *Los Angeles Times* that "the federal funding for the project will improve the lives of millions of people, and I don't see why the citizens of Southern California don't deserve a mass transit system that every other major metropolitan city in the nation enjoys." The Administration accompanied the budget with a booklet that singled out the proposed Los Angeles subway as an example of "highly expensive systems, paid for by all taxpayers for the benefit of a few, which we no longer can afford."

Nevertheless, as a result of my limitless trips to the nation's capital with other RTD representatives and an earnest program of information and education for lawmakers and policy architects, Reagan's request for revoking Metro Rail funds was ignored by Congress. It was allowed to lapse on April 15, 1986.

THE SYSTEM WITH NINE LIVES

Two months after Congress rejected the President's plea to rescind Metro Rail funding, United States Transportation Secretary Elizabeth Dole placed a call to Senator Pete Wilson. She informed him that a green light had been given to begin tunneling the first 4.4 miles. Jubilation immediately broke out at City Hall and the RTD. Holding a press conference on the corner of First and Hill streets, where the Civic Center station was envisioned, a proud Mayor Bradley said, "I wouldn't be happier if the Dodgers, the Raiders, and Lakers all won world championships this year." The mayor popped the cork and champagne was passed out to transportation officials and onlookers.

The *Herald Examiner* reported that "Patsaouras, who guided the project through its oftentimes bleak and most difficult negotiations with the federal government, broke into a brief Greek dance." There was no music, only the one playing in my head. I opened my arms like an eagle and danced for myself, not the audience. The brief subtle steps were a triumphant release of my years of tension. I had fulfilled my mission. Raising his cup of champagne, Supervisor Hahn urged everyone to save their plastic cups, directly assuring them that they would be good for a free ticket on the subway.

Celebrating the Metro Red Line Full Funding Grant Agreement. Photo: courtesy of Metro

Celebrating the Metro Red Line Full Funding Grant Agreement: with Mayor T. Bradley, Supervisor K. Hahn, Councilmember N. Holden, and Supervisor D. Dana. Photo: courtesy of Metro

Funding for the first 4.4 mile starting line totaled $1,167,600 broken down as follows: (in millions) UMTA, $176; Federal gas tax, $428; Federal funds for construction, $10.6; State of California, $213; LACTC, $176; Los Angeles City, $34; Private Sector (Benefit Assessment Districts), $130.

Waxman, however, once again in August 1986 tried to sidetrack Metro Rail with a surprise amendment in the House, saying that he didn't act sooner "because I thought the Reagan Administration would stop it." But when Secretary Dole agreed to a funding package on July 11, he tried to block it in the House Rules Committee. When that failed, he introduced his surprise amendment that was meant to stop Federal money for the subway until a new Environmental Impact Report was completed. As reported by the *Los Angeles Herald Examiner*, I remobilized and sought to defeat the amendment in its second hearing in the House.

In September Waxman admitted he struck a deal with me to support Metro Rail but told reporter Linda Breakstone that his position "evolved to one of distrust for the entire project." He claimed that he lost confidence with RTD planners because "they used political considerations instead of safety, technical, or practical reasons" in designing Metro Rail. He did not act earlier because he believed the project would never be approved.

The deal struck with me was threefold: RTD would not tunnel through Fairfax, a technical committee would evaluate the 4.4 miles of the 18.6-mile system, and a safety study would be completed for the rest of the proposed route. All commitments made by the RTD were carried out.

Signing the Metro Red Line Full Funding Grant Agreement. Photo: courtesy of Metro

Metro Rail Groundbreaking, with Chris Stewart, Kenneth Hahn, Tom Bradley, Nate Holden, and Gilbert Lindsay. Photo: courtesy of Metro

SCRTD-Metro Rail Groundbreaking, 9/29/1986. Photo: courtesy of Metro

Congressional Representative Ed Roybal inserted a new twist to Waxman's actions, stating that "if he doesn't want it in his district, we ought to look at putting it in East Los Angeles where most of the people live, where jobs are needed, and where they really need transportation."

Waxman's efforts failed.

VIGNETTES

It has been written that it was "a boneheaded decision to bypass the Hollywood Bowl on the Red Line's route into the San Fernando Valley." Boneheaded was Congressman Henry Waxman's decision to stop the Red Line going through Fairfax, raising phony safety issues. The RTD Board under my leadership overturned General Manager J. Dyer's recommendation to build a station at Highland/Hollywood. Marvin Holen and I strongly favored building a station at the Hollywood Bowl in the original Red Line route. The vote was 6–4. The station was designed by Frank Gehry depicting a horn instrument. The Los Angeles Philharmonic Board of Directors had adopted a resolution declaring their intention to share in the construction costs of the station. However, when Waxman got involved, the route was reconfigured, placing the station at Hollywood/Highland, and bypassing the Hollywood Bowl.

*

It was customary, when Congress members or Senators were visiting LA to learn firsthand the need for federal funding for Metro Rail, to give them a helicopter tour over the congested freeways. Republican Congressman Silvio Conte from Massachusetts was the ranking member of the House Appropriations Committee and a key vote on the Red Line funding. Conte, in one of those helicopter tours, asked if he could fly over the Dodger Stadium. After flying over the stadium multiple times he was taken to lunch to Rex Restaurant, which at that time was one of the more exclusive Italian eateries in Los Angeles, and where scenes for the movie "Pretty Woman" were filmed. According to Barry Engelberg, Government Affairs executive for the Southern California Rapid Transit District (RTD), Conte looked at the menu and said: "Garbage." He said that he would cook lunch. After explaining to the Matre'd who Conte was and how important he could be to the future of Los Angeles, Conte marched off into the kitchen. After waiting "for what seemed like an eternity," out came Conte with some lasagna looking dish. "Enjoy" he said. "This is one of my mother's favorite dishes."

*

Jamie Whitten from Mississippi, chairman of the House Appropriations Committee, was average height and somewhat overweight. On the way to a meeting with Whitten, Mayor Bradley asked if arrangements had been made for a photographer. After a twenty-minute meeting, Whitten requested a photo with the mayor. The photo revealed an undersized Whitten trying to put his arms around a towering Bradley. After the meeting, Barry Engelberg said that Whitten's staff had all the heavy lifting. Bradley then said, "Oh, they like us now."

*

In one of my many trips to Washington, DC, I testified before a Senate Committee along with California Senators Pete Wilson and Alan Cranston. After the testimony, on the way to the airport, one of the lobbyists accompanying me received a call from Senator Cranston's office. "The Senator would like to see Patsaouras." When I walked into Cranston's ostentatious chambers, Cranston was majority whip at that time, I was very impressed and moved to sit down. Cranston said, "No need to sit down, Nick. I know you are a successful fundraiser and I just want you to host a fundraiser for me."

Cranston was an obsessive fundraiser, and as a result he was involved in a national scandal. Cranston was one of the "Keating Five." The Keating Five were five United States Senators accused of corruption in 1989, part of the savings and loan crisis. The five Senators included Cranston, CA, Dennis DeConcini, AZ, John Glenn, OH, John McCain, AZ, and Donald Riegle, MI. They were accused of intervening in 1987 on behalf of Charles H. Keating, Jr., chairman of the Lincoln Savings and Loan Association, being investigated by the Federal Home Loan Bank Board (FHLBB). I did not hold a fundraiser for Senator Cranston.

*

In a conversation I had with Allan L. Alexander who was very interested in transportation issues and especially the subway plans through Beverly Hills, Alexander told me the Beverly Hills City Council and the community were opposed in the mid-1980s to the subway going through their city, with the main concern being the perceived potential for crime. Meanwhile, traffic was getting gridlocked and development in the Westside was booming, promising even more congestion.

When Alexander was elected mayor of Beverly Hills in 1990, he appointed a five-member committee to study traffic and crime. Two members were opposed to having a station in Beverly Hills and three were in support. They analyzed the question of crime and whether crime travels. The Metropolitan Atlanta Rapid Transit Authority (MARTA) had done a study at that time on the issue of crime and concluded that it does not. The subject of crime was studied again in 2006–2007. Mayor Stephen Webb, who was member of the committee of five in 1990, appointed an eighteen-member committee chaired by two former mayors, Allan Alexander and Mark Egermam, with the task to recommend where the alignment would go if the subway were to come to Beverly Hills, would there be one station or more stations in Beverly Hills. They were also tasked to study the issue of crime. The committee met for nine months. The committee met with Metro, the Police division, and it seemed quite clear that there was not a problem. There was also a traffic consultant that advised the committee. Since the Atlanta study, UCLA had also done a study on crime and whether crime travels, concluding unanimously it does not.

A HISTORIC DAY FOR LOS ANGELES

With band music heightening the atmosphere and 1,200 guests in attendance on September 29, 1986, shovels with the RTD logo turned the dirt at the future Civic Center station at First and Hill streets.

"I will never feel prouder than I am today," Bradley declared. "It's a historic day for the city," I asserted. The ceremonies officially marked the start of the Metro Rail project. Pointing to me, the mayor summarized it all with appreciative remarks. "This is a tribute to tenacity, in the face of what many said couldn't be done and shouldn't be done, was done."

However, Reagan had another shoe to drop, and he dropped it. Five months following the official groundbreaking, he vetoed the $88 billion highway bill that included $870 million for Metro Rail. The money was earmarked for the project's first leg, totaling $203 million, and $667 million for the second phase. The President singled out the Los Angeles system funding, calling it a "budget buster." It was a questionable project, he said, and termed the legislation that supported it to be "a textbook example of special interests and pork barrel politics." To break the veto an improbable two-thirds majority in the Senate was needed. What was termed as a "bare-knuckles showdown" ensued with Republican Senators, including California's Wilson, meeting privately with Reagan.

They could not be manipulated by the White House's heavy hand and joined fity-four Democrats to vote for the override. On April 2, 1987, the Senate voted 67–33—exactly a two-thirds majority. Later, Elizabeth Dole reported that the President had spent more than ninety minutes negotiating with the Republican Senators. "Have I got a vote in here, or not?

Blue Line Grand Opening: with LACTC Commissioner C. Reed, Supervisor K. Hahn, Mayor T. Bradley, Supervisor Ed Edelman.

Opening day of the Blue Line. With Los Angeles County Supervisor Ed Edelman. July 14, 1990. Photo: courtesy of Metro

Mayor Eric Garcetti's rail plan for the 2028 Summer Olympics in Los Angeles. Courtesy of Jake Berman of 53 Studio

US Representative
Julian C. Dixon

Any volunteers?" No one stepped up. Wilson said, "In good conscience, I couldn't support him on this issue." The House had voted overwhelmingly for the veto override on March 31, 1987.

After my labyrinthine journey, Los Angeles was finally on its way to world-class status, capable of adding the one missing jewel it lacked—a world-class Metro Rail system. The "starter line" (4.4 miles of the Red Line) opened on January 30, 1993, and the entire Red Line was completed in 2000. It runs between downtown Los Angeles and North Hollywood with landmark stops at Grand Central Market, the Los Angeles Convention Center, Staples Center, MacArthur Park, the Pantages Theater, the Walk of Fame, and Universal Studios. Over time the transportation network helped transform the Downtown region into a "live, work, and play area."

Champions of the first phase will be remembered for creating a reality out of a hopeful need to turn Los Angeles into a world-class city, and for supporting Mayor Bradley to realize his campaign promise. Besides me, they included Senator Pete Wilson; Congressional Representatives Glen Anderson, Julian Dixon, David Drier, and Norm Mineta; Los Angeles County Supervisors Kenneth Hahn and Ed Edelman; John Dyer, RTD feneral manager; Rodney Rood, vice chairman and assistant to the chairman of ARCO, and Christopher Stewart, president of the Central City Association.

On June 23, 2000, the 7th/Flower Streets Metro Station was dedicated to Congressman Julian C. Dixon, the stalwart supporter of the campaign to secure federal funding for the subway.

Only a small number of public projects are burdened with similar vulnerabilities, kindling anguish, heartbreak and a myriad of negative probabilities. Certain tales are properly disregarded in history's closet. But this Metro Rail narrative must be kept alive and retold because it is a tutorial on how improbable goals are attainable if one has audacity and tenacity and a yearning for the hunt.

* * *

Historian **KEVIN STARR** in his book *Coast of Dreams* published in 2004 wrote, "Here was being envisioned through public transit an entirely new organization of the Southland; and no one played a greater role in fashioning and implementing this vision of Tom Bradley than Nick Patsaouras." With its fleet of 2,600 buses, its 1.3 million boardings per day in more than eighty cities, the SCRTD was the largest transit district of its kind in the nation.

"Here, truly, was an empire to shape, and Patsaouras was an empire builder. Here, also, were the tools with which to bring into being—through transportation—the next stage of Los Angeles's development, and Patsaouras was a bold dreamer, desirous of bringing Los Angeles to world prominence as an achieved urban environment. Whatever its eventual format (and fixed rail may very well make a comeback), no one will be able to write the history of public transit in Southern California—its successes and failures alike, its relevance or irrelevance as social experiment, its utopian and dystopian dimensions, without reference to Patsaouras. Like Robert Moses of New York, Patsaouras exercised a species of appointed authority beyond that of elected government. Like Moses, Patsaouras sought, sometimes singlehandedly, to use public works to bring into being a highly personal, deeply felt vision of regional urbanism.

"Transportation systems and public works, Patsaouras believed, had more than a functional importance to metropolitan Los Angeles. Like the Eiffel Tower or the skyline of Manhattan, transportation expressed, perhaps better than any other form of public activity, the particular genius of the region. As fact and symbol, metropolitan Los Angeles was about the mobility of people in society across space and, as Patsaouras knew from personal experience, as movement across classes and social conditions. Transportation was the one thing everyone had in common, and it offered a compelling symbol of civic aspiration and unity. Transportation also needed to be more efficient, and it needed to be more public. Freeways and the automobile alone could not fully satisfy Patsaouras's notion of a collective civic ideal: his vision of metropolitan Los Angeles as an integration of urban nodal points. Fixed rail was a necessity.

"From the start, Patsaouras knew he was fighting a battle of metaphor and identity as well as the more gritty realities of day-to-day politics. Metropolitan Los Angeles—indeed, all of Southern California—had built its social identity around the automobile. It was an intensely suburban model, one prizing individual choice, point-to-point transportation at will, good roads and the monumental freeway system, and, above all else, privacy: the right to choose where to go and when to go, and with whom, the right to be along in one's car, the expectation that one could live anywhere and work anywhere one chose, as long as one could afford an automobile. This vision of reality, this cluster of preferences, demanded a certain level of affluence. The miracle was that Southern California had been providing millions of citizens with this level of economic well-being since the end of World War II. If asked what their civic or communal symbols were, millions might readily answer: their roads and freeways, the long processions of automobiles in which they joined daily. For all its disassociations, its emphasis on the solitary choosing self, this infrastructure—cars roads, freeways—constituted for millions one of their most primary and fundamental experiences of society and civilization as a larger force."

LEWIS MacADAMS wrote in the *LA Weekly*, "In this century there have been only two other decisions as profound in their implications for the city as the commitment to mass transit: the decision to bring water from the Owens Valley via the Los Angeles Aqueduct in 1908 and the decision to create the freeway system in the years immediately before and after the Second World War. Leadership in all three instances came from men whom historian Mike Davis (author of *City of Quartz*) calls 'the visionary engineers': William Mulholland, Lloyd Aldrich (whose 1937 manifesto published by the Arts Club of Los Angeles charted the freeways), and Nick Patsaouras."

Patsaouras stood by the Metrorail subway system when many other officials were questioning its cost and usefulness in a city wedded to freeways. —*Los Angeles Times*, April 1993

MTA HEADQUARTERS AND TRANSIT CENTER

Thus, in all these ways we will transmit this City, not only not less, but greater and more beautiful than it was transmitted to us.

—*Athenian Oath of Citizenship*
Taken more than 2,000 years ago by the Citizens of Athens

In the 1970s and 1980s the Southern California Rapid Transit District was housed in a leased jumble of dilapidated buildings at 425 South Main Street, in the heart of Skid Row. It had grown over the years by breaking into adjacent buildings with space that was not improved and, in some cases, not air conditioned. There were no windows in a 500,000-square-foot space, with very wide corridors making the building inefficient. Most importantly, there was no parking, making it necessary for security guards to accompany female employees to their cars across the dangerous Skid Row. The building originally was the data center for Security Pacific National Bank, and now people were working there. RTD employees didn't want to stay around past 5:00 p.m. because people were sleeping on the sidewalks. They did not want

MTA Headquarters, Patsaouras Transit Plaza and East Portal. Photo by Shervin Khazra

to park their cars anywhere near Skid Row. Staff turnover was high. Employees hungered for another safe location. It's generally less expensive for public agencies to own rather than lease their buildings. In 1987, the *Los Angeles Herald* Examiner ran a story by political and investigative reporter Linda Breakstone with the headline "RTD pays penthouse rent for Skid Row digs."

I joined the RTD board of directors in 1981, and in 1989 I convinced my fellow board members that we should consider moving into our building instead of paying rent, because the RTD as an institution would be in existence for many years. I said, "Such an Intermodal Center with RTD as its anchor could become LA's fundamental urban regional public-transit structure for the next one hundred years." It became, therefore, obvious that the board had the obligation to look into moving into its own facilities.

Velma Marshall, RTD real estate director, was charged to lead a staff committee to identify existing buildings that were for sale. According to Gary Spivack, assistant general manager for operations, "There was a great deal of interest in finding buildings in the core of downtown that could be adapted to RTD's needs for expansion as well as accommodate current staff. But the available buildings were old, not earthquake safe, and certainly could not meet the RTD's needs for expanding requirements. We needed extensive computer facilities because all of the modeling work done for the rail was performed at the Caltrans building and they were not too happy about sharing their resources because RTD's models took up to twenty-four hours to run at that time." A decision was then made to look into the feasibility of building new headquarters. Marshall hired John Bollinger for this task and to specifically help prepare a request for proposal for new headquarters. Bollinger remembered, "I received an invitation from [Nick] Patsaouras to meet him at the Jonathan Club. I went to the Jonathan Club not knowing who else was going to be there other than Patsaouras, but Alan Pegg, the general manager, was also there. Patsaouras reiterated his vision and turned to Pegg, 'Give him all the support that he needs and get this going, and if I hear that you are not supporting him,' Patsaouras kind of intimidated him a little bit, 'you'll have to answer to me.' I was both impressed and a little bit in awe of what Patsaouras said."

Bollinger developed the RFP and sent it out to the private sector in November 1989 requesting development of properties on and around rail sites. Initially, there were sixty responses. Each developer had a different site, many along the Metrolink lines. Bollinger and his team went through a systematic process of narrowing the list to ten developers, then to three. Frank Gehry's design was affectionately referred to as "the Gumby" because its lack of straight lines, no corners, and its angled top presented a striking resemblance to the Claymation character, Gumby. AC Martin, Richard Keating, and Barton Myers were members of some of the teams that submitted proposals. Patricia Flynn of Coopers & Lybrand was engaged to review the economic analyses. Yvonne Burke, before she was elected Los Angeles County supervisor, Amy Freilich and David Farrar of Jones Day were hired as legal counsel.

In September 1990, RTD agreed to give exclusive rights to negotiate to Catellus, once the real estate arm of Atchison, Topeka & Santa Fe Railway, for the construction of a joint development project that would include RTD's new headquarters and an intermodal center at Union Station in downtown Los Angeles. Legal counsel for Catellus was Cindy Starret of

View from MTA Headquarters. Photo: Shervin Khazra

Latham & Watkins. The joint development was possible because Gov. George Deukmejian had in 1983 signed SB 1159, a bill authorizing the RTD to engage in joint development ventures. Gordana Swanson, member of the RTD board of directors, was very supportive of the move, "Of course it makes the most sense to have the headquarters at the nexus of all transit systems. It was like having the administrative headquarters of LAX at LAX. It has to be at Union Station. We need to have a presence there. If we believe in the power of transit, we need to vote with our feet."

The Gateway Center, as it was named later, is on a 6.5-acre site on the east side of Union Station. There was a negative perception in developing in that part of town. Although city planners had made attempts to invigorate Union Station, real estate experts had been growing skeptical about development in the neighborhood because of competition from other areas of the city, including City West and South Park. In an interview with *Downtown News* I said, "I'm very proud of overcoming this negative perception. When I proposed the move, some of the realtors and brokers dismissed the idea. This will open up development to the whole east side of the city. It will provide a catalyst for expanding economic opportunities at El Pueblo (Olvera Street), Little Tokyo, and Chinatown."

Today, the Metropolitan Water District of Southern California headquarters, the California Endowment, First 5 LA, Mozaic at Union Station Apartments, the LA Plaza-Village mixed-use complex, La Plaza de Cultura y Artes, and CoreSite Los Angeles Data Center are at and around Union Station, because the RTD had the vision and the courage to move where, after all, it belonged.

My vision to create a transportation hub with the construction of the MTA headquarters was wholly realized when, in February 2011, the Metro Board of Directors voted to purchase

Union Station for $75 million from Catellus Operating Limited Partnership. Richard Katz, Metro board member and Art Leahy, chief executive officer, spearheaded the purchase proceedings, thus fortifying my objective to see the area become a major economic driver, with new businesses and employment opportunities.

The office market in downtown Los Angeles had collapsed in the early 1990s, and there were many arguing that it was wasteful to invest money in a new building when many Downtown office buildings were vacant. Jack A. Keyser, chief economist of the Los Angeles County Economic Development Corp. commented that, "there was overbuilding in the 1980s." The AON building on Sixth Street was offered to the RTD for purchase. However, it would need extensive seismic and life safety upgrades. More importantly, it had ten thousand square feet of floor space, which means a single department would occupy two to three floors. And it was blocks away from a subway station. The offer naturally was rejected. John Cushman of Cushman & Wakefield was very critical of me. I heard that Cushman would comment derisively around downtown, "The Greek wants to shift the center of downtown to Union Station."

One planner told the *Los Angeles Times*, "It's unfortunate that we live in a city where you can spend billions of dollars on rebuilding downtown and then end up having one of your most important public agencies locate their headquarters in an Edge City." Other critics had objected to the site of the new high-rise, away from the other downtown skyscrapers. They were quoted in the *Los Angeles Times*: "It's going to be the Transamerica of the 21st Century," said an architect, referring to the lonely high-rise at the southern edge of downtown. But I was adamant that the RTD would not bail out office building speculators.

The Union Station parcel was chosen for the RTD headquarters not only for economic factors but also because of its proximity to several modes of transportation, including Amtrak trains, the Metro Red Line subway, the El Monte Busway, and commuter rail lines. Today the Pasadena Gold Line, Metrolink, regional and local bus service, and vanpool, carpool, and taxi services are also there. Spivack pointed out that originally Catellus was going to own the land underneath the headquarters and the RTD would own the building. The RTD refused, and as result there was a land swap, so the RTD owned the building and everything underneath it.

The *Downtown News* commented, "The development provides one of the few bright spots in an otherwise dim downtown real estate market. But, perhaps more important, the commitment by RTD signifies a new pro activism by the public sector to steer downtown development toward Union Station, the region's major outlet for mass transit."

Bill Fulton, editor of the *California Planning and Development Project*, was quoted in a September 1995 article about the Gateway Center in the *Los Angeles Times*: "The project's location makes a powerful statement about the region's changing transportation priorities. For the first time in a lot of years, we're building a skyscraper next to railroad tracks instead of next to the freeway." In the same article, he said, "Admirers say Gateway will become not only an important transit nexus but a civic treasure in the tradition of the great public works projects of the 1920s and '30s. The project, they say, will revive a forgotten but historically important part of Downtown and create a new, public place for a city with many communities but few communal gathering places."

Noted architect Scott Johnson was quoted in the *Los Angeles Times*, "Over the next fifty years, public transportation, with the improvements that are happening right now, will reinforce the importance of transportation hubs as development zones. The argument persists that we've always had in Los Angeles: should there be centers?" He added, "My own view is absolutely. We need public symbols. We need places that, no matter what edge of the city we live in, we all pay respect to and we all unify behind. Unity in our diversity is more important than ever."

The agreement between Catellus and RTD was signed in June 1991. There were seventy-two agreements that Spivack along with Jeff Lyons, the RTD's capable counsel, successfully negotiated. Catellus would be the developer and Pankow Builders Ltd. would be the general contractor. During the negotiations, I thought that Catellus's proposed plan prepared by the architectural firm HOK was treating the buses not important enough. The plan called for a big parking structure above ground, with a little bus plaza inside the parking structure. RTD planning staff asked, "How can we redesign this, so that the bus plaza is important?" "Well, you place the parking garage down below it. It is more expensive, but that creates a plaza, similar in concept to big piazzas and plazas in Italy."

Under the agreement, the RTD retained control over the design aspect of the project. It was mutually decided that a new plan and new vision were needed, and new architects and planners should be brought aboard. There was an architectural competition with Directors Marvin Holen, future Los Angeles County Supervisor Don Knabe, and Los Angeles City Councilman Richard Alatorre serving as jurors. McLarand, Vasquez & Partners was selected as the architect for the RTD Tower. Ehrenkrantz & Eckstut Architects and Laurie Olin, Urban Planner and Landscape Architect, were selected to design the Transit Center and Plaza.

Before the final agreement was signed, I was invited to have lunch at the Beverly Hills mansion of billionaire Stewart Resnick, with the owner of the 425 S. Main Street building. Resnick and his wife Lynda, own several businesses, including Teleflora, Fiji Water, and POM Wonderful. They are also known for their philanthropy, including the Lynda and Stewart Resnick Exhibition Pavilion at the Los Angeles County Museum of Art. He tried to convince me that the move was not economically sound, saying he could make tenant improvements, and may lower the rent, etc. It was a fruitless attempt to change my mind. It is interesting that the day the RTD moved out of the building, the bank took over the building and it stayed vacant for many years until developer Tom Gilmore bought it as part of the Old Bank District project.

David Farrar, the RTD's outside legal counsel, suggested that we form an entity that would focus on the design and construction of the headquarters. That entity, a joint venture between the RTD and Catellus, would get the approval of the full RTD board for the scope, the budget, and the schedule, and if there were no substantial changes the new entity would not have to go to the RTD board for approvals every month. There would be a design-build partnership. At that time, nobody was talking about design-build. Farrar, in suggesting the nonprofit entity, said, "I could see that one of the big problems that public agencies have always had in doing major project development is the tendency of the press to want to find something to criticize at every stage. We saw that as being an impediment to being a successful project, major decisions have to be made very quickly or the negativity from the project will compound."

In the fall of 1991, the RTD board, in partnership with Catellus, created the entity and named it Union Station Gateway Inc. John Bollinger was appointed as president. The USG board consisted of six members: three from the RTD and three from Catellus. I was one of the RTD representatives, along with Richard Alatorre and Antonio Villaraigosa. Representing Catellus were Vernon Schwartz, Ted Tanner, and Rob Vogel. I served as chair. Vivien Bonzo later replaced Villaraigosa when he was elected to the California Assembly and Nelson Rising replaced Schwartz when Rising became president of Catellus. The success of the USG board as an independent and separate authority later served as a template for the formation of the Foothill Construction Authority in charge of the Gold Line, and the Exposition Construction Authority in charge of the Expo Line.

USG would have discretionary authority to make decisions that needed to be made every day, as things progressed. The meetings were public, anybody could attend and provide comments. It was a single purpose entity to make sure the headquarters was built properly, as opposed to having a multipurpose entity, the full RTD board, where the issue of the building would often become submerged in a complex and busy agenda.

Outside counsel Amy Freilich explained, "I've now spent my entire career doing public-private partnerships and what I've discovered is that they are always the same. The one thing that I think that project had that I've seen others fail, that don't have is public leadership. There needs to be somebody that steps up and says, 'I'm willing to take the heat and push through' and I saw Patsaouras was that person. I learned a lot from that experience because I think that it is always about risk, it is always about trust, it is always about control... but fundamentally I think it is about leadership, and about having a vision and the ability to see it through." Robin Blair, deputy director of planning said," "If staff doesn't believe they have the support, they're going to let everything go. If you get a chance to do the right thing and you have someone like Patsaouras, who is going to defend you, then you'll take chances."

Freilich continued, "I remember there was language in the statute giving RTD the authority to do joint development and that was unique in California. We chose design-build and that was critical. I've always thought design-build for public projects makes the most sense, because it allows to put all the risk in one party, in this case Catellus, and not creating all the finger pointing."

The USG board was proved to be a wise concept. Decisions were made fast, and there was very close supervision. As a result, the $300 million complex consisting of the headquarters, Transit Center, Plaza, and East Portal was built on time and on budget. This was the first time in the RTD's history of construction. Pankow president Tom Verti, said, "The project was built on time and on budget with no claims or delays. What you'd call the project of a lifetime."

After construction of the RTD complex had begun, an event occurred that created chaos and uncertainty. As discussed earlier, the office market downtown was in a recession, with a 33 percent vacancy factor. A much-respected developer, Ray Watt, who had served as undersecretary of the US Department of Housing and Urban Development under President

Richard Nixon, had bought the Thomas Cadillac property west of the Harbor Freeway and had prepared plans for a thirty-story office building. He had obtained all the permits, and he had bought the steel for the building, stored in the City of Commerce. He had spent close to $50 million, and he suddenly found himself in the middle of a catastrophe.

Watt approached his good friend Mayor Tom Bradley and convinced him that the Los Angeles County Transportation Commission should move into his building. In a closed meeting, the LACTC on January 27, 1993, had directed staff to initiate negotiations with Watt to build a $111 million headquarters, even while a separate $145.5 million RTD building was under construction with excavation 60 percent complete and $12 million non-recoupable already expended. On March 3, 1993, the transportation commission voted unanimously to establish a panel to investigate whether to construct two headquarters buildings. The panel consisted of a Los Angeles County Supervisor, a Los Angeles City Council member, and a representative from the Los Angeles County division of the League of California Cities.

The Los Angeles County Metropolitan Transportation Authority was created by legislation by state Assemblyman Richard Katz signed by the governor on February 1, 1993. It merged the two feuding agencies, the Los Angeles County Transportation Commission and the Southern California Rapid Transit District, effective April 1, 1993. Councilman Richard Alatorre, who chaired the MTA board, argued against construction of two headquarters. "It's one entity; why have two buildings to perpetuate something that the merger was to bring to an end?" he asked. "The RTD has already broken ground." Before making a decision, the commission staff evaluated several options, including purchasing the building the commission leased at 818 W. Seventh Street, building next to headquarters at Union Station, or building its own structure on Watt's property. Neil Peterson, executive director of LACTC, said the agency decided to pursue the Watt project. In March, Peterson said, "I do not believe it is necessary for the two agencies to be united under one roof, even after the merger." This was a bizarre statement, considering there would not be two agencies but only one as of April 1, 1993.

Fortunately, in a special MTA Board meeting on June 9, 1993, the two buildings concept was voted down. Director Larry Zarian, the mayor of Glendale, moved and Director James Cragin, a Gardena City Council member, seconded to: "Terminate all negotiations for the lease or construction of a headquarters project at locations other than Gateway." However, that motion failed. Director Mark Ridley-Thomas successfully added an amendment to Zarian's motion, seconded by Chairman Alatorre: "That approval be subject to the Catellus Gateway proposers providing a written guarantee that the MTA would not be responsible for any cost overruns due to construction." That decision cleared the road to proceed with full force to design and construct the $300 million complex.

The RTD issued through Orrick Sutcliff & Herrington thirty-year general revenue bonds to finance the construction of the tower, including the parking and related improvements. According to Rodney Johnson, deputy executive officer for finance at MTA, "There were ensuing 'refinancings,' with no 'new money' bonds being issued." Final maturity of the remaining bonds is in 2027, when MTA will be housed in rent-free facilities!

The funding for the intermodal center was a combination of federal, state, and local funds. Construction had started for the intermodal center with just a letter of no prejudice from the Federal Transit Administration, but not the full $145 million dollars. Therefore, the controller-treasurer agreed to issue certificates of participation and other short-term instruments to fund the construction of the project, which could then be rolled over when the actual funding became available. The project was funded by the Federal Government as part of a demonstration project.

John Bollinger said "Patsaouras kept pushing, to keep the project going in spite of the fact that the only real money was $10 million to $15 million yearly funding from the federal government. Pankow was taking risks and ordering material and equipment." Catellus's Rob Vogel said, "So we're digging this hole, and Pankow is like going, 'How far can we commit, because we saved a boatload of money by buying all the reinforcing steel up front?' They were saying 'They, RTD, are not going to let us bill for this, so how are we going to keep doing that?'" Ted Tanner said, "There was trust between Catellus and the RTD. There was camaraderie among those involved, teamwork, instilled from the beginning by Nick. This teamwork and trust were the main reasons the project was built on budget and on time."

I had a similar experience in 2007 with the Los Angeles Police Administration Building, with Ron Tutor as the general contractor, when I was asked by Mayor Villaraigosa to oversee the project. Tutor would proceed with work at his own risk because there had been developed from the beginning a trust between the city and Tutor. As a result, that $500 million project was built under budget and on time.

I chaired a kickoff meeting with the MTA headquarters architects, engineers, artists, and planners. I indicated that I expected the consultants to do their best work. They should not be worried about external players trying to force their own ideas or the eventual criticism by the press. "I'll take all the bullets and arrows. You don't have to worry. Do your job and do it right. I expect great design, because great design does not mean expensive design. Let's finish the project successfully, then you can take your bows and kudos. Do the good work and credit will come. Once we are done, the press can't do anything about it." Landscape architect and planner Laurie Olin years later said, "Nick gave us enough rope to hang ourselves." I added, "I expect a signature complex, not admired on a postcard or viewed from a helicopter, but a people's space." The vast majority of us experience a tower from ground level. Only helicopter passengers see the top floors of a skyscraper. Urban theorist Jane Jacobs spoke of a need to maintain "eyes upon the street." This means buildings need active ground-floor uses.

During the meeting, I posed the question: "Who is the conductor?" Faces looked surprised and perplexed. I explained "We have great violinists, piano players, trumpet players, etc., but where is the symphony? I would like you to spend one day, all of you, architects, planners, engineers, landscape designers, artists, etc., and explain to the group your individual vision. I expect a seamless, coordinated design." Visitors to the Transit Center would agree that the group was successful in achieving a design that is seamless, harmonious, calming, pleasant, and functional. I believe that the public may not be aware of the details, but it has a great experience passing by or relaxing in multiple places.

After the meeting, the architects came with plans and schemes that did not satisfy my vision. Of course, they were eager to get started, protesting that there would be delays of the project, but I was undeterred. One day I received a call from architect Stan Eckstut, who was based in New York. He told me, "Nick, I think I got what you are looking for. I'd like to fly over and show you." The next day Eckstut came and presented a picture of the Rockefeller Center in New York. Immediately excited, I exclaimed, "That's it." The RTD headquarters is at the north end of a vibrant, very public plaza, with the East Portal and other developable buildings, in the future, on either side of the plaza. In fact, there are foundations for future buildings, so there is no need for excavation.

In one of the design charrettes taking place at the then vacant Harvey's Restaurant in Union Station, Laurie Olin was having a hard time with RTD bus operations personnel. Steve Nakada the project manager for Eckstut remembers, "There was a heated discussion. The operations people said, 'There is no way you are going to have trees up against the curb. It will never work,' and one of the guys actually said to Laurie, 'I'm going to cut your goddamn trees with a chain saw, if you plant these there.' Laurie reached across and grabbed the guy by his tie, and people had to break them apart. It was a very tense meeting." There were also complaints that the buses would not be able to negotiate the turns because of the arroyo design. I walked in, saw the model and I said, "Brilliant." A compromise eventually was reached, and the palm trees were placed back enough to satisfy all concerns. According to Vogel, "Laurie Olin did not equivocate. He understood that you have to be creative with ADA requirements, material costs, and building costs. Internally, Eckstut argued with Olin. They argued that's not really what they thought they were going to do, blah, blah. Well, once Patsaouras said, 'Brilliant,' then everybody shut up."

In another situation Eckstut wanted only one bridge over the arroyo, according to Robin Blair, MTA director of planning, who remembers as follows. "I said, 'No, there really needs to be two bridges because of the means of getting to the bus stops,' and he would yell and scream at me. Eckstut said, 'No. I'm going to go directly to Nick.' We had this meeting and he presented it, and I sat on the side. After about forty minutes of presentation, Eckstut looked over and said, 'Robin, what do you think?' and Blair said, 'I'm going to need two bridges,' and I said, 'Stan, design two bridges.'" The arroyo, which imitates a dry river, came about because of ADA requirements that were just coming into effect, and so the way to deal with the arroyo was to make it an ADA ramp to meet all the rules without creating a whole series of ramps.

I had learned through my experience with the media and the different governmental agencies while lobbying for Federal funding for the subway, and therefore I set from the very beginning the ground rules on how the bidding process would proceed, even though it was a public-private partnership. Vogel wanted to award contracts to subcontractors the way a private sector entity does, because "It's design-build." I told Vogel, "You cannot do that, because based on my experience, there will be audits, considering public funds are involved." Vogel was not happy, but he came around. I instructed Vogel, "You, the president of USG, counsel, the cost estimator, and other appropriate parties, review the bids and select accordingly. And above all else, you document the reasons for your selection, so there is a paper trail."

At the end of the project, after the audits by the funding agencies were complete, Vogel told me years later, "Nick, you were godsend. The Feds audited the books and they did not find any irregularities. Thank you very much." Bollinger added, "The Feds audited everything above $10,000 and more. We showed competitive process, we had everything documented and they gave us a clean bill of health."

I had insisted there would not be interviews, bragging about the designs, and definitely "no leaks." According to Bollinger, "The project was not publicized because it would not appear on the monthly RTD agenda. USG had received authorization and approval up front from the full RTD board for scope, budget, and schedule and did not have to get any more approvals. Otherwise, the press would question and second-guess every decision. In addition, the project was far enough from downtown that people did not pay attention." The *Los Angeles Times* had not focused on the building until it was practically finished. A critic quoted in the *Times* and other publications called the building a "Taj Mahal," an unfortunate and erroneous characterization. It should be pointed out that the funds used for construction of the building could be used only for construction and not for operating expenses, subsidies of fares, or the purchase of buses or trains.

State Sen. Quentin Kopp, chairman of the Senate Transportation Committee, said, "I was flabbergasted. I was in awe of such conspicuous consumption." A comment from another politician feeding into the public's perception that government is inefficient and wasteful. That senator is the same person who brought us the high-speed rail, between Los Angeles and San Francisco, a disastrous project with astronomical cost overruns and unbelievable delays.

I knew that sooner or later the media and critics would focus on the costs, and I therefore had asked the consultants to take a survey of the construction costs of ten private sector downtown office buildings of similar size. The construction cost of the RTD tower fell within the middle range. "Italian marble" was a nonsense criticism. There was only $500,000 worth of Italian marble in the $145 million building, and that was for a special application. In fact, the Italian granite was cheaper than the domestic variety. Of the building material used, 95 percent was American, with only the following exceptions. The escalators were manufactured by Mitsubishi Company of Japan, the lowest responsive and responsible bidder. The stone panels for the Headquarters curtain wall were fabricated and imported from Savona, Italy, with an estimated $200,000 saved by using the Italian firm. The granite in the lower level was used as an anti-graffiti material, saving maintenance costs. When a visitor walks in the offices above the public spaces, they will notice it is just a landscape office design, similar to any standard office building.

Critics also brought up "English brick." There had been a discussion about the type of material to be used in the plaza. Concrete or asphalt were options but were dismissed for costs, durability, and maintenance. It was decided to use brick. But before proceeding, it was decided to test brick with buses not only running over them but also turning on them. An area with American brick was built at the northeast section of Union Station. Unfortunately, the American bricks could not withstand the weight and movement of the buses and they would be pulverized.

Someone then suggested we consider using English bricks because roads in England paved with bricks have stood the test of time. It was decided that a group would fly to England for research. Although I was the chair of the USG board, I refused to go because I did not want to give the media a reason to call the trip a "junket." The English bricks were cheaper than the American ones, and thirty years later they have withstood the test of time. The brick were laid on sand, and they can be picked up individually with a knife and replaced. Thus, maintenance is simple, in contrast to cracked concrete or asphalt.

Steve Nakada, the project architect, pointed out, “Patsaouras had instructed the consultants that he wanted a building, a plaza, a public space to last one hundred years. There was a hundred-year criterion in the specifications that were in the contracts. Operations has its maintenance manual, so like building systems, periodically you need to check for any movement, check the waterproofing. If there is sand loss all you need to do is throw sand on it. It is a paving system that is not new. Part of the research was seeing how the Europeans did this. This is no different than the Appian Way that the Romans used, where it’s granite cobblestones on sand. The bricks really require very little surface maintenance. Oil does not penetrate the clay pavers. The bus tires pick it up and take the grease out of there. The only concern is sand loss, and that is why periodically casting sand right over the bricks is necessary. Dallas-Fort Worth International Airport uses the same system for airplanes. Right on the tarmacs they have concrete pavers, and you have these huge airplanes just taxiing around. The reason they have it is because sometimes they need to repair the utilities fast and they can’t wait for concrete to cure. They lift the pavers overnight, they change the utilities, they put the sand and the pavers back, and the next day it is in use. It is a great system if it is maintained properly, and I think anybody who comes to LA admires this signature brick paving plaza. It is the largest installation of brick paving in the country, on a suspended deck, and the pattern is very unusual. The pattern actually comes from the Chumash and Gabrielino Indiginous Americans, who used to reside here, from their basket weaving patterns.”

There were many challenges for a complex and complicated project such as this. During the early design stages of the tower, when the USG board was working to get the green light from the full RTD board for the costs and scope of the project, there were objections regarding the need for a child-care center for the employees. Interestingly, the objections came from the female board members. At the time childcare centers at public facilities was a novel concept.

Los Angeles City Councilwoman Joy Picus introduced the Child Care Policy in City Hall in the late 1980s, and after persistence and perseverance, she established a child-care center in City Hall, and it was named after her. Again, I did not give up and convinced my colleagues that it would be great for morale and instill loyalty in the employees. A free-standing childcare center exists today next to Alatorre Park. There is a waiting list to enroll, and it is operated by a private contractor. The *Los Angeles Times*, in a story regarding child-care centers, wrote in January 2023, “The lack of availability and affordability (of child-care centers) has forced many parents, especially mothers, to put their own careers on hold.”

However, I was very vigilant, always questioning why, when, and how every dollar was spent, asking for justification for small or large costs. I give a lot of credit to Bollinger, who was a stickler for detail and documentation, although that did not make Bollinger popular with some members of the team. Bollinger was assisted by a very competent and experienced cost estimator, Iskander Abdulla, who gave very detailed monthly presentations to the USG Board. Los Angeles City Councilman Bill Rosendahl, referred to me as, “A bulldog, the taxpayers’ watchdog.” Vogel said, “Nick was very, very tough. I mean if I heard him once, he said it a million times, 'no change orders.'" There were only three change orders. The steel modifications as a result of the 1994 Northridge Earthquake and two minor ones because of design improvements. For a project of this magnitude, it is almost unheard of.

And Villaraigosa said, "Nick was so tough with consultants and contractors, I would sometimes hide under the counter. I was so embarrassed. However, that was one of the reasons I asked Nick, ten years later, to oversee the Los Angeles Police Administration Building when Ron Tutor was the general contractor. Nick is tough, gets things done, high integrity, loyal and independent."

On January 17, 1994, when the steel frame was four to five levels above ground, the devastating Northridge Earthquake hit Los Angeles. The whole building code changed. One had to do with different welding and the stiffening requirement was huge. We did not have to change the foundation. At the ground floor, the columns are all clad in stone, massive. Those are box beams that could be made only in Belgium. Herrick Company, an American firm, subcontracted $200,000 to the Belgian steel company to acquire special structural shapes and reduce cost. They made them in Belgium, they put them on ships, took them all the way through the Panama Canal, and we had to get numerous nighttime permits to get them to the site, but because we had already started construction, that was the only real cost-effective way we could come up to meet the new codes.

As Vogel said, "We had meetings in the Building Department, and they said, 'You are going to build the tower and the East Portal to the new code, but it's up to you as to whether you do what you've already got in place and you go back and retrofit.' So, that took a nanosecond to figure out no retrofit."

Bollinger remembers: "At that time, there were not enough inspectors, so we came up with a deal whereby we were willing to pay extra to bring consultants that the City would agree to use as inspectors. That helped move the construction forward with no delays. There was also a strike against MTA. They struck the site briefly, but we showed them that the workers were union. That also helped to move the project forward without delays."

The decision was made to design and construct the building as an "essential services facility," considering it is important for the building to operate during a human-made or natural disaster. Such a building is designed for a higher seismic event with uninterrupted power and communications. Essential buildings are fire and police stations, emergency operations centers, California Highway Patrol offices, Sheriff's offices, and emergency communication dispatch centers.

I had made sure from the beginning that there was a line item of $5 million for art in the budget, emphasizing that art must be an integral part of architecture, and not an afterthought. People later asked, "How could you afford this?" My reply, "It's part of the budget that the full board approved."

The need for an aquarium in the East Portal was questioned, and for cost savings it was suggested to be eliminated. First, the cost of $300,000 was a line item in the budget. Second, I fought fiercely to have it built, pointing out that children from certain communities do not have the opportunity to see real fish. It has been gratifying to see during school days children with their noses at the glass wall of the aquarium, admiring and getting excited watching

Bus shelter at Patsaouras Transit Plaza. *Reunion*. Artists: KimYasuda and Noel Korten. Photo: courtesy of Metro

Aquarium at Metro Transit Center. Artists: May Sun and Richard Wyatt. Photo: courtesy of Metro

the fish. It is a seven-thousand-gallon undulating aquarium. Artist May Sun stocked it with coastal saltwater and native Pacific fish. In fact, the original design for the aquarium was twenty times bigger, located at the south end of the Plaza along the 101 Freeway. It was downsized and relocated as part of the value engineering process.

The procurement process for the art was unique at the time, in that there was full outreach in the community. Artists were engaged from within the Los Angeles area. The person responsible for the art program was Tamara Thomas, an exceptionally talented individual as anyone visiting the complex will attest by observing the beauty and variety of the art. Unfortunately, Thomas died at a very early age.

The artwork links the MTA building to the 1939 Union Station. Public art is on a scale not seen here since the Works Progress Administration projects of the 1930s. Seventeen artists were selected. Michael Amescua adapted the Latin American craft of paper cutouts into the medium metal for the "Guardians of the Track," elegant, patterned metal fences, guardrails, and wall motifs decorating the Plaza. The bus shelters are etched glass and ribbed wings and vine-like structures, metal work so complex that an out-of-state firm that builds roller coasters was used.

The pedestrian connection between the Plaza and the intersection of Cesar Chavez Avenue and Vignes Street was originally a Spartan design with limited enhancements, an oversight remedied by then City Councilman Richard Alatorre. The Councilman requested more prominent and striking improvements along the pathway. Three tiled fountains by Roberto Gil de Montes, Elsa Flores, and Peter Shire now decorate the passageway, creating a mini park experience, affectionately referred to as "Alatorre Park." It is one of the most traveled corridors in the Gateway complex. Inside the building, at the entrance to the cafeteria, Margaret Nielsen's panoramas of memory are captured in postcards from Los Angeles past, the glamorous 1930s and 1940s.

Patrick Nagatani's mural collage "Epoch" at the boardroom entrance, a series of 1887 photographs by photo pioneer Eadweard Muybridge, that show a naked man in motion drew complaints and was covered. Some workers were shocked, others were amused. At the man's feet are postcard images of trolleys, trains, and antiquated modes of transportation. Around him are NASA photographs of space.

National TV stations and media covered the

Artwork by Michael Amescua at Patsaouras Transit Plaza. Photo courtesy of Metro

Fountain at Richard Alatorre Park/ Paseo Cesar Chavez. Artists: Elsa Flores, Peter Shire, Roberto Gil de Montes. Courtesy of Metro

James Doolin's mural, *Los Angeles, circa 1870*, at Metro Headquarters. Photo: courtesy of Metro

Los Angeles After 2000. Artist: James Doolin. Photo: courtesy of Metro (MTA building at lower right)

controversy. I told the media, "Personally, my view is that the Sistine Chapel has ten times more nudity than this. Art should provoke debate." The ACLU of Southern California sent a letter condemning the covering of the mural as censorship and an "unconstitutional abridgement of free speech under the 1st Amendment." Eventually the curtain was removed, eliciting applause from dozens of employees.

In the lobby of the building, visitors can admire James Doolin's bird's-eye-view murals. Visions of Los Angeles transportation are used as a device to cut through time and space from "Circa 1870," where a train moves toward a new century, to "Circa 1910," a city falling in love with cars, to "Circa 1960," a sprawling smog covered metropolis, and "Circa 2000," a mural at the third floor that envisions a city of the future with the MTA building and the Hollywood sign clearly seen.

City of Dreams/River of History in East Portal of Metro Transit Center.Artist, Richard Wyatt. Photo: Courtesy of Metro

At the East Portal, next to the escalators leading down to the subway, are the "lightsticks" by artist Bill Bell. Fleeting, images of freight trains and cars, historical figures, and movie stars. The "persistence" of vision retains the image in memory after it has passed in front of the eye. I am pictured here, running after a bus.

In the East Portal, on the west wall are faces painted on the huge mural, "City of Dreams/ River of History" by Richard Wyatt depicting the multiethnic faces of Los Angeles. They are images of Indigenous Gabrielino, Latinos, and Angelenos. The faces of vanished Angelenos also appear etched on the glass of the aquarium nearby. The mural contains the face of a young Latino modeled after the face of Antonio Villaraigosa. The artist was asked, "Where am I?" by Board member Antonio Villaraigosa, as he looked at the artist's mock-up of the mural and the mix of faces. The artist returned later with a different mix of faces and a new child's face modeled after a much younger Villaraigosa.

The floor of the East Portal is decorated by now internationally famous artist May Sun with bronze images of turtles, trout, and sycamore leaves that once swam or floated in the Los Angeles River. Sun designed a serpentine tile bench along a water sculpture that depicts a riverbed set in rocks from the river itself, medicine bottles and other artifacts unearthed from the original Chinatown, which stood where the train station now stands. The river theme is carried by Laurie Olin in his Arroyo design. Fountains, fences, grills, and walls of Kasota stone are part of the traveler's experience as they descend hurriedly to catch their train. Beneath the bridges and planters are arboreal tile murals by Wayne Alaniz Healy and David Rivas Botello. Painted tile birds and animals are seen among the trees and bridges, and there is also "La Sombra del Arroyo" or "Shadow of the Stream" by the East Los Streetscapers.

La Sombra del Arroyo. Artist(s): East Los Streetscapers. Courtesy of Metro

The MTA headquarters, designed by McLarand, Vasquez & Partners Inc., is a twenty-six-story tower with 628,000 square feet of space. The building, with its mix of Moorish-Spanish, Art Deco, and Modern, its chandeliers and tile mosaics, imitates Union Station and, as such, carries on the architectural tradition expressed in Los Angeles earlier times, creating a building that is quintessentially "Southern California."

The design emphasizes the pedestrian quality of the building's base, with detailed architecture scale relating to the historic Union Station. The project includes an arts program in the tradition of the Beaux-Arts, where artwork is combined directly into the architectural design.

During the preliminary stages of the design, the 350-seat board room was to be on the west side of the building with spectacular views of the Los Angeles skyline. I vetoed this choice and insisted that the employee cafeteria instead be placed there because the employees

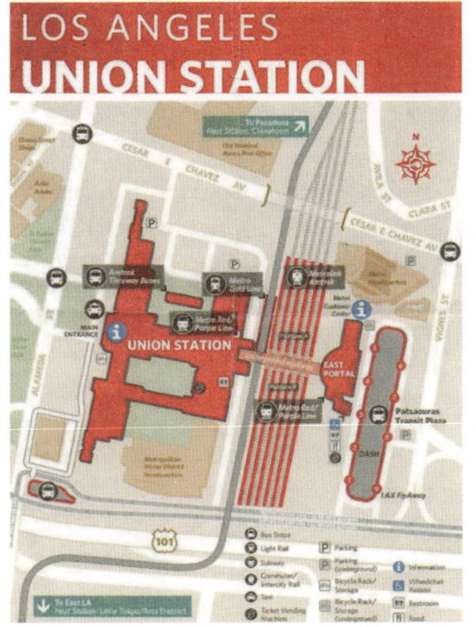

Union Station site plan. Courtesy of Metro

Dome of East Portal at Metro Transit Center. Photo: courtesy of Metro

deserve to spend their lunchtimes enjoying a beautiful view. Besides, the board members go there once or twice a month, whereas the employees go there every day.

The construction of the building was filmed in the 1994 children's video, "There Goes a Bulldozer," in which Dave Hood climbed a tower crane. In the *Star Trek: Voyager* episode "Future's End," a digitally altered image of the building was used to represent the 1996 headquarters of villain Henry Starling (Ed Begley, Jr.). The building was again seen, this time on a matte painting depicting a building on the Mari Homeworld in the *Star Trek: Voyager* episode "Random Thoughts" in 1997.

The architect for the Intermodal Transit Center was the Ehrenkrantz & Eckstut Architects. The project managers were Steve Nakada and Allen Terry, exceptionally talented architects. Unfortunately, Terry died young. Because of his dedication to the project and his excellent design, a commemorative plaque was placed in the arroyo to honor him. The associate architect for the East Portal was RAW Architecture. The Transit Center is one of the most important urban development and transit projects in the nation.

The Plaza accommodates more than a dozen bus lines and offers transit users and nearby office workers an inviting and richly varied outdoor environment with plazas, gardens, landscape walkways and art. The Transit Center serves Metro's Red, Purple, and Gold Lines, Amtrak and Metrolink, while the Patsaouras Transit Plaza in the East Portal area offers essential bus connections with about 1,500 arriving and departing buses very day. Those services include Megabus, FlyAway, Greyhound, Bolt, USC Shuttle, and local service from Metro and other municipal lines including Foothill Transit, Antelope Valley Transit Authority, Santa Monica Big Blue Bus, Los Angeles Department of Transportation's Dash, and Orange County Transportation Authority.

The East Portal is a grand concourse that links the Plaza and Union Station. Its impressive semicircular space and dramatic canopy of steel and glass recalls America's and Europe's historic stations, as well as provides all weather protection for transit users. "The East Portal is this half cylinder half dome, and it is not air conditioned. It acts as a thermal chimney, and it actually takes air from the subway. It has got a sun-shading device, tetrahedrons, and it is able to keep the temperature at a very ambient cool temperature because the walls are five feet thick and it has got a double layer of skylit dome. The pattern of the sun-shading device has actually come from Arabic geometries. A lot of local stone was used. The Cold Springs granite comes from the Sierra Nevada Mountain range. The limestone from Minnesota. It captures uniquely the Southern California sunlight. The stone comes out of the earth and it is in layers, so if you cut the stone in one way, you actually see the veins in one way, but if you cut the stone that way, you have what is called the fleuricut, it has all these swirls. This stone is used as an accent around the windows and openings," Nakada said.

The Transit Center is about 92,000 square feet, with 2,500 parking spaces in four levels below ground. Part of the garage is below Vignes Street. The tower and the Intermodal Center were completed in October 1995. On February 28, 1996, the MTA Board of Directors voted to rename the Gateway Transit Plaza the Patsaouras Transit Plaza in my honor.

"The naming of this beautiful plaza after Nick Patsaouras is appropriate since his dedication and hard work over many years was in large part responsible for its completion," MTA

Board Chairman Larry Zarian said. "This is a fitting tribute for a man who gave of his time and expertise to complete this project for the people of Los Angeles." MTA Board Member Richard Alatorre said, "Nick Patsaouras has spent ten years spearheading this project and overseeing the design and construction activities. He had a dream with a vision of creating a transportation hub serving both bus and rail passengers for generations to come. He deserves this recognition."

In an interview with the *Los Angeles Times* in September 1997, I was asked, "You see the Gateway Center next to Union Station as an important civic statement. How does a piece of transportation architecture make us feel better about Los Angeles?" To which I replied, "History tells us that it does, whether it's Rome, Paris, Athens, or Los Angeles. Great public buildings have always created a sense of pride and public unity. But it's important that public buildings are accessible and people friendly."

At the ten-year anniversary ceremony, Board Member Marvin Holen said, "This is a building of beauty and function, located in the right place. Not to have built it would have diminished the treasure that is Union Station. It was built with very great care for taxpayer money and it's a landmark building for Los Angeles. Everyone is proud of it."

On November 1, 2020, there was an addition to the Patsaouras Transit Plaza. It is used by lines that run on the El Monte Busway and offers an easier, quicker, and safer connection to Union Station. The new platform features full Metro station amenities, including a shade canopy, ticket vending machines, seating, closed-circuit TV surveillance, electronic message signs, ADA-compliant elevators, and a pedestrian bridge. A notable project improvement is the new pedestrian bridge that directly connects the busway station to Patsaouras Plaza. California

Foreground: "Wind Bridge" connecting a busway station to Union Station and Patsaouras Transit Plaza. Artist: Ned Kahn. Photo: courtesy of Metro

artist Ned Kahn designed the 750-foot-long bridge, *The Wind Bridge*, dressing it up with stainless steel panels that move with the wind and reveal patterns of light and shade. The bridge is lit at night to reveal patterns of silhouettes against illuminated surfaces inside the bridge.

The project was named by *Engineering News Record* among California's 2021 "Best Project Winners." It received the honor for Best Airport/Transit Project in Southern California. ENR is widely regarded as one of the construction industry's most authoritative publications.

VIGNETTES

Steve Nakada, the architect of the Gateway Transit Center and East Portal, recounts an experience he had at the arroyo of the Patsaouras Transit Plaza. "I think one of the nicest emotional experiences I've had was actually in the arroyo after it had opened up. There was a grandmother who had about six children, probably half of them were not her own, but she was in the arroyo with these children and it was a safe place. You could vaguely hear the buses whirling around, but here her kids were playing before going to board the bus, but she could watch the kids. I watched her, and then she got up and got right into the bus. That to me rang very loud and clear that the agencies had done their job, that we had created something that was a great amenity for the public."

*

The negotiations for the RTD headquarters between RTD and Catellus were very tough and exhaustive for both sides. In one meeting, RTD Operations Director Gary Spivack and RTD Counsel Jeff Lyons were negotiating with a vice president of Catellus, who was very difficult to close the deal. At one point, the vice president, according to Spivack, told Lyons and Spivack, "Take everything I got because I have nothing left from the company to offer." They walked out of the negotiations. The rest of the Catellus team, embarrassed by this demonstration, pleaded with Spivack and Lyons to return to the table.

SOUTHERN CALIFORNIA RAPID TRANSIT DISTRICT

A Bold New Bus Era | The California State Assembly on August 22, 1964, enacted legislation creating the Southern California Rapid Transit District to serve Los Angeles, Orange, Riverside, and San Bernardino Counties. RTD was charged with creating a heavy rail public transportation system for Southern California as well as planning for bus improvements. In 1973, RTD began narrowing its service area when the Orange County Transit District took over Orange County service.

In 1976, the California State Legislature adopted Assembly Bill 1246 by Assemblyman Walter Ingalls, which created the Los Angeles County Transportation Commission to oversee public transit and highway policy in the county. The law required the transportation commission to approve all plans and funding for transit projects and operations and highway

With Supervisor Michael Antonovich.

improvements. The rival agencies, the RTD and transportation commission, were merged with the formation of the Los Angeles County Metropolitan Transportation Authority on February 1, 1993. The merger was the result of Assembly Bill 152 by Assemblyman Richard Katz. It took effect April 1, 1993.

In 1980, Baxter Ward, a two-term county supervisor and former TV news anchor was up for re-election. A key issue in both the City and County at that time was energy, which was slowly spinning into a national crisis for President Carter. It was an opportunity for me to step forward as an electrical engineer, experienced in energy management and transportation. The notion that my professional experience could carry the day was naïve. I envisioned a race in which an immigrant could stitch together different constituencies, ethnic communities, and civic groups in which he held membership—such as the San Fernando Valley Wine and Food Society, cultural organizations, the Jonathan Club, and a Northridge college relationship—and gain needed support.

These were hopeful thoughts that lacked political practicality. I did not consider how important campaign funding was for success in the largest local governmental operation in the nation. At the time, each of the five county supervisorial districts encompassed nearly 1.5 million residents, nearly three times more than a congressional district. In 1980, the County annual budget was $4.45 billion; today it is more than $40 billion. A candidate may have the right message, but to convey it funding is needed—and lots of it. Without it no candidate stands a chance.

Also running in the June 1980 primary election was Mike Antonovich, a stalwart of the Republican Party with name recognition and a political base as a state assemblymember from Glendale and with heavy support from the development community. Since 1911, local offices in California technically have been considered non-partisan, but Antonovich also had the powerful backing, financial support, and endorsement from the lone Republican incumbent supervisor, Pete Schabarum.

Antonovich, with 44 percent of the vote, and Ward with 41 percent, were the two top finishers in the primary and advanced to the November runoff. Even with scarce funding, I received 9.2 percent of the vote. About one in ten people had connected with me.

Heading into the November general election, both Ward and Antonovich, who finished first with 44%, courted me. I met individually several times with both but realized if I were to be effective after the race, I had to be able to work with someone who would listen. Ward was a lone wolf; my voice would eventually not be heard if I endorsed him. Antonovich, despite our party differences, was very attentive.

After conducting their polling, they concluded that my votes were solid, and my endorsement would be important. I endorsed Antonovich who went on to unseat Ward by a margin of 55.2 percent to 44.8 percent in the general election.

Sure enough, it was written and discussed that my endorsement had significantly contributed to Antonovich's becoming the new county supervisor in 1980. He served for nine terms—the second-longest tenure of a Los Angeles County supervisor behind only the forty years served by Supervisor Kenneth Hahn—until he was forced out of office in 2014 by term limits.

In February 1981, I got a call from Kathleen Crow, Antonovich's Chief of Staff, asking if I would be interested in serving as his appointee on the RTD Board of Directors. I was taken aback because as an electrical engineer I thought I could be more useful in matters of energy. Also, as a self-employed businessman I could be effective in any involvement with the business part of the county. I told her, "Let me think about it."

At that time, I was friends with Marvin Holen, whose wife served with me on the LA Ballet Board of Directors. I knew that Holen served on the RTD Board of Directors as an appointee of Supervisor Edmund Edelman. I called him and said, "Marvin, I was offered a seat on the Board of Directors of RTD, but I don't think I would be interested because what do I have to do with running a bus company?" At that time, RTD was the operator of the bus system in the Los Angeles area. Marvin said, "Let's have dinner." At dinner he told me what a terrific challenge RTD would be. RTD had received federal funding for preliminary engineering for the subway. I was convinced. I called Antonovich's office the next day and accepted the seat on the board.

I served as Antonovich's appointee for more than fifteen years on the boards of the RTD, the Los Angeles County Transportation Commission, and the MTA. I will always appreciate that Antonovich trusted my judgment and never questioned throughout all those years any of the decisions I made as his representative on the boards. I am also grateful that he gave me the opportunity to be involved in crucial civic issues in those historic years.

For me, the opportunity to serve on the RTD's eleven-member board of directors and subsequently on the MTA board was a privilege and a blessing. Serving as president of the RTD board from 1983 to 1986, and again from 1990 to 1991, set the course of my life from then on.

In 1983, the board President Michael Lewis indicated he was not going to run again for president. I decided I would be a candidate. I approached my fellow board members expressing my interest and outlining my vision and ideas. I was successful in securing five votes of support. Two weeks before the election, Lewis called me and told me that he had changed his mind, and he was going to seek the presidency again. "That's fine Mike," I said. "What, are you still going to run?" a surprised Lewis asked me. "Yes Mike, and may the best man win," was my response.

Five minutes before the election Lewis invited me to his office and asked. "Are you still running?" I responded, "Mike, as of this morning I checked with my five votes and they are still with me." "You are going to lose," Lewis said. I leaned across the table, looked Lewis straight into his eyes, paused for fifteen seconds and said, "Mike, if I were afraid to lose I wouldn't be here!" A few minutes later the first item on the agenda was the election of officers. I won by a vote of six to five!

Seeking the presidency took conviction, confidence, and courage.

From then on it was an odyssey of hard work, excitement, disappointments, victories, and losses and above all my opportunity to become a small part of Los Angeles's history and fabric. During my presidency (1983–86), I focused on securing funding for Metro Rail, the RTD's participation in the transportation plan for the 1984 Summer Olympics, and labor negotiations.

According to the *Los Angeles Times* in 1997, historian Kevin Starr called me "the most influential transportation activist of this generation."

LABOR PEACE

Labor negotiations were underway in the spring of 1985. California Gov. George Deukmejian was putting pressure on the RTD and its five thousand drivers to agree on a new contract before a cooling-off period expired April 21. "If the district and the union fail to reach an accord during this period, it will represent nothing more than a cruel slap in the face to the daily riders" the governor said in a letter dated April 4, to me as RTD board president and Earl Clark, head of the United Transportation Union. When negotiations fell apart in late January, both sides asked the governor to intervene by appointing a panel to study the dispute and by asking the Court to issue a sixty-day injunction against a walkout. Clark said the union would do all it could to reach an agreement, while I said I hoped a deal could be reached if the union met the RTD halfway. "The district has gone as far as it can," I said. "We are not in a bargaining position anymore. What they see is what they get."

On April 17, 1985, the RTD and the bus drivers union announced an agreement had been reached on a new contract. The announcement was made after two days of bargaining that went virtually around the clock and four days before the end of the court-imposed cooling off period. Los Angeles Mayor Tom Bradley, remarking that RTD negotiations had always

Announcing labor settlement in 1985, first since 1969. With Union Chief Earl Clark. Photo: courtesy of Metro

RTD Poster Night at Dodger Stadium, 7/28/1990. Photo: courtesy of Metro

unraveled and led to strikes said, "I'm ready to shout hallelujah! Bravo to Nick, John (Dyer), and Earl (Clark)."

The RTD also reached agreements with the Brotherhood of Railway, Airline and Steamship Clerks, a union that represented 700 clerical employees, and the Amalgamated Transit Union, which represented eighteen hundred mechanics. "This long-term contract," I said, "gives RTD the opportunity to predict its costs. It is within the budget and therefore would not force us to increase the bus fares." It marked the first time since 1969 that the RTD arrived at labor contracts without a strike. There had been five strikes previously. I called the accord "a truly a landmark agreement, the longest in RTD's history."

"We've never had a ratification vote like this before," an excited Earl Clark said. "It`s a beautiful package. We're proud of it."

What brought this new era in labor relations to the transit system? The key element was a new RTD negotiating philosophy and strategy, devised and aggressively implemented by RTD General Manager John Dyer with my total support as board president. Jerry Long of the mechanics union said, "Dyer rolled up his sleeves and worked with us." Dyer said, "We cannot try to game the union leadership and the unions. They are intelligent. They talk to each other, and they know if they're being snookered." The relationship between the RTD and the unions was very different when Jack Gilstrap was RTD general manager during the 1970s. "Not once did he (Gilstrap) ever sit down in negotiations with the leaders of any union," Long said.

SECOND TIME AROUND

I served again as president of RTD in 1990–91. I focused at that time on improving the RTD's poor image—bus riders were unhappy and employee morale was low. The RTD was widely perceived as inefficient and tardy, with dirty buses, lousy bus service, and rude drivers. Along the way, RTD had lost territory and funding. Ridership was declining. I took a page from the public relations playbook of Lee Iacocca who was best known for reviving Chrysler Corp., and embarked on a number of programs, calling news conferences weekly. The RTD public relations staff told me the media would ignore the programs and initiatives. How wrong were they!

THE TRANSIT RIDER BILL OF RIGHTS

- Freedom of choice—Consumers should have the opportunity and freedom to choose their means of transportation.
- A safe journey—Safety is a primary concern.
- Courtesy—Everyone should be treated with courtesy and respect.
- Convenience and reliability—Meet schedules.

- Access to transit stops and vehicles—The RTD is committed to making its fleet 100 percent accessible to seniors and wheelchair users.
- Timely and accurate information—Every rider has the right to correct and timely information.
- Quality service—Every rider has the right to expect that the vehicles will be well-maintained, clean, and free from graffiti.

The inclusion of the "right to timely and accurate information" was the result of my personal experience seeking information from RTD. As a college student, I rode the bus, and once in a while I had to call RTD for information. The public telephone booths, when one could find them, were the only place where one could use the phone. Unfortunately, I often found myself in a cold telephone booth calling RTD for information, but waiting for a long time before anyone would answer, and sometimes with no answer at all.

When I became president in 1990, I would hold monthly meetings with the executive staff. In one such meeting, I turned to General Manager Alan Pegg and said, "Alan, could you please call information and ask how to get from here to Ventura Boulevard and Sepulveda in Encino?" Perplexed, Pegg stared at me and said, "What do you mean?" I replied, "Alan, I need to get to the Valley, and I need to know which lines and where the bus stops are." Pegg dialed the number, and the phone kept ringing and ringing and ringing. One could see the tense faces of all present in the room and a deafening silence, which made the phone's incessant ringing even more unnerving. I turned to Pegg and said, "Alan, how would you like to

Announcing RTD Transit Rider Bill of Rights: With RTD General Manager Allan Pegg and Police Chief Sharon Papa. Photo: courtesy of Metro

be stranded on a cold rainy night in a telephone booth and you can't get an RTD operator to help you? What would it take for an operator to answer after two rings?" Pegg replied, "Eight to ten extra operators." "Alan, get it done," I said.

As board president, I visited all RTD departments, including the operators. News of the board president making the rounds in the building went through the building like a "firestorm," according to the board Secretary Helen Bolen. I told the operators they were the voice and ears of the agency and we depended on them. Tears came down some of their faces, probably because no one had bothered to appreciate them thus far. I carried this customer service protocol to the Los Angeles Department of Water and Power when I served as president of its board of commissioners a few years later.

The *Transit Rider Bill of Rights* received worldwide recognition, with requests for information coming from Houston, Toronto, Montreal, and Melbourne, Australia.

DIVISION OF THE MONTH

A division of the month was determined by division-wide performance comparisons of criteria applicable to both Transportation and Maintenance. For transportation these indicators included: total days of absenteeism, traffic accident frequency, occupational injuries, number of canceled transportation and late transportation assignments, and bus-related customer complaints.

The performance criteria for equipment maintenance included improvement of miles between road calls, improvement of accessible service, occupational injuries, improvement in coach cleanliness, absenteeism, number of maintenance-related complaints, and the number of out-lates—buses that leave the maintenance yard late for service—and cancellations.

The outstanding division flag flew for a month on the division's flagpole below the California flag. The announcement of the Division of the Month was made at the division at 4:00 a.m., rain or shine, by me as board president and General Manager Pegg. I visited each of the fourteen operating divisions, from downtown Los Angeles to Pomona, collecting suggestions, ideas, and complaints. Most executives had never visited a division before. As a result of my direct style, bus maintenance improved. As the program went into effect, the average number of buses unavailable to hit the road dropped 14 percent. The average number of miles between breakdowns climbed 20 percent. Morale among employees improved. Bus drivers were calling out the names of stops more than 70 percent of the time compared with the month before. Interviews with drivers indicated that I had made an impact according to the *Downtown News.*

"He is trying to get better morale," said Jesus Jimenez, an RTD driver for ten years. "We needed someone like that. Before drivers weren't stopping [at stops] and were not calling out stops." Tony Cabada, a fifteen-year RTD veteran said, "In comparison with other people, we've had before, he cares. He's the only board president who's come to the division." Compared with the year before, 76 percent fewer bus runs were canceled on a daily basis, daily weekday ridership was up 3 percent, and the rate of reported crimes had declined by about a third.

AMBASSADOR CORPS

The district put "SCRTD ambassadors" aboard its buses to listen to passengers' comments and complaints. The program included the president, directors, general manager, assistant general managers, and RTD employees of all levels. The ambassadors rode the buses wearing special badges. While aboard the bus, they would greet passengers, talk about the district, and gather suggestions. I had said, "It's critical that RTD management, which makes key decisions affecting millions of riders, take to the buses and converse with them on a one-on-one basis." I noted the Ambassador Program was another element of the district's *Transit Rider Bill of Rights*. Each ambassador rode the selected bus line at least one day per week.

TOLL-FREE HOT LINE

A new 800 toll-free hotline was set up to respond to complaints and suggestions and to assist RTD patrons. And I noted at the time, "The establishment of this toll-free number is part of the RTD *Transit Rider Bill of Rights*. We wish to communicate more with our customers so we can hear what they have to say." The new toll-free number did not alter the service of the telephone information section on routes of buses. I wanted the toll-free number to accommodate complaints, suggestions, and requests for assistance, representing an expansion of our new RTD customer-oriented policy.

PEOPLE MOVING LA IN THE 1990S—"NOW IT'S YOUR TURN AT BAT"

"What does it take to get Los Angeles moving again? My intention in initiating this program is to allow the public an opportunity to propose solutions that would ease our commute crisis and improve the quality of life for all of us," I stated in announcing the contest. A total of 1,100 ideas were submitted, and ninety were singled out for praise, including proposals to install toll booths along roads to encourage carpooling and raise transit money, to allow bicyclists to take their bikes on the Blue Line, and to establish zones where bus rides are free.

The judges found merit in Diana Cheng's proposal to display bus route numbers on the front, side and back of the bus. This excellent suggestion was one among others that were implemented. Peter L. Eason's plan to ease traffic by screening accidents from rubbernecks earned him a shirt, a bus pass, and his name and idea on a commemorative brochure, as was the case with other winners. Officers from the California Highway Patrol, Los Angeles Police Department, and the Los Angeles County Sheriff carry dark polyethylene drapes to shield accident sites from view. (This plan has been successfully implemented in Japan.) RTD board member Norm Emerson, chairman of the contest judging committee said, "One of my favorites is a proposal to allow neighborhoods to adopt a bus, putting their name and community identity on the sides of the bus. This would encourage more people to take the bus but also encourage riders to keep the bus clean.'

Following are some of the other proposals:

Sue Dwiggins: A radio frequency dedicated to traffic news, using call-ins from car phones for up-to-the-minute developments.

Margaret Presley: Post bus timetables at bus stops for lines that run infrequently.

Dorothy Beffman: Encourage bus ridership by having bus schedules and maps more readily available to the general public. All schedules should be available at supermarkets, post offices, libraries, schools, and colleges and major sporting facilities.

George Endress: Place a Happy Miles sign at the front of the bus. A pleasant greeting to bus passengers is sure to brighten their day and will bring goodwill.

Kathleen Rodriquez: Publicize an 800 number so passengers can register their complaints about poor service (another idea implemented).

LA'S NEWEST ATTRACTION

RTD was perceived to be a closed, insular agency, inaccessible, unfriendly to both the customers and the public at large. I initiated LA's Newest Attraction, whereby the public would be given tours of the RTD facilities: towering robots hoisting bus transmissions at RTD's Central Maintenance Facility, computerized trains inching across the Blue Line's Central Control Facility screen, and a state-of-the-art computer center at which a dispatcher tracks buses. Thousands went on these tours to get familiar with the RTD's operations. They would leave impressed, informed, and with an appreciation of the challenges and issues such a huge organization has to confront every day twenty-four hours a day.

THE RIGHT THING TO DO

The program was a special educational project, addressed to teachers, and sponsored by the *Los Angeles Times* and the RTD. Its purpose was to educate students about transportation choices and the environment The project included using the *Times* in the classroom together with newspaper-based teaching strategies for a total of fifteen weeks.

WE'RE PUTTING OUR MONEY WHERE OUR MOUTH IS

RTD press conference. Photo: courtesy of Metro

If the bus was more than fifteen minutes late, the ride was free. Period! The program was intended to boost ridership and public confidence. However, when I first proposed the program, it was met with a lot of skepticism both from the board and staff. I originally proposed ten minutes, and when staff expressed concerns, I said, "Make it fifteen minutes. The public will not register how many minutes, but *late and free*." Next issue was the cost. After much deliberation, the Board voted to approve the program on a four-month trial period at a cost of $2.4 million. "It's time we put our money where our mouths are," I said. "There is a public perception that you cannot depend on the RTD. I believe that if we can break that mostly erroneous perception, our ridership will go up." RTD Board Member Gordana Swanson, who abstained from the vote to introduce the program, said, "In general, I am not in favor of experiments that take up such time and energy. I'm not sure that in the end this program really does much for the average rider."

RTD had set aside $600,000 to cover free fares for the first month, but the actual cost proved to be much less, only $61,000 dollars. "These numbers are phenomenal," I said in a downtown news conference. "The cynics and the bureaucrats said we would lose our shirts, but we have proved them wrong. It's a great day for the RTD." Out of a total of thirty-four million passengers who rode RTD buses, only fifty-nine thousand were granted free rides under the program. That translates to 0.18 of 1 percent. In the first month of the program, bus ridership gained 5 percent, a goal some thought would take a year to accomplish. Drivers had more self-pride. At the end of the trial period, many drivers who had been the most vocal skeptics were the first to demand that the policy be continued.

In response, in a 1991 *Los Angeles Times* story under the headline, "The Man Who Loves the RTD," Joan Taylor wrote, "RTD President Nick Patsaouras has made recent visible improvements in RTD bus driver attitudes, clean bus interiors and improved schedules."

I rode the bus as a college student, and after a few years was head of the bus company. But I was still running after the bus. I made a point of riding one at least once a week, taking notes on graffiti, rattles, missing signs, and suggestions from bus drivers.

Tom Chorneau of the "Los Angeles Daily News" wrote in a blog post, "RTD President Nick Patsaouras admits he is trying very hard to change the image of the bus agency. But last week at a press conference, even he had to laugh at his thinly veiled attempts to get good press." I had called a press conference the previous week to open my first quarterly "State of the District" meetings with the public, patterned after the corporate world's shareholder meeting. "At these meetings, from now on, we are going to deal directly with the issues and deal directly with our public," I said. "We will deal with the good and the bad, it is our intention not to shy away from anything." Unable to hold back a big grin, I looked up at the reporters with a small shrug, "It just so happens that today, we have only good news," I said with a laugh.

*

There was a meeting at the RTD headquarters where the Los Angeles County Transportation Commission brought in to present a prototype pair of Metro Blue Line light rail passenger seats. The commission was building the Blue Line, which RTD was to operate. The upholstery of the seats was designed by a British company and the colors were a combination of black, gray, and brown. According to Armando G. Ramirez, deputy to Councilman Richard Alatorre, "Patsaouras said, 'we don't live in cloudy England, but in sunny Los Angeles.' As a result, the colors were changed to the current vibrant colors. Patsaouras then said, 'Are the seats vandal proof?' 'Oh, yes sir.' He turned to his colleague Charles Storing and asked, 'Charlie, do you have a knife?' The boardroom became dead silent. Patsaouras walked down from the dais, approached one of the seats, slashed it, and said, 'And you call this vandal proof?'"

*

During the RTD investigations by the major news media in 1985, Linda Breakstone of the "Los Angeles Herald Examiner" requested the files of all board directors, looking for conflicts of interest and expenses claimed. Helen Bolen, the board secretary, gave Breakstone ten files. Breakstone pointed out that the file of the president of the board was missing. Bolen explained that I was not claiming any expenses, not even for mileage. Breakstone filed a front-page story, above-the-fold line, detailing the expenses of directors and staff, and mentioned, "Patsaouras does not claim expenses." I was prudent not to claim any expenses. It was a time when senators, House of Representatives members and White House officials would visit Los Angeles to have a firsthand look at the traffic from a helicopter. After the helicopter flight there would be lunch or dinner. I did not want to host the officials at McDonald's or Denny's, but I always chose a decent restaurant so that I would not have to justify the costs. It was a wise and prudent decision that I am still very proud of. In fact, I never took trips within the United States or abroad at government's expense to "inspect" the transit systems, as many others were doing at the time.

THE UNIVERSAL CITY METRO STATION

Chronicle of a Standoff | In the mid-1980s Bill Fain, prominent architect and urban planner, was planning for the Music Corporation of America's Universal Studio Complex. Quickly, it became apparent that the intersection capacities would determine the density that MCA could put on the property. The densities translated into value per square foot of the land value, land residual. When the Southern California Rapid Transit District proposed the Red Line subway, which runs 14.7 miles between downtown Los Angeles and North Hollywood, it had Universal City/Studio City Station with a park-and-ride facility.

When Lew Wasserman heard about the station "he went ballistic," according to Fain. Known as the alleged king of Hollywood, Wasserman had changed nearly every facet of show business. As president of the media conglomerate, he had led the takeover of Universal Pictures in 1962 and controlled Universal Studios. Now he demanded that the RTD change its plans to meet his own needs, rather than those of the public.

Wasserman, Fain said, was so sharp he understood that if people were going to come at rush hour to get on the subway to go downtown, the facility would become a parking lot. Therefore, the value of his property would go down. This was before the sale of MCA, in 1990—so he was staging his property to be part of a bigger package that would increase the value of MCA stock.

Fain was the primary associate of William Pereira who had more than four hundred projects to his name, including the Transamerica Pyramid in San Francisco. When I was president of the RTD, I had collaborated with Pereira on the design of the Wilshire/Western and Wilshire/Normandie subway stations.

Wasserman was a true connoisseur in the world of power politics. An inflexible deal maker and powerful fundraiser for the Democratic Party, he was also instrumental in guiding Ronald Reagan to the presidency of the Screen Actors Guild, the governorship of California, and eventually the White House.

The RTD's plans distressed him, so he naturally gravitated to political action. He called Mayor Tom Bradley and groused into the telephone: "I'm not coming down. You come here!" He was referring to the Black Tower in Universal City, the offices of MCA. I, in turn, got a call from the mayor to meet him at MCA the next morning. I invited John Dyer, RTD general manager, to come along.

The next morning, Bradley, Dyer, and I were at MCA chatting when Wasserman walked in. He extended a feeble handshake, then perched atop a credenza, his fidgety feet tapping the side of the furniture. Dyer began a short presentation only to be abruptly cut off. In a loud rumble, Wasserman said, "I don't want a station." His notorious ego suffocated the room. In my view he was acting like a bully. He tried to intimidate with threatening words and coercive mannerisms. Wasserman pressed on. "I'm not paying for anything." He was referring to a property tax mechanism for benefits received from specific public improvements. This fee, known as a benefit assessment, is paid by property owners for proximity to subway stations already built (see Benefit Assessment Districts chapter).

I had faced bullies before. Their reputation mattered little. "Very well," I said. "Tomorrow morning, I will call a press conference and announced that MCA does not want a station at Universal." I paused momentarily, then quickly cautioned. "RTD will proceed with its plans to locate a station at Universal. We have worked hard, spent time and money defending the benefit assessment program all the way to the State Supreme Court." I told Wasserman that regarding the assessment fees, which other property owners paid, he may have them voted down through a special election, if one was called.

Then I turned and walked toward the door. "Nick, come back, let's talk," Bradley said, moving after me. Wasserman sat frozen, stunned by the evolving scenario. He did not expect this counter, not here in his building, from a young immigrant, at that. "I respect your interest in protecting your shareholders," I resumed, facing him. "At the same time, I have to protect the taxpayers."

The outcome of the meeting was that Fain had to work with Dyer for more than a year, holding monthly meetings with Ray Remy, Bradley's chief of staff, acting as facilitator. They developed plans with the new connection road to the freeway; now the Universal Terrace Parkway comes right down, connects, and goes straight on the freeway. Through the resources of transit, they were able to increase the capacity of the road system at the same time.

THE MTA DEAL WITH MCA

Compromise or Public Betrayal? | The Los Angeles County Metropolitan Transportation Authority's plan for the Red Line subway had called for the Universal Studios station to be on Lankershim Boulevard near the front entrance to the theme park, but half a mile downhill from most of its major attractions. Lew Wasserman, president of the Music Corporation of America, which owned Universal Studios, wanted it at the top of the hill closer to the entertainment giant's Universal CityWalk and Universal Studios amusement park. MCA was nurturing the theme park business and had determined a station at the top was valuable. George Mihlsten, a Latham & Watkins attorney representing MCA, said: "By the time the movie titan arrived at this decision, the alignment for the station had been set. So, Wasserman was determined to go to the White House in search of a change in the alignment."

As expected, the MTA opposed a location change for the station. First, the design had already been completed. Second, a station on top of the hill created serious concerns over the curve radius, the depth of the station, and the steep climb from the station to the park entrance. Third, the required changes were costly, estimated at $41.6 million, and construction and design would delay the project at least two years. Additionally, federal grant agreements would have to be renegotiated. At stake were tens of millions of dollars in federal funds that could be jeopardized if the subway's Red Line extension delays continued. Nevertheless, if MCA's proposal was to be seriously considered, MTA would have requirements of its own. Wasserman's company should defray much of the new costs. But, once again, company officials were intransigent and insisted they should not be forced to assume the full bill.

"It made more sense to put the station right at the tourist attraction," Larry Spungin, president of MCA's development division, told the *Los Angeles Times* in February 1994. The plan by MTA was fatally flawed, he said, as it was first designed twelve years earlier. Without changes, MCA warned it may not pay the company's $6 million share of a benefit assessment district tax.

However, to provide time for MCA to find the funds, the transit authority set a thrity-day deadline, although it was pessimistic over the possibility of Wasserman's success. The transit authority's Planning and Programming Committee approved the extension unanimously, cognizant of the fact that waiting even one month for a decision on a station site was estimated to cost the transit agency $520,000.

Mihlsten told the *Los Angeles Daily News* that MCA "thinks it's important to have the extra time. We believe that a package can be created in the next two to four weeks." He also said that MCA appealed to congressional leaders and the US Department of Transportation with lobbyists who now planned a return trip.

Lobbying the conventional sources that provide transportation funding was not enough. MCA also embarked on a questionable course, using its White House connections, in the hope of snaring earthquake relief funds, money from President Clinton's discretionary fund of $550 million.

On January 17, 1994, at 4:31 a.m., a magnitude 6.7 earthquake centered in Northridge left seventy-two people dead and caused some $20 billion in damages. Los Angeles Mayor Riordan had asked Wasserman and other Los Angeles corporate chiefs to help push an earthquake relief bill through Congress. Now Wasserman was exploring the possible use of those discretionary funds for the Universal subway station.

When Riordan heard $42 million had been set aside for the Universal Station, he asked the MTA's chief federal government lobbyist, Arthur Sohikian, if he knew anything regarding that. "At this point, it is still at the discretion of the President how he spends that money," Sohikian replied. "But yes, that has been discussed, Mr. Mayor."

I informed Supervisor Michael Antonovich of the plan to raid the earthquake relief funds. Antonovich's reaction was swift: "Using the emergency funds for anything other than the quake is wrong and a misuse of money," he told the *Los Angeles Daily News* on February 11, 1994. Antonovich also told the *Los Angeles Times* that "raiding the last resources available to many desperate victims is not wise or ethical public policy." This was a response directed to Riordan. Antonovich comments over the embarrassing MCA plan persuaded transit officials to call off any action related to the relief funds. In fact, Universal's untimely move created adverse results. Tom Epstein, special assistant to the president for political affairs told the *Los Angeles Times*, "It (the discretionary funds) cannot be used for the subway project. Anybody who has an understanding to the contrary is mistaken."

Christine Hanson, a spokeswoman and lobbyist for MCA, admitted that the company was seeking federal funds to offset the relocation costs but not pursuing revenue targeted for disaster relief. "We are not looking for earthquake funds in any way, shape, or form," she said.

Two days after the MCA statement, Bill Boyarsky wrote in his *Los Angeles Times* column, "I know that MCA Inc. runs an earthquake ride in its Universal Studio amusement park, but that's no reason to spend federal earthquake relief money to build a subway station there." The *Los Angeles Times* decried the mere idea of raiding earthquake relief funds for "self-serving, profit-driven purposes." On February 20, 1994, the newspaper editorialized: "To Universal/MCA officials may we all say, 'for shame,' for their efforts to grab for their corporation pocketbook monies generated to help alleviate the misery, pain, and suffering inflicted by our January 17 earthquake!"

Boyarsky also reminded readers that when the Metro Rail route was laid out, a stop at Universal City was proposed and MCA opposed it. "Nick Patsaouras and then Mayor Tom Bradley visited MCA boss Lew Wasserman and asked him to reconsider." His response, "We don't need a subway here." Consequently, transit planners found a site north of Universal City and began the expensive task of buying the property and designing the station. "Then MCA changed its mind," Boyarsky wrote. It asked MTA to move the station to Universal Studios.

Lobbied heavily by a corps of MCA lobbyists, MTA eventually voted to have its Washington activists work with MCA lobbyists to find federal funds for moving the subway station closer to Universal City.

Meanwhile, Riordan, the city representative on the MTA board, held a meeting at City Hall in search of a compromise that would keep the subway station in the planned site, but link it to the Universal CityWalk, Universal Studios, and the Cineplex Odeon theater complex with a $20 million "people mover" tram. Riordan appointed Ted Stein, his senior policy advisor and Encino lawyer/developer, to lead negotiations. Stein was also president of the Airport Commission who later testified before a federal grand jury about events surrounding his hiring of Webster L. Hubbell as a lobbyist for Los Angeles International Airport for $8,250 a month. Stein reportedly said that he hired Hubbell to help convince federal officials that the airport should be allowed to transfer $58 million to the city's general fund, an illegal action under regulations of the Federal Aviation Administration. Special prosecutor Kenneth Starr focused on whether Hubbell did the job he was paid for. "Did he earn his money, is the unanswered question," Starr told reporters.

Riordan was determined to end the deadlock over the Universal Station, but he first had to resolve a conflict-of-interest issue. He had received $12,500 in campaign funds from MCA. MTA board members are barred by state law from participating in any action affecting companies or individuals who made campaign contributions over the previous twelve months. The *Los Angeles Daily News* reported on February 19, 1994, that Riordan returned the campaign contributions to MCA. Riordan called his compromise "a sensible solution to what could have been a difficult problem," the *Daily News* reported. "The last thing we need is a protracted dispute over something that should have been so obvious."

I did not applaud the agreement ending the controversy of the subway station in Universal City. I wrote the following in an Opinion piece for the *Los Angeles Times* on March 20, 1994, under the headline:

MTA Deal with MCA Sells Out the Public. "Transit agency's concessions to the entertainment giant over subway station sets a dangerous precedent that will prove costly to the taxpayers."

"The company had been lobbying to force the MTA to make a costly change in plans and build the Metro Red Line station half a mile nearer to its hilltop entertainment complex," I wrote. "This complex includes Universal Studios and the CityWalk shopping center and will clearly benefit from easy access from a subway station.

"The dispute ended with an agreement reached Feb. 23 that will leave the station on Lankershim Boulevard at the Hollywood Freeway. In return for MCA's withdrawal of its objections, the transportation agency agreed to:

- "Build two additional station entrances on the east side (the MCA side) of Lankershim and a tunnel under the street connecting them to the station for an estimated $2 million. From there, MCA can build its own 'people mover' to haul its customers up the hill to its parks, movie houses, and CityWalk.
- "Spend about $4 million to widen Lankershim and add new ramps to and from the Hollywood Freeway to make it easier to get to the station—and incidentally to MCA's entertainment businesses.
- "Buy the adjacent MCA-owned property it needs for the entrances, parking, and other amenities surrounding the station for $8.3 million if the appraised value is confirmed. The transportation agency was planning to condemn and purchase this property anyway.
- "Most significantly, not collect the assessment fees that property owners near enough to benefit from the station would otherwise be expected to pay. In the case of MCA this amounts to about $6 million."

But as a result of the MCA deal, MTA did not have the moral, ethical or legal grounds to demand benefit assessment taxes from the property owners near the stations of the second and third phases of the Metro rail benefit assessment taxes. Consequently, MTA forfeited $45 million that the taxpayers ultimately paid.

"Some will claim that the agreement imposes a $20 million cost contribution for the people mover to be paid by MCA. Hogwash! The agreement specifically leaves the decision on whether to build the people mover up to MCA 'in its sole discretion,'" I wrote in the opinion piece.

But a people mover—a tram-like shuttle—had been opposed by MCA executives. In my view it was never the intention of MCA to build it. I disagreed with the concessions provided to MCA by the transit board. Similar concessions to private companies have been vetoed in the past. It's an issue of fairness.

Following the bravado surrounding the Riordan compromise, Spungin said MCA would have to conduct tests to determine whether a people mover was possible. "No, I don't think we can guarantee it," he told the *Los Angeles Daily News*. The people mover was never built.

Originally, the MTA had planned parking for 2,500 cars, but instead agreed to 575 spaces, affording MCA the opportunity to provide paid parking for subway riders while generating substantial income.

I also wrote in the *Los Angeles Times* commentary: "Let's look at the $8.3 million land deal. The agreement gives MCA all air rights and easements to develop its people-mover. But we have also granted the company the right of first offer should we seek to develop the land, for example, with housing and shops. This will prevent us from soliciting competitive offers to help develop our landholdings." This political settlement gave away hard-won rights of a public agency for absolutely nothing in return.

Tim Lindholm, Metro's deputy chief program management officer, told me how he comprehended the process that eventually led to the Universal bridge. "In the 1990s when Metro was planning the Red Line Universal Station there was dispute between Universal and Metro ostensibly about eminent domain and Metro developing a large parking lot adjacent to Universal Studios." Metro, Lindholm said, entered into a legal settlement with Universal that allowed the station and parking lot construction to proceed with both parties splitting the projected $8 million cost of a tunnel under Lankershim. The $4 million from Universal was fixed.

In 2000, Metro sent the project out to bid and the cost came back too high, about $12 million, so the bids were thrown out and Metro went back to the drawing board with value engineering. A year later, bids were solicited again, but Metro ended up with the same results as before. "At that point," Lindholm said, "Metro pretty much gave up and the project was quiet for about a decade." But Universal did not forget and stated its position clearly. Legally and politically Metro was obligated to build an undercrossing. "Metro pivoted to building the bridge you see today," he said. Construction started in 2014 and the bridge opened in 2016. The final cost: $28 million. Universal's share: $4 million. The $24 million was funded through Proposition A, the county's half-cent sales tax.

I remember having breakfast with my friend Murthy Krishniah, Metro's chief engineer, and he was very concerned that he would have to answer the tough questions about the bridge cost overruns from the Metro fiscal watchdog, Supervisor Gloria Molina.

Political compromises are made daily with parties accepting something slightly different from what they really desire. But when the compromise does not provide a pragmatic solution but simply surrenders rights and benefits—especially public rights and benefits—it becomes a damaging concession. In the case of MCA, which received public advantages unavailable to others, it was a breaking of the rules. Was it a compromise then, or a public betrayal?

THE DEMISE OF THE EAST LOS ANGELES SUBWAY

One must wonder: Why does West Los Angeles have both a subway and a twenty-two-mile light rail line and East Los Angeles has a six-mile light rail? The answer is Machiavellian politics and delays due to corruption.

In May 1993, President Clinton's Transportation Secretary Federico Peña, held a news conference at Evergreen Park in East Los Angeles to announce that the Federal Transit Administration was awarding $1.23 billion for the construction of a 6.8-mile Eastside subway and extension of the subway west on Wilshire Boulevard and into the San Fernando Valley. A final environmental impact statement was approved by the transit agency, an arm of the US Department of Transportation, in September 1994. The Los Angeles County Metropolitan Transportation Authority proceeded with the design of construction documents, relocation of utilities at Third and Alameda streets and real estate purchases.

The saga of the $65 million Eastside Extension construction management procurement began in July 1994 with the issuance of the original Request for Information & Qualifications (RFIQ). That process was halted, however, as the MTA considered alternate management concepts. Failing to arrive at any, another RFIQ was released in July 1995.

In response the MTA received four bids:

- Metro East Consultants (a joint venture of O'Brien-Kreitzberg Inc. De Leuw & Company, Telacu Industries Inc./Cordoba, and Hoctief (MEC)
- Jacobs Engineering Group Inc./Mott McDonald Hatch/ACG Environments (a joint venture) (JMA)
- Bufete Industrial/Stone & Webster (a joint venture)
- Bechtel/Vanir (a joint venture)

MTA's chief executive officer Joseph E. Drew, on March 13, 1996, recommended Metro East Consultants. Supervisor Gloria Molina's deputy Gerry Hertzberg earned the nickname "the riffleman" after he was seen riffling through the files of construction staff's desks trying to figure out how the staff recommendation was made. Hertzberg brought to Molina's attention that, even though the evaluation committee had scored the references section, no reference checks had been conducted. Because of concerns raised by Molina, staff's recommendation was deferred in March and again in April.

On April 24, the recommendation was pulled from the agenda by Drew, and eventually was thrown out after an investigation by the agency's inspector general found serious irregularities. The Inspector General walked into the boardroom, collected the board reports, and told us, "everyone in this room is under investigation." Meanwhile, at the same meeting, the board proceeded to approve the purchase of a number of parcels for the Eastside Extension and architectural/engineering services for the Little Tokyo and First & Lorena stations.

To ensure a cleaner selection process the board decided in April to spend $375,000 to bring in seven tunneling and construction experts. In June 1996, MTA issued an amended RFIQ for construction management services. The outside construction industry experts met a number of times in the first week of August and ranked the proposers as follows:

1. JMA
2. BECHTEL
3. MEC

On October 17, 1996, Drew recommended for the second time MEC to the construction committee, overturning the opinion of the seven independent experts. At the construction committee meeting, Molina presented a chart showing the expert panel's rankings. A few moments after Molina spoke, committee members discovered that Leroy Graw, the fired director of construction contracts, who had managed the evaluation process, was in the room. Graw declared that he and his boss, MTA construction chief Stanley Phernambucq, originally prepared a staff recommendation for Drew's signature that the board choose JMA. Graw said he was fired soon after he made that recommendation in late September. The committee voted 3-to-1 to reverse Drew's decision and recommend JMA, the team ranked first by the panel of outside experts.

On October 23, 1996, the full MTA Board met to consider the recommendations by MTA staff and the MTA construction committee and to award the contract. However, at that MTA board meeting, the MTA inspector general stated that an "investigation into certain activities" of MTA staff and personnel involved in the procurement process had been undertaken. The MTA inspector general requested that the decision on the award of the Contract be postponed to a later date.

Meanwhile, the inspector general had sequestered executive Michael Gonzalez in the Hilton hotel downtown, now Wilshire Grand Centre, fearing for his personal safety. González had discovered that the document properties in the report was not authored by MTA staff and he had reported that fact to the inspector general.

It was discovered later in depositions that Drew had changed the board report recommending MEC via a bogus report written by a board member's consultant and given to Drew on a diskette at a gas station meeting point in the San Gabriel Valley.

In November 1996, US Congressional Representatives Esteban Torres, Lucille Roybal-Allard, and Xavier Becerra urged Drew not to proceed with his recommendation of the team ranked last by a panel of experts to supervise the project, warning "The agency could lose credibility in Washington. To ensure that the project continues to receive federal funding MTA should award the contract to the firm ranked first." They said a criminal investigation by the agency's inspector general had "unnecessarily delayed the decision-making process." Drew stood by his recommendation of MEC, but "he would put the matter before the board for a vote on December 18th." On December 4, Drew unexpectedly announced his resignation because of "political infighting and public hypercriticism." The board at its December 18 meeting continued the item to a special board meeting on January 10, 1997.

Key board members who had been in Washington, DC, in December 1996 to discuss the future of the subway were increasingly questioning whether to continue tunneling. They wanted to study whether the MTA should proceed with plans to extend the subway to the Eastside, Mid-City, and across the San Fernando Valley, or instead build aboveground rail lines. "We should finish what we started and then rethink everything else," county supervisor and MTA Board member Zev Yaroslavsky told the *Los Angeles Times*. Others still stood by promises to build a subway at least through the Eastside and Mid-City, fearing the loss of millions of dollars in federal funds earmarked for the Metro Rail Project. "I will stick my neck out. There are segments of the city where a subway is a necessity," the *Los Angeles Times* quoted me as saying.

Metro East Consultants filed a lawsuit against MTA that was discussed in closed session on January 10, 1997, and as result the award to JMA was deferred to January 22, 1997. Mayor Riordan attempted to defer the award again by a substitute motion, to send the decision to one more panel of experts, but that failed. Instead, the board awarded the contract to JMA on a vote of eight to one. Councilmember and board member Richard Alatorre was the lone dissenter. Board members Riordan and John Fasana abstained.

On September 25, 1997, the Eastside subway was still on track, and a contract was awarded to relocation consultants. But clouds were gathering above the Eastside subway. Cost overruns and the consent decree that Riordan had signed with the Bus Riders Union in 1996 (which he later admitted was a huge mistake) alarmed the FTA, and as a result the agency demanded in 1997 a financial work out plan that would address how Metro would meet its freshly signed consent decree obligations while continuing to build rail. FTA held up any federal funding until Metro complied.

The MTA board, at the recommendation of Riordan, appointed a former colleague of his, Julian Burke, as chief executive officer, on August 26, 1997. Before Burke joined MTA, he was a successful corporate turnaround specialist with Victor Palmieri Associates. In January 1998, Burke asked for board authorization to suspend and implement the demobilization of:

- Eastside Extension of the Metro Red Line
- The Pasadena Blue Line
- The Mid-City Extension of the Metro Red Line

County supervisor and MTA Board director Michael Antonovich introduced a motion to direct the chief executive officer to terminate all subway extensions and all subway contracts for the Eastside and Mid-City projects immediately. The motion failed, with board members Zev Yaroslavsky and Larry Zarian in favor. The board voted then that the chief executive officer suspend for at least six months the Eastside Extension and return to the board in six months or less with a report to the board of any feasible funding options for the remobilization of the project. Board members Antonovich, Yaroslavsky, and Zarian were opposed.

In March 1998, Yaroslavsky announced that he was launching an initiative campaign to end local funding for Metro Rail subway extensions. The announcement sent shock waves to Wall Street. It would ban the use of the transit sales tax for any subway construction beyond the North Hollywood line. Yaroslavsky put Wall Street and bond buyers on notice that any further borrowing by MTA to finance extension of the subway could be invalidated by the voters in November. The initiative basically froze any plans for future projects.

County supervisor and MTA Board member Gloria Molina criticized Yaroslavsky, saying that the initiative did not offer an alternative transit system for residents east of downtown Los Angeles. "All it says is: Tough luck, no subway for you." Molina, to save the Eastside Extension, in April 1998 accused Burke "of manipulative management." In a forceful letter to her MTA colleagues, she wrote, "If management is going to continue to dictate to board members without their consultation, then the agency should call it what it is, a complete receivership and let dictatorship take its course. To continue to pretend that we are in charge of this sinking organization with a manipulative management operation is totally disrespecting the important responsibility we have to taxpayers." Molina was outraged that Burke's two hunderd page "restructuring" plan offered no options for restarting the three mothballed rail projects.

Yaroslavsky said his initiative would redirect sales tax money that had been going to subway to light rail lines, busways, and improved bus service. Peter Bianchini, director of Standard & Poor's Western Regional office in San Francisco, said the measure "could limit (MTA's) sale of new debt, if it includes for subway extensions. It seems pretty clear if it passes, they can't do it."

Then Assembly Speaker Antonio Villaraigosa said he had been concerned about the agency's commitment to building a heavy rail system. "There is no question in my mind that heavy rail is not the best investment of our precious transit resources. Light rail, busways, and improved bus service are a better solution to the area's transportation needs."

In November 1998, Los Angeles County voters approved Proposition A, the MTA Reform and Accountability Act that was sponsored by Yaroslavsky, and barred the use of county sales tax money for all future subway projects. That was the final nail in the Eastside subway's coffin. The Westside killed the Eastside subway.

However, Molina was determined to bring a rail line to East Los Angeles. She worked with the Eastside congressional representatives and especially Lucille Roybal-Allard to salvage the funds that had been designated for the aborted subway. The six-mile Light Rail Line from Union Station to Atlantic Boulevard in unincorporated East Los Angeles opened in November 2009. In recognition of these efforts, the Metro board voted in March 2023 to name the East Los Angeles Civic Center Station, Gloria Molina Station.

THE LOS ANGELES 1984 SUMMER OLYMPICS

The Traffic Nightmare that Wasn't | The 1984 Summer Olympics (officially the Games of the XXIII Olympiad) were held from July 28 to August 12, 1984, in Los Angeles, California. In the mid-1970s, only two cities made serious bids for the 1984 summer games, Los Angeles and Tehran, Iran. Tehran withdrew its bid in June 1977 as the Iranian Revolution erupted.

1984 Summer Olympics in L.A. Photo: J. Halicki

Announcing the RTD Olympic Service Plan: With Mayor Tom Bradley. Photo: courtesy of Metro

RTD bus stop sign, the colors of the 1984 Summer Olympics in Los Angeles.

That left Los Angeles's bid and it was accepted by the International Olympic Committee. The official announcement was made in Athens, Greece on May 18, 1978.

In March 1984, a spat developed between the Los Angeles Olympic Organizing Committee and the Hellenic Olympic Committee. Peter Ueberroth, LAOOC president, made an announcement that, "The problem with Greek officials—who objected to using the Olympic flame to raise money—was only 'a misunderstanding' and had been clarified to the satisfaction of both parties." He also said $3,000 contributions for those wanting to sponsor one kilometer of the run would be accepted through April 10, 1984.

Mayor Tom Bradley, while in Athens, in early February 1984 during his trip to Greece to establish the LA–Athens Sister City affiliation, explained to the Greeks that "the commercialization of the torch" was a misunderstanding, because the funds would be used for philanthropic purposes. Bradley participated in a meeting with the International and Hellenic Olympic Committee to "resolve the misunderstanding." The HOC issued an angry statement seeking an explanation to Ueberroth's comments. In a telex sent to the HOC, LAOOC declared that it had stopped accepting new contributions. The Greeks, led by Spyros Fotinos, the mayor of the city of Olympia, objected to the commercialization of the New York–Los Angeles Olympic Torch relay (see Los Angeles–Athens Sister City section).

The Olympic flame, carried by a torch, is lit several months before the Games at Olympia, the birthplace of the Olympics, where the Ancient Olympic Games took place. The flame is lit by a holy priestess using the sun's rays and a parabolic mirror. The 1984 Summer Olympic torch relay began in New York City and ended at Los Angeles Memorial Coliseum, crossing thirty-three states and the District of Columbia. I was proud to sponsor my daughter Tanya so she could be a participant, running with the Olympic torch for a short distance in Los Angeles. Rafer Johnson, winner of the decathlon gold medal at the 1960 Summer Olympics, was the final torchbearer. With the torch he ignited the flame that passed through a flammable Olympic logo igniting all five Olympic rings. The flame then passed up to a caldron atop the Coliseum's peristyle to signal the beginning of the 1984 Summer Olympics.

The chairman of the Los Angeles Olympic Organizing Committee was Paul Ziffren, a close advisor and confidante to Bradley. The committee selected Ueberroth as president with Yvonne Brathwaite Burke casting the tie-breaking vote. Harry L. Usher was appointed as executive vice president and general manager.

There was considerable concern about traffic in Los Angeles during the Olympic Games. Many had feared there would be terminal gridlock in which thousands of fans would be stuck in traffic jams while athletes performed to empty stadiums. To the contrary, traffic conditions improved. What happened?

After years of planning and coordination, a transportation plan was implemented for sixteen days. Under the overall umbrella of the Integrated Planning Group, more than fifty federal, state, county, and local agencies coordinated their Olympic planning efforts. The California Department of Transportation's Olympic Task Force, functioning through the Traffic Control Subcommittee of the Olympic Security Coordinating Committee, coordinated and stimulated the development of Olympic transportation plans with the California Highway Patrol, the Los Angeles City Department of Transportation, the Los Angeles Polic Department, the Los Angeles Olympic Organizing Committee, the Southern California Rapid Transit District, and numerous other government and private transportation planners and operators.

SOUTHERN CALIFORNIA RAPID DISTRICT DELIVERS GOLD MEDAL PERFORMANCE

- Unlike past Olympiads, where events were scheduled in a central location, the Los Angeles Games were held in twenty-three venues, spread over a distance of 200 miles.
- In 1984, the Games were held in a city that did not have a rail rapid transit system
- About seven hundred thousand visitors were expected to arrive in Los Angeles each of the sixteen days of the Games.
- The most popular sporting events were scheduled at Exposition Park (track and field), USC (swimming and diving), and UCLA (tennis and gymnastics), and all three had severe parking shortages and the worst traffic.
- The RTD was expected to carry 40 percent of all spectators attending the Exposition Park and Westwood venues. Substantial bus demand was also expected at other major venues, including the Rose Bowl in Pasadena, the Forum in Inglewood, Dodger Stadium, the Long Beach and Anaheim Convention Centers, Loyola Marymount University, and Santa Anita Park Racetrack in Arcadia.
- Moreover, the RTD was given the charge by the LAOOC to provide this special Olympic service *without the use of tax dollars.*

I had been appointed by Paul Ziffren to the Olympic Citizens Advisory Commission, and under my direction, the RTD planners, General Manager John Dyer, and Chief of Bus Operations Art Leahy devised a complex transportation plan after consulting with the Integrated Planning Group. The RTD opted to start from scratch a second bus fleet that would provide special direct service to the major Olympic venues. The RTD's 550-bus Olympic fleet ranked as the fourth largest public transit district in California. Its operation required more than one thousand workers, including four hundred temporary drivers who had to be hired and trained. Many RTD administrative employees left their desks and worked in the field as passenger assistants, providing fare exchange and information, and supervising bus traffic and security at the various terminals.

The system's efficiency was tested repeatedly over many months and was proved most notably at Exposition Park during the opening and closing ceremonies. Platoons of buses arrived or departed from the Coliseum about every ten seconds. To help expedite travel, reserved bus lanes were established, and freeway ramps near Exposition Park were open only to buses. The operators of the buses could radio up to the minute status reports to the State Traffic Coordination Center, enabling quick responses to traffic bottlenecks. At the Coliseum, the LAOOC constructed two bus facilities at the east and west ends so that the RTD could drop off and pick up passengers at the door.

To inform the public of the special Olympic bus service, the RTD implemented an Olympic communications program. More than one million free RTD Olympic service brochures were distributed worldwide. Buses were identified by Olympic emblem decals on the front and rear of the bus. "The traffic Armageddon predicted to loom over the region during the Games never materialized, largely because of the SCRTD Olympic service plan," said Bill Forsythe, director of transportation for the LAOOC.

The 1984 Summer Olympics have been dubbed the "Capitalist Games" because they relied on corporate sponsorships and were the most financially successful modern Olympics. In addition to the private financing, there were low construction costs because organizers decided to use existing venues and facilities as much as possible. The only venues that had to be constructed were the Velodrome in Carson and the Olympic Swim Stadium at USC.

Robert Janovich, Los Angeles zoning administrator, remembered having a case involving UCLA. They wanted to have the athletes live on the campus, which was against the zoning code. Eventually I got to the point where I told them, "Well, you can do that if you have them learning how to be citizens."

The games generated more than $225 million in profit. Some of that went to the US Olympic & Paralympic Endowment for athletes' use and $93 million went back to Los Angeles to what is now the LA84 Foundation.

THE SCRTD $5.1 DEFICIT FROM OLYMPICS BUS SERVICE

Because the 1976 Summer Olympics in Montreal had left that city more than $1 billion in debt, Angelenos objected to any government financing of the 1984 Summer Olympic Games. Los Angeles City Councilmember Robert Ronka proposed that the issue be placed on a ballot for the citizens to decide. Councilmember Ernani Bernardi proposed a charter amendment to control spending. Bernardi told Bill Boyarsky of the Los Angeles Times that if the International Olympic Committee would not go along with the cost controls, "the IOC had better find another pigeon."

Ronka and Bernardi had pledged to initiate a petition drive to place their charter amendments on the ballot if the City Council failed to approve them. Bradley was consequently forced to propose to the IOC that Rule 4, the one concerning financial responsibility, be waived. The General Assembly of the IOC approved the waiver on October 8, 1978, by a vote of seventy-four to three. The Los Angeles City Council approved the contract on October 12, 1978 by a vote eight to four with Councilmember Marvin Braude providing the eighth vote after a last-minute meeting with Bradley the night before at the Getty House. The council, to ensure there would not be any financial responsibility for the city, placed Charter Amendment N on the November 1978 ballot, forbidding Los Angeles from spending taxpayer monies on the Games. The ballot was approved by 74 percent of the voters. The Charter Amendment included language of the cost-control ordinance written by Councilmember John Ferraro.

Unfortunately, neither Peter Ueberroth nor Harry Usher honored the spirit or the letter of Charter Amendment N. As a result, the taxpayers were saddled with a $5.1 million bill. While costs were well under budget, a shortfall in revenue and ridership resulted in a $5.1 million deficit in the RTD's Olympic budget.

- The late withdrawal of the Soviet bloc countries, in response to the American-led boycott of the 1980 Summer Olympics in Moscow in protest of the Soviet invasion of Afghanistan, resulted in lower than projected ridership.

- Because of the lower number of spectators, the RTD sold fewer Olympic souvenir sets—consisting of twenty-four bus tokens, each with an official Olympic design—than expected. The number of the tokens and revenue projections were established in close cooperation with the LAOOC.

I approached Ueberroth and asked that the LAOOC honor its commitment to shun public subsidies to finance the Games. Ueberroth referred me to Harry Usher. I knew Usher, from our early mornings exercise at the Jonathan Club gym. As RTD president, I attended a two-hour meeting on October 9, 1984, with officials from both sides in the controversy present. The RTD got sympathy, but no cash from LAOOC. Usher said after the meeting, "We are not under any moral or legal obligation to the RTD. But we recognize the excellent operation they had during the Games."

Los Angeles County Supervisor Kenneth Hahn and Bradley asked the county supervisors to officially "urge reconsideration." "If this matter is not settled," Hahn said, "and the RTD riders have to pay for the deficit...it will be the only sour taste left by the XXIIIrd Olympiad." In the end, taxpayer money was used to support the Olympic Games, despite the repeated pronouncements and promises by Olympic officials—a small amount, but nevertheless real. Meanwhile, Peter Ueberroth and Harry Usher received big bonuses.

Hopefully the mayor, the Los Angeles City Council, and the LAOOC will be more careful when making statements such as, "There will not be any public subsidies used to stage the 2028 Olympic Games."

RTD/MTA TRANSIT POLICE

Poor Decision, Grave Results | In a November 2016 editorial, the *Los Angeles Times* wrote, "Voters this month passed Measure M, a permanent sales tax increase that will fund one of the nation's most ambitious and expensive transportation system expansions. . .The MTA hopes Measure M projects will eventually triple the number of regular transit riders. But Metro cannot hope to get more people into trains and buses unless the agency addresses a fundamental problem: Too many people are scared to ride public transit. During public forums on Measure M, people repeatedly asked why they never saw law enforcement or security officers at stations or around buses. Almost 30 percent of past riders left the system because they did not feel safe, according to a recent Metro survey. For years Metro's leaders downplayed concerns over safety."

And that was 2016. Today no day goes by that some former transit rider does not complain to me, knowing my past relationship with the Southern California Rapid Transit District and Metropolitan Transportation Authority that they don't feel safe, telling me they never see a law enforcement officer on the buses. Dedicated police forces such as transit, airport, and campus/school police have specialized training and provide a higher degree of safety, specifically addressing the unique needs of their environments. Transit safety in Los Angeles has suffered due to the purely political decision to disband the dedicated Transit Police force in favor of a contractual relationship with the Los Angeles Police Department and the Los Angeles County Sheriff's Department.

There were several political agendas at play that led to the decision to disband the Transit Police in 1997. A dedicated funding stream for transit security was established due to an earmark in the Transportation Sales Tax that could only be used to enhance security on the system. Millions of dollars were now available to law enforcement agencies providing security to the transit system. Sheriff Sherman Block saw an opportunity to establish the largest policing contract in the history of his department, both in size and revenue stream. He had a built-in advantage in swaying votes on the MTA Board, since all five of the county supervisors were members of the MTA Board and those transportation dollars would go to the county coffers if the sheriff's department provided security services to the transit system.

Mayor Richard Riordan, who controlled four votes on the MTA Board, also saw an opportunity to tap into those funds and enhance his ability to keep a campaign promise of "3,000 more police officers" to expand the size of the LAPD by merging the existing MTA Transit Police Officers into LAPD. It represented an immediate boost of additional officers during a very difficult recruiting period. He also saw the opportunity to funnel transit dollars into the LAPD budget.

A Request for Proposals from the LAPD and the sheriff for police services was conducted, which clearly showed those agencies to be far more expensive. Their pay and benefit packages were far more costly than the MTA Police Department. The justification for moving forward anyway was the "economy of scale" argument that MTA would no longer have the overhead of their own command staff and police chief, and MTA would get additional services such as bomb squad and SWAT, as needed. No one wanted to acknowledge that those services were already provided at no cost, as part of existing mutual aid agreements.

Despite the very fact that Transit Police officers were specifically recruited, screened, and hired to work exclusively for the transportation system and spent additional time attending transit-specific police training upon graduation from their State-certified basic academy training, the politicians determined that LAPD and LASD personnel were better qualified to provide policing services. Neither of those agencies' personnel was familiar with the transit system or had any transit specific law enforcement training, and perhaps most importantly, no particular interest or desire to work that type of assignment.

Once the move was made, both the LAPD and the sheriff put their best foot forward and ensured they maintained high visibility due to the intense media coverage of the switch in policing agencies. However, as time went on, they had difficulty getting officers to work the assignment, and it became almost exclusively an overtime detail with no long-term commitment. The transit system was not viewed as a coveted assignment and the turnover of personnel was frequent. Although never acknowledged publicly, it became known as a dumping ground for mediocre officers.

The MTA should never have given up their police department. They relinquished their ability to recruit, hire, and train the type of employee they wanted to work for them. They gave up the ability to deploy personnel as needed, provide additional training as new issues arise, develop policies reflecting their priorities and values, the ability to sanction or remove officers who engage in inappropriate conduct, and most importantly, the ability to control costs though labor negotiations. The current increase in crime on the transportation system and the correlating decrease in ridership is a predictable outcome when facts are disregarded in favor of politics.

History proves the facts. In September 1990, the *Los Angeles Times* ran a headline, "Riders applaud RTD's beefed-up security." RTD had Miracle on Broadway squad, a police force that patrolled the bustling Broadway retail strip. Its mission was to protect RTD passengers both on buses and waiting for buses. According to the Downtown News, "The force reduced crime along Broadway." The officers boarded buses at random, or at the request of drivers. According to MTA Police Chief Sharon Papa, transit police officers were garnering so much positive media attention that LAPD command staff demanded that Papa discontinue the foot beats.

When they were told "No," they attempted to get the city attorney to rule that RTD police did not have any authority to walk foot beats on LA city sidewalks.

As RTD board president at the time, I, along with Papa, during an intense meeting had to remind them that RTD police were State-certified peace officers and had jurisdiction anywhere there were properties owned, operated, or utilized by the Transit Agency, and that included bus stops on city streets. The LAPD had to back off, but not before stating RTD was making LAPD "look bad."

In August 1991, a police station opened in Sunland as the headquarters of a thirteen-officer Safe Community Alert Awareness Team. It was very successful according to Chief Papa, "People are saying it's nice to see transit police in the Valley." Some police officers rode the buses in plain clothes, but the high visibility of uniformed officers was to let people know who the transit police were. Uniformed RTD transit police officers, foot-patrolled on Van Nuys Boulevard, between Oxnard Street and Sherman Way, near bus shelters, where large numbers of people congregate and where much of the crime occurs.

As I said at the time, the idea of deploying foot patrols came in response to complaints from merchants and bus riders about safety in the neighborhood. The most persistent problems faced by the alert team had not been violent incidents but drinking in public and rude teenagers. I was asked by other San Fernando Valley City Council offices to extend the foot patrols in their districts because of the noticeable success. An RTD driver said the bus patrols show that the drivers are not the only authority on the bus. "Before they never thought we had any type of security. Now they kind of watch out." Chief Papa commented, "LAPD has their hands full. They don't have the time to target crime at bus stops or on buses."

The success of the Safe Community Alert Awareness Team resulted in establishing similar teams in East and South Los Angeles and Sun Valley. The teams proved to be more effective because they were more mobile and could saturate an area or bus lines for a few days, then move to another area. A clearly marked black and white police car drove the line simultaneously, so any arrestees could be immediately transported for booking. Passengers appreciated the uniform presence on board and along the bus routes.

In December 1992, the RTD Board selected the RTD transit police to patrol the Red Line subway, passing up an LAPD bid that would have cost $4 million more. Marv Holen, RTD board member, said the "Decision was of great significance, because it helps define the MTA. It establishes transit security."

The success of Chief Papa was attributed to her own style of community policing for the transit system and in deploying her resources in innovative and effective ways. In an interview with the *Los Angeles Times*, Papa explained that transit policing is based on a different philosophy. "Most local law-enforcement agencies are response-oriented. They don't have a lot of prevention programs. Our officers are not catching people breaking the law; they need to prevent laws from being broken. Our most high-profile community-police effort is our foot-beat team downtown. They are not there to handle the shoplifters. They are making sure panhandlers aren't hassling passengers at the bus stops or that illegal vendors aren't blocking buses from getting in and out of stops."

When questioned about graffiti prevention, Chief Papa explained, "We have twenty officers assigned full time to what we call our Graffiti Habitual Offenders Suppression Team. The taggers focused on RTD buses because they viewed them as rolling billboards. We were laughed at by the LAPD and the Sheriff's department. They asked, 'you've got a task force working a misdemeanor crime?' But not every crime impacting a community is based on major felonies and drive-by shootings. We were the pioneers in combatting taggers, so much so that we ended up training other law enforcement agencies. We were the only ones with a database." The graffiti suppression team was established when vandalism exploded on the transit system.

Although an isolated crime was a misdemeanor, the aggregate cost to the transit agency increased from two million dollar in cleanup costs to ten million. Several transit police officers were former bus operators. One of those officers would drive the bus and a couple of passengers were undercover officers. When taggers "bombed" the bus, the officers took them into custody and used the same bus to take them to jail.

RECENT CONDITIONS

In a March 2023 editorial the *Los Angeles Times* stated, "Disorder, rising crime and declining confidence in the system pose an existential crisis to Metro." According to an office of inspector general audit, Sheriff's deputies were assigned to Metro to ride the trains only 12 out of 178 weekly shifts, providing little visibility on the system. When Sheriff Robert G. Luna was asked on March 23, 2023, at the Jonathan Club to explain the lack of safety on Metro buses and trains, he candidly replied "I'm short- staffed."

In a March 22, 2023, letter to the editor of the *Los Angeles Times*, Chief Papa wrote, "The MTA Board of Directors made the unwise political decision to disband the dedicated MTA Transit Police Department in favor of a contractual relationship with LAPD and LASD. The lack of consistent dedicated personnel specifically hired, trained, and deployed to work in such an environment has greatly contributed to the crime problems and quality of life issues. Bigger isn't always better. The chief safety officer of MTA was quoted in your reporting as being told, "LA police were not going to have a bus company tell them how to deploy their resources. That statement clearly sums up the problem."

In June 2023, the Metro board voted to consider recreating its own Transit Police Department to take over the responsibilities currently under the LA County Sheriff, LAPD, and Long Beach Police Department within three years.

VIGNETTE

Neil Peterson, Chief Executive Officer of the Los Angeles County Transportation Commission, described launching the Los Angele–Long Beach Blue Line in 1990—Los Angeles's first new rail project in nearly four decades:

"One of the issues that I remember really well is when we were building the Blue Line, it was a time period when gangs were really big, and the Bloods and the Crips were the two major gangs, and they were heavily in the Watts and Compton area, and the Blue Line was going right through that area.

In our wisdom, we decided that we should paint the cars blue and red which, of course, are the two colors of the Bloods and the Crips. I can remember people coming up to me saying, 'You gotta be kidding me. This is going to be graffitied to hell, there are going to be incidents, there are going to be all kinds of problems, this is going to be gang warfare.' And then I went around, and I talked to the Chief of Police in Los Angeles, the Sheriff, California Highway Patrol, and I asked, 'What would you do.' All of them said the same thing. They said, 'The only way to deal with this is to have a massive show of force on day one so that you establish this as neither one of their territories and that becomes clear.' So, I followed that advice.

THE SUMITOMO DEBACLE

Rail Car Polemics and Racist Attitudes | "The Sumitomo Debacle" was a huge, messy affair that began with the Los Angeles County Transportation Commission's procurement in January 1992 of forty-one automated rail cars for the Green Line that inflamed a national debate over foreign trade and domestic unemployment. The months leading up to the initial contract with Sumitomo were filled with announcements of job layoffs in the area, many related to aerospace and manufacturing and the closure of the General Motors plant in Van Nuys, which employed 2,200 autoworkers. President George H. W. Bush had returned from fruitless trade talks in Japan.

It was a time of high unemployment and a recession. The economy was in bad shape and there was the perception that Japan was restricting entry to its markets by American products and contractors. A great deal of anti-Japanese and Japan-bashing were going on. Local government officials and the public strongly and loudly voiced their concerns over the awarding of the rail contract to a foreign company. The comments were pretty ugly at times. Politics definitely played a role in the pro-America stance and regarding the union's concerns with fully automated, driverless rail cars. Los Angeles City Councilman Joel Wachs set up a hot line that fielded calls that were anti-Sumitomo and some overtly racist references to Pearl Harbor. Councilman Zev Yaroslavsky was applauded when he said, "Never again!" to union workers who had come to protest the Sumitomo contract.

Richard Katz, chairman of the state Assembly Transportation Committee and a potential mayoral candidate, made the comment that the Los Angeles County Transportation

Commission was giving a "Christmas gift to the city...one of the biggest white elephants ever seen." Under these circumstances, the commission, on December 18, 1991, voted seven to four, to affirm the use of driverless cars for the Metro Green Line, a 19.3-mile-light rail line between Redondo Beach and Norwalk.

The commission also awarded a contract to Sumitomo Corp. of America to build forty-one cars at a cost of $121 million, $67 million above the original estimate. Sumitomo's chief lobbyist was former Governor George Deukmejian, now in the same camp as his foe in the 1982 and 1986 gubernatorial elections, Tom Bradley. The projected cost of the Green Line had initially been $814 million, but at this point was already more than $1 billion.

Staff engineers and outside consultants had expressed in private briefings with Commissioners that the driverless cars were "the most complex transit vehicles they have ever worked with."

"The driverless cars do not get passengers there any faster and they don't get them there any more often or cheaper than conventional trolleys," said Gerry Hertzberg, Supervisor Gloria Molina's alternate on the commission. Councilman Zev Yaroslavsky challenged Mayor Tom Bradley to reverse the decision. Bradley responded angrily, "It was time critics come into the 20th century," he said. "If you don't like vision, if you don't like taking risks, you should get off this board." Bradley, the driverless system's proponent, also chastised staff engineers for questioning its cost effectiveness.

A number of elected officials, including Bradley, expressed the strong desire that the transportation commission use its financial clout to hire and buy from local companies and require outside firms to open local offices and hire local workers. William Agee, chief executive of Morrison-Knudsen, a construction giant that was branching into transit car manufacturing, told Bradley that Morrison Knudsen could assemble the cars at the soon-to-be closed General Motors Corporation plant in VanNuys and hire local workers. Agee also called for an investigation of the commission.

A month later, on January 17, 1992, bowing to intense political pressure, even though Sumitomo had more experience than Morrison Knudsen, the only US rail car manufacturer, the commission—in an auditorium packed with outraged union members, local business representatives, and other opponents—voted to cancel the contract with Sumitomo based on a motion introduced by county Supervisor Michael Antonovich. Antonovich's motion included a six-point plan to develop a standardized Los Angeles rail car that could be used along various routes in Southern California and that could be built by a US company at a local assembly plant. The plan would leave open the potential to have driverless cars in the future. There was also a vote to explore bus and rail car-making facilities as a way to offset lost aerospace and other jobs in Southern California.

Bradley was strongly opposed to Antonovich's plan, which he considered a political move. One of the major arguments for canceling the contract was the need to harness infrastructure investment for more local and domestic jobs and to jumpstart the local economy. I had championed that proposal eighteen months before with the *Jobs Creation Initiative*. I commented to Rick Orlov of the *Los Angeles Daily News*, "The politicians who exploited the process—for laudable objectives—have rendered a disservice to the community. It has opened wounds that will take time to heal. If they had paid attention to this earlier, we could have had a deliberative, thoughtful debate rather than risk tearing the city apart." I was referring to one union member's testimony that, "The Japanese have handed us another Pearl Harbor."

Deputy Mayor Mark Fabiani accused Yaroslavsky, Wachs, and Holden "of whipping up xenophobic sentiments all over Southern California. There is certainly no shortage of demagogues on the City Council who are eager to exploit anti-Japanese sentiments."

I strongly believed the public expected the taxes for transportation projects to include a reinvestment in the local and national economy, with new projects relying on local and domestic companies and workforce. The public wanted to know that an economic return on their transportation investment was a top priority.

In June 1992, the commission agreed to seek new bids without specifically requiring the creation of any local jobs. It approved an eighty-five-car order for the Gold Line extension to Pasadena in addition to providing vehicles for the Green Line. The order required that the cars be mostly American made, but it did not mandate that any of the cars or components be made in Los Angeles or California. Instead, the Commission would award bonus points to bidders offering to hire local workers, foster new American transportation businesses or new products from existing firms. These bonus points would be added to scores to each bidder's technical management skills and price. Commissioner Mas Fukai said he was disappointed by the new plan. "The LACTC canceled its order with Sumitomo because the company would not create many local jobs but did not mandate that bidders on the new contract at least match Sumitomo's projected 370 jobs," Fukai said.

As the one who had proposed using the commission's multi-billion transportation plan to create local jobs long before the Sumitomo controversy, I responded that the commission's new plan was the only one that would work in the marketplace and said, "It's a healthy thing to do, to rely on the free market. That way you develop a healthy industry that is based on what the market will continue to support for a long time, not one imposed by regulation. That won't last."

Ironically, nine months after the imbroglio with racist undertones forced the transportation commission to cancel the contract to buy Green Line cars from Sumitomo, it voted nine to zero to approve the purchase of fifteen Blue Line-style cars from Sumitomo because it was unable to find any other company to build cars to its specifications on its schedule. The new cars, which weren't driverless, cost $2.975 million each—the same price as each driverless car under the canceled contract—and more than twice the $1.3 million the commission paid for the original identical Blue Line cars in 1985.

Meanwhile, six domestic aerospace and defense companies teamed with three international rail car manufacturers and one US maker to submit bids on building the new eighty-five Los Angeles standard cars. The specifications for the cars called for them to be compatible with the Metro Blue Line and upgradable to driverless technology.

The four bidding teams were:

- Northrop Corp. with Bombardier Inc.
- Lockheed Corp. and Hughes Aircraft Co. with Morrison-Knudsen
- TRW Corp. and AAI Corp. with Siemens Duewag Corp.
- Rockwell Corp. with Sumitomo Corp.

The contract was awarded to TRW Corp and AAI Corp. with Siemens Duewag Corp, a German company with a California manufacturing facility. Siemens converted a former steel works plant in Carson into a rail car shell plant that employed many local workers.

As the leading advocate of defense-rail industry collaboration I was pleased that my vision of two years earlier had been fulfilled saying, "These partnerships will create thousands of local jobs."

JOHN DYER

Rationalizing His Way to a Mature Rail Structure | At the Southern California Rapid Transit District, I worked hand in hand with John Dyer in securing funding and implementing the Red Line subway. He was a master in understanding the funding process in Washington. He knew his way in the corridors of Congress, not only in relationships but in legalities. He was one of a kind. Dyer was brought to Los Angeles from Miami by the RTD Board after voters passed Proposition A in 1980, establishing a countywide rail transit system financed by a half-cent increase in sales tax in Los Angeles County.

Dyer was a tough negotiator with RTD unions, and he developed one of the strictest transit employee drug and alcohol abuse policies in the country. George Takei, an RTD director when Dyer was general manager, fondly remembers him. "He had a way of rationalizing the world. When a staffer said 'No, that can't be done,' Dyer would say, 'Well, let's rationalize.' That was his favorite word, and that really impressed me that he looked at a problem and did not go with the bureaucratic solution."

Ironically, Dyer, while he was the director of the Miami-Dade Metropolitan Transit Agency, secured funding for the Miami Downtown People Mover that was designated for the Los Angeles Downtown People Mover, a project that Congresswoman Bobie Fiedler killed. Dyer led the efforts for the planning and operation of the public transportation system for the 1984 Olympic Games in Los Angeles.

Unfortunately, Dyer was misunderstood and badly treated. I remember that in 1987 in one of the community meetings in the San Fernando Valley to discuss Metro Rail, Bobie Fiedler accused Dyer of being investigated by the Grand Jury. This was an absolute lie and an attempt at character assassination for purely selfish interests and advancement. The truth was that the Board of Supervisors had asked for a Los Angeles County Grand Jury investigation of RTD only as it related to management practices in general, not specifically about any individual.

In another case, Dyer was mistreated by the RTD Board of Directors. RTD was the center of investigations, starting by the now defunct *Herald Examiner*, followed by the *Los Angeles Times*, and the *Valley Daily News*. I went to the *Herald* with fellow RTD Director Marvin Holen to find out what was their real objective, and we were told, "Dyer was focusing solely on the subway and neglecting the buses. Once Dyer would resign, the stories would stop." At a special RTD Board meeting that afternoon, Dyer was asked to submit his resignation. Obviously shaken, Dyer asked if he would like to have the evening to think about it and

John Dyer explaining initial route of Red Line with
Hollywood Bowl Station. Photo: courtesy of Metro

discuss it with his wife, Beth, whom he adored. I witnessed in that meeting the display of complete lack of empathy, appreciation, and gratitude for good work and an example of the heartless killer attitude of a self-centered politician. One director said, "John, you don't understand. You go upstairs, sign a letter of resignation, and bring it down here while we are waiting."

John Dyer deserves to be remembered and respected for his expertise, professionalism, enthusiasm, and work ethic. Because of his leadership and expertise, Los Angeles has a subway system.

He is watching, smiling, from above because, in large part thanks to him, Los Angeles has a mature rail network.

CHAPTER FOUR

THE CHALLENGES WE FACE

CLEAN ENERGY

We're making this analogy that AI is the new electricity. Electricity transformed industries: agriculture, transportation, communication, manufacturing.

—ANDREW YAN-TAK NG

When Mayor Antonio Villaraigosa appointed me to the Los Angeles Board of Water and Power Commissioners in 2005, his first directive was, "Get me 20 percent renewable by 2010," which he emphasized with a very hard hit to my thigh. I established a committee solely addressing renewables where staff would report bi-weekly on challenges of and progress toward the 20 percent goal. It was accomplished by 2010.

One of the renewable projects completed in June 2010 was the Pine Tree wind farm in the Tehachapi Mountains, which was designed and constructed under the leadership of Aram Benyamin, then assistant general manager of the power systems for the Los Angeles Department of Water and Power. Pine Tree, which consists of ninety turbines spread over 8,000 acres, provides up to 135 megawatts of green wind power for Los Angeles. It displaced 215,000 tons of greenhouse gas emissions per year and cut 8 tons of nitrous oxide and 11 tons of carbon monoxide.

During my Presidency at LADWP, I became aware of the many challenges renewable resources face. In addition to the fact that power is produced only when the wind is blowing or the sun is shining, there are logistic, political, and environmental concerns, such as: lack of transmission infrastructure, ideal wind sites, the turbines produce noise and affect wildlife, and the need to acquire rights of way.

Henry Martinez, former LADWP executive, told me about a proposed solar project near Desert Center in Riverside County on the edge of the Joshua Tree National Park. "There were four agencies and local tribes that opposed the project because it's sacred land," he said. The project was abandoned.

In March 2010, the LADWP abandoned an eighty-five-mile-long Green Path North transmission line after it encountered stiff opposition from community and environmental groups. The line—which would have gone through Big Morongo Canyon Preserve north of

Palm Springs, Pioneertown near Yucca Valley, Pipes Canyon, and part of the San Bernardino National Forest before connecting with power lines in Hesperia—was designed to bring electricity generated by solar, geothermal, and wind projects in the southeastern California deserts and Arizona to Los Angeles.

In the past, fuel was brought to power plants. Now the utility goes where the fuel is. Transmission lines have to go where the wind is blowing and the sun is shining. Utilities have both challenges and opportunities to upgrade rather than install new transmission lines.

Grid transmission lines are rated on the basis of maximum ampacity and temperature limits. If cooling during high wind or low ambient temperature are not accounted for, then there is unused capacity on many overhead transmission lines. Dynamic Line Rating (DLR) is a changing transmission line rating based on local conditions, thus providing additional ampacity to a transmission line. The US Department of Energy has identified DLR as a transmission and distribution infrastructure solution to defer upgrades and increase distributed power. DLR is one of the solutions known as Grid Enhancing Technologies.

- https://inl.gov/national-security/dynamic-line-rating
- The Federal Energy Regulatory Commission (FERC) Order 881 (https://www.ferc.gov/news-events/news/ferc-rule-improve-transmission-line-ratings-will-help-lower-transmission-costs) may also allow additional capacity using weather conditions to calculate the maximum transfer capability of transmission lines.
- The Department of Energy is doing a study to expedite transmission line upgrades and buildouts. - https://www.energy.gov/gdo/national-transmission-planning-study as part of the Infrastructure Investment and Jobs Act (IIJA).

Mayor Eric Garcetti launched Los Angeles's Green New deal in 2019 to set aggressive goals for the city to address the climate emergency and place the city on course to be carbon neutral by 2045. In June 2022, Garcetti committed to 100 percent clean power by 2035. Under his direction Metro committed to fully electrifying its bus fleet by 2030 and the Los Angeles Department of Transportation would do likewise for its fleet by 2028. Garcetti also led the efforts to reduce the city`s reliance on dirty energy sources, including completely divesting from coal power by 2025 and building out the largest public electric vehicle charging network of any city in the country.

A major focus of the decarbonization efforts of Los Angeles is the transition from fossil fuel-based power generation to renewable energy sources, such as solar, wind, and hydroelectric power. The LA Green New Deal goal of 100 percent renewable energy by 2035 is an ambitious target that requires a complete overhaul of the city's energy infrastructure and investment in sustainable energy solutions. Transportation decarbonization will also encourage the energy transition in the city and help formulate holistic strategies that are focused not only on reducing emissions, but also on the ultimate outcome to create a more sustainable, resilient, and environmentally friendly community.

The National Renewable Energy Laboratory released a study that concluded that Los Angeles is capable of achieving 100 percent clean energy by 2035. To achieve that goal, NREL

With Vice President Al Gore and Sylvia.

recommends solar farms, wind turbines and batteries, solar panels on rooftops, electric cars, and electric heat pumps in houses. It also recommended investing in energy efficiency and demand response programs, whereby the utility pays its customers to use electricity during times of day when solar and wind power are in abundance. The cost of LADWP's electrical generating system powered by 100 percent renewable energy by 2035 would be approximately $86 billion. Under this scenario, critics say that LADWP power rates will triple. If the Department were to set a goal of 80 percent renewables, there would be a savings of $30 billion by 2035, thus the rates would only double. The NREL study determined that LA will need to add 470 to 730 megawatts of solar, wind, and batteries every year for the next twenty-five years. Under the NREL plan, LA would shut down its gas-fired power plants in El Segundo, Long Beach, Wilmington, and Sun Valley. Those gas plants would be replaced partially by renewable energy and hydrogen.

If we were to decarbonize, then more clean energy is needed. Despite record investment in renewables in the beginning of 2023, wind-turbine supply chains have struggled. Rising costs, caused partly by higher interest rates, have resulted in developers abandoning once profitable projects. In January 2024, European energy developers Equinor and BP announced they were canceling the contract for a massive offshore wind project in New York because of interest rates and supply chain disruptions. In 2023, Danish energy company Orsted canceled two wind projects off the New Jersey coast, citing negative economic conditions. Obstacles are the slow approval, which delays projects for years that can tie up capital, resulting in lower returns, and protectionism, which raises costs and threatens shortages. Solar panels are more than twice as expensive in the US as elsewhere, mostly because of the anti-dumping duties on Chinese suppliers.

In October 2023, California Governor Gavin Newsom traveled to China to promote decarbonization, but he has eviscerated the solar industry in his home state. The utilities and organized labor persuaded him and the Public Utilities Commission to sharply reduce incentives for solar installations in 2022. As a result, rooftop solar installations have taken a nosedive in the state. An analysis by the California Solar & Storage Association discovered that solar installations in the state have dropped 77 percent to 85 percent since April 2023, when the gutted incentives took effect. In November 2023, the Public Utilities Commission, whose members are appointed by the governor, voted to dramatically reduce solar incentives again, this time for apartment buildings, schools, and small businesses. In Los Angeles, much of the city's sustainability and decarbonization efforts are outlined in the Green New Deal pLAn (https://plan.lamayor.org/sites/default/files/pLAn_2019_final.pdf), which replaces the Sustainable City pLAn 2015. The first four-year update includes:

- The Virtual Net Energy Metering pilot program, which aims for multi-family buildings to go solar—this program allows property owners to shared benefits of an on-site Renewable Energy Generation Facility (REGF) with their tenants and provide community solar programs and expansion of savings to low-income and rental households through solar rooftops and shared solar programs.
- Bus and transit corridor improvements to encourage modal shifts and facilitate transportation decarbonization.
- Expansion of the curbside charger program to include the private sector between 2022–2028. In 2021, FLO, a leading North American charging network, was awarded a California Energy Commission BESTFIT grant for an EV charging pilot program to equitably deploy public charging infrastructure. BESTFIT is a grant program for innovative charging solutions.
- BlueLA is the country's first, all electric vehicle (EV) sharing program focused on disadvantaged communities.
- Cash for Clunkers Program supports vehicle trade-in, which provides a payout capped at $1,000 or $1,500 for low-income people if their vehicles fail emissions tests.

Lynn Feng, Mobility and Decarbonization consultant, says that clean energy is currently responsible for 86 percent of Los Angeles's Greenhouse Gas emissions reductions, in hopes of 100 percent renewable energy by 2045. Key benchmarks for this sector include investments in key upgrades to transmission and distributions systems, ending coal-based electricity generation in the fuel mix by accessing transmission from the Intermountain Power Plant in Utah, and the cancellation of plans to repower Once-Through-Cooling (OTC) gas power plants. LADWP is projected to have approximately 68 percent renewable energy by 2028, but according to LADWP executives, arrangements can be made to serve the Olympic Load (housing, events, etc.) using 100 percent renewable energy. The Intermountain Power Project is a partnership between Utah and Southern California municipal utilities and serves as a renewable energy hub through its solar, geo-thermal, wind, and hydropower potentials. IPP will also be able to store hydrogen fuel in underground salt caverns. Target date October 2024. (https://ww2.arb.ca.gov/sites/default/files/2020-07/ladwp_cn_fuels_infra_july2020.pdf).

Because IPP is near the only major geologic salt dome formation in the west, it is the ideal location for clean energy technologies. LADWP is the largest purchaser of electricity from IPP. IPP Renewed is a project that includes the retirement of the existing coal-fueled units at the IPP site and the eventual use of renewable energy-powered electrolysis to split water into oxygen and hydrogen, storing the latter in underground salt caverns for use as fuel to drive electricity-generating turbines. A key feature of IPP Renewed is the utilization of "green" hydrogen. Green hydrogen is produced by electrolysis and not from fossil fuels. It's a process extracting hydrogen from water—using wind, solar, and geothermal. Hydrogen can be stored for many months, compared with only hours for storage of electricity in batteries, thus saving energy produced from renewables whenever they are abundant.

Los Angeles County has been making significant strides in its journey toward sustainability and carbon neutrality, guided by a series of ambitious targets and innovative strategies. The plan focuses on increasing the use of renewable energy, reducing per capita vehicle miles traveled, promoting transit-oriented development, and converting fleets of city and school buses to zero-emission vehicles.

Antelope Valley Transit Authority is the first agency in North America with an all-electric bus fleet. Three transit agencies in Southern California plan to have an all-electric bus fleet by 2030: Santa Monica, Long Beach, and Los Angeles Department of Transportation. LA Metro as of 2023 had forty-five electric buses. The Orange Busway (G Line) operates with an all-electric bus fleet. The Los Angeles Unified School District is planning to operate 180 electric buses by 2026, said Christos Chrysiliou, FAIA, director of architectural and engineering services. Forty of them will have vehicle-to-grid capabilities, meaning that when they are not on the road, their massive batteries will be used to store energy and send it back to the grid when needed.

A key aspect of Los Angeles's approach mirrors best practices seen at the national level, such as the formation of interagency committees. These committees focus on diverse practice areas, including EV infrastructure deployment, stormwater management projects, and oil and gas reform, showcasing the city's holistic approach to environmental challenges. Another noteworthy element of the city's strategy is its robust partnerships with local entities and organizations. These collaborations are not only more feasible at a local level but also highlight the crucial role of civic engagement in the planning process. By involving community stakeholders, LA enhances the effectiveness and impact of its sustainability initiatives. This comprehensive approach, blending strategic collaboration with transparency and governmental accountability, reflects LA's firm commitment to realizing its ambitious sustainability goals, setting a standard for urban environmental responsibility.

The Washington, DC, Department of Energy and Environment announced in December 2023 that it had formally adopted the Advanced Clean Cars II Rule, a standard set by California in 2022. Under the regulations, automakers will be required to sell only zero-emission vehicles beginning in 2035 in an effort to curb carbon emissions and fight global warming. The nation's capital joined eleven other states that have adopted California's model.

Electrification has been introduced and advertised as a "green solution" and often to serve the purpose of reducing greenhouse gas emissions. However, it's worth noting that transportation electrification will significantly affect the energy landscape, which underscores the importance of renewable energy integration into the EV ecosystem.

With transportation electrification, the increased electricity demand is inevitable, which also leads to challenges for peak demand (and triggers opportunity charges for EV adopters).

The first step toward electrification should start with a grid stability assessment and upgrade. New technologies such as vehicle-to-grid are positioning EVs as energy storage units, which will help balance supply and demand on the grid, but as of now, this technology has not been widely adopted.

The integration of renewable energy sources, in this context, becomes crucial for maximizing the environmental benefits of this shift, securing energy independence, and ensuring sustainability in growth. The nature of renewable energy provides a resilient solution to fundamentally reduce greenhouse gases and transform the transportation sector. The development of renewable energy, especially for EV charging, can help stimulate the transportation industries and contribute to economic growth and technological advancement, too.

As we tackle the challenges of climate change, the synergy between sustainable energy production and the electrification of transportation is becoming increasingly crucial. This shift to green technology isn't just about adopting cleaner power sources; it's about thoughtfully managing how our transport systems interact with the electric grid, especially in light of more frequent power outages. One of the key concerns is the growing need for fast- charging infrastructure for EVs. Although Los Angeles, and many other cities have a good base of slower chargers, expanding the fast charger network is essential for the widespread adoption of EVs. However, this expansion brings its own challenges, such as added pressure on the electric grid, which could lead to service disruptions, less reliable power supply, and potentially costly updates to the grid.

According to Feng, because of the unpredictability in the growth of EV usage and the existing demands on the power networks, we could underspend on crucial updates and new technologies. To counter this, she said, we need to strategically invest, particularly in areas with a high concentration of charging stations. This helps prevent bottlenecks and encourages EV charging during less busy times to manage peak electricity demand. As we add more EV chargers, Feng said, the overall load on our power infrastructure increases, which could strain our current systems. EV batteries offer an innovative solution—technologies such as Vehicle-to-Grid and Vehicle-to-Vehicle can turn these batteries into valuable assets, enhancing our grid's efficiency, reliability, and balance. In general, the drive toward electrification in the transportation sector requires expansion of charging infrastructure, she said. In Los Angeles, however, EVs will probably not have a significant effect on the grid in the short term, because EV charging most often takes place overnight. In fact, the California Energy Commission estimates that EV charging will account for only a small percentage of power usage during peak hours, 5 percent in 2030 and 10 percent in 2035. (https://calmatters.org/environment/2023/01/california-electric-cars-grid/). According to a study by the International Council on Clean Transportation, the utilization rate of Level 2 and DC chargers will increase from two to three hours a day in 2020 to eight hours a day in 2025 (https://theicct.org/wp-content/uploads/2021/06/LA-charging-infra-feb2021.pdf). But regardless, future grid upgrade needs should be acknowledged.

Level 2 EV charging is faster than the basic Level 1 charging, but lower than Direct Current fast charging, Level 3. Level 2 chargers use a 240-volt power supply, similar to what household appliances such as electric dryers and ovens use.

Transportation electrification plays a vital role in aligning with environmental, social, and governance, or ESG principles. Reducing greenhouse gas emissions is a major goal in many cities, including Los Angeles. Companies and agencies, no matter big or small, are aiming to meet their ESG targets and net-zero goals, and a key part of these efforts is reducing their Scope 1 through 3 emissions. One effective way to do this is by electrifying the fleets used for transporting passengers and goods, either owned directly by the entities, or indirectly by their contractors.

Scope 1, 2, and 3 refer to different levels of an organization's greenhouse gas emissions. Scope 1 includes direct emissions, which come directly from sources that are owned or controlled by the organization. Scope 2 refers to indirect emissions from purchased energy, because while these emissions occur at the place where the energy is generated, the emissions are generated because they are consequence of the organization's energy use. An example of this could be the emissions from the generation of electricity that a company purchases and uses for keeping regular operations of business. Scope 3 is a broader category that includes all other indirect emissions that occur in an organization's value chain, such as the emissions from the organization's employee's business travel.

Achieving ESG goals and reducing emissions from different scopes require diversified strategies based on the nature and source of the emissions. Scope 1 emissions can be reduced by optimizing direct operations to be more energy efficient and switching to cleaner energy sources. For example, an organization could transition to EVs fleets. Scope 2 emissions could be reduced by utilizing renewable energy or investing in energy efficient buildings and processes. Mitigating Scope 3 emissions would require engaging with energy suppliers, designing processes with lower lifecycle emissions and changing consumer behavior to reduce emissions associated with the use of the company's products and services.

I definitely see mass adoption of EVs in Los Angeles in the very near future, in concurrence with rapid charging infrastructure roll-out and fleet conversions. In fact, some studies have been done for local agencies to help them develop EV transition plans and facilities design. But it is important to note that with the advancement of technology, societal needs will also change, and the mobility future in cities like Los Angeles will continue to evolve. Therefore, in my opinion, embracing innovation while prioritizing sustainability, equity, and safety will be key for cities aiming to create efficient and inclusive transportation networks.

More broadly speaking, agencies in Greater Los Angeles and the rest of Southern California have been frontrunners in integrating transportation technologies and pioneering innovative solutions: the city of Los Angeles's electric-vehicle-sharing program, Metrolink's Southern California Optimized Rail Expansion capital improvement program that integrates Intelligent Transportation Systems and Clean Air Vehicles, the Los Angeles County Metropolitan Transportation Authority`s microtransit service, San Bernardino County Transportation Authority's hydrogen-powered passenger train, Southern California Edison's Charge Ready Program, and a Mobility-as-a-Service study in 2021 by Southern California Association of Governments to look at obstacles and actions towards a fully integrated mobility solutions platform.

- Intelligent Transportation Systems refers to the application of advanced technologies—including computer, electronics, and communication in transportation systems. The goal is to improve transportation safety, efficiency, and sustainability. This includes systems such as traffic management software, real-time traffic data collection and analysis, adaptive traffic signals, electronic toll collection, and advanced traveler information products. ITS has been fairly popular in recent years, and has become a preferred tool to integrate multiple transportation modes and travelers' information, manage real-time traffic and incidents, as well as determine dynamic pricing for toll lanes.
- Mobility-as-a-Service is a concept that integrates various forms of transportation services into a single accessible on-demand mobility service. It combines services such as public transport, ride-sharing, car-sharing, bike-sharing, and taxis, allowing users to plan, book, and pay for multiple types of transportation within a single application and with integrated payment systems. The Smart Columbus project in Columbus, Ohio, is one of the most famous and well-regarded examples of MaaS in the US However, generally speaking, the development of MaaS in America lags significantly behind significantly East Asian countries, for a number of reasons including its car-centric culture, the low acceptance of public transit, diverse regulatory landscapes, cybersecurity and data-sharing concerns and lack of central support.
- Microtransit is a form of demand-responsive transport service that operates in shared passenger vehicles. Unlike fixed-route public transit services such as buses or trains, microtransit services use smaller vehicles (vans or shuttles) and do not follow a fixed route or schedule. Instead, they adjust routes based on user demand, often facilitated by a digital platform (like an app). Microtransit services are designed to provide more flexible and efficient transportation options, especially for first/last-mile connectivity and in areas with lower population density. Microtransit can be a hit or miss, depending on the geographical location, travel behavior, and operations management. Microtransit can be expensive to operate, too. Although some agencies have decided to terminate their microtransit pilots after experiencing low ridership and high operating costs, others have decided to cancel all of their fixed-route buses and operate with sole microtransit services. So while this is a good technological addition, tailored evaluation and solution will be needed to respond to the local realities.
- Connected and Automated Vehicles are advanced vehicles equipped with technologies that enable them to communicate with other vehicles, transportation infrastructure, and external systems, as well as having the capability to operate without human input, Automated Vehicles. The connectivity in CAVs allows for real-time data exchange, which can improve safety, traffic efficiency, and environmental sustainability. Automation ranges from partial (where the driver still controls the vehicle but is assisted by technology) to full (where the vehicle operates without any human intervention). An example of this exists in Orlando, Florida. In August 2023, the city's Lynx transit system launched a six-month pilot project in which two automated shuttle buses will provide free service during off-peak hours on part of its Orange Line.

WATER

The earth, the air, and the water are not an inheritance from our forefathers but on loan from our children. So we have to hand over to them at least as it was handed over to us.

—Mahatma Gandhi

Los Angeles has had a strange and storied relationship with water, which is as fluid and fascinating as water itself. Mayor Antonio Villaraigosa appointed me in 2005 to serve on the Los Angeles Board of Water and Power Commissioners when he took office. Villaraigosa also appointed David Nahai, who later became the DWP general manager. Nahai, who has also served on the State of California's Los Angeles Regional Water Quality Control Board, has been involved in water issues for many years, and he provided his expertise and knowledge in the development of this book's discussion on water.

Michael Gagan, public advocacy strategist, told me some interesting historical facts about water. For example, the Los Angeles Charter prohibits the city from serving water outside the city boundaries. Gagan explained that it was not to protect the interests of the existing

Sources of LA water supply. Courtesy of LADWP

consumers of Los Angeles water, but an inducement to surrounding communities to voluntary annex to the City of Los Angeles. As a matter of fact, water in Los Angeles has been a deliberate and very successful tool in the growth of the city. The city's use of its water supply as a tool of annexation was viewed with increasing alarm by a lot of the cities surrounding Los Angeles, and that is one reason why coastal communities from the Palos Verdes Peninsula to Malibu voted in 1947 to create the West Basin Municipal Water District and then to join the Metropolitan Water District of Southern California so that they would have a supplemental water supply to ward off Los Angeles. The same situation is true with respect to the formation of the Central Basin Municipal Water District. Many of the cities in southeast Los Angeles County that are not part of the city of Los Angeles were groundwater pumpers, and so they could go without a supplemental supply all the way through the 1950s. They successfully warded off efforts by the city to expand, including the cities of Vernon and Huntington Park.

Los Angeles as a region is not blessed with much water. The usual annual rainfall is around fourteen inches (although this varies widely from year to year depending on drought conditions). It is estimated that Los Angeles could not support more than half a million people with its own indigenous water resources. So, how do nearly 4 million people live here, with the taps always flowing with only periodic governmental mandates to conserve water?

The fact is that Los Angeles is a semi-arid area heavily reliant on water from hundreds of miles away: the Owens Valley via the Los Angeles Aqueduct, the Colorado River via the Colorado River Aqueduct, and the Sacramento-San Joaquin River Delta via the State Water Project. And the history of how water was brought to Los Angeles from each of these faraway places has been the subject of numerous books and a movie—stories of ambition, intrigue, betrayal, and engineering marvels and larger-than-life figures such as William Mulholland.

WATER SUPPLY CHALLENGES

The future of Los Angeles's water supplies faces numerous challenges, including:

- Significant reduction in Los Angeles Aqueduct flows due to environmental reallocations of water to Mono Lake and the Owens Lake dust mitigation project.
- Uncertainty about the yield of the State Water Project until San Francisco Bay Delta environmental issues are resolved.
- Pumping limitations due to San Fernando Valley groundwater contamination.
- Changes in precipitation, snowpack, and available water due to the effects of climate change.
- Population growth.

The history of the relationship between Los Angeles and water is still being written even now, especially as a result of the calamity of climate change.

THE LOS ANGELES AQUEDUCT

Many Angelenos drive on Mulholland Highway as it winds through the Santa Monica Mountains and take in the breathtaking views of the San Fernando Valley without having the faintest idea of who William Mulholland was. Yet he was probably the most pivotal person in the history of Los Angeles simply because, without him, there would be no Los Angeles as we know it today. A lowly Irish immigrant, he rose from a ditch tender in the late 1870s to be the first superintendent and chief engineer of the Los Angeles City Water Company in 1886. He was just thirty-one years old. The city eventually took control of the water company and made it the Los Angeles Water Department, with Mulholland as superintendent. He brought water to Los Angeles, which had a population of about 9,000 when he arrived, and gave birth to a metropolis, which is now the second-largest city in the US and an economic powerhouse to rival most countries.

Mulholland had learned that the Eastern Sierra contained beautiful, lush, green landscapes fed by snow from the majestic mountains that rose on the east and west sides of the Owens Valley like mighty sentries guarding the rich valley. That snowmelt and rain gathered to fill the one-hundred-square-mile Owens Lake. Mulholland envisioned that water being delivered to Los Angeles through a gravity-fed aqueduct. First, the city needed to gain dominion over the water rights. Posing as ranchers and speculators, agents of the Water Department bought up great swaths of land in the Owens Valley.

With the water rights thus secured, the Water Department built an aqueduct to bring water from the Owens Valley to Los Angeles—a 233-mile series of canals, pipelines, and tunnels operated completely by gravity without a single pump and with the added bonus of generating electricity along the way. Construction of the aqueduct started in October 1908 under the supervision of Mulholland and opened in November 1913.

In the 1930s, as a hedge against the possible abandonment of the planned Colorado River Aqueduct, Los Angeles decided to extend the Los Angeles Aqueduct to the Mono Lake Basin. Work on the 105-mile extension was completed in 1940, and water diversions began in 1941.

The aqueduct was built, but not without controversy. Locals in the Owens Valley, feeling conned and cheated, used dynamite to blow holes in the aqueduct and diverted water back into Owens Lake. The resistance fizzled, and Los Angeles continued to take water. Within thirteen years the one-hundred-square-mile Owens Lake dried up completely and became the worst dust bowl in the entire nation. To date, after much litigation and various regulatory orders, Los Angeles has been forced to spend billions of dollars trying to mitigate the pollution emanating from that huge dust bowl, and the pain is not over yet. As part of that effort, Los Angeles has had to undertake measures such as shallow flooding, thus reducing the amount of water Los Angeles can import from the area. On top of this, there is constant pressure for Los Angeles to leave more water in the region for local development and use by farmers, businesses, residents, tribes, and others.

The city's diversion of water from Mono Lake is still the subject of heated disputes as local interests allege that the actions of Los Angeles are reducing the volume of water in the lake to dangerous levels. The extensive effects of climate change, with its consequential shrinking of the snowpack in the Eastern Sierra Nevada, has added to the local pressure. Consequently, Los Angeles can no longer count on the volume of water that flowed so cheaply and abundantly in the past.

By the early 1920s, it had become clear that Southern California did not have enough supplies to meet growing demand. Without additional investment, water shortages were on the horizon. As the Los Angeles metropolitan area grew in the early 1900s, Mulholland and others began looking for new sources of water. The Colorado River Aqueduct was another brainchild of William Mulholland. In 1941, the aqueduct began delivering water to Southern California.

THE COLORADO RIVER AQUEDUCT

Catherine Mulholland in her book *William Mulholland and the Rise of Los Angeles* wrote that the city of Los Angeles was so concerned the growing outlying areas would demand access to the city's water supplies, that the city decided to find additional water supplies just to preserve its own.

By 1923, Mulholland and his engineers were looking east to an even larger water supply than the Owens Valley—the mighty Colorado River. The plan was to build a dam on the Colorado River 155 miles downstream from Hoover Dam and divert its waters into a series of tunnels and canals across hundreds of miles of mountains and deserts. In 1924, the first steps were taken to create a metropolitan water district, made up of Southern California cities. The Metropolitan Water District of Southern California was incorporated on December 6, 1928, and in 1929 took over where Los Angeles had left off, planning for a Colorado River Aqueduct.

The MWD is composed of twenty-six member agencies: fourteen cities, eleven municipal water districts, and one county water authority, which collectively serve the residents and businesses of more than three hundred cities and numerous unincorporated communities in six counties in Southern California. The MWD is a supplemental water supply for its member agencies, most of which have other sources of water. The State Water Project and the Colorado River are MWD's principal sources of water.

The 242-mile Colorado River Aqueduct was the largest public works project built in Southern California during the Great Depression. The Colorado River was originally placed on the city of Los Angeles property tax roll, because it was going to be a decade before the MWD could sell water, considering it was going to take so long to build. And, when the revenues were insufficient, Los Angeles came to the rescue with its property taxes. The aqueduct was approved in 1931 and financed with $220 million in bonds approved by voters that same year. Construction started in 1933 with 35,000 workers toiling in the desert. It opened in 1939.

There can be no doubt that water from the Colorado River has helped transform Southern California. The water sustains people, farms, businesses, tribes, and wildlife. However, while demands on the river have grown, the river itself has not. It is suffering from a twenty-three-year drought caused by climate change.

Two of the largest dams in the United States by volume, both on the Colorado River, Hoover Dam at Lake Mead and Glen Canyon Dam at Lake Powell, provide power for millions of people. However, dams have what is called a dead-pool level, which is the depth at which water will no longer flow downstream, as well as a minimum power-pool elevation, which is the depth at which the turbines in a dam can no longer produce power. Today, there is a real concern that these levels may be breached if adequate water is not left in the river.

The Colorado River's drainage basin covers parts of seven states: the Upper Basin states of Colorado, Wyoming, Utah, and New Mexico; and the Lower Basin states of California, Arizona, and Nevada. Access to the river's water was divided among these seven states in 1922, in an agreement known as the Colorado River Compact. Today, its operation is dictated by the Law of the River—the many agreements, federal laws, court decisions and decrees, and regulatory guidelines that govern the use of the river.

The Lower Basin states receive their water deliveries every year from massive reservoirs, in particular Lake Powell and Lake Mead. As stated above, if water levels fall too low in these reservoirs, they could reach "dead pool," cutting off a lifeline to some twenty-five million people.

The Colorado River is drying up because of a combination of chronic overuse of water resources and a historic drought driven by climate change. The dry period has lasted more than two decades, draining Lake Powell and Lake Mead to levels not seen since they were first filled decades ago.

In the face of this dire predicament, in May 2023, after nearly a year of wrangling and under the threat that the federal government would impose a solution, California, Nevada, and Arizona finally reached an agreement to use less water from the Colorado River over the next three years.

The states agreed to conserve at least 3 million acre-feet of river water through 2026—about 13 percent of the amount they receive. In exchange, farmers and other water users were expected to receive compensation from the federal government. The agreement would affect the water supplies of about nineteen million Southern Californians in six counties who receive imported water from the Metropolitan Water District. However, the impact in the immediate future was not expected to be severe because in 2022 rains and atmospheric rivers greatly boosted supplies from the State Water Project. A wet winter eased the emergency, but the relief was expected to be short-lived. Although the bounty from the State Water Project will help offset the losses from the Colorado River Aqueduct in the short term, the State Water Project can no longer be counted on to supply the region with inexpensive, unlimited water over the long haul.

THE STATE WATER PROJECT

California experienced a second economic "gold rush" after World War II ended in 1945. Attracted by plentiful jobs, people flocked to California. It was soon obvious that the increased population and commerce required more water. Groundwater basins were also being rapidly depleted to irrigate the burgeoning agricultural sector. In 1945, the California Legislature authorized an investigation of statewide water resources. In November 1960, the Burns-Porter Act, the ballot measure that gave birth to the State Water Project, was narrowly passed by voters.

The State Water Project brings drinking water to twenty-seven million people and provides irrigation for 750,000 acres of farmland. It remains the nation's largest state-built water and power generator and conveyance system. Its centerpiece is the 444-mile-long California Aqueduct, which delivers water all the way to Southern California into the waiting arms of the Metropolitan Water District. To reach Southern California, the water must be pumped nearly two thousand feet over the Tehachapi Mountains. The A.D. Edmonston Pumping Plant is the highest single-lift water pumping plant in the world. The State Water Project itself is the fourth-largest power generator as well as the largest power consumer in California, with a net usage of 5,100 gigawatt hours (a gigawatt equals one million watts) of hydroelectricity annually. The State Water Project was built and is operated by the California Department of Water Resources, which delivers the water to twenty-nine water agencies, including the MWD. In turn, MWD provides water to its twenty-six member agencies.

Approval of the State Water Project was not smooth. Northerners claimed the water was theirs and did not want their water being taken by the South. Even the MWD, a huge beneficiary of the project, initially opposed the project out of concern that its share of Colorado River water could be reduced as a result. The MWD withheld its endorsement of the Burns-Porter Act until days before the vote. The *San Francisco Chronicle* fiercely fought the proposition. California's North-South rivalry was on full display during the campaign. Today, the State Water Project faces a myriad challenge, all of which are intensifying.

To begin with, the water is transported through the Sacramento-San Joaquin River Delta, which has been described as California's most crucial water and ecological resource—the largest freshwater tidal estuary of its kind on the West Coast, providing important habitat for birds on the Pacific Flyway and for fish that live in or pass through the delta. More than thirty-five native plants and animals that live in or pass through the delta are now listed under state or federal endangered species acts. Many factors account for the decline of native fishes: loss of habitat, changes in the volume and timing of flows, changes in water quality. Clearly, robust environmental protections are absolutely necessary. However, they do put pressure on water supplies. California has struggled for decades to find a balance between diverting delta water for agricultural and urban purposes and allowing it to flow through the delta to support the ecosystem. This see-saw balancing act has been referred to as the "fish versus farmers battle," with environmentalists advocating for the protection of endangered species and the fragile delta ecosystem, while agricultural interests and water agencies push for greater water exports from the delta.

Add to this the effects of climate change. The delta, like the Los Angeles Aqueduct, is fed by the Sierra Nevada snowpack. Rising temperatures are already causing alarming decreases in snowpack. The mountain snowpack, which consists of snow that accumulated during wet winters, provides as much as a third of California's water supply. The snowpack releases the water slowly during the springs and summers. Warmer temperatures melt the snow faster and earlier, making it more difficult to store and use throughout the dry season. With climate change, we can expect a "boom or bust" precipitation pattern, referred to as "climate whiplash," in which the snow or rain will come in great bursts, followed by prolonged dry spells, making water deliveries erratic and unpredictable.

To compound matters, the delta faces daunting infrastructure challenges. One issue concerns levee instability. In the late 19th and early 20th centuries, some 1,100 miles of levees were built to enable farms to be established on hundreds of thousands of acres of tidal marsh land. Many such "islands" have sunk over time, increasing pressure on the levees, which are at risk from rising sea levels, floods, and earthquakes.

For many decades federal, state, and local agencies that use delta exports have been exploring a longer-term solution involving new water conveyance infrastructure and ecosystem improvements. The proposed solution has gone by several names: Peripheral Canal, California WaterFix, and Delta Conveyance Project. However, its purpose has always been the same—bypassing the delta as water is moved from Northern California to San Joaquin Valley farms and Southern California residents. Its design has changed several times, from a canal to twin tunnels and most recently a single tunnel. The Peripheral Canal was part of the original State Water Project plan. It was a series of proposals starting in the 1940s to divert water from California's Sacramento River, around the periphery of the San Joaquin-Sacramento River Delta, to use farther south. But voters rejected a 1982 ballot measure to build the canal.

The 2015 WaterFix proposal consisted of five tunnels: three north tunnels that would each be fourteen miles long and two main tunnels that would be about thirty miles long. In 2019, the state redesigned the project, calling for twin tunnels, each forty feet in diameter and thirty miles long. The new WaterFix, with an estimated cost of $15 billion, would have relieved environmental pressure on the delta area, but it was abandoned. In 2022, WaterFix was renamed Delta Conveyance Project and scaled back to a single tunnel thirty-six feet in diameter and forty-five miles long. The proposed tunnel, which would cost an estimated $16 billion, would reduce freshwater flows to the delta by diverting them to Southern California. In December 2023, the state Department of Water Resources approved the project, along with its final environmental impact report, signaling the beginning of a process to seek permits to build the tunnel.

Proponents claim that the tunnel would help California adapt to worsening cycles of drought, capture more water, and alleviate some of the infrastructure concerns. Opponents believe that the tunnel will degrade the delta even further and that efforts and funds should instead be devoted to increasing local water resources in Southern California communities.

Regardless, the tunnel would take many years to build, if it survives legal challenges. In the meantime, Los Angeles must confront the fact that its sources of imported water—the

Los Angeles Aqueduct, the Colorado River Aqueduct, and the State Water Project—are no longer cheap, abundant, or dependable. Los Angeles must take steps to attain some degree of water self-sufficiency if it is to be the master of its own fate.

Following is what Los Angeles has done, is doing, and must do to realize that goal:

LOS ANGELES WATER INDEPENDENCE

The city of Los Angeles is required to adopt an Urban Water Management Plan every five years to comply with California's Urban Water Management Planning Act. The act became effective January 1, 1984, and requires that every urban water supplier that provides municipal and industrial water to more than three thousand customers prepare and adopt an UWMP every five years. The 2020 UWMP is the last adopted plan and continues to serve as the city's master plan for reliable water supply and resources management.

Mayor Eric Garcetti in October 2014 issued Executive Directive No. 5 aiming to meet the challenges of the drought. Under the directive, the city was asked to conserve an additional 20 percent on top of the 17 percent to 18 percent that had been achieved at that point. The directive also charged the city to irrigate 85 percent of its golf courses with recycled water by 2017. "By January 2017 there was a full 20 percent reduction in water usage from two years before," said Martin Adams, DWP general manager.

Previous generations every thirty or forty years built the next "big thing" providing water to the region. Our generation has to look for projects that deliver more water resources. Executive Directive No. 5 accelerated those local projects, so that those that were on the twenty-year horizon are now on a ten-year horizon. Los Angeles must strive to substantially reduce its dependence on imported water because it will otherwise expose its citizens and businesses to the vagaries of a water delivery system that will be costly, unreliable, and, quite possibly, incapable of functioning as intended.

Los Angeles had a number of reservoirs—Silver Lake, Encino, Rowena, Stone Canyon, Hollywood, and Van Norman that are now out of service because of earthquake damage or water-quality problems. The Upper and Lower Van Norman Reservoirs in Sylmar were damaged by the 1971 Sylmar earthquake and replaced by the Los Angeles Reservoir, which was built between them on more stable ground and is the only reservoir presently in operation. "The other reservoirs would require the DWP to construct treatment plants. The neighborhoods objected to these plants, and consequently DWP decided to cover the reservoirs," said Adams. The process of covering the reservoirs started in 1989. The reservoirs can be brought back to service in an emergency with the exception of Silverlake.

The Los Angeles County Board of Supervisors, on December 5, 2023, approved a plan that specifies how the county must stop importing 60 percent of its water and sourcing 80 percent of its water locally by 2045. The plan has a number of goals: improving reliability of the region's water supply, collecting and storing groundwater, increasing the quality and resilience of small systems, mitigating the effects of wildfires on the water supply and managing watershed sediment.

TEN STRATEGIES TO SECURE THE CITY'S WATER:

Conservation: Reducing water consumption in the city is tantamount to producing a new water supply. Los Angeles has done well in this regard—the city has grown by more than one million people in the last few decades; yet our water use has actually declined. Still, we can and must do better. DWP has been highly successful in cutting water use by adopting a five-prong approach in tough times:

1. Enacting the Water Conservation Ordinance, which prohibits wasteful practices (such as restaurants serving water without a customer request, washing cars in driveways) and restricts outdoor irrigation.
2. Deploying a team of DWP professionals to educate the public and to enforce the law.
3. Mounting a public campaign with an extensive outreach and information strategy to change behavior.
4. Adopting shortage-year rates designed to encourage conservation and discourage waste.
5. Creating a system of rebates and incentives to reward responsible conduct, such as a turf replacement program.

However, there is a downside to conservation. First, one of its consequences is loss of revenue to DWP, which then necessitates rate increases to offset the funding shortfall. Second, it means less water in the sewage system, which has an adverse financial effect for the Sanitation Department.

Infrastructure repairs: Water pipes and treatment systems throughout the United States are deteriorating. California's systems, designed to serve sixteen million, now have to cater to nearly forty million people. An estimated 240,000 water main breaks occur in the United States every year. This is a waste of billions of gallons per day. We must make the needed investments to upgrade our water pipes and infrastructure. Sensing technologies have made impressive advances in the last few years. We need to make better use of them. For us, in Los Angeles, any loss of water from leaks and breaks is truly lamentable. Felix Rohatyn, in his book *Bold Endeavors*, eloquently describes how "an activist government led by bold leaders with vision and perseverance, made far-seeing investments that helped to shape America. …Decisions which in their time were attacked as costly, unmanageable, and unnecessary."

New building standards: We have made good progress in Los Angeles with ordinances that require water-saving appliances to be incorporated in development. So much more can be done by way of legal mandates, especially with respect to gray-water systems, cisterns, and other design features to conserve water. These can be combined with incentive programs, but we must ensure that these programs are administered equitably. Otherwise, those who have the wherewithal to take advantage of the rebates and incentives end up paying less to the utility, leaving those who cannot do so paying more since the utility's fixed costs stay the same.

Wastewater recycling: "The Los Angeles River could supply water to the whole city for a year, but the fifty-one-mile river falls 794 feet, about half the elevation loss of the entire 2,340-mile Mississippi River in a fraction of the distance. The Los Angeles River is steep, and when it rains hard the water goes rushing downstream, and hours later it is in the Pacific Ocean," according to Adams. The DWP has been looking at all opportunities to collect that water. Recaptured stormwater that is allowed to seep into the ground ultimately becomes drinking water.

Recycling programs treat wastewater so that it can be used safely for irrigation, industrial purposes, and groundwater replenishment. Los Angeles has used recycled water since 1982 for irrigation of landscaping at various locations, including Griffith Park and the Mount Sinai and Forest Lawn memorial parks.

Before my service on the DWP board in the mid-2010s, the department historically had not been a friend of recycled water. The department had tried once before and got burned, when Jerry Gewe was assistant general manager of water operations. Gagan remembered the Pavlovian comment the water executives of the department would make any time he raised the recycling issue, "You know, we don't want another Gewe situation." Gewe was set up by the City Council and the policy leaders who told him, "Oh, yeah. We love recycled water." Gewe went public, and all he wanted to do was to use recycled water for irrigation. The irony is, "Indirect potable reuse" got a new name: "toilet to tap."

Hearings on the recycling project's safety were held in 1995. The Los Angeles City Council approved it unanimously, so did the Los Angeles Regional Water Quality Control Board, the state Department of Health Services, and the state Environmental Protection Agency. In 2001, mayoral candidate Joel Wachs, who had approved the project in 1995, screamed during a mayoral debate I attended, "Go tell someone in the Valley that they have to drink toilet water."

The political climate started to change with the election of Antonio Villaraigosa. In June 2008, the mayor held a news conference in City Hall with me and DWP General Manager David Nahai, when the protections built into the plan to recycle treated sewage effluent into drinking water were explained. In 2019, Mayor Eric Garcetti made recycling a key part of his Green New Deal plan for Los Angeles. The plan calls for 70 percent of the city's drinking water to come from wastewater plants by 2035.

Recycling has to be a crucial element of any program to produce new water. Enough progress has been made, but we are lagging behind other places, such as Orange County and Israel, as I was able to observe during my visit to Israel with Villaraigosa when I was president of the DWP board. Los Angeles has spent billions of dollars building facilities to treat our wastewater (secondary and tertiary levels) only to dump it in the ocean. Other jurisdictions have long discovered that wastewater is an asset and have devised ways to use it safely and affordably. As the saying goes: "It's not waste unless it is wasted." As of 2023, it is still the policy of the city that all discharges of wastewater to the ocean must cease by 2035. This initiative is called Operation Next at DWP and Hyperion 2035 at Los Angeles Sanitation. Operation Next is a water supply initiative being developed by DWP in partnership with LA Sanitation and Environment that aims to improve the overall water supply resiliency and reliability for Los Angeles and increase local water supplies. "Operation Next will allow the city of Los Angeles to develop a new source of advanced purified water for beneficial reuse. The program aims to maximize the supply of advanced purified recycled water from the Hyperion Water Reclamation Plant in Playa del Rey," said Adams. This is an essential step to provide water security for the city. The highly treated water can be stored in groundwater basins or introduced directly into the water system under recently adopted regulations for Direct Potable Reuse. Currently, the city's objectives also call for the following measures:

- Reduce imported water by 50 percent by 2025.
- Source 70 percent of water locally by 2035.
- Reduce per capita potable water use by 22.5 percent by 2025 and 25 percent by 2035.
- Capture 150,000 acre-feet of stormwater by 2035.

However, attaining these necessary results will require a great deal of resources and political courage.

Rainfall capture: It is estimated that 60 percent of the rain that falls on Los Angeles is lost. It hits impervious surfaces—roofs and streets—enters a vast storm drain system and runs to the ocean untreated. Consequently, the rain carries the pollutants on our streets—such as cigarette butts, motor oil, and animal waste—straight to the ocean. Therefore, it is a water quantity and quality problem. This is a central Los Angeles paradox: In a place so heavily dependent on imported water, our own rainfall is treated like a nuisance to be disposed of as quickly as possible. We must create and implement stormwater capture projects large and small to keep more of our rain. Of course, we also have to recognize that we live in a flood-prone area and must strike a balance to protect against flooding. Fortunately, in 2018, Los Angeles County voters approved Measure W. Los Angeles City Mayor Eric Garcetti played a crucial role in the passage of Measure W, which provides nearly $300 million a year for projects that increase local water supplies, improve water quality, ease the risk of flooding, and beautify neighborhoods. This is a huge boon to the effort to battle urban runoff pollution and to augment our water supply. To date, Measure W has been a considerable success facilitating the construction of numerous projects. Still, improvements need to be made in the administration of Measure W to ensure that disadvantaged communities properly benefit as funds are approved and that there is adequate accountability and oversight, considering Measure W monies that go directly to cities within Los Angeles County.

Aquifer remediation: The San Fernando Valley groundwater basin provides an important source of groundwater supply for the cities of Los Angeles, Burbank, and Glendale. The basin acts as a large, natural underground reservoir. In Los Angeles, roughly 10 percent of our water comes from our own aquifer in the San Fernando Valley. It is a real pity that this irreplaceable resource is suffering from volatile organic compounds and perchlorate contamination. Remediating the basin is crucial to advancing the city's water supplies.

Approximately 70 percent of Los Angeles's wells in the San Fernando Valley have been idle for decades because contaminants seeped into the aquifer. In the 1950s, the Valley was home to automobile, defense, and aerospace manufacturers. Their storage and disposal of metals, solvents, and other waste allowed carcinogens to trickle into the aquifer. In 1974, the Safe Drinking Water Act mandated strong testing and monitoring standards for drinking water. Because the basin was terribly contaminated, it was designated as a Superfund site. Some of the major polluters, including Honeywell and Lockheed Martin, agreed to fund cleanup projects.

During my tenure at DWP, the department embarked on a study to characterize the contamination of the San Fernando Valley groundwater basin, as part of the necessary remediation activities. The study was completed in 2015. It has been a long and arduous process, but finally in June 2021, DWP and Honeywell signed an agreement to expedite the remediation of groundwater in the basin. The agreement calls for Honeywell to design, fund, and construct groundwater treatment facilities. The United States Environmental Protection Agency is monitoring Honeywell's cleanup work.

The city has completed a $634 million project to bring that resource back online. The project creates giant filters enabling Los Angeles to regain access to up to 87,000 acre-feet of water each year. Half of the cost, about $310 million, has come from Proposition 1, a $7.5 billion water bond measure approved by the state's voters in 2014. The project partly advances Garcetti's Green New Deal goal of reducing the purchase of imported water by 2025 and producing 70 percent of the city's water supply locally by 2035. Once fully restored, the San Fernando Valley groundwater basin will be an aquifer that can provide drinking water to more than 800,000 Angelenos.

Agriculture: The bulk of the water used in California is consumed by agriculture. In the past, the agriculture sector has been slow to adopt irrigation techniques that save water. In addition, farm runoff has been a source of contamination to surface water and groundwater resources. On top of this, over-pumping of groundwater in many farm areas has led to surface subsidence and degradation of groundwater assets. Much remains to be done, and prescriptive laws such as the Sustainable Groundwater Management Act, a three-bill package that the California Legislature passed in 2014, will bring improvements.

Financing: Utilities need funds to carry out the measures referred to above. The funding for projects must come from either local rate increases, voter initiatives, such as Measure W or Proposition 1, the Water Quality Supply and Infrastructure Improvement Act of 2014; or federal sources. Rate increases in Los Angeles are notoriously difficult to achieve, and other pots of funding are hard to find. Additional ways to raise money need to be devised. One promising approach may be to develop public-private partnerships that facilitate the building of projects while ensuring that water remains an asset of the public. Also, more needs to be done to attract investment for companies involved in the water industry. Small companies can invent, innovate, and survive only if they have access to capital. For various reasons, capital does not flow as easily to companies in the water world. We need to tackle the investment challenge by identifying the causes and removing the roadblocks.

Encouraging innovation: Innovation is dependent on investment. Many great ideas and companies wither and die for lack of financial sustenance. To counteract this problem, we must facilitate investments, but we must also support the work of our universities and incubators. In this connection, the work of the Los Angeles Cleantech Incubator, a project spearheaded by Kelli Bernard, deputy mayor over economic development for Eric Garcetti, deserves mention. Many startups, including water companies, benefit from the services the incubator offers. One of its services is to help startups navigate the public sector. A utility such as the DWP can't afford to invest ratepayer money in a nascent technology, or a product being marketed by a startup, or something that may be obsolete in a year or two.

Desalination: The technology of removing salt from seawater has progressed immensely. Effects on marine life have been somewhat eased by subsurface intake systems that pull the water through the sand, and desalination plants have become more energy-efficient. Thus, for some locations and some communities, desalination can be an attractive alternative. However, it remains the most expensive of the water production options, requiring the construction of large facilities at the coast, with attendant environmental, financial, and political risks. It also makes little sense to treat our wastewater to a high degree, dump it in the ocean, and then suck it back out to desalinate it. All the other measures referred to above are less expensive and easier to attain. For these reasons, desalination is not at the top of the water production list here in Los Angeles. However, this may change as a warming climate and other pressures continue to take their toll on our water resources.

"The DWP looked at desalination at the Hyperion Water Reclamation Plant next to the Scattergood Generating Station. The advantage was there was power at Scattergood and seawater intake. However, it was very expensive water, almost $2,500 an acre-foot, in comparison, the Department purchases water at a cost of $1,000 an acre-foot," said Adams. There are places in the world that do it a lot cheaper, but they don't have the environmental regulations Los Angeles has to comply with. Israel, for example, does a lot of desalination. The difference is Israel uses a large filtration screen, whereas Los Angeles has a very small screen because the screens were picking up plankton.

San Diego built a plant in Carlsbad, the biggest desalination facility in the United States, at a cost of $1 billion. Since opening in December 2015, it has provided about fifty million gallons of pure potable water a day. "Los Angeles would need ten of those plants to supply the entire city with water," said Adams. The reason San Diego built the plant was to reduce its reliance on MWD.

Conclusion:
Los Angeles's relationship with water is in a state of flux. Perhaps this has always been the case, but it is even more so today because we must envision a water future with more reliance on our own resources. To accomplish this, we will need bold, visionary, and courageous leadership. Every initiative outlined above is fundamental to our future.

VIGNETTES

As told by Ron Gastelum, former general manager of the Metropolitan Water District of Southern California:
"The city of Los Angeles almost killed the State Water Project. The State Water Project was not going to go ahead if the Metropolitan Water District of Southern California would not agree to sign onto a contract. Joseph Jensen, chairman of the MWD board for twenty years representing Los Angeles, was not going to sign because the city did not need the water. Los Angeles was going to be paying the lion's share of it from property taxes, considering the city was the most developed area, and it had for many years underwritten the development outside. It was a question of equity in their minds.

"Governor Pat Brown, who was very focused on getting the State Water Project built, called Los Angeles Mayor Norris Poulson and said, 'We need your help. This is for the good of mankind.' Jensen got a call from Poulson and overnight the city of LA said 'Okay, we'll sign on.'"

The water supply contract between the California Department of Water Resources and MWD was signed November 4, 1960.

As told by Jeffrey Kightlinger, former general manager of MWD:
"William Mulholland was going to build the Colorado River Aqueduct by himself in the early 1920s. William 'Billy' Mathews, who was general counsel of the Los Angeles Department of Water and Power at the time, asked Mulholland, 'How much money are you going to need for this Colorado River Aqueduct?' Mathews then looked at the math and said, 'The City of Los Angeles can't quite do it. There is not enough assessed valuation to float bonds to do it all.' But he said, 'If you bring in the suburbs, the Pasadenas, the Glendales, that'll work.' So in 1928 Mulholland put together the state legislation that created the Metropolitan Water District. There were thirteen cities. Colton and San Bernardino voted no because of the route of the aqueduct. One of the routes was to go right through the pass between Mount San Gorgonio and the San Jacinto Mountains. However, the choice was to go under the San Jacinto Mountains and bypass Colton and San Bernardino. As a result, these two cities dropped out. Voters approved a $220 million bond measure for the aqueduct in 1931 during the peak of the Great Depression.

"In the mid-1940s San Diego joined the MWD. San Diego had always wanted to build its own aqueduct, but the city kept dithering on it, waiting and waiting. And finally President Franklin Roosevelt said, 'I want secure water. We've got Navy bases down here. We're fighting

the Japanese, and enough of this nonsense of them thinking about building an aqueduct in the future.' The MWD annexed San Diego for free to the chagrin of Los Angeles and other cities. Harry Hopkins, an advisor to Roosevelt who supervised the Work Projects Administration, signed the papers in the mid-1940s."

As told by Martin Adams, former general manager of DWP:
"Congress passed the Safe Drinking Water Act in 1974. The DWP operated the aqueducts but the water was not filtrated. Water would cascade into the city and go into the reservoirs. It would be chlorinated and then served to the public. The act forced DWP to build a filtration plant that was completed and put in service in 1986, dedicated by Mayor Tom Bradley. It was the largest direct filtration plant in the world. Anheuser-Busch founded a brewery in the middle of the San Fernando Valley in 1954 because of the quality of the Los Angeles aqueduct water."

CHAPTER FIVE

ARCHITECTURE

"I don't think that architecture is only about shelter—it should be able to excite you, to calm you, to make you think."

—ZAHA HADID

I've been absorbed and fascinated by the art of architecture since my boyhood days in Athens. Strolling next to the resplendent Parthenon, built almost 2,500 years ago, I came to realize that humans can design and create enduring buildings that can be powerful symbols that embrace culture and environment.

The Parthenon profoundly inspired me. Beyond its practical purpose of bringing people together, I was moved by its harmonic proportions and its artistic sculptures, all of which have been copied throughout the centuries. It was constructed as a symbol of victory and has since been praised as a monument to democracy.

With these thoughts, along with my many years of experience as an electrical engineer—which involves designing the power, lighting, and communications systems for buildings working with architects—I developed a deeper appreciation and interest in architecture. Furthermore, I became engrossed with the architectural history and its creative process in Los Angeles. Indeed, for many years I witnessed the local architectural profession produce structures in a multitude of forms, many becoming stunning landmarks receiving the praise of peers and critics. I have long held that architecture is more than the built environment; it showcases our values. It is the way we see ourselves and the way we want others to see us. No cultural form is more public or communal than architecture. Great civic buildings can tell us some interesting and important things about the places where they are and the people who built them.

In Los Angeles, nearly all architectural styles can be found. The Mediterranean climate and appealing landscape attracted architects and allowed them to experiment with different designs. As I observed in the 1970s and 1980s, oil companies, department stores, banks, and insurance companies became the main clients for architects. But creativity was not necessarily their main objective. In the private sector, executives selecting the architect for a project often chose a "name" architect. If the commission failed, the excuse could be, "Well, we chose the best."

This was true in the public sector as well. To protect their jobs, bureaucrats looked for "well-connected" professionals rather than taking a chance on young talent with exciting designs.

A case in point was the 1990s, when it became crucial to build more classrooms for elementary and high school students. Multi-billion-dollar bond measures to finance their construction were successful. Alas, a creative building program was not! The program was delegated to former Seabees, the construction wing of the United States Navy. As expected, the program was conducted with military efficiency. However, for all this multi-billion-dollar investment, the city got little that contributed to enhanced civic life. Absent was architectural excellence and vision—as well as any interface with the communities in which the schools were situated. Disregarding this once-in-a-generation opportunity to revitalize and uplift Los Angeles's many neighborhoods, poor urban planning and unimaginative architecture resulted in a portfolio of cookie-cutter and cheaply built stucco "boxes" that, with very few exceptions, were almost immediately forgotten, adding little to the social and aesthetic betterment of the city.

The Parthenon was not only an architectural feat, but it was also built to last. Through bombardments, neglect, vandalism, and earthquakes, it has remained standing, thanks to the sophisticated methods of construction. The Medici laid the groundwork for the renaissance in Florence. The creativity in art and architecture persists today. I wish Los Angeles architects, public and private institutions, and patrons of the arts had emulated the great feats of engineering, architecture, and artistry of the ancient Greeks and the Medici when Los Angeles was experiencing a construction boom over the last forty years.

Los Angeles Unified School District Board Member Yolie Flores Aguilar, who served from 2007 to 2011, called the new buildings "monstrous, with the look of an institution. They're impersonal."

The campus construction undertaken by the Los Angeles Community College District received similar criticism. A great opportunity was lost.

We love our designs from early modernists such as Irving J. Gill; twentieth-century masters including Frank Lloyd Wright, Rudolph M. Schindler, and Richard J. Neutra; and current global stars such as Frank Gehry and Thom Mayne.

In 2017, *Architectural Digest* identified nine of the best academic buildings around the world, and two were designed by Los Angeles architects: the Moody Center for the Arts at Rice University in Houston, Texas, designed by Michael Maltzan, noted for its forward-thinking creation of collaboration spaces and openness; and the Bloomberg Center of Cornell Tech on Roosevelt Island, designed by Mayne, which generates all of its own power on campus and is the largest net-zero building in the nation.

Yet, despite this distinctive pedigree, Los Angeles suffers from an inferiority complex.

Celebrity architects, such as those listed above, found much of their best work elsewhere. Interestingly, even Gehry once complained that he could get hired anyplace on earth other than Los Angeles.

Los Angeles' feelings of not measuring up may have been stirred by competitive San Francisco. It had a skyline. Los Angeles did not. Consequently, we razed Bunker Hill and many parts of downtown to erect glass-and-steel towers. Charming Victorian houses, beloved and preserved in San Francisco, were replaced in Los Angeles by office towers.

Although Los Angeles is undoubtedly the cradle of architectural talent, this endowment was generally ignored. The world was carefully scoured in search of "big name" architects to recruit.

Craig Hodgetts—a founding dean of the School of Design at California Institute of the Arts, who has held visiting professorships at Yale, MIT, and a tenured professorship of architecture at University of California, Los Angeles School of Architecture and Urban Design—agreed. He told me, "We haven't cultivated our own architects in a way that gives them the sort of scale or influence that will let their ideas be heard."

The absence of this opportunity frustrated him. "One would have hoped that the clientele had gotten more sophisticated and would open to the younger guys, such as Tom Wiscombe, Andrew Zago, Heather Roberge, and Georgina Huljich, all of whom are very talented. "These are the people who put SCI-Arc on the international map because these remarkable people are on the faculty, but no one will hire them," he said with a sigh.

I reviewed my own records and determined that foreign architects have been involved in important local projects. They include Coop Himmelblau (Austria), Central Los Angeles High School Number Nine, now the Ramon C. Cortines School of Visual and Performing Arts; Jose Rafael Moneo (Spain), Cathedral of Our Lady of the Angels; Arata Isozaki (Japan), the Museum of Contemporary Art; Renzo Piano (Italy), the Los Angeles County Museum of Art's Resnick and Broad pavilions; Rem Koolhaas (Netherlands), the Audrey Irmas Pavilion at the Wilshire Boulevard Temple; Peter Zumthor (Switzerland), LACMA's David Geffen Galleries; Ma Yansong (China), "Star Wars" creator George Lucas's Museum of Narrative Art in Exposition Park; and Herzog & de Meuron (Switzerland), the Los Angeles think tank Berggruen Institute's campus in the Santa Monica Mountains.

Additionally, non-Los Angeles architects have also been deeply involved in major local projects, such as Richard Meier (Getty Center); Diller & Scofidio (the Broad contemporary art museum); Moshe Safdie (Skirball Cultural Center); Pei Partners (the 1993 expansion of the Los Angeles Convention Center and Library Tower, now the US Bank Tower); Hardy Holzman Pfeiffer Associates (the renovation and expansion of the Central Library).

LOCAL ARCHITECTS CAN TRIGGER A NEW RENAISSANCE

I have come to believe that the abundance of local talent in architecture, if suitably engaged—as shared with me by numerous authorities—could have revitalized architecture in Los Angeles and triggered a new renaissance. But the button to activate this effort had to be pressed by the business leadership, the boards, and the bureaucratic executives. As an example, and to my personal dismay, the Southern California Rapid Transit District failed in the early 1980s to kick-start a resurgence of great architecture when it built Metro stations. The unfortunate outcome of that endeavor resulted in mediocre stations. It becomes even more painful when one considers what could have been created, and so I took appropriate action (see *Transit Oriented Development* section).

Hodgetts expressed his own regrets. His group had won a competition for modular classrooms with a stress skin, fiberglass roofing system that "blows everything else away," he told me. A prototype was built for LAUSD. But then the administration changed and those coming in decided to buy iPads for students. "Lost was the first investigative process of our project, and it was a bureaucratic unwise decision. The architecture has been instrumental in the new restaurant culture," Hodgetts also shared with me, pointing out that an openness has resulted through interior renovation. "It's about social interaction, it's engaging. It's not just food and aesthetics, but the environment in which people are actually enjoying their food," he said. "Restaurant culture and café culture are main drivers of cultural awareness."

When Hodgetts asked the chef of the Broad museum restaurant if he could work in somebody else's kitchen, he replied: "Oh, no! I couldn't work in somebody else's environment." Using consultants, he designed his own back-of-the-house layout. Hodgetts insisted in our discussion that renovations to the interior of meaningful restaurants have become today's focus for architects. "I can't even think of a restaurant built from the ground up other than the chains, like IHOP and Taco Bell."

American architect John Lautner helped develop the Googie style, a type of futurist architecture influenced by the car culture, jets, and the atomic age. The term "*Googie architecture*" was coined by a design critic after seeing Lautner's 1949 Googie's Coffee Shop on the world-famous Sunset Strip, a popular meeting place for celebrities. The style—which featured upswept roofs, geometric shapes and bold use of neon and steel—became popular among roadside businesses such as coffee houses, motels, and gas stations.

Ships Coffee Shop on Wilshire Boulevard in Westwood was part of a small chain that embraced iconic Googie architecture, as did the Norms restaurant chain, which continues to operate 23 locations in Southern California. Interestingly, the Norms on La Cienega Boulevard

Norms restaurant on La Cienega. Photo: S. VanDerKamp

in Los Angeles, opened in 1957 and is the chain's oldest operating restaurant. Hodgetts's developer had bought the property and was going to demolish Norms. But the nephew of the developer intervened. "You can't tear that down. It's one of the finest representations of the culture then," he insisted. Hodgetts studied the building in detail, the tile work with the logo embedded, the terrazzo floor—all precise, making a huge difference, he told me. "Maybe the public was not aware of the fine features," I gathered, "but the aura made everyone feel good. To me, they came across at a subliminal level and evoked effusiveness, power, optimism, and happiness."

Were McDonald's restaurants another example of Googie, I asked Hodgetts. "Not the original," he said. "The latter ones after everybody said, 'No, that's not architecture.' Our cultural guardians, like the *LA Times*' Sam Hall Kaplan, opposed any architecture that was exuberant. They thought that cities must be more orderly."

Unremarkable buildings began to infest the city, with function and efficiency opposing life and freedom. Architecture greatly affects creativity, something some social sentinels in the press failed to recognize. Architect Pedro Birba, who served on the Los Angeles Board of Building and Safety Commissioners and is an American Institute of Architects/Department of Housing and Urban Development national award winner for housing design, recalled for me the period in 2001–02, when LAUSD received $2.4 billion in bond money approved by voters in 1997 allowing the school construction program to shift into high gear.

He recalled what Kathi Littmann, a construction management expert who headed the district's campus building efforts, said at a meeting of architects, "The district was going to try to build the airplane while we were in the air and flying it backward." Littmann's description hit Birba, an architect on the project, with great impact. "It meant that we were going to be in for a serious, painful process.

The district had very lofty goals. They talked about a commitment to design and a commitment to sustainability, and a lot of commitments, and then they proceeded to shoot themselves in the foot relative to all of that, starting with probably the most fundamental one, which is site planning." His exasperation was unmistakable. "I think that we might as well have been making sausages as opposed to trying to make architecture," Birba said.

Decision-making was flawed, he said, and despite the presentation of three elaborate site plans, an LAUSD design team strolled by them, pointed to one, and that was the extent of the review. "Five minutes," Birba said. "The decision was made in five minutes without discussion." Later he received a call "from some bureaucrat" who told him, "You have to change the design, and it has to be this other type of design, and by the way, you're doing it on your nickel."

I asked him if that encounter was typical of LAUSD. Birba's response was blunt. "From that experience, from talking to a lot of my colleagues who experienced a lot of the same frustrations, it was clear that, at least from an architect's point of view, the school district was saying one thing, but consistently doing something else relative to design, relative to commitment to good architecture."

It was my feeling that the school district had the opportunity to be a Medici, to create great buildings, using the billions provided by bond measures. Instead, it settled for minimal results with little if any architectural gains. "LAUSD could have created buildings that would have been real catalysts for change in the communities that they're in, and instead what we've ended up with is a series of self-contained fortresses that are more black holes than anything else in the communities that they serve," Birba said.

THE SPREAD CITY CONTINUES TO SPREAD

Bill Fain's interest in the city is its urbanistic aspects; he plans for the expansion of the city's neighborhood revitalization—a whole series of urban interventions. And he is local, having grown up on the Palos Verdes Peninsula. Los Angeles is a "spread city," he said, constantly moving outward from the core. "We're very much like London, an Anglo city, as opposed to a continental city where the middle class lives in the center of the city," he told me. "Our middle class tended to migrate outward."

After architecture school at the University of California, Berkeley, he left for New York to work for Mayor John Lindsay's Urban Design Group, where he found a mega-city taking a proactive approach toward development. Los Angeles, Fain said, does not share this positive attitude. "It's more reactive. Wherever a developer, a very influential business executive, or a group of executives, want to do something, the city will bend the rules to accommodate, instead of looking at all the infrastructural issues, like streets and transit. Here we tend to back into solutions," he told me. "We don't try to anticipate and be out in front of certain development decisions."

Fain spoke about interviewing with celebrated professionals such as William Pereira, Charles Luckman, and Albert C. Martin, but was attracted to Pereira because it was not just the buildings that he was involved with but the environment and space-making. He described how visionaries like Pereira were able to shape the city and improve the environment and quality of life at a time when a more active public sector thrived because of Calvin Hamilton, the visionary but controversial Los Angeles planning director and his centers concept.

Fain emphasized that Los Angeles's emerging young architects are particularly talented, and the city has two Pritzker Prize winners—Mayne and Gehry—and he does not think that there are many cities with this pedigree. "This illustrates that the city does promote a high degree of individuality and creativity, probably one of the best cities in the world in that regard," he said. "On the other hand, in terms of community development and in developing public places and in rallying around communities, it's not as far ahead as you might say other cities are."

I asked him to expand on that statement. Fain's response was very much in line with his desire to revitalize neighborhoods. "Los Angeles has a kind of culture that honors our privacy, home, private domain, and car. Everything tends to support this." There has been some slow progress in creating changes to this ethic by moving into public transit and making certain areas denser. "At the basis of this, your environment begins to shape the way you think. The public place that was represented at the public square, turns out that it's just another mall," Fain said.

I recalled for Fain that once, looking down from a tower on Bunker Hill, I saw a lot of open space, but all within walls. Only the tenants of those buildings knew they existed. He said he regarded those spaces to be private, or semi-private. "Two sides need to be totally publicly accessible."

"Why do we import architects for large assignments when Los Angeles has such great creativity and innovation?" I asked. "We have evolved into a great world city and a very important economic region," he said. "Commensurate to that and to stress its importance worldwide, architects from all over the world are invited. We are world class, and we draw from the world for our talent."

Eric Owen Moss is an architect. But he can also be called a philosopher, or an innovator. Or an urban revitalizer. Moss was born in Los Angeles, earned two master's degrees in architecture, held chairs at Yale and Harvard, and appointments at Columbia, the University of Applied Arts Vienna, and the Royal Danish Academy of Fine Arts in Copenhagen. He has also taught at SCI-Arc and served for a dozen years as its director. Moss is widely recognized for his prized visionary designs around the world.

His company, Eric Owen Moss Architects in Culver City, joined forces with developers Frederick and Laurie Samitaur Smith to transform an abandoned industrial neighborhood in Culver City into a campus for creative-minded companies. Called the Hayden Tract, it has attracted successful design, film, internet, and digital media companies.

Moss discussed with me over lunch the "Bilbao effect," the result of Gehry's design of the Guggenheim Museum Bilbao of modern and contemporary art. Bilbao, Spain, is the main urban area in what is defined as Basque Country, where a strong separatist movement existed for decades. In fact, the political strife threatened the museum. Gehry, according to Moss, spoke about threats to blow it up.

The museum transformed Bilbao. It also excited Moss, who told me that it was "a kind of hypodermic for architecture and the use of architecture in a powerful commercial way." Modern architecture, he said, was, in a way, an adversary of commerce, as something that was trying to make a revolution as opposed to confirming the status quo.

"Oddly enough, a fairly radical piece of architecture turned out to be a way of reiterating the commercial status quo of cities, so architecture became a very different kind of tool," Moss explained to me. He didn't know what a suitable classification might be used to identify Gehry and the magic of his design. Perhaps a hustler, or a huckster, or an entrepreneur— "whatever pejorative or commendation you want to put on his work—it turned out to be a magnet."

I shifted the discussion to Los Angeles and how it compares with other cities. "Los Angeles is just warming up," Moss said. "For all the work that you've done, and all the projects you've been involved in, Nick, I think, Los Angeles is ahead of most cities, almost entirely." The future is bright, as well. He spoke about the enormous space the city has, and room to do all kinds of things. "What are you going to do in Manhattan? Or on Market Street in San Francisco? By and large, those cities defined themselves, to some extent, in the 19th or 20th centuries. Half of our space is little asphalt parking lots," he said, quoting the visionary Tom Gilmore, a downtown Los Angeles developer. "What is not clear is exactly how it will be done and who will do it."

"Do you see problems that might be detrimental to growth in the local political structure?" I asked. "Chicago and New York have different political structures," Moss said. "One of the problems is that LA is a piecemeal city, a happenstance city, so the council districts are little fiefdoms. The mayor has relatively little power to organize and direct policy."

Los Angeles is an open city in many ways. When you start talking about big policy, urban policy, there's lots of room to make a future, Moss told me. "The question is, is there a political and a conceptual way to implement it?" Moss said the future of Los Angeles is ahead of it, but it may be ahead in perpetuity unless it does something, and it must have a way of doing it. He emphasized that Los Angeles was a special place for experimentation in architecture and it could be the same for planning, on a big scale. "I wouldn't call it planning," he said. "I would just call it 'big scale architecture,' but with big policy implications."

Moss referred to the planning elements in the city and said they happen by accident or as a function "of a particularly unusual sponsor or client." In that category he placed Cardinal Roger Mahony, the longtime archbishop of the Roman Catholic Archdiocese of Los Angeles, who built a new cathedral using contemporary architecture, the Cathedral of Our Lady of the Angels, and the Walt Disney Concert Hall advanced by Lillian Disney and her initial gift of $50 million. Reaching further back, he included the Chandler family, which owned the *Los Angeles Times*, and Eli Broad, the philanthropist and art collector.

Curiously, Moss told me that when Los Angeles was an interesting, innovative, experimental city in architecture, Broad, "the famous art collector had nothing to do with it. He had no role in supporting, understanding, sponsoring, or anything." Considering the direction of our dialogue, he said, "This is less an architectural discussion, really, than a policy discussion." What was missing, he said, is a bigger idea about what the city could be, how the city continues to build itself. "What you find in Los Angeles is infrastructure and, sadly in a way, what defines the city are train routes, old and new, pieces of freeway, power grids, the river, things like that." Civil engineers created these defining elements.

"Nick, you're a guy who can make projects happen in the city. We need fifty guys like you, and there aren't fifty guys like you, and someone in the Department of Interior, and a president who can use infrastructure in American urbanism to really remake the country. We have to go back to Roosevelt to find somebody who used infrastructure in American urbanism to really remake the country. "I think the promise of LA is the frustration of LA. I mean your book, how to make projects in American cities, in Los Angeles, could sell at the Harvard Business School."

I asked Moss how he saw Los Angeles in fifteen to twenty years. "I'm very optimistic," he said. "It's a city that continues to spread laterally. I think we came to the end of big suburban housing projects and will come back to the city. I think it's a higher-density city." "Specify the density," I said. "Is it Manhattan density?" "No, because I think Manhattan buildings are big and high, but they are small. Actually, they are too small in plan." Moss clarified that bigger buildings and different kinds of construction can be made, that have to do with different uses of energy and different ways of inhabiting them. In other words, I summarized, density in a horizontal way, and open green space.

"That makes more sense to me. There are different ways of working now, and therefore, very different kinds of spaces that are completely workable," he said. When very big buildings have very big spaces between them, very different issues of connection, of landscape occur. "It's a different kind of a world." Moss concluded.

Architect and preservationist Brenda Levin has been called Los Angeles's most notable revitalizer of historically significant buildings. The *Planning Report* identifies her as the person who "has done more to protect and celebrate the city's built environment than anyone else."

In 2010 she received the highest award from the Los Angeles chapter of the American Institute of Architects, the Gold Medal, and it was said that she was the person who "pioneered the preservation and revitalization movement in Los Angeles, a city that not too long ago had little appreciation of its past."

With these tributes in mind, I asked Levin to ponder with me the revitalization of Los Angeles' buildings and the adaptive reuse program and reflect on the individuals who made it all possible. "The people who transformed downtown had a vision before planners and politicians," she said. "I truly believe that real estate developer Wayne Ratkovich established a mentality about preserving existing buildings and adaptive reuse of them, not being precious preservations, but really understanding that they needed to take on a new life." He went against every traditional common-sense thought, Levin said, when he gambled on the ground floor of the Oviatt Building with Rex il Ristorante, an elegant Italian restaurant, in 1980. Nobody was on the streets of downtown at the time. Further, ground-floor space was used for banks, which operate 9 to 5, close before the bad people came on the street, and that would be it. "Wayne went against all of that, created this unbelievably high-end expensive restaurant." Ratkovich was also known for saving the Art Deco-style Wiltern theater, the Fine Arts Building downtown, the 1920s vintage drive-in Chapman Market in Koreatown, and 5900 Wilshire, a thirty-story office tower across from the Los Angeles County Museum of Art.

Ira Yellin, a civic leader and longtime champion of downtown Los Angeles, best known for his restoration of Grand Central Market, was another. He and a group of investors bought and restored downtown's landmark Bradbury Building, the Million Dollar Theater, and the old Metropolitan Water District headquarters. Levin affirmed for me that Yellin understood Grand Central Market "as being a social, political, and economic engine for new immigrants in Los Angeles, and its history in providing those business opportunities with individual stalls that went from German immigrants to Jewish to Chinese to Vietnamese to Hispanic. It has really followed the waves of immigration in Los Angeles."

The Bradbury Building, built in 1893, has always held for me a special appeal with its extraordinary skylit atrium, access walkways, stairs and elevators, and ornate ironwork. Levin told me she remembered walking into the five-story building for the first time with her husband, David Abel, publisher of the *Planning Report*. "From the exterior, the building looks like nothing," she said. "You walk in, and you are just completely blown away. It's just this incredible icon so everybody speaks about it. I always used to have these conversations with Sam Hall Kaplan about Broadway that it's exactly the kind of street that when you go to another city in Europe or elsewhere, South America, anywhere, you seek out, you go to the public market, you go where there's lively street music and vendors, and it's not a fearful experience, it's one that you seek out."

Bradbury Building. Photo: LA Conservancy

She believes that the key to downtown's transformation was the City Council's Adaptive Reuse Ordinance which was approved in 1999 and allowed commercial buildings to be converted to residential. "Tom Gilmore planted himself on the corner of Fourth and Main, the most ridiculous district to think about putting residential. With the ARO, it made it possible to renovate these buildings in an economic way. Young people wanting to be where there's a buzz, transformed downtown more than anything else."

I reviewed the latest census data and was amazed by the growth of residents in the downtown area. As a visionary and planner, I sought Levin's opinion on the role demographics will play in architecture, because of the young.

She agreed that a role will be played but cautioned that "we've been talking about it for decades and wishing for it to happen. I think my sort of slight distrust of our city is that we're not very good planners, that we don't have a good tradition of really thinking about things comprehensively."

Although a lot of thought has gone into the downtown plan, she thinks that we must focus on open space, invent pocket parks, and undertake small interventions that could happen and have profound effects. "The city has always been a project-by-project city, and a developer-by-developer city, and the vision thing, call it whatever you want, has never been anything that this city valued," she said.

There are three great periods in Los Angeles architectural history, Michael Maltzan told me. The first wasn't huge, but it was important. Frank Lloyd Wright, often called America's best architect, was in Los Angeles, and Rudolph Schindler and Richard Neutra came to the city from Austria largely to follow him.

"Wright," Maltzan said, "had seen an extraordinary opportunity here, where the culture and climate allowed him to build in progressive ways that he couldn't do in other cities. As a result, he created a range of work that we still look at as being some of the most important early modernist work in the city and had influence."

Maltzan, originally from Long Island, first came to LA as part of a student research trip with the Harvard Graduate School of Design in 1987 and returned a year later to work in Gehry's office on the design of Walt Disney Concert Hall. He founded his own firm in 1995 and later worked on a major renovation of the Hammer Museum in Westwood. Through an international competition he and the engineering firm HNTB were selected to design the Sixth Street Viaduct. Known as "the Ribbon of Light," it was the largest bridge project in the history of Los Angeles.

I asked him what the second great architectural period was. He told me it was postwar, and it was experimental, using materials that were previously unavailable, manufactured products such as steel frames, composite in-fills, and new mechanical systems. When I asked him who was involved, he listed Gregory S. Ain, Peter Koenig, Craig Ellwood, and Charles and Ray Eames. "The work really exploded because it created a new vision, that inside-outside living could take place through new means and methods of construction, new forms, much lighter space. You could build something that dealt with the way society was changing."

Then the third period was when a group of young architects, notably Gehry, who was the oldest, Mayne, Moss, Hodgetts, Hsinming Fung, Robert Mangurian, and Frederick Fisher conducted a series of exhibitions, taught at universities, and created SCI-Arc.

Maltzan said that Victor Gruen might have been the only person who was able to have one foot in both pots. Gruen understood that there was in the invention of structures like shopping malls a way to create a new version of public and community space that resonated with how Los Angeles and other contemporary cities were evolving. "Even Jon Jerde grew out of that sensibility," he said, noting that there was a huge amount of dynamism around those ways of rethinking how the city worked.

It was a period when California was going through major changes, with big demographic shifts. The postwar economy made it difficult for younger firms to design larger commercial and institutional buildings. "So, they became more experimental with cheap materials and new types of materials created as a part of the war effort," Maltzan said. "They became their laboratory, creating an architectural culture of experimentation with big implications, even if the structures they made were small."

Los Angeles architecture attracted national attention. New York, Boston, and Chicago were not doing much, and more media coverage was given to Los Angeles, which was showing a direction for architecture that had a future, one that was going to be more exciting, that would challenge conventions.

And architects were drawn here, I presumed. "Indeed, in my generation, this was the place where it was happening," Maltzan said. Among the transplants he named were Greg Lynn, Neil Denari, Wes Jones, and Mark Wai Tak Lee of Johnston Marklee & Associates.

Some have not made a name in the field, I noted, and asked for an opinion. "Because there is less of that in the 20th century intensity of building going on, there is less room for young experimental firms to thrive," Maltzan said. "They tried to make a practice by being academics first, and through competitions, through experimental projects, build a portfolio." The academic side can tend to hold people back initially because it doesn't translate easily to actual practice, he said. A void was created in Los Angeles. Although the city is filled with very talented architects, there's very little to show for it.

INVENTING A LIFE IN LOS ANGELES

Los Angeles was America. That is what Michael Rotondi's father, an Italian immigrant, told him. "This is the place where you could invent a life and realize all of the things that you imagined were possible in the old country," he remembered being told. His father's family remained in New York. "Let's go to the coast," that's what he called California. He wanted to invent his own life. New York with the family was like the old country, he reasoned. He even had the same seat at the dinner table he had in Italy. In Los Angeles, he told Michael, "I sit anywhere I want."

Rotondi was born in the Silver Lake/Los Feliz area. He has said he fell in love with isometric drawing in junior high school and realized his affinity for precision. In 1972, he and fifty other students left Cal Poly Pomona to attend the newly founded SCI-Arc where he rose from student to teacher, to graduate school director, and finally to second director of the institute.

Because of his innovative asymmetry and industrial concepts and materials, he became a prominent figure in the Los Angeles postmodernism school. His professional career included stints with established firms and independent collaborations with the likes of Hodgetts. In 1991, Rotondi founded a new firm, RoTo Architects, with Clark Stevens and Brian Reiff. His buildings "evoke kinetic mechanisms that fold, twist, and split open. ...They express the architect's feelings, thinking and mood at the time they had been designed," according to an interview in *ArchDaily.*

I asked Rotondi specifically about the Los Angeles vitality and the architectural opportunities that work here. "I've always thought it was advantageous that the umbilical cord from Europe never made it over the Rocky Mountains," he said. "Everybody was content. Architecture was changing a bit postwar but was still importing from other places, from Japan with more openness." Rotondi spoke of Schindler and Neutra and said that Wright was still European in his outlook even though he had an eclectic Midwestern attitude. He considered Ray Kappe to be the most important architect of the postwar era initially in Los Angeles because of the spatial ingenuity in his houses.

I spoke with Kappe, who was an important educator, teaching architecture at the University of Southern California, and founding chair of the architecture department at Cal Poly Pomona.

After a notorious dispute with his dean in the fall of 1972 (student protesters wore T-shirts emblazoned with Kappe's face), he and faculty members Thom Mayne, James Stafford, Glen Small, Ahde Lahti, William Simonian, and his wife, Shelly Kappe, founded the alternative educational experiment that would become the SCI-Arc. Rotondi was a student at Cal Poly then.

Kappe's disagreement with his dean was over an environmentally designed program with landscape and planning courses. When SCI-Arc was started, fifty students left Cal Poly, joining twenty-five others from around the country, to study with Kappe.

Mayne, who is now an internationally known architect, credits Kappe for bringing in faculty with strong personalities and unique ideas. "He had an incredible tolerance for radically different views. Debates were often emotionally filled and unusually open, with screaming and yelling," Mayne said.

I asked Kappe if he was surprised by the new school's quick acceptance. Not at all, he said, noting that accreditation came in four years, which was amazing for a school like that. "We were doing stuff that other schools weren't doing, and so we were more leading than following."

In a 2011 feature in *CA-Modern* magazine by Dave Weinstein, long before the internet made it possible, Kappe had said that "Los Angeles could be transformed by encouraging telecommuting and tele-shopping with goods delivered not by truck but through underground tubes. Instead of cars, people would get around hands-free in tiny, computer-controlled vehicles."

He envisioned a city divided into four-square-mile neighborhood grids, with businesses and cultural centers clustered near freeways. Free of traffic, neighborhood streets would become greenbelts. His concept, as Kappe related to me, was to have the freeway system generate so much more than it does, and his proposal was to get electric cars the size of the Smart car and "we'd get about ten to forty times the number of cars on the freeway." It would all be computer controlled. Naysayers told him then that computers were not sophisticated enough to do that. Was Los Angeles a good place for architecture? I asked.

Kappe's answer was direct. "There's lots of things that can be done here besides architecture, in urban design issues and planning, and so it seems that LA has so much more opportunity to grow. It's a great place for architects. But it is hard. It's very competitive now. If you're not a good marketer, it's tough. If you haven't really driven yourself, it's difficult."

During his sixty-year career, Kappe used custom homes to pioneer techniques for mass housing. The more than one hundred homes he designed were spacious and innovative. He was a pioneer in prefabrication, building several of his houses out of pre-manufactured parts that were trucked to the site and hoisted by cranes into place. His practice was in Los Angeles, and the only other local firm he considered to be on this scale was A.C. Martin.

Rotondi told me that Kappe's houses were "extraordinary special inventions that he did intuitively. It wasn't didactic, it wasn't theoretical. People will be doing dissertations on his houses."

In the 1970s, the architecture in Los Angeles became very experimental, Rotondi said, and it was possible because nobody had any expectations. "Nobody was publishing, and [architectural historian] Esther McCoy, who was first to write about Schindler and Neutra, argued with people on the East Coast to publish us."

Kappe was the perfect first director at SCI-Arc "because he was a very progressive parent," Rotondi said. He didn't judge. When told that the graduate students were "mixed up" and Rotondi must do something with them, he expressed uncertainty. What did he know? Many students were his age.

Kappe's response: "Worst that could happen is you'll screw it up. Don't worry about it."

These days, he made it known, that people are afraid to make mistakes. "Nick" he said, "people might say you had courage when you started your own business at twenty-five. You didn't need courage because you were out in front. The people that need courage are the ones that are behind, sucking the dust." I knew that SCI-Arc experimented with social and educational principles. I asked Rotondi to explain the contributions it made to the city.

"At first we talked about creating a society within the school and through our projects, through a competitive society against the standard rather than each other, and then cooperate with each other because we were trying to survive," he said. The desire was to keep that concept alive beyond SCI-Arc. "Our influence produced a lot of young people who are very optimistic."

Rotondi's father was the executive chef at Patsy D'Amore's Villa Capri in Hollywood, a favorite spot for Frank Sinatra and movie stars James Dean, Marilyn Monroe, and Jimmy Durante. Although he didn't follow in his father's footsteps, the restaurant culture did influence his desire to learn more about restaurants.

Mayne co-founded Morphosis in 1972, and after Rotondi joined the firm five years later, they created the minimalist architecture that gave Nicola restaurant in Silver Lake an elegant environment. Then came the popular 72 Market Street Oyster Bar and Grill in Venice, launched by actors Tony Bill and Dudley Moore. Morphosis also designed Angeli Caffe on Melrose Avenue, a concept that was a contemporary version of a historical Italian café where someone felt comfortable getting up and walking around and talking to other people, Rotondi said. "It was designed to get people to feel like they were in a public space."

In delving further into how Rotondi imagined a restaurant's architectural style, he said that there was no fixed way to do a restaurant "because it was one of a kind. We talked with the chef about the social life he wanted in the restaurant, and it became clear that every chef we worked with saw the restaurant as a public living room."

Morphosis's next restaurant project after Angeli, was Kate Mantilini in Beverly Hills, Rotondi said. He received a call from Marilyn Lewis, the fashion designer, film producer, and owner of the Hamburger Hamlet restaurants, who asked if he wanted to do a restaurant. "Yeah," he said, "but not a Hamlet." "Perfect," Lewis quickly replied, "because I want to do a one-of-a-kind restaurant." She wanted a roadside steakhouse for the future named after the 1930s Los Angeles boxing promoter Kate Mantilini, who was the mistress of one of Lewis's uncles. And Lewis wanted a clock in the design. Mayne and Rotondi studied watch mechanisms and motors and fashioned a motorized model of the solar system projecting through a skylight in the ceiling. It was a unique orrery with a sundial on the roof.

Mayne and Rotondi transformed a former Wells Fargo branch on Wilshire Boulevard into a local landmark—a restaurant with a large, open interior dining room filled with sunlight and walls layered with collages.

Ma Maison, the brainchild of Patrick Terrail on Melrose and the launching pad for celebrity chef Wolfgang Puck, was elevated to a lifestyle and marketed to the Hollywood crowd, but it was very informal, with plastic chairs. I knew Terrail and I hosted events there.

Rotondi drew parallels between Puck's experiments with food and the architecture at Ma Maison. Both are languages, he said. "The food that began to emerge at that time was very much like the architecture we would look at. Ma Maison was an epicenter, and you could trace a lot of restaurants back to that point."

It has been written that from Gehry's Santa Monica studios emerged a circle of architects called "Gehry's Kids." They included Rotondi, Mayne, Moss, and Frank Israel, all of whom sought to keep pace with combinations of new construction, recycling, and industrial materials. This was the best way to serve a city whose built environment had become a shifting stage set.

"Gehry," Rotondi told me, "In his heart of hearts is a socialist." Even though Gehry has earned millions, in the beginning he was trying to make buildings social as well as experimental, he said. "He's a sculptor who worked in architecture and he was still interested in doing social buildings."

Instead of reaffirming the status quo, "Mayne and I would question the way people lived together, played together, worked together, and based on a contemporary moment, how to design all of that to be a part of the evolutionary paradigm."

SCI-Arc claims to be dedicated to educating architects who will imagine and shape the future. "Do you have some in mind who can do that?" I asked Rotondi. "There are a lot of great young guys who can do that," he replied, citing Patrick Tighe, Lorcan O'Herlihy, Herwig Baumgartner, and Scott Uriu. "Andrew Zago will be influential theoretically, and Peter Zellner and Tom Wiscombe are talented, motivated and courageous."

With an eye on tomorrow, Rotondi speculated that young people who see the world falling apart have a survival instinct that has a positive appeal: "I don't have to accept the world that my parents want me to inherit. I can invent my own." Things change from within and incrementally, he told me. "But you must have people with a mind-set that things can change."

TRANSFORMING ARCHITECTURE AND WINNING A PRITZKER

Mayne was an iconoclastic architect who turned theory into practice, the *New York Times* wrote almost two decades ago. In so doing he helped define the Los Angeles architecture boom.

A winner of the 2005 Pritzker Architecture Prize—often referred to as the Nobel Prize of architecture—Mayne added respect to the art of architecture in Los Angeles. Originally from Connecticut, he studied architecture with a social agenda and a planning focus at the University of Southern California, but it wasn't enough, he once said. He needed "a more tangible solution."

In the hope of reinvigorating architectural education, he helped found SCI-Arc in 1972. Then, with colleague James Stafford and Rotondi, he created Morphosis, a Greek word that implies an architecture dedicated to transformation.

In a conversation with him, I said that young people these days do not want the traditional suburban life with a house, a pool, and a yard. They want to be able to move for employment. "They will come more to the center, and urbanize, thus forcing the builders and developers to rethink what they are building. They are looking at public transportation, thinking of pedestrian lifestyles, bikes, and open space. The change, I believe, will come from the young," I said. "Absolutely," Mayne replied. "The suburb is not a useful environment for that group. They want a cosmopolitan life, a city, and connections. These are the things you need to make a city come alive, with street life. They are a perfect audience because with that comes buying power, restaurants, bars, shops, and cafés. The majority of the population is going to be interacting, and that is exactly what cities are. That literally is a definition of cities."

The ancient Greeks called the city *polis*, meaning a society characterized by a sense of community.

Los Angeles is complicated, the concentrations that are not downtown are more interesting, Mayne told me. He knew because he had been through the cycle himself, having lived in a little apartment above a bait and tackle shop by the Venice Pier. "I was living at the ocean, teaching and working in Santa Monica, driving two miles a day, barely needing a car." Many of his friends, academics, architects, and artists lived the same way. "That's changed a bit now. The ocean is not as accessible and is more expensive, but that's also good for downtown because, finally, you're looking at where concentrations are. It's a big city, so it has room for multiple concentrations of people."

Eli Broad, who made a fortune in home-building and insurance, was planning to build a contemporary art museum next to Walt Disney Concert Hall. Broad asked Mayne to work on a design for the downtown site but it turned out to be a failed partnership. The *Architect Newspaper* quoted Mayne as saying he did not want to produce a building of which he wasn't proud. "We demanded having a major public space, and Eli said, 'No public space,'" Mayne told me. "That's the problem when you have nobody speaking for the public, when you have a weak political system, and nobody is interested in challenging it." If you challenge Broad, you're gone, Mayne said. "I did that. When I left the project, I wrote him a letter; someday it will be shown."

Mayne was unreserved about Los Angeles. "This is a city that will always be vibrant, with an artistic community. I have no idea where it will go, but the near future is going to remain a very vital base because of the institutions." Candidly, he told me that there's a vibrancy about Los Angeles in terms of its creative atmosphere that just comes with the city. "This is why you are here." He loves Boston and Paris, he said. But he could not possibly live in Paris. "It would be the most boring place in the world because everything's fixed. They know what's correct. They're not looking for solutions. It's not a place of creativity and exploration."

Mayne said that someone told him that we no longer live in a society, "we live in a market." He told me it was totally true. "Today, when you read about a play, a film, a piece of art, it shows up first in the Business section. What the hell does that have to do with culture?" Van Gogh and Caravaggio died poverty stricken, he remembered. The market value of art is irrelevant for a cultural item and is only appealing to somebody who's primarily interested in business.

The architectural pedigree of Gehry and Mayne elevated the city's status internationally, I resolved. "Are there successors?" "There will be a lot of them," he said. "Neil Denari is starting to be one of these people. And Tom Wiscombe is going to be very successful." He also mentioned Ma Yansong of Beijing, and Hernan Diaz Alonso, director of SCI-Arc.

"There's always going to be another wave."

EXPLORING CONTEMPORARY LIFE

Neil M. Denari was born in Texas, emerged in New York with a series of theoretical projects on the collapse of the machine aesthetic of Modernism, and launched his practice in Los Angeles in 1988. As an architect and a teacher, he explores the realms of architecture, design, urbanism, and all aspects of contemporary life.

We began our chat examining public transportation because he did a project for the redesign of Westwood Village, in collaboration with Roger Sherman and Edwin Chan, creating a different type of potentiality and structure, he told me. "It's an underperforming world, a giant market with UCLA, but nobody is making a commitment to making something happen."

I participated as former Metro board member in a forum regarding the Westwood Village Plan in 2011. Other participants were Dana Cuff, UCLA; Chris Hawthorne, architecture critic, *LA Times*; Aaron Betsky, director of the Cincinnati Museum of Art; Mark Robbins, Dean, Syracuse University School of Architecture; and architects Neil Denari, Roger Sherman, and Edwin Chan, the designers of the Plan.

I bemoaned then the lack of cooperation between the big partners, MTA and UCLA, saying, "MTA and UCLA should have formed a partnership five years ago to create a master plan of the city block from Wilshire north to Gayley and Westwood boulevards." Again, another example of poor urban planning; and as a result of this multi-billion-dollar investment, the city got little that contributed to enhanced civic life.

He had taught at SCI-Arc and was its director before becoming a tenured professor at UCLA.

He called Los Angeles a horizontal sprawling place with traffic, and that's why architects he knew would never live here. At the same time, they did want a world of layers of potentialities, such as lifestyles, and ways in which someone can inhabit the city. "We're talking fifty years out, with big vision and big plans, and we get a taste of it now," he said, turning to me. "That's been your mantra."

"Indeed," I said. "My pursuit and mantra were relentless as we promoted the subway to create a backbone, followed by various important lines that were built." I explained that the subway system in New York is more than one hundred years old. Ours is rather young. Had we not started in the 1980s, we would not have a rail system because Washington had changed and stopped providing support.

There are neighborhoods in Los Angeles, but they do not function like those in New York because of the structure. "Here you have to deal with distance; you have to shrink the city to survive, but then you give up so much of the richness because it is so spread out," Denari said.

"The beauty of public transit and the rail system is that they connect the neighborhoods and that will make the city great," I said. "Los Angeles will be a phenomenal city in fifty years. Young people are mobile. They want new employment challenges every two or three years. That's why downtown is exploding. There are nightclubs, restaurants, and cafes. And there are museums and transit cores.

"LA will become a hybrid city," he said.

"Yes, a better city, not like New York, where you can go anywhere with the subway, but a hybrid city with great weather and more choices," I said. "We can still live in Encino, but we also live in a loft downtown and enjoy the edginess of the arts district."

"What's the future of LA? somebody always asks me," Denari said. "Everybody wants a sustainable world, but how do we get there? Nature and life can kind of commingle here. It's not about density as it is for other types of cities."

Denari—who has been exploring the spheres of architecture, design, urbanism, and global cultural phenomenon—seeks out projects that demand new and innovative solutions. "For a long time, the sustainable thing was a conservative thing, and it was going to prevent aesthetic development, and stunt progressive ideas in favor of just reproducing known models."

Denari has worked in New York and Los Angeles, so I asked him to compare them in terms of the environment and architecture, and the opportunities for architecture. "In New York, everything goes in cycles, and everything operates in terms of periods," he said. "Global wealth allowed New York to return to its inherent logic. It made sense for people to invest in New York to see recovery after 9/11, but also because of the markets there." But it's a tough city as an environment, he added, although opportunities were fantastic. "I'm going to speak personally; I think that there's this weird convention that you are not as well liked where you are from—more liked when you are from the outside. Frank Gehry and Thom Mayne took a long time to come back to their projects. I've done more work outside LA. Opportunities to design public buildings do not exist in Los Angeles, Denari lamented. "We don't have a competition program to do schools and libraries. They are in a bureaucratic system that rejects creativity!"

Scott Johnson, who has designed a few skyscrapers in Century City, said self-confidence is an essential trait for architects.

"I'm a designer, I like to design buildings," he told me. "And designers tend to breed self-assurance, not always accurately, but self-assurance nevertheless in order to conceive, design, engineer, and construct their designs and, in the process, convince a wide variety of stakeholders." There is a relationship between buildings and ideas, he said. Most people would have difficulty looking at buildings and connecting them to ideas. So, the architect frequently thinks it's his or her job to connect the idea and the place. "In a sense, we become critics of our own work."

Johnson studied at Stanford, the University of California at Berkeley, and the Harvard Graduate School of Design. He has lectured and taught at SCI-Arc, UCLA, Berkeley, and the University of Southern California, where he once served as the director of the Master of Architecture program.

In 1983, he joined Pereira Associates as the principal and design director. Five years later, he and co-worker Bill Fain, whom he had met at Harvard, acquired the firm, and renamed it Johnson Fain.

"Donald Trump called from New York," Johnson told me, and asked if we were the "*Die Hard* guys," referring to the movie, which featured the Fox Plaza building in Century City. Fox was the first high-rise building for Johnson in Los Angeles. After that building, he received numerous additional commissions.

After Johnson and Fain assumed control of William Pereira's company, they had two or three years of work before the economy crashed. Domestic work was minimal and in the mid-1990s, they began international work, traveling to China and Southeast Asia with projects that were urban, mixed-use, high-density. They were big enough and centrally located such "that they could be thought of as a critical piece of the city with a significant public impact."

Whether they were public or private projects, the firm thought of them as de facto public projects, he emphasized. "Our challenge was to explain to the equity holders, or our clients, that even a private project needs to open up and address broader community issues."

Johnson described for me the changes in architecture in today's world, and the role of the Internet and instantaneous communications. "We're all working with computers now and we can prototype a building thirty-five different ways, if we choose to. With 3D printers we push a button and when the clay dries you have a three-dimensional object that reflects what you are proposing."

"A good architect is both a visionary and a collaborator. He would not be comparable to, say, the first violinist at the Los Angeles Philharmonic, but rather like Dudamel, the conductor of a virtuosic set of great musicians, singers, and instrumentalists, who guides the vision, establishes the tempo—and works to bring it all together." He insisted that when these many talents are of one mind and heart, and the client supports that, then a great work of architecture can be the result.

"Nick," he said, "you have raised the question about form versus civic purpose. In architecture, the computer has unleashed a torrent—an encyclopedic capability—to articulate form in an infinite number of ways. It provides freedom to create. But with freedom, one could argue, comes responsibility. With freedom comes a bounty of opportunities to conceive, refine and make structures people centered."

I wanted to explore that point further and asked if, with all that knowledge, from an architectural point of view, could it serve the public? "We're a diverse and pluralistic society, and there is no turning back," Johnson said. "Our underlying critique of successful architecture should address that. Our efforts should be more universal, inclusive, and solution based. We should be able to look deeper into the process of form-making than just surfaces, materials, and aesthetic strategies and decide whether all this adds to the value of our shared space."

I admire buildings that are open and observed that downtown buildings have open space, but it's often at a different elevation than the pavement. The open space is often on a rooftop or a setback, visible only when one looks down from taller buildings. How can that be justified?

"Los Angeles is still a ground-level city, I mean you are often in your car on the ground level and the car is the dominant form of circulation now and in this place. In earlier times, we were doing more walking, but we were still on the ground level," Johnson said. "In other cities in Europe and Asia, and New York as well, the land is so built-up and costly that the roof becomes valuable. The roofs are landscaped. They become gardens, amenity areas, social spaces and they are either publicly or privately accessible."

Johnson said, "Los Angeles was very slow to embrace urbanization because of its suburban legacy and reliance on cars. It's a matter of how we think about and use public space." He also spoke of how we build enormous boxes to contain parked cars all the while the Metro transit system is expanding, driverless vehicles and ride-share programs are growing, and air taxis are being prototyped. Building codes require commercial buildings to have significant onsite parking. "We're ending up with all these garages that, in time, will be converted to other uses or demolished," he said.

DOES AN INDIVIDUAL GOOD LIFE MEAN A BETTER COLLECTIVE LIFE?

"The hope of what Los Angeles embodied was represented through the private sector," architect Roger Sherman told me. "It's a paradox of some sort where the city—the possibilities of the city—were represented through lifestyle, through what it afforded in terms of single-family lifestyle as opposed to a collective lifestyle."Basically, it implied that a good life for each individual would accumulate into something that was good for the collective, he said."If everybody could have a better life individually, then somehow the collective would be happy," he told me.

As principal of Roger Sherman Architecture and Urban Design in Culver City, his work and research dealt with how new modes of collective life may be produced by harnessing the self-organizing logics of cities.

The reason he came to Los Angeles, he said, was not by desire, but by circumstances. It provided him with the opportunity to put forth very strong architectural ideas about the city and about living here. About what it embodied through residential architecture.

With a grin, he told me that he saw himself as having a decidedly libertarian bent, although he's a strong Democrat. "I'm a weird hybrid," he confessed to me. His arrival in Los Angeles occurred during a transition point in 1998, when the fulcrum was shifting, he said. It was in the 1970s and 1980s when corporations were seen as good citizens, I pointed out. It was generally believed that what was good for the corporation was considered good for the community, and vice versa. Regulations have tightened and personal interests have become self-interests, he said. That has made it difficult both for architects to have the freedom they used to enjoy and for the public sector to succeed at commissioning projects of the ambition that was emblematized in single family residential architecture.

Sherman came to Los Angeles because he won the design competition for the West Hollywood Civic Center in 1987. After two or three years the project was aborted "largely because of the self-interest of citizens." He pointed to a young and inexperienced City Council that did not realize the importance of building consensus behind something that would be a collective benefit. "It didn't understand that you needed to sell the community, to persuade it," he said. "The community was of a mind that happiness was predicated upon individual comfort—how it affected them selfishly or individually." And that was because West Hollywood residents were predominantly renters who did not see a long-term legacy or benefit of the Civic Center, he said. Renters felt they would be there for two to five years and move someplace else. Consequently, the funding was overturned.

It was with that bracing, vigor, and intensity that Sherman was introduced to Los Angeles. He noted that it is a theme that continues to pervade the politics of the city, whereby similar projects are kept from being realized. "It is true that even in the culture of patronage that you have mentioned, Nick, the notion of self-interest still lurks there," he said. "In other words, patrons forget the fact that it's the public benefit that matters and instead think about their own personal legacy."

"Looking into the growth history of Los Angeles, the thought that I have always had is to what extent has there been a close alliance between development interests and political interests and how developers have been able to influence political policy, and development policy. It has made it difficult for the city to achieve real highs in the quality of what it builds and to consider those things as legacy projects."

My deep thoughts on Los Angeles and its development, its multitude of seasoned and emerging architects, its expansive landscape and its cherished weather, are that Los Angeles will continue to blossom as a world-class city with new and exciting growth that optimizes quality and serves the public good. With transparency and safeguards, the public and private sectors must continue to ardently engage in creating and sustaining the vision of the city, with open space and a walkable infrastructure.

We don't have to reinvent ourselves. We simply must preserve and enrich our historic urban vision, with character and good design.

CHAPTER SIX

HOMELESSNESS

"People who are homeless are not social inadequates.
They are people without homes.
—Sheila McKechnie

As is the case with most Los Angeles residents, I was aware of the increasing problem of homelessness throughout the city and that the city and Los Angeles County had for years tried and failed to address the issue, so I was willing to get involved when Mayor Eric Garcetti asked for my help with his homeless housing initiative, "A Bridge Home," in October 2019. The program was intended to create temporary housing with mental health and other services provided for people experiencing homelessness across Los Angeles.

Homelessness is recognized as one of the most pressing problems facing greater Los Angeles, as it is in many cities around the United States. Much is being made of the increasing ranks of homelessness, now estimated at 60,000 to 70,000 countywide. A key factor in homelessness is that, despite significant efforts to build affordable housing and place people experiencing homelessness into such housing, the number of unhoused people continues to rise. What is not well recognized is that, although thousands of people are being housed annually, a greater number of others are falling into homelessness due to high – and rising – housing prices, overall demand for housing well over supply, loss of affordable housing units due to demolitions or conversions (often to condominiums), a complex and lengthy funding and development approval process, and community opposition to affordable housing in certain areas.

Historically the number of individuals experiencing homelessness was even higher in the past: in the 1980s countywide numbers exceeded ninety thousand. The majority were white, single, older men. Subsequently, Blacks and Latinos became most of the homeless population. An aggressive housing development program largely funded by redevelopment dollars in the 1980s and early 1990s reduced those numbers by nearly 50 percent. Efforts to address homelessness were stalled by the recessions of the mid-1990s and late 2000s. In the 1990s for the first time the ranks of homeless moved from being predominantly single adult males to a mix of males and females and a growing number of households with children, complicating the rehousing program by requiring a shift from small, efficient, and single-bedroom units to more expensive multi-bedroom family units. The recessions also reduced public revenues, affecting funding streams for affordable housing when the need continued to grow.

The lack of affordable housing, the Great Recession December 2007 to June 2009, stagnating income, and high rents contributed to the homelessness crisis. The opioid epidemic and other substance use, and misuse problems, compounded the rehousing problem, requiring the addition of medical, mental health and rehabilitative services to housing developments.

SKID ROW

Homelessness really is a change in how we think about a very basic human value. As an immigrant, I believe what makes this country unique is that there is a fundamental belief that if you work hard, play by the rules, and commit to making progress for your family and for yourself, then you can be somebody, that you can achieve something. That is what the United States is known for. That is why people want to come here. That is why people stay here and that is why they succeed.

The other side of that value is that if you do not work hard, if you are not lawful, then there is something wrong with you. So, fundamentally, the undercurrent around homelessness is this belief that if you are homeless, then it is really your fault because you haven't been able to find a job or a career, you haven not figured it out on your own, and therefore, there is a fundamental sense that the homeless are failures.

It is not articulated this harshly, but there is a belief that there is something wrong with homeless people, because this country allows a person to go from nothing to amazing things. It is the expectation of a homeless person to decide on their own when they're ready to join the rest of us.

We are also a very compassionate country and a very forgiving country, and so when an individual says, "I'm ready to take action to improve my life," then society says, "Okay, we'll help you." There is a large part of the homeless population that has given up on the idea of being helped. So, the question as a society that we need to ask ourselves is, "Is what we're doing okay?" Is it okay to have a sector of our community that essentially is never going to be housed, never going to be in a way of life that is not just about survival every day? Or are we going to say, "Even though you are not ready, even though you are not willing or interested, we are going to try to help you anyway. We are going to try to provide you with assistance to get out of being homeless, and we will take care of you. The only expectation is that you are going to move inside an apartment."

When the United States or Los Angeles did not think about homelessness, it was because they had this belief that you had to take care of yourself. During that time, we said "You can choose to be homeless. But, if you choose to be homeless, I just don't want to see you. If you want to live that way, perfect, that's your choice. You're free to choose in this country. I just don't want to see you. I don't want to smell you. Just go away." So, what Los Angeles did strategically, very intentionally as a public policy, as a way of eliminating the view of this population, it created Skid Row.

It covers fifty city blocks immediately east of downtown Los Angeles. It is officially known as Central East. It has been plagued for decades by poverty, drug addiction, and mental illness.

Skid Row did not just happen. A district was formed to say, "Here, if you want to live like that, you can, and so we will bring services to this community that keep you alive." That is all it is. "We will provide you shelter if you want it, provide you food, and you can do whatever you want in that area and stay in that area." It was created in the last century, and it was maintained as such.

More and more services came in. It was reinforced by do-gooders and churches that said, "We care for the homeless, so let's go down there and feed them." It was created by folks saying, "We need to house them." It was all concentrated in this area, and so it became more intense, denser, more concentrated. If you never went downtown, you never had to see it. You knew it was there. It was part of the folklore to say, "You don't want to end up in Skid Row." It represents something in our language. It is the worst place one could end up. It is a place for the people who have given up. It is where people go to die. It is Skid Row, and as a society we said it was okay. A lot of cities deliberately created similar areas, such as the Bowery in New York City and the Tenderloin in San Francisco. We are a case study of how Skid Row was formed with good intentions.

Since the mid-2000s, there has been a discussion about the right thing to do. *Los Angeles Times* columnist Steve Lopez's frequent and biting columns on homelessness contributed to bringing the issue up front and center of the discussion. The debate also was driven by the fact that homeless people had decided to go out beyond Skid Row. They have done that because the circumstances that create homelessness had persisted, and there's now a stratification that exists in the homeless community. Among the homeless, the worst place you could end up is Skid Row, so they'll say, "Whatever happened to Johnny? I haven't seen him around." And they say, "Oh, he ended up on Skid Row." To them, it was the worst place to end up because living in Hollywood, under a freeway in the San Fernando Valley, or in Venice Beach, as difficult as that life is, it's still not the worst place you could be.

Numerous studies have reported that about one-third of homeless people in Los Angeles have serious mental health issues. That is attributed to the deinstitutionalization movement in California under Gov. Ronald Reagan in the 1960s, when many state health hospitals closed, forcing many people who needed care into the streets. Under the California Mental Health Act of 1967, or the Lanterman-Petris-Short Act, which Reagan signed into law, the mentally ill were moved from psychiatric hospitals into "community clinics." The Mental Health Systems Act of 1980, signed by President Jimmy Carter, provided grants to community mental health centers that included a provision for federal grants "for projects for the prevention of mental illness and the promotion of positive mental health." In 1981, President Ronald Reagan, who as governor had reduced funding for California mental institutions, signed the Omnibus Budget Reconciliation Act of 1981, repealing most of the Mental Health Systems Act.

Despite the claims of homeless advocates, media attention directed to homeless persons made it increasingly clear that many of them were, in fact, seriously mentally ill, according to Dr. E. Fuller Torrey, a psychologist and schizophrenia researcher. In 1981, Life magazine ran a story titled "Emptying the Madhouse: The Mentally Ill Have Become Our Cities 'Lost souls.'"

In Los Angeles, Miguel Santana, in addition to his experience as an executive dealing with homeless issues, first as deputy chief executive officer in charge of homeless for Los

Angeles County and later as chief administrative officer of the City of Los Angeles, he also has firsthand experience helping the homeless.

In my interview with Santana, he recounted that he started doing work around homelessness when he was in college, helping at shelters. "Our job was to keep people alive during the winter months," he said. "That's all we did. We prepared food, we put out cots. When it got dark during the winter, they would line up, they would come in, we would feed them, they would sleep. By seven in the morning, they were gone, and I would see them again the next night. I did that for four years, first as a volunteer, then as manager of the program. What was interesting is that we saw the same people repeatedly, and they looked very different the first day we saw them versus the last day we saw them."

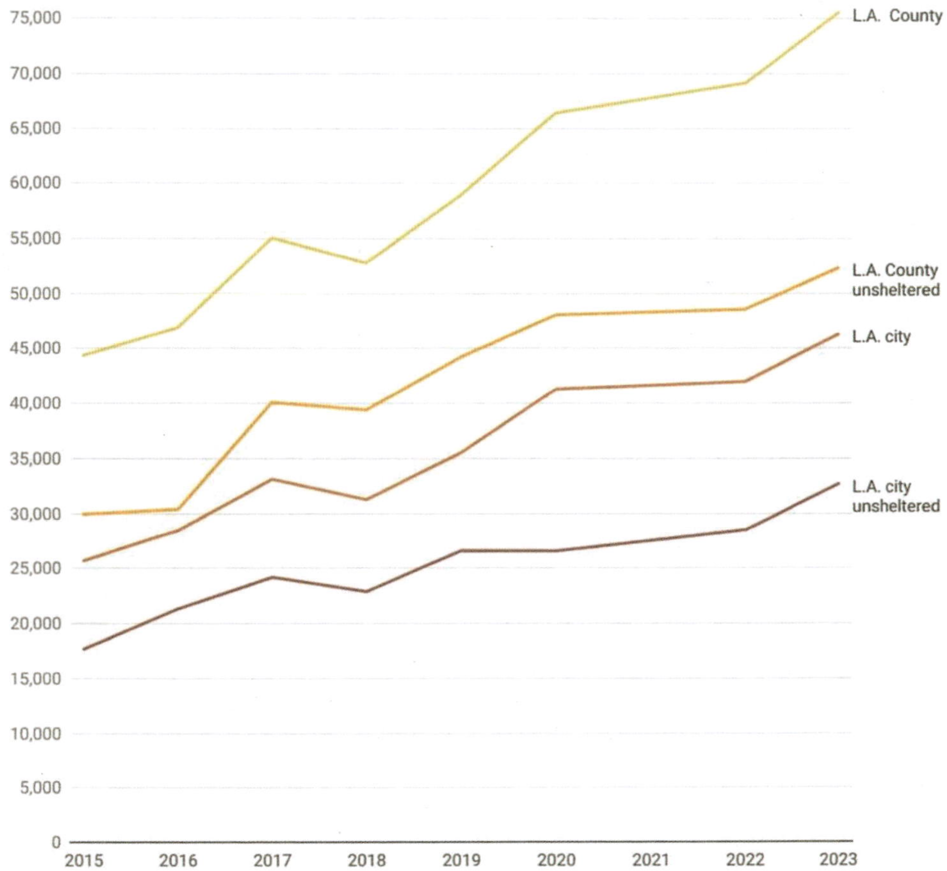

It became apparent to Santana that the best time to help someone who is homeless is the first day that they are homeless, when they are still terrified of what they are experiencing. Human beings can adapt, and once we adapt and it becomes a lifestyle, then we cannot imagine something different. It is hard for us to imagine something different, what it used to be like and what it can be like, as we shall see later in the case of Mr. Livingston. When all our instincts are focused on just survival, then we get caught up in that world.

Santana admitted that he "left this experience feeling good that I helped. But really did I help? Because we were not connecting them to an end game." This early encounter with homeless people proved invaluable understanding for Santana in dealing with the issue when he became an executive.

According to Santana, when he was deputy chief executive officer of Los Angeles County, homelessness was seen politically as a Vietnam, a war that one can never win. All five county supervisors agreed this was an issue that couldn't be won, but politically it was impossible to ignore. The person who led the effort to confront it, who made it part of the county agenda, was David E. Janssen when he was the county's chief executive officer. Janssen served on the United Way of Greater Los Angeles board, learned about this issue, and was motivated to act.

The county was experiencing a tremendous increase in revenue in the early 2000s, so Janssen proposed in a very bold way that the county set aside $100 million of this bounty of new revenue to address the homeless problem in Los Angeles County. Janssen worked very hard behind the scenes to persuade the supervisors to do that, but they did it how the board is used to doing things. And so, the first thing they did was divide the amount by five. So, the supervisors thought that "If we're going to get $100 million, then I can decide how my $20 million gets spent." Instead of having a comprehensive approach to homelessness, there were five individual approaches. Janssen was committed to getting something done, and so he accepted that solution because fighting the "divide by five" would be too hard. However, the homeless are not divided by five.

County Supervisor Gloria Molina was appalled by the number of homeless families and children, and so she initiated a pilot program, which became institutionalized, on how the county addresses homeless families. As soon as a family is identified as being homeless, a case manager will give that family that same day a voucher to go into housing, and if the best housing they can get is a motel, then that is what they get.

There are many entitlement programs that exist for poor families. A poor family through a centralized case management system is connected to existing, federal, state, and local funded resources. That family is moved from the motel to a home, then connected to the Welfare to Work Program. It may sound simple today, but Molina was very committed. She would drive around seeing homeless families, and was appalled at the number of children in homeless families who died. Molina changed the way the issue was dealt with. She questioned, "Why do I have to wait for that family to show up at my office?

We need to go to them." She believed that serving the homeless is different from other social services. "When a child is involved, we need to get out of our offices and go get them, talk to them where they are, and change the rules," she said. "Before you fill out an application, let me move you into housing right away. Not make an appointment and we'll see you next Tuesday, which is the way the county normally functions."

Homelessness in the city and county has been treated as "a hot potato" issue. Molina, when she was on the Los Angeles City Council, insisted that the city sue the county for failing to address homelessness. She settled that lawsuit as a county supervisor, and the settlement resulted in the creation in 1993 of a joint city county powers authority called Los Angeles Homeless Services Authority (LAHSHA). LAHSA was supposed to bring the city and county under one umbrella to solve the problem. Homelessness is an issue in which the city deals with the effects of it: crime, dirty streets, and people living in squalor. The city oversees building housing, and the county is in charge of the services. Services are the most important part of it. The city cannot manage the service program because it does not do that, and the county cannot deal with the homeless problems in the streets. It was a "hot potato," with both sides blaming each other.

County Supervisor Zev Yaroslavsky was the focal point because he represented much of the city. He was being really pushed and criticized by the advocates over the fact that the county was not working with the city to address homelessness. This was in the mid-2000s. There was a summit between Mayor Antonio Villaraigosa and Yaroslavsky, with no cameras, just on their own, as a joint effort to address homelessness together. The fact that they would be in the same room was kind of a historical event, and the expectation was that the meeting would inspire a new era of partnership. This meeting happened, but not much resulted from it.

At that time, for several reasons, there was hostility between Villaraigosa and Yaroslavsky. A lot of it was driven by the fact that Steve Lopez was writing stories about homelessness, about whether anyone was in charge. He wrote a lot about Nathaniel Ayers and held all governments accountable for the failure of the system. Lopez first encountered Ayers, a gifted musician who was homeless, in Skid Row, who was not only homeless but also mentally ill. Lopez developed a bond and friendship with Ayers, and as a result he wrote a book about Ayers, *The Soloist*.

According to Santana, Yaroslavsky wanted to do something about the problem inspired by "Housing First," the idea that you cannot get sober, you cannot get mental health treatment, you cannot deal with your chronic diabetes if after you go talk to your shrink, after you go to rehab, the place that you go is a street corner, because you need housing first, before you could do anything else. You need to feel safe. Then, once you are in housing, then we can start dealing with all the issues and causes that got you to be homeless in the first place. It is the opposite of how homelessness was approached at that time.

Homelessness was this idea that if you want housing, we will give you housing, but you are required to promise sobriety. You must agree to get medication and treat your mental illness. You need to get a job. We are not going to give you the housing for free because we are Americans, and that means that you have to roll up your sleeves first and we will help you when you are willing to help yourself.

"Housing First" throws that out and says, "It doesn't matter if you are willing to do any of those things. The only decision you must make is to move inside."

Yaroslavsky in 2007 approached homelessness by saying, "I want to do that here in Los Angeles. I want a pilot here in, and I'm going to go to the hardest place. I'm going to do it in Skid Row." He was criticized and some people said, "Well, it is easy for you to say that. You want to provide housing for fifty people and you're going to put it in Skid Row, which you don't represent. Why don't you put them in Brentwood or on the Westside?"

Los Angeles Councilwoman Jan Perry, whose district included parts of Skid Row, told the *Los Angeles Times* that she would prefer to give first chance at permanent housing to people already in emergency shelters. Other critics said the program would not address the root of the issue, such as drug or mental health problems.

In October of 2007, Yaroslavsky convened a regional conference of homeless experts, administrators, and Los Angeles County representatives to examine the persistent and expensive problem of homelessness in the county. The conference culminated in strong support for a Permanent Supportive Housing approach. The project was influenced by New York's Project 50. In November 2007, the Los Angeles County Board of Supervisors unanimously approved the project with a $3.6 million budget. Project 50 had been expanded to house 133 participants and had an 80 percent retention after four years.

There were thousands of people in Skid Row. How do you pick who gets this opportunity? At the center of this approach was the Vulnerability Index, which basically asked questions, such as, how long have you been homeless? How many times have you been arrested? How many times have you been in an emergency room?

There was an evaluation based on the answers, appearance, etc. that gave the person a number, and so if you are the first person on that list, you have the highest likelihood of dying because that means you have everything off the charts. You are sick, you have an addiction, you suffer from severe mental illness, and your probability of death is high. You get the first house that is available. There was a partnership with Skid Row Housing Trust, which housed them in units on Main Street that they had available in Skid Row. According to Santana, the first person on the list was Mr. Livingston. He was originally from New Orleans and had been homeless for most of his life. The case workers had to diligently work with him to find out what his name was, and they finally got him an ID.

Santana chaired conference calls with all county managers, and they would ask, for example: "What does Mr. Livingston need?" "Well, he needs an ID." "Who is going to call the Registrar to try to get his birth certificate in New Orleans?" The goal was to eliminate the bureaucracy and figure out how to manage these people. The reasons, according to Santana, why it was important to do that were: first, they were trying to create a new model, and second, they wanted to understand what it really takes to help somebody like Livingston. Waiting for Livingston, who had been homeless for more than twenty-five years, to show up at the office, was not going to happen. They had to go to him in a very persistent and compassionate way. The decision to move into that housing was his. It took almost three months to persuade him to go inside. The first night he came in and asked, "Am I the only one with the keys to this apartment?" "Yes." He replied, "I don't believe you."

So, he left and went back outside. Here was a man who had been homeless for decades, and had no trust in anybody. He would rather sleep outside than to be in an apartment where he did not believe that someone would not come in. One day, the case worker persuaded him to go back in, and the locks were changed in front of him. "Here, Mr. Livingston. You're the only one with the keys. Nobody can come in." He stayed, and he re-created his tent inside the apartment. He re-created the space that he had outside inside. For him, deciding to move into a room, an apartment with four walls and a ceiling, was the boldest decision he could possibly make. It was the hardest decision of his life. Then, after time, he started getting mental health treatment, saw a doctor, and began dealing with his addiction issues.

In 2009, Santana prepared a cost analysis to show how much these fifty people cost the county living outside versus inside. It is expensive to put them inside, but it is more costly when they live outside because they are the ones in the emergency room, they are the ones in our jails, they are the ones that businesses complain about, they are the ones that the police respond to. It was a pilot program. Yaroslavsky said, "We're ready to say this pilot project worked. We know that it's cost effective. It's very expensive, but more cost-effective than having them outside."

As the deputy chief executive officer, Santana was tasked with writing a report with his staff and present it to the Board of Supervisors recommending the expansion of Project 50 countywide. Santana wanted to turn Project 50 into Project 500, then 5,000 and so on.

He presented the program to his former boss, Supervisor Molina and to Supervisors Mike Antonovich and Don Knabe. At the time, Mark Ridley-Thomas had just gotten elected to the Board of Supervisors. Santana remembers Antonovich asking, "So, can they use drugs and alcohol in their apartment?" "Yes, they can," and he said, "Why would we subsidize somebody's drug use?" "Because you're subsidizing it now outside." In this housing approach, all the homeless people must do is agree to go into housing. It is housing first, before everything else. Anybody can drink inside their apartment. There are no conditions. So, if he or/she is an alcoholic and they are drinking inside, it is cheaper for the county when he/she drinks inside than when he/she drinks outside, and we all get to experience their drunkenness. At least inside he/she is on his/her own. Yaroslavsky's motion in May 2009 to expand the Project 50 countywide failed on a four to one vote.

The city of Houston applying the "Housing First" initiative was successful in housing 25,000 homeless individuals without requiring them to abstain from drug use. Almost all those people remained in the housing after two years.

JONES VS. CITY OF LOS ANGELES

The next phase of homelessness really came about because of the new development that was occurring downtown, and suddenly new people were moving in who were witnessing the homeless problem, and it was becoming part of their consciousness. Steve Lopez started writing about that. The most significant thing that occurred is that the city was sued over its so-called Safer Cities Initiative, which sought to use law enforcement, under the broken windows theory, to start cleaning up downtown and Skid Row. People were getting arrested. During the first year of the initiative on Skid Row, the Los Angeles Police Department issued twelve thousand citations, about twice the citywide average. Most of those citations were for pedestrian violations. Residents and service providers complained that police stopped, detained, cited, and arrested Skid Row residents for trivial violations, such as jaywalking or littering, making it more difficult for people to leave the streets behind.

The lawsuit filed by the American Civil Liberties Union of Southern California and Carol Sobel for the National Lawyers Guild, sought to end the enforcement of Section 41.18(d) of Los Angeles City Code. It alleged that people's belongings were being taken from them and thrown away, their IDs and medications were being confiscated, and their civil rights were being violated. Essentially the city was sued for simply trying to keep the neighborhood clean. The case was known as Jones v. City of Los Angeles. Six homeless individuals, unable to obtain shelter on the night when they were cited or arrested, filed an Eighth Amendment challenge to the enforcement of a City of Los Angeles ordinance that criminalized sitting, lying, or always sleeping on public streets and sidewalks and in all places within Los Angeles city limits. One of them was Edward Jones, a homeless man who slept on the streets with his mentally ill wife, who required constant care.

In April 2006, the US Ninth Circuit Court of Appeals issued a historic decision in the case of Jones v City of Los Angeles ending the criminalization of homelessness. Writing for the majority, Judge Kim M. Wardlaw stopped enforcement of the Los Angeles city code that allowed police to arrest people for sleeping on the street when there are no available shelter beds. Judge Wardlaw wrote that the Eighth Amendment of the US Constitution prohibits the city from punishing involuntary sitting or sleeping on public sidewalks. That is an unavoidable consequence of being homeless or without shelter in the City of Los Angeles.

On September 19, 2006, Los Angeles and the ACLU reached a compromise. According to the deal, homeless individuals would be allowed to set up tents and bedrolls between 9 p.m. and 6 a.m., though not within ten feet of a business entrance. City lawyers had negotiated the proposed settlement with the ACLU after a court-ordered mediation.

Councilwoman Jan Perry used discretionary funds to hire a retired judge of the Ninth Circuit of Appeals, William A. Norris, and Edward Lazarus to represent her at the mediation. On September 20, 2006, acting on a motion by Perry in a closed meeting, the council voted ten to three to reject the settlement and to appeal the Ninth Circuit Court of Appeals' ruling in Jones v. City of Los Angeles.

In October 2007, the Los Angeles City Council approved a settlement that banned LAPD officers patrolling Skid Row from conducting unconstitutional searches of homeless individuals and required that officers undergo training to search and detain people. Attorney Carol Sobel said, "This is an important step protecting the rights of the poorest residents of our city. Now the work begins to see it is put into practice. Two years ago, Mayor Antonio Villaraigosa launched the Safer Cities Initiative, billing it as a multifaceted, enlightened approach to deal with homelessness that would include supportive housing and transitional services. But no new housing or services have materialized."

In 2023, in a friend-of-the-court-brief, Los Angeles City Attorney Hydee Feldstein Soto described the Ninth Circuit's approach as unclear and unworkable. "Sidewalks currently serve two often incompatible functions: housing tens of thousands of unsheltered residents (and their personal belongings), and also providing access and a right of way for pedestrians, [wheelchair-using] travelers, school children seeking safe passage to and from school, business owners and customers relying on accessible store fronts and residents seeking to access services from municipal, state, and federal government offices," she wrote.

Suddenly, the city couldn't respond to the encampments. The encampments started to grow, and they spread from Skid Row to throughout the city. The homeless who now live under the freeway overpasses got comfortable knowing nothing could happen. They brought in a couch, and then moved in, and the encampments became bigger and bigger, and now the homeless problem is visible everywhere. Folks started thinking, if you get a blue tarp and cover your stuff and you claim it, then the city cannot touch it, even if it is trash.

Tents started popping up creating a sense of permanency. The outcome of the lawsuit was that the city's ability to make the problem no longer visible is less limited, and suddenly people in the San Fernando Valley, the Westside, South Los Angeles, and the Eastside were saying, "What's going on? Why are there all these homeless people here?" Well, the reality is that they had always been there, they just were not visible. Now they were visible because the city was not able to act. Outside of the fact that there was a lawsuit, the resources were limited. There was a strong drumbeat about having to do something about homelessness. Santana, the chief administrative officer for the city, wrote a report that asked one simple question: How much does homelessness costing the city of LA? It turned out that the city was spending more than $100 million a year. The county asked the same question, and its spending on homelessness was more than $1 billion a year.

Santana was widely criticized for writing the report because he was basically stating that the city and county were failing. He was told, "What are you saying? We're doing all this great work on homelessness." Santana's response was: "No. I mean, maybe, but there's still a lot of homeless people, but if the city is spending $100 million a year, why don't we spend that money to actually solve homelessness?"

In June 2014, Mayor Eric Garcetti made a commitment to First Lady Michelle Obama to eliminate homelessness among veterans by 2016. He did it in a public meeting. He said, "I promise to do this," and he signed a pledge. It was an initiative that the First Lady had asked many mayors to do, and Garcetti committed to it." His spokesperson Connie Llanos said in September 2015, "The city should be able to bring the veteran homeless population to functional zero by next summer." A commitment that was not fulfilled, unfortunately.

Legislation by US Rep. Henry Waxman and Sen. Dianne Feinstein prohibited an enhanced-use lease covering any land or improvement of the Veterans Benefits and Services Act of 1988, a decision that aggravated homesless veterans. I can attest to the gravity of the situation because I oversaw in 2019 the construction of a homeless shelter in Westwood to house veterans when I was asked by Mayor Eric Garcetti to get involved with the A Bridge Home program. The program was running into significant cost overruns and delays, and Garcetti knew I had experience advising previous city and county leaders on projects facing difficulties in meeting construction deadlines and budgets.

US Reps. Ted W. Lieu and Jeff Miller cowrote H.R.5936, the Los Angeles Homeless Veterans Leasing Act of 2016, which authorized the Veterans Affairs secretary to enter into a lease at the West Los Angeles Veterans Hospital to provide for permanent supportive housing for veterans. Lieu had started working on this issue in April 2007.

Meanwhile, Los Angeles City Councilman Huizar was being forced to address homelessness because he was running in 2015 against Molina, who was no longer serving on the County Board of Supervisors and wanted to return to the City Council, and homelessness ranked as the top issue in downtown. Huizar decided to ask for a committee to oversee homelessness. Council President Herb Wesson made Huizar the chair and Councilman Marqueece Harris-Dawson the cochair. They made a bold commitment to have the city adopt a comprehensive plan around homelessness.

New county supervisors Hilda Solis and Sheila Kuehl, elected in 2014, were very interested in working with the city, and under Santana's leadership a plan was developed. Part of the plan was the commitment "Each side is going to stay on its own lane." The central issue to solving homelessness is coordination. The most symbolic thing that happened to this plan was that it was adopted on the same day by the City Council and the Board of Supervisors. The reason why that was important was because neither side wanted a story that said that the city took a bold step on homelessness, or that the county did so. There was a whole series of recommendations in that plan tied around the lessons learned. The center of it was "Housing First."

The housing measure HHH approved by the voters in 2016 is the child of Project 50.

AFFORDABLE HOUSING

The biggest problem we face in dealing with homelessness and housing affordability today is that no one is managing the bureaucracy. For whatever reasons, our elected leaders do not have managerial backgrounds, and they do not seek out managers with real management expertise. As a result, the bureaucracy is crawling at a snail's pace, if they move at all. They have no direction, no leadership, and nothing gets done. Below are two examples.

The City of Los Angeles has been stalling (they call it "reviewing") a fully funded private proposal to build transition housing for "emancipated youth" for eight years, with no end in sight.

Los Angeles County is saying that a conditional use permit to allow student housing in a housing zone next to a university in Willowbrook will take twelve months to approve.

Elected officials, in addressing the homeless crisis in our city, have all been parroting for the last twenty years, "Expedite the Permit Process" to house the homeless population and build affordable housing. It's a simplistic answer to a serious problem. Mayors have relied on advice for homeless issues on deputies whose backgrounds are community organizers, attorneys, psychologists, planners, and bureaucrats who have risen to their positions through seniority. None has gone through the process of building anything, and thus, despite spending billions of dollars and employing thousands, the crisis gets worse by the day. Encampments are all over the city and the multibillion transit system is close to being considered obsolete because the paying riders have unwillingly ceded the system to drug users and the criminal element.

In November 2016, voters approved a $1.2 billion bond measure, Proposition HHH, to fund the development of supportive housing in the City of Los Angeles, with the intent to create ten thousand new apartments over a decade for people experiencing homelessness. Six years later, with the city's homeless population one-and-a-half times what it was when the measure passed, some wondered whether Prop HHH should be considered a success or failure. Los Angeles City Controller Galperin noted in an audit that the city initially thought HHH housing would cost $350,000 to $414,000 per unit, depending on the number of bedrooms. Yet, in 2019, the median per unit cost had grown to $531,373 with more than 1,000 units projected to cost more than $600,000. The city's Housing Department said the HHH program will produce 8,600 units by 2026, whereas the voters were told the number would be 10,000.

WHY THIS CRISIS IN BUILDING AFFORDABLE HOUSING?

A developer may seek funding from the city or county as well as the state and federal governments. But rather than apply to the various agencies simultaneously, the developer must secure funding from the city and county first, before being able apply for state funding. And the developer may not be able to apply for federal funding until being awarded the state funding. If the developer's application is not selected, he/she must wait until the next round of funding to reapply, which could take from several months to a year. In addition to the lengthy process of securing funding, the city's approval process can add to the timeline because developers must wait for multiple departments to sign off on their plans, a process that can take up to a year.

Nothing adds to cost more than time. The time that it takes to go through the process. Miguel Santana, a veteran public servant who is experienced, knowledgeable, pragmatic, and emotionally attached to the issue of homelessness, believes that "our system to resolve homelessness is so complicated that whether you are a service provider or a developer or a councilmember, you are a slice of a very big pie. The system is uncoordinated and unaligned."

PROPOSALS TO REDUCE THE COSTS OF AFFORDABLE HOUSING

There are numerous ways the state, the county and the city can reduce the cost of affordable housing, including the following:

- Coordinate all plan checks, permit, and other approvals needed from not only the Department of Building and Safety and City Planning, but also from the Bureau of Engineering, the Los Angeles Department of Water and Power, and the Fire Department.

- Appoint a person or small team of people with authority to move all city approvals and decisions on a guaranteed, preset timeline.

- Reduce or eliminate multiple approvals by the City Council and mayor. The Housing Department should not be required to secure City Council/mayoral reapproval of a loan unless the project or loan terms have substantially changed since the initial approval.

- Implement the planned universal application process as soon as possible, before the next funding rounds at the city, county, or Housing Authority of the City of Los Angeles.

- When approvals can't be provided across all local funding sources at the initial application, ensure that applications that meet a certain threshold can be funded in the next round(s) solely via updates to pro formas, not require a full re-application.

- Clarify the Housing Authority rental subsidy timeline and availability, and coordinate decisions.

- Make accessibility/certified access specialist review and approvals to the Department of Building and Safety and reduce subjectivity in approvals.

- Shorten the Housing Department's process for approving draws and releasing funds, including commitment to funding draws within three days of approval and the ability to wire funds instead of cutting and mailing checks.

- Reduce and better define the timeline for city attorney review and approval. Assign a dedicated city attorney to each project, and ensure the developer is notified of the assigned attorney, so that other funders can be informed.

- Streamline the funding applications and approvals for all local sources of funds, with a universal application for capital funds and rental subsidies.

- Identify less traditionally desirable sites to drive down acquisitions' costs. Design creativity can make sites work advantageously.

- Add density to existing structures, such as Star Apartments.

- Use of modular/container at significant scale, more than 500 units. Cost efficiencies should allow for custom design of common/community spaces and intimate scale in a large building.

- Pre-permit standard design components for partial or complete housing products, such as bathroom and kitchen units, to control risk costs related to entitlement process.

- Modify regulations to allow building on sites adjacent to freeways. Eliminate the 500-foot exclusion rule from infrastructure for nonprofit developers.

- Examine alternative living arrangement unit types, such as co-living, which potentially reduces the number of expensive bathrooms and kitchens per resident.

- No Parking Minimums—LA City Zoning 12.21A4 (a).

- No Apartment size minimums—HCIDLA/Affordable Housing Guidelines, LADBS Code CH. 12.

- No private open space requirements (balconies)—LA City Zoning 12.21G.

- Strike down unit calculations—LA City Zoning RD1.5, R3, R4.

OTHER POTENTIAL SOLUTIONS TO ADDRESS HOMELESSNESS

Changes in how affordable housing is added to the supply need to be considered to reduce homelessness more effectively.

More attention needs to be paid to creating mixed-income housing. Integrating affordable housing into mixed-income developments allows for increased community acceptance and allows innovative, non-cash ways to finance affordable housing, including housing bonuses that will enable a developer to create additional market rate units in numbers that exceed the affordable component (state law, for example, allows a bonus up to 35 percent of total units in exchange for 11 percent to 21 percent of the units being restricted to affordable price ranges, depending on the level of affordability).

Purchasing existing affordable housing where affordability covenants are close to expiration or negotiating extensions of those covenants. Modest upgrades and rehabilitation would be substantially less expensive than new construction and eliminate the delay in waiting for new construction units to come online.

Increasing emergency stay-in-housing or rapid rehousing rent subsidy programs for households being priced out of their housing. Avoiding displacement, or minimizing the period of displacement, avoids additional costs associated with service provision, including physical and mental health or substance abuse issues that often are severely exacerbated by a period of homelessness.

Streamlining the approval process for developments that include affordable housing, making them ministerial rather than discretionary, which invites public hearing delays, redesign to address community issues, the intent of which is often to stymie housing development, and extensive carrying costs.

Creating an affordable housing development entity for Los Angeles city and county. The current Los Angeles Homeless Services Authority has very limited powers, it is mostly a funding intermediary for social services. The agency was created in the early 1990s to settle litigation among the city, county and Community Redevelopment Agency that originated with the city suing the county over the low rate of general relief payments to extremely low-income individuals and households. The county counter-sued and accused the city and CRA of being responsible for the loss of affordable units through redevelopment, code enforcement actions, and down-zoning in communities, reducing the capacity of the city for housing development and compounding a demand-supply imbalance. The underlying issues of inadequate general relief payments and zoning caps remain unresolved.

The elected leaders must show fortitude in dealing with the NIMBYs.

HOMELESS SHELTERS IN CITY PARKS

Few cities possess the natural beauty of Los Angeles, from its coastline to the rugged mountains. Fewer still enjoy a climate that allows such a great variety of plant life. Our city could be a botanical garden on a metropolitan scale, with the most extensive tree planting, the lushest parks, and the longest greenways. In cities whose quality of life we admire, parks and greenways are widespread. San Francisco devotes more than 8 percent of its land to parks, Seattle more than 15 percent. In New York City, the figure is as high as 17 percent. And in Los Angeles? A paltry 4 percent. Parks are not a luxury or an extravagance. They bring enormous economic benefits, including increased property values, greater attractiveness for corporate relocation and tourism, commercial uses such as filmmaking, and improved air quality (see Greenways section). We can remake Los Angeles into a city valued by its residents and remembered by visitors not as a city of asphalt, concrete, or homeless shelters, but as one of of trees and open space.

Case in point is the property at First and Broadway, which is proposed to be used for homeless shelters. The city had spent tens of millions of dollars to purchase the land from the state and the county, and millions more to demolish the existing structures and prepare environmental impact reports and architectural and landscape designs. After an international design competition, the landscape architecture firm of Studio-MLA founded by Mia Lehrer was awarded the contract to design the park. The firm had designed a superb park, and the budget was funded by so-called "Quimby fees," which are paid in lieu of dedicating land to the city for park and recreational purposes, but the funds were raided to be used at other sites. The property is in front of City Hall, in the heart of Los Angeles. The proposed park would have been connected to the Gloria Molina Grand Park, a place for celebrations, festivals, concerts, and where families can spend a day in the park (considering downtown is lacking desperately needed open space). The site is directly across from the former *Los Angeles Times* headquarters, but since the Times escaped to El Segundo, the newspaper has no vested interests to protect, thus it has been unusually mum. It is a travesty, an affront to the citizens of Los Angeles that our city leaders have allowed it to happen.

Echo Park is another place where the community has been deprived of a natural wonder. Then-Councilman Mitch O'Farrell's office arranged for the park's closure in 2021 and erected a fence after a huge homeless encampment housing more than two people was cleared from the area. Hugo Soto-Martinez unseated O'Farrell in the November 2022 council election with a campaign promise to remove the fence. In March 2023, the fence was removed to the consternation of the neighbors. "I'm disappointed the councilman didn't work with the community to really listen to our concerns," one neighbor said. "We fear that the quality of the park environment will be degenerating and go back to what it was before the fence went up." "No worries," Soto-Martinez said. He promised to send homeless outreach workers into the park seven days a week, while having a team of unarmed responders available at night. The "Homeless Industrial Complex" at work again.

Additional parks with open space converted to homeless shelters: Griffith Park; Lafayette Park; North Hollywood Recreational Center; Alexandria Park; Ken Malloy Harbor Regional Park; Strathern Park West; Arroyo Seco Park; and Eagle Rock Park.

In July of 2023, Judge Milan Smith Jr. of the US Ninth Circuit Court of Appeals, wrote: "There are stretches of the city where one cannot help but think the government has shirked its most basic responsibilities under the social contract: providing public safety and ensuring that public spaces remain open to all. One-time public spaces like parks—many of which provide scarce outdoor space in dense, working-class neighborhoods—are filled with thousands of tents and makeshift structures and are no longer welcoming to the broader community."

THE HOMELESS-INDUSTRIAL COMPLEX

Each day, the homelessness scene is worsening, acquiring a bleak permanence. In Los Angeles County, one in 150 residents, or 69,000 people, experience homelessness. Good intentions, legislative action and numerous directives are doing little to lessen the problem. Funding from local, state, and federal sources is continuously made available.

As I got absorbed by the problem and comprehended the intricacies and complexities facing our society, I was startled by what slowly became apparent: a "Homeless-Industrial

Complex" had developed, and vested interests were gradually and methodically influencing public policy.

Miguel Santana was honest when he said at a forum organized in the spring of 2023 by the Urban Land Institute to discuss homelessness, "We have created a system not for the homeless, but for the interests who benefit from that system."

Michael Shellenberger, in his book San Fran-sicko, claims that: "And it was Democrats, not Republicans, who played the primary role in creating the dominant neoliberal model of government contracting to fragmented and often unaccountable non-profit providers that have proven financially, structurally, and legally incapable of addressing the crisis." Like the Military Industrial Complex, the present system to end homelessness reinforces the existing failed structure.

I can fully attest to this because when Mayor Eric Garcetti asked me to oversee the design and construction of homeless shelters as part of the A Bridge Home program, I was stunned when I witnessed a common expression become an embarrassing reality: the tail wagged the dog.

Providers supplying services arbitrarily added unreasonable requirements and demands, resulting in skyrocketing construction costs and delays in housing. The Los Angeles Homeless Services Authority which funds and administers the providers, was flapped by the tail.

During my tenure, I did not observe any LASHA representative attend a single meeting when I oversaw the A Bridge Home program to assess and evaluate plans when providers presented them. I saw variable and excessive requirements added that were stricter than the requirements of the Building and Safety Department or the Fire Department. Of course, safety must always be a high priority, but it does not have to be overplayed simply to add to the costs. Consequently, prices rose sharply, and tangible results remained elusive. I heard it said: "We are not assuming the operation of the shelter unless everything on our list is taken care of," thus delaying the opening of the project. Intriguingly, the building "check list" appeared after the Certificate of Occupancy was issued by the Building and Safety and the Fire departments. Meanwhile, four homeless people have been dying in the streets every day. In retrospect, I should have overstepped my authority and demanded more accountability from the shortsighted bureaucrats, even for issues beyond my jurisdiction. The homelessness crisis was outpacing the current program because it allowed the providers to set the rules.

The old axiom, "throwing money at a problem," was thought to be all that was necessary to fix it. When that didn't work the response was to throw more money at it, and then even more, thereby establishing the blueprint for a public strategy that did not address the problem but multiplied special interest fervor and constant funding.

It was my direct observation that what was implemented did not mitigate homelessness; it provided a crude response to the symptoms. Concurrently, it contributed to growing a zealous industry.

Garcetti's fiscal year 2022–23 budget included $1 billion for homeless programs, twenty times the amount directed at homelessness when he took office in 2013. In fiscal year 2021–22, the budget also included $1 billion for the homeless. Meanwhile, the population in Los

Angeles experiencing homelessness has surpassed New York City's to become the largest in the nation.

Mayor Karen Bass, who replaced the termed-out Garcetti in December 2022, has indicated a plan to spend $1.3 billion to address homelessness in fiscal year 2023–24.

In a recent report, provided in part by the Homeless Data Integration System, an average of $8.1 billion every year for the next twelve years must be invested "To create the housing, shelter and supportive services needed to adequately address and solve homelessness in California."

But I have been asking myself, "Are the pathways to ending homelessness handicapped by a system that constantly seeks inroads to greater public investment, while organizations like the Los Angeles Homeless Services Authority fail to anticipate needs and simply react with short-term responses and fabricated data?"

An audit released in August 2019 by Los Angeles City Controller Ron Galperin stated that LAHSA "failed dramatically to meet the goals of its contract with the city of Los Angeles." Galperin told the *Los Angeles Times* that even though LAHSA doubled its staff of outreach workers in fiscal year 2017–18, it missed seven of nine goals, and five out of eight the following fiscal year. The goals that were set by the city were not unreasonable. Quite frankly, he disclosed, they were set at a low bar to begin with. "If you can't meet the low bar, that's a problem," he said.

He also said that LAHSA provided the controller's office with four versions of its outreach numbers, each one significantly different. Further, the audit showed that LAHSA took credit for placements into permanent housing made by other agencies and inflated numbers by counting individuals that fell in and out of homelessness during the year. A chart in the audit showed the percentage of homeless people placed into shelters dropping from 64 percent in the first version to 19 percent in the last, according to Doug Smith, senior writer for the *Los Angeles Times*.

When LAHSA was created in 1993, the city and county were each supposed to fund the agency with about $2.5 million a year to pay for homeless programs and services, according to a report from the Luskin Center for History and Policy at the University of California, Los Angeles, The Making of a Crisis: A History of Homelessness in Los Angeles.

In 2003, LASHA adopted "A strategic planning process for Bring LA Home: The Ten-Year Plan to end homelessness in Los Angeles." Since 2003, LASHA's budget has skyrocketed as fast as the number of homeless people that have flooded our neighborhoods. In the fiscal year 2022–23, LASHA's budget was astounding: more than $845 million with $40.3 million budgeted for administrative costs and 340 employees. In comparison, in fiscal year 2014–15, the budget was $71.4 million. City and County officials have finally started asking for a review of LAHSA's financial operations to assess how the funds are being spent and have questioned whether LAHSA is the best way to continue to move forward. In July 2021, the Los Angeles County Board of Supervisors voted to establish a Blue-Ribbon Commission on Homelessness to address the crisis, saying it is time for sweeping changes to the system.

In an August 2023 Los Angeles City Council budget meeting, the mayor's homelessness czar admitted that "The city could be paying for weeks for an empty (hotel) room." This was the result of city officials not having direct access to LAHSA's data, despite the fact the council is providing LAHSA with millions in funding to improve data access. Councilmember Marqueece Harris-Dawson said, "It feels like we're flying blind with the people's money." The Council's fiscal watchdog, Councilmember Monica Rodriguez said in frustration, "These types of problems with LAHSA's data have been going on for six years."

I was especially discouraged when an audit released in February 2021 by California State Auditor Elaine Howle reported that the state has the nation's largest homeless population "likely in part because its approach to addressing homelessness has been disjointed." At least nine state agencies administer and oversee forty-one different programs that provide funding to mitigate homelessness, yet no single entity oversees the state's efforts or is responsible for developing a statewide strategic plan, according to the audit. Most telling was the auditor's biting comment that the state's plan to mitigate homelessness is not designed to achieve this because, if that was done, then nine agencies and forty-one different programs would no longer be needed, federal and state funding would dry up, and public employee union jobs would be lost.

Katy Grimes, an investigative journalist and editor of the California Globe, in reviewing the audit, said the biggest problem of all may be the state's failure to track funding provided to combat homelessness. "There is no single state entity that comprehensively tracks the sources of funding, the intended uses, or related expenditures for these programs," nor does the state "track how much funding is available or spent toward addressing homelessness statewide," she wrote. These audits directly underscore my view of the presence of the "Homeless-Industrial Complex." It also corroborates my assertion that this complex has manufactured a revolving door, in perpetual motion, which draws in more money and returns little, if any, results.

In local action, Measure ULA, placed on the November 8, 2022, ballot by a coalition of housing advocates and labor unions, passed with about 57 percent support in the election. The measure established a new Homelessness and Housing Solutions Tax within the city of Los Angeles, imposed on the sale or transfer of real property valued at more than $5 million, to fund affordable housing and tenant assistance programs. This represents another revenue stream directed to homelessness by increasing the city transfer tax on property valued at more than $5 million, but less than $10 million. The seller will pay the tax. It is estimated the so-called documentary transfer tax will generate $1 billion a year.

After her election in November 2022, Los Angeles Mayor Karen Bass declared a state of emergency on homelessness with the Inside Safe plan. The plan is intended to move people out of encampments by leasing apartments and motel rooms across the city. This will be done through "master leasing," which involves the city leasing an entire building then subleasing units to people living in the streets. Bass made a campaign commitment in 2022 to move 17,000 unhoused residents by the end of 2023 from tent cities to hotel rooms and eventually to permanent housing.

Through this program, unhoused people can move into housing units, bypassing the customary rejection of those with housing vouchers or bad credit. But it is not a panacea. The gap will continue to exist between the number of people who need affordable housing and the amount of available housing units.

To ramp up her fight, at Bass's recommendation the City Council approved the purchase of a fifteen-story downtown hotel for $83 million to create "permanent interim housing." The city-owned residential building would house homeless people for up to a year before they find their own apartments. It will also offer an array of services on the ground floor, such as substance abuse counselors, mental health clinicians, and public health workers.

With the Los Angeles County-sponsored Homeless Initiative (Measure H) approved by the voters in 2016 generating revenue from a one-quarter-cent sales tax over ten years (from 2017 to 2027)—the first revenue stream dedicated to addressing homelessness—the number of outreach workers doubled. So did the city and county funding from their general funds.

Every year the Homeless Initiative spending plan is a significant portion of the county's overall spending to address homelessness, which exceeded $1 billion in fiscal year 2021-22.

Despite all the billions spent to address homelessness, the homeless population continued to grow, jumping 9 percent in Los Angeles County and 10 percent in the city according to a survey by LASHA in 2023. The count estimated 75,000 people were living in interim housing, car, van, RVs, tent, or makeshift shelter in Los Angeles County, compared with 69,000 the previous year.

The Garcetti administration had spent billions to improve the homelessness situation. However, since the 2015 count, homelessness has increased by 80 percent in the city. The city has registered an increase in seven of the last eight annual counts. There was no count in 2021 because of the COVID-19 pandemic.

Va Lecia Adams Kellum, chief executive of LASHA, told the *Los Angeles Times* in June 2023: "The city and county are NOW [the author's emphasis] working with coordination, collaboration and strategic focus." That's an incredible comment to make in 2023 and a strong indictment of the powers that be, considering LASHA was created in 1993 so the city and county could coordinate, collaborate, and focus their efforts and the agency has been spending millions of taxpayer dollars annually all these years.

An audit released in December 2023 by Los Angeles City Controller Kenneth Mejia stated that "LASHA's dysfunctional system is insufficient for addressing the wide problems of LA's homelessness emergency." In another section of the audit the controller said, "The woefully inadequate amount of both interim and permanent housing resources, as well the antiquated and inefficient methods of data collection and housing referral processes, significantly inhibit efforts by the city to respond to the crisis with the urgency that it requires."

Councilmember Traci Park said the city has been relying on bad policy. She told the *Los Angeles Times*, "It is clear to me that we have done so far has not worked. Despite throwing billions of dollars at this problem over the last number of years, we have failed to address the growth of encampments on the streets."

After $40 million had been spent in Mayor Bass's Inside Safe program in her first six months in office, with an additional $260 million authorized by the City Council, only 1,400 people had been housed in Los Angeles motels and hotels, and only seventy-seven had secured long term housing, as reported by city officials to the city's Budget and Finance Committee in July 2023.

According to the Los Angeles NBC4 News investigation on November 30, 2023, under the Inside Safe program the city has spent more than a year, $67 million to move 255 people into permanent housing; and about 4 percent of the 46,000 unhoused, about 1900, into motel rooms, at a cost to the taxpayer of about $3,300 a month per person.

The *Los Angeles Times* reported on July 7, 2023, that the hotel workers union United Here Local 11, in negotiations over new contracts for thousands of hotel workers, was demanding that the hotels endorse a measure set for the 2024 ballot that would require hotels in Los Angeles to rent vacant rooms to the homeless. The union was also urging hotels to agree to impose a 7 percent fee on all guest room rates to create a fund to assist hospitality workers in obtaining affordable housing. According to Los Angeles City Councilmember Traci Park, "The measure would have catastrophic consequences for tourism. The thought of putting individuals, many of whom have serious mental health and substance abuse issues, [in hotel rooms] without on-site services is a recipe for disaster."

There is such disarray in the homeless efforts that even the front-line workers, those folks who search out people on the street, make contact, earn their trust, and guide them to temporary housing, are facing burnout and high turnover. It is reported that more than half of them quit after less than two years.

Bass said that "Caseworkers from nonprofits are moving so slowly because we have worked them beyond capacity…they basically cannot manage it."

According to a *Los Angeles Times* editorial on June 4, 2023, "Nonprofit homeless service organizations that employ the front-line workers work mostly on contracts with government agencies— such as the Los Angeles Homeless Services Authority—to provide homeless services. Those contracts are funded with county, city, state, or federal funds that nonprofits say are routinely underfunded." The editorial notes that these front-line workers are paid so little that they face their own struggles to stay housed in the high-priced Los Angeles County market.

Meanwhile, the LASHA Chief Executive Officer's annual salary is $430,000.

The study quoted by the newspaper was performed by the Rand Corp., commissioned by the nonprofit Social Justice Partners Los Angeles. It recommends, among other things, that government funders cover the full cost of services that an organization provides. It also suggests that workers get basic cost of living increases in their contracts.

When President Eisenhower spoke of the "Military-Industrial Complex," he was criticizing the compounding problem of unnecessary defense spending, the result of vested interests.

It is my observation and conviction that we have a "Homeless-Industrial Complex"—whereby special groups are enjoying benefits and privileges from the billions allocated to address our existing homelessness issue—and that vested interests continue to flourish.

Under these existing arrangements the job will not be done. Even with the billions allocated and spent on homelessness, it has become apparent that the more we spend each year the more the homeless count grows. Money alone will not solve homelessness. We must decide how to spend it, where to spend it, and on whom to spend it. Time is running out, 2027 is around the corner, and the decision makers must account to the citizens who voted for Propositions H and HHH.

Miguel Santana, in the 2023 Urban Land Institute forum to discuss homelessness said, "There is no one in charge of homelessness!"

In March, 2024, U. S. District Judge David O. Carter ordered a comprehensive independent audit of all homelessness programs funded or run by the city of Los Angeles.

The time is now for corrective program direction, and one not engineered by those interests benefiting the most from homelessness, otherwise Los Angeles may always have an increasing number of homeless people.

VIGNETTE:

Miguel Santana was working for William T. Fujioka, Los Angeles County's chief executive officer, and was overseeing the partnership with Skid Row Housing Trust, which housed homeless in units that they had available on Main Street in Skid Row. During that time, developer Tom Gilmore was gentrifying Main Street. According to Santana, "Tom didn't support this program because the Skid Row Housing Trust Project was on Sixth and Main, and he said, 'We don't need more homeless people here.

We're done taking the homeless for the entire city. Put them somewhere else.' However, we worked out a compromise with Tom because there was this beautiful Victorian building on the corner of Sixth and Main that Skid Row Housing Trust owned. Skid Row Housing Trust committed to refurbishing the outside of the building and make improvements. As a result, we were able to convince Tom to support the project."

CHAPTER SEVEN

PROMOTING THE ARTS

Art washes away from the soul the dust of everyday life.

—PABLO PICASSO

The most perfect structure ever built, the Parthenon, stimulated my love for art and beauty. As a young boy living adjacent to this acclaimed monument, I was inspired by the ingenuity of the ancient builders and artists. Frequent visits broadened my sense of art and enhanced my admiration for the brilliance of the carved marble under the blue Athenian sky, the flawlessness of the physical beauty, and the satisfaction it conveyed to the mind and the eye. The sculptures seemed alive, the temples flawless, the environment preserved. A motivating equilibrium prevailed.

Years later, when visiting my son Alexi, who was studying philosophy at Oxford, I was disheartened when I saw the Parthenon Marbles at the British Museum—sculptures violently hacked by Lord Elgin and carried off to London in 1801 in what the Guardian reported as "a blatant act of serial theft." Greece's decades-long campaign for the antiquities' reunification has been reinvigorated, an undertaking I strongly supported. My father also played a central role in expanding my exposure to the arts. At an early age, I was frequently taken to the Athens Symphony and museums.

This love and understanding of the arts and their influence on society convinced me to pursue programs that make art accessible to all. As Dr. Seuss, the children's author, said, "Be who you are and say what you feel because those who mind don't matter and those who matter don't mind." In 1984, as President of the Southern California Rapid Transit District, with the support of fellow director George Takei, I convinced a reluctant board of directors to require half a percent of the cost of a subway station structure to be allocated to the "Arts-in-Transit" program.

Consequently, artwork in various media—painting, sculptures, engravings, murals, holograms—are among the art form types found in the Los Angeles subway, light rail, and busway stations today. In addition, coveting even greater artistic impacts, computers, rotating art displays, stained glass and sound-and-light presentations have been utilized. More than 1,000 artists have already added their talents to this program, and their number is growing as new rail lines are added to the system. Among them is Frank Romero, a pioneer of the Chicano art movement. Romero painted Going to the 1984 Olympics, owned by Jim and

Gold Line Bridge. Artist, Andrew Leicester. Courtesy of Foothill Gold Line Authority

Azusa Horticultural Paradise at Azusa Citrus Station. Artist, Lynn Goodpasture. Courtesy of Foothill Gold Line Authority

Mural at Wilshire/Western Station by Richard Wyatt.

Rachel Garrison. Romero was commissioned to create a commemorative poster in 1990 for the grand opening of the Metro A line (Blue Line).

It was a challenging mission. In those years, when it came to art and transportation, the naysayers abounded. In their opinion, the mission of a transportation agency was simply to take people from one point to another. My determination succeeded in creating what may finally be regarded as an elongated museum that runs along the rails and busways of the county. Metro now provides an opportunity for artists and architects to work together from the beginning on the design of subway and light rail stations.

The acclaimed Metro's Young Artists program was initiated in the 1990s. Kehinde Wiley, at age seventeen, was one of fourteen young artists chosen to participate in the program, and he created a large-scale mural that was reproduced and placed on 2,000 buses. Later, Wiley was selected by President Barack Obama to paint a portrait of the former President to appear in the Smithsonian National Portrait Gallery.

Early on in my career, after establishing my engineering business in Los Angeles, I had joined the Fraternity of Friends of the Music Center, eventually becoming a Music Center Founder. I also became a member of the Los Angeles Opera Associates and was a member of the Board of Directors of the Los Angeles Ballet, which actively promoted young aspiring dancers and staged multiple performances at the Music Center.

Following a visit to Moscow's subway stations celebrated for their art and design, I walked in the Union Station passageway only to notice walls plastered with advertisements and frayed posters peeling, representing an unsightly image of Los Angeles for the tens of thousands of passengers who crisscross the area daily. It was an ugly picture that had to be rectified. I called Art Leahy, CEO of Metro, and suggested to him the creation of an art gallery in the tunnel. Leahy, in turn, summoned Maya Emsden, head of the creative services group at Metro, to take the lead. She secured a federal grant to procure and install professional quality backlit artwork panels for an ever-changing gallery of art exhibitions designed to appeal to

Lightboxes along the passageway connecting Union Station East to Union Station West, displaying rotating photographic artwork.

every age group and taste, with a variety of Los Angeles landmarks represented. Showcased is the work of contemporary artists, including portraitures, landscapes. and thematic exhibitions, all part of the Photographic Lightbox Series set to celebrate its tenth anniversary in 2024. This area of Union Station is cherished, notably by the artists and the public, and the diverse art exhibitions displayed have received national awards. The concept of the wall-mounted lightboxes as a rotating arts program has been carried out at the Historic Broadway and Grand Arts/Bunker Hill Stations of the Metro Regional Connector.

I was cognizant of Emsden's dedication and capabilities, and of her prior work as a member of the Los Angeles County Transportation Commission (LACTC). In the early 1990s, she was frustrated over the proposal by insistent engineers to use barbed wire along the Green Line and called on me for assistance. I convinced Neil Peterson, executive director at Metro, that barbed wire represented a discreditable and unsuitable endeavor on the part of the public transit operation. The barbed wire at the Green Line was never installed.

Emsden told me that she came to Los Angeles from New York, where her work was diverse, refurbishing various underground stations. In Los Angeles she concentrated on making stations localized, reflecting the neighborhood. "The art was clearly a way to do it, in really innovative ways," she added.

She remembered that I had strongly advocated art programs at Metro that enhanced the customer experience. It was this vision that led to the design criteria with elements of variability and continuity—with art being the focal point. Metro Art encourages ridership and connects people, sites, and neighborhoods throughout Los Angeles County.

Renée Petropoulos was the lead artist of a design team that incorporated art enhancements into the Metro Green Line station in El Segundo. Petropoulos designed customer seating areas at five transit plazas and selected final station colors and materials. Working with four other diverse local artists, Daniel Martinez, Richard Turner, Carl Cheng, and Charles Dixon, all of whom grew up in the Los Angeles area and had a strong connection to the city, she coordinated their efforts closely with the architects. She was also the lead artist on the Los Angeles Metro's Orange Line, which she imagined as a ribbon weaving through the San Fernando Valley. A Los Angeles contemporary artist and a professor at Otis College of Art and Design in the Graduate Fine Arts, Petropoulos' work includes the acclaimed large painted ceiling at the downtown Los Angeles Public Library.

"It was not just a painting," she clarified. "It was site specific, meaning that we had to think about what else was in that building." She had to reason how to sit a square in a symmetrical building because today "we're an asymmetrical society." Further, she explained, she designed the painting to include names of Los Angeles writers who had been published but were not in the collection of the library. Now they all have books in the library.

During our discussion, I reflected on decisions I had made early in my career. When I ran for Los Angeles Mayor in 1993, I considered mass transit, joint development, greenways, and adaptive reuse of historic buildings in downtown Los Angeles as important programs to pursue. I recall Los Angeles County Supervisor Ed Edelman expressed a different opinion. Transportation was only the moving of people from one point to another, claimed the Supervisor. I disagreed. "Billions of dollars were directed to transportation, and it was an opportunity to rebuild the city," was my response. Because of this, Metro flourished and the lives of millions have been directly and positively affected.

Petropoulos lamented the absence of significant art programs in schools. "They have not put art where it should be; theater and music are a bit better than the visual arts. People can become more civically minded through engagement in the arts. You look at a work; you talk about it, people become conversant. It breaks down the isolationism that now exists."

Pulitzer Prize winner Christopher Knight, the art critic for the *Los Angeles Times*, reinforced that New York is the consumption center for Los Angeles's new art.

"Manhattan is the marketplace," he explained to me, "it is not for production." It was too expensive for young artists, he stressed. So, they moved out of the city and headed west to Los Angeles, for the most part, where the weather was better and where a lively artist community existed.

"Will Los Angeles ever compete with New York as a marketplace for art?" I asked. "Not as long as Wall Street is in Manhattan," Knight responded. It is a base for collectors. "If you're going to spend $100,000 on a painting made in Los Angeles, buying it in an art gallery in New York will gain you access to other arrangements, other deals."

"It used to be a slur that LA was the city of sprawl," Knight stressed, "but sprawl became one of the great cultural virtues because it made the city too big to gentrify." Neighborhoods are always changing, and in the many years he has followed the art scene, he admitted art galleries have been all over the place. At one point it was on La Cienega, then downtown, Santa Monica and Culver City, mostly adjacent to wealthy communities. "It just keeps morphing." If a Los Angeles art neighborhood changes, it will just mushroom somewhere else, he added. "Manhattan is an island when it is full."

Berlin, he noted, in terms of sprawl, is like LA "When the wall came down suddenly there was this whole vast area of East Berlin that opened up, not exactly urban, not exactly suburban, with lots of opportunities—so galleries started opening up all over the place."

Los Angeles, he said, has become the microcosm of the global macrocosm. "Los Angeles, the city said to be without a center, is a city with multiple centers. The rest of the world is becoming more like LA rather than like New York. Culturally, that's significant for LA. So, you're painting a picture of Los Angeles as a great city," I chimed in. "Oh, absolutely," Knight responded. "LA is the model for Beijing. It's the model for Mexico City. Although originally built to look like Paris, it became more like Los Angeles."

I also commented on the Los Angeles Unified School District buildings not integrating art with architecture. Knight called it a complicated issue when an architect and an artist are in conflict. The architect feels he is good enough on his own and does not need help from an artist to do his job. Coordination, skill, and leadership are critical.

"Who would have thought Los Angeles would have made such great progress in the past twenty years with restaurants, galleries, the arts," I added. "We are witnessing history. The younger generation sees things differently today. They want to be mobile, free, and want to use their income for experiences at restaurants and galleries, not mortgages and the pool man."

Knight also said young people are starting small galleries and are being involved with artists but are never institutionally involved. "Institutions tend to pay a lot of lip service to younger generations, but it's mostly patronizing." Agreeing, I commented on an art gallery my daughter Tanya had in Venice, California: C.A.V.E. Gallery (Center for Audio and Visual Expression) which supported for several years new contemporary art that was fresh and energetic.

The enduring benefits of art are incalculable, I learned from my father, and I, in turn, carried this lesson forward.

Los Angeles has always loved the arts. For years, Hollywood has been celebrated globally for its creative process that has both entertained and explored issues that profoundly touched many lives. But the city's international character as an art hub was thwarted until now.

"Right now, I would argue that Los Angeles is the cultural capital of the world," Ann Philbin, the former director of the Hammer Museum at the University of California told me in a recent discussion about the city and the arts. Philbin's acclaimed cutting edge program showcases young and emerging artists, as does her signature Made in LA Biennial which focuses on artwork created in the region. Named director in 1999, Philbin developed a strong and original institutional identity and built a national and international reputation for thematic contemporary exhibitions, scholarly historical exhibitions, and contemporary artists' projects. "LA is the place where creativity is," she continued. "If you think about it on a per capita basis there are more creative people here—whether it's the film industry or the visual arts industry, or music—this is the place." Artists are coming to the city from all over the world, and not just the young ones, but those who have had successes.

She recounted for me her two decades of involvement in New York at a time during the 1980s, and 1990s when it was full of artists. They took over Soho and built the East Village. Then real estate became so expensive, artists could not live there anymore. New York became a place where art was sold, and Los Angeles became the place where art was made. When she came to Los Angeles, she became aware of how nonexistent was a system to afford support for artists, a network of spaces, galleries, and museums, thus leading to the creation of the Hammer Projects providing many small spaces for artists to show in a museum.

The Museum of Contemporary Art (MOCA), established in 1979, actively promotes the creation of new work and presents 'the most significant and challenging art of our time,' along with the Hammer and the Los Angeles County Museum of Art (LACMA), the largest art museum in the western United States, brought a lot of light to shine onto the city, said Philbin.

The artist ecosystem is filling in, she said, supported by artists and institutions and galleries. Collectors are also involved. "One thing we are still working on is philanthropy, a very important part of the ecosystem.

She added that philanthropists don't necessarily understand that to become a great city, institutions must be supported, like the ballet, music, and the arts. "What makes a great city is the culture."

I referred to music's innovative approach as supported by Esa-Pekka Salonen, the former music director of the Los Angeles Philharmonic, and Gustavo Dudamel, the current music director, considered among the most distinguished conductors of our day, and asked Philbin if contemporary art is important in our society today. "People are interested in the things that are being made in the moment," she replied. "Yes, of course, the fact that Dudamel is doing that, and the fact we are going to see that happening more and more at the Music Center—and certainly it is happening in the museums—contemporary art has become especially important to young people because they want to see what artists of their generation have to say."

She explained that New York has always been a hierarchical city interested in history, and before that, Paris was the center of culture, but the focus on contemporary art is Los Angeles. "We are just reclaiming our history in Los Angeles, our history of the 1960s and 1970s." When the Getty did Pacific Standard Time it was all focused on those years, she said, "and it was mind blowing to people what had happened here that had never been codified, never been historicized."

She was especially fond of the show at the Hammer called Now Dig This! when African American artists of those years in Los Angeles divulged that this was an incredible community with amazing artists. "The Museum of Modern Art (MoMA) took the show to New York and bought twelve works from it—thus becoming a canon in our history where a show came out of a Los Angeles university museum."

Lewis MacAdams was a poet, activist, conservationist, and the founder of the Friends of the Los Angeles River, but he was also a journalist who loved the city and wrote more than a dozen cover stories for *LA Weekly*. He later worked with an influential magazine in art design and the art world, and he befriended Ed Ruscha, the artist who was said to have made the ordinary extraordinary. "When I think of art in Los Angeles, I think about Ruscha," he told me.

"Ruscha has become an international star in the global art world," he said. "He is LA, and was incredibly influenced by LA," and greatly roused the way people see the city, he added. Recognized for paintings incorporating words and phrases, Ruscha was also linked with the Pop Art movement and the Beat Generation. MacAdams said Ruscha will be remembered more than most of the area's political figures because he helped define the way you look at what the city is. "I believe the series of photographs of parking lots, and things like that, depict a way that no one before looked at LA. There's no other city like LA" he reasoned, telling me that it is still a young city, that "all of the deals have not yet gone down."

"It used to drive me crazy that nobody understood how much was happening downtown regarding art and culture," Sue Laris, former publisher and editor of the Los Angeles Downtown News, told me. "It's just crazy." Everyone thought just two things were happening, the Music Center and maybe something else, she said. "I used to tear my hair out." The arts and culture scene are essential to the future of downtown, she added.

For years, she printed "More Every Week" and "More Than 100 Things to Do Downtown LA" She hired someone to specifically track the events. She pointed to the dozens of locations that hold important events, "zillions of art galleries, tours, music, theater, dance, opera," and she insisted that they must be listed weekly.

How correct was Georgia O'Keeffe, one of our most significant artists, when she said, "Whether you succeed or not is irrelevant, there is no such thing. Making your unknown known is the important thing."

Richard Koshalek was standing on a train platform at Grand Central Station in New York reading the *New York Times*. "Holy smokes," he uttered, "I've never heard of these people. I don't even know about the museum." The article he read stated that the candidates to be the director of the museum of Modern Art in Los Angeles (MOCA) were Pontus Hulten from Paris, Martin Friedman from Walker, Henry Hopkins, and him. His support of the team of artists had worked unknowingly on his behalf. The final interview came down to two people, Hulten from the Pompidou Museum and Koshalek, both of whom were brought to Los Angeles. Hulten, a world-renowned figure who had worked government-backed museums and didn't quite understand fundraising, had once commented to Eli Broad that MOCA would cost a lot of money, only to be told, "don't worry, we're men of deep pockets," was selected to be director and Koshalek to be deputy director and chief curator.

Fifteen months later, directing the yet unbuilt museum in LA, Hulten decided to give up that position to organize the arts and cultural program for the 1989 World's Fair in Paris. It was at the request of French President Francois Mitterrand, he had said. "Not so," recalled Koshalek. At a meeting in New York, Hulten had pulled out a letter saying it was from the French President. "I've got to return to Paris," he had claimed. "Obviously, I could not reject such an offer," he also told the *Los Angeles Times*.

The letter was a fake, Koshalek revealed to me. "It was Pontus's way of saving face." A subsequent news release issued by William Kieschnick, MOCA board president and hief executive officer of Atlantic Richfield Co., and Eli Broad, board of trustee's chairman, announced that Koshalek would assume the museum directorship.

The biggest force behind MOCA was Tom Bradley, Koshalek related to me. "He was an extraordinary man with a vision for the city. He believed in the city. He knew that ideas and new institutions were critical and that a total commitment was required."

While walking through Little Tokyo's historic district Koshalek was fascinated by a run-down building that was being used as a police car warehouse. "I want this building," he pleaded with the mayor. Fred Nicholas negotiated a 99-year lease with the City of Los Angeles and MOCA for $1 per year. Eli Broad, the construction and insurance magnate and founding chairman of MOCA "went nuclear" when he heard Koshalek's intentions. "It's obscene, Richard, nobody's going downtown to see contemporary art in a warehouse. You're going to embarrass MOCA." Broad agreed to let Koshalek go forward only if he found the money. A portfolio of prints known as the Eight by Eight for the Temporary Contemporary, the name given to the building, was produced and successfully marketed.

Famous architect Frank Gehry was hired by Nicholas, and he renovated the building imaginatively, leaving the interior intact except for new entrance doors. A partially shaded plaza was formed at the dead-end street by a canopy of chain-link fencing and steel trusses. In the interior he created two large open gallery spaces illuminated by wire glass skylights and a row of clerestory windows along the south wall. Some 40,000 square feet of exhibition space were offered. On November 17, 1983, with a Shinto purification ceremony, the museum was inaugurated. Writing in the *New York Times*, Joseph Giovannini said that the museum represented an important turning point for the redevelopment of downtown Los Angeles. "The long anticipated, much publicized, already controversial museum of art was opened, and its impact on Los Angeles is beginning to be felt immediately." He added that the actual location of the Temporary Contemporary is potentially brilliant, if unexpected: at the edge of a warehouse district in which many Los Angeles artists work.

"To a certain degree," Koshalek disclosed to me, "that's the beginning of the Arts District. It was the precedent."

From the beginning MOCA adopted a multidisciplinary approach to contemporary art. Exhibits consist mainly of contemporary American and European art created after 1940. In 1996, it was renamed The Geffen Contemporary at MOCA after receiving a $5 million gift from the David Geffen Foundation. The latest addition to Geffen Contemporary occurred in 2019. Thanks to a $5 million gift from MOCA trustees Wonmi & Kihong Kwon, a performance space that hosts free concerts, screenings, readings, conventions, and other events. The beguiling name, Temporary Contemporary, had an interesting origin, Koshalek confessed to me. When he sought a permanent permit for occupancy, he faced a bureaucratic bundle of requirements. So, he asked for, and finally obtained, a temporary permit for occupancy to be active for three years or so—a temporary permit for a contemporary museum.

Koshalek ended his sixteen-year tenure as director of MOCA in 1999 and was subsequently appointed president of Art Center College of Design in Pasadena. The *Los Angeles Times* called him an energetic, visionary administrator, credited with building one of the world's leading showcases for contemporary art almost from scratch.

Paul Schimmel was convinced that Los Angeles was a significant center for new contemporary art in the United States. "This was its place," he told me. Schimmel was MOCA's curator of contemporary art for twenty-two years, until 2017. "In the 1950s, there were loyal collections, family collections, representing hundreds of years of collections." He referred to Norton Simon as a "great collector, very influential to a whole generation." But he was disheartened by the Arensberg collection's being split between the Philadelphia Museum of Art and Claremont College, which now displays the works at the Huntington Library in San Marino. The collection included works by Marcel Duchamp, Henri Matisse, Pablo Picasso, Georges Braque, Salvador Dalí, Marc Chagall, and Vasily Kandinsky, among others.

He referred to major private collections, like J. Paul Getty, Armand Hammer, and Norton Simon, which became public institutions. "Los Angeles is not a place of older collections, most museum collections—that includes LACMA and MOCA—are collections of a collector."

The game changer was CalArts (California Institute of the Arts), he said. CalArts was formed in 1961 as a merger of the Chouinard Art Institute and the Los Angeles Conservatory of Music—institutions that had become financially distressed. Walt Disney, longtime friend of both Nelbert Chouinard and Lulu May von Hagen, the chair of the Conservatory, had trained many of his studio's artists at the two schools for a fee that would be deferred until Disney could afford to pay. He coordinated the merging of the two entities to continue the educational mission of the schools. Disney had claimed that "we don't make movies to make money, we make money to make movies." CalArts became renowned internationally for the education of professional artists by bringing out visionary creative talent, offering more than seventy comprehensive degree programs in the visual, performing, media, and literary arts.

Schimmel said despite its remote location "in the middle of Timbuktu" (actually, in Santa

Clarita), it started from the ground up and had substantial private funding. "It embraced visions to have the best filmmakers, the best artisans, the best animators, the best people who are practicing in the arts."

He explained to me that his first show at MOCA was Helter Skelter and was very successful. Critics agreed. It was LA Art in the 1990s, and featured works by sixteen local visual artists and ten writers. Spanning different generations, backgrounds, disciplines, and formal practices, the artists focused on a common vision of alienation, dispossession, perversity, sex, and violence.

Los Angeles may not be as high in the commercial art market as New York or San Francisco, Schimmel estimates, but it is certainly very high in the creativity world. The high commercial markets include London, Paris, Chicago, Berlin and Tokyo, and Beijing and Shanghai are bubblish in a way.

"I like to think that Hollywood is running interference for creative artists who live in Los Angeles," he related to me. But entertainment and art are not the same, he pointed out. "People who confuse it really don't know anything about entertainment, and they certainly don't know anything about art." The entertainment world is not really very helpful to being truly a free spirit and creative person in visual arts only because artists will look at actors and say, "these are no role models."

I asked Schimmel to reflect on David Hockney, the artist who the *Los Angeles Times* called "an emblematic Los Angeles celebrity," that impacted the art scene. Hockney was born in Bradford, England, and wanted to move to Los Angles, which he did in 1964, after watching Laurel and Hardy films, impressed by the shadows they cast on the screen. In Bradford, the sun did not cast long shadows. A painter, draftsman, printmaker, stage designer, and photographer, he contributed to the pop art movement of the 1960s and is today considered one of the most influential British artists of the twentieth century.

"David does his own thing," responded Schimmel. "He lives this extraordinary life of an Englishman in Hollywood, returning to England to visit his mother when she was alive, although he had said 'I hated it there.' Reports said he never stayed more than two weeks. He was in some ways a little bit more of a foreigner from Los Angeles." A 1972 work of Hockney's, Portrait of an Artist (Pool with Two Figures), was sold at a Christie's auction house in New York in 2018 for $90 million. In 1966, David Hockney made a series of prints to illustrate a selection of renowned Greek poet Cavafy's poems, including I*n the dull village*.

Ernest Fleischmann, the determined organizer who dominated the Los Angeles Philharmonic for nearly thirty years and transformed it into one of the nation's top orchestras through the force of his demanding personality, shocked the musical world in 1987 when he called for the end of orchestras, according to Mark Swed, classical music critic for the *Los Angeles Times*. According to Swed, what was needed were larger communities of musicians who take on a variety of musical tasks throughout their towns, playing early music, new music, movie music, chamber music, whatever is wanted. The noted critic said this was in line with CalArts' collaborative and community-centric ethos.

Steve Lavine, the third president of CalArts (1988 2017), told me when he arrived in Los Angeles the Philharmonic did not have a big enough audience to mount its own music series.

So, CalArts music group would present it. Fleischmann hated it. "He knew he needed us because his budget couldn't handle it, but he hated the fact that we put students on the same stage as his professionals."

The music scene was very fragile at that time. Then, Fleischman did a remarkable thing. In 1992, he hired in Esa-Pekka Salonen, the Finnish composer and conductor to be the music director of the Los Angeles Philharmonic. "Young, radical conductors weren't being hired then, now everybody wants one," said Lavine.

Lavine related to me the work of Betty Freeman, the Beverly Hills philanthropist who hosted legendary salons where her guests heard the best new work from established and emerging American composers. "In a way, it was the center of the new music," he added. Almost always, the performers were faculty or students from CalArts. She actively supported numerous modern composers, including John Cage, Philip Glass, Pierre Boulez, and John Adams.

When he came to Los Angeles, dance was the weakest of the arts by far. "Bella Lewitzky was almost the only person to keep a dance company going." Interestingly, when the Ballet Russe de Monte Carlo broke up, dancers came to Los Angeles to become involved in the movie and music world. In the 1950s, local ballet training was unprecedented. In 1970, Lewitzky became the founding dean of the dance program at CalArts. Ballet mystified Los Angeles for many years. Numerous local attempts were undertaken to create a local ballet company only to fail within a few years. Even celebrated dancer and choreographer George Balanchine attempted with Ballet Los Angeles in the 1960s without success.

In 1974, John Clifford, a dancer from Los Angeles who had performed on television's Danny Kay Show and Dinah Shore, was a George Balanchine protégé. Balanchine was the father of American Ballet. Clifford became the founder and artistic director of the original Ballet Los Angeles. The Music Center had been dedicated ten years before, but at that point was "just for the LA Philharmonic and had no real interest in dance," Clifford told me. When he joined the New York City Ballet, there were six dancers from Los Angeles, Clifford said, and there were famous dance teachers locally. If there was an outlet for them locally, he surmised, they would not have to go to New York. "A Los Angeles ballet company could rival New York and San Francisco. He envisioned a resident ballet company at the Music Center. Clifford was a genuine ballet star, the first American male guest artist to dance with the Paris Opera Ballet. As a choreographer, he created new ballets for Les Ballets de Monte Carlo, Teatro Colon in Buenos Aires, Deutsche Opera Ballet in Berlin, Zurich Ballet, Maggio Danza in Florence, Italy, and has staged his works for the Ballet du Nord, France, the Rome Opera Ballet, and Ballet British Columbia. In the United States, he had created eight works for the New York City Ballet, and had been commissioned by ballets in San Francisco, Miami, the Pacific Northwest, Dallas, Santa Fe, North Carolina, Atlanta, Chicago, Oakland, and Sacramento. Clifford's Los Angeles Ballet desired residency at the Music Center. A new member of Clifford's board was known optometrist Bernice Brown, who informally set up a meeting with Dorothy Chandler, founder of the Music Center and the namesake of its first venue, the Dorothy Chandler Pavilion.

"I'm going to tell the truth," he confided to me. "Dorothy Chandler had read about my coming back to Los Angeles." At the meeting, he admitted to her that one reason for his return was the Music Center. "Well, you know, I had a bad experience with Stanley Holden (the former Royal Ballet principal character dancer), and his wife, Judy." It appears that Holden's dancers had interfered with the orchestra members over shared studios, and space. The relationship went sour. "You know, I don't like ballet. I really am not going to help. Good luck." That brusque remark ended the conversation, but not the aftershocks.

Clifford subsequently held performances with his Los Angeles Ballet at the Ambassador Auditorium in Pasadena, Shrine Auditorium, the Pantages Theater, and virtually every theater and University of note in Southern California. For ten years, everyone raved over them except for *Los Angeles Times*' Entertainment and Arts writer Martin Bernheimer. Chandler was the widow of the publisher of the *Los Angeles Times* and director emeritus of the Times Mirror Company. Clifford`s ballet tours fittingly received accolades. Anna Kisselgoff, a reporter for the *New York Times* on June 30, 1981, wrote, "Anyone who wondered what happened to John Clifford, one of the New York City Ballet's most popular and exciting dancers of the 1960s and early 1970s, had a chance to find out this weekend at the Brooklyn Academy of Music, where Mr. Clifford's Los Angeles Ballet made its New York debut last night."

"Nick, the reviews we got in the *New York Times* were unbelievable," Clifford remembered. "We had a big two-page Sunday spread." The ballet company performed one hundred times a year in LA and toured internationally with praiseful results. He finally got into the Music Center and performed The Nutcracker at 92 percent capacity. "We were representing Los Angeles nationally and internationally well," he told me. Good reviews were carried by the Los Angeles Examiner, Variety, The Reporter, and all Hollywood trade papers. But the *Los Angeles Times*' Bernheimer and Lewis Segal chipped away with constant negativism. "I believe that Dorothy Chandler did not want us to succeed," he said.

In July 1982, it was announced that the Joffrey Ballet would become the resident dance company of the Music Center. The announcement was made after a meeting of the center's Performing Arts Council Board of Governors. The Joffrey would continue to maintain a base in New York as part of its agreement with the Music Center. Politics had danced into the ballet. Clifford provided his own insight to me on this intriguing development. Ron Reagan, Jr., the president's son, who had dropped out of Yale University and had decided to study ballet, had become a regular member of the Joffrey Ballet's traveling troupe. This most likely played an unexpected role in the Music Center's decision.

The general manager of the Joffrey, Philip Semark, disclosed to Clifford the reason they got residency. "It was Nancy Reagan."

Clifford told me that to help her son, Nancy Reagan got David Murdock, a multimillionaire developer and member of President Reagan's Kitchen Cabinet, to give the Music Center $2 million to help the Joffrey get its residency. "If the Music Center did not get the $2 million, we would have been the resident company," he stated. "It was rotten timing."

I probed further, asking if Clifford thought his company's demise was the result of the *Los Angeles Times*, Nancy Reagan, Dorothy Chandler, or was it due to the absence of interest?

"Interest was there, and it was amazing, as you know, Nick, as a member of the Board." He attributed 75 percent of the downfall was due to the money that was given to the Music Center. "I don't want to get into politics, but it's the facts." He spoke about the women's group that supported Clifford's company, called the Los Angeles Ballet Guild. It was a flourishing social club, with fashion shows. "Cary Grant gave us an award, and the women loved it." Jody Jacobs, the then society editor of the *Los Angeles Times*, called the president of the social club to say that her newspaper could no longer cover them, nor the Los Angeles Ballet. Limited space, Jacobs said, and they were only going to cover the Joffrey events. "When the 160 women of the Guild got the news, they broke into tears."

When Clifford's ballet folded, his *Los Angeles Times* nemesis, Martin Bernheimer, wrote on January 27, 1985: "Clifford thinks matters might have been different if he had enjoyed a happier relationship with the Los Angeles press in general, with this ogre. But his press has been bad at worst, uneven at best, in other locales, too . . . if negative reviews killed the Los Angeles Ballet, that is regrettable. The alarming alternative to negative reviews, unfortunately, would have been dishonest reviews."

As fate would have it, in July 1983, the Joffrey Ballet announced that Ron Reagan Jr., a corps de ballet dancer—not a principal or soloist— resigned from the company to pursue other interests.

Clifford offered his opinion to the board of the Music Center, saying that they would not get any more money from Murdock, or the Reagans. He held that The Joffrey would last a couple of years and they will be gone because it's not the kind of repertory Los Angeles wants. His ballet had Balanchine as its base and had included the famous Alexandra Danilova, the Russian-born prima ballerina, and Coppelia, the definitive comic ballet of the Romantic era. Alexander Minz from the American Ballet Theater danced in the Nutcracker, and brought in the legendary Alicia Alonso, the Cuban 'prima' ballerina assoluta and choreographer whose company became the Ballet Nacional de Cuba. Clifford's sense of Joffrey's role is that it is best fitted for a second company in a city. "It's a good alternative program," he related to me. "They didn't do classics; they really specialized in kitschy rock and roll ballets. They didn't do Balanchine."

Eight years later, in 1991, the Music Center decided not to renew the contract of the financially troubled Joffrey Ballet, ending Joffrey's role as a resident company of the downtown Los Angeles Performing Arts Center. The company also failed to meet a deadline to show that it is in sound financial health. I was very well aware of the superb reviews Clifford had received outside of Los Angeles and asked why the negative reviews in his home city? "Snobbery, basically snobbery, Nick," was the quick response. "I thought about this my entire life. LA has a second city complex for the arts. It's great if something is from San Francisco, or New York, or Paris." "New York has been responsible to a certain point, regarding Los Angeles," I added.

"Every country has it," replied Clifford. "In Paris, if you're not Parisian, you don't exist. Jean Stone, wife of best-selling biographical novelist Irving Stone and his researcher, had the greatest line regarding San Francisco." Paraphrasing Stone, he said "San Francisco built their opera house before they paved the streets." Italians there had a long history of supporting opera and the arts. LA is a different world, Clifford continued. "It didn't get around to having the LA Opera until after we folded."

Clifford continued his work with a chamber-sized touring ensemble Ballet Los Angeles and became the artistic director of the Los Angeles Dance Theater. In 2003, at the request of Warner Bros Studio, he created a dance-musical production of Casablanca, The Dance, based on the classic film, Casablanca. This $4 million dollar extravaganza premiered in Beijing, China at the historic "Great Hall of the People" as the opening event of their yearly Drama Festival. Over 15,000 people saw the three-performance run to standing ovations.

Constantine (Stan) Karos, the Beverly Hills attorney and producer, knew very well what a negative press review could do to a production. He supported a play by Dale Wasserman, best known for his book, *Man of La Mancha*. Karos's client, the actor Victor Buono, was involved in Wasserman's work, Playing with Fire. "I got involved when they wanted to perform in a ninety-nine-seat house which was an equity waiver situation," he told me. That meant the charge for the seats was little. Anything above that moved the production to another level requiring more money for the actors and the production.

Karos believed that Buono, who had earned Academy Award and Golden Globe Award nominations for his role in What Ever Happened to Baby Jane? deserved better. So, he undertook the play's production at the Westwood Playhouse. Some of the investors included Karos' brother-in-law, Telly Savalas, and me. "It was a first-class production," he remembers. Gardner McKay, literary critic for the Los Angeles *Herald Examiner*, in a rave review, said the play was destined for Broadway. Not so, according to Sylvie Drake, theatre critic and columnist for the *Los Angeles Times*, who totally panned the production and nearly killed it. "We couldn't sell tickets," lamented Karos. "People were put off by Drake's review, and we were on the hook for four weeks. But it was a wonderful production and a wonderful play."

Heidi Duckler was dubbed the "reigning queen of site-specific performance" by the *Los Angeles Times*, and for good reason. "We danced everywhere," she told me. "Nobody did that, nobody had heard of doing that." When she started her company in the 1980s, she didn't want to dance in theaters, so she chose alternative sites, like laundromats, gas stations, libraries, and anywhere they could—even the Los Angeles River. Her reputation soared. Locations became an integral part of her company's performance.

With delight, she shared with me the reason she chose site-specific locations for her performances. She referred to artist Robert Rauschenberg and his belief that "painting

Seeing Los Angeles in new ways. Heidi Duckler dancing at Disney Concert Hall. Courtesy H.Duckler Dance

relates to both art and life." Rather than filling stages with decorative objects and props, she decided to go to the real world where these objects are found.

"When I did Laundromatinee, we rehearsed in a laundromat," she explained, "and people who were doing their laundry became engrossed in the work process. These were not people that go to the theater or the opera." Her rehearsals had dancers on top of washers and dryers.

She applied and to her surprise received a National Endowment grant, a Masterpiece Award. People in Washington were convinced that such a performance in a laundromat could be a masterpiece.

"Avant-garde?" I probed. "Is that how you would characterize your dance?" "Well, I'd call it contemporary, but it's very collaborative, it's sort of multi-disciplinary with different artists and different disciplines all collaborating together." Instead of trying to transform a space, she seeks to organically develop within the space, thus creating a site-specific work rather than an outdoor performance.

In 1995, she produced and choreographed a multi-media performance under the Glendale Boulevard Bridge in Atwater Village called Mother Ditch— a translation of Zanja Madre, the Indian name for what later was to be called the Los Angeles River. Her dancers, Elizabeth Nairn and Eli Nelson, provided the centerpiece of a forty five-minute performance that was a tremendous logistic feat, wrote reporter Robin Rauzi, of the *Los Angeles Times*. While dancers performed in the water a sixteen-person choir sang words drawn from Joseph Conrad's "Heart of Darkness," accompanied by eight accordions and revving engines of twenty motorcycles.

She recalled the work of Bella Lewitzky and called Bella's dance company "very Los Angeles modern" with lots of support. Duckler said she was supportive of Lewitzky's desire to build a Dance Gallery and her outreach to the community to raise awareness about the value of dance and about having a place for dance. Los Angeles today has become more sophisticated, explained Duckler, it is easier, "We have a downtown now, there's a more active artistic scene, and the population is more innovative. Additionally, dance companies band together, they are not as competitive.

"Do we still compare ourselves to New York?" I asked, recounting a nagging past narrative related to the arts. "No!" she replied. "We're pretty content with who we are, our sense of identity."

Vascular surgeon George Andros had an interest in ballet since the age of five. He marveled at the beautiful music and scenery and was instantly enamored by this art form. When he and his wife, Marie, moved to Los Angeles from Chicago they attended a symphony performance at the Music Center. It was 1971, and he found embedded in the program a solicitation envelope. "Since we were interested in the symphony, we placed a check for $25,000 in the envelope for a founder's membership," he told me. Tennis players at the time, Andros' locker was across the aisle from Z. Wayne Griffin, governor of the Los Angeles Music Center Performing Arts Council.

"Hey, George," said Griffin, who also produced General Electric Theater, a weekly dramatic series in the 1950s that was hosted by Ronald Reagan for eight years. "I hear you gave some money to the Music Center. You did something that's never been done before, you became a founder through our donor's letter." Griffin asked him to be a board member of the opera company, but Andros declined. A year later Griffin introduced Andros to Charles Luckman, once called the boy wonder of American business, former president of Pepsodent and partner with William Pereira in the notable Pereira-Luckman architectural firm—and member of the Los Angeles Ballet Board of Directors.

"I hear you're interested in the arts," Luckman said, and introduced Andros to Jim Jacobson of Prudential who was president of Los Angeles Ballet. As a result, Andros went on the Board in 1978, and a few years later when Jacobson became chairman, he became president. Not long after, Andros became chairman of the board, and he invited me to join the board.

The ballet company, under Clifford, performed at the Music Center, a feat that made Andros proud. "We had to chip in plenty, and we did two years of The Nutcracker there, trying to bridge the gap between a company not being originally a part of the Music Center, but growing into the Music Center family," he told me. He said they were overwhelmed by the power of Nancy Reagan and David Murdock who maneuvered to make Joffrey the Music Center's resident troupe in support of the younger Ron Reagan. "That's how we came to fall apart," he acknowledged. The donor base was lost, and people drifted away. Clifford's new Los Angeles Ballet began to grow in Glendale.

Andros admitted to me that he was dismayed by "the lightweights," those who did not really understand that the full ballet concept must include starting a school, educating, building the community, and attracting and keeping the best dancers.

In 2009, Glorya Kaufman boldly and affluently injected herself into the Los Angeles dance scene. She donated $20 million to the Los Angeles Music Center to establish the Glorya Kaufman Presents Dance series. She is the widow of Donald Bruce Kaufman, who with Eli Broad, co-founded Kaufman & Broad, a publicly traded real estate development and construction company.

Andros said that is what money buys you. "We went and saw the Corella Ballet, which was wonderful." While he praised the event, he lamented the approach. "You don't build your local company, you don't build your local school, you don't build your local audience. You build nothing.

The 1984 Olympics Arts Festival was a seminal moment for LA. Not only did the world become aware of the city's cultural relevance, but it sparked a newborn desire to overcome the local existing disparity in fine arts.

Barry Sanders, chairman emeritus of the Los Angeles Parks Foundation and winner of USC's Thornton School of Music 1999 Medal of Honor, has been a major player in the Los Angeles music and art landscape for many years, including board membership on the Los Angeles Philharmonic, the Los Angeles Opera and the city-wide Ring Festival, the Los Angeles Performing Arts Center (formerly "The Music Center"), the Music Center Foundation, and The Walt Disney Concert Hall Corporation.

He related to me that establishing programs befitting Los Angeles was dependent on economics. Coordination, partnerships, and stipends were pursued and events that turned a profit were kept. "LACMA would never coordinate with what it was doing with the Music Center, which wouldn't coordinate with Getty. The idea that you could sit around a table and say, 'We're doing this, why don't you do something similar?' was a breakthrough."

In 1984, the arts festival adjunct to the summer Olympic Games showcased imported talent which provided more than 400 performances by 145 theater, dance and music companies, representing every continent and eighteen countries, including Britain's Royal Opera of Covent Garden, the National Theater of Greece - in a Greek-language performance of 'Oedipus Rex,' Australia's Circus Oz, and Japan's erotic modern dance company, Sankaijuku.

Lectures and debates blossomed. "The city was engaged on all bases, and it was united," he recalled.

From the 1984 Olympic experience, the Los Angeles Festival was born in 1987, which staged several ambitious citywide programs of international arts and culture. But then its budget was slashed for the 1993 festival. Artistic director Peter Sellars and executive director Allison Sampson had noted that the international touch would be lost due to monetary reasons. Participation was limited to Los Angeles-based artists.

Regarding the Los Angeles dance scene, Sanders was on the Music Center board during the Joffrey ballet, which failed because of the exhaustion of its repertoire. He recalled the "ugly fight" over stage time because of the Philharmonic, although "there was nothing going on at the Music Center."

"The Music Center was never conceived by Dorothy Chandler as a performing arts organization, it was a fundraiser," he disclosed to me. In 1989-90 Los Angeles experienced a depression, Sanders said. The aerospace industry faced serious trouble with the end of the Cold War. Donations dropped off.

Esther Wachtell became president of the Music Center in 1988, and was an expert fundraiser. She told the *Los Angeles Times*, that "The president of the Music Center will always have to have a major role in fund-raising because in fact the primary responsibility is the financial health of this place, but I intend to separate the functions so that I do not have to concern myself with the day-to-day operations."

The newspaper also reported that as president, Wachtell became the chief operating officer of the Music Center, encompassing the Los Angeles Philharmonic, the Center Theatre Group (the Taper and the Ahmanson), the LA Music Center Opera, the Joffrey Ballet, the Music Center Chorale, and the Music Center Education Division. The budget was projected to be more than $70 million in 1989.

"They fell short," remembered Sanders. "Resident companies who had money only from their board members were in a crisis." "What did they do?" I asked.

"It's an interesting story not truly known," he replied. "The prohibition on fundraising would go away, and while the Music Center would still seek funds from ARCO and the Bank of America, and all other people they raised funds from, for the first time the resident companies had to create development departments and hire fundraisers."

However, confusion ensued. The Philharmonic Company was in serious economic trouble, Sanders said, not being able to meet its enormous budget. When it went to ARCO to seek funds they were told, "We just gave." The resident companies were also knocking on their door. Additionally, of the money the Music Center raised in the name of the Philharmonic, 50 percent would go to Music Center overhead and education programs and the other 50 percent would be split among the Center Theater Group, the Opera, and the Philharmonic.

Stephen Rountree served as president and CEO of The Music Center from 2002 to 2014 and was also CEO of the Los Angeles Opera from 2008 to 2012, a position he held concurrently. For four years, up until 2019, he was the managing director of the Center Theatre Group, considered to be Los Angeles's leading nonprofit theatre company, which includes the Mark Taper Forum, Ahmanson Theatre, and the Kirk Douglas Theatre in Culver City.

He spoke to me about the "genius of Dorothy Chandler," who created a performing arts center which was the landlord and the glue that brought resident companies together, and who also was able to get the Los Angeles County Board of Supervisors to agree funding it. "The force of her personality and her intelligence was fascinating," he added, "being able to create an institution that thrived." Stephen Roundtree spoke about Esther Wachtell, who followed Chandler at the helm of the Music Center and the scandal widely reported by the *Los Angeles Times*. "There was embezzlement and so on, not her, but the people who worked for her," he said.

Roundtree stated that Andrea Van de Kamp became chair in 2003 of the Board of Governors of the Music Center and oversaw the Development Committee, which raised funds to build the Walt Disney Concert Hall. "She re-energized the Music Center, reorganized everything with a lot of help from people like Stuart Ketchum and Steve Hinchliffe," he added. She also hired Roundtree.

He also touched on Gordon Davidson, the artistic director of the Mark Taper Forum who helped establish Los Angeles as a West Coast capital of regional theater and challenged audiences with socially conscious plays, and Ernest Fleischmann, the German-born American impresario who served for thirty years as executive director of the Los Angeles Philharmonic. Davidson was an artistic director for the Center Theatre Group, originally selected in 1967 to be the artistic director of the then new Mark Taper Forum. He is credited with transforming LA from a backwater theater setting to "a wellspring for new works that won Toney Awards and Pulitzer Prizes," according to the *Los Angeles Times*. He became theater's most prominent face having produced more than three hundred works and directing more than forty plays.

Roundtree explained that he was part of the Walt Disney Concert Hall team with Bill Siart and Jack Burnell, after Fred Nicholas had left. Nicholas was the first chairman, guiding the development of the building, creating the program and architectural infrastructure for the Concert Hall including the selection of the architect, Frank Gehry and the acoustician, Nagata & Associates.

Nicholas, a friend of mine since the late 1970s, had combined a successful legal career with his real estate involvement to become an institution builder in the arts in Los Angeles. Consequently, he was widely known as "Mr. Downtown Culture," for his role in building MOCA, the Geffen Contemporary, and the Walt Disney Concert Hall. Nicholas was also a trustee of Art Center College of Design in Pasadena, California, for approximately nine years, having joined the Board at the request of Richard Koshalek, former director of MOCA. "I was very close to Tom Bradley," Nicholas told me, "And I think he was responsible for the beginning of MOCA because Marcia Weisman, an early art collector, encouraged him to start a museum." Bradley made it possible for MOCA to gain access to the land.

Regarding the Geffen Contemporary, Nicholas confided to me that he hired Gehry to design the architecture for two warehouses. So good was the project that people liked it better than the regular MOCA, added Nicholas.

For almost a decade Danielle Brazell persistently nudged City Hall to support the Los Angeles nonprofit art scene. In 2014, she was appointed by Mayor Eric Garcetti to head the Department of Cultural Affairs, the progressive arts and cultural agency of the city which supports and provides access to visual, literary, musical, performing, and educational arts programs. Further, the DCA makes funds available to arts organizations and individual artists. Brazell explained why she felt the arts were so important in Los Angeles. "It connects the city and the people to the past. The city is incredibly dynamic, constantly evolving." "This is a global city.

We are an exemplary manifestation of cultural diversity. There is no shortage of commitment from our intra-agencies, there is no shortage of commitment from our artists," she added. She praised the efforts of other city departments and pointed to the Metro in the Arts program.

"What we lack is support for noncommercial creative production, affordable live-work space for artists," she summarized. The absence of community platforms to celebrate their cultural identity and expression was also on her mind.

It was always difficult not to notice Merry Norris, a dear friend of mine, called the "godmother of art and architecture in Los Angeles." Alissa Walker of Curbed Magazine wrote that she dressed head-to-toe in prerequisite black, draped in whimsical accessories, with an asymmetrical bob that tucked around her chin like a piece of site-specific sculpture." Wherever she went a crowd gathered. And she always occupied the center. Norris began to enhance her fascination with art and design while serving as a patron and docent at the Santa Barbara Museum of Art in the mid-1960s. And then she began to collect. In the early 1970s, she married William Norris, who was running for California state attorney general, a race he lost. The couple relocated to Los Angeles and shared their mutual interests in arts and politics.

Over lunch, she confided that she took trips to New York to attend art auctions and bidding and to visit galleries. Although Los Angeles had many good artists, she was repeatedly told that nothing was really happening there. I cited what Fred Nicholas had told me, that while he had as clients almost 80 percent of LA galleries, there truly was no activity.

In 1984 Mayor Tom Bradley appointed her to the city's Cultural Affairs Commission. "I wasn't sure what that was, but it sounded like a nice honor."

Norris eventually became chair of the Commission and changed the way LA designed public buildings, reported the *Los Angeles Times*. By enlisting architects, she oversaw a revamp of the city's design standards, resulting in transformative civic landmarks such as the Central Library expansion in Downtown, and contextual neighborhood outposts like fire, police, and water and power stations.

"The Commission did not have an architect on staff but occasionally borrowed one from Recreation and Parks who showed little interest," she told me. "Everything looked like Taco Bell," she said. So, she went seeking help from celebrated architect Jon Jerde who put together a group that had an architect advising her at every commission meeting.

Kinetic Light. Artist, Paul Tzanetopoulos. Courtesy of LAWA

She mentioned George Takei, the actor best known for his role as Mr. Sulu in the original Star Trek television series, a very valuable member of the Commission. Takei, a member of the Rapid Transit District (RTD) Board of Directors, strongly supported my art program for Metro stations which, he said, gave meaning and identity to the stations, a sense of place. "The station artwork gives the ridership a sense of continuity with the community."

Norris was widely known as a co-founder of the city's MOCA and was instrumental in founding the influential architecture school, SCI-Arc, and served on its board of trustees. When the Community Redevelopment Agency offered land on Bunker Hill if enough money was raised for an arts museum that had community support, Norris accepted the challenge, saying. "That's when I became a fundraiser."

Norris cited the "percent for art" fee whereby 1.5 percent of all construction, improvements, or renovation projects undertaken by the city be set aside for public art projects, while a similar fee must be set aside by private developments. However, using her husband's contacts with ARCO she brought in Bill Kieschnick, the company president and chief executive officer, who eventually stabilized MOCA, while serving as the museum's board chairman.

She also told me about Lennie Greenberg, who with her husband were major art collectors. "Lennie was a fundraiser volunteer," she said, and eventually became president of the board.

Norris also mentioned Marcia Weisman, the sister of Norton Simon, an avid modern art collector. With her husband, Fred, she hosted many parties and lectures in their home and a community of collectors formed around these conversations. She is credited for her generosity and the founding of MOCA, which contains much of her collection. But Norris confided that Weisman "took credit for everything, making everybody crazy because she didn't do anything but have these fabulous parties at her house. That's exactly what she did." Her monetary contributions to MOCA were the smallest amount, she continued. "It was just ludicrous."

One of the public art components supported by Norris was the Kinetic Light Installation in 2000 by Paul Tzanetopoulos as part of the LAX Gateway Beautification Project—pylons consisting of structural steel support frames encased in a layer of translucent, tempered glass. Fifteen pylons forming a 560-foot "gateway" circle at the intersection of Century and Sepulveda Boulevards are an average of one hundred feet high and twelve feet in diameter. Eleven pylons along the Century Boulevard median between Aviation and Sepulveda Boulevards are six feet in diameter and ascend in height from twenty-five to sixty feet.

Tzanetopoulos's overall concept was centered on the pylons functioning as both beacon and gateway to Los Angeles. The colors, he said, metaphorically work from the airport out to the greater Los Angeles community—and beyond.

Japanese-born architect Ted Tokio Tanaka, aware that Los Angeles had very few architectural landmarks, designed giant three-dimensional LAX letters for the airport entrance, as part of the beautification program.

By applying creativity and aesthetics, builders and architects can design cultural symbols and acclaimed works of art. Concurrently, they can revitalize a city's image and enhance its reputation by transforming or renovating faded and dilapidated buildings.

That is what Los Angeles had in mind when a subdivision was adopted in the Municipal Code known as the Adaptive Reuse Ordinance in 1999. It sought to facilitate the conversion of older, economically distressed, or historically significant buildings to apartments, live/work units, or visitor-serving facilities. ARO was part of my plan when I ran for mayor of Los Angeles in 1993.

Tom Gilmore caught on quickly. The ARO became a catalyst for the downtown Los Angeles residential boom. Seeing the opportunity, developer Gilmore began his Old Bank District Renaissance project at Fourth and Main Streets and saw investment pour into the city's historic core.

Bordered by the Jewelry District, the Fashion District, Gallery Row, the Toy District, and the Civic Center area from Main to Spring between 4th and 5th Streets, the area became Gilmore's residential conversion project. But waking up Downtown LA was not enough for Gilmore. He had visions for a contemporary art museum in the heart of the historic core. Along with business partner Jerri Perrone they opened the Main Museum in 2016, which was focused on Los Angeles art and organized around a residency program rather than a permanent collection. "I don't know if the museum was part of the process or the culmination," Gilmore told me. "We were focused on the arts, and we have a lot of artists here." At the time, he said, we were seeing the next generation of artists because we were building new lofts, and the Art District was starting to head in a different direction. He was driven by the concept of embedding culture into the fabric of these buildings, he related. He had seen in New York how Tribeca and SoHo changed when the artist community was edged out by commerce. He sought to reinforce and enable the artistic community and an artistic culture which he considered inherent to the city. "There are geographic and cultural differences between one museum and another," he continued.

I added that the museum envisioned by Gilmore was an artists' house rather than a place for exhibits. Gilmore agreed and cited the Main's opening show where Suzanne Lacy—known for her work in performance and social practice—taught Andrea Bowers, an artist whose politically minded practice is rooted firmly in drawing, how to be a performance artist. "It was an extraordinary artistic event that began a broader conversation about the nature of art in contemporary society," he said.

Asked about his personal motivation, Gilmore replied that he was evolving. "The strength I bring to the table is my strong level of naiveté and my desire to get from here to there." "Los Angeles is on an extraordinary trajectory," he added. "I'm seeing it through the eyes of many people. I believe we are the most forward-thinking city in America."

In May 2019, the noncollecting, nonprofit Main Museum which opened three years earlier in the beaux-arts building, was leased by Gilmore to the ArtCenter College of Design for $1 per year for ten years with the option to renew. It is used as an exhibition and event space, staging shows, talks, and other public programs.

Michael Amescua uses a blowtorch on quarter-inch sheets of used metal to create art, breathing three-dimensional innovative life to Mexican symbols and myths. His decorative and functional art elements grace the entry to Metro Headquarters and the Patsaouras Transit Plaza.

He draws inspiration from the Latin American custom of papel picado, or paper cutouts, often viewed at religious celebrations and festivals."What I do is cut steel," he told me. "I don't tell people I'm an artist, I tell them I'm a welder. Then eventually in the conversation I say that I do art with it." And art can come from a passing shape, from a scrap of paper, from a spider's web, Picasso had noted: "The artist is a receptacle for emotions that come from all over the place."

Amescua has completed important commissions for the Los Angeles County Metro, the Los Angeles International Airport, Paseo Colorado in Pasadena, the Los Angeles Zoo, McCambridge Park in Burbank, Montebello Transit Center, the Los Angeles Department of Water and Power, and the Los Angeles County Chatsworth Courthouse.

He holds a degree in anthropology from Occidental College and has been a longtime artist in residence at Self-Help Graphics in East Los Angeles. He had taken classes in art and responded to a call from Sister Karen Boccalero—a Franciscan nun who began making prints with Latino and Chicano artists. Printmaking is an artistic process where images are transferred from a matrix onto another surface, most often paper or fabric. Her vision, Amescua told me, was to have us do art that represents us. She created Self-Help Graphics and taught East LA teenagers the art of photography, painting, sculpture, and printmaking from a specially outfitted van.

He told me that working with steel is certainly a niche of his, but he is also "shrinking them down" to jewelry size, not cutting them with a blowtorch but with water or laser. The work he did for Metro can be downsized to a broach of a pendant.

Art is a journey, he said. There's a lot of highs and lows, but it's also a lot of fun. He would advise young artists to get into the moment every time they sit in front of an easel or when they hammer something. Technology is making a difference in art, he stressed. "When I did that thing at Metro for you, I had four guys working for me and now because of digitizing I have one person." He paused momentarily. "Digital images can be as good as great artists. But there will always be art and there will always be a craft."

"I'm not your typical artist," Sandy Bleifer admitted when we met to discuss her work and her long-term engagement in community events. "Actually, Nick, you were kind of the person who got me started in a lot of community activities," she told me.

Bleifer is a Los Angeles native who studied art and classical music at the University of California, Los Angeles, and has been active as an artist-in-residence in local schools, is the co-author of teaching materials on art appreciation, and has worked since the mid-1970s on collages using handmade papers, and widely known for her experimental uses of paper to evoke land and seascape imagery as well as social issues.

Bleifer envisioned doing more than just creating art with her life. When she went to Japan to attend a paper-making conference and saw the lunch boxes and photographs at the Peace Memorial—dedicated to the legacy of Hiroshima as the first city in the world to suffer a nuclear attack—she created a whole body of work by making 35 paper sculptures from molds of her leg to depict the ravages of war.

She told me that when she returned home, she decided to use her talent as a tool for social action, embarking on an ambitious plan to bring about social change by approaching the built environment. Working as a real estate specialist on behalf of tenants and buyers, she founded a company in 1996 to pursue the creation of a vibrant residential and business community in the neglected historic and industrial sections of downtown. She brought the Arts Organization to Tom Gilmore's first building, as well as a theater and a charter school. "It was all about making changes."

She described today's art world as a kind of a reflection of the gallery scene. "So many wealthy people bank their money in the art world when the stock market is unreliable. The art system, at the highest level, creates an investment system," she continued. "The big galleries are in cahoots with a lot of the museums to validate the artist." Then a second validation is required, she said, provided by the auction system.

"Fortunately, there's a lot of roles for artists in our community," Bleifer reflected. "A lot of my work now is about the environment and environmental degradation. If I could use my

Images graffitied on the Berlin Wall. Artist, Sandy Bleifer. Courtesy Sandy Bleifer

artwork as a lever, and trigger, that's what I would want to do." When I asked her about the future of art in Los Angeles, Bleifer replied that artists need to be in residence. "You must have that creative environment, that spectrum of economics, patronage, and that feeling of accomplishment. You must have that ladder within the art system to keep it vibrant."

I was fortunate to meet Milton Katselas, director and producer of stage and film, and develop a close friendship over the years - attending his classes at the Beverly Hills Playhouse, over lunches, and visiting the exhibits of his paintings, sculptures, and photography. I spent many Saturday mornings at his master class for professional actors, not to learn about acting, but to be inspired by his enthusiasm, to be entertained by his humor and wit, and to reflect on his philosophical soliloquies.

Katselas founded the Beverly Hills Playhouse in 1978 and had a wide range of students, including famous actors Gene Hackman, George Clooney, Alec Baldwin, Tom Selleck, Michelle Pfieffer, and his good friend Jeffrey Tambor among others. Doris Roberts, best known for her role as Ray Romano's mother in the television series Everybody Loves Raymond, was a friend of Katselas since their years as students at the Actors Studio in New York City. She was attending his master class almost every Saturday, where I often saw her. Another participant in the Saturday morning master class was Thaao Penghlis, Australian-born actor of Greek heritage and best known in the United States for roles in daytime soap operas such as Days of Our Lives, Santa Barbara, and General Hospital. Penghlis starred in the 1980s remake of Mission Impossible and guest-starred on numerous crime dramas, also doing stage acting.

With Milton Katselas,left and Jeffrey Tambor

Katselas was trained under Greek American Elia Kazan and Lee Strasberg. He was nominated in 1969 for a Tony Award for directing the Broadway production Butterflies Are Free, and in 1972 directed the movie version starring Goldie Hawn and Eileen Heckhart, who won an Academy Award for her role. He also directed the 1973 movie 40 Carats with Liv Ullman.

Katselas had a strong magnetic personality. His thirty years in Hollywood raised him to guru status in the eyes of hundreds of actors. He gave a standoffish impression, but to those of us who knew him well, he was warm, funny, and kind.

According to Bill Fujioka, chair of the board of trustees for the Japanese American National Museum in Los Angeles, in 1942, the United States government ordered the relocation and incarceration of over 128,000 individuals of Japanese heritage from their homes and placed in ten concentration camps built in desolate areas of America. Many of these individuals were American citizens. This gross violation of civil liberty and social justice was driven solely by racial fear and discrimination. The Japanese-American National Museum (JANM) was established not only to preserve the history of Japanese-Americans, but to ensure their stories are retold to hopefully prevent what happened to this community never happens

President George W .Bush presented the Presidential Medal of Freedom to Secretary of Transportation Mineta on December 15, 2006. Courtesy of FHWA

again to any other community. JANM was built on the site where thousands of individuals of Japanese heritage were forced onto buses and taken to concentration camps. This site is ground zero for the Japanese-American civil rights movement.

An early supporter and champion of JANM was secretary of transportation Norman Mineta. He proudly served as the Chair of the Board of Trustees for JANM for many years prior to his death. Secretary Mineta and his family were removed from their home in San Jose and taken to concentration camp located at Heart Mountain, Wyoming. This experience forged his passion for social justice, equality, and democracy. Following the bombing of the world trade center on September 11, 2001, pressure was being applied to profile members of the Muslim community.

Secretary Mineta, who was the US Secretary of Transportation at the time of the bombing, fought back against this action stating that he would not condone an action that was like what was tragically imposed on his family and community in WWII. Secretary Mineta's story in one of many from the Japanese American communities throughout the United States.

I had the privilege to work with Congressman Mineta when I was leading the efforts to secure federal funding for the Los Angeles subway. Congressman Mineta was an affable, unpretentious individual, very effective and influential in Washington, DC.

In 2023, Metro named the Regional Connector Little Tokyo Station the Norman Mineta Station in Congressman Mineta's honor, a well-deserved recognition.

VIGNETTE:

While serving on the Board of Directors of the Los Angeles Ballet, I befriended the great architect, Charles Luckman. In one of our lunches at the Jonathan Club, Luckman gave some advice to the young engineer. He said," Nick, when I would go to meet corporate clients, even if knew the answer to a question, I would respond, 'I don't know, and I'll get back to you.' It made me look human."

CHAPTER EIGHT

THE EDGY NARRATIVE BEHIND THE STORY

There is nothing so powerful as truth—
and often nothing so strange.
—DANIEL WEBSTER

PACIFIC PALISADES OIL DRILLING

One of the richest men in the world didn't care about money. Armand Hammer cared more about prestige, power, and the ability to influence. That's how Rick Jacobs described his boss, the legendary entrepreneur, to me over lunch. At one time, Jacobs was vice president of Occidental Petroleum Corp, a company ruled exclusively by Hammer. He was viewed as one of the most powerful and clever capitalists in the world, the man who had successfully fashioned business ties and friendships with generations of government leaders on both sides of the Iron Curtain. For some, he had become a conduit between the Soviet Union and the United States on crucial issues. Hammer was an entrepreneur, and he owned an oil company. It was natural that the oil-rich bluffs of Pacific Palisades would capture his attention. To ultimately get political support for the right to drill, he shrewdly engineered a campaign to influence the Los Angeles City Council and Mayor Tom Bradley. So many top politically connected lobbyists were brought in to persuade key decision makers, the operation was described by some as a well-oiled blitz.

Drilling in Pacific Palisades had been steeped in politics for years, creating a bitter civic debate. It first surfaced as a major campaign issue between then-Mayor Sam Yorty and opponent Bradley in 1973.

Occidental had struggled unsuccessfully to develop the Palisades field since its geologists found oil-bearing sand in 1966. The *Los Angeles Times* had reported that this discovery had led Occidental geologists, using known geologic information and seismic soundings pounding the surface and listen to sound waves come back to center their attention on the Palisades area.

Calculations indicated the Palisades field could yield a minimum of 25 million barrels of oil and a maximum of 60 million. At the 1987 price of oil, the maximum find would bring in more than $900 million and industry experts said oil prices would rise during the projected twenty-year life of the Palisades field. Occidental's 1987 revenues totaled $17.1 billion.

In 1981, the *New York Times* Magazine reported that "Julius Hammer, an immigrant from Russia, was a dedicated supporter of Lenin and the Communist Party," and that Julius named

Armand after the arm-and-hammer symbol of the Socialist Labor Party of America. The father was also the founder of the American Communist Party. "Armand Hammer went to Russia at age twenty-three in 1921, just after graduating from Columbia College of Physicians and Surgeons," Jacobs told me. "He claimed that he went because he thought it was a great opportunity to do business. I had known that Hammer originally claimed the trip was intended to recoup $150,000 in debts."

Journalist Edward Jay Epstein had written in his 1999 book: *Dossier: The Secret History of Armand Hammer*, that "His father had lent money to the Soviets and Armand went try to collect it, but on the way, he met Boris Reinstein, (a member of the Socialist Labor Party of America) who introduced him to Lenin." This relationship and the many extraordinary deals Hammer negotiated with the Soviets and with nations that have usually been hostile to the United States turned him into the "epitome of success of American capitalism." One lucrative deal was the commitment by Hammer's company to ship one million tons of concentrated phosphoric acid to the Union of Soviet Socialist Republics annually for twenty years, thus providing Soviet agriculture with the liquid fertilizers it desperately needed to improve crop yields. The deal, according to Hammer, was worth no less than $20 billion.

Hammer had described to Jacobs his initial meeting with Lenin. He said he wanted to help the Soviets with the famine problems they faced. "I don't need that," Lenin replied, "I need businesspeople." As a result, Hammer received an asbestos mine concession in the Urals. Then they created Amtorg Trading Organization, the first trade representation of the Soviet Union in the United States.

Amtorg was established in New York in 1924 by merging Hammer's Allied American Corporation with Russian cooperative societies. The company was controlled by the People's Commissariat for Foreign Trade and served as a de facto trade delegation and a quasi-embassy. It handled almost all exports from the Soviet Union and supplied Soviet industries with technical news and information about American companies. In the first five years it had negotiated contracts with major American companies such as Ford Motor Company, General Electric, International Harvester, DuPont de Nemours, Radio Corporation of America, and more than a hundred other companies. Some sources have said Amtorg served as a front for Soviet intelligence service operations in the US. Intriguingly, of the company's first six presidents, one died under suspicious circumstances and four were executed during political purges.

Hammer became the Soviet gateway for many American companies. In one conversation with Lenin, he said: "I want a pencil concession because you're teaching everyone to write, but you don't make pencils." Only the Eberhard Faber Pencil Company in New York made them at that time. Hammer hired workers from Eberhard Faber, brought them to the Soviet Union, and set up "Hammer pencils." Soviet leaders, at least through Leonid Brezhnev, learned to write with Hammer pencils. In 1926, Russia no longer wanted Hammer's capitalistic endeavors and he lost his pencil concession to the government.

Jacobs recalled that "only two people believed that the Soviets would pay off their war bonds, Hammer and Averell Harriman, the US Ambassador to the Soviet Union during World War II and the subsequent Cold War, and governor of New York. "They bought up everything for pennies." He related to me how Hammer set up a bank in Paris, and how the Soviets paid off "because they had to get into the financial markets. So, he made another fortune."

The Soviet state suffered the consequences of a devastating civil war and needed money to build a new society. So, it decided to raise funds from the sale of priceless masterpieces that had been amassed by the old regime. Hammer moved quickly. He set up the sale of Russian antiques (for which the Soviet government gave him a 10 percent commission) and organized the sale of "Romanov treasures" in New York's largest department store, Lord & Taylor, which had no relation to the imperial family, according to Natalya Semyonova, a historian and author of "Selling Russia's Treasures."

The great entrepreneur acted inventively, according to Jacobs, when "he hired a guy to masquerade as a Russian prince and had him selling Russian stuff in stores like Macy's." In Project: University Art Museums and Galleries in Virginia, America, & the World, Lisa M. Gerben writes a darker account of how Hammer became involved in the Russian art business. "The Soviet government had acquired tons of artifacts from the wealthy that they had not been able to export due to embargoes and pending lawsuits from those who had their family heirlooms stolen. Stalin put Anastas Mikoyan in charge of foreign trade, who then enlisted Hammer to assist him in selling some of the art."

Hammer set up a gallery in New York called L'Ermitage Galleries to sell the art, but it was generally unsuccessful and nearly went bankrupt several times. Innovative Hammer sent word to midwestern department stores that he had privately acquired a Romanov treasure and wished to "exhibit" it, which really meant sell it, and split profits with the store. Hammer said that the show was much like a 'traveling circus.'"

It was later determined that the treasures were not authentic Romanov. When they had "been sold off to the everyday person shopping in the department store, Hammer resorted to creating counterfeit works of art and selling them off as the real deal," Gerben wrote.

In the early 1970's, Hammer's attention turned to oil. He had acquired a controlling stake in Occidental Petroleum in 1956, and the company won exploration rights in Libya in 1965. His negotiations with Libya's ruler, Muammar Gaddafi, contributed to the growth and power of the Organization of Petroleum Exporting Countries, thereby radically changing the oil business around the world. Occidental became the main channel of Libyan oil, and the biggest independent oil company in the world.

But it was the 1985 vote by the Los Angeles City Council that created the divisive environmental-political acrimony for years over oil drilling in Pacific Palisades. The council had voted ten to four in favor of Occidental's plan, and ultimately received Bradley's signature to the surprise of many because the mayor had vetoed the project six years earlier. I clearly remember the City Hall hallway whispers that Hammer had reached high into the political, business and labor establishments for his strategy on the bureaucracy. He had earlier put on the Occidental board the city's former administrative officer, C. Erwin Piper, and used as a lobbyist Bonnie Reidel, a former city planning commissioner.

He also elicited support from former Gov. Edmund G. "Pat" Brown and US Senator Alan Cranston and convinced a few wealthy Jewish businessmen that the Palisades project would enhance Israel's security by making the US less dependent on Arab oil.

A move that was considered controversial was Hammer's hiring of the influential law firm of Manatt, Phelps, Rothenberg & Tunney, packed with powerful Democratic players. The firm included Charles Manatt who was once chairman of the Democratic National Committee; John Tunney, former US Senator from California; John Emerson, ambassador to Germany during the Obama Administration and head of US Senator Gary F. Hart's primary election victory in California in the 1984 presidential campaign; Mickey Kantor, Vice President Mondale's California campaign chief and later US Secretary of Commerce; Maria Hummer, significant City Hall lobbyist for Occidental, and pollster John Fairbank.

The notion at the time, Jacobs told me, was that the opposition "couldn't hire anybody, we hired everybody." Included were George Kieffer, who chaired the appointed commission charged with rewriting the charter of the city of Los Angeles, and Joe Cerrell, prominent public relations, and political consultant. Kantor was especially significant for Hammer. He oversaw the lobbying campaign and knew what buttons to push—and when.

In 1982, Bradley lost the California governor's election to George Deukmejian by a razor-thin margin of some 100,000 votes, or about 1.2 percent of the 7.5 million votes cast. In the expected rematch against Deukmejian, four years later, the mayor needed to be on the winning side of environmental matters. In a news conference held at a gas station with Jim Birakos, deputy executive officer of the South Coast Air Quality Management District, he assailed the failure of oil companies to control sulfur emissions and the state's meager sulfur and sulfate policies.

When Bradley initially opposed Occidental's project, he pointed to the need to stabilize the fragile cliffs above the drilling sites with a water drainage system and to insure the city against suits should the system cause a landslide. All of that was done. A trapped Bradley could not equitably veto the City Council's vote for Occidental when it resurfaced in 1985. Typical of high-stake City Hall outcomes, according to Joel Sappell, writing for the *Los Angeles Times* in 1985, "There also were campaign contributions—tens of thousands of dollars given mostly to lawmakers friendly to Occidental." While recipients denied being swayed, Councilman Joel Wachs, an Occidental opponent, said some of his colleagues were not being candid. "Of course, they were influenced by the contributions," he told the newspaper. "City Hall gave a new meaning to the expression 'voting your pocketbook,'" another council member quipped.

Hammer was known for using money to gain influence, not only in the Soviet Union but also in the United States. In 1976, he pled guilty to secretly donating cash to Richard Nixon's Committee to Re-elect the President and escaped prison by appearing for sentencing in a wheelchair, accompanied by elaborate heart-monitoring equipment, according to a July 21, 2015, article by journalist Steve Sailer, in Taki's Magazine. "He wanted a pardon," Jacobs told me. "That's all he wanted because he said, 'I was never guilty.' We got one for him in 1989. (George H. W.) Bush gave it to him."

I met Hammer through Rosemary Tomich, a member of the Occidental Petroleum board of directors, and an ardent advocate for education, social, and women's causes. One of the reasons I believe Tomich befriended me was the fact I was advisor and confidant to Councilwoman Peggy Stevenson, a key vote in the oil drilling fight. Another reason, I was very close to presidential candidate Michael Dukakis and Hammer wanted a presidential pardon.

I had lunch with Hammer several times and had the opportunity to admire the paintings displayed in his offices on top of the Occidental headquarters in Westwood. Hammer and his brother Victor, who had studied art, began collecting art readily available at an inexpensive price since well-to-do Russians left behind their belongings when they fled the country after the Bolshevik Revolution.

Hammer gave his collection—featuring old master paintings and drawings and works on paper by Honoré Daumier and his contemporaries—as well as galleries for traveling exhibitions to the Hammer Museum when it opened adjacent to Occidental headquarters in November 1990, a month after his death. Today, the Hammer Museum is one of three public arts institutions of the School of the Arts and Architecture at UCLA. Jacobs said that Hammer "traded for art, he traded for everything."

During our discussion, Jacobs likened Hammer to circus tycoon P. T. Barnum, an icon of American ingenuity and promotion, known widely as "the greatest showman." He told me of how he tried to maneuver into a position of prominence in 1986 after the KGB arrested U.S. News & World Report journalist Nicholas Daniloff on espionage charges. "Hammer managed to get into a receiving line with Reagan in the White House," Jacobs said. He told the president that he was going to Moscow to try to get Daniloff out. "Great," Reagan said. "He went to Moscow, and he said, 'I talked with Reagan, and he told me to work on this." After intense discussion between the US and Soviet governments, Daniloff was allowed to leave without being charged.

Jacobs disclosed to me that "honestly, the Palisades thing was one of the most cynical things I've ever seen." Yet, he began to see Hammer's point of view. "He had a deal with Mayor Yorty to drill for oil in exchange for some land for a park. So, he thought he was right." He felt he was not being treated properly.

Joy Picus, who was elected to the Los Angeles City Council in 1977, recounted for me how she was "targeted by the most powerful man in Los Angeles to change my vote and approve his project." The earlier council vote was nine to six in favor, and Picus was on the opposing side. "Occidental had sixty days to hold its nine votes, and get one more," she explained to me, emphasizing that she was considered by Occidental to be the possible tenth vote. "I was taken out for lunch, dinner, breakfast, and everything, and every lobbyist in town, anyone who knew me or had a relationship with me, was in my office."

Picus recounted for me the day Hammer paid her a visit. Using a scale model of the area in the Pacific Palisades to explain the project, he "told me how he had wined and dined with kings and queens and heads of state and attempted to persuade me to change my vote."

"I don't support it," she told him. Hammer left. She justified her decision to me, saying she was very uncomfortable. She said she was "a nice Jewish girl that grew up not to be able to say 'No' to important people when they asked for things."

That evening, Picus continued, she attended a women's political event at the home of Elizabeth Snyder, the first chairwoman of the Democratic Party in California. There she related the Hammer episode to Catherine O'Neill, cofounder of the watchdog group Women's

Refugee Commission "Joy, Armand Hammer doesn't give a fig about the oil, he wants to win, and you are standing in the way," O'Neill told her.

Bradley had perceived a sense of fairness in stating his support in 1985. When he vetoed the project six years earlier, he stated objections that were ultimately satisfied by Occidental. Pat Russell, City Council president and a former project opponent, had become supportive of business interests and considered it unfair to block drilling in the Palisades, while wells pumped oil on the Venice waterfront and elsewhere in the city.

I also recall the issue of equity being raised at the time. Questions arose about the rich against the poor, about the elitists wanting to preserve their view of the ocean and to hell with everybody else.

When the Soviets announced their boycott of the 1984 Summer Olympics in Los Angeles, Bradley was hopeful that a personal visit by him to Moscow might change minds. According to Jacobs, Hammer talked a lot with Bradley and "wanted to put him on a secret trip to Moscow."

Hammer later checked with his Moscow sources and advised the mayor that no one would meet with him once he got there. On May 13, rather than being on a plane to Moscow, Bradley met us at the home of Jim and Helen Birakos to reminisce of our trip to Greece to establish the Los Angeles-Athens sister city affiliation.

Two years after the 1985 vote, there was a major political shift on the City Council. Four council members who had supported Occidental were out. Russell and Stevenson lost in their reelection bids, David Cunningham Jr. retired, and Howard Finn died. Their successors had taken stands against drilling in the Palisades.

I remember well the political shift at City Hall and the momentum it provided to Councilmen Zev Yaroslavsky and Marvin Braude who, at the time, were weighing a measure for the November 1988 ballot that would ban oil drilling on Los Angeles beaches.

The drilling controversy raged and spilled into the courtroom. Ignoring its staff recommendation, in July 1987, the California Coastal Commission approved the Occidental drilling plan on a seven-to-five vote, aware that a legal challenge would follow. Two months later, No Oil Inc. and the Pacific Palisades Residents Association filed a lawsuit against the commission, alleging that the panel approved the plan without giving opponents an adequate opportunity to present their views. It also claimed that the commission did not have a required environmental impact report and was in violation of a city mandate that such exploration be done in conjunction with actual oil production.

In November of that year, a ruling by California's Second District Court of Appeal upheld the Los Angeles City Council's 1985 approval for Occidental to open a coastal oil field estimated to produce sixty million barrels of oil and $100 million in taxes for the city over the next thirty years.

In the November 1988 election, voters narrowly approved the anti-drilling measure co-sponsored by Yaroslavsky and Braude—Proposition 0. It received 52.3 percent of the votes, while Occidental's opposing measure, Proposition P, the LA Coastal and Public Protection Act, was rejected by a two-to-one margin.

This was considered the most expensive campaign in the city`s history. According to Jacobs, "the Hammer team organized the African American ministers and the whole thing was, well, rich white people can drill for oil in poor black people`s backyards, but they won`t let them drill for oil in their own backyards." Proposition P, according to Jacobs, was Kantor's idea, basically stating that oil drilling would be prohibited in Santa Monica Bay and that city revenue from any oil produced by Occidental would go to police, fire, paramedics, and other government services.

"We pretended that Occidental was not involved in the proposition," Jacobs told me, "Then, just before the election, Hammer personally made the company take out a full-page ad in the Los Angeles Herald-Examiner that he signed about why Proposition P should pass and the other should fail."

"He couldn't contain himself," Jacobs stated regretfully. "I think we could have won."

VIGNETTE

As told by Joel Bellman, a former Los Angeles Herald-Examiner editorial and oped columnist:

"While the Los Angeles Times *occupied prime real estate in the downtown Civic Center only a couple of blocks from City Hall and the County Hall of Administration, the Herald's building sat on the edge of Skid Row, adrift in a sea of vacant lots. Its circulation had fallen to less than a quarter that of the Times. And unlike the Times, it was patronized and indulged, more than feared and respected, by the local business and political communities.*

Against this backdrop, Dr. Armand Hammer, chairman of the Occidental Petroleum Corporation, surely thought he had little to fear from the Herald-Examiner editorial page.He was heading into the home stretch of his twenty-year effort to sink a few slant-drilling oil wells at the base of the Pacific Palisades cliffs across Pacific Coast Highway from Will Rogers State Beach. All that seemingly stood in his way was the November 1988 ballot, on which a pair of measures, Prop. P (for "petroleum") and Prop. O (for "oceans") were battling it out.

Prop. O was a citizens' referendum mounted by two Westside City Council members, Marvin Braude and Zev Yaroslavsky, intended to overturn the city's 1985 approval of Hammer's drilling plan. Reasoning that you can't beat something with nothing, Occidental decided to sponsor its own counter-initiative, Prop. P, to reaffirm political support for the drilling—and to hedge their bets, because even if Prop. O passed, as long as Prop. P got more votes; the drilling plan would still go forward.

The problem: how to sell Angelenos on an oil company scheme to drill near a popular beach. Solution: create a front group, the Los Angeles Public and Coastal Protection Committee; recast beachfront oil wells as the Palisades Inland Energy Project; keep Occidental's name out of it or just refer vaguely to "a local firm;" keep any Occidental personnel off the initiative campaign's executive committee; and identify Occidental attorney and lobbyist Mickey Kantor only by his outside title as chairman of the California Conservation Corps. Lastly, bury the fact that roughly ninety percent of Proposition P's campaign donations came from Occidental Petroleum.

Fortunately, in October 1988, Los Angeles County Superior Court Judge Thomas Johnson decided that the law and "common sense" demanded that Occidental come clean with its involvement and ordered Proposition P ads to reveal that the oil company was their hidden backer.

Occidental had already won approvals from Mayor Tom Bradley and the Los Angeles City Council, hired some of the city's biggest lobbyists, and locked up the editorial endorsement of the Los Angeles Times. *It's amazing they even bothered wooing the Herald Examiner at all. Yet there they were, only a few weeks after Johnson's ruling had exposed their machinations, a delegation dispatched by Hammer to sell our editorial board on the coastal drilling scheme.*

In those days, my office dress was strictly casual unless we had guests to meet with; then I wore a suit. But on this day, I'd completely forgotten the scheduled meeting and was in my Levi's and work shirt. I was unprepared when Kantor—who was personal friends with Bill and Hillary Clinton and would go on to become Clinton's US Trade representative and secretary of Commerce—showed up with a pin-striped-suit lobbying delegation. Joining him were top Bradley confidants H. H. Brookins, bishop of the First African Methodist Episcopal Church, and Samuel Williams, president of the Los Angeles Board of Police Commissioners, the first Black president of the State Bar of California, and a senior partner in the powerhouse law firm of Hufstedler & Kaus.

Kantor took one look at me in my denims and didn't miss a beat. He immediately took off his coat, loosened his tie, rolled up his shirt sleeves, and began talking about his early career in legal services representing farmworkers. He could sure read the room.

But after that icebreaker, Mickey got down to business. While Brookins and Williams sat there stone-faced, Kantor, who lived on the Westside, declared that it was about time the privileged (white) Westside shared the burdens and responsibilities of "resource recovery" the way other (Black) parts of the city had done. Think of all the essential services—public safety, parks, libraries, street repair—denied to the inner city that those oil royalties would fund. In a blatant ethnic pitch aimed at the Jewish community, he touted the benefits of energy independence that would protect against future OPEC and Arab oil embargoes. Appealing to tight-fisted fiscal conservatives, he invoked a veritable gusher of new public revenue with no new taxes—while hinting at the city's costly legal exposure should voters "renege" on earlier approvals granting Occidental's coastal drilling rights.

The harder Kantor pressed, the more we pushed back, and it was surely obvious by the time they left that their pitch had fallen on deaf ears. Our editorial board was unanimous in opposition. This was a major local issue, and virtually all the media opinion leaders in town, with the sole exception of KNX Newsradio, had already endorsed Occidental's drilling plans, as did most of the local political establishment. As the major outlier, we knew our editorial had to be long and substantive to have any credibility at all. But with our deputy editorial page editor, the principal environmental writer, out on indefinite leave, who would write it?

Editorial writers normally work solo, but this assignment clearly demanded some collaboration, and the task fell to me and my colleague Cheryl Heuton (who, with her future husband Nicolas Falacci, would go on to become a successful creator and show runner of the hit 2005–2010 CBS television series, Numbers.) With the election less than two weeks away, we had to work fast.

Within an hour or two, we were done. After a light edit, it was typeset for the following day's edition, and Kantor and Co. woke up to read our 1,800-word editorial, "No on Oxy's Prop. P: Don't let the sales pitch fool you.""Within a few hours, the editorial page editor, Jim Kinsella, came out to inform us that Hammer was so incensed at our editorial that he'd personally called Frank Bennack, chief executive of the Hearst Corp, which owned the Herald Examiner, *in New York and threatened to withdraw Occidental's advertising if the paper didn't recant its opposition. Bennack reportedly shrugged and said he had no editorial control over a local paper. But instead of withdrawing his advertising, Hammer took out an ad in the paper denouncing the editorial and touting Proposition P.*

On Election Day, the public rendered its verdict: Proposition O had passed with 52.33 percent of the vote, and Proposition P was defeated, with 65.62 percent of the electorate voting against the coastal drilling plan.

Two years later, Hammer would die at the age of ninety-two, his dream of coastal oil drilling off the Palisades unfulfilled. Six months after his passing, Occidental Petroleum Chairman Ray Irani would announce at the company's annual shareholders' meeting that it was formally abandoning the Palisades drilling project."

THE NORTHRIDGE EARTHQUAKE

It was in the early morning hours of January 17, 1994, a federal holiday—Martin Luther King Jr. Day—with most people in bed when a magnitude 6.7 earthquake struck the densely populated San Fernando Valley, about twenty miles northwest of downtown Los Angeles. The earthquake's epicenter was a few miles from my home in Tarzana, which my family and I had to vacate for several days because of damage to walls and the fireplace. Buildings, shopping centers, and portions of freeways collapsed.

Los Angeles Mayor Richard Riordan, just six months on the job, was jolted out of bed at 4:31 a.m. and found himself on his back on the carpeted floor of the Bel Air home of his future wife Nancy Daly. He tried to call the police and fire chiefs, but the lines were dead. Even the mobile phone in his Ford Explorer didn't work. Frustrated, he hurriedly dressed in a gray sweatsuit and running shoes and scurried off for City Hall, eighteen miles away. The hasty drive was perilous because roads and bridges were damaged and confused drivers scrambled for safe routes.

When he finally arrived, he parked in the City Hall garage and rushed to the Emergency Operations Center—a bunker-like quarters four floors below ground where some tousled department heads were gathering. Riordan was surprised by the lack of personnel and equipment. "Basically, the room was divided up with the LAPD on one side, the Fire Department on the other," he told the Los Angeles Daily News. "And we had no real plan on how to respond." Wooden tables with rotary phones were set up and paper maps were pinned to the wall. Only a few television sets were available.

"As I walked around the room and asked about our emergency plans, it dawned on me that no one had the slightest idea what to do. It was shocking, but not necessarily surprising,"

Riordan wrote in his 2014 memoir, The Mayor. He said that during the transition into office, his team found many city agencies were disorganized and utilized outdated technology.

The news at the operations center painted an alarming picture for the San Fernando Valley. There were reports of widespread damage with multiple deaths and injuries. The city's transportation manager, Bob Yates, identified on a wall map where bridges and overpasses had collapsed. Later, Riordan wrote, "We learned that scores of buildings had been leveled, and one oil main and as many 250 gas lines had ruptured, igniting a number of dangerous fires." Detours were ordered around the La Cienega bridge which included three intersections in Culver City and necessitated state permission, a two-year feat under normal circumstances. Riordan ordered the takeover of those intersections ignoring state and city ordinances and told staff if someone complained to give them his home number. If it is ethical and practical, he reasoned, he would ignore the law.

Riordan noticed that Police Chief Willie Williams was nowhere to be found. His wife had panicked because falling furniture almost hit her, it was reported to Riordan. He told a staffer to "pick him up and drive him here as fast as you can," according to the Hollywood Reporter. Noticing that some members of the press overheard the discussion about Williams, he told them, "If you like LA at all, you will not report on it because we don't need people to lose faith in their leaders."

More than three million residents were left without electricity. Electric transformers exploded and in Sylmar entire city blocks were said to be ablaze. Toxic chemicals were reported to be leaking from a sixty-four-car freight train that derailed between Chatsworth and Northridge. Two of the aqueducts carrying the city's water from the Sierra Nevada Mountains had ruptured.

At 5:45 a.m., Riordan officially declared a state of emergency, which followed a similar declaration by California Governor Pete Wilson, who also asked President Clinton for federal aid.

"In the middle of this," Riordan wrote, "I noticed we didn't have food in the operations center. It was one problem I could immediately fix, and I sent an aide to the Original Pantry, the twenty-four-hour downtown diner that I own. Within forty minutes, a breakfast of scrambled eggs, pancakes, and French toast arrived at City Hall."

On January 18, Riordan met downtown with Wilson and a group from the California Department of Transportation to discuss repairing the freeways and asked, "What did the architects and engineers you had out yesterday suggest?" When he heard that no one had gone out to do assessments, Riordan decided to send private engineers and architects to begin the survey. While no looting was reported, the mayor initiated a dusk-to-dawn curfew for the first two days. The National Guard then arrived and began street patrols.

In freezing Washington, DC, John Emerson, President Clinton's deputy director of intergovernmental affairs —with a primary responsibility to be the president's emissary to California—told me that when reports of the earthquake reached the nation's capital, he hurried to see Clinton. "I went straight to the Oval Office and walked in. George Stephanopoulos was there with the president, as was Press Secretary Dee Dee Myers. They were monitoring the earthquake." (Emerson was later US ambassador to Germany during the Obama administration.) Immediately they called James Lee Witt, director of the Federal Emergency Management Agency. "You guys got to get out there today," Clinton said, so Witt and Emerson, along with, Federico Peña, secretary of transportation, and Henry Cisneros, secretary of Housing and Urban Development, headed for Andrews Air Force Base and boarded a jet for Los Angeles. Because of the cold at Andrews, and the three inches of snow on the tarmac, the Air Force jet had to be de-iced—an uncanny circumstance considering their destination had recorded 85 degrees on that same day. Myers held a White House news conference to say the president was sending four officials to Los Angeles. Riordan responded by saying he welcomed the "A+ team" to his city. The president vowed to help victims deal with the earthquake and its aftermath.

Emerson described to me his plane's flying path to Burbank-Glendale-Pasadena Airport that night, which took him over Palmdale or Lancaster to land from west to east. "No lights were on in the cities below, but you could see the 14 Freeway going north with nothing but red lights." It reminded him of an apocalypse movie, with everyone streaming out of Los Angeles. The entire San Fernando Valley was dark. When the plane landed, Riordan was there to greet them, along with the chief of the Office of Emergency Services, and the police and fire chiefs. FEMA had already set up headquarters at the Hilton in Pasadena. Three aftershocks of at least magnitude 5.0 or more rattled the area that night.

Two days after the earthquake, Clinton arrived, aboard Air Force One in Burbank. "This is a national problem," he said. "We have a national responsibility, and we will be in it for the long run. This is not something where all of us from the federal government just showed up while this is an issue in the headlines." Later, at a news conference with Riordan, Wilson, and US Senators Dianne Feinstein, and Barbara Boxer present, as well as numerous other officials, the president said he had walked the crowds that day and saw public workers who had slept only two or three hours in three days, working on the roads, water lines, and gas lines. "We saw countless numbers of people who had lost their homes, who didn't know when they were going to be able to go back to work. We saw children asking us to help fix their schools so they could go back to school."

Clinton had issued a disaster declaration the day the earthquake struck, and in addition to the federal team already present, he said that about 1,500 federal personnel in California, Washington, and Texas, were working on quake relief. Clinton was unambiguous when asked what he was willing to do. "We have no intention, none, of letting this be a short-term thing. We will stay with you until this job is finished." The president was determined to provide special attention to California because he loved the state, said Emerson, adding that Clinton often joked about making it his second home.

Then Los Angeles Councilman Hal Bernson, dubbed "Mister Earthquake" at City Hall because he was the most avid proponent of seismic safety on the City Council and had spearheaded a slew of safety-minded ordinances, including the retrofitting of thousands of unreinforced masonry buildings, told me that "the earthquake lasted about ten to fifteen seconds," and that was fortunate. "It was a short-thrust fault," he said, "not too far below the surface." It was very violent, he added, explaining that it had the highest acceleration rate and a vertical gravity rate of 1.9—"both of which have never been equaled anywhere that we know of."

He lived in Granada Hills and could not get out of bed because the shaking was too violent. "I thought we were going to die, I really did." Glass was everywhere from heavy mirrored doors that crashed after being pulled away from closets. It was bedlam, he said, the refrigerator came away from the wall and was in the middle of a kitchen, which was littered with groceries as all cupboards stood wide open. His yard had three levels, with the swimming pool above the patio and the lower yard. "Half the swimming pool was in the lower yard," he mentioned as we reminisced.

Feeling a heavy responsibility, Bernson called Riordan immediately after the quake to discuss recovery strategies, Greig Smith wrote in his 2010 book *If City Hall's Walls Could Talk*. Smith was an aide to Bernson and later a Los Angeles Councilman. He said that Feinstein had also flown in to meet with Bernson to determine the level of federal aid needed. The councilman sought the mayor's immediate guidance as well as his concurrence during the declared emergency. When Bernson and Smith entered Riordan's office they were directed to a couch since the mayor conducted all his business around a coffee table. He had an office without a desk. As they sat, Riordan said, "You have to hear this." He played a funny routine from a comedy album by a team called Hudson & Landry. Bernson sat in disbelief for ten minutes, then turned to Riordan.

"Excuse me, Mr. Mayor, our city is in shambles, people are living in the parks. The federal government wants directions, we have serious work to do." Riordan, raptly listening to the comedy routine, had his trance interrupted. He shook his head and said, "Oh yeah, that would be a good idea, what do you have in mind?"

Damage was widespread, as buildings, shopping centers, parking lots and portions of major freeways all collapsed. At least fifty-seven people died, while thousands more were injured. At the Northridge Meadows apartment complex, sixteen people were killed, all of whom lived on the first floor, when the three-story, stucco-and-wood structure fell on them, in a pancake effect.

Los Angeles motorcycle officer Clarence Dean died when he drove off an interchange from Interstate 5 to Highway 14 that collapsed during the earthquake.

Art Leahy, former chief executive of Metrolink, the regional commuter rail service, and once head of the county's Metropolitan Transportation Authority, discussed with me the agency's emergency response to the earthquake. At the time, he was MTA's chief operating officer, living in Glendale. He felt the strong tremor, saw his chimney fall off and the TV coming out of the cabinet, and heard car alarms blaring because of the shaking. He ran to his car which had a radio and called the radio dispatcher

"What happened?" "Don't know," was the response. "Do we run service?" "Yes, mobilize everything. We don't know what happened, we don't know the epicenter, we don't know if there's going to be evacuations. Mobilize everything." Leahy jumped in his car and headed for the Southern California Rapid Transit District headquarters. While driving he went through a mental checklist and thought of the subway, remembering there's hydrogen sulfide down there, a colorless gas that is poisonous and flammable. It can kill.

He called radio dispatch. "No one goes in the subway without gas detection and breathing apparatus until we get clearance. And don't operate until we do a complete inspection."

And then he exclaimed, "The subway's only a year old, our billion-dollar subway and I've just shut it down on my authority." Radio dispatch called Leahy to inform him that Alan Pegg, MTA's executive officer for administrator had called Chief Executive Frank White regarding damage to the RTD headquarters at 425 S. Main Street in downtown Los Angeles—known widely as the "Skid Row headquarters." In turn, they authorized vacating the building.

Leahy saw a problem—that is where the radios were. If the building were abandoned, there would be no communication. "Put the CEO's order on abeyance until I get there," he told radio dispatch. It crossed his mind that first, he shut down the subway, then he put the orders of superiors on hold. There was no time to linger on these points.

He said he arrived at the headquarters—the building he hated—and parked across the street, fearful of aftershocks. "When there's a quake the building goes dark. There are no windows." Moreover, he recalled reading a passage in the building's earthquake report that said: "In the event of a maximum expected magnitude quake, of more than 30 seconds in duration, the lateral movements of the walls of the building become disharmonious." When buildings become disharmonious, vertical hinging occurs which can cause major risks. He walked into the building with a silent prayer, "Please no vertical hinging." Leahy climbed the stairs to the fourth floor where the radio was. An hour after the quake, thirty people had also arrived, including top managers in transportation and maintenance. Reporting stations were inspected and put back into service, getting 93 percent of the bus service operational that day.

Early the day after the earthquake, Emerson told me, he and his Clinton administration colleagues were taken to the Rose Bowl to board military Black Hawk helicopters, he and Witt on one and Secretary of Transportation Peña and Secretary of Housing and Urban Development Cisneros on the other, with sliding doors open affording the opportunity to look down. Destruction on a catastrophic scale is what he witnessed. In one exchange in Santa Clara the whole freeway had crumpled, and a portion of the 118 Freeway had collapsed, as had the 10 Freeway by La Cienega Boulevard. He noticed that almost every single house in the San Fernando Valley had a tent pitched in the backyard. People were afraid to sleep in their houses, or in some instances, they could not, he added.

He was struck by another singularity: it was a beautiful day with eighty plus degrees and clear skies—a typical January Indian summer day—the weather evidently apathetic to nature's quaking behavior. But every once in a while, Emerson said, looking out at the hills on the north side of San Fernando Valley he would see big clouds of dust slowly rising. "What's going on down there?" he asked.

"Oh, aftershocks," was the response. He realized, he told me, "That one of the consequences of an earthquake is airborne bacteria that can cause respiratory ailments, so we immediately got hold of the Surgeon General's office and leadership was dispatched to deal with these issues." People were told to wear masks. At night, they returned to the hotel, except for Cisneros. He went to big parks where people had pitched tents and visited with them through the night.

The federal officials visited places in the Valley, Santa Monica, and Hollywood where they witnessed buildings and houses knocked off their foundation. Emerson walked on the

118 Freeway and saw where the freeway disappeared, dropping suddenly ten feet. California State University Northridge suffered major damage. Everywhere walls were knocked down, apart from picket fences.

In the university library, bolts the size of saucers were stripped, having been lifted off by the force of the building as it was shoved upward. "We later found out that the earthquake was a thrust fault, where it moved up and down, rather than a slip fault, which moves sideways," Emerson said. The library literally was lifted off its foundation and dropped back down again."

The earthquake sent people looking for food stamps, but there were concerns. Food stamp outlets were packed and Los Angeles county sheriff Sherman Block, along with county Supervisor Gloria Molina, called Emerson to convey their concerns about possible fraud.

"We opened huge food stamp places at big centers like Costco and supermarkets," Emerson said. Worries about fraud persisted. Emerson decided to deal with this issue later, putting the need to provide food and housing ahead of doubts over dishonesty. "People were allowed to sign under penalty of perjury whether they were eligible or not to obtain food stamps."

I wondered about financial relief for impacted quake victims and Emerson responded that two avenues were made available, one from FEMA and the other from the Small Business Administration (SBA). "FEMA would provide three to six thousand dollars just to help individuals through the next few weeks, to get out of their houses and into rental housing and pay expenses. Proof, of course, was needed regarding where people lived and if their house was red tagged." Because it would take valuable time to obtain documents, Emerson decided to have people sign under penalty of perjury and get the loan quickly, prosecuting possible fraud cases later. "You know, Nick, over a two-to-three-week period over 600,000 people got checks," he said.

Meanwhile, the SBA was offering loans up to $1.5 million at very low interest rates to rebuild businesses with fewer than one thousand employees. The San Fernando Valley had hundreds of businesses with 250 to 500 employees and not many with more than one thousand.

"We changed SBA policy. For a company with more than 250 employees the cap was lifted and whatever money was needed was made available," Emerson said. "Two months later, with Hillary Clinton on the scene, a check was given to an employer of 500 people who were able to rebuild, and he wouldn't have, had we not changed those rules."

Rebuilding houses was another issue that had to be resolved. SBA policy was to lend up to $250,000, but that was not enough for Emerson. "This is Los Angeles," he reasoned. "Property is expensive. Because of the earthquake and demand, construction costs would climb." He discussed this with SBA director Erskine Bowles, who changed the regulation. "Usually in Washington to change regulations takes forever," Emerson said. "We went ahead and did what was needed operating on the tenet that it's better to ask forgiveness than permission."

Peña had an idea on how to expedite freeway rebuilding in record time. Contractors were offered financial incentives to finish construction early. For example, Emerson said, the administration told the contractor that if it completed the freeway in less than 120 days, it would receive a $1 million bonus for each day—in other words if the job is done in ninety days the contractor would receive a $30 million bonus. "Sure enough, it was miraculous breakthrough. Those freeways were rebuilt in ninety days because of a creative change in government policy."

I had envisioned quickly building a busway along the Expo right of way to get traffic moving again because the earthquake's destruction of the 10 Freeway rendered traveling from West Los Angeles to downtown difficult. It was fortunate that Riordan and Wilson had joined forces and essentially removed red tape that hindered public works projects, allowing the freeway to be built within three months.

At the time of the earthquake Los Angeles was in the midst of a severe recession with unemployment in double digits. The peace dividend had caused the aerospace industry, a major employer in the region, to collapse. "What we did," Emerson said, "was pump $16 billion into the regional economy in a six-to-nine-month period. President Clinton had a big hand in helping Los Angeles bounce back." Rocky Delgadillo, Riordan's deputy mayor for economic development, said, "We used the earthquake to create jobs."

He said they knew that $750,000 worth of contracts would create fifteen permanent jobs. A full court press was activated to obtain grants. Then members of his team were sent out to get those who suffered damage to apply. Riordan got some credit for this effort, but Gov. Pete Wilson got more. City Council President John Ferraro had a better approach: Give credit to everyone and get the money with the lowest possible interest rate. "I remember we had an event with Hillary Clinton in the Valley because we had the largest ever Small Business Administration loan to a medical device company which had its building collapse; $9 million dollars at 3 percent," Delgadillo said.

Ron Brown, then secretary of commerce, came here and said, "Look, I want minorities and women to participate," Delgadillo recalled. He was asked how this was to be done. "You figure it out," Brown said, and provided a grant. (Brown, the first African American to hold the position of Secretary of Commerce and chairman of the Democratic National Committee, later died with thirty-four others in a 1996 plane crash in Croatia.)

The grant went to the Minority Business Opportunities Committee, a partnership between the city and Commerce Department that was created just weeks before the quake to help businesses owned by minorities and women. In 1994, a City Council proposal to accept the $767,500 seemed benign, but it came with the condition that Delgadillo be hired as project manager under a $100,000, one-year contract. Councilmember Rita Walters saw it as an intimidation tactic by the federal government, but Councilmember Richard Alatorre said Delgadillo was the best person for the job. The motion passed on a ten to four vote. By July 1995, the Minority Business Opportunities Committee had helped more than ten thousand minority and women run businesses receive a total of $1.1 billion in earthquake-related work.

In reviewing activities in the White House when the earthquake hit, Emerson told me of its "Greek connection," referring to Stephanopoulos. When the president decided to send a team to Los Angeles, Stephanopoulos told Emerson he must also go. Known as "the twins," because he did the work of two people, Stephanopoulos was on top of everything. Emerson described him as "Calm, cool, collected with amazing judgement and an incredible ability to understand volumes of information."

Furthermore, Emerson said Stephanopoulos was, like Clinton, equally adept at politics and policy. "That's why they connected so well during the campaign."

Wilson had come under fire from the Clinton administration for his slow pace in safeguarding vulnerable freeway bridges from earthquakes. In response, the governor authorized the use of emergency powers to speed the work on some spans within Los Angeles County. The new authority made it easier to hire outside engineers to retrofit some fifty bridges damaged by the quake—amounting to 8 percent of the six hundred bridges identified as being vulnerable.

The *Los Angeles Times* reported on February 18, 1994, that Caltrans' chief bridge engineer, James E. Roberts, said, "It's a start. We'll be able to reconstruct and retrofit these bridges simultaneously and hope to get more from him later." Without the governor's action retrofitting the structures with jackets of steel reinforcements would not be completed as quickly as rebuilding or refurbishing of bridges. The *Los Angeles Times* had reported one week earlier that 80 percent of the 1,313 bridges statewide had been identified as being vulnerable to earthquakes. Wilson had said it was uncertainty whether the procedure to rebuild and refurbish bridges could be expanded to regions not directly affected by the earthquake.

In retrospect, the epicenter of the 1994 Northridge Earthquake turned out to be the Los Angeles neighborhood of Reseda—three and one-half mile south of Northridge. It left more than 100,000 people temporarily homeless, fifty-seven dead, and about 9,000 injured, including 1,600 who were treated at hospitals. The quake also damaged 66,546 buildings and left 48,500 without water or power for at least a day.

Many changes were implemented in the aftermath of the 1994 Northridge Earthquake, including the passage of legislation to reinforce freeway bridges and update building codes to help ensure the region is better prepared for another major seismic event. Some twenty years after the Northridge killer quake, Los Angeles Mayor Eric Garcetti signed into law a mandatory building retrofit ordinance to ensure the city's most vulnerable buildings were strengthened to prevent loss of life in a major earthquake. The ordinance was introduced by then City Councilmember Gil Cedillo. Garcetti praised Cedillo's work along with that of Lucy Jones, a world-renowned seismologist and public voice for earthquake science and earthquake safety in California.

Cedillo at the time of the Northridge quake was general manager of the Service Employees International Union Local 660, Los Angeles County's largest union. He recalled working with the office of then Councilmember Richard Alarcon. They took three hundred volunteers on buses to the San Fernando Valley, where they were deputized by FEMA, trained, and then sent out to evaluate and "red tag" buildings accordingly.

Garcetti had vowed to "make good on our promises to take action before it is too late." Aware of coming earthquakes, he required building safety retrofits before they struck. By strengthening the buildings and protecting the community, lives can be saved, and social and economic effects can be avoided. Key to ensuring life preservation and economic resiliency in a major earthquake, the ordinance focused on two of the most vulnerable types of buildings: those made of nonductile reinforced concrete and soft first-story buildings that have wood frames and large openings on the first floor for tuck-under parking, garage doors and retail display windows. Some 13,500 soft, first-story buildings were identified by the Department of Building and Safety and about 1,500 nonductile, reinforced concrete buildings were affected according to a study released by the University of California, Berkeley. The city's first-ever chief resilience officer, Marissa Aho, was charged with implementing recommendations of the report, titled "Resilience by Design."

In a February 15, 2023, opinion piece in the *Los Angeles Times*, Jones expressed alarm about what a magnitude 7.8 earthquake—like the one that hit the Turkey-Syrian region—would do to Los Angeles. Reuters reported that the death toll from the February 6, 2023, earthquake had surpassed 50,000.

Jones wrote that when an earthquake of the same strength happens on the San Andreas fault, we will see death and destruction, perhaps not as extensive as seen in Turkey, but much worse than most people expect." The founder of the Dr. Lucy Jones Center for Science and Society and author of The Big Ones: How Natural Disasters Have Shaped us (and What We Can Do About Them?), also said that rather than the post-earthquake usable buildings many people think are guaranteed by the building code, the current code asks only that our building try not to collapse.

Buildings are only as good as the building code in place at the time they were constructed and the degree to which that code was enforced, she wrote. "Problems with enforcement of the code in new construction and the lack of retrofitting of old, bad buildings will contribute to the California death toll when the next big earthquake comes." Jones said that our engineers and scientists have developed standards for a "functionary recovery' code—that is, a building code that aims to give us structures that can be repaired after a major tremblor, whose function can be recovered. "Needless to say, functional recovery is a safer standard for human survival as well as building survival," she wrote.

There were lessons that were learned from the Northridge quake. Michael Gurnis, director of the Seismological Laboratory at California Institute of Technology, said researchers have learned more about where earthquakes are likely to happen, and how danger to human life and damage to property might be mitigated when they do occur. Northridge was a devastating earthquake for Los Angeles, and there was a massive amount of damage, Gurnis says in a 2014 Caltech article titled "Lessons from the Northridge Quake." "But in some sense, we stepped up to the plate after Northridge to determine what we could do better. And as a result, we have ushered in an era of dense, high-fidelity geophysical networks on top of hazardous faults. We've exploited these networks to better understand how earthquakes occur, and we've pushed the limits such that we are now at the dawn of a new era of earthquake early warning in the United States."

All of that, he said, was because of the Northridge Earthquake.

EAST LOS ANGELES PRISON CONTROVERSY

There was an urgency in the mid-1980s to build a state prison in Los Angeles County—an urgency that turned into a vigorous political debate and gave birth to a mothers' grassroots movement.

For some, the dominant justification for the prison was the issue of fairness. After all, Los Angeles County sends thousands of inmates to prisons every year but had no state prison of its own. Backers wanted the facility to be built in East Los Angeles. Residents of East Los Angeles opposed the plan, saying it was neither fair nor impartial, but heavily tainted with racism against the Mexican American community near the projected prison site. It had happened before. Government planners had used public projects to dissect East Los Angeles with five freeways and clear it of housing.

I knew Frank Villalobos, chairman of the Coalition Against the Prison in East Los Angeles, as he had been an architect of Red Line Subway stations, and I was aware of his involvement in the Eastside community. I had been the electrical engineer of the new state prison, named the California Reception Center, for the architecture firm, Dworsky Associates. Greg Serrao the project manager for Dworsky, said, "The team was not aware of the communities' strong opposition to the project. The construction documents were issued to the state for bidding. The state, under separate contract, cleared the site, and removed hazardous materials, which made the site ready for construction."

I wanted to learn more about the community's concerns and arranged an interview with Villalobos. "Our community had already taken more than our share," Villalobos told me. He had organized a community protest in Sacramento against the prison's location in August 1986 when bitter fighting in the Legislature pitted elected officials who supported the prison against those who sought to keep the prison out of their districts.

Villalobos, FAIA landscape architect and president of Barrio Planners, also disclosed to me a little-known story involving then Gov. George Deukmejian, the leading advocate for the East Los Angeles site. According to Villalobos, Deukmejian, while flying home to Long Beach, looked over East Los Angeles and sighed, "Well, look at that, that's a pretty site for a prison."

To establish veracity, Villalobos said, "It was in the newspapers," As a matter of fact, he added, Mayor Tom Bradley, who ran against Deukmejian for governor, saw the story and called the comment disdainful. "We knew Bradley was with us and against an Eastside location." Bradley backed a proposed prison site in Saugus.

Through my association with Richard Alatorre and Art Torres, who were state legislators at the time, I had befriended Villalobos in the 1970s, a time when few from the Westside or the San Fernando Valley would cross Broadway and enter the Eastside. In the view of many, Villalobos had become a "godfather" of East Los Angeles, a perceptive fighter protecting the rights of his community.

Villalobos informed me of another fascinating personal narrative. In 1982, when Governor Jerry Brown was considering building a prison in Los Angeles County, one possible site considered was thirty acres at Santa Fe Avenue at the end of Twelfth Street. The owner, Crown Coach, was known for its yellow school buses. At the time Villalobos was working on the Plaza del Sol project, the first indoor mall conceived for East Los Angeles. While at City Hall to present the idea at the Planning Department, he overheard architects presenting their concept for a prison. "You remember, Nick," he said, "it was open counters in those days, just one big table, and you could hear the person next to you." The conversation he heard covered the number of prison beds, traffic, no requirements for an environmental evaluation." "God put me there," he told me, because it was how he became aware of the prison plan for East Los Angeles.

So, he went to then Assemblywoman Gloria Molina. "Are you aware of that?" he asked. She explained that the Japanese community was building a museum and Deukmejian had promised them money if Torres agreed with the prison location. Alatorre had also been contacted, according to Molina. "Pitting allies against each other," Villalobos said, angered by the politics. "The Japanese community had been wonderful to us. We related to each other. We did not want disunity."

Villalobos sought out Steven Kasten, a realtor in Lincoln Heights, and Carmine Botho, both presidents of Boyle Heights chambers of commerce. Molina and many nonprofit organizations joined them in creating the Coalition Against the Prison in East Los Angeles.

Torres and Alatorre were the powerhouses, and people were reluctant to go against them, Villalobos said. When the Mothers of East Los Angeles were organized to fight the prison, Torres' mother and father joined the group, to Villalobos's relief. "When we marched with 8,000 people against the prison, Art and Richard were with us," Villalobos said with a smile.

"The turning point for us was Sen. David Roberti, an Italian neighborhood guy," Villalobos said. Roberti met with him and Monsignor John Moretta of Resurrection Catholic Church, and after heated discussions "with the F word" tossed around, Roberti said, succinctly, "The real danger in putting another prison in East LA would bring you down and create a penal colony for you. We don't want that. You will become a free society if I can help it."

Deukmejian and his staff badly underestimated the resentment of East Los Angeles residents, who already had three large county jails in their neighborhood. Nevertheless, state prison officials maintained that the only acceptable site for them was the industrial area just across the river from predominantly Latino Boyle Heights. East Los Angeles consists of six square miles of unincorporated county territory, as well as Los Angeles neighborhoods such as Boyle Heights.

East Los Angeles, which is known as an immigrant gateway community, had struggled with existing public sentiments against Mexican Americans and anti-immigrant rhetoric and numerous legislative initiatives targeting them. Alatorre, born and raised there, had been elected to the State Assembly and had quickly developed into the most influential Latino politician in the state. He had embarked on his lifelong drive to gain equality and racial justice through equitable Mexican American political representation.

Through Villalobos, the prison discussions led to meetings, and meetings gave birth to organized protests. Suddenly, mothers coalesced to fight it. A prison near their homes was unacceptable. Molina, who in 1982 became the first Latina elected to the state Legislature, drew wide attention to the prison plan and began to rally support in opposition. So did Moretta who guided the mothers and named them Mothers of East Los Angeles. With church funds, he bought white sheets and had them cut into mantillas, scarves to be worn to symbolize nonviolence principles. Swiftly, they joined the Coalition Against the Prison in East Los Angeles, directed by Villalobos, Kasten, and Botho. An unceasing protest, visible and determined, was set in motion.

I was fully aware that Deukmejian had piloted the largest prison expansion in state history, from twelve to twenty-eight sites, and mentioned it to Molina. "It was awful," she said, "and they had decided to put the new state prison in my district." "Who cares?" she said facetiously, mocking their assumed conversation. "Put it there, the least number of voters, a bunch of Mexicans."

"Deukmejian was a nice man, but his aide was a tough-talking guy who wore boots and was rough," Molina told me, as she reminisced. "He cut all the deals for Deukmejian." When the subject of another site was suggested, Steven Merksamer, the governor's chief of staff, rejected the proposal, declaring to a reporter, "It's not under discussion. This is the best site."

Molina told me how it became necessary to appeal to powerful Assembly Speaker Willie Brown, a Democrat, for support. "Tough luck," Brown told her. "That's the way it goes. Somebody's gotta eat it, and it is yours." Provoked, Molina called on her friends in the Assembly for support, got it, and began to beat up on the administration with every opportunity. "They couldn't get it out of committee," she remembered, blocking the bill. "It was killing, killing Willie and Deukmejian and everyone who supported a prison for East LA."

The battle lines were clear from the start, and both sides had powerful advocates. Sen. Robert Presley (D-Riverside) had introduced a bill in 1985 to allow the state to move ahead quickly with the purchase of the controversial prison site, but it fell one vote short of passage in the Senate. He blamed several Republicans who departed early to attend a $1,000-a-plate fundraiser featuring President Reagan at the Century Plaza Hotel in Los Angeles.

Torres, a state senator whose district included the proposed prison site, pleaded with his colleagues to turn down the purchase because of a precedent it could set in allowing big state projects without thorough environmental reviews, according to Leo C. Wolinsky of the *Los Angeles Times*. "Forget about the fact that you are going to put a prison in my district," Torres said. "Think about your own constituents in your districts and let that be on your conscience." Torres unsuccessfully attempted to block Presley's bill by rewriting provisions on the floor to require a full environmental review before the property could be purchased. "They shoved other things down our throats in East LA, like freeways," Torres said. "I'm sure they will have the power to shove a prison down our throats." I asked Molina, "Were there helpful legislators you specifically remember?"

"Art Agnos would not fold, neither would Burt Margolin. Many others gave me their strong support," she said. "Unfortunately, that's when Richard Polanco got elected, in 1986." Polanco was elected to fill the seat vacated by Alatorre, a supporter of the protest, after he became a Los Angeles City Councilman. Molina then described for me how an interesting scenario was staged. Polanco was sworn in at noon, had a little reception for lunch, then rushed off to the Assembly Judiciary Committee to be sworn in and to vote at 1:30 p.m. His vote got the prison bill out of committee. "It went to the Assembly floor, and I lost," she lamented.

After the Assembly vote the bill went to the Senate and "flew through there," Molina said. It landed on the governor's desk. Later, Merksamer called and told her the governor wanted to see her.

"First time I met Deukmejian," she told me. "He invited me to sit down." She noticed all her bills, good bills that had passed almost unanimously with bipartisan support, dealing with such things as high school dropouts, were in front of him. She was handed a yellow pad. "Write down which bills you want me to sign," Deukmejian said. "All of them." "I would be happy to sign all of them. But I need you to accept the prison in East LA," was the governor's response. "I can't," Molina said. "I just can't."

It was an unbearable meeting, she disclosed to me, "sitting there with the governor, being hijacked, and realizing that all my bills were going to get killed." "I can't," she repeated. "Well, I am going to sign the prison bill anyway, you know that. I want you to accept it." "I can't," Molina repeated. Merksamer intensified the anxiety in the room with his own declaration. "You will have all your bills vetoed. The prison bill has already passed the legislature, all we want you to do is accept it." Shaking her head, she repeated her stance, and resentfully watched as her bills were vetoed while the prison bill was signed.

In 1986, Molina successfully ran for and became a Los Angeles City Council member, taking the fight against the prison to City Hall. She persuaded the council to hire the law firm of O'Melveny & Myers to defend a lawsuit filed by Villalobos and his associates against the prison site. A $1-million allowance for the defense was authorized. Villalobos recounted for me all the work done by the city attorney and how the community had won the support of the National Resources Defense Council.

A foremost point of disagreement was Deukmejian's position that a required environmental assessment for the East Los Angeles prison site would be undertaken only after the property was purchased. Two other prisons that would be authorized in the same bill—one in Del Norte County and another in Madera County—would have full environmental studies before any steps were taken to purchase property.

Roberti, the Senate president pro tem, had become a visible and insistent opponent of the East Los Angeles site. He suggested creating a three-member panel to make a judgment on the timing of an environmental review. The committee met and voted 2 to 1 for a review after the purchase. It was the no vote of a Cal Poly Pomona professor that gave the prison opponents the right to go to court. "If it was unanimous, if there had been three votes against us," Villalobos said, "they would have built it."

The East Los Angeles prison opponents now had funds and attorneys in place to escalate their fight.

Attorneys and lawsuits translate into money and time, and the California Department of Corrections feared the dispute would result in a decade-long stall. It sought an alternative, as Villalobos related details to me. "Sen. Roberti comes in and sits with Willie Brown and we're sitting at the negotiating table with Torres and Molina. Mothers of East LA are also there.

Polanco is a persona non grata, an unwelcome person, and nobody wants to talk to him. He had stabbed us in the back."

Remarkably, a second site for the prison was invented: Lancaster. A speedy, unannounced visit to the Lancaster city manager led to a discussion with the local Chamber of Commerce and the second prison site idea appeared acceptable. Lancaster emerged as an official site when the Legislature approved a "pain-for-pain compromise" to put one prison in the largely Republican high desert area and another in the Democratic East Los Angeles area. However, the protests would not diminish.

But in June 1991, a legislative conference committee voted to transfer $130 million earmarked for the East Los Angeles prison to an alternative site in the San Joaquin Valley, a decision that the Mothers of East LA ecstatically celebrated as a victory after a six-year battle.

"My heart is bursting with joy," Juana Gutierrez, a fifty-nine-year-old mother of nine who helped form the group in 1985, told the *Los Angeles Times*.

However, it remained unclear whether Governor Pete Wilson would go along with the committee's decision when the budget was finally presented to him. "Tens of millions of dollars had been contractually obligated," Bill Livingstone, the governor's press secretary had said. "He's not planning to make any decision until the budget is completed and on his desk."

Pressures mounted. The Latino Legislative Caucus in Sacramento yearned to block construction funds for the East Los Angeles prison, thereby attracting additional attention from the governor who faced his own budget crisis. Assemblyman Polanco, once deemed a proponent for the prison, now chaired the caucus, which advocated blockage of the funds to build it. It was this action that later earned him the mothers' group forgiveness.

Indeed, on Monday, Sept. 14, 1991, the governor signed legislation aimed at opening a new prison in the Antelope Valley and ending plans for the bitterly opposed East Los Angeles prison. The action terminated a divisive battle between the "sagebrush" site and the "barrio" site. The measure that Wilson signed was written by Sen. Torres.

The Mothers of East Los Angeles generated headlines and gained support, becoming a formidable force in political circles and a valuable resource for others who sought social justice. When it was announced that a hazardous waste incinerator was going to be constructed in the City of Vernon, adjacent to homes, schools, hospitals and churches, Assemblywoman Lucille Roybal Allard gathered support from Mothers of East Los Angeles which quickly organized protest marches. Eventually, the mothers sued the US Environmental Protection Agency for failure to provide an environmental impact report. Fierce opposition to the incinerator led to the proposal being dropped in 1991.

How mothers mobilized to protest, and how they generated local and national headlines by fighting against all odds, and winning, is a political playbook with strategies and winning plays for others to follow. The Mothers of East Los Angeles became a legend.

THE WAR AGAINST SMOG

Comedian Bob Hope used to say that in Los Angeles you can wake up in the morning and hear the birds…coughing.

In the summer of 1943, during World War II, a major dose of unbearable air pollution alarmed the populace. Four years later, on June 10, 1947, California governor Earl Warren signed a statute passed by the state Legislature that allowed counties to create their own smog-fighting agencies. Later that year, Los Angeles County became the first to do so when it formed the Los Angeles County Air Pollution Control District. It was also the first of its kind in the nation. The epic "war against smog" began.

But no one knew what smog was. The word was coined to refer to smoke and fog due to its opacity, and odor. On smoggy days in downtown Los Angeles, one couldn't see across the street. Los Angeles's elected leaders—especially the county supervisors—exerted political will and unparalleled creativity to counter this infamous phenomenon.

With the backing of the supervisors, the Air Pollution Control District immediately launched the most vigorous and massive assault ever against this dangerous environmental occurrence. Obvious sources of visible air pollution were controlled first, such as open burning dumps and smokestacks. Next came restraints on industrial dust, smoke, vapor, mists and fumes, and the banning of the backyard incinerator. Every home had one, and during evenings household trash was burned making every home a source of billowing black soot. By 1958, rules enacted by the district had achieved dramatic results: Oil refinery fumes were cut from 800 tons a day to 150 tons a day, industrial smoke was reduced from one hundred tons a day to twenty-five tons a day, and the banning of the county's 1.5 million backyard burners resulted in the elimination of eight hundred tons of pollution a day. Despite pollution controls on stationary sources, the smog problem persisted, and even worsened. The auto industry purposely ignored the local plight.

I have known Jim Birakos since the early 1970s. For more than twenty-five years he provided leadership on air pollution issues, so much that the *Los Angeles Times* wrote, "when you speak of smog in Los Angeles the operative name is Birakos." He explained that scientists for the Air Pollution Control District discovered evidence of a unique and complex chemical reaction occurring in the atmosphere: Emissions of hydrocarbons and oxides of nitrogen were reacting in the presence of sunlight to irritate the eyes, sting the nose, and reduce visibility, in addition to numerous other complications.

Jim Birakos outlining the AQMD plans for the 1984 Summer Olympics

I had worked with Jim on many occasions from my early years at the Southern California Rapid Transit District, when reducing the number of cars on the road was an important strategy in fighting air pollution. And we operated in tandem when he evaluated sites and times for the 1984 Summer Olympics in Los Angeles—to avoid scheduling athletic events during elevated smog—and I guided the transportation system with new customized routes and the creation of a temporary transit system of venue-to-venue shuttles, express buses, and park-and-ride lots. For the sixteen-day Olympic period, a city with a global reputation for traffic, freeways, and smog was transformed into a more efficient, accessible, and healthy community.

As Birakos explained to me, the air quality problem that afflicted Los Angeles was caused mostly by motor vehicles, and it had a real name: photochemical smog. The air district's senior scientist, Walter Hamming, along with Margaret Fox Brunelle, had taken their discovery to Arie Jan Haagen-Smit, an Air Pollution Control District consultant and professor at the California Institute of Technology whose interest was smog's effect on crops. "Haagie" later became known as the father of photochemical smog controls and was first the chairman of the California Air Resources Board in 1968. (Birakos disclosed to me a little-known but important historical fact. In 1967, Governor Ronald Reagan appointed the air district's control officer, Louis J. Fuller, to that post. After conducting the California Air Resources Board's first meeting in Sacramento, Fuller loathed traveling and changed his mind. In turn the Air Pollution Control District recommended Haagen-Smit for the post.)

THE NUMBER ONE SMOG CULPRIT

Los Angeles was always considered to be a haven for the private motor vehicle: a sprawling, attractive landscape made famous by Hollywood and adorned with beaches, mountains, alluring deserts—a picture-perfect postcard, from all angles. One could go skiing in the mountains and swim at nearby beaches on the same day. Although the private car made Los Angeles a perennial summer holiday, it also turned the city into an environmental nightmare.

The private car was the perfect smog maker. It spewed contaminants that were the perfect smog mix. Ten percent of the gasoline in the tank in an uncontrolled car ended up raw in the atmosphere thus forming the reactive hydrocarbons. Also emitted by internal combustion engines were the oxides of nitrogen. The sun then provided the energy to create the photochemical reaction that resulted in high smog levels, quantities unmatched anywhere in the world. Los Angeles's early morning brilliance disappeared, and so did the blue skies. There were days when cars traveled with their headlights on in downtown Los Angeles, at high noon.

The Los Angeles County Air Pollution Control District, with vigorous political support, developed and adopted more than one hundred rules and regulations that included prohibitions for sulfur compounds, combustion contaminants, carbon monoxide, gasoline loading, storage of petroleum products, solvent usage, and fuel burning equipment. A unique engineering permit system was created and implemented to prevent problems. Specific conditions to ensure compliance were carefully spelled out, and a surveillance and enforcement program was instituted to confirm the strict operations of plants. The district's enforcement division would write up 350 companies each month, with all ending up in the courts. Its black-and-white units with red lights and sirens and officers dressed like highway patrolmen photographed and cited smoky trucks for visible violations. The early leadership at the District under S. Smith Griswold, Lou Fuller, and Bob Chass brought innovative changes and control over industrial sources. Yet smog persisted, with levels climbing rather than falling.

The public was getting tired of the annoying diatribe over smog and the daily negative reports and front-page disclosures. Then Board of Supervisors chairman Warren Dorn, a former mayor of Pasadena who won his board seat on an anti-smog platform, brought in Birakos to resuscitate the beleaguered agency. Birakos was the senior information and education officer for the county under the chief administrative officer and president of the county's public information officers' association. Birakos was elevated to division director at the Air Pollution Control District and was charged with influencing changes in the control program and regaining public support for the agency, which was viewed as ineffectual by an annoyed public and a stubborn press.

I led the campaign in 1992 at the Southern California Rapid Transit District to replace diesel buses with ultra-clean compressed natural gas buses. The CNG buses are about 1,000 times cleaner than diesel. Los Angeles now can claim that it operates one of the largest clean-air fleets in the United States. In another major milestone, Metro operates all-electric buses on the Metro G (Orange) Line in the San Fernando Valley.

In 1967, Los Angeles County's population had doubled from the war years to seven million residents, and the number of private cars had tripled to more than 3.5 million. Healthful air quality in Los Angeles depended on controlling the motor vehicle. But the "Big Four" automakers—American Motors, Chrysler, Ford Motor Co., and General Motors, along with their trade group, the Automobile Manufacturers Association, not only refused to help but also plotted to delay the use of pollution-control devices for motor vehicles.

THE CONSPIRACY OF THE AUTOMAKERS

In 1947, Kenneth Hahn became the youngest person, at age twenty-six, to be elected to the Los Angeles City Council. Two years later, he complained that due to smog he could hardly breathe in his office and called for a report on the worsening smog conditions, his first step in a long journey of combatting smog and in supporting all anti-smog measures.

A year after being elected to the Los Angeles County Board of Supervisor in 1952, he wrote to Henry Ford II, chief executive officer of Ford Motor, to ask what his company knew about automobile pollution and what plans the company had. The response provoked Hahn and the anger never left him. Incredibly, Ford had written that there really was no problem and, therefore, no need for research. Years later, Hahn still remembered, "The Ford engineering staff, although mindful that automobile engines produce gases, feels that these waste vapors are dissipated in the atmosphere quickly and do not present an air pollution problem."

Hahn continued his writing campaign for fourteen years, again being told at one point by an auto company president that its cars don't pollute, but they might discharge a puff of smoke though that was the fault of the driver.

But the Air Pollution Control District knew better. Then Director S. Smith Griswold had told the supervisors that automotive pollution control devices had been available for decades, having acquired specific data from studying patents. Further, it was discovered that in 1953 the automakers had made a joint cooperative agreement, supposedly to pool their research on air pollution and come up with a solution. In essence, however, it was agreed that no manufacturer would break ranks and introduce control systems.

Hahn saw it for what it was: a clear-cut conspiracy. A resolution by the Board of Supervisors in January 1965 asked the US attorney general to initiate an investigation and take legal action to prevent the automakers from engaging in "further collusive obstruction." A federal grand jury convened in Los Angeles for eighteen months. There was debate over whether the grand jury should seek a criminal or civil indictment, and the civil route won out. Major players, including Lloyd Cutler, a well-known attorney at the Washington, DC, law firm of Wilmer, Cutler & Pickering who represented the Automobile Manufacturers Association and consumer advocate Ralph Nader, friend of the Air Pollution Control District, briefed Justice Department officials on the possibility of a major antitrust suit.

In 1969, while testifying on an upcoming rule before the district board, Birakos was asked to investigate a rumor that a solution to the smog conspiracy was in the works. Indeed, on September 11, 1969, the Justice Department announced that the case would be settled by consent decree. "What was the purpose of that decree?" I inquired. "There were no admissions of guilt," Birakos replied. "In other words, the automakers promised they would stop doing what they said they were never doing."

Hahn was furious. He wanted the automakers to go on trial in Los Angeles. He asked Thomas Lynch, California's attorney general, to file a separate antitrust action but was told that the seal on the grand jury records hampered the process. "I received a call from Hahn asking me to hurry to his office," Birakos told me. "When I arrived, he introduced me to the foreman of the grand jury, Martin Walshbren, who was also agitated over the consent decree." There was a roomful of grand jury evidence, he said, and if the Justice Department had sought an indictment, the grand jury would have brought it.

THE MOTHER OF ALL SMOG BATTLES

Two years before the consent decree, the mother of all smog battles with the auto industry was set on the biggest stage of all, the floor of the House of Representatives in Washington, DC. Pending was the Air Quality Act of 1967. Tired of California's intervention in the affairs of their industry, the automakers crafted an amendment that would have the state's program dictated by Washington.

A month earlier, in meetings with members of the Senate Subcommittee on Air and Water Pollution, chaired by Senator Edmund S. Muskie (D-Maine), Birakos and other officials had argued for separate, tougher laws for California because it faced the worst problems. Senator George Murphy (R-California) wrote and presented an amendment that passed the Senate unanimously, providing California a waiver from the federal law and the right to impose more restrictive automobile emission standards.

The automakers wrote an amendment to be guided by Representative John Dingell (D-Michigan). Known as the Dingell Amendment, it replaced the Murphy Amendment. If adopted by the House, clean air could never be restored in Los Angeles. The supervisors directed Birakos to launch an intensive campaign against the Dingell Amendment and to take the fight to Washington, DC, Birakos immediately began a crusade calling for the defeat of the Dingell amendment. He teamed up with investigative reporter Al Wiman and Joe Pyne, the era's confrontational radio and television talk host heard nationally, to produce "Breathe of Death," a series targeting the Dingell Amendment that aired over a two-week period on KLAC, the area's only talk radio station. More than a half million pieces of mail were received by the district and the station, and an airline and a moving van company volunteered to deliver the hefty mail bags to Washington, DC. In a distinctive first, all thirty-seven members of the California congressional delegation were present when the mail bags were emptied on the Capitol steps, an act photographed and published by news outlets around the nation.

Birakos recalled for me additional steps that were taken in Washington as the House debate drew closer. He said that for days votes were sought in every Congressional office building, the Capitol rotunda was plastered with large photographs of Los Angeles during a smog siege, and each representative was given a can of "Genuine Los Angeles Smog." Slowly, calculatingly, the nations' attention was drawn to the upcoming floor fight. Cutler, known as the Capitol mandarin, headed the lobbying assault for the automakers, often before or after Birakos's visit to congressmen.

A key suggestion by Senator Robert Kennedy (D-New York) swung the vote in California's favor. One morning in the elevator, Kennedy told Birakos to contact Southern leaders and demand they support California's "state's rights." Together, they prepared a list of key Congressional players, and Birakos searched them out, reporting to Kennedy daily results and obtaining more political insight.

Later, during the bitter floor debate, Dingell said, "There has been a great deal of smog today and not all of it is in California." He called the state's rights issue a red herring. Angrily, he said, "I have tried to clear up the smog of misunderstanding, ignorance and misrepresentation which has surrounded this amendment through the efforts of certain persons in California." When the final vote came, the Dingell Amendment was defeated—just by a handful of votes. The federal standards would not apply in California if the state had more stringent rules. Consequently, each year California implemented more stringent standards, and the federal government followed. The California waiver forced the auto industry to control its polluting products. Every automaker was required to make two types of vehicles, one for California and another for the rest of the nation. It was a political slugfest and a victory won against all odds.

Before the House debate, Los Angeles County supervisors had sought the state's help in the Dingell Amendment fight, but their request was rejected by Governor Reagan who considered it to be a lost cause. After all, he claimed, Washington was governed by a president and a Congress from the same party and would not reject its own committee's amendment. But it did. When victory came, he sent the California Air Resources Board executive officer, Eric Grant, to Washington. At a victory celebration held by the California Heritage Society, Representative Chet Holifield, dean of the California congressional delegation, got wind of Grant's presence and promptly asked him to leave.

"The return to Los Angeles was memorable," Birakos told me. He was met at the airport by the supervisors and a band. For his efforts in defeating the Dingell Amendment, which promised the state`s air quality would constantly improve, Birakos was named to the list of "25 People who Changed Los Angeles" by Los Angeles Magazine.

AUTO INDUSTRY CONTINUES TO STALL

Clearly, the victory for California in Congress was a major turning point. It might even be said that the battle against smog was won during a smoglesss, cold, and rainy day in Washington, DC, on November 2, 1967. It took constant pressure against the auto industry, and the United States Environmental Protection Agency, which was formed in 1970, and the California Air Resources Board, to keep the program honest and moving forward. For example, the auto industry wanted the standard to be an average of all cars coming off the assembly line, a position supported by the California Air Resources Board. The Los Angeles County Air Pollution Control District demanded that each vehicle must meet the standards. Again, Los Angele County prevailed.

Because of constant local pressure cars became cleaner, and the rest of the nation and the world benefitted. In 1970, the lead in gasoline was phased out, a dangerous pollutant that at high levels can cause behavioral problems and even brain damage in children. Although lead did present health concerns, the immediate reason for its removal was that it poisoned the catalytic converter which had become the heart and soul of vehicular emissions control.

From the very beginning controlling emissions from motor vehicles was a priority for the Air Pollution Control District, so much that it had established its own motor vehicle control laboratory. However, it was felt that California, with ten percent of the national car market, could be a significant pressure point for Detroit, and the district sponsored legislation that created the Motor Vehicle Pollution Control Board. The air district's lab was turned over to the new entity. Seven years later, in 1967, the board was merged by law with the Bureau of Air Sanitation to form the California Air Resources Board.

I knew that public transit made a major difference in the quality of our air and the use of natural resources. More people are moved efficiently, compared with the Los Angeles habit of having one person per vehicle. Further, a bus emits only 20 percent as much carbon monoxide per passenger mile as a single-occupant car, and only 10 percent as many hydrocarbons, per passenger mile. Trains emit only 25 percent as much nitrogen oxides per passenger mile as a single-occupant car, and nearly 100 percent less hydrocarbons and carbon monoxide. That was the driving force for me.

Despite California's pressure, automobile manufacturers failed to meet standards with their early control systems (from 1967–1970) after only a few thousand miles—another disclosure made by Birakos and the Air Pollution Control District. Further, to meet the tough laws, operation of the car's engines was altered through leaner carburetion and changes in injection timing, which resulted in a 50 percent increase in the discharge of oxides of nitrogen. It took half a dozen years to bring this contaminant to the pre-control level.

POLITICAL PRESSURES ON THE AIR POLLUTION CONTROL DISTRICT

During the 1970s, claiming that smog knows no political boundaries and incapable of implementing the tough Los Angeles regulations, San Bernardino, Riverside and Orange counties pressed the legislature to create a regional air agency in the four counties. In Birakos's mind this was a political move undertaken to derail the tough Los Angeles program. Behind the concept was an attempt to take political control of regional air pollution control. Twice the legislature passed bills to create a mandatory regional air district, but both measures were vetoed by Governor Reagan.

To avoid interference, in 1975 a voluntary agency composed of the four counties (Los Angeles, Orange, Riverside and San Bernardino) was created, but it was short lived because a county could easily withdraw from the agency. In 1976, the legislature again passed a bill creating a regional air pollution district, and this time Governor Jerry Brown, making good on a campaign promise, signed the measure forming the South Coast Air Quality Management District.

SMOG AND THE 1984 LOS ANGELES OLYMPICS

The 1984 Summer Olympics put Los Angeles through an intriguing and compelling smog examination. The charter of the Olympic Games requires Olympiads to be held "under conditions as perfect as possible." Would Los Angeles meet that challenge? "What did we do to silence skeptics, and there were many," I asked Jim. "A few years before the Games of 1984, and in order to win the bid, we developed charts comparing Los Angeles with previous Olympic cities," he told me. "We showed that Tokyo and Mexico City, specifically, had pollution levels worse than Los Angeles during their Games."

For the period of the Los Angeles Games, big business and industry, including refineries and chemical plants, were asked to voluntarily cut production by 20 percent, and they did. Events were scheduled around anticipated high smog levels, as identified by Birakos. For example, athletic events at the Los Angeles Memorial Coliseum were held in the morning, stopped at noon, and resumed in the afternoon when smog had been swept away, traveling its regular inland route.

To prevent problems for the athletes, air monitoring equipment was set up at each site. If pollution levels rose to the unhealthful category, events would be postponed. For soccer, held in Pasadena—an area of high pollution levels—all matches took place in early evening when smog had moved eastward. Of great concern were the men's and women's marathons. But they were scheduled for early morning and late afternoon when smog levels were low, and they were routed through beach communities that are rarely affected by air pollution.

Sports Illustrated scoffed at Birakos's comment regarding anticipated levels of smog during the marathons. "James N. Birakos, offers comforting assurances concerning apprehensions that Olympic marathoners might suffer from oppressive smog and heat. In so doing Birakos makes a statement that, coming from an Angeleno, is truly remarkable. The statement amounts to a testimonial to LA's fiercest intrastate civic rival. Pointing out that the starting times for the Olympic marathons—8 a.m. on Sunday, Aug. 5 for the women's and 5:25 p.m. the following Sunday for the men's—are scheduled during periods of traditionally low smog and that the LA course hugs the Pacific much of the way, Birakos says, unflinchingly, "In that part of town, the quality of air, even in the summertime, is comparable to what they have in San Francisco. " Despite the stringent planning, the sky fell on Los Angeles just days before the start of the Games. A severe smog attack blanketed much of Los Angeles. The *New York Times* reported that of the first twelve days of July, an Olympic month, the first eleven had smog alerts. The winds were feeble, the inversion layer was at surface levels and the potent sun cooked up the contaminants. "Everything was perfect for smog," Birakos was quoted as saying. And indeed, the smog siege raised new worries regarding the Games.

Supervisor Hahn called for a smog summit to bring together top business and industrial leaders, chambers of commerce, and refiners, and to ask for more sacrifices, lest the Games be remembered for pollution and not athletic achievement. The day of the summit, with the conference room at the Hall of Administration packed, Hahn welcomed attendees and said he had special things to say, new strategies and proposals for immediate smog abatement. The pleas worked. With Birakos in strong support, additional voluntary reductions were applied, and the support of business and industry was honorably noted. The image of the city, the reputation of the Games and the leadership of Los Angeles mayor Tom Bradley and Hahn was conserved. It appeared that even the ancient Olympian gods collaborated. Slowly, gradually, the smog siege lifted, and the grand 1984 Summer Olympics were held without the slightest air pollution problem.

NEWER MOTOR VEHICLE STRATEGIES

Methanol and natural gas as motor vehicle fuels were advocated in the 1980s. Methanol never became a dominant alternate fuel, but the oil companies recognized the coming mandate and significantly cleaned up gasoline. In the 1990s, the California Air Resources Board adopted a landmark regulation aimed at both vehicles and the fuels used by them. Through a Low Emission/Zero Emission Vehicle program, auto manufacturers were required to develop incrementally cleaner cars with a mandate to finally produce an electric zero-emission vehicle. The ZEV regulation is an integral part of California's long-term solutions to improve air quality and reduce the state's effects of climate change. Again, none of this would have been possible for California were it not for the defeat of the Dingell Amendment.

The US Environmental Protection Agency recently compared 1970 vehicle models with new cars, sports utility vehicles, pickup trucks, heavy-duty trucks, and buses and said they are roughly 99 percent cleaner for common pollutants (hydrocarbons, carbon monoxide, nitrogen oxides and particulate emissions).

Yet despite control successes, Los Angeles still has days of poor air quality. The world has turned its focus on the crucial challenge of climate change. Carbon pollution from burning fossil fuels is rapidly changing the Earth's climate. The transportation sector is one of the largest sources of carbon pollution and new carbon emissions standards for passenger cars and trucks, heavy duty trucks and buses are in the works.

CALIFORNIA'S SMOG CHECK PROGRAM

In 1984, the state added another important weapon to its smog-fighting arsenal: the California Smog Check program. It requires vehicles to be tested every two years to ensure they meet emissions standards. Those that fail must be repaired in accordance with federal and state guidelines until they pass the smog check. Two California committees were established, one to develop the test equipment, headed by Ron Sommerville, the San Diego County air pollution control officer, and another to guide its acceptance statewide, headed by Birakos. When the first facility was opened in Los Angeles, Bradley and Birakos held a news conference at the site to explain its purpose and the significant role it would play to help clean the area's air.

But diesel vehicles were not included in the program. Yet diesel vehicles discharged cancer-risk pollutants that are seven times greater than all the 181 other air toxic substances followed by the Environmental Protection Agency. Birakos called for a meeting in Los Angeles with diesel manufacturers. Fearing new measures, the manufacturers did not show up. Immediately thereafter, Birakos held a second news conference with Bradley and Hahn at truck stops and gas stations and stated that diesel vehicles may be banned in Los Angeles. Everyone showed up. The program to control diesel emissions got its start.

SMOG IMPROVEMENTS AND CLIMATE CHANGE

Fifty years after the smog fight began, cleaner air is within sight. Smog alerts are no longer a daily occurrence, although Los Angeles suffers a handful every summer. But growth is still a never-ending challenge. It can sabotage every advance we have made in air quality if it is not properly checked.

Cleaner cars are the answer, but the developing population of cleaner cars will continue to be a problem. Although smog will linger and go away slowly, much like it came, the most immediate and growing threat today to the environment, public health, and the economy, is climate change. California has taken pioneering action to help reduce greenhouse emissions that are warming the planet. I am deeply concerned about those people and groups that mischaracterized the science of climate change to create uncertainty about its existence and causes. The answers lie in creating more renewable energy and cleaner modes of transportation.

Climate change is real, and the science is clear. Humanmade greenhouse gas emissions affect our planet. The debate, although not as passionate as in previous years, is reminiscent of the dispute over the danger of cigarette smoking.

LOS ANGELES INTERNATIONAL AIRPORT

The crisis after 9/11 Lydia Kennard was the executive director of Los Angeles World Airports when terrorists attacked our nation on September 11, 2001. Of the four hijacked flights, three were bound for Los Angeles International Airport.

On the morning of the attack, she was home in Pasadena getting ready for work when Michael DiGirolamo, deputy executive director of operations, called her. "Lydia, a plane flew into the World Trade Center. The Federal Aviation Administration has ground-stopped all aircraft." The call abruptly ended. "OK, which World Trade Center, Los Angeles, Chicago, New York, where?" She was not told. Kennard rushed to her car and headed for LAX, listened to the radio and began calling the office. The North Tower of the World Trade Center in New York was in flames. By the time she hit Dodger Stadium a second plane had slammed into the South Tower. Both towers eventually collapsed.

"At LAX, we had about one hundred thousand people that had to be managed. Some were on aircraft, others in terminals ready to depart, or getting off planes, and there were fifty thousand people that work there every day," she told me. "It was my call. I had to evacuate the entire airport." And she did. Immediately, with extraordinary calmness and attentiveness, airport employees began getting people out. But that did not mitigate the intensifying circumstance. She was informed by the FAA that 5,000 or more aircraft were in the air at that moment. If it could not be determined that an aircraft was under domestic control, F16s around the country would shoot them down.

News reports were incessant, and they continued to shock; the Pentagon was hit. Kennard, her memory rigidly locked on that shocking day, recounted moment-to-moment events for me. For planes destined for Los Angeles that were not close, pilots were directed to land at the nearest airport. "They had to get down, out of airspace," she said. "Additionally, at that moment, there were 198 aircraft on the ground at LAX and we had to get the passengers out and determine where to put them."

The chaotic day became more frenzied when recollection of the "millennium bomber" came to mind—the thirty-two-year-old Algerian who was arrested in December 1999 with materials for a powerful explosion in the trunk of his rental car and plans to bomb LAX on the eve of the millennium celebrations. Los Angeles was an important icon to be protected and high security had been established. "Of course, you had compounding concerns,"

I pointed out, "families of the victims, and friends of the flight crews, had gathered at LAX since three of the hijacked planes were headed here."

She explained that her staff acted adeptly, arranging a hotel in Century City to house the families, away from reporters who would naturally hound them. "And the press," she said. "We knew reporters would be all over us." A twenty-four-hour press room was created on the west side of the airport with news conferences every four hours. Thankfully, helpful data were disseminated by reporters regarding airport operations. People who had been dropped off at the airport had to leave on their own, but there was no panic. Everything ran well, until the "testosterone wars."

The Federal Bureau of Investigation, Los Angeles Chief of Police Bernard C. Parks and Los Angeles County Sheriff Lee Baca all maneuvered for jurisdiction over the airport. Parks called it a local issue, while Baca claimed it was under his purview and the FBI sought overall authority. Kennard pointed out that LAX is a twenty-four-hour 365-day operation. "Lots of noise, lots of cars, and everything," she told me. As the airport was relieved of people, so was the noise. Her office overlooked the central loop road. Suddenly, police sirens blared, and emergency and black and white vehicles and motorcycle officers thundered around the airport. "I panicked," she confessed to me, and phoned DiGirolamo. "What's going on?" "Oh, don't worry about it," DiGirolamo said.

Later, it became clear to her that this was just a testosterone rush. This was a moment for the bold and the brave, an opportunity to show "they are going to go and get the terrorists. This was a male concept of wanting to protect and thwart the terrorists, and they were surged. They were just wired." "It was just a show?" I asked her. "Sirens and emergency vehicles at midnight?" "It was test," she politely called it. "These guys were running around with their sirens because they could, and because it was their macho thing."

Worried about car bombs, the FAA issued an order prohibiting parking in structures within five hundred feet of the terminal. This made LAX totally vulnerable. It was concluded that the airport may soon open, but the parking structures would not. Structural engineers appeared to testify that the terminals could withstand a bomb blast from the parking structures.

"Wait a minute," Kennard responded. "People's lives in a parking structure are as valuable as people's lives in the terminal." She realized that the engineers cared as much about the infrastructure as they did about people. After an animated debate, she declared that the parking structures would stay closed. "We couldn't take that risk," she insisted. A controversial busing system began operating within twenty-four hours. People were forced to park in outside lots and get bused into the airport. For at least a week it was an acceptable alternative. Then hotels and the airlines began to clamor for the reopening of the parking structures, saying that people were losing their jobs. Kennard was unmoved. Her recurring comment to me was that she was not yet comfortable because LAX was the airport target of the country, if not the world.

Meanwhile, Parks and Baca continued their strange sparring with Kennard becoming a conduit for them. Baca complained that Parks had not given him a copy of a security report, insisting that this was a local issue, and his. Clashes persisted until, in frustration, she communicated her displeasure. “I’m trying to run an airport and you have to deal with your interpersonal relationships,” she told them. “Did pressures intensify to open the airport?” I inquired.

Indeed, it had become an uncomfortable situation. The day after the terrorist attack, Wednesday, September 12, 2001, DiGirolamo told her they were going to reopen the central terminal area loop road by 6 p.m. “We made a decision to do this,” he said. “Who’s we? I didn’t make the decision,” Kennard said. “We did,” he responded, “Parks, the FBI, everybody says we can do it, we can secure the airport.”

“We’re not!” Kennard said. “I’m not there, I’m not comfortable.”

Agonizing over developments, she conferred with her chief of staff who assured her that the decision to open was hers. She had always sought consensus, but she did not want to be pressured into making the wrong decision. She told Ted Stein, president of the Board of Airport Commissioners, that she must be directed by the commission to open LAX, if that is what they wanted. Mayor James Hahn had appointed Stein to the board in August 2001, and his appointment was approved by the City Council.

Hahn was stranded in Washington, unable to return and City Council President, Alex Padilla, now a US senator, was acting mayor. Speaking under the bridge between City Hall and City Hall East, in the shadow of high-rises, Padilla explained the risks the world faced and how Los Angeles was going to be secured. Without skipping a beat, he repeated his remarks in Spanish.

Demands to open the airport led to a public airport commission meeting. Kennard related events as they unfolded. “In a surreal way, just before taking the votes, Police Chief Parks, the FBI, and the CIA rushed into the hearing room. We dismissed ourselves and moved to executive session where we were informed that new information from Afghanistan was uncovered suggesting that LAX was still a target.” “Don’t open the airport up!” they said. Kennard felt vindicated.

On September 13, 2001, the airport was finally opened, and two months later private vehicles were allowed back into the central terminal area. In the center of the Theme Building there is a permanent memorial to 9/11 called “Recovering Equilibrium,” a compass-shaped art piece that features words and phrases reflecting national perceptions, rights, and ideals. But Kennard’s days as the airport chief were numbered.

According to an October 6, 2005, article in the Los Angeles Daily News, “Kennard, LAWA’s whip-smart former executive director, was run out of the job in 2003 after enduring years of an imperious Airport Commission led at the time by developer and attorney Ted Stein, who was doing the bidding of then-Mayor James Hahn until the investigations of pay-to-play contracting led to his resignation.”

The newspaper said that Kennard was too decent to make a federal case out of her maltreatment and didn’t really have to. Everyone in the region shared her skepticism over Hahn’s $11 billion LAX modernization plan. “Her resignation was a loss to Los Angeles,” the Daily News noted.

LAX MODERNIZATION

Kennard was replaced in December 2003, by Kim Day, whose main task was to ram through Hahn's LAX modernization, although it appeared unlikely that the plan could ever be fully carried out.

I specifically recall a period in 2004 when Los Angeles World Airports executives were preparing to present to the Los Angeles City Council the airport's master plan for approval. One of her executives asked Day to ignore Councilmember Antonio Villaraigosa's concerns because "we have the necessary votes." And she did, dismissing Villaraigosa and discounting the comments he made during a council meeting. A big mistake.

When Villaraigosa was inaugurated as mayor on July 1, 2005, he dispatched to the airport Robin Kramer, his chief of staff, and Tom Saenz, his chief legal counsel, to fire Day. She pleaded for a meeting with the mayor and an opportunity to apologize. Day later resigned. There was no alternative. I knew the mayor did not forgive those who slighted him.

The caustic management style of Stein, a detrimental factor in Kennard's tenure at LAX, was not the only matter that had stigmatized Stein. According to Chip Jacobs, bestselling author and journalist, Stein "allegedly pressured several large engineering companies to donate to the anti-Valley secession campaign that Hahn backed or face interference next time they came seeking work." The *Los Angeles Times* also reported on April 2, 2004 that officials at URS Corp. had "told federal authorities that a lobbyist for the company had solicited the donation at the behest of Ted Stein, Hahn's appointee as president of the airport commission, and that the lobbyist had said they would face serious problems if they did not contribute." The newspaper also said that Lydia Kennard, then the airport's executive director, told an auditor that she was troubled by the possibility that Stein had played too large a role in selecting contractors. Stein had treated his volunteer airport post as a full-time job, at times sitting with staff members to interview potential contractors.

Dan Garcia, a longtime local political insider, had been Mayor Richard Riordan's designated leader of an earlier LAX expansion effort but was removed in 1998 as the president of the city's Airport Commission. Riordan's plan called for nearly doubling LAX capacity to about one hundred million passengers a year. It would have added 4 million square feet of cargo space, at an estimated cost of $8 billion to $12 billion, a tab that would make it one of the most expensive public works projects in the country.

In less than a year after Hahn took office July 1, 2001, LAX had spent about $10 million studying how to improve the world's eighth-busiest airport. His expansion plan had stirred discontent and remained stalled in controversy. More burdens had been placed on the airport. A few years earlier Riordan, on the pretense that the airport owed the general fund money for services such as fire protection and traffic control from 1920 to 1970, had $31 million transferred to the city. The FAA demanded the funds be returned. Still litigated was an earlier transfer of $58 million. That money represented condemnation payments, plus interest, from the state of California to the Department of Airports for city land the state needed to build the 105 Freeway between LAX and Norwalk.

Unwilling to comply, Riordan caused the city to forsake more than $117 million in federal grants urgently needed to improve safety and security at the airport. With the terrorist attack of September 11, 2001, safety at airports was given a renewed focus, leading to a fifth alternative to the LAX modernization plan, which was approved by the City Council in 2004.

I had known Lydia Kennard for a number of years, having worked with her father as the electrical engineer on numerous projects, including the trauma center at Martin Luther King Jr./Drew Medical Center. Robert Kennard, a talented architect, was a close friend of mine and a man of the highest integrity, a great human being. Mayor Villaraigosa knew I was friends with Lydia Kennard and when he decided to appoint her to replace Day as the executive director of Los Angeles World Airports, he asked me to talk to Kennard because she was apprehensive to return after her previous experiences.

The mayor was aware that Kennard held an educational pedigree matched only by few other city executives, including a law degree from Harvard, and despite pressure from politicians, her own deputies and airline executives, her insistence for safety won praise nationwide. I addressed Kennard's concerns and issues, and after Villaraigosa assured her that she would be totally independent, she returned as the city's airport chief in October 2005.

Villaraigosa also moved quickly to settle five potential litigation obstacles that LAX faced so that the airport master plan could move forward. The settlement, deemed historic, was subject to ratification by the Los Angeles Board of Airport Commissioners, on which my wife, Sylvia, served. The settlement was hailed widely as a major milestone in the development of airports in Southern California.

LAX is being reimagined in 2023 through a $15 billion Central Improvement Program that will modernize terminals, create a safer airfield, improve access, and provide connections to regional transportation. Major infrastructure improvements have been underway since 2017, during Mayor Eric Garcetti's administration, with state-of-the art facilities and an Automated People Mover train system.

In one of my meetings with Deborah Flint, who was appointed by Mayor Eric Garcetti in 2015 to be chief executive of Los Angeles World Airports, she discussed the design of the upcoming Automated People Mover. Instinctively, I asked if there would be a wow-factor, a striking feature for visitors. Flint advised her staff accordingly. Garcetti, on a visit to the airport, emphasized the wow-factor regarding the people mover. When the Request for Proposals (RFP) was issued to contractors competing for the project it included under the Evaluation Criteria, the following request: "The extent to which Proposer's overall architectural vision for APM Fixed Facilities, as set forth in the referenced submittals, incorporates at least one architectural design feature providing an iconic statement or a 'Wow-Factor' that will be memorable for users of the APM System or other members of the public. The signature feature can be part of the Guideway, Stations, Mezzanine, or Pedestrian Walkways."

As the city brilliantly demonstrated in 1932 and 1984, Los Angeles is once again preparing to embrace the world for the 2028 Olympic Games. Los Angeles International Airport, the entry point for many, will roll out the welcome mat.

PRIVATE AND SERVICE CLUBS

Outlawing Intolerance and Racism | Three decades after the Civil War young progressive Republicans in Los Angeles organized politically in 1894 to back Morris M. Estee in his bid for governor of California. Despite their vigorous campaigning and downtown torchlight parades, their candidate lost. However, during the year-long political drive the sustained camaraderie bonded the men, all white Protestants. They decided to preserve that solidarity by staying together. After all, it was said, they had plenty of liquor still in the cabinet. So, in 1895 they filed with the state to become a social nonpolitical organization. But what would they call themselves? They studied the prominent symbolic names of their time: Yankee Doodle (from a pre-Revolution song); Brother Jonathan (the personification of the newly independent American people after the Revolution). "Brother" was used by men who shared common interests. Jonathan was also the default name then, as John Doe is today. He was portrayed as a sly and cunning figure. The iconic Uncle Sam is based on a combination of the two American characters: Yankee Doodle and Brother Jonathan.

Nat B. Read, author of the Jonathan Club Story, a public relations consultant and club member since 1995, told me that Jonathan was "a yahoo, badly dressed, a hick, a ploughman, but somehow he always came out on top." Read compared him to Columbo, the television detective who "appeared dumb but had wisdom that got the best of all the well-dressed, educated people." Consequently, the caricature Jonathan's name was bestowed on the once modest club. Eventually, the Jonathan Club became an esteemed, established organization that embraced some of the most influential figures in California history.

During Abraham Lincoln's time, the Republicans were the liberal party and passed laws that granted protections for Black Americans, and advanced social justice. The conservative Democrats largely opposed expansions of federal power. With the passage of time, the parties shifted platforms.

Likewise, the Jonathan Club did not preserve its initial liberal bearings. With time it also shifted dramatically. "Let the record be clear," Read admitted, "we were an ant-Semitic, racist, misogynist club. No Jews, no blacks, no women, and the very fact that we can talk about that now so openly is testimony to the fact that we really, really did change."

Indeed, the fluidity of time altered shared perceptions. Society changed in many ways in respect to racial biases. About 1987, Read explained, "The entire house of cards of private clubs collapsed everywhere." He referred to the Cosmos Club in Washington, DC, the California Club, Jonathan Club, and Kiwanis, and Lions all changing in one year. "We admitted women, a few black members, we already had a few Jewish members. We had been very selective, but we were a restricted club, no question."

THE TRANSFORMATION WAS NOT SMOOTH

On May 28, 1987, Los Angeles mayor Tom Bradley signed an ordinance sponsored by Los Angeles City Council member Joy Picus to ban discrimination based on "sex, sexual orientation, race, color, religion, ancestry, national origin or disability" at most of the city's large private clubs. It applied to any club with more than four hundred members that "takes payments for meetings attended by non-members." The ordinance opened the door for women and minorities to become members of clubs that had long excluded them.

Picus told me the Washington Post, as well as other news outlets closely followed her motion and the City Council's public hearing where the ordinance passed unanimously. At one point she came up with a phrase she considered to be the best of her sixteen-year political life, a felicitous slogan that described august private clubs and their members: "princes of privilege in their palaces of power."

Bradley told the *Los Angeles Times* that "the city should be proud of this action. This is an open society and by the actions which we take today, we are assuring that we take one more step in removing any vestige of discrimination or discriminatory practices in our city." Interestingly, the mayor of Los Angeles was always made an honorary member at the Jonathan Club, but not in the case of Bradley.

"Was that because he was black?" I inquired. "Yes, that's my understanding," Read said. A year after the Los Angeles action, the US Supreme Court ruled that cities may, in certain cases, force large private clubs to admit minorities and women. It said that "clubs which serve meals and rent facilities to outsiders are more like business establishments than intimate social groups and therefore have no right to escape anti-discrimination laws."

A few years ago, the magazine, LA Confidential, quoted an old adage: "The people who run Los Angeles belong to the Jonathan Club; the people who own Los Angles belong to the California Club." A block away from the Jonathan Club sits the competing California Club which calls itself "LA's premier private social club." It also practiced racial intolerance. The *Los Angeles Times* reported on February 1, 1988, that "there had been a long period of outright hostility to blacks in the California Club. Some members say that as late as the early 1970s, a member who one day brought a black guest to lunch in the main club dining room found that no one would serve them."

A PRIVATE CLUB FOR JEWISH MEMBERS

The Hillcrest Country Club golf course, across the street from 20th Century Studios at 10000 W. Pico Blvd., opened in 1920—the first Los Angeles country club for the city's Jewish community. In what may be considered a counterbalance move, it came at a time when Jews were not permitted to join other private clubs.

In April 1987, state Board of Equalization member Conway Collis told the *Los Angeles Times* that Jewish clubs were just as guilty of discriminatory behavior as other private clubs. He also said Jewish lawmakers and other officials in Sacramento had long been subject to sharp questioning when they sought to end racial, religious and sex discrimination at gentile clubs in Los Angeles, San Francisco, and other cities. Then Hillcrest Club president Mark B. Levey said that although his club has had some women as associate members, it had never enrolled a woman as one of its regular members. With about two dozen non-Jewish members, he said Hillcrest had taken steps to ensure that it was nondiscriminatory. He said by-laws would be changed to admit women as regular members in response to the Los Angeles ordinance outlawing discriminatory policies by clubs.

At Hillcrest, movie moguls would gather and outbid one another with gifts to the United Jewish Welfare Fund and other Jewish causes, Neal Gabler wrote in *An Empire of their Own*. Many of Hollywood's biggest stars in the 1940s were members of the exclusively Jewish club, including Milton Berle, Jack Benny, Danny Kaye, George Burns, George Jessel, Al Jolson, Eddie Cantor, and the Ritz Brothers. Author Frank Rose in his book on the William Morris Agency described the Hillcrest as a "preserve of Hollywood's elite. All the great moguls had belonged to Hillcrest—Louis B. Mayer and the Warner brothers and Harry Cohn of Columbia and Adolph Zukor of Paramount."

It was said that Eugene Wyman, an attorney, and once Democratic state central committee chairman and one of the party's chief fund raisers (he raised millions for the presidential campaigns of John F. Kennedy, Lyndon Johnson and Hubert Humphrey, and gubernatorial candidate Edmund G. Brown) would invite a few Jewish businessmen to Hillcrest and close the meeting room doors. "No one will leave until we raise our goal of $250,000," he would say—a lot of money for the 1960s and 1970s.

Hillcrest was also known for its Round Table of Comedians, where Hollywood's top comedians—including Benny, Burns, Jessel, Groucho Marx, Kaye, Berle, and Don Rickles —got together for a regular Friday lunch to socialize and try new material out on their friends. Marx once proclaimed that he would not want to be a member of any club willing to have him as a member. Danny Thomas, a Catholic of Lebanese descent, was the first non-Jew invited to join Hillcrest. Benny quipped: "At least they could have picked a guy who looked like a gentile!" Frank Sinatra and Sidney Poitier were also prominent non-Jewish Hillcrest members.

HENRY E. HUNTINGTON

Although the Jonathan and California clubs are similar in many ways, they differ in others. Read said that the California Club, established in 1888, was older by seven years, and is said to have a more prestigious membership, while the Jonathan Club has the most impressive amenities, among the very best in the country, with thirteen floors of athletic, dining, and overnight facilities.

The first headquarters for the California Club was in the second-floor rooms over the Tally-Ho Stables on the northwest corner of First and Fort (Broadway) Streets, where the LA Law Library now stands. In 1896, the Corfu Hotel next door at 132 South Spring Street went broke. With dining and overnight facilities, a kitchen, and meeting rooms, it was a perfect location, so the Jonathan Club moved in.

In 1904, Henry E. Huntington, the railroad magnate who owned the Pacific Electric Railway as well as substantial real estate interests, planned to build the largest office building west of the Mississippi, "a grand empire building," Read said. As the building neared completion, Huntington informed the architect he wanted the two top floors to be suitable for a social club, and not offices. Huntington invited the California Club to move into his Pacific Electric Building at Sixth and Main streets, but it declined because the club was planning its own building overlooking Pershing Square. Huntington then extended the offer to the Jonathan Club, of which he was a member. The hundred or so members believed that moving from 132 South Spring Street to the top two floors of the city's most prestigious building would increase their stature and reputation. So, for twenty years (1905–25), they were Huntington's tenants in a luxurious location, and the club membership grew. Huntington became Jonathan Club president for twelve years (1904–16).

Although he did not attend a single board meeting during his final six years, he remained the acknowledged figurehead president so his celebrity name would be an enduring Jonathan appeal. Nonetheless, the relationship finally soured and the Jonathans decided to construct their own building.

A MAJESTIC BUILDING

William P. Jeffries, founder of Jeffries Banknote Company, came along, "a man who imagined in a gigantic sphere," Read said. As club president (1923–30) he persuaded the Jonathans to build a thirteen-story building at Sixth and Figueroa streets. And he would raise the money. He got subscribers for two bonds and built an elegant structure using the architects, Schultze and Weaver, of the Waldorf Astoria and the Los Angeles Biltmore. The Jonathans moved into the new building in 1925.

Built on a hotel concept with old ruffle brick, punctuated with keystone arches and balconied windows, it quickly became the center of attention. Its ornate ceilings were designed by a man who was trained at the Vatican, Giovanni Battista Smeraldi. In addition to its ultra-elegance, refinement, and the rich décor, it had a parking garage within the building. Although it was a men's club, "upstairs" they would have mixed affairs. To get there they would have to ride the same elevators as women—which, the Jonathans felt, ruined the male bonding experience. So a women's elevator was added, along with a tunnel, to take women from the garage to the floor reserved for mixed couples' events.

"It was in 1985–86 that the question of women members came up," Richard Oxford told me. Oxford was a member of the board of directors and Jonathan Club president. Aside from the separate elevator for women, there was a separate dining room—not for women members who didn't exist—but for spouses and guests. "We had widow members of the club, but they were not full-fledged members and couldn't vote" he said, "and they still had to take the women's elevator."

I was introduced to the club by an architect friend, Robert Oltman, who told me the Jonathans had gym facilities and opened at 5 a.m. I was an avid early morning exerciser, and

The Jonathan Club.

I belonged to the Century West Health Club. Because my main activities were downtown, I joined the club. An additional attraction for me was the Jonathan Club's beach facilities in Santa Monica, because my children were very young at the time and enjoyed going to the beach.

The Jonathan Club is considered a good place. It has survived for over 1.25 centuries. For me, the club has been my second home over the last four decades, a place where I meet with business, political, and social acquaintances and friends any time of the day, including early breakfasts, midday lunches, dinners, and after-dinner drinks and exercise in great athletic facilities.

I vividly remember the conflict over women membership. "We were very fond of our tradition to swim in the nude, and in nude sunbathing," Read said of the members. "When women were finally admitted, they were told they were in, paid the same dues as men, but two places remained out of reach for them: the second-floor tap room and the swimming pool." An adjustment was made for women to use the pool on Sundays. That was not enough for the newly admitted women. After all, they were paying the same dues but didn't have the same privileges. It was agreed by the men that this was discriminatory, so they lowered the dues for women.

One early female member, aviator Brooke Knapp, said she believed that the club on its own volition would eventually permit women to use the facilities. She worried that by pressing on such details the city may create a backlash that will slow women's progress not only at the Jonathan but at other private clubs as well.

But for Los Angeles, patience had run out. On January 8, 1988, the *Los Angeles Times* reported that the Jonathan Club and the City of Los Angeles had filed dueling lawsuits. The club asked the federal court to invalidate the anti-discrimination ordinance, and the city sued in Superior Court to compel the club to let women members use its bar and grill.

The Jonathans challenged the constitutionality of the 1987 ordinance, charging that in moving to integrate the men's bar and grill, the city was interfering with the club's internal affairs. The club's attorney, John R. Shiner, argued that the ordinance was "being misused to bully private organizations." The club's general manager, Charles R. Walter, Jr., called it a "frivolous lawsuit," and said the city should be spending taxpayer's money to aid the homeless or to address other problems such as ocean and air pollution.

Then City Attorney James Hahn and Controller Rick Tuttle strongly chastised the Jonathan Club. Tuttle said it was outrageous for business leaders who belong to the club to continue to degrade women. "A 'no women allowed' policy in the club's dining room is no more tolerable than a policy of 'no Jews allowed,' or 'no Blacks allowed.'"

In its centennial 1895–1995 publication, *Jonathan: A Celebrated Club*, Sally R. Guthrie stated that "in spite of the adverse publicity demand for membership in the Jonathan Club continued to be strong. After a survey that brought an enormous response, the Jonathan Club bylaws were changed in several areas, one of them granted Resident membership to women. Also, despite heated opposition, the vote was more than two to one in favor of the bylaw change." Women now sit on the board and run committees and have also served as president of the club.

THE JONATHAN BEACH CLUB

The Roaring Twenties became the challenge of the Thirties for the Jonathan Club, Guthrie wrote. In truth, it was more than a challenge, it was an ordeal.

Jonathan Club President Jeffries was given the board's proxy to vote the stock of the Jonathan Club Building Company. With the Great Depression Los Angeles suffered the same financial affliction as the rest of the country, but Jeffries saw opportunity. Real estate prices were low. In April 1930 the Jonathan Beach Club was formed. Taking unilateral action, Jeffries had bought in 1927 the Edgewater Club and surrounding properties on the beach at Ocean Avenue and California Incline in Santa Monica. Upset by his autonomous move, the club members fired him as president, yet they recognized his many contributions and named him president emeritus. As some members feared, the lengthy Depression broke the Jonathans.

Along came Asa Call, later described by the *Los Angeles Times* as the "last undisputed baron of the power structure," with unmatched behind the scenes clout. He was the legendary chairman of Pacific Mutual Life Insurance Co. Call told the Jonathans he had a plan to save them and in turn make himself a lot of money. He created The Jonathan Club using the same bylaws and officers and began to buy up debt, "which was easy then, offering ten cents on the dollar," thus becoming the major creditor for The Jonathan Club.

As prearranged, he demanded payment of the debt from The Jonathan Club, which told him it could not pay. Given the opportunity to seize the assets, The Jonathan Club was sold on the courthouse steps to Asa Call. In other words, Jonathan Club bought The Jonathan Club. Call then negated the role of second bondholders, leaving $1.5 million which was enough to save the club. Call, of course, took his cut. The second bondholders were not happy. In appearance, nothing really changed. The Jonathan Club's magazine at the time made no mention of this activity.

In the 1940s the unhappy second bondholders went to court, calling the earlier action "patently absurd fiction," according to Read. The Jonathan Club's centennial publication notes: "Too much credit cannot be paid to LeRoy M. Edwards, then Jonathan president, for his legal acumen and his devotion to the Club which enabled it to reorganize itself on a sound financial bases, with all of its properties owned in fee."

The Beach Club provides its members with an oceanfront destination to dine and relax by the shore. Amenities include three acres of private beach, an indoor pool, an outdoor kid's pool, a full-service spa, five paddle tennis courts, and a gym. The Club, the Jonathans say, is cradled in the rolling bluffs where members have enjoyed their own piece of the Pacific seashore.

But the surf became less enjoyable for Jonathans in 1985, when the California Coastal Commission decided to approve the club's expansion of an existing parking lot and paddle tennis courts on the condition that all members of the public be given equal opportunity to access the club. Signs at the beach site proclaimed: "Jonathan Beach Club, Members Only."

In January 1985, the Santa Monica Planning Commission approved the club's expansion plans but voted to ask the city attorney to investigate the club's membership practices and send a letter about the issue to the Coastal Commission. The letter and the investigation were voted down in February 1985.

Yet the office of the state's attorney general pointed out that if the Jonathan Club was discriminating against women, minorities, or people of any given religious faith, it was in jeopardy of forfeiting its lease and that land may go back to the state, the *Los Angeles Times* reported on August 1, 1985. Oxford, then The Jonathan Club president, and the club's lawyer, John Shiner, told the Times the commission had exceeded its authority in tying approval of the 13,664-square-foot expansion to the policy statement.

Controversy over the club's membership policies had plagued it for years. "We do not discriminate against people that apply to the club. We don't have any women. We do have minorities," Oxford told the Times. He also explained that the "fight with the Coastal Commission was over the mean high tide line. Essentially the Beach Club property extended to the mean high tide line. But they put in a breakwater in Santa Monica and a new high tide line was the result."

A coalition of minority and women`s groups—including the Anti-Defamation League of B'Nai, B'rith, and the NAACP (as well as Mayor Bradley)—protested, alleging exclusion of women and minorities from exclusive clubs such as the Jonathan. The group marched in front of the club's Santa Monica Beach facility in July 1986. The issue finally ended up in state's Second District Court of Appeals, which in January 1988 upheld the authority of the California Coastal Commission to require the club to agree it would not bar members because of race, sex, or religion. The Jonathan Club was required to drop any discriminatory membership policies before expanding its beach facility in Santa Monica. The club appealed that ruling to the state Supreme Court which on May 6, 1988, refusing to overturn the appellate court decision. The Jonathan Club filed another appeal, this time to the US Supreme Court. On October 11, 1988, the high court refused to reconsider the state appeals court decision.

During the Prohibition era, from 1920 to 1933, when the 18th Amendment banned the manufacture, transportation, and sale of alcoholic beverages, Huntington along with a battalion of cops raided the California Club, Read said. In turn, he shut down the bar at the Jonathan Club. Interestingly, The Californians were holding a formal event with a replete buffet when the club was raided. They were crossed, Read said. "The cops ate the shrimp off the buffet table. It offended their sense of who's who."

The Jonathan Club's building, a Los Angeles landmark, was built during Prohibition, so there were no bars—at least not on the plans or the blueprints. The elevators stopped at the twelfth floor, the last official floor. But there were "things" on the roof, Read said. There was a solarium and a fan room for bringing up air through the building. And there was a casino and a bar. "That was where all the good stuff was, locked up there behind a false wall on the thirteenth floor—and that's where the good times were," Read said. The same architects had built the Biltmore, and they built all kinds of ruses for prohibition as well.

The police could arrive at what the Jonathans called the Sky Bar by taking the elevator to the twelfth floor, then climb a staircase—allowing plenty of time for members to put up the wall. "We were never raided during Prohibition," Read said with a wink.

THE CLUB REBUFFS THE DOWNTOWN PEOPLE MOVER

The Downtown People Mover, a 2.9-mile system of automated vehicles operating on a fixed guideway—powered by electricity without exhaust emissions—was proposed for Los Angeles in 1973. The project was designed to move people to activity centers throughout downtown, and to make Union Station a major transfer point for bus riders whose destination was not downtown. The people mover would pass under Bunker Hill and link two huge parking garages for commuters, one at Union Station and the other at Los Angeles Convention Center. The cost was estimated at $259 million. Backers said the project would have numerous benefits, including the reinforcement of the downtown economic strength.

In November 1974, California voters approved Proposition 5, which allowed vehicle fuel taxes and fees to be used for mass transit guideways. The Los Angeles Community Redevelopment Agency was successful in securing a $125 million grant from Proposition 5 to fund construction of the LA People Mover, according to Project Manager Albert Perdon. Mayor Bradley and I strongly supported the anticipated state-of-the art system, but it was met with hostility and opposition by the Jonathan Club and then Republican Representative Bobbi Fiedler.

Of the thirteen planned downtown stops, one was at Fifth and Figueroa Streets, and another at Seventh and Figueroa Streets. The Jonathan Club, through its counsel, John R. Shiner, referred to the area as "the disputed segment" in the final environmental impact report for the people mover in June 1980. The segment also included Arco Plaza, where the oil giant had its world headquarters in one tower and Bank of America occupied the second tower. Coupled with a major subterranean multilevel shopping center, those offices generated considerable pedestrian traffic.

The station contemplated for the site would be aerial, equipped with elevators, escalators, and stairs with safe and convenient access from city street and adjacent buildings with pedestrian bridges. People Mover vehicles, with seating for 50 passengers and standing room for up to 120 others, would stop there for less than a half minute and would be visually prominent.

The Jonathans disputed the cost and benefit of the contested segment. It said the City Council had abandoned its duty to make these findings, and it did not allow adequate time for review. Further, in its view, the environmental impact report failed to cite specific economic, social, or other reasons to support the determination that significant impacts would be mitigated to the extent feasible. It made no comment regarding the expected significant increase in retail sales primarily due to trips to retail places and restaurants in the "disputed segment." Known for being vigilant guards of their interests, the Jonathans always strove to defend what they considered their domain. They decided the project must be stopped. They did not want "this people mover going in front of the club." So, they sued the city of Los Angeles.

Fiedler, also a fervent foe of Metro Rail funding, urgently rang the death bell for the downtown people mover in Washington. Consequently, the program died in 1981. Interestingly, the grant to build the LA system was diverted to the Miami-Dade County Department of Transportation and Public Works which built its Metromover, a free, elevated downtown people mover.

SERVICE CLUBS

Years before joining The Jonathan Club, I had been an active member of a Los Angeles Sertoma Club chapter. Formerly known as Sertoma International, Sertoma, Inc. is an organization of service clubs founded in 1912. The name is an acronym for Service to Mankind, and I was attracted to the club because the local chapter sponsored community projects to assist youth and to benefit other community needs.

My participation in Sertoma consisted mainly of spending time on weekends with underprivileged youth and with senior citizens.

A friend of mine, Sotos Kappas, who played Greek music with his bouzouki in Greek restaurants, festivals, and other events, accompanied me to local senior citizen centers to entertain the residents. Although we were both young men at the time, it gave us great pleasure to see the joy that Greek music provided to the elderly, many of whom were in wheelchairs and lacked access to other forms of entertainment. The music provided not only entertainment to the seniors, but also offered health benefits. It has been proved that

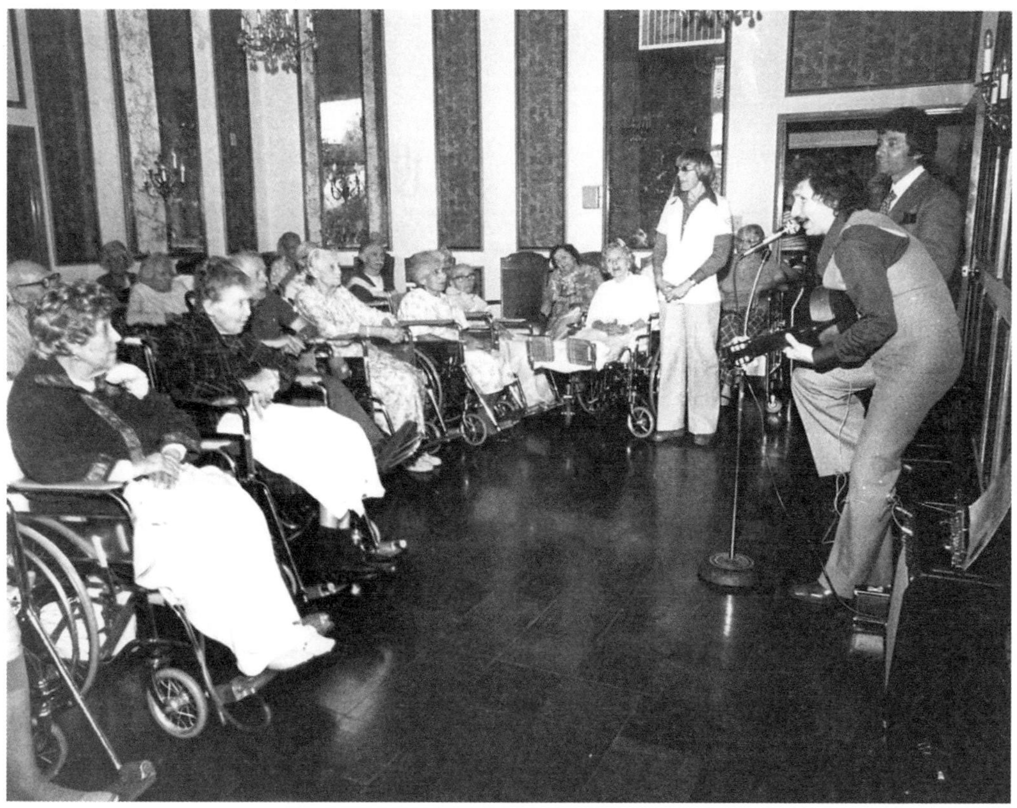

Entertaining senior citizens, with musician Sotos Kappas.

music keeps the brain engaged throughout the aging process. It reduces blood pressure and pain and improves sleep quality and mental alertness. "Music therapy" was practiced by the ancient Greek physician Hippocrates in 400 BC.

For a period of time, I also belonged to the Rotary Club, the global network of clubs of business, professional, and community leaders who volunteer their time to provide service to others. It was an enjoyable experience, but I decided to spend my limited free time on more civic-focused activities.

The word virtue had two faces: virtue in the sense of excellence—striving to be one's best—but also service to others. Sacrifice for one's family, neighbors, and country is essential to the good life. —ARISTOTLE

CHAPTER NINE

DINING OUT IN LOS ANGELES

A bottle of wine contains more philosophy than all of the books of the world.
—LOUIS PASTEUR

While Los Angeles reinvented itself over the last half century into a world-class city with its surging skyline, distinctive art galleries, and celebrated musical attainments, a newer experience in dining blossomed with an haute cuisine and restaurant hospitality that matched and surpassed respected culinary capitals of the world. For years the city was said to be a wasteland when it came to food, a destination to be dismissed if one sought a lasting gastronomic encounter. Then talented and creative chefs and restaurateurs saw opportunity in a flourishing Southern California with its diverse population and innate yearning to always be the best.

"California cuisine" made its debut, a process less about cooking styles and more about fresh and sustainable ingredients with an attention to seasonality and an emphasis on the bounty of the region.

Whether haute cuisine, nouvelle cuisine, novo cucina, or California cuisine, it became all available in grand style in Los Angeles, as well as the best of Mexican and Asian culinary experiences. Los Angeles is a world-class city that proudly expresses itself with world-class cuisines and wines.

My interest in food and wine considerably expanded in the 1970s when a friend, David Jay Flood, an architect and aquatics commissioner in the 1984 Olympics, invited me to join the Wine and Food Society of San Fernando Valley. Meeting a half-dozen times a year for black tie events in special restaurants, we savored a six- to seven-course dinner and fine wines, with each course and wine informatively explained during the evening. And there were other less formal events throughout the year revolving around the enjoyment of good food and fine wine. Sojourns followed to the California wine country, raising my awareness and interest in wine, and creating the motivation to learn more. Trips to the wine regions of France, Italy, Germany, and Croatia ensued, and of course always to Greece to taste the Greek wines as they evolve.

In the 1970s, there were only a few exclusive restaurants in Los Angles, but the gripping account of the city's culinary progress, and my love for good food and wine, kept me abreast of the local history and included myriad discussions with recognized and prominent participants in this never-ending story.

I was fortunate to have enjoyed since the late 1970s the fine food and ambience of the restaurants I highlight, and to have met the owners and/or chefs of many of these great places.

I heard from Donato Poto, who along with Chef Michael Cimarusti coowns Providence, the stylish establishment that scored the No. 1 spot on Jonathan Gold's 101 Best Restaurants list, and twice a Michelin-starred restaurant, that food is certainly the topmost consideration of diners, but hospitality is the critical factor. "Food needs to evolve, and restaurants need to evolve, that's the biggest thing right now happening in Los Angeles," Poto told me. Providing excellent food and unrivaled service in an appealing setting remains his constant pursuit. Restaurant hospitality is his domain. Poto has been called the consummate front of house personality. Born on Italy's Amalfi Coast, years of study and practice in hospitality cultivated his effortless tableside manner and understanding of customer inclinations. Chef Cimarusti, with his ingenious and contemporary style, has elevated the seafood-centric restaurant to be among the best in the nation with tasty dishes that "embody what a restaurant should aspire to be," according to the late Gold.

When building Providence, Poto asked former patrons of Patina restaurant—the flagship establishment of Chef Joachim Splichal which opened in 1989 on Melrose Avenue—the current Providence location, what they disliked about Patina. "The lighting, that it was a little noisy when they talked," was the response. So, Poto worked with the architect to create a "restaurant high-end, fine dining, to make it so people can talk without being bothered by loud noise." He told me that he wanted them to hear the good sounds, "which is the glass, the silverware, the little chit-chat from far away that doesn't bother you." At the same time, they wanted to make the restaurant "feel full and energetic." Patina used to have African lemonwood on the wall, and it was taken out because sound bounced off of it. It was replaced with padded Italian fabric. Poto explained that today the chef-driven restaurants in Los Angeles compare favorably with New York and San Francisco and many talented chefs are equally here as they are in those cities. When he arrived in Los Angeles in the 1980s, he quickly realized that changes were underway in the local restaurant industry. The culinary landscape began to change a bit earlier, in 1973, when Ma Maison opened on Melrose Avenue. But it did not become a magnet for Hollywood's elite until Wolfgang Puck, twenty-five years old, became its new chef two years later.

Patrick Terrail, a Parisian with a background in hospitality, came to Los Angeles after managing a hotel in Tahiti. The beautiful weather awakened his French enthusiasm for a casual restaurant with a terrace. He opened Ma Maison for $40,000 raised in part from actors Gene Kelly and Mel Stewart and producer Fred Weintraub. His wallet, he said, determined the restaurant's design. Cast-off chairs made of wood from a rental place were obtained and a French liquor company gave him umbrellas with their name on it. The dirt parking lot became an Astroturf-lined patio. His French chef had canned sardines on the menu and beef belly as a special, which was good for the first seven orders but waned quickly after sitting for a couple of hours. Obviously, Terrail needed an inspired, creative chef. From contacts in Europe, he was told about Puck who was living in a flophouse in downtown Los Angeles and worked in a restaurant at the ARCO Towers.

"When I came to LA," Puck told the Hollywood Reporter in 2015, "everything was imported in cans—white asparagus, peas." He was surprised having lived in Provence. "This is so crazy! We are in a climate where you can grow things, and you cannot find anything." He began to source arugula and fresh vegetables. It was his love for farm-to-table cuisine, for using ingredients sourced from the local farmers markets, pairing California's produce with French technique that eventually created a new type of cuisine, "California nouvelle." Terrail shared that love with Puck, and they hit it off. "My first paycheck from Ma Maison bounced," he recalled. "Terrail became the showman out front, kissed the women and made the flower arrangements. I learned from him not to be shy with the customers," Puck added.

Practical reasons dictated everything they did, recalled Terrail. The Rolls Royces and expensive cars were parked in front to be better watched, inexpensive cars in the back because it would be cheaper to fix them if they got scratched. Puck's magic became known and quickly the patio was packed with the likes of Jack Nicholson, Burt Reynolds, Fred Astaire, Elton John, Rod Stewart, Ringo Starr, Stevie Wonder, and Marlon Brando. Not only was the restaurant a hub for some of the biggest celebrities of the time, but also businessmen and lawyers dominated the space, wrote the Hollywood Reporter.

Terrail said Ma Maison was sold out for ten years straight. Upstairs gin rummy was being played on Fridays from lunch on, with wives joining husbands for dinner. Absent traffic, customers from MGM, Universal, or Warners got there in fifteen minutes. Puck remembered Jack Lemmon, who would arrive a half-hour before lunch, sit at the bar and have two martinis, and have two more with lunch. Orson Welles, said Terrail, ate at Ma Maison every day. Very much into food, he would arrive at 11 a.m. and would ask what the day's special was. Puck would try new dishes on Welles, like sausage with truffles inside or a warm lobster salad, which later became popular. Ma Maison was a discrete place; the restaurant's phone number was unlisted. If you did not have the number, you didn't belong there, was the enduring philosophy.

My office then was located a few blocks away from Ma Maison, and I would often see Welles walking to the restaurant. When a friend visited me for lunch, I suggested we, too, should walk to Ma Maison. The distinguished Terrail, I remember, was very well dressed, a red carnation on his lapel and sporting clogs for shoes, but he also sported an arrogant behavior for those he did not recognize.

It was noontime on a gorgeous day and the restaurant was empty. But Terrail directed us to the darkened bar area. When I voiced my concern, Terrail shook it off and said, "That's it!" My response was pithy. "My money is as good as Streisand`s or Spielberg`s. Let's get out of here!" And we did.

A few months later, attending a reception in Beverly Hills catered by Ma Maison, Terrail spotted me and said, "You're the guy who walked out of my restaurant." "Yes, you directed me to your dungeon." "You have an accent," Terrail said. "You're a genius," I responded. "I'm Greek." Terrail continued the conversation, with new warmth in his voice. He pursued the discussion in perfect Greek. His mother was Greek. The Greek connection resulted in a genial bond. Thereafter, without reservations, I would have the best table at Ma Maison. In the ensuing years I hosted a number of events at Ma Maison, including a major fundraiser for Greek

Orthodox Patriarch Diodoros of Jerusalem who was visiting Los Angeles to raise money for repairs to the Holy Sepulcher Church in Bethlehem. Terrail donated exquisite food and wine.

With Bishop Anthony, Patriarch of Jerusalem, Diodoros, and President of the LA City Council John Ferraro in City Hall.

Ma Maison's closure was the result of an unfortunate and bitter split in 1982. Puck told Terrail he had found the perfect location to make pizzas since "Los Angeles has no good pizza places." A new company was going to be created, with a 50-50 split. Terrail looked at Puck and said: "I'm always going to own 51 percent." Spago (Italian for 'string', suggesting spaghetti) was opened by Puck in 1982 on the Sunset Strip. His meteoric fame and star status were the result of his culinary achievements, which include two Michelin Stars.

Piero Selvaggio, who along with Mauro Vincenti and Evan Kleiman is known as the man who changed American cuisine, arrived in Brooklyn in 1964 with his family from Modica, Sicily, and worked in the kitchens at New York University. At seventeen, he bought a one-way bus ticket to Los Angeles where an uncle worked as a manager at Chasen's, the exclusive restaurant that attracted stars like Liz Taylor and Gregory Peck. He became a busboy at Chasen's while attending college during the day.

Rather than pursue a journalism career, he found refuge in restaurants, rising from busboy to manager. At age twenty-five, he wanted his own restaurant. With a partner, he took over a beer bar, a place "so ugly and depressing," that he almost changed his mind. Yet in 1972, he opened Valentino's at that spot to highlight Italian food, which meant heavy sauces, garlic, pizza and straw-flask Chianti and checkered tablecloths—more American-Italian than Italian. Nevertheless, business picked up, but the partners split and Selvaggio became sole owner. A regular customer, a gastronome, told him the best part of the restaurant was Selvaggio's passion and determination. "The food was awful and the wine banal," according to Silvia Donati of *Italian Magazine*. It was suggested that he travel to Italy and learn from the source.

Taking the gourmand's guidance, Selvaggio went to Italy in 1979 and was "awakened," he later said. "I began to realize that Italian cuisine is really about simplicity and quality." He gained understanding of the decisiveness of the chef, the elegance of food, and why the restaurant needed a person to guide customers through a gastronomic voyage, according to writer Donati. He became that guide. Upon his return, Valentino was transformed. Only authentic and high-quality ingredients were used, and he introduced fresh mozzarella, burrata, real prosciutto, extra virgin olive oil, risotto, and balsamic vinegar, and white truffles—items on every Italian restaurant menu today but considered exotic at that time. Provoked by the gastronome's comment on the restaurant's banal wine, Selvaggio was determined to build America's best and biggest wine list. At one point he had up to 100,000 bottles in his cellar, matched only by a few cellars in the world—and they were all in Italy. For years Valentino has held the coveted Wine Spectator Grand Award.

I asked Selvaggio about French food. It was axiomatic that French food was the best in the world. It was the epitome of what food could aspire to be. "In French cooking the big thing is technique," he said, "in Italian you need product. We are into farm to table." He spoke about L'Orangerie, LA's iconic and long established haute French restaurant that closed in 2006 after twenty-nine years, and L'Ermitage, which opened in 1975 as a restaurant for the rich and closed in 1991.

"In Los Angeles things have evolved to shy away from fine, fancy restaurants," Selvaggio told me. "French restaurants were stuffy, long affairs, and people didn't have time anymore for a three-hour dinner." Selvaggio stressed that restaurants are where people entertain, where they celebrate, a home away from home, and in Los Angeles there is the need to constantly replenish them because these places strongly impact the community. In the 1990s, successful places were many, like Spago, Rex and Valentino, some good French restaurants, and the graceful influence from the East with Japan becoming a big part of the restaurant community. China would follow. San Francisco, Selvaggio added, held on to the old-school style with fish restaurants, traditional ones and high-end French ones.

Los Angeles had moved forward with open kitchens, freshness, simplicity and atmosphere. Primi Un Ristorante was a prime early example. Selvaggio had decided to deconstruct the inviolable sequence of Italian courses and focus on the first courses, the primi. In 1986, he opened Primi, where I first met Donato Poto, on Pico Boulevard to become the most innovative Italian eatery of its time. He had five young chefs in the kitchen who competed with each other to experiment and provide a tapa style concept, food on small plates. Patrons would have daisy-shaped pasta with gorgonzola, saffron, poppy seeds, and a number of other plates of cheese, duck, and an exclusive Umbrian olive oil. A series of ten plates were often taken to a table with food changing with the season.

Gérard Ferry built L'Orangerie on a vacant parking lot in West Hollywood, making it a bastion of the elaborate French "haute cuisine" in the southland. Only nine different chefs cooked at the prestigious kitchen. Regular diners included Ronald and Nancy Reagan and numerous movie stars who always knew that absolute privacy would be afforded. L'Orangerie's signature dish was eggs with caviar.

Jean Bertranou opened L'Ermitage in 1975, and it quickly became an institution. He believed that French cooking was an attitude, not a formula and brought the French spirit into Los Angeles kitchens. "While Julia Child enabled people to master the art of French cooking, Bertranou enabled us to master the flavor," wrote Ruth Reichl, *Los Angeles Times* food editor, upon L'Ermitage's closure. When Puck opened Spago in 1982 he said "Bertranou is the one who showed us what could be done, that something more was possible in Los Angeles." According to reporter Reichl, before Puck preached the gospel of freshness, Bertranou found someone to grow haricots verts—the sweet tiny green beans of France—since they were not available in Southern California. Further, the ducks didn't please him, so he started a duck farm, smuggling eggs for his farm by camouflaging them as Easter candies. "In my part of France," he said to a friend, "we are all smugglers."

Chef Angelo Auriana was raised in Bergamo, Italy, and often saw on television scenes from the United States, mostly New York, where food presentations captured his imagination. He told me he dreamt of places like California, Malibu, and movie stars. In October 1984, he received a call from a gentleman who needed a chef in Miami. "Look," the caller said, "I have this ticket in front of me with someone else's name, but he doesn't want to go. Would you be interested?" A month later, with passport and visa in hand, he landed in Miami. In 1986, he visited Los Angeles to see the city. Selvaggio summoned him. "Angelo, can you make a risotto?" "Absolutely, how do you like it?" The risotto was made and presented. "When do you want to start?" asked Selvaggio.

Auriana returned to Florida to give notice and came to Primi to eventually become a leader among the young chefs in the kitchen. A year later, the chef at Valentino left. Selvaggio called his young Primi chefs to dine together. There he announced that Angelo would be the new chef at Valentino. With Chef Auriana at the helm, the 1990s were considered to be the best years for Valentino. Yet it was his first day at the restaurant that unlocked food's evolution for him. "Mr. Piero, why this is not an Italian restaurant, but a continental restaurant?" he asked of Selvaggio. "Well, see, continental means that we're bringing Europe to the United States," was the response. The wine list proved his point. All the Barolo producers were present, including the French Burgundy and Bordeaux. "We were the nouvelle cuisine, an eclectic style originated in France, but now transitioned into Italian," Auriana told me.

Italy was also transitioning, defining the concept of a total cuisine with refinements in food, table setting and service. The move was spearheaded by Gualtiero Marchesi, the accepted father of contemporary Italian cuisine—who considered cooking a science that could turn into art, but only by the very best. A good friend of Selvaggio and widely known as "the maestro," he began in the art district of Milan, a place called Brera (thus the name of his restaurant), serving after-hour meals for starving artists. Himself a musician with studies in the Conservatory in Milan, he attracted artists and musicians from Teatro alla Scala. Marchesi focused on simplicity and ingredients, then technique and embellishment, and brought his cuisine to the table staging final delivery and meat cutting in front of customers. Like a musical score, each dish was clearly recognized and made to achieve harmony. Auriana said that the maestro taught them, four or five chefs who ended up at Primi. "He opened the window. We were all from Bergamo, Milano, Lombardy. We had a white canvas to experiment, but not to imitate."

Matteo Ferdinandi was born in the small town of Chioggia in the Venetian lagoon, had studied geometry, and was preparing for a career in civil engineering. His family of bakers sent him to London to learn English and while there, for pocket money, he worked in a restaurant in Mayfair. His passion for the restaurant business won over geometry. Meeting people in the dining room, talking about culinary arts, service, wines, and beverage enticed him, he said to me, as did the other elements of success in restaurants, such as public relations, finance, fundraising, and design. When he came to Los Angeles in 1992, he worked for Harry's Bar in Century City and gained his first exposure to the American way of doing business.

"What was missing," he added, "was the authenticity of what Italian food is really like." In Italy, from town to town, people ate different food. He did not know what people ate in Padua, 15 miles from Venice, or Verona, twenty-five miles away. He eventually transferred to Prego in Beverly Hills. Puck's managing partner, David Robins, interviewed Ferdinandi, who was later told by Wolfgang that he needed him at Spago in Las Vegas with Celine Dion's arrival. He worked directly under Puck and learned from his mentor all the important aspects of the business. After four years, Puck called him to say he was opening Cut at the Beverly Wilshire and wanted him back in Los Angeles. He returned and did Cut and Sidebar, basically creating the front of the house service.

But he told me he wanted his own place. In his opinion, Auriana was then—and still is—the only Italian chef who understood Italy's culinary culture, heritage, history, and the technique, and had the dedication and driving force. Together, in 2013, they opened Factory Kitchen, a new northern Italian trattoria in the trendy arts district east of downtown Los Angeles. "We are a little bit old fashioned, but it was the perfect time to do exactly what we did growing up, the enlightening and the nouvelle cuisine of Marchesi." Officine Brera followed, built in an old, converted warehouse with a high roof in downtown Los Angeles, with an industrial decoration style. Auriana's risotto Milanese, according to Jonathan Gold, was creamy and subtle as might be at a trattoria in the Milan district of Navigli, and it becomes magical when you spoon in a bit of roasted bone marrow. The menu was inspired by the cooking found near the foggy banks of the Po River.

STRUGGLE FOR SUPERIOR CUISINE

The cuisine battle between the French and Italians underwent momentous alterations in the mid-1980s when France's nouvelle cuisine was introduced to the West, but only to face an Italian counterpart—nuovo cucina. Rex il Ristorante in Los Angeles became the protagonist on the Italian side. With culinary refinements and countryside appeal, all displayed in a formal dining room overseen by tuxedoed waiters and captains, it quickly became a centerpiece and was used for many weddings and big Hollywood parties. Rex was the elegant restaurant where Richard Gere takes Julia Roberts by limousine in the movie "Pretty Woman."

After sixteen years of praise, the restaurant closed its doors in 1997. Mauro Vincenti, the front of the house icon, and his last chef, Gino Angelini, brought gastronomic passion and knowledge to Los Angeles. In October 2001, Angelini opened his own restaurant, Angelini Osteria, in the heart of Los Angeles. Rated forty-six among the 101 best restaurants in Los Angeles by Jonathan Gold (who said the spaghetti alla norcina with strands of hand-cut pasta in a sauce of summer truffles from Umbria was the best meal of the year for him).

I asked Angelini the reason people moved from French to Italian cuisine. "The Italian cuisine is simpler," he said. "And you can eat every day. The French is for celebration, for something special. And the food is heavier." He explained that the French make vegetable stock, and chicken and fish and meat stock. His grandmother never made broths, or reductions—au jus. She did not have demi-glace. She made the meat stock with the meat. "When we cook meat on the grill, we don't serve sauce, we put extra virgin olive oil, salt and pepper." He also said that unlike the French, Italians do not eat a lot of meat, they don't put cheese with fish, nor cook with vodka. He remembers Christmases when they had cappelletti, lamb, lasagna, and ricotta from sheep in his hometown of San Clemente in the Emilia Romagna region of northern Italy. He spoke highly of the success of Wolfgang Puck and his success with the California cuisine. If you go to an authentic Italian restaurant in Italy, they will do forty people for dinner, he said. When he visited Spago in Beverly Hills he went into the kitchen and saw they were making pasta for 400 people a night. Ruth Reichl, author and former *Los Angeles Times* restaurant critic, said, "The 1980s were halcyon time: LA was the most interesting place to eat in the country."

LOS ANGELES CUISINE LEGENDS

Before the ushering in of the California cuisine, cuisine nouvelle, and nuovo cucina, Los Angeles had dozens of legendary restaurants where Hollywood drank and ate, places for those who wanted to see and be seen—but only a few were truly exclusive.

Perino's at 3927 Wilshire Boulevard was opened by Alexander Perino in 1932 with a $2,000 loan in the midst of the Great Depression. At 19 he had emigrated from Piedmont, Italy, to the United States, worked his way as a waiter in various restaurants, including the then newly opened Biltmore Hotel. His chef and friend for a lifetime, Attilio Balzano, created a cuisine of high-class Italian and French food. Quickly a loyal celebrity clientele made Perino's famous.

With his fastidious approach to detail, Perino featured 150 separate entrées on the menu and 270 different wines. He moved his restaurant to 4101 Wilshire Boulevard, designed by Paul Revere Williams, the trailblazer African American architect. It featured a main dining room and two private rooms with a sitting capacity for 360 people. It was known that the stars loved Perino's, and that Cary Grant, Marilyn Monroe, Alfred Hitchcock, Dean Martin, Joe DiMaggio, and Elizabeth Taylor were regular customers; that Bette Davis had a permanently reserved booth; that Frank Sinatra occasionally performed at the Steinway piano in the restaurant bar; that Cole Porter composed songs on the back of menus; and that regulars were also Richard Nixon and Ronald Reagan.

Perino's was the place where the AXIOS philanthropic organization met in the 1980s. The membership was composed mainly of Greek Americans, and we would invite monthly guest speakers from the academia, business, entertainment, and political fields. Scenes from the movie Scarface were filmed at Perino`s. Perino's shuttered in the 1980s, despite several failed attempts to revive it. The historic building was torn down in 2005 for an apartment complex.

Chasen's was another famous Los Angeles landmark, located at 9039 Beverly Boulevard on the border of Beverly Hills. Launched in 1936, it became the site of the Academy Awards party for many years. Originally named Chasen's Southern Barbecue Pit, it was opened by vaudeville actor and comedian Dave Chasen and his partner, Joe Cook, with a $3,500 advance from New Yorker Magazine founder and editor Harold Ross. At first it was nothing more than a shack with six tables, a six-stool bar and eight-stool counter, mainly serving chili and ribs.

Within a year it became a full-service restaurant with uniformed waitresses and a menu with over thirty-five items. The name was shortened to "Chasen's," and the famous clientele grew its reputation. Regular customers included Walt Disney, Leopold Stokowski, Cary Grant, Jack Benny, Jackie Gleason, and W. C. Fields. The list was long, and involved the day's biggest celebrities, such as Reagan, Nixon, Sinatra, Gregory Peck, Bob Hope, Jack Lord, Jack Nicholson, John Travolta, and Mel Gibson. Established customers simply signed for their charges and a bill was later mailed. As a matter of fact, Reagan proposed to actress Nancy Davis in Chasen's in 1952. John F. Kennedy had also savored the famous chili.

And the chili was famous, indeed. Elizabeth Taylor had several orders of Chasen's chili flown to the set of Cleopatra in 1963 while filming in Rome, Chasen kept his chili recipe a secret and would make it himself on Mondays for the entire week. The restaurant closed on April 1, 1995, falling victim to change. In Europe restaurants last for generations, but in Hollywood they became a fad. It was said that people did not dine anymore, they stopped "gourmet-izing." They just eat.

Scandia, I remember, was another exclusive place, a magnificent Scandinavian restaurant along Sunset Strip founded in 1947 by Ken Hansen. His sister-in-law Teddy Hansen became the hostess, and the restaurant became famous as an extravagant global cuisine spot. Hansen was a Copenhagen native who worked his way up in restaurants and was determined to operate the best restaurant in America.

An eclectic menu featured dishes from Scandinavia and beyond and waiters prepared sizzling steaks and crisp Caesars tableside. Scandia had its own butcher and items were given names like Hamlet's Dagger, (fried lobster and tartar sauce) and Viking Sword, a brochette of broiled turkey breast. A collection of 30,000 bottles of wine featured top grade French and California reds. Impeccable service was a Scandia gift, as was the restaurant's maître d' Frode Benedictus Christensen who seemed to remember everyone, even after one visit. Scandia ruled the Strip, and one critic wrote that no one is very sure of the definition of a great restaurant, but everyone is sure that Scandia is one. The real world was not kind to Scandia. Heavy food was no longer fashionable in the late 1970s. Hansen sold the restaurant to a fellow Dane in 1978, but its glory days were over. It finally closed in 1989.

Alexilion Restaurant located at 10960 Wilshire Boulevard in Westwood was an elegant, first-class restaurant specializing in Greek cuisine, a welcome new venue to the restaurant scene in the 1970s. However, the restaurant, with the entrance in the parking lot behind the Tishman high-rise, was not easy to find. Alexilion is the Greek word for parasol, and Parasol was the name of a chain of Southern California coffee shops owned and operated by Angelo and Ann Pappas, both leaders in the Greek American community and close friends of mine. Alexilion emphasized in its decor the Greek gods and goddesses. It had a very comfortable cocktail lounge, a spacious, grand dining room with semi-circular booths in dark red suede, soaring walls covered with luxurious fabric and with interpretations of ancient Etruscan murals, and with copper service plates adding to the elegance of the table settings.

The menu included successful versions of the classical Greek appetizers, entrees, and desserts, with starters such as taramosalata (fish roe–based dip), tzatziki (thin slices of cucumber in garlic-tinged yogurt), avgolemono soup (egg-lemon soup), saganaki flambé (fried kasseri cheese), stuffed grape leaves, and Greek peasant salad. The entrees included familiar Greek chicken and lamb dishes, moussaka, souvlaki, veal, and shrimp. Desserts and Greek coffee were a special treat, including baklava (thin layers of filo dough encasing a honey-sweetened nut filling), ravani (a sponge cake soaked in orange liqueur with chopped almonds and orange peel), as well as a delicious chocolate mousse torte.

The Brown Derby was shaped like a derby hat, an image synonymous with Hollywood's Golden age Located at 3427 Wilshire Blvd. (across the street from the Ambassador Hotel), the restaurant was designed by Carl Jules Weyl, the art director of the film Casablanca, and opened in 1926. Founded by Wilson Mizner, the property owner was Herbert K. Somborn and Jack L. Warner had put up the money. The Derby became a tempting alternative to the studio commissaries. It was said that the cobb salad originated at the Derby when Sid Grauman (Grauman's Chinese Theater) came to the restaurant late one night asking for something to eat. Chef Robert Cobb tossed together leftovers, lettuce, watercress, chicory, and romaine, topped with diced turkey, blue cheese, hard-boiled egg, sliced tomatoes and avocado. He

Original Brown Derby on Wilshire Blvd near Ambassador hotel

tossed everything in a bowl with French dressing. The restaurant's walls were lined with framed caricatures of the stars who were regular customers. The Derby was a small restaurant and suffered from acoustic problems with sound bouncing off the semicircular ceiling traveling across the room. The Brown Derby closed in 1985, replaced by a stripmall called the Brown Derby Plaza.

Dan Tana, a Serbian American restaurateur, actor, and former professional footballer (soccer), who knew war and hardship in the transforming years of Yugoslavia, eventually played as a striker for Red Star Belgrade. When on a game trip to Belgium he defected, eventually going to Canada and the United States, illegally and without a passport. Recognized by a fellow Serb while a dishwasher in Los Angeles, he was introduced to the Yugoslav American football team. The team arranged a job in a San Pedro tuna cannery and a soccer contract, allowing him to stay in the country legally. While attempting to transition professionally from playing to acting, he worked at various restaurants. At La Scala, he associated with Matty "Matteo" Jordan, Joe Patti, and Piero Selvaggio, each of whom launched successful Italian restaurants.

In 1964, twenty-nine-year-old Tana opened his own eatery by taking over Domenico's hamburger restaurant on Santa Monica Boulevard in West Hollywood, renamed it after himself and adopted the New York-style Italian concept, hiring Chef Michele Diguglio to run the kitchen. With deep, red-painted walls and matching red leather booths, and Chianti bottles dangling from the ceiling, it quickly became known for its delectable Italian food and steaks, along with classic pasta dishes.

Celebrities became fond of Dan Tana, and located next to the Troubadour, the restaurant hosted many notable musicians. In August 1980, the entire restaurant burned down. Linda Ronstadt, staging The Pirates of Penzance on Broadway, hearing that Tana faced a long delay in securing building permits, asked her then boyfriend California Governor Jerry Brown to help, and with his intervention the restaurant was able to reopen in six weeks. In 2009, Tana sold his restaurant to Sonja Perencevic, a budding restaurateur.

Le Dome, West Hollywood's chic French restaurant, was cofounded by Elton John in 1977, the brainchild of Michel Yhuleo and Eddie Kerkhofs. The building at 8720 Sunset Blvd., was formerly the design studio of William Haines, and later the location for Don Loper, the costume and necktie designer. Perched above the Strip it provided a panoramic view of city lights. A large bar was the featured central hub with smaller rooms emerging out from it. The thrust of the menu was Continental, with prime rib chops and tandoori chicken thighs, and a harlequin soufflé, wafting the scent of Grand Marnier. After 20 years of operation, La Dome closed. In 2003, construction tycoon Ron Tutor bought the Dome and renovated it. It closed in 2007.

La Scala, Beverly Hills, was opened in 1956 by Jean Leon, who was born on the northern coast of Spain as Ceferino Carrion. Stowing away on a merchant vessel bound for New York, he bused tables for four dollars a day. The Korean War offered him the opportunity for citizenship with two years of service and Carrion jumped at the chance. He moved to Hollywood, changed his name to Jean Leon, and landed a job at Villa Capri, a restaurant off Hollywood Blvd. He befriended patrons like Frank Sinatra, Marilyn Monroe, Gene Kelly, and James Dean. With Dean he made plans to open their own high-end Italian restaurant, but the actor died in an automobile accident. Leon decided to go forward, took out a loan, and opened La Scala. It was an instant success in Hollywood circles.

Known for its innovation, La Scala was the first restaurant to make its own pasta and to serve white truffles. From a vineyard he purchased outside of Barcelona, Leon made his own Cabernet Sauvignon and Pinot Chardonnay. It was a popular place with visiting politicians, with six US presidents having been served there. I hosted at La Scala Senator Paul Tsongas from Massachusetts on one of his visits to Los Angeles and Kitty Dukakis when Governor Mike Dukakis of Massachusetts was running for president. In 1989, Leon moved his legendary La Scala restaurant and La Scala Boutique to 434 Canon Drive in Beverly Hills. Jean Leon died in 1996, and his daughter Gigi took over the operation.

L'Escoffier at the Beverly Hilton in Beverly Hills was an elegant French restaurant on the eighth floor of the hotel, named after Master Chef Auguste Escoffier. Opened in 1955 with French singer Paula Desjardins flown from Paris by Conrad Hilton to entertain attendees, the restaurant closed in 1994 and was rebranded the Stardust. At its peak, diners were treated to fashion shows from top designers. L'Escoffier was a favorite of mine for special occasions, a place where Sylvia and I could have a great dinner in an elegant setting and dance to music we enjoyed, and it is where the Southern California Association of Electrical Engineers had the annual dinner party when I was president.

Romanoff's, Beverly Hills, opened in 1939 on Rodeo Drive, when the area was known for trendy restaurants rather than a shopping destination. It was the work of Harry F. Gerguson (born Hershel Geguzin), known as Michael Romanoff, a conman and actor born in Lithuania. He claimed to be a member of Russia's royal House of Romanov, widely known to be untrue, but treated by the press as a humorous deception. He talked Charlie Chaplin, Humphrey Bogart, and James Cagney into supporting his restaurant pursuit. The French menu included filet mignon, eggs Benedict, frog legs, and crab-stuffed tomatoes. The chocolate soufflé was considered to be especially good, as was a special dessert, Strawberries Romanoff. The restaurant closed after a New Year's Eve party in 1962.

Musso & Frank Grill at 6667-9 Hollywood Boulevard has often been called "the genesis of Los Angeles." Opened in 1919 by owners Joseph Musso and Frank Toulet, it is the oldest restaurant in Hollywood. Four years later, they sold the restaurant to Joseph Carissimi and John Moss.

Today, Musso & Frank Grill continues with its original character of high ceilings, dark wood paneling, and red booths, and waiters and bartenders dress in the same red coats. Many patrons claim to have heard the ghosts of the past at the bar. Charlie Chaplin's favorite spot, a booth, often suggests a strange presence and a change in variations and temperature. The restaurant claims that many writers, such as Nathaniel West, F. Scott Fitzgerald, and Bill Lippman, created literary works in the high-back booths. In 2013, the *New York Times* named Musso and Frank Grill as one of the ten top "World's Greatest Old Dining Institutions."

Coconut Grove, at the Ambassador Hotel on Wilshire Boulevard, opened in 1921. Occupying twenty-four acres, the lavish hotel attracted high-profile guests and many Hollywood celebrities. The original nightclub was called Zinnia Grill and had murals painted on black satin walls. The lavish Coconut Grove seated 1,000 in tiered seating with boxes that could be reserved on an annual basis. Guests walked down a stately staircase to a ballroom decorated with mechanical monkeys swinging from full-size palm trees, purchased after Rudolph Valentino's movie The Sheik.

Chef Henri would often include citrus fruit and fresh California produce with traditional Continental dishes prepared in a California style, creating a French-California fusion cuisine. In 1930, the Ambassador hosted the second Academy Awards and then did so seven more times. Countless celebrities frequented the Ambassador, and the Grove hosted performers galore, like Bing Crosby, Merv Griffin, Richard Pryor, Barbara Streisand, Judy Garland. Lena Horne, Nat King Cole, Frank Sinatra, the Supremes, Benny Goodman, Liza Minelli, Vickie Carr, Sonny and Cher, and Liberace. Many heads of state and US presidents stayed at the Ambassador, and many US presidents, too. On a sad June 5, 1968 day, Senator Robert F. Kennedy was assassinated in the pantry area after giving a victory speech following the California Democratic presidential primary election.

Los Angeles Unified School District built the Robert F. Kennedy Community Schools, (called the RFK Community Schools), a complex of public schools, designed for 4,200 students, which can be filled by students within a nine-block radius. At a cost of $578 million to build, it is said to be the most expensive public school in America.

Taix French Restaurant was founded in 1927 by the Taix family that arrived in Los Angeles from the Hautes-Alpes region of France in 1870. They opened a hotel in downtown Los Angeles at a time when French immigrants represented 20 percent of the city's population. Today it is the location of the city's Chinatown. The casual restaurant featured French country meals served at long communal tables. The brick building had a tin ceiling, hanging chandeliers, and dark wood floors. It quickly became popular with civic center government workers. The subterranean wine cellar at Taix housed one of the top collections of French and California wines with more than 700 vintages. Interestingly, during the days of Prohibition, the original Taix purchased wine for medicinal purposes and served it quietly to wealthy patrons. In the 1970s the restaurant hosted cooking classes and shows and chef Hubert Ballard taught special cooking techniques and the history of French countryside foods.

The original Taix on 321 Commercial Street, near Union Station, closed in 1964. The new Taix, located at 1911 W. Sunset Boulevard in the Echo Park area, continues to serve simply prepared foods at moderate prices. It was a popular destination before and after the Dodger games and continued operations until 2022, when it closed. The site was slated for redevelopment as a mixed-use project.

Michael's was opened by Michael McCarthy in Santa Monica in 1979 when he was twenty-five years old and had degrees in French cooking, wines, and restaurant management. He wanted his restaurant to be a fun place with a sense of openness and spontaneity. He converted a 1930s three-bedroom house, painting walls a creamy color and adding French doors that opened into a verdant garden.

From the beginning Michael's offered a cuisine that constantly evolved. Outstanding wines are listed on the wine menu, and Michael's has over 800 labels from California, France,

Italy, and other wine-growing regions, as well as the latest vintages from McCarthy's own Malibu Vineyard. Feeling that Michael's grew organically from his own life experiences, McCarthy focused on the freshest farmers' market products, and his dishes changed to accommodate whatever was sold in the local market at the time. He got rid of the restaurant's white tablecloths and fine silver and simplified his flower arrangements. Michael's earned the right to be considered an icon, according to the Michelin Guide, and it continues to operate at the original site.

LA Nicola was the brainchild of Larry Nicola who was called an innovator and trendsetter and one of Los Angeles's most synergistic and diverse restaurateurs. In 1980, he opened LA Nicola, across the street from The Nicola Twins Market—a family business since 1944 where Fountain Avenue meets Sunset Boulevard. Quickly the restaurant became "a gathering spot for an eclectic Silver Lake crowd of yuppies, artists, celebrities, and regular folks," according to the *Los Angeles Times*.

After twelve years the restaurant closed, and a new restaurant, named Nicola's, opened downtown with a 110-seat dining area as well as a large patio with take-out food. Because of the Los Angeles riots, Nicola said, the restaurant did not make it; it was an economic disaster and was sold. From downtown he moved to Beverly Hills, to Nic's Beverly Hills, and continued to grow his Martini Lounge and installed the Vodbox, a walk-in freezer (twenty-eight degrees Fahrenheit) at the back of the restaurant that housed more than fifty different vodkas on thirty shelves. Guests enter to taste vodka wearing faux fur coats and hats to keep warm, provided by the restaurant. "It's like you were in St. Petersburg on a winter's night," he told me. "Each vodka has a different taste." Los Angeles food is getting simpler, he said. "You can only taste three or four bites. People like to share, so smaller plates with a variety of food are good and when you have a cocktail you can pick up an olive, or an oyster, or something like that." Nic's closed in 2016.

The Polo Lounge in the Beverly Hills Hotel, known as a center of power dining in Los Angeles, a preferred place of stars, Hollywood power brokers, politicians, and world leaders, was named after the polo fields on which it was built. The hotel is known as the "Pink Palace" from the special pink it was painted back in 1948. The trailblazing African American architect and first African American member of the AIA, Paul Revere Williams, designed the hotel's Crescent Wing, as well as reimagined the Polo Lounge when the hotel was renovated in the 1940s. Williams was also the creator of the hotel script and front signage.

Both the hotel and the lounge have had roles in politics, such as the Watergate Scandal in 1972. The leaders of the Committee to Re-Elect President Richard Nixon, US Attorney General John Mitchell, Jeb Magruder, and Fred LaRue, were staying at the hotel. Watergate burglar G. Gordon Liddy called Magruder at the Polo Lounge, a call Magruder had to take outside the lounge for security reasons. When Governor Bill Clinton would visit Los Angeles, I would meet him for drinks or dinner at the Polo Lounge and had many memorable conversations and the opportunity to develop a close relationship with him.

Bistro and Bistro Garden were opened by a German immigrant, Kurt Niklas, who was maître d' at Romanoff's. When Romanoff's closed, Niklas was encouraged by director Billy Wilder to open his own restaurant. Niklas opened the Bistro on North Canon Drive in 1963, bankrolled by such luminaries as Jack Benny, Frank Sinatra, and Tony Curtis. The restaurant immediately attracted "the Beautiful People," including actors, producers, politicians, the Kennedys, and Ronald and Nancy Reagan. In 1979, Niklas opened the Bistro Garden nearby on the same street as an informal setting best known as a place where ladies would have lunch, including First Ladies Nancy Reagan and Barbara Bush. Jackie Collins was inspired to write her novel Hollywood Wives there. The Bistro closed in 1994 and presently is Mastro's restaurant on the second floor. The Bistro Gardens location in Beverly Hills became Spago, the flagship restaurant of Wolfgang Puck.

Bistro Gardens relocated in 1990 to Coldwater and Ventura Boulevards in the San Fernando Valley to an elegant venue with a "garden" atmosphere that often served as a film set for TV and movies. The owners, Greg and Carolyn Niklas Pappas, grew up in restaurant families. Greg is the son of our family friends Angelo and Ann Pappas of Alexilion and other Los Angeles area restaurants, and Carolyn is the daughter of Kurt Niklas of the Beverly Hills Bistro and Bistro Gardens.

Bistro Gardens closed its San Fernando Valley location in 2020 after thirty years, a victim of the COVID-19 pandemic, but the Pappas family of Bistro Gardens remained in the food business with Bistro Kitchen and Catering, a service offering deliveries of fully cooked meals ready to be reheated at home.

Jimmy's was located at the border of Beverly Hills and Century City. It was founded by Jimmy Murphy, an Irish immigrant, and was a popular restaurant with entertainment talent and executives, politicians, attorneys, and businesspersons working in Century City. It was the place where Washington politicians would have lunch or dinner and where they would hold small fundraisers. I held various fundraisers there for Vice President Walter Mondale when he was running for US president, and I was the campaign's Southern California finance chair. Charlotte Conway, Nelson Rising's sister and a fundraising star at the time, would arrange dinners at Jimmy's when Senator Ted Kennedy visited Los Angeles. She would arrange for me to sit next to Senator Kennedy at these events. These were great opportunities to get to know the Senator and develop a friendship I valued. Before opening Jimmy's, Murphy was maître'd at the Bistro and was persuaded to open his own place by Johny Carson and Don Rickles in 1978. The formal restaurant emphasized French and California cuisines. It closed in 2000.

La Serre, a French restaurant specializing in haute cuisine on Ventura Boulevard at Coldwater, was for many years the most prestigious restaurant in the San Fernando Valley. It opened in 1974, and quickly developed a reputation for French cooking in charming, small dining rooms with rustic brick floors and filled with plants. With an interior décor that created intimate areas suitable for privacy, La Serre attracted diners from the various studios as well as from business and entertainment. The restaurant closed in November 1991 as a result of the recession. Mistral, a French Bistro, was opened in 1988 by one of the owners of La Serre just blocks away.

TOP-SHELF WINES BECOME THE RESTAURANT'S CRITICAL FOCUS

Most fine-dining restaurants make a small profit on their food items but more than 80 percent profit on alcohol sales. Wine lists are wide-ranging with various vintages and price points, featuring everything from a $15 sauvignon blanc to a $15,000 bottle of rare Burgundy. In a successful restaurant the sommelier plays a major role. He must gain the trust of the customer and provide an objective wine assessment and recommendation. Cultured and elegant, he stimulates a patron's interest in food and drink.

David Osenbach, the wine director of the Michelin-starred Providence, is such a person. His 600-label wine list is curated to marry well with the seafood-centric cuisine and tasting menu. In reviewing wine with me, he said, "There are three different types of people at the restaurant: the adventurous who want to find something new and interesting, those who know enough to appreciate the wine they like and want it, and the people who want to spend money on a bottle of wine that doesn't go at all with the entrée they are eating. There used to be a time when people dreaded having the sommelier come to their table, afraid he was trying to sell them something. That has changed, now they actively embrace his presence."

Views on wine vary depending on the culture of the sommeliers. California wine versus French, he said, depends on individual regions. "Bordeaux has been beaten down almost because it priced itself out. It's like $5,000 a bottle of first growths. California Merlot still has that sidewise backlash of a few years ago. Pinot noir became the darling of everything." Osenbach noted that Chardonnay is another good wine, although there was an oaky chardonnay backlash. Oak is something it needs, he claimed, otherwise it turns into a tropical fruit salad mess. I inquired about Paso Robles and its position in California wines. "It is having its moment," he replied, "and Lodi, as well." Regarding New Zealand, sauvignon blanc is big, he added, as is pinot noir. Australia is a different story because "it decided to make a ton of cheap wine and flood the market, and then everyone said when they think of Australian wine they think of Yellow Tail."

Providence is an example of a successful restaurant that has a capacity of eighty to eighty-five guests, and on a busy night, they will do 120 wine pairings. There are fifty people on staff, equating to one staff member for every two guests. As Osenbach told me that if you go to a restaurant with fantastic service and mediocre food, the restaurant will be remembered. However, if the food is fantastic and the service is mediocre, the restaurant will not be remembered.

Ken Bleifer, a fellow member of the Wine and Food Society of the San Fernando Valley, knows wines and restaurants. His father, an actor in the 1930s, knew about Los Angeles's best eating places and drove by them, never really tasting their food because "he couldn't afford it," he told me. He recalled the dominance of French restaurants in the 1980s, and how the Italian places took over the Los Angeles scene after 2000. French restaurants, for the most part, are quiet places, while Italian eateries are busy and noisy and raucous at times, and that's what people like. "Quiet restaurants don't make it," he said.

Bleifer shared with me how with the advance of food, wine became a big part of the dinner, and then people looked at wine as a separate entity. Wine societies opened up, then competitions, then tastings, he related. He pointed to Robert Parker and the Wine Advocate and credited him for putting wine on the map as early as 1982. Wine merchandising grew. A French restaurant once carried Montrachet Domaine de la Romanee Conti in the 1960s for $75 a bottle. Today a 2009 bottle of that wine sells for $16,000.

The California wine industry, probably next to Bordeaux and Burgundy and Rhone, is the second-best wine producing area. Italy may also be second-best. The development, he said, of little boutique wines where they would produce maybe 400 cases, and you had to subscribe, had to be on restaurant wine lists. They couldn't be found in stores. "It piqued the interest, maybe involved a little snobbery, but it was good for the economic development of the California wine industry." When Bleifer, a nephrologist, started collecting wine decades ago, he did not think of it as an investment. He simply loved wine and, like many connoisseurs, ended up buying much more than he could ever drink. Later he began selling a portion of the 4,000 bottles stashed in his wine cellar. A dozen years back he sold two bottles of Burgundy purchased for $80 in 1983 for $4,700. Bleifer told me that wine investing required buying prestigious labels, such as from France's Bordeaux region, and holding them for years. Every bottle that is uncorked lifts the value of the remaining bottles.

WOMEN RULE THE KITCHEN

Top restaurant kitchens are not the province of men. Talented women chefs abound and are prominent in the Los Angeles food scene. As a matter of fact, a new female-led era is dawning, according to the late Jonathan Gold, and it's about time.

Nancy Silverton, chef and restaurateur, rented a house in Tuscany thirty-three years ago, and promptly became obsessed with Italian cuisine. Three decades later, she became one of LA's most notable chefs as the owner and coowner of multiple restaurants across Los Angeles—namely La Brea Bakery and Michelin-starred Osteria Mozza. Now she splits her time between California and Umbria cooking and learning and celebrating the abundance of the Italian countryside.

Suzanne Goin, a celebrated chef and restaurateur from Los Angeles, ran three fine-dining restaurants, Lucques (now closed), Tavern, which she runs with partner Caroline Styne, as well as four Larders. Goin's background includes positions in acclaimed restaurants in the United States, including Ma Maison, L'Orangerie in Los Angeles, Al Forno in Providence, Olives in Boston, Chez Panisse in Berkeley, and Alain Passard's Arpège in Paris. Her work as executive chef at Campanile put her on the culinary map in Los Angeles and laid the groundwork for her first restaurant.

Evan Kleiman, chef and author, radio host and restaurant owner, has been the host of "Good Food" on KCRW since 1997 and was inducted into the James Beard Who's Who of Food and Beverage in America in 2017. She grew up in Los Angeles and earned a bachelor's degree and master's degree at UCLA. She opened Angeli Caffe in 1984, which served Italian food before closing after twenty-eight years.

Mary Sue Milliken came from Chicago and Paris where, with her longtime collaborator Susan Feniger, founded the critically acclaimed City Café in 1981. They moved to a larger space on La Brea Avenue and renamed the establishment CITY Restaurant. In 1985, they opened the Mexican restaurant Border Grill in the original City Café space, before moving it to Santa Monica in 1990. Milliken and her partner opened Ciudad, now closed, in Rex's former space in Los Angeles in 1998. The success of their restaurants often led Milliken and Feniger to be recognized for their important role in the changing of Los Angeles's culinary landscape.

Suzanne Tracht is considered a driving force in the Los Angeles culinary scene as the chef/owner of Jar, one of mayor Antonio Villaraigosa's favorites, a modern chophouse revered for its timeless setting, and exceptional steaks, braises, and seasonal sides—including Suzanne's sumptuous pot roast. She is highly respected for the purity of her cooking, especially her signature braises.

Odette Fada earned a degree in culinary arts in Italy and worked with Gianfranco Vissani in Orvieto and Rome, she became chef for the renowned Rex Il Ristorante by Mauro Vincenti. Fada has cooked for Italian enthusiasts as well as Oscar parties and the Grammy Awards, all while searching for the finest Italian ingredients available.

Sossi Brady, along with Serve, has redefined the Lebanese Armenian kitchen in Hollywood since the mid-1990s, according to Jonathan Gold. A splendid array of small dishes, called mezze, roast chicken and barbecue quail, as well as fried sardines and grilled sausage, are outstanding features as are Lebanese wine and housemade jallab. The Lebanese kitchen is the most cosmopolitan in the Middle East.

Xiomara Ardolina left Cuba as a child in the 1960s, and in 1979, opened the nouvelle-inspired place in La Cañada called the Epicurean. In 1991, Xiomara Restaurant debuted in Old Pasadena, where the kitchen dealt primarily in California cuisine. The plates were as big, the greens drizzled with raspberry vinegar, the chicken breast sliced and splayed. With the opening of the second Xiomara near Hancock Park in 2003, she repositioned the venture with dishes from the place of her birth: roast pork leg with juicy caramelized plantains, and ropa vieja, a slow-cooked beef stew, by making it with duck and spooning it over manchego-spiked polenta. It later closed.

Genet Agonafer, a former flight attendant, caterer, and now proprietor of one of LA's most beloved Ethiopian restaurants, and sole chef of Meals by Genet, an upscale gathering place at the heart of Fairfax's Little Ethiopia district. Covid played a disheartening role for Agonafer. Before the pandemic, she would regularly arrive at 5 or 6 a.m., prepping all day for an onslaught of customers was often, especially on weekends. Sometimes, she says, she would work eighteen or nineteen-hour shifts. Then she shifted to carry-out menus.

Josie Le Balch grew up in Southern California with a very French upbringing, especially during mealtime. Her father was a celebrated chef from Brittany and started one of LA's first cooking schools in the early 1960s. He also had an eponymous restaurant, Chef Gregoire on Ventura in Sherman Oaks. It is said the chef failed to show one day ,and she, then fourteen, filled in. She became known as chef-owner of Josie Restaurant in Santa Monica for her farmers' market approach to American cooking "with French and Italian influences." Then she opened Josie Next Door to reveal a quirkier side: beer and bacon caramel corn, deviled eggs, booze-cured salmon, and dry-rubbed pork riblets.

Indeed, women in Los Angeles's kitchens are many and very talented. Only a few have been mentioned. Many more are expanding the culinary tastes of Los Angeles, changing with the seasons and over time, as good food should.

ETHNIC RESTAURANTS

The dining scene in Los Angeles has increasingly shifted in recent years to reflect ethnicity as the result of the region's pluralism and demographics. Los Angeles has become a culinary mecca, with a wide variety of cuisines, including Italian, Middle Eastern, Asian, Mexican, Central and South American, Caribbean, and Greek. In fact, Los Angeles is a hotbed of sushi in America. This is one benefit of the geographic sprawl, with some examples of this variety below:

Bestia, Bavel, Brera Ristorante, Factory Kitchen, Bridgetown Roti in the Arts District.
Damian, Holy Basil, Hayato, and Sushi Kaneyoshi in downtown Los Angeles
Skaf's and Mini Kabob in Glendale.
Great Greek, Carnival, and Anajak Thai in Sherman Oaks.
Louka in Beverly Hills and Taste of Tehran in Westwood.
And Rocio's Mexican Kitchen, a nondescript, Michelin star gem in Bell Gardens.

Food is certainly one of the "lifestyle arts" that distinguishes Los Angeles, along with others starting with "f," film, fashion, and finance, as well as architecture, aerospace, music, and now video games.

CHAPTER TEN

OVERSIGHT OF PUBLIC PROJECTS AND AGENCIES

You will not find a more tenacious fiscal watchdog than Nick. Nick has a proven track record of scrutinizing large-scale projects.

—LA COUNTY SUPERVISOR GLORIA MOLINA TO THE LA TIMES

THE $1.6 BILLION WHITE ELEPHANT

I-405 widening | In 2009, the Los Angeles County Metropolitan Transportation Authority awarded a design-build contract to Kiewit Corp. to build a ten-mile-long, high-occupancy vehicle lane on the northbound 405 Freeway between the 10 and 101 freeways. The cost was estimated at $1.03 billion. According to Metro's engineers, the drawings were incomplete and were not ready to go out to bid. But the Metro Board of Directors ignored staff's concerns and awarded the contract at the urging of US Representatives Brad Sherman and Howard Berman. They informed the board that "There is $149 million federal funding available and use it or lose it," meaning the federal funds would be available contingent on construction beginning in 2009. It was an opportunity for members of the board to have a groundbreaking with all the fanfare, knowing that they might not be around when it came time to pay the piper. But the homeowners in the area suffered for five years during construction, and the taxpayers ended up with a $1.6 billion "white elephant."

Metro was tasked with procuring and managing the project, even though highways were not its core competence. In order to backfill their lack of highway experience, Metro partnered with the California Department of Transportation, or Caltrans, to support the construction phases of the project, but Metro retained managerial control. The lead designer was HNTB Corporation. The project became bogged down with numerous problems right from the beginning. Richard Raine, Kiewit project manager, said, "There were hundreds of changed conditions in the field. Design approvals were slow and difficult. Additionally, the scope of utility relocation ballooned." In 2011 and 2012, Metro had already closed a ten mile stretch of the 405, creating havoc for residents of the San Fernando Valley working in West Los Angeles. Detours, delays, highway shutdowns, and streets clogged with traffic became part of the everyday life in the area for five years.

In May 2013, Eric Garcetti was elected mayor of Los Angeles. In August of the same year I received a call from Borja Leon, Garcetti's deputy for transportation, requesting a meeting with the new mayor. I met with Garcetti in his City Hall office, and he told me he would appreciate my overseeing the completion of the 405 HOV lane, because the project was close to two years behind schedule and saddled with serious cost overruns. I told Garcetti, "Mr. Mayor, our relationship has been strictly professional. When I was board president of the Los Angeles Department of Water and Power and you were president of the City Council, we would meet to discuss issues as they related to LADWP matters. Mayor Villaraigosa asked me to oversee the LA Police Administration Building because we are very good friends. My friendship with Mayor Villaraigosa goes back twenty-five years, and he has seen me in action while we both served on the Southern California Rapid Transit District board (the precursor to Metro). Why are you asking me to undertake this difficult and demanding task?" Garcetti's response was "First, people I trust, trust you. Second, you get things done. Third, you are not transactional. And fourth, your name is a brand in this city." After the conversation, I agreed to serve and went to work immediately as an unpaid volunteer.

I started my involvement by chairing a biweekly meeting with Metro, Caltrans, Kiewit, and representatives of the architect and construction manager. I had a history of overseeing mega-scale projects for the Los Angeles County and the City of Los Angeles over a span of more than fifteen years, many with similar problems I was now asked to mitigate. Given the crucial nature of the work and the importance of keeping the projects on a budget and a timeline, the meetings started at 8 a.m. sharp, a fact quickly understood by all involved. The reason I insisted that it would be the first meeting of the day was so there would not be an excuse for late comings, because "I was detained in another meeting."

At the very first meeting, the project managers of Metro and Kiewit almost had a fistfight. "I don't trust you," they yelled at each other. These men had been working together for four years and one could cut the vitriol, anger, and mistrust between them with a knife. I stepped in and said, "Hold it. This is a new beginning. We will leave all sentiments and bad feelings at the door, and we will work as a team from now on." I then turned to Raine, Kiewit's project manager, and asked him, "Richard, what can we do for you?" Raine was visibly surprised. Obviously, he did not expect such a question. I continued, "I am a fair man, and I don't expect answers right now. Bring your list at the next meeting."

I got a call from Raine that afternoon asking if we could meet for coffee. I invited Raine to meet me at the Jonathan Club in downtown Los Angeles. At the meeting, Raine told me, "Mr. Patsaouras, we have been working on this project for close to four years, and not once we have been asked 'what can we do for you?' I promise I'll get together with my team and we'll have the list at the next meeting. I'll also bring a list of achievable but aggressive dates for major accomplishments such as opening of ramps and major traffic switches." At the next meeting, Raine, passed me the lists. Raine reminisced sometime later, "I remember vividly what happened next. Patsaouras took our lists and without looking at them, slid them across the table to Metro's project manager and directed him to implement all of the things on the list."

It was a simple yet clear action that set into motion a long overdue joint effort to meet the milestones enumerated in the list. The meetings were used to check in on the status of the goals and for clearing roadblocks. The parties were finally working jointly toward the same goals. Things started happening, and at a much faster pace.

My practice was to place "TIME IS MONEY" at the top of the agenda page. The bottom of the page read: "Accountability/ Communication/ Coordination/ Integrity /Responsibility/ Responsiveness/ Transparency / Trust." In the meetings, Raine often mentioned, "Finally there is urgency." As a result, I added "urgency" to the credo on the agenda. Below are two examples that illustrate the meaning of this type of urgency.

There was work to be done at the Skirball Center Drive on-ramp/off-ramp. A dispute among Caltrans, the Los Angeles Department of Transportation, or LADOT, and LA Bureau of Public Works had been going on for months. When the issue was raised in one of the biweekly meetings, I instructed the Metro project manager to go out in the hall and ask all those involved to come over at 10:00 a.m. The project manager was flabbergasted, amazed and hesitant to place the call. "How can all these people come within an hour's notice?" he asked. I told him, "Go in the hall and place the call, please." He came back ten minutes later and said, "They will be here at 10:00 a.m." I listened to the point of view of each of the three entities and after twenty minutes, based on logic, my technical knowledge and experience, I said, "Caltrans is right."

Another case involved the Getty Center. Getty and LADOT disagreed as to the number of traffic lanes along Getty Drive. The issue had been going on for more than two years without resolution. I requested that Getty and all parties meet at LADOT headquarters at 9 a.m. on Monday November 25, 2013. Within two hours of the request, I was forwarded an email sent from Getty to the mayor's office asking, "Who is Patsaouras, what authority does he have to call a meeting and who attends?" I did not bother to give a long explanation and justification. I punched the caps lock on my computer and wrote, "I AM THE TAXPAYERS' WATCHDOG. I WILL SEE YOU ON MONDAY AT 9:00 A.M." Within twenty minutes in that meeting the issue was resolved and LADOT prevailed.

Getty had been the big gorilla so far in the process, and they were shocked that somebody had stood up to them. When reviewing the costs, I noticed a number of change orders totaling $15 million under "Getty betterments." When I asked the construction manager why she had been eager to please Getty with taxpayers' money, she answered in a timid, apologetic manner, "Well, it's Getty." She and the rest in the group were at awe of Getty, and Getty was running the show within their geographic area.

The person who "gave" the taxpayer's money to Getty worked for the construction management firm that was a "body shop." Their employees seemed to not have pride of ownership or public interest. The contract was not a fixed fee contract, so the longer the project dragged on, the more money they charged because they were paid by the hour. That firm had been awarded a very small contract in February 2009 to provide technical assistance to staff. That contract ballooned from a few hundred thousand dollars to $140 million as of 2016. The company was still involved with the project in 2023.. It was given twenty-five projects by Metro without board members ever questioning the staff's recommendation every time they came before the board for approval.

The same company that managed the 405 widening had also provided construction management services for the Crenshaw/LAX Transit Project (K Line). In fiscal year 2015, the company charged Metro $627,456.00 for a resident engineer and $118,783.00 for an administrative assistant.

The Metro Board had voted in June 2013 to award a $1.27 billion contract to Walsh/Shea Corridor Construction for the Crenshaw/LAX (K) Line, an 8.5-mile alignment to be completed by September 2018. The lead designer was HNTB Corporation. The K Line was four years behind schedule and ultimately cost the taxpayer nearly $2.45 billion, including $600 million in change orders and claims. A staggering $288 million per mile! By comparison, the 21.9-mile Blue Line, in today's dollars, costs $100 million per mile. The six-mile Gold Line, Eastside, which is partially underground, costed $147 million per mile in today's dollars.

When I asked who was going to pay for the cost overruns of the 405 widening project, Carrie Brown, the Caltrans district director for Southern California, said, "Certainly not the Feds, and Caltrans has no money. Metro has the money, and, above all, they mismanaged the project." And, in fact, Metro paid.

During the time the new working relationship developed, a lot of progress had been made and it seemed possible that the opening of the freeway could happen sooner than the November 2014 projected completion date. The projected opening was moved first to September and then July. I approached Raine and asked him, "Based on the progress thus far, how about May?" Rain responded, "Nick you are crazy, but I'll check with my team and Omaha [Kiewit headquarters] and I'll let you know." At the next meeting, Raine advised me that they would try to deliver the project the weekend before Memorial Day 2014, provided Metro, Caltrans, and the city agencies cooperated.

Mayor Garcetti in his first State of the City address said, "When I took office, I right away called my old friend, Nick Patsaouras, and I asked him to expedite the project. I'm pleased to announce that the 405 will open the weekend before Memorial Day. Mind you, opening early did not cost the taxpayers a nickel, and there were no overtime charges."

According to the *Los Angeles Times*, at the opening ceremonies in May 2014, Los Angeles County Supervisor Zev Yaroslavsky said, "People in this part of town have put up with a lot, and it's finally time for the public to begin experiencing one of the major benefits of this project. . . . I've been asked many times 'Was it worth it?' It was very much worth it. I wish it had been on time and on budget."

Former Metro chief executive Philip A. Washington gave the typical bureaucratic cheerleading comment: "Traffic would have been much worse if we had not done anything."

There were construction cost claims because of defective and incomplete drawings and delays. The original claim of $518 million was filed by Kiewit in May 2014, the same month the carpool lane opened. Metro settled the claim with Kiewit for $300 million. The settlement was funded through the sale of bonds financed by Proposition C, a half-cent sales tax that Los Angeles County voters had approved in 1990, and certainly not for the 405 Freeway cost overruns in 2016.

Suspiciously, the Metro Board approved the settlement less than two weeks after voters approved Measure M, a new half-cent sales tax. A number of officials, including former

Metro board member Yaroslavsky, questioned whether the announcement of the settlement had been withheld pending the election. Martin Wachs, an urban planning researcher at the RAND Corp,. told the *New York Times*, "I certainly do believe that the announcement timing was influenced by the Measure M vote."

Was $1.6 billion Worth It?

On December 20, 2016, the *New York Times* published an article by Adam Nagourney with the headline, "Los Angeles Drivers Ask: Was $1.6 billion worth it?" And the categorical answer is NO!

The *New York Times* quoted Los Angeles County supervisor and MTA board member Yaroslavsky as saying, "It was the most disruptive project" he had seen during his forty years in public life. "I doubt the project would have been undertaken in the first place, if we'd known it would cost $1.6 billion…It was a nightmare of a project." Bob Anderson, an engineer who was on the community advisory board for the project said in the same story, "As far as improvement, I don't see anything. Was it worth a billion dollars? I doubt it. Was it worth $1.6 billion?" The homeowners in the area suffered for five years , and the taxpayers ended up with a $1.6 billion "white elephant." "In the long term, it will make no difference to the traffic pattern," Marcia Hobbs, who has lived her whole life in Bel Air, told the *New York Times* "I haven't noticed substantial cutbacks in traffic. As a matter of fact, I would say it was the opposite." According to a study by Metro, congestion is as bad, even worse, during the busiest hours of 4:30 p.m. to 6:30 p.m.

In July 2011, Christopher Hawthorne, the *Los Angeles Times* architecture critic, wrote, "It's striking, though, that amid all this handwringing we've barely paused to ask the most basic questions about what the widening project means for the city and how we navigate it or how we think about the relationship between architecture and mobility in a city planned for more than half a century around the primacy of the car To begin with: Is widening the 405 really something that we should be spending $1.6 billion? Will it actually make traffic through the pass better? And if so, for how long? As soon as you open up new lanes, drivers adjust: A few more decide to take the newly widened route each day, and before long the congestion is just as bad as before."

In an oped piece in the *Los Angeles Daily News* in June 2022, veteran public servant Rick Cole wrote, "Yet now that the brutal racism, colossal waste, and utter failure of these monstrosities (freeways) is increasingly recognized, the tide may be turning against the displacement, pollution, and climate arson consequences of widening urban highways. Just as the 405 quickly filled up after Metro spent $1.6 billion to widen it, these costly projects will invariably fail to reduce congestion."

In July 2015, Hawthorne wrote another piece in the *Los Angeles Times*. It said, "As it snakes over the Sepulveda Pass, the expanded freeway should feel like a unified corridor, a streamlined platform for dramatic views. Given typical traffic patterns on this part of the 405, among the busiest stretches of highway in the country, it should look as good to drivers going three miles per hour as sixty-three. Instead, it's a hodgepodge. The walls near the Getty Center don't match the ones fronting the Skirball Cultural Center, at the top of the pass, or those farther south, approaching UCLA. If the new 405 were a house, it would be covered with stucco, glass, shingles, and tile, with little Tutor half-timbering thrown in for good measure. The expanded 405 might be the first LA freeway project to look haggard and disjointed the day it opened."

Throughout the centuries, architecture has been used to bridge the gaps between physical or psychological obstacles. Most of these bridges are also regarded as landmarks. Golden Gate Bridge links the northern tip of the San Francisco Peninsula and Marin County. West Los Angeles and San Fernando Valley are almost two cities by themselves, and the 405 is the link between them. It was a lost opportunity to connect these two places architecturally, aesthetically, and figuratively with the 405. Bridges do more than connect two pieces of land. They ignite the imagination and inspire us with their beauty.

East Los Angeles has been blessed with the Sixth Street Viaduct, designed by the famous local architect Michael Maltzan. A lost opportunity was the design, or rather the lack of design, of the bridges that replaced the 405's three major bridges at Mulholland Drive, Skirball Center Drive, and Sunset Boulevard. The 320,000 daily drivers stuck in traffic on the 405 can only look at utilitarian bridges, if they notice them, which replaced the unimaginative bridges designed in the early 1950s by Caltrans engineers. Instead, if there were some visionaries at Metro, those daily drivers would enjoy looking at great architecture that would bring some serenity and peace to their heart and mind, while stuck in traffic.

Again, "Was $1.6 Billion Worth It?" The answer lies within the decision of Metro, which is spending tens of millions of dollars to study a transit system to alleviate the traffic between West Los Angeles and the San Fernando Valley that will cost $15 billion to $20 billion to construct, with most of the funds not identified as of yet.

Cost overruns such as this, and all Metro projects are excessively over budget, necessitate projects in other communities being postponed or eliminated altogether. In addition, the inability to complete projects on time and on budget ultimately leads to higher fares and taxes, as it also takes away from service upgrades, and long overdue improvements are scaled back or canceled.

THE ELON MUSK VIGNETTE

In August of 2013, Elon Musk, the billionaire chief executive of Telsa and Space Exploration Technologies, unveiled ambitious plans for his "Hyperloop," a transportation system that according to Musk, is similar to the old pneumatic tubes used to send mail and packages within and between buildings but would operate under much less pressure to save energy. Musk claimed that a trip between Los Angeles and San Francisco would take thirty minutes travel time. He had approached newly elected Mayor Eric Garcetti about the possibility of building the hyperloop system parallel to the 405 Freeway, one of the nation's most crowded highways, to connect the San Fernando Valley and Los Angeles International Airport. The mayor at that time had asked me to oversee the construction of the troubled widening of the 405, which was experiencing years in delays and horrendous cost overruns. Garcetti suggested that I meet with Musk to hear what he had to offer. The mayor arranged a meeting for me at Musk's Space X facilities in Hawthorne, where I was welcomed by an affable Musk who gave me a tour. As an electrical engineer, I had spent countless hours in laboratories in my college years, but still I was impressed by what I witnessed. Vast open space, clean as a surgery room, full of rockets, satellites and groups of engineers and scientists huddled in front of computers and other equipment, a science fiction movie.

After the tour, Musk invited me to lunch at the facility's dining room, where the employees can eat gourmet food prepared by great chefs and continue their technical discussions. Musk explained the Hyperloop involves transporting passengers in aluminum pods through tubes, using air cushions to achieve near supersonic speeds. Each capsule would carry twenty-eight people, and a ticket could cost $20 for a one-way trip. He claimed that his Hyperloop would cost $6 billion versus $68 billion for the same phase of the bullet train connecting Los Angeles and San Francisco.

According to the Los Angeles Times, *in fact, it was the high cost of the high-speed rail project that prompted Musk to research the Hyperloop in the first place. "How could it be that the home of Silicon Valley and JPL—doing incredible things like indexing all the world's knowledge and putting rovers on Mars—would build a bullet train that is both one of the most expensive per mile and one of the slowest in the world?" he said. I explained to Musk that, based on my experience, constructing a rail system purely on technical terms is relatively simple. However, the challenges are politics, the relocation of very old infrastructure, street conditions, disruption of business operations, land acquisitions, community opposition, etc.*

Of course, as expected, the media greeted the Hyperloop with headlines such as, "Seriously, Elon Musk? Are you Kidding Me With This Tunnel? What Is This?" or "Sorry, Elon Musk-Your Hyperloop is going nowhere" or "Hyperloop: Transportation Nirvana, or a Pipe Dream." And he was derided when he went head-to-head with the National Aeronautics and Space Administration when he unveiled SpaceX, his space launch company. We tend to ridicule visionaries and dreamers throughout history, men and women ahead of their times. But their tenacity, persistence and perseverance, failure after failure, and not giving up, at the end those ideas have made our lives better and safer.

Unfortunately, when it comes to transportation systems, the United States finds itself behind Europe. In May 2023, Hyperloop Transportation Technologies, won a bid to build a prototype in Italy in collaboration with Zaha Hadid Architects. The Venetian Motorway Concession, known as CAV, awarded Hyperloop Transportation Technologies $85 million that could lead to a hyperloop along a portion of the twenty-five-mile route from Padua to Venice.

RIBBON OF LIGHT

Sixth Street Viaduct | The Sixth Street Viaduct, the largest bridge project in the history of Los Angeles, was dedicated to the people of Los Angeles on July 9, 2022. It is a transformative infrastructure project for the City of Los Angeles, replacing the original 1932 bridge, uniting the Boyle Heights community to the east and the Arts District and downtown to the west. The bridge is the east/west backbone of the region, the bow tying Whittier Boulevard at the east and, with a small jog, Wilshire Boulevard to the west.

Press conference regarding 6th Street Bridge. Mayor Antonio Villaraigosa, Edward McSpedon HNTB Executive at the podium, and Gary Moore, General Manager of BoE. Photo: courtesy of E. McSpedon.

6th Street Viaduct. Photo: Shervin Khazra

The original bridge was diagnosed with alkali-silica reaction, causing it to become structurally deficient and in danger of failure in a magnitude 7.3 or stronger earthquake. The deterioration was often attributed to the concrete used in its construction, which made use of sand collected from the Los Angeles River.

The new bridge rests on thirty-two seismic base isolators equipped with triple friction pendulum bearings at its twenty-three columns and abutments. This configuration allows the structure to move up to thirty inches independently in situations involving seismic activity and can withstand a magnitude 9.0 earthquake, which scientists predict happens once per millennium.

Initially, the City of Los Angeles's Bureau of Engineering and the California Department of Transportation, or Caltrans, suggested a standard utilitarian bridge. However, Mayor Antonio Villaraigosa demanded that the city conduct an international design competition, and his instructions were, "Dream big and make the new bridge an iconic and lasting landmark for Los Angeles." The project was conceived and green-lighted during the Villaraigosa administration in 2012. Therefore, it was disheartening to observe at the dedication ceremony politicians, who were not even in office at that time, self-congratulating, lobbing kudos among themselves and city engineers, and not once mentioning Villaraigosa's name! This was an example of politics at its worst.

The successful team of HNTB, infrastructure engineers; Hargreaves Associates, the landscape architects; and internationally recognized architect Michael Maltzan as its leader saw the bridge not just as a replacement, but as a multimodal project, one that accommodates cars and incorporates significant new bicycle lanes. In addition, it increases connectivity for pedestrians to access the viaduct, not only at its endpoints, but along the entirety of the span, linking the bridge, the Los Angeles River, and urban landscapes in a more meaningful relationship.

The bridge is 3,500 feet long (two-thirds of a mile), thirty to sixty feet high and one hundred feet wide, with ten concrete arches of varying heights along either side of the entire length of the bridge. "To open up the roadway with generosity to the sky, the arches point outward nine degrees," Maltzan said.

The structure's generous spans create large recreational green spaces below that were planned to include a twelve-acre park, soccer fields, fitness facilities, a playground, basketball and volleyball courts, a dog park, and picnic areas. An arts plaza and amphitheater on the west side of the park were designed by Hargreaves Associates. The new bridge spans the Los Angeles River, eighteen railroad tracks, the 101 Freeway and several city roads. Groundbreaking took place in 2016, with a contractual opening date of September 22, 2020. Extensive delays and cost overruns plagued the project. As a result, Mayor Eric Garcetti asked me in May 2018 to get involved and rescue the project. I had helped the mayor with another troubled project, the widening of the 405 freeway, also in a volunteer capacity.

In 2013, the city had entered into a Construction Manager/General Contractor, or CMGC, contract with Skanska Stacy and Witbeck (SSW) "as a bridge construction expert." CMGC is a contracting method that involves the contractor in the design process. This approach forms a partnership with the city, the design consultant, and the contractor to maximize the scope of work delivered within the project budget, which in this case was $482 million. The primary objective of the CMGC project delivery method is to fully engage the contractor in the design process in a collaborative environment to work with the design consultant to create an innovative, cost-effective, and high-quality project for the city.

SSW was paid $4 million for pre-construction services to ensure constructability, provide design input, incorporate preferred means and methods, and identify and address ambiguities and conflicts in the contract documents. In addition, CH2M Hill was hired as construction manager.

During the preconstruction activities, Caltrans, a founding partner that eventually would inspect the project, had numerous concerns with the design and other issues that could result in exorbitant additional costs and possibly jeopardize the project. CH2M Hill negotiated with Caltrans on behalf of the city unsuccessfully and in a protracted fashion, City Engineer Gary Lee Moore said. Moore had to step in, and the situation was so alarming that the mayor's political assistance was required to clear the project with Caltrans. According to a city memo in August 2018, "Current disputes are between SSW and the engineering designer HNTB." The memo pointed out that the opening had been rescheduled to August 24, 2021, meaning it was 336 calendar days behind schedule.

When I became involved in the project, I found out at the very first monthly meeting that the root cause of the problems was the lack of trust between SSW and the Bureau of Engineering. "I don't trust you," they repeatedly told each other in the monthly meetings. There was an incredible turnover of both SSW and HNTB personnel, as much as seventy percent within months of the start construction. There was also strong animus between the SSW project manager and the Bureau of Engineering project manager. The management teams of all parties involved were very weak, without prior experience in large, complicated projects such as the viaduct. As a result, the project suffered to the end.

Every time the Bureau of Engineering pointed to a construction conflict, the Pavlovian response from SSW was, "You should have done a Bridge Information Modeling." The city did not hold SSW accountable for the terms and conditions stipulated in the CMGC agreement and the pre-construction services SSW provided for $4 million. When I asked for a copy of the record documents of the three-year effort, I was handed very few and incomplete documents, especially from the pre-construction activities construction manager, CH2M Hill. During construction, the city hired TYLin, as construction manager. There was no discipline, pride of ownership, accountability, or sense of urgency.

As an electrical engineer, I did a cursory review of the electrical drawings and found many serious mistakes. I discovered that electrical services were shown within the right of way of the driveways. There are hundreds of conduits embedded in the concrete deck of the bridge, terminating in the electrical switchboards. If not corrected on time and the deck was poured, the conduits would have to be rerouted, causing an extensive delay and horrendous extra costs. I requested a meeting with HNTB's electrical engineer to discuss the electrical service locations and other issues. The engineer who came to the meeting spoke a different engineering language because he was a traffic signals engineer. I asked questions, but I was given ambiguous, wrong, and uninformed answers.

My desire to seek answers to questions on issues of concern was met with displeasure. On July 10, 2018, HNTB sent a letter to City Engineer Gary Lee Moore complaining of my behavior. "Mr. Patsaouras has demonstrated a lack of respect to our staff. ...One example of this behavior was during a meeting, held on May 22, when Mr. Patsaouras asked questions regarding the electrical design. ...During the following meeting, held on June 13, Mr. Patsaouras reacted negatively to the emailed responses regarding light fixtures in metal cabinets, fault current designs and electrical specifications." And to further undermine the serious concerns and add salt to the injury, the letter said, "Further, while your representative may ask any question he desires, we are challenged to understand how the referenced questions dealt in any way with critical project issues."

It took months for the Bureau of Engineering staff and SSW's very capable utilities manager, Robert Thorpe, to resolve the electrical services locations, among other mistakes. I personally had a number of meetings with the Los Angeles Department of Water and Power in order to resolve their issues. The meetings were open to the public and were taped in order to avoid such misinformed, nonsensical, and self-serving comments.

In reviewing the list of change orders, I noticed that 90 percent of the reasons for the change orders were listed as "unforeseen conditions." I requested an explanation from the construction manager, TYLin, and the Bureau of Engineering. They eventually revised almost all of them as "errors and omissions."

Early on, I determined that the city was not being represented properly either by the construction manager or the scheduler. The schedulers of SSW and the city never agreed on the schedule of the project. SSW was making extensive changes to the project schedule every month, and had been doing so since the beginning of the project. I asked Gary Lee Moore to attempt to enlist the services of an excellent construction manager and scheduler, Bill Lacher. Lacher had successfully worked with me on the Police Administration Building.

Once on board, Lacher held SSW accountable to the schedule and other construction issues. SSW planned the falsework supporting the deck based on "typical" conditions. They were overlooking differences in bridge geometry and site topography.

Meanwhile, the Bureau of Engineering's review times for submittals were taking too long. TYLin's staff was "too light." There were only three full-time, experienced people and, although capable, they were not adequate for processing the reviews and submittals in a timely manner. One of the consultants commented that "The city team and SSW do not respect or trust each other, and they do not communicate well. The city team's responses are usually through letters, which circulate and distract from productive staff time that should be spent moving the project forward. There should be more face-to-face dialogue."

In early meetings, the blame for SSW not being able to proceed with work over the 101 Freeway was placed on Caltrans being unreasonable and recalcitrant, especially the main inspector. I asked Mike Aparicio, the SSW executive, whether he had met the inspector who they blamed over the last two years for their problems. The answer was no. I then suggested that Aparicio have a cup of coffee with that "unreasonable" inspector. At the next meeting, when Aparicio was asked whether the meeting took place, the answer was again no, so I insisted that the meeting take place. Eventually the meeting took place, and since then "Caltrans was the best." However, cooperation between SSW and the city was minimal, if any.

The schedule was a moving target, and the conflicts between SSW and HNTB were constant. I suggested that both parties cut their losses and try to see if a "global settlement" could be reached.

SSW and the city entered into a Supplemental Agreement Change Order. It stipulated that, for a lump sum, SSW would guarantee the opening date and there would not be any claims or disputes, both known or unknown. There were milestone dates within the document, and if progress of work was not in accordance with the milestone dates, payments would be suspended. There were liquidated damages in the event the milestone dates were not met. To my astonishment, I discovered, for this project and others, that the liquidated damages the city was requesting from its contractors were laughable, to put it kindly. I insisted on meaningful liquidated damages, a strong incentive for SSW to adhere to the agreed-upon schedule. A requirement of the change order was the replacement of SSW's project manager.

The viaduct opened July 9, 2022, two years late and with a final construction cost of $588 million, one hundred million dollars over budget. Funds came from the Federal Highway Administration, Caltrans and the city. The cost overruns were paid by the city, tapping the general fund and transportation funds, thus forcing City Hall to scale back city services and postpone or cancel other capital projects.

The project became a landmark immediately the day it opened to the public. The *Los Angeles Times* in an article, "6th Street bridge: A civic wonder that reflects LA's promise and its simmering problems," included quotes from a few visitors to the bridge. "It's like the first time we have something, because I feel like Boyle Heights is always being left out," one visitor said. Another visitor said, "In the whole scheme of things, it's just a street that crosses another street and gets you from one thing to another. But if you grew up here, it's part of you. It's our bridge." A person speaking in Spanish said, "It's beautiful and it's free."

In an editorial the *Los Angeles Times* said, "The 6th Street Viaduct has become a spot for family strolls, bike rides, scenic views, even quinceanera photos and a podcast recording. This is no mere roadway connecting Boyle Heights and downtown. It's an opportunity to rethink LA transportation infrastructure and public space. . . .What if Los Angeles closed the bridge to car traffic several nights or days each week? The bridge is already a visual landmark. What if it became a cultural landmark as well marking the beginning of a new era in Los Angeles, one that elevates people over cars."

The arches lighted with LEDs are visible from miles away, making the bridge a civic beacon. Michael Maltzan put it this way: "The rhythm of elements frames a sequence of views of the cityscape, which engender an almost "cinematic" experience—leaning into the old viaduct's prominence in on-screen portrayals of Los Angeles Iconic structures that are inseparable from identities of their cities—such as the Eiffel Tower, the Statue of Liberty, or the St. Louis arch—are not just major landmarks, they are also observation points from which we see those metropolises differently." There has been effusive press coverage of this project, including international reports from Canada, England, Japan, Germany, and other countries.

A BRIDGE HOME

Urgent Program for the Homeless | On April 17, 2018, Los Angeles mayor Eric Garcetti declared a shelter crisis, which allowed the city to take immediate action in establishing additional shelters to address the health and safety of the city's homeless population. His fiscal year 2017–18 budget included the A Bridge Home—Emergency Temporary Housing initiative that established homeless shelters across the city. Garcetti issued an executive directive on May 30, 2018, ordering each general manager or head of department or office to streamline their application, entitlement, review, procurement, inspection, permitting, certification, and construction processes for the establishment of temporary emergency homeless shelters. The program was implemented at large by the General Services Department, which provided construction services, and the Bureau of Engineering which provided design and construction management services.

The mayor's office was represented by Apryle Brodie, senior project manager. The program, however, ran into problems within a year of its inception. Cost overruns, delays, difficulties in negotiating leases with public agencies and lack of direction hampered the program. Only four shelters had opened by September 2019 since the launch of the program in April 2018. In October 2019, Garcetti again requested my services as "Mr. Fix it," saying, "Patsaouras is a 'czar' whose expertise could help remove obstacles to a network of homeless projects." Despite bringing together senior staff from across the city's departments to work on the homelessness crisis, I had a 'suspicion' that it might be necessary to bring in an outside person who had a proven track record of bringing things in cheaper and quicker. "He [Patsaouras] is a dogged outside expert who won't settle for excuses. Anybody who has been in a meeting with him knows that. He has a clear mission to cut through any red tape that he can find, and always finds something. Patsaouras will work as an 'unpaid volunteer.'"

I accepted the responsibility because I was well aware that poverty and homelessness are interrelated. I felt I could contribute in a small way to address one of the most challenging ills facing the city. I attended two meetings to get an understanding of how things were going so far. The first meeting, conducted by the deputy mayor of homelessness, was limited to a brief slide presentation and some participants reporting quickly on what they were working on. It lasted less than an hour. The other meeting took place in the C. Erwin Piper Technical Center in a small conference room where the General Services Department and Bureau of Engineering representatives were having a nice chat, very informal, with no structure.

Right away, I realized there was no sense of urgency, communication, accountability, and responsiveness. I established monthly meetings starting at 8 a.m. and attended by all general managers, including representatives from the chief legislative analyst's office, the chief administrative officer's office, the Department of Water and Power, and the Fire Department. The meetings lasted until noon without scheduled breaks. I knew from experience that a break stops the momentum, intensity, and tempo of discussions. With the assistance of Brodie, a very capable, responsive, and responsible individual, I prepared a very extensive agenda. Detailed oral and written reports were required from each department head and field managers. The first meeting was opened by the deputy mayor of homelessness, but around 9:15 a.m. she whispered to me, "It's getting late." I looked at her with astonishment and said out loud, "The meeting will last till noon, and you may go." She never attended another meeting. The attendees right away understood this was not "business as usual."

A Bridge Home projects by state law were to operate for three years. Therefore, the leases negotiated were to be of three-year duration. One of the first tasks I had to deal with was negotiating a lease with the California Department of Transportation for a property in San Pedro. However, the Federal Highway Administration had partly funded the asset, and the agency's approval was required. Brodie said the Federal Highway Administration had not been responsive for months and A Bridge Home staff was demoralized. It was one of the reasons Garcetti's office asked for my assistance. While overseeing for the mayor the Sixth Street Viaduct project, I had developed a working relationship with Caltrans Southern California District 7 Chief Deputy Director Shirley Choate. I asked her if she could intervene with the Federal Highway Administration. Within two weeks, the agency gave the clearance to Caltrans.

In another situation, Caltrans was requesting as part of the lease that the City of Los Angeles be responsible for all the contaminants that may exist under the property for ever, long after it vacated the property. The city attorney had run into a wall for months and could not get Caltrans to be reasonable. I requested a conference call with all those involved. The attorney for Caltrans was still recalcitrant. I tried to reason with her to no avail. After a few minutes, I said, "If we don't have an agreement right now, I'll call a news conference and tell the governor that all his proclamations about homelessness is hot air." Caltrans gave in.

The Los Angeles County Metropolitan Transportation Authority had agreed to lease a particular parking lot along the Orange Busway in the San Fernando Valley for a shelter. Along the way, they changed the lots to be leased, then they claimed that the project would interfere with the construction activities for the planned "betterments" for the transit line. Metro's chief program management officer sent a letter to the city that the lot would not be available, end of discussion. Meanwhile, the city had spent hundreds of thousands of dollars of staff time, and architectural and engineering services on the site.

I requested a meeting with Metro. It took place at the mayor's conference room attended by fifteen individuals, including the Metro chief program management officer and five of his colleagues. After the self-introductions, I asked the chief engineer why, considering the line is eighteen miles long, they could not include in the contract that work for this particular small block be scheduled to be done when the A Bridge Home shelter vacates the property after three years. "Hmm, that's a good idea" was the response. The meeting had started at 10 a.m. sharp. Including the self-introductions, stating the issue, and its resolution, my watch showed it was 10:17 a.m. The contract for the 'betterments' was being negotiated in 2024!

However, negotiating the leases was the easy task. The General Services Department, which was constructing the project, had a budget, but did not adhere to it. Costs were 40 percent over budget. Its representative stated more than once in the monthly meetings that they could not deliver the projects in four months per the mayor's directive. Their projects were two months behind schedule. The drawings were incomplete, full of errors and omissions, which I brought to the attention of the Bureau of Engineering. The Bureau had to replace the consultants.

The city paid higher fees than it needed to, and still got poor services. The architectural and engineering fees were calculated on a time-and-material basis, reaching $500,000 to $600,000 per project. I pointed out to Bureau of Engineering staff there is practically no architecture considering the design involved was setting a few trailers or tents on concrete pads. Therefore, the fee should not exceed $200,000 per project. Future projects not contracted were designed successfully with fees ranging from $200,000 to $250,000.

At the end of 2019, Garcetti issued a directive that all projects must be completed by June 30, 2020. I knew that the General Services Department would not be able to come through, so I decided that the work must be done by the private sector, and I asked the city engineer for a list of prequalified contractors. I was presented with a ten-year-old list that included contractors that I knew were involved in mega projects. I pointed out that these contractors would not bid on a $5 million project, and I wanted to establish a new list. I was given a document with about thirty requirements for a contractor to pre-qualify for this type of work. That would mean the mayor's timeline could not be met, and hundreds of homeless people would have to wait months to be housed. In studying the document, I realized that most of the requirements were to be addressed after the award of a contract. I requested a meeting with Bureau of Engineering staff and the city attorney, and at the conclusion of the meeting it was determined that a new list could be formed within two weeks.

One of the successful contractors was Ford EC Inc., a very responsive and responsible contractor that despite the COVID-19 pandemic's challenges delivered the projects ahead of schedule and within the budget. Ford's project manager, Arash Daghighian, was one of the best I had encountered. He was in constant communication with me, working to find ways to move forward rather than focusing on problems and how to get change orders. He was committed to the cause and was a team player. He told me that "being part of the city's team and building the emergency A Bridge Home shelters was not only essential, but also a true sign how Angelenos can work together." I was convinced again that if you provide clear goals and direction, support staff, and have confidence in them, they will go the distance to deliver and be proud of their work.

When Jose Fuentes came in as the new Bureau of Engineering construction manager, the projects moved in the right direction with urgency. He brought commitment, expertise, and dedication to the program. Field project managers Marcelino Ascensio, Javier Gonzalez, and Mariet Ohanian proved to be very responsive, responsible, and capable once they were given direction and what was expected of them. Apryle Brodie made my task that much easier, because of her superb work, responsiveness, and great sense of urgency. Meg Barclay of the chief administrative officer's office was excellent in advising the team, finding new revenue sources, and keeping up to date with new relevant legislation. The projects were delivered on budget and on time, despite the rocking start, because of the team's efforts, trust, urgency, and open communication. Eighteen projects with 2,600 beds were delivered by June 30, 2020.

The heading of the agenda page read in capital letters: "TIME IS MONEY," and at the bottom, the credo:

"Accountabilty/Communication/Coordination/Integrity/Responsibilty/Responsiveness/Transparency/Trust/Urgency,"

Followed by an inspirational quote: *"Some men see things as they are and ask why. I dream of things that never were and ask, why not."* —ROBERT KENNEDY

THE LOS ANGELES POLICE DEPARTMENT ADMINISTRATION BUILDING

In 2007, Mayor Antonio Villaraigosa asked me to oversee the construction of the new Police Administration Building. The wedge-shaped, eleven-story, five-hundred-thousand-square-foot tower was being built across First Street from City Hall. The mayor had served with me on the Board of Directors of the Southern California Rapid Transit District. He trusted me

New LAPD Administration Building. Photo: wmedia

and knew my capabilities, commitment, integrity, and loyalty. I accepted the assignment because he was a good friend and I wanted him to succeed. Meanwhile, I was given condolences for having to work with Tutor-Saliba Corp., the general contractor of the Police Administration Building. The mayor advised the city's chief administrative officer, Bill Fujioka, of his decision. Fujioka cautioned that "If Ron Tutor, [president of the project's general contractor], heard that Nick would oversee the project, he may pull out. That would be a catastrophe because Tutor-Saliba was the only bidder." The announcement of my involvement was delayed until after the signing of the contract.

My team consisted of representatives from the City of Los Angeles Bureau of Engineering; the Bureau of Contract Administration; the Fire Department; the Department of Transportation; the Bureau of Street Services; the offices of the Chief Administrative Officer and the Chief Legislative Analyst; Sharon Papa, LAPD assistant chief in charge of operations; and architects, engineers, and other consultants hired for the project.

Los Angeles Times columnist Steve Lopez had written a very derogatory article regarding Ron Tutor in January 2007, a few weeks before the first oversight meeting. The headline was, "Watching a hole in the ground fill with money." In the article, Lopez wrote, "The city initially estimated that the new 11-story cop shop would cost $177 million and then adjusted to $200 million, but they are still moving dirt around and the price is up to $231 million. Add the planned parking facility a block away and add furnishings, and the original estimate for the whole project was $302 million, but that was increased to a projected $340 million. Then in September, the City Council approved an increase to $396.8 million and was warned by city staff that the tab could be $420 million before long.

"The building is constructed by Tutor-Saliba, a contractor with a long history of high-profile disputes with public agencies." "For me this is less about Tutor and more about this thoughtless, shoot-from-the hip, throw-deals-on-the table-without-thinking way that the city of Los Angeles builds its major public facilities," City Controller Laura Chick told Lopez. "Not long ago, she said, the new LAPD site was supposed to become a park and the cops were supposed to move to Little Tokyo; then all of a sudden that was scuttled. It was mindless and, thoughtless, and last minute. We've got all this money, so let's figure out where we're going to put it, and let's screw the park."

Lopez was correct that the Bureau of Engineering, as I make the case in other sections of this book, often is wrong in estimating construction costs and mismanages projects, causing serious problems for other city departments. But Lopez was wrong about Tutor-Saliba's performance in the Police Administration Building. The project was completed on budget and ahead of schedule.

After self-introductions in the first meeting, Tutor-Saliba's project manager, Ghassan Ariqat, went on a rant about how unjustifiably Tutor was being judged and blamed for the cost overruns, delays, etc. mentioned in Lopez's article. I let him vent and when he finished, I looked at him across the table and I asked,

"Sir, have we met?"

"No."

"Have we talked over the phone?"

"No."

"Do you know anything about me?"

"No."

"Sir, take all this garbage you have been giving us for the last ten minutes and throw it out of the door. This is a new project and a new beginning. I expect us to work as a team, with a common goal. The city gets a great project on time and on budget and Tutor-Saliba makes a profit." That, in essence, set the theme of for what was expected from all parties.

Also at that meeting, I sensed that the outside construction manager was inexperienced and unqualified. However, I decided to give him another chance. At the second meeting, my suspicions were validated, and I informed City Engineer Gary Lee Moore of my concerns. At the third meeting, the principals of the company attended the meeting, and they themselves decided to change the construction manager for the project. They sent him to their Los Angeles Unified School District and engaged Bill Lacher, to whom I attribute the success of the project along with Ariqat. Having overseen as a volunteer close to a dozen state, county and city projects, I have concluded that contractors are as good as the plans they are given by the owners.

In reviewing the construction documents, I detected discrepancies, lack of coordination among the disciplines, code violations, errors, and omissions. I therefore, requested the architect and the consultants— structural, civil, mechanical, electrical, heating, ventilation, and air conditioning/life safety controls, etc.—to coordinate and review their work based on the bid documents. Within a month, many pages listing errors and omissions were given to the contractors for pricing. They submitted a change order of close to $350,000. It was the best money spent. Some of the errors and omissions were very serious, but it was easy to correct the mistakes on paper, rather than tearing down walls and floors during construction, which would have cost millions of dollars in change orders and delays.

At the beginning of the project, during excavation, I requested that the fire marshal, the HVAC/life safety controls contractor, the architect, and the engineers meet biweekly to discuss the designs. They were very surprised because they thought it was too early for such coordination. However, I had learned in overseeing the former Los Angeles County/USC Medical Center (now the Los Angeles General Medical Center) that early coordination was necessary. At the medical center, there were a lot of problems in getting the HVAC system to work in conjunction with the life safety controls. Johnson Controls had to bring personnel from around the country to make the systems work towards the end of the project. In the case of the Police Administration Building, the Fire Department had a number of requirements that, had we waited, walls would have to be torn down, control panels relocated, hundreds of feet of conduits and wiring rerouted, etc.

Again, give the contractor a good set of drawings and a competent project manager, and he will deliver the project on time and on budget. Los Angeles County would have had a disaster with the Harbor/UCLA Medical Center, a project that I also oversaw, because of incredibly bad drawings and lack of coordination with the utility companies. In the Harbor/UCLA Medical Center case, the public works managers had to request an additional $45 million from the county Board of Supervisors before the project was even sent out to bid.

In fact, because the managers were both scared and ashamed, I personally had to meet with Supervisors Yvonne Brathwaite Burke and Don Knabe to request the additional funds. If the project had been constructed as originally designed, it would have stayed empty for close to two years until Southern California Edison Co. could bring power to the site.

In overseeing the Police Administration Building, I met with LAPD Chief William Bratton and Assistant Chief Papa to discuss special requirements and the progress of construction, so there would not be any surprises once they moved in.

We were able to work as a team from the beginning and trust each other. Ariqat would proceed with work at Tutor-Saliba's risk before the architect and engineers approved the shop drawings or responded to the requests for information, or RFI.

I instituted a process that had never been used before, and unfortunately is not applied by public agencies, either because of ignorance, laziness, or both. I had asked to review all the RFIs of the previous month. Obviously, I could not review each and every one, but I cherry-picked a number of them to make a point. In the process I discovered that when the contractor was asking to delete a piece of equipment or modify the design, resulting in savings, the response to the RFI was "OK." I then posed the question, "If it were the other way around, and we had to add that piece of equipment, would we pay the contractor?" The answer was, "Yes, of course." Therefore, I asked "Why should not the city receive a credit?"

The individual credits may have appeared insignificant, but cumulatively it was a sizable sum. For example: "Roller shade deletion on north side—$2,200.00" and "Power strip deletion from telecom racks—$5,150.00." At the end of the project, Tutor-Saliba owed the city $850,000 in credits!

At the beginning of construction, an alarming event took place. I received a call from the general manager of building and safety, Andrew Adelman, advising me that he could not issue a building permit as "Police Headquarters" because the building was not designed as "an essential services facility." I immediately called Mayor Villaraigosa to inform him accordingly. A meeting was convened in the mayor's office attended by Villaraigosa; City Councilman Bernard Parks, chair of the committee in charge of the LAPD; Deputy Mayor Marcus Allen; Adelman; City Engineer Moore; and myself. One option was to stop construction and redesign the building systems to qualify the building as "essential services facility." That would entail an exorbitant cost and considerable delays. City officials decided that, since there are no jail facilities as such, instead of referring to the building as "Police Headquarters" to call it "Police Administration Building."

It is unfortunate and ironic that, after all the brouhaha, many expensive studies, political posturing, buying a building at a premium from a very well connected investor in order to temporarily house large number of forces of the LAPD that never happened anyway, demolish a historic landmark because of seismic concerns, and consequently a significant property in front of City Hall staying vacant since 2018 to date, and losing the opportunity to create a public square for Los Angeles, the new LAPD building cannot be called Headquarters but Administration Building because the Bureau of Engineering failed to design the building as an "essential services facility." The media erroneously refers to the building as "Police Headquarters." Fire and police stations, emergency operations centers, the California Highway Patrol offices, sheriff's offices and emergency communication dispatch centers are "essential services facilities."

The Police Administration Building was completed ahead of schedule and below budget because of the team effort and trust displayed from the beginning by all parties, but especially Tutor-Saliba. The building achieved Gold Level certification. Its striking design by Paul Danna has received a number of awards. The building was dedicated on October 24, 2009.

PERFORMANCE AUDIT OF THE CONSTRUCTION OF THE PAB

In overseeing the construction of the Police Administration Building, I found glaring deficiencies and irregularities in the management practices of the Bureau of Engineering. Therefore, I asked City Controller Laura N. Chick to audit the project.

Following are general comments from that audit:

- It is astounding that voters keep being asked to approve multi-billion-dollar bond measures without including language to set aside a small percentage of the bond money for regular audits of these projects. For example, out of a total current budget of $454 million, this audit cost 0.03 percent of the total budget and provided thirty-two recommendations on how we need to do it better and more cost effectively.

- For more than a hundred years the city has been conceptualizing, planning, and building its construction projects much in the same way. It is time for the city to be thinking outside the box and adopting more flexibility and modern approaches that cost the city less in the long run.

- As I have found in several other audits, the city must do a much better job at the front end of the negotiation process. We found many limitations and obstacles in how the contracts were written that may have resulted in increased costs.

- The audit follows the convoluted path of this project from $303 million in 2004 to $454 million in 2007 (including general fund expenditures).

- The Bureau of Engineering did not utilize all available mechanisms in the cost negotiation process with the project architect and the project construction management firm. As a result, it is not clear whether the Bureau of Engineering obtained the most favorable rates for these two agreements.

PARTIAL KEY FINDINGS

- The Bureau of Engineering's design-driven construction change orders do not distinguish between an error and omission (I encountered the same issue when I oversaw the mega-project Sixth Street Viaduct many years later.)

- It is unclear whether the Bureau of Engineering obtained the most advantageous contractual rates with the construction manager due to the limited documentation and definitive policies regarding rare negotiation protocols.
- The Bureau of Engineering inappropriately used the project manager's reimbursable expense allowance to procure services from the architect.
- The Bureau of Engineering did not follow its own procedures when procuring and administering the architectural and engineering contracts.
- The contract type used by the Bureau of Engineering may not be the best type for architectural and engineering services.
- The architects' agreement contract terms contain limitations.
- The Bureau of Engineering did not sufficiently negotiate the original agreement and subsequent amendments with the architect. Project delivery Manual Section 6.4 follows California Government Code Section 4526, stating that is illegal to procure professional services using a method that constitutes a bid. However, the Project Delivery Manual further states that the price of a proposal can be considered, but that it shall not be dominant or the only criterion. Our view of the qualifications evaluation score sheets revealed that competing firms had very close scores. Utilizing cost as one of the criteria could have resulted in the selection of a different design firm with potentially much lower cost to the city.
- The Bureau of Engineering did not obtain a list of hourly billing rates for key personnel and activities as part of the requirements of the Request for Qualifications as defined by Project Delivery Manual Section 6.4. This further limited the bureau's ability to consider cost as a review criterion, as these rates for key personnel and activities could have been utilized as the basis for cost negotiations.

Among the audit's thirty-two recommendations were the following:

- In price negotiation with a consultant who was not selected based on price, consider conducting a pre-analysis of the consultant's proposed rates to establish reasonableness prior to finalizing the contract.
- Enforce policies and procedures and require consultants to provide the first cost proposal to initiate cost negotiations.
- Consider asking firms to submit a cost proposal when responding to a Request for Qualifications. (I had instituted this requirement at the Los Angeles County Metropolitan Transportation Authority in the early 1990s and years later at the Los Angeles Department of Water and Power, whereby the price was submitted in a sealed envelope to be opened after the selection of the wining team, resulting in tens of millions of dollars in savings.)

LAC + USC MEDICAL CENTER

In 2002, I was chairman of a committee that included Jerry Epstein, a developer of Marina del Rey, and A. Redmond "Rusty" Doms, head of Karsten Realty Advisors, to oversee the construction of the new Los Angeles County + USC Medical Center. I had been asked by Los Angeles County supervisor Gloria Molina to get involved as an unpaid volunteer because she and I had served on the construction committee of the Los Angeles County Metropolitan Transportation Authority, and as a result she knew my technical knowledge and capabilities, and she trusted me.

The new 600-bed hospital replaced the 1,200 Art Deco landmark County/USC Medical Center in Boyle Heights, which was damaged by the 1994 Northridge Earthquake. The new hospital was a compromise that ended a three-year stalemate between state lawmakers, Molina, who wanted a 750-bed facility and the majority of the county Board of Supervisors, who pushed for a 600-bed hospital.

LAC + USC Medical Center. Photo: G. Hauser

Supervisor Zev Yaroslavsky had claimed that a 750-bed hospital "would bankrupt the County." Molina`s position was supported by a task force headed by Dr. Robert Tranquada, a former dean of the Keck School of Medicine of USC, and endorsed by Mark Finucane, head of the county Healthcare System. The compromise proposed by Molina called for a 600-bed facility to be constructed at the County-USC site, with a smaller satellite facility to be built in the San Gabriel Valley city of Baldwin Park. As then state Assemblyman Gil Cedillo said, "The board never would have considered the 150-bed annex had it not been for Molina 'hanging-in there' in the face of her colleagues' unanimous opposition."

Construction of the 600-bed, 1.5-million-square-foot hospital was finished on time and on budget, with zero claims, because of the trust and cooperation between the county staff led by the capable Jacob Williams, who unfortunately died at a very young age, and the general contractor, a joint venture of McCarthy-Clark-Hunt led by Richard Heim.

In March 2013, Los Angeles County announced that it was authorizing the construction of a new 150-bed hospital it its LAC + USC Medical because the Center had been overcrowded since it opened in 2008, running at around 95 percent capacity. Molina told veteran reporter Marc Haefele, "I should feel vindicated, but it`s been bitter, harsh and painful," because she had fought for the 150 extra hospital beds for more than fifteen years.

LOS ANGELES DEPARTMENT OF WATER AND POWER

Owens Valley; with LADWP Commissioners David Nahai and Mary Nichols, and Mayor Antonio Villaraigosa.

When Antonio Villaraigosa launched his campaign for Los Angeles mayor in 2005, I told him that I would be involved in the campaign providing counsel, fundraising and serving in the transition team with the understanding that I would not serve in any official capacity, either in the administration or as a commissioner.

One Friday afternoon in July 2005, Villaraigosa called and asked me to serve on the Department of Water and Power Board of Commissioners because he needed "a watchdog," experienced in overseeing multibillion dollar budgets and heavy construction and a trusted friend. I reminded the mayor of our agreement and told him therefore I would not accept. The mayor told me, "The mayor is asking you." I still refused. Then Villaraigosa told me, "A friend is asking for your help." I accepted. DWP is the nation's largest municipally owned utility, providing safe, reliable and affordable electric and water services to nearly four million people.

In my first meeting as an LADWP commissioner, in the opening remarks I did not spend time on the traditional niceties, but I went on a forty-five-minute litany of "lessons learned" during my sixteen years of service as an RTD/MTA board member. The other commissioners and the staff looked surprised and puzzled. It was the precursor of what was going to be a true oversight of an agency mired in scandals, inefficiencies, corruption, and the ratepayer be damned. Even board president Mary D. Nichols sent me an e- mail in January 2006, a few months later. "I would like to get some ideas about how to manage this place. The overlap, confusion, deference to union, lack of accountability, it's terrible. I thought you were too harsh at first about the need for 'culture change,' but you were right."

WASTE AND ABUSE

In January 2006, *Los Angeles Times* columnist Steve Lopez wrote, "A good deal of what Nick Patsaouras told me Tuesday about Los Angeles Department of Water and Power, which he oversees as a board member, is unfit to print . . . his rage over the Department's expenses, which include big bucks for lobbyists, writing teachers and, if to send him over the edge, bottled water. That's right, the company that pumps the water to your tap apparently doesn't always drink the stuff itself. During the same two-year period that DWP forked out one million dollars to convince us its tap water is top of the line, it also spent $31,160 for Sparkletts bottled water. If it had been Perrier instead of Sparkletts, I think Patsaouras might have gone into cardiac arrest. Patsaouras blew a gasket over $2.2 million the water agency spends on lobbyists. Patsaouras also wondered why the agency needed to spend $180,000 to teach employees how to write. 'How do they get in?' he wondered. He ranted for several minutes about what he called a six hundred-thousand-dollar audiovisual equipment contract 'to move some speakers around for in-house speeches.'"

I was surprised to find out the meetings of the board of directors that oversees a five-billion-dollar corporation lasted one hour to one hour and a half. The board met bi-weekly, on Tuesday at 1 p.m. It had only one committee, an audit committee that met once a year to ratify the legally required audit of the department by an outside auditor. I led the effort to institute fifteen committees, among them the Contracts Committee, chaired by me.

Traditionally at DWP and other agencies, staff would go before the board and request an approval "today, otherwise the sky would fall." The item would be among multiple items on that day's agenda. Therefore, there was very little time for discussion and questions. The Contracts Committee expected items to be presented for consideration well in advance before they would go to the full board. Committees would meet at 9 a.m. on the morning of the scheduled board meeting, which allowed ample time for discussion and, if necessary, to ask the staff to come back with a fuller explanation. Millions and millions of ratepayers' dollars were saved that way.

We instituted a Customer and Community Relations Committee that enacted programs to help and expedite customers' issues and calls. (No impersonal response on the other line, if you finally get them to answer the phone.) There was an Electrification of the LA Harbor Committee that pioneered the electrification of the docks in the Port of Los Angeles. There was an Economic Development Committee to promote "social justice and equity," twenty years ahead of its time! And a Security/Emergency Preparedness, Response and Threat Assessment Committee formed by Commissioner Lee Kanon Alpert. Thanks to the Energy and the Environment Committee, Villaraigosa was able to celebrate a major LADWP milestone: 20 percent of its power came from renewable sources in 2010. Unfortunately, all these committees were eliminated in subsequent years.

The department's $5 billion dollar budget had been approved with very little discussion, sometimes on a consent calendar. I requested that a full day be devoted to discussing the "power" section, another full day to discuss the "water" section, a third day to discuss "joint operations," and a fourth day for more discussion and approval. There was $110 million savings in the first budget year the Villaraigosa commission was in charge.

When I joined the LADWP Board of Commissioners in 2005, I noticed in the first extensive budget hearings I instituted that the overtime charged by the employees in every department was outrageous, so policies and monitoring were established. I requested a written and oral report by each division manager to be presented to the Board and the public monthly. It was difficult to justify unjustifiable overtime in public. Overtime was eventually reduced to a minimum, primarily for field crews who had to restore power and water services in extreme weather.

Alas, overtime was embedded in the agency's culture. In a scathing report in February 2023, the inspector general wrote, "Written policies regarding overtime are largely nonexistent.

Individuals self-reported overtime work without any apparent effort by respective managers to assess whether the time was actually worked or whether the use of overtime was appropriate. The study revealed systemic issues and failures by the department to effectively manage overtime in the public's best interest." Former General Manager Martin Adams said, "The utility has not had an overarching effective overtime policy for years."

DECEPTION

On March 3, 2009, Los Angeles voters rejected Measure B, a controversial ballot measure that would have created the largest solar project in US history. The "Green Energy and Good Jobs for LA Solar Initiative" called for installing 1,500 acres of silicon panels atop city buildings at a cost of $3.6 billion. The solar energy panels would be installed, operated, and maintained by DWP on properties within the city and city-owned airports and produce at least four hundred megawatts of electric generation by 2014. The solar power installations would be the property of DWP, and all work would be done by DWP employees.

City Council President Eric Garcetti introduced the Measure B motion to the council and Chief Legislative Analyst Gerry Miller reported that it could be implemented without voter approval. But City attorney Rocky Delgadillo issued an opinion stating that only voters could approve the plan. Garcetti and eleven of the fourteen other City Council members backed Measure B. Only Councilmembers Bernard Parks, Dennis Zine and Greig Smith opposed it. The council was strongly criticized in the media, especially in the *Los Angeles Times*, because it rushed the twenty-five-page proposal onto the ballot without reading it or knowing how much it would cost. The measure was placed on the ballot with no engineering and operational input from DWP and no consideration of the overall cost. A *Los Angeles Times* editorial advised the City Council to "sober up."

It was conceived in backroom discussions by a handful of power brokers. The measure's sponsor was the International Brotherhood of Electrical Workers, the DWP Union. The measure would have given IBEW a near monopoly over all the work. City Controller Laura Chick said, "The whole political process stinks." In December 2008, *Los Angeles Times* reporter David Zahniser broke a story about how Garcetti had hidden from his council colleagues a report calling the plan "extremely risky" with open-ended costs.

Mitchell Schwartz, who had managed Barack Obama's presidential campaign in California and was a lobbyist for CH2M Hill, a company that was accused by the DWP of overbilling and fraud, filed an unsuccessful court petition to water down the "con" language opposing Measure B in the official voter guide. I was among eight people, including Ron Kaye, former editor of the Los Angeles Daily News, who had signed the ballot argument in opposition. We were dubbed "The Solar 8" and were defended by Noel Weiss, an attorney activist. We were sued over innocuous ballot language. Schwartz had asked the judge to take out wording in the voter pamphlet warning that the solar plan would give monopoly to IBEW.

Los Angeles County Superior Court judge David P. Yaffe, who heard the case, said, "The proposition is so vague and so encompassing that speculation about just about anything is fair game." Yaffe refused to remove language that warned that "no competitive bidding" would be used under the solar program. And he declined to take out wording that warned that the DWP would use "outdated technology" for the initiative. The "Solar 8" had prevailed over Mayor Villaraigosa, the City Council and the powerful DWP Union.Voters defeated Measure B by a margin of 50.5 percent to 49.5 percent even though supporters spent $1.6 million, and foes spent only $74,451.

FRAUD

About a century ago, scouts from Los Angeles went to Owens Valley, on the eastern side of the Sierra Nevada to purchase land quietly, posing as ranchers and farmers, hiding their intentions. It did not take long for residents of the Eastern Sierra to figure out that the water rights were purchased on behalf of LA. The scheme became the subject of the 1974 classic film Chinatown. By taking water from the Eastern Sierra, LA has turned Owens Valley into a dust bowl.

There have been efforts since the 1990s to make amends for taking the region's land and water. DWP focused on the environmental and economic damage caused by the water grab. The DWP under the leadership of General Manager David Freeman in 1997, reached an agreement with the Great Basin Unified Air Pollution Control District to combat the powder-fine dust from the dry 110-square-mile Owens Lake bed. The estimated cost then was $120 million. As of 2024, the cost has exceeded $2.5 billion.

Dominick Rubalcava, DWP commissioner in 1997, said Freeman came to the commission and said, "I have a settlement for the Owens Lake issue." His settlement, in summary, was a determination that Owens Lake could be remediated for about $120 million and that it could be done within two and a half or three-years. He had brought in a number of experts to verify those conclusions. Rubalcava was doubtful. "Freeman brought in lawyers who negotiated a settlement with all litigants, the plaintiffs in the lawsuit against the department, and he strongly recommended the settlement," he said. "I had had the benefit of being there after severe rainstorms. I had had the benefit of being there when there were dust storm conditions. I understood the size and the complexity of the issue, and I was 100 percent convinced that he was wrong both on the money side and on the timing side. So, when the matter was presented to the commission, it resulted in a four to one vote. I was the only commissioner who voted against the settlement."

"That to me is a perfect example of how external forces have distorted the mission of DWP. I have seen elected politicians pander to the public, promise the moon, knowing that they were not going to be around when the projects were done, and they were not going to be around when a single mother in South Central or East LA with two or three kids on a fixed income was going to have to deal with a DWP bill that was going to double." Rubalcava said.

In January 1998, the DWP awarded a sole source contract to CH2M Hill for $550,000 to act as an expert witness on dust mitigation to resolve legal issues related to Owens Lake. From then till April 2006, CH2M Hill had been program manager, designer, and construction manager. In July 1998, a Memorandum of Agreement was signed by the City of Los Angeles and the Great Basin Unified Air Control Pollution District. The Agreement was the result of a settlement of issues with the Owens Valley State Implementation Plan adopted by Great Basin in July 1997.Warning signs of the ballooning costs surfaced in the early 2000s. The City Council learned in 2002 from the city administrative officer that water increases would be required to cover the high costs of the Owens Lake dust mitigation project.

The Council in 2004 hired the RAND Corp. to study the city's proprietary departments -- the airport, the port and the DWP. It was recommended that the city leaders focus on high-risk contracts, monitor performance after awarding contracts, and balance fraud prevention with more fraud detection. According to the *LA Weekly*, former councilwomen Cindy Miscikowski and Wendy Greuel and City Controller Laura Chick testified before a blue-ribbon task force formed to enact RAND's recommendations. "It was an open-ended, fix-it-no-matter what-it takes situation," Miscikowski said.

"City Chief Administrative Officer Bill Fujioka called for oversight of the proprietary departments, but council approval was so poorly managed. It set in motion a never-ending money pit with no oversight. Fujioka wrote to Mayor James Hahn in 2004, "The cost of the Owens Lake Dust Mitigation Project has dramatically increased since its inception. A more cautious approach to oversight may be justified."

Chick was apprised of the cost overruns, but she chose to ignore the issue. According to *LA Weekly*, Chick privately briefed mayoral candidate Antonio Villaraigosa early in 2005 about the ballooning costs, but took no action, despite being personally contacted by DWP employees acting as whistleblowers. When Chick was asked by an *LA Weekly* reporter whether she intended to audit the contract, she replied, "I don't know."

According to *LA Weekly*, Richard Harasick, who was overseeing the Owens Valley project for DWP, wrote to Jim McDaniel, chief operating officer of the water system, in December of 2005, "What was not really contemplated was the operation's organization and costs. What you are seeing is just a general lack of full support of the project by our own staff." McDaniel then wrote to General Manager Ron Deaton, "Equipment material, final layout and the overall quality were not under the direct control of the DWP and were not up to its standards." Deaton went to the commissioners and said, "We didn't know what we were getting into." These facts were confirmed by a third-party audit by GCAP Services, Inc. a few months later. On November 1, 2005, during a marathon eight-hour board meeting, Harasick stated that the CH2MHill contract had reached $120 million. Harasick said, "CH2M Hill provides 'shadow analyses' of Great Basin's air-quality findings in addition to designing, then overseeing construction. I remarked, "So the fox is watching the chicken coop? This is an outrageous conflict of interest." "They are protecting their design," Harasick replied. "They should be protecting us," I said in exasperation.

It became clear to me that an outside "forensic" audit was needed. I told the newly elected Mayor Villaraigosa that unless we get control of "this fiasco" we will own it in six months. I asked DWP Commission President Mary Nichols to place an item on the agenda to issue a request for proposals for "a forensic" audit of CH2M Hill and DWP staff. Nichols refused to place the item on the agenda, saying that "we can have staff do the audit." That was absolutely absurd considering we needed to audit the staff management practices. There was an exchange of e mails between Nichols and me. I wrote on December 30, 2005, "Mary, you and the other members can vote as you like. I want it on the agenda and it can go up or down quietly, otherwise I'll make my speech AGAIN. I'm getting tired to chase you to place the item on the agenda under 'commissioners' items.'" Nichols replied on December 31, "Please take me up on my suggestion that you and I meet with the city attorney to discuss options before we put anything out. Or give me one good reason—other than YOU want to grandstand—why this needs to be on the agenda."

I had the same problem when I was serving on the RTD Board, and the president refused to place an item I was interested in on the agenda. I learned then from the board secretary Helen Bolen that, "if the board secretary receives an item signed by the majority of the board members, the item automatically goes on the agenda." I advised Nichols I would resort to such an action if the RFP to audit CH2M Hill was not on the agenda of the next Board meeting.

In January of 2006, LADWP solicited proposals to assist in reviewing the department's management of CH2M Hill's performance on two Owens Lake Dust Mitigation Program professional services contracts and to identify and propose alternative contracting practices to achieve maximum value from its professional services contracts. In the same month, an RFP was issued for construction management services and terminating CH2M Hill as of April 6, 2006. GCAP Services, was selected to conduct the performance review, which commenced May 31, 2006. GCAP issued its final report May 7, 2007, and some of the nineteen findings were:

a. The procurement process did not include sole source justifications or engender full and open competition.
b. Standard protocols for project management and project controls were not consistently incorporated into the management of the Owens Lake Dust Mitigation Program.
c. The department did not verify that labor rates proposed by CH2M Hill, and its subcontractors were fair and reasonable.
d. The department's invoice processing procedures for the Owens Lake Dust Mitigation Program are duplicative, incomplete, and inefficient.
e. Contract compliance monitoring was very limited on the project and no effort was made to ensure that Minority Business Enterprise and Women's Business Enterprise programs were serving a commercially useful function.
f. There was no evidence that the department reviewed design costs over the course of the project.
g. CH2M Hill invoiced direct costs for subcontract management and also invoiced markups on subcontractor costs.
h. Markup on subcontractor costs were found to be excessive.

However, the most egregious act was the instructions from CH2M Hill to subcontractors outlined in a letter, the "smoking gun," uncovered by GCAP in CH2M Hill's files, how to defraud DWP.

DWP made repeated efforts to settle with CH2M Hill with no success. CH2M Hill executives were arrogant and dismissive. The DWP board decided to sue CH2M Hill in US District Court, Central District of California, Case No. CV08-04154CAS, pursuant to subdivision (a) of section 54956.9 of the California Government Code.

The lawsuit accused CH2M Hill of overbilling the utility over a seven-year period. The lawsuit alleged that CH2M Hill conspired to defraud the DWP by preparing and approving numerous invoices that "artificially inflated the value of the work performed by CH2M Hill and its subcontractors." Then General Manager David Nahai said that "LADWP would seek at least $13.5 million, plus punitive damages and $10,000 for each allegedly false claim submitted by the company." The DWP lawsuit accused CH2M Hill of breach of contract, fraud and providing negligent representation. Relying on the state's false claims act, the DWP intended to seek triple damages in the billing case. CH2M Hill settled in August 2009 for $2.9 million. A lot of lessons to be learned by politicians, bureaucrats and contractors.

CUSTOMER SERVICE

Below is a list of accomplishments and initiatives performed under my guidance as the DWP board president:

a. Establishment of LADWP Ratepayers' Bill of Rights to assure the ratepayers right to reliable service, the right to privacy, the right to courtesy, the right to quality service, the right to clear air, the right to clean water, the right to green power, and the right to participate in programs and rebates.

b. The LADWP's Customer Service Division received two 2008 Quality and Productivity Awards, honoring excellence in service from the LA City's Quality and Productivity Commission:

1. LADWP's Customer Contact Center earned the Record-Breaking Customer Contact Service Levels award that showcased the stellar improvements in the percentage of customer calls answered within sixty seconds. The Call Center reached its goal in 2018 by answering 92 percent of its customer calls within sixty seconds, and by reducing the number of abandoned calls by 90 percent.

2. The Remittance Processing Center was honored with the Check 21 Processing Method award that highlighted the efficiency gains and cost savings realized by automated imaging and processing of the customers' payment checks. With the implementation of the Check 21 system, LADWP's Remittance Processing Center is saving millions of dollars by depositing electronic checks to the City Treasurer for same-day investment.

c. Initiated the work in 2008 to increase the number of participants in the Low Income,

Life Support and Lifeline Rate Program from 154,000 customers to more than 300,000 customers by 2011.

d. Amendment to Rule No. 14

Under LADWP rules, the Department is the sole owner of all water service connections.

In mid-March 2008, *La Opinion* newspaper published an article with the headline "Evictions are Order of the Day." The article described the experiences of several residents of the Encanto Apartments at 7660 Lankershim Boulevard in North Hollywood, and appeared to demonstrate actions taken by an agent of the landlord that were intended to force the tenants in the building to abandon their residences before the end of their tenancy. Among the accusations by residents was the following charge: "Every day they are turning off our water without notice, they have left us without water for up to five hours."

I used to read *La Opinion* every day to improve my Spanish and to give news conferences in Spanish as well as English. When I read that this crime was committed, I became incensed remembering my childhood days, when poor people were powerless and mistreated. I met with Deputy City Attorney Julie Riley to get a briefing on the law. Riley contacted the Metro Field Office and, upon her request, the master meter for water service for 7660 Lankershim Boulevard was turned "on" and locked to prevent the landlord from turning off the master meter. LADWP staff reported that the master meter had been in the "off "position.

It appeared that the landlord's practices described in the *LA Opinion* article were not isolated incidents. As a result, the Board on May 1, 2008, amended Rule 14 with a number of resolutions, including the following:

1) BE IT FURTHER RESOLVED that it is a crime, both under federal and state law, to interfere with the operation of a public water system with the intent of harming persons.

VIGNETTE

Mayor Richard Riordan tried to privatize the DWP. According to S. David Freeman, former General Manager of DWP, "Duke Power Company and Louis Dreyfus were going to take over all the generating plants and operate them privately." When Freeman came in as general manager in 1997, he opposed it, and with the help of City Councilmembers Jackie Goldberg, Ruth Galanter, and others, stopped it. Ron Deaton, who was then chief legislative analyst, "worked with me. He believed in the utility." Freeman said. "I found David Wiggs had been hired as a consultant by Riordan, and they were doing memos on bankruptcy," Freeman told me. When Freeman became General Manager, he reduced the work force by 1100 people with early retirement and brought order and confidence in the utility.

LESSONS LEARNED

You can't let your failures define you. You have to let your failures teach you.

—BARACK OBAMA

Over the last thirty years, I have overseen as an unpaid volunteer, and as a member of the board of directors of the Southern California Rapid Transit District, the Los Angeles County Metropolitan Transportation Authority, the Los Angeles Department of Water and Power a number of City, County and State projects including:

MTA Transit Center/Headquarters;

LAC + USC Medical Center;

UCLA/Harbor Medical Center addition;

LAPD Administration Building;

405 Freeway widening;

Riverside-Figueroa Bridge replacement;

6th Street Bridge;

A Bridge Home, a program to provide emergency housing shelters for the homeless.

KEYS TO A SUCCESSFUL PROJECT DELIVERY

Phase 1 - Development

Avoid irrational exuberance for project outcomes (*1).

Avoid unfounded political "talking points" about project outcomes.

Note opportunism: stakeholders promoting projects for individual gains.

Phase 2 - Planning/Design

From concept planning through opening to public service takes an average of 13.5 years, thus planning assumption may not hold true (*2).

Be aware that funding conditions and timeliness—local, state and especially federal funding often are unpredictable.

Engineering/design—the quality and quantity of resourcing has a paramount impact.

Construction contracting—market conditions, project risks and competitiveness are rarely considered in the development of construction plans and contracting methods.

Phase 3 - Delivery

Sponsor's talent capacity in managing its selected consultants and specialists often are lacking skillsets and/or experience for specific project complexities.

Ensure the quality of sponsor's selected consultants and contractors.

Sponsor effectiveness in the timely resolution of third -party agreements, right-of-way/ real estate acquisitions and utility relocations is critical. They are called the "killers" of public projects.

Board of Directors and Executive management's continued project support is essential 'it takes a village.'"

(*1) Initial project utilization forecasts accompanied by cost estimates and schedules, have limited factual basis at completion.

(*2) Project scope, creep-betterments and dealing with unknown conditions as design progresses are major risks.

I came to the conclusion that after having overseen a number of projects, the public projects are over budget and not on schedule mainly because of poor sponsor management and inaccurate construction documents. The managers of these projects are not paid well enough; their compensation is as low as one- third of managers in the private sector. As a result, public projects are constructed well over budget and with extensive delays. One recent example is the Crenshaw/LAX Transit Project (K Line). The project took four years longer to complete than originally scheduled and ultimately cost the taxpayers nearly $2.45 billion, including $600 million in change orders and claims, for a staggering cost of $288 million per mile. This was mainly because of an inexperienced and unaccountable sponsor's manager.

When Arthur Leahy was CEO of Metro, I cochaired with the knowledgeable and dedicated Metro chief engineer Murthy Krishniah a task force to determine the appropriate compensation of the executive officers. Assisted by a consultant expert on compensation, with a plethora of data and statistical comparisons with the private sector, a comprehensive report was presented to the Metro board of directors. The report clearly proved that the compensation of the executives had to be adjusted to attract experienced managers. After very little deliberation, the report was shelved. Consequently, most Metro`s projects are over budget and not on time. According to Federal Transit Administration reports dated July 28, 2022:

"Why do Sponsors end up with a Comprehensive Settlement?"

- Many unresolved claims with questionable or questioned merit.
- Insufficient justification or supporting documentation.

- Sponsor Independent Estimates much lower than Contractor Price.
- Inadequate and/or inexperienced Sponsor staff.
- Pressure put on project team to settle claims backlog.
- Experienced contractor negotiates with inexperienced Sponsor team.
- Contract requirements not enforced."

PROFESSIONAL SERVICES FEES

According to federal guidelines, "Qualifications-Based Selection is a procurement process established by the United States Congress as part of the Brooks Act and further developed for public agencies to use for the selection of architectural, consulting and engineering services for public construction projects. It is a competitive contract procurement whereby consulting firms submit qualifications to a procuring entity (owner) who evaluates and selects the most qualified firm, and then negotiates the project scope of work, schedule, budget, and consultant fee. Price is not the determining factor in selection. Price will be taken into consideration under Qualifications-Based Selection but not for the purposes of the public owner`s determination of the most suitable and qualified provider of construction services."

While serving on the Los Angeles County Metropolitan Transportation Authority Board of Directors, I determined that the agency was not receiving the best price after the selection of the consultant The fee for a particular project would be posted, estimated by the agency`s personnel. The posted fee proved to be consistently very high, and it was the bar for fee negotiation. I suggested that part of the submittal contain a sealed envelope that would include:

- All applicable direct labor, all applicable labor surcharges such as taxes, insurance and fringe benefits, as well indirect costs, overhead, general and administrative expenses, other direct costs, and profit.

- The Price Proposal submitted shall describe the number of hours proposed by labor category, and fully burdened rates for all proposed personnel, including subcontractors. This information is required to support the Proposer`s execution plan.

My suggestion was rejected right away because "It violated the Federal guidelines for procuring professional services." However, I persisted and asked the county counsel to render an opinion. After the agency consulted also with outside attorneys, it was determined that the requirement for a sealed envelope containing the price to be opened after the selection process was legal. I felt that the process forced the bidders to provide sound, accurate and thoughtful costs. As a result, millions of taxpayer dollars have been saved, considering the billions of dollars the agency has spent every year since the adoption of the policy 30 years ago.

When I served as president of the Board of Los Angeles Water and Power Commissioners, I instituted the same policy, which is still in effect.

RATEPAYER ADVOCATE

You have power over your mind, not outside events.
Realize this, and you will find strength.

—MARCUS AURELIUS

Measure I, which appeared on the March 2011 ballot, asked voters to create an Office of Public Accountability within the Los Angeles Department of Water and Power, the nation's largest municipal utility. It included a ratepayer advocate who would review proposed increases in water and power rates. I was the driving force behind the ratepayer advocate proposal when I was president of the DWP Board of Commissioners.

As board president, it became obvious to me that the public and elected leaders were not getting all the information in a timely manner as they should have. Everything that was done was driven by the political agenda of DWP management and the unions, and not the public concerns. When I first proposed the ratepayer advocate, my proposal met with resistance from City Hall and fellow board members. I appointed DWP board members Wally Knox, a former California State assemblyman, and Edith Ramirez, who would later serve as chair of the Federal Trade Commission under President Obama, to a task force that would hold a public hearing on the proposal. The public was totally in support of the proposal. However, Knox and Ramirez voted the proposal down because of pressure from Los Angeles City Hall.

But I did not give up. In fact, after consulting with Karen Gorman, inspector general of the Los Angeles County Metropolitan Transportation Authority, I included in the proposal clauses that would authorize internal investigations, oversee audits, root out corruption, and enforce ethics. I notified the City Council that if it failed to place it on the ballot, I would collect the necessary signatures to place it on the ballot. Councilwoman Jan Perry, chair of the council's Energy and Environment Committee, which oversaw the DWP, started a conversation with me and instructed the chief legislative analyst to draft my proposal for a ballot initiative.

An event in the summer of 2009 forced the council to move forward the ratepayer advocate proposal. "Well, then to me the tipping point was ECAF (Energy Cost Adjustment Factor) in 2009, the rate proposal for renewables," said Rafael Prieto, of the chief legislative analyst's office. The DWP uses the ECAF to pass through the costs of natural gas and other fuel costs to the customers. The ECAF charge was unfrozen in 2006, but increases were capped at 0.1 cents per kilowatt-hour per quarter, unless the board increased the limit. As a result of the cap, the DWP had almost $500 million in under collection. The board voted for an increase.

The president of the Board of Commissioners at that time, Lee Alpert, told me in March 2017 that he had called the chief financial officer in and said to him, "Look, it's a terrible time in the economy. Can we take the predictability factor out for this one time only, and if we need to increase it again, we can increase it." The City Council rejected Alpert's proposal and instead called for an independent review. The study came out showing that the DWP needed more rate increases. On November 5, 2010, Chief Operating Officer Raman Raj told me,

"Honestly, it was the proposal from the mayor's office to take 2% or 3% out of it, and make it into a common surcharge. . . . That was a disaster, that was a true disaster, and from there it went downhill completely. The ECAF became a political issue." Raj told the City Council members he would stop the city transfer if they did not approve the rate adjustment. Both City Council President Eric Garcetti and Council member Perry appeared before the DWP Board and asked the board not to hold the transfer hostage to rate increases. Each year the DWP transfers about $250 million to the city's general fund as surplus. Critics have challenged the transfers in court saying the surplus is a "tax," according to Proposition 218, and therefore voter approval is required. Both the Superior Court and state Courts of Appeal ruled that the transfers of DWP surplus to the city's general fund are lawful.

Prieto of the chief legislative analyst's office came to the conclusion: "We need to have a ratepayer advocate, no more (holy grail). ...There was overwhelming support for a ratepayer advocate. The ratepayer advocate idea was strong. We prepared the proposal in the fall of 2010. Councilwoman Perry played a critical role in pushing our office, very supportive."

The proposal went before the City Council in November 2010, and it voted to place it on the March 2011 primary election ballot. Los Angeles voters overwhelmingly approved it by a margin of 77.6 percent to 22.4 percent. When the proposal was before the City Council for a vote, Garcetti approached me as I was sitting at the back of the council chambers and said, "Nick, we have to delete the section of Inspector General, otherwise the union will mount a campaign against it." I made the decision that the ratepayer advocate was better than nothing, and I would wait for an inspector general another day. Well, that day came on April 11, 2022, when Garcetti, who was then mayor, announced that DWP had selected its first inspector general.

The inspector general provides review and oversight of contracts, whistleblower complaints, ethics and internal policies and responsibilities, mirroring my 2009 proposal. Garcetti's action was precipitated by corruption scandals that engulfed the DWP and also involved the city attorney's office under Mike Feuer. Federal prosecutors charged that city lawyers helped arrange outside legal representation for DWP customers involved in a class-action lawsuit against Los Angeles over erroneous charges in an attempt to control the terms of the settlement. Former DWP General Manager David Wright was sentenced to six years in prison after pleading guilty to one count of bribery in January 2022. He admitted soliciting bribes, destroying evidence, and being part of several "corrupt schemes" at the utility. Other DWP officials were charged with and convicted of similar crimes. Privately, a LADWP official revealed to me that the scandal has cost the city more than $120 million.

LOS ANGELES BOARD OF ZONING APPEALS

In February 1981, I got a call from Fran Savitch, a top aide to Los Angeles Mayor Tom Bradley who was in charge of appointments to city commissions. Savitch asked if I would be interested in being appointed to the Board of Zoning Appeals because Howard Finn had resigned from the board to run for City Council in the north east part of the San Fernando Valley. The mayor, according to Savitch, wanted to fill that vacant seat with someone with a technical background, who was involved with the community, and who lived in the San Fernando Valley. I agreed to serve on the Board of Zoning Appeals just two weeks after Los Angeles County Supervisor Michael Antonovich had appointed me to the Southern California Rapid Transit District Board of Directors. The Board of Zoning Appeals met on Tuesdays and RTD met every other Thursday. (The Board of Zoning Appeals was later absorbed by the Planning Commission as a result of Mayor Richard Riordan's charter reform.)

The Board of Zoning Appeals was composed of five members appointed by the mayor and confirmed by the City Council. It was a quasi-judicial body, which meant the members could not discuss the cases with anyone from the public, especially lobbyists, or among themselves before the meetings. The board addressed specific cases that appealed to it. It was not a policy-making body. Its charter mandate was to determine whether the zoning administrator erred or abused his or her discretion. The board, in case of a variance to the zoning code, had to make five statutory findings.

The appeals varied, including variances for over-height-fences, setbacks from property lines, configurations of tennis courts, homeowners opposing the operations of new hotels and restaurants, alcoholic beverage conditional use permits, and adjustment of density from one portion of a property to another. The five statutory findings were rigid, and whereas to neighbors who oppose a project or to the applicant who is suffering some hardship, the resolution was very simple and clear, the board had to make all five variance findings to grant or deny the appeal. In contrast with a variance, the board had discretion when it reviewed applications for conditional use permits, such for example to grant a restaurant a permit to serve liquor.

Serving on the board, although it was at times frustrating, was in general a challenging and rewarding experience. There were rarely cameras or reporters at the board meetings, and therefore little public awareness of the proceedings, but some of the board decisions involved many millions of dollars.

According to the *Los Angeles Times*, "Some City Council aides considered the sessions so difficult that they tried to send co-workers." Following are three cases that give a sense and flavor of the proceedings and dynamics.

In May 1992, there was a case in which the owner of an auto-repair shop wanted to add another bay. The zoning administrator had refused to grant him a variance unless he paid for widening the street and putting in new curbs, at a cost of half a million dollars. The zoning administrator explained that because the city could not afford to widen the street to the Department of Transportation's specifications, it was customary to require developers to pay for road improvements. According to an *LA Weekly* reporter present, I went "ballistic' stating, "The future of this city is not going to be about the car! More cars, more highways, widening more streets are not going to solve our transportation problems. We can't allow the Bureau of Engineering and the Department of Transportation to have a blank check to plan our city." The board unanimously overturned the zoning administrators' decision.

In the second case, an influential lobbyist was making the case to expand the shopping center at Beverly and La Cienega boulevards, across the street from the Beverly Center.

Nearby homeowners had appealed the decision of the zoning administrator saying there was not enough parking, and the expansion would increase traffic congestion. The lobbyist pinned a site plan on the blackboard and said, "We propose to add (a specific amount) of extra parking spaces." My office was a few blocks from the shopping center, and I occasionally would go to the Rexall drugstore. I was therefore familiar with the site. In addition, considering that my profession required reading architectural plans, I knew right away from looking at the site plan on the wall that the lobbyist's statement was wrong. I asked the lobbyist to count the parking spaces. The room was full, with more than one hundred homeowners. There was deafening silence and bewilderment on the faces of all in the room, especially the zoning administrator and the applicant. The lobbyist said, "Commissioner it will take a lot of time." To which I replied, "We have all day." With a red face and stuttering, the lobbyist apologized for "misspeaking." The proposal was withdrawn.

The lesson here is that before one appears before a body one must do some homework and find out the background, education, profession, etc. of each member of the body. Another fact that became known then is that the zoning administrators do not necessarily know how to read plans. They just know how to interpret the zoning code.

The third case involved Rebecca's restaurant in Venice, which is closed now. This was a popular restaurant whose interior was decorated with Frank Gehry's trademark design, "fish." Two giant stuffed crocodiles hung from the ceiling. I happened to be visiting the restaurant when I noticed that the valets were charging for parking. This violated one of the conditions that the board imposed when it granted the restaurant's conditional permit. Board members believed that only free valet parking would keep patrons from parking on residential streets.

The *Los Angeles Times* reported my reaction on this case as follows, "When Patsaouras found the restaurant had also improperly stored its trash bins, he was livid," say those familiar with the case. 'When you do not abide by these conditions, you offend me and you offend the city,' Patsaouras told the restaurant's operators. He led a campaign to revoke the permit and close the restaurant -only relenting when he was assured that the owners had learned their lessons. Patsaouras was 'a hero' recalled one woman who lived near Rebecca's. Another Venice local, Bonnie Faulkner said to the Times. 'Nick Patsaouras stood up for the neighborhood against the moneyed interests.'" The owner of Rebecca's, Bruce Marder said, "The punishment was out of proportion to the offense, I don't understand why he has to rant and rave." Marder said he spent sixty thousand dollars in legal fees to keep Rebecca's open.

I served on the Board of Zoning Appeals for twelve years, and when I started to get restless, I knew it was time to move on. After one board meeting, I walked into the mayor's office and told Bradley, "Mr. Mayor, thank you for the privilege and opportunity you gave me to serve the city, but it's time for new blood." When I left, my commendation said I was the "emotional engine" of the board.

CHAPTER ELEVEN

PRESERVING LOS ANGELES HERITAGE

Heritage is not just about preserving buildings; it is about safeguarding the stories and memories they hold.

—UNKNOWN

LOS ANGELES CITY HALL

When the most destructive earthquake in the history of Los Angeles struck on January 17, 1994—the magnitude 6.7 deadly Northridge tremor—it seriously damaged historic City Hall but did not bring it down. However, the city's emblematic structure was almost demolished at the time. I was perplexed to learn from Dan Rosenfeld, a real estate developer who, at the time, had been asked by Mayor Richard Riordan to organize the city's real estate holdings as Los Angeles assistant manager of assets that Riordan had proposed to tear down City Hall.

From 1981 to 1992, I spent every Tuesday in this beautiful building as a member of the Board of Zoning Appeals, in addition to many meetings with Mayor Tom Bradley while we were planning and lobbying for funding for the Los Angeles Metro Rail.

To make City Hall safe from earthquakes and to restore it would cost about $300 million, Rosenfeld said. "Riordan didn't want to do it. He thought it was a big waste of money. He wanted to move City Hall up to Bunker Hill, and either buy an existing building or build a new one."

"In other words, the celebrated centerpiece of Los Angeles, featured in hundreds of movies, its image engraved on LA police badges and official documents, would cease to exist?" I asked Rosenfeld, seeking clarification. That was Riordan's desire, he said. Rosenfeld remembered Riordan calling him and oddly remarking that everyone is committed to keeping this building, adding, "Can't we just replicate it out of fiberglass?" Rosenfeld had ample knowledge about renovating buildings from his time as deputy director of real estate assets in the Gov. Pete Wilson`s administration. He had led the revival of the historic core of downtown Los Angeles. In 1990 he opted to renovate an old department store in what was then a chancy block of Broadway to the state Junipero Serra office building.

There was apprehension about what Rosenfeld called Riordan's "managerial idiosyncrasies," explaining that the mayor was swayed by the person he spoke with last. "I remember several people would call and say, 'Hey, I just shared a cab with Mayor Riordan, and he wants me to look at real estate, or whatever.'" One of the people that had contacted him was Stuart Ketchum, a real estate developer and Music Center board member, who had opposed

Los Angeles City Hall.
Photo: wikimedia

starting work on the proposed Walt Disney Concert Hall until final funding for the project was guaranteed. Obviously, he had captured Riordan's ear.

Kenneth Reich, reporter for the *Los Angeles Times*, wrote on November 23, 1995, that Riordan and City Controller Rick Tuttle named a fourteen-member panel to take a fresh, hard look at how to retrofit—or even replace—Los Angeles's quake-damaged City Hall. Ketchum was named the panel's chair. Ketchum had stated that replacing City Hall was one of the options. On the panel were seismic experts, a contractor and architect, bankers and businesspeople, real estate brokers, along with Nelson Rising, a longtime adviser to Bradley.

Months later, the advisory panel recommended a scaled-down $165-million project, sacrificing earlier plans to modernize the building and confining the work to preserving its safety. It foresaw the eventual reoccupation of all City Hall floors, except for the observation deck on top.

"I remember standing as I was reading the panel's report," Rosenfeld related to me, "when Ketchum said, 'Well, this shouldn't cost $300 million. Why do we have all these elevators? Use the stairs. And why do bureaucrats need air conditioning? We can cut $50 million out of this project.'"

John Ferraro, president of the Los Angeles City Council, and Councilwoman Rita Walters, as well as other seasoned observers, considered the building to be the city's noteworthy heritage and it was their responsibility to preserve it, to 'bite the bullet' and do it right. Ron Deaton, the city's respected chief legislative analyst, also pushed for the building restoration and retrofit despite objections over costs. City Councilwoman Cindy Miscikowski said his work and support truly ensured City Hall's existence.

Linda Dishman, former longtime executive director of the Los Angeles Conservancy, the largest membership-based preservation group in the country and the primary institution for preservation in Southern California, recounted for me why Riordan wanted a new City Hall. He simply did not want to spend all that money to retrofit it. However, the idea of a new City Hall died quickly, she told me, "I think City Hall is just beloved. Most people know what their City Hall looks like. They may not know that we have a historic downtown, or a historic neighborhood, but they've learned about City Hall from Dragnet or from a variety of things they saw on television."

Dishman believed that buildings visible from the freeway are easier to save. Riordan's idea about a new city hall "died a pretty sudden death" within a few months, she said.

The retrofitting of City Hall was very much alive and plans to proceed unfolded. In 1995, the building was closed, and nine hundred city employees were relocated to other offices, most moving across the street to City Hall East. Moving expenses, rent for other locations and furniture cost the city $22 million. Consultants on the project sought to modernize the building with new electrical fixtures, heating, and air conditioning. Although I was pleased the building was being restored and retrofitted, the constant, enduring concern I had, of course, was over the padding of the budget, a favorite pastime in this town. My uneasiness proved accurate as I witnessed projected costs, initially $165 million, continuing to spiral upward.

Reich wrote in the *Los Angeles Times* that Riordan recused himself from participating in decision-making on the project because he and the building's architect, Christopher C. Martin, were partners in a downtown office building. Consequently, Ferraro became the most influential elected official in all deliberations. For some, the temporary headquarters were comfortable, but Ferraro said he preferred to return to the 1928 building. The temporary location was nice, "But in my view, it's still not City Hall," he told the *Los Angeles Times*.

By 1999, a nonstop restoration was underway. Almost three hundred workers labored two shifts a day, six days a week. Retrofitting involved, among other things, installation of more than five hundred base isolators in the basement and beneath columns. Reinforced concrete shear walls to fortify the upper parts of the building were poured, and viscous dampers—big shock absorbers—were utilized.

The steel-with-brick-infill tower walls were upgraded with reinforced steel and concrete. The shear walls run the full building height and resist lateral earthquake forces. Importantly, the project added a four-foot-wide moat around the foundation, allowing the ground to move under the building during an earthquake. According to the *Los Angeles Times*, steel slides within the foundation act as bearings if the earth shifts. The eighteen-inch-deep moat had a cover at ground level and was landscaped. To strengthen the building, it was estimated that thirty thousand cubic yards of concrete, three thousand tons of structural steel and five thousand tons of reinforced steel and 68,467 pounds of dead-weight were added to the structure.

Structural engineer Nabih Youssef, known for his expertise in seismic retrofit, said an "integrated" concept using the latest seismic innovations to protect a building very close to a dangerous fault zone had been followed. City Hall was the tallest building in the world ever to undergo base isolation as part of a seismic retrofitting. After three years of seismic retrofitting, on Thursday, June 29, 2001, the Los Angeles City Council moved back into what its president, Ruth Galanter, called "the real City Hall." The cost for the project was $299 million. The council chamber was formally named for its former long-term president, John Ferraro.

At the time, James Hahn, who three days later was inaugurated as mayor, said the work expanded beyond retrofitting and brought broad modernization to the 1928 building. He told Reich of the *Los Angeles Times* that "some people said we shouldn't rebuild City Hall, that it would be too expensive, we ought to tear it down, maybe we should just relocate to a building elsewhere downtown." "What a loss that would have been! Thankfully, cooler heads prevailed," he said. Remarkably, outgoing mayor Riordan skipped the opening ceremony.

Project Restore raises private funds each year to complete the restoration of architectural finishes in the building that were not funded by the federal "seismic safety" grant. Greg Fisher, deputy to Councilmember Jan Perry and downtown historian, told me the ancillary benefits of retrofitting were many, including installation of a magnificent glass and iron chandelier that was put up in 1928, only to be taken down in 1933 after the devastating Long Beach earthquake struck. killing 115 to 120 people.

I asked him how it was found after so many years. Fisher said that Brenda Levin, an architect and advocate of historic preservation who spent eight years restoring City Hall to its original splendor, knew exactly where it was: in boxes in the basement. "It was put together and rehung." It made the place look less cavernous, less unfinished, he said.

Federal grants totaling $126 million and proceeds of a bond measure to upgrade city buildings to earthquake standards, which was approved by Los Angeles voters in 1990, financed much of the work. Although every council member praised the new chamber, Laura Chick, city controller-elect at the time, pledged to review the retrofitting costs.

Identified as a "modern American" masterpiece, it was designed by three of the city's architectural and design celebrities: John Parkinson, John C. Austin, and Albert C. Martin, Sr. Parkinson provided the concept, Martin the structural design and Austin the working drawings and general administration of the project. In the 1960s, the firm A.C. Martin designed the Los Angeles Department of Water and Power building that faces City Hall. These two buildings frame the Gloria Molina Grand Park.

Classical Art Deco design elements dominate the building, especially the tower topped by a step pyramid. As an engineer, I've had a special interest in roof design for many years. Some believe that it was influenced by ancient temples, because King Tutankhamun's tomb was discovered in 1922 and ancient things became fashionable at the time. However, I have a different opinion. Greek King Mausolus built his tomb about 350 BC in Halicarnassus, a

Atlantic Richfield Tower Photo: Courtesy of L.A. Conservancy

Eastern Columbia Building Photo: Courtesy of L.A. Conservancy

tomb so impressive it was regarded as one of the Seven Wonders of the Ancient World. From King Mausolus we get our word 'mausoleum.' The structure stood almost 150 feet tall, and its spectacular roof was pyramidal.

According to Clark Construction, the general contractor, with AC Martin Partners the designer, the retrofitted City Hall can withstand a magnitude 8.2 earthquake.

"Its architecture, and particularly its Spring Street entrance and grand rotunda, have helped City Hall stand out as a visually striking location in scores of television productions and feature films," said Phil Sokoloski, vice president of integrated communications for FilmLA. "The building remains a captivating shooting location."

For the late City Councilman Tom LaBonge, "City Hall was his second home," his wife, Brigid, said. She recalled the days when her husband would drive around the city with the family, noting that for years no buildings were allowed to be taller than City Hall.

As a matter of fact, from 1928 until the late 1950s, it was the tallest building in Los Angeles and shared the skyline with only a few structures having decorative towers, including the twelve-story Richfield Tower on South Flower Street and the thirteen-story Eastern Columbia Building on Broadway.

A 1905 municipal ordinance set the maximum height at 130 feet. Subsequently, there were so many requests for variances the city voters approved a City Charter amendment effective 1911 establishing the 150-foot height limit that remained until 1958.

The first "skyscraper" constructed after the height limit was rescinded was the eighteen-story United California Bank building at Sixth and Spring streets, built in 1961. It is presently an apartment building. The thirty-story One Wilshire high rise followed in 1966, and then the forty-story Union Bank Plaza on Bunker Hill at Fifth and Figueroa streets, built in 1968.

Paul Gleye, an architectural historian, said that the idea that the height limit arose from earthquake concerns was a popular misconception. The San Francisco earthquake occurred in 1906.

The truth is that Los Angeles residents did not want their city to become another Manhattan. The main factor was aesthetics, Gleye said.

Los Angeles's representational persona, a few years from its 100th birthday, star of television and film, lies in splendor embraced by modern structures. Its observation level on the twenty-seventh floor provides a panoramic view of the City of Angels, while viewers far and wide can look at the civic center and see the majesty of City Hall and feel the pulse of its city.

Los Angeles City Hall was designated a Los Angeles Historic Cultural Monument in 1976.

LOS ANGELES CENTRAL LIBRARY

An Essential Rebirth | I have been particularly interested in the Los Angeles Central Library for more than fifty years. My consulting engineering office for many years was at the six story Beaux Arts building previously known as the Pacific Mutual Building and now known as PacMutual at Sixth and Olive streets. I would see the library building almost daily as I walked back and forth between my office and the Jonathan Club, which is on Sixth and Figueroa and is the place I used as my gym, daily parking, and venue for my social, professional, and political meetings and events for decades. I therefore followed with great interest what was happening with the library building over the years.

The Central Library, dedicated in 1926, was designed by architect Bertram Grosvenor Goodhue, FAIA. The library sits where the State Normal School was built in 1881, which later evolved into the University of California, Los Angeles. The person who helped lay the Los Angeles Public Library groundwork was Charles F. Lummis, a journalist and activist for Indian rights and historic preservation, who was appointed city librarian in 1905. Lummis' acquisitions brought acclaim to the library's special collections on the history of California and the West. Lummis was a scholar, before entering Harvard University, his minister father had taught him Greek, Latin and Hebrew. He resigned as head librarian in 1911 and established the Southwest Museum.

The library building includes architectural elements of Egyptian, Spanish Colonial, Roman Byzantine and various Islamic civilizations and displays formal minimalism. The second floor of the library has a high-domed rotunda full of light and color, and at the center of the dome is an illuminated globe chandelier with the signs of the zodiac. Twelve murals on the walls painted by Dean Cornwell in 1933 depict the history of California.

There was a plan since the late 1970s to tear down the Los Angeles Central Library, sell the property, and build a new library, according to Donald Spivack, deputy chief of operations and policy for the Los Angeles Community Redevelopment Agency. Architect Charles Luckman had recommended the replacement of the library and had drawn plans in the late

Central Library
Photo: G. Hauser

1970s for a high rise building to house the new library. Luckman once told a writer for The New Yorker, "I am firm in my belief that architecture is a business and not an art." Interestingly, there was a letter published in the *Los Angeles Times* from a person from New York. It said, "Dear Editor, I heard about this proposal to tear down the Bertram Grosvenor Goodhue public library in Los Angeles. That is just a horrible idea. It is one of the most important buildings, if not the most important building in the city. Please save it, if not for yourselves, at least us New Yorkers."

In the late 1970s, the city had prepared an environmental impact report to demolish the library. Meanwhile, the historic preservation committee of the Los Angeles chapter of the American Institute of Architects had produced in 1978 a historic study of the Central Library and how it could be preserved, written by Margaret Bach, founding president of the Los Angeles Conservancy. Preservationist John Welborne, Bach, architect Barton Phelps, and Atlantic Richfield Company executive Rodney Rood attended a presentation at the library for its demolition. AIA filed a lawsuit that put the brakes on the demolition plans. Welborne created the Citizens Task Force for Central Library Development. Welborne and Barton Phelps wrote a speech, and they started to talk to the business community.

Chris Stewart, president of the Central City Association of Los Angeles, reluctantly allowed Barton Phelps to speak before his group. As result, the CCA endorsed the idea of preserving the library. The group was gaining momentum, and it brought aboard one of the great civic leaders in Los Angeles, Steve Gavin, to be the spokesperson.

The Luckman plan engendered strong opposition, and it brought together a group of concerned citizens who wanted to fight to save the building, but who also realized there was a need to have an ongoing preservation organization that would focus not only on advocacy but also on education. This was the genesis in 1978, of the Los Angeles Conservancy, which has more members than any other historic preservation organization in the country. From the beginning, the conservancy was highly active in terms of education, partly in the belief that not everybody realizes that Los Angeles has a lot of historic resources, and not everyone understands yet that we need to save them. Therefore, the conservancy's education component was strong. This fits in with the overall preservation movement nationally. Many local and state preservation groups were founded in the 1970s to promote preservation, such as Pasadena Heritage, founded in 1977, a year before the conservancy. The conservancy's work on the Central Library was very focused on trying to get a win-win solution. According to Linda Dishman, former president of the conservancy, "The librarians had wanted to tear down the building, build a new office building, and have a state-of-the-art library. The Conservancy never argued with what they wanted."

Robert Harris, dean of the School of Architecture at USC said, "By 1985 the building was decrepit, with limited automation, and shabby, without adequate HVAC system. The librarians had a big problem. Over time the interior of the library had been decimated. As they had more staff, they had to make another little office, the books were getting larger and larger, so the reading spaces were getting smaller as they added stacks, and the office arrangements were unpleasant. So, the librarians and the library staff were eager to have a real library building. They were interested in having it replaced somewhere where there was more ground."

In 1980, developer Robert Maguire and former ARCO Chairman Robert O. Anderson arranged for their companies to contribute $300,000 for a study to determine how the sixty-year-old building could be preserved. At the end of 1981, Mayor Tom Bradley, Luckman, Ed Helfeld, CRA Administrator, and Lodwrick Cook, ARCO chief executive officer, met in Cook's offices on the fifty-first floor of ARCO Towers to discuss the future of the library. As relayed by Helfeld after the meeting to Don Spivack and others, "Cook looked out of his window and said, 'This is not acceptable. We've got to fix it.'" From that time forward the conversations were about how to restore the library. The primary barrier was that the library was housed in a very inefficient building. The discussions evolved ultimately into a plan to restore the library building, which is a landmark, and use it for non-library functions with few exceptions and build a new library next to it.

THE FIRES

In 1986, two arson fires at the Central Library, a big one on April 29 and a smaller one in September, caused about $24 million in damage. In total four hundred thousand books were destroyed. On May 22, 1989, a temporary library opened in Los Angeles Design Center, a ten-story Art Deco building, at 433 South Spring Street. According to the library archives, on April 29, 1986, Carlton Norris, an ARCO executive looked down from the thirty-second floor of the ARCO Tower and saw the fire coming from the west side of the Central Library. Norris had an extraordinary love and appreciation for libraries. With the approval of Cook, phone banks were immediately set up on an empty floor of the ARCO building.

The ARCO Tower was across Flower Street from the library and one of the twin fifty-two story towers completed in 1971. They are the tallest twin towers in Los Angeles. ARCO occupied the northern tower, which is now known as the Paul Hastings Tower. On April 30, 1986, ARCO invited the library administration to occupy the thirty-fifth floor of its tower. This would be the genesis for a major private and public effort to reach out and engage Angelenos in restoring what had been lost.

The efforts to save the books from fire and water damage united the city. More than 1700 volunteers worked tirelessly to salvage the surviving books. Cook and Bradley helped form a Save the Books Blue Ribbon Committee. The campaign raised $10 million to replace books damaged in the fires. Televangelist Gene Scott, who had a well-known television show, hosted a Save the Books fundraiser telethon. Cook showed up wearing a cowboy hat and boots and danced to "Just a Gigolo," while City librarian Wyman Jones played the piano. The two-day telethon raised $2 million. When the expanded library opened on October 3, 1993, the rotunda was named for Cook, who founded and was the first chairman of the Library Foundation of Los Angeles.

Martha Katsufrakis, a member of the Board of the Library Commissioners at the time of the fires, recalled, "We were at City Hall wondering what to do, a knock on the door and a man walked in, Eric Lundquist, who explained he had been at Stanford, had heard about the fire, flew down to LA and was offering his service to help save the books. Obtain every frozen food locker to freeze the books as soon as possible." Katsufrakis, who is proud of her service, including helping design the carpet in the children's section, believes that because of Cook's firsthand role as chair of the Save the Books campaign, others got involved in the effort, such as ABC-TV sponsoring an Essay Contest, "What the Library Means to Me."

I would like to pay tribute to Martha's husband and my dear friend, Peter Katsufrakis. A Greek American, the affable and innovative Los Angeles small claims court judge built a reputation as an advocate for the little guy. Peter recalled in a *Los Angeles Times* interview that when he took over small claims every Friday was called "store day." "All these big companies would come in with up to fifty claims apiece—most of them defaults, where the defendants didn't show up, and they'd just get an automatic judgement from the clerk. The judge wouldn't

Televangelist Gene Scott offered his studio space for a forty-eight-hour "Save the Books" telethon that his University Network co-sponsored with ARCO. Pictured at the telethon from left to right are: ARCO Chairman and CEO Lod Cook, Central Library Director Betty Gay Teoman, Assistant City Librarian Tom Alford, Library Commissioners Martha Katsufrakis, Ronald Lushing, City Librarian Wyman Jones, and Gene Scott. Photo: Los Angeles Public Library Institutional Collection

even hear the cases," he was quoted as saying. Judge Katsufrakis eliminated the 'store day' issuing orders limiting each plaintiff to two cases per session, and his transformation of the Los Angeles small claims court garnered national attention.

There is a misconception that people decided to save the library because of the fires. Not true. The library was really saved in 1981-82—politically. The construction drawings were in progress in 1986. In fact, architect Norman Pfeiffer and Central Library Director Betty Gay Teoman were reviewing the plans for the first and second floors of the existing library when the April 29 fire occurred.

CREATIVE FINANCING

In the early 1980s, the city was eager to find a way to finance the project without having to dip into the general fund. According to Spivack, that was a problem in the early 1980s because of the passage of Howard Jarvis' Proposition 13, which limited property taxes, and therefore there were no funds available for renovation or new expansion. Ed Helfeld came up with the idea to turn the city-owned library over to the CRA for $1. (When CRA was dissolved in 2012 along with all other redevelopment agencies in the state, the library reverted to the city.) The CRA would then market for development the unused density of the existing library and the expansion.

Transfer of development rights and transfer of floor area rights (also known as air rights) are economic incentive programs to help direct new development away from sensitive areas, including land parcels containing historic resources. These programs allow property owners to quantify and sell unused development rights from their sites to other landowners so they can increase the density of new construction in more appropriate locations. Nelson Rising, senior partner of Maguire Thomas Partners, proposed in 1983 that the concept of air rights transfer be expanded to include in addition to the small Engstrom apartments site across from the library, the new Gas Company Tower at Fifth Street and Grand Avenue, which freed the old Gas Company headquarters at 810 South Flower to be converted into lofts.

However, the pads for the different buildings would not allow the size of buildings planned because the City Charter caps the floor area ratio at 13:1 on each site. To resolve the issue, the City Council adopted a separate ordinance for the library expansion sites: the Library Tower, the Gas Company Tower, 550 South Hope Tower, One Bunker Hill, the pad for the plaza west of the library and the Bunker Hill steps. The ordinance allowed adding up the density for these sites and then distributing it in whichever way made sense, so long as it they did not exceed 13:1 of that sum. That allowed the seventy-three-story Library Tower to be built directly across the street from the library, where the Engstrom apartments were located. The Library Tower has limited parking beneath it because of the size of the pad on which it was built. The balance of the parking is beneath the Maguire Gardens next to the library. The building today is the Los Angeles headquarters of US Bank.

The 550 South Hope Tower was not part of the Maguire Thomas Partners deal, but its timing and the need for additional revenue and to maximize the use of the density on the

The Gas Company Tower. Photo: Shirley Bleviss. Courtesy of Angels Walk LA

Library Tower. Photo: Shirley Bleviss Courtesy of Angels Walk LA

library site, brought it into the entire city-CRA- developer deal. The tower was built on the land previously occupied by the Church of the Open Door.

As part of the deal, One Bunker Hill received funding for some interior building upgrades plus the reconstruction of the portion of the building facing Fifth Street, where the former ramp to Hope Street and retaining wall had to be removed for the Library Tower. Part of the remodeling added street level retail and a second level retail deck, for which additional development density was required.

Maguire Thomas Partners paid for the Library Tower building, the Bunker Hill Steps, and the landscaping. Maguire Thomas Partners and the developers of the 550 South Hope building paid for the plaza west of the library. They secured the rights to build a garage underneath and construct a park on top of it, which became the Maguire Gardens. CRA bought a parking garage at Fourth and Olive streets to provide parking for library employees, who used to park where the gardens is now.

Maguire Thomas Partners signed a pledge that, in addition to buying the development rights from the library parcel for the Library Tower and Gas Company building, the company would guarantee it would begin paying the property taxes as of a certain date, whether the buildings were completed, per the agreed schedule. With that pledge, the CRA was able to issue the bonds that would pay for the library. The final cost to renovate and expand the library was $213.9 million. All but about $33 million was paid for by the library deal.

According to Spivack, when the environmental analysis on those towers was performed, it could not get approved. The primary reason was the traffic impact. CRA determined that the traffic was not because of the towers, but because of the parking. Therefore, if the car park were to be moved away from the towers, it would solve the problem. A series of traffic studies was conducted to determine how much parking could be built at the Library, Library Tower,

Bunker Hill Steps. Photo: Shirley Bleviss. Courtesy of Angels Walk LA

and Gas Company Tower sites, and how much would have to be diverted to allow the projects to be approved. By reducing the at-site parking to 60 percent of code and moving the rest to a remote location, the projects could be approved.

Maguire Thomas Partners agreed to fund the first major garage, located remotely, and therefore reduce the number of parking spaces on site, which would allow the environmental report to be approved. Maguire Thomas Partners built a parking structure at Seventeenth Street and Grand Avenue. It turned out that the garage was not necessary because, even at the downtown parking requirement of half the city code—which was allowed within a defined traffic zone bounded by the Hollywood Freeway, Harbor Freeway, Hill Street and Olympic Boulevard—there was overbuilt parking.

Groundbreaking for the $350 million seventy-three-story Library Tower was held June 23, 1987. It was the tallest building west of Mississippi until 2016, when it was dethroned by the Wilshire Grand Center at Seventh and Figueroa streets, the Los Angeles headquarters of Korean Air, designed by Chris Martin, partner of AC Martin Partners. Henry N. Cobb and Harold Fredenburgh of I.M. Pei & Partners designed the Library Tower. It was a joint venture of Maguire Thomas Partners and Pacific Library Tower, a subsidiary of the Los Angeles energy and real estate giant Pacific Lighting Corp. Each company had 50 percent equity in the project.

The Bunker Hill Steps, a staircase that provides a pedestrian route from Bunker Hill to the Los Angeles Central Library, were designed by landscape architect Lawrence Halprin. Robert Graham's 1992 sculpture of a woman, "Source Figure," offering water stands in the middle of a round fountain at the top of the stairway. The Bunker Hill steps were designed to resemble Rome's Spanish Steps. The original Bunker Steps were constructed in the late 1920s, about the same time the Central Library was built. They provided access to the business district for the Bunker Hill residents. The original steps were below the seventy-three-story Library Tower. The new Steps were built between the 444 South Flower Building and the Library Tower.

Maguire Thomas Partners also bought from the city all the land around the library that did not have any buildings on it. That provided Maguire with sufficient additional air rights to build the second building of the Library Square Redevelopment Project, the Gas Company Tower. Construction started in 1988 and the building opened in 1991. The Gas Company Tower had a large enough pad to meet its (reduced 60 percent of downtown code) parking requirement.

The Gas Company Tower was designed by Richard Keating of Skidmore, Owings, and Merrill, and today is the Los Angeles headquarters of accounting giant Deloitte.

With close to $125 million received from Maguire and funds from other sources such as city bonds and foundations, the central library was renovated and expanded between 1988 and 1993. The architect was Hardy Holzman Pfeiffer Associates. Brenda Levin collaborated in planning the restoration of the Goodhue Building. She was responsible for the first phase of the renovation and the Rotunda level that included adapting two of the original reading rooms for new use as the children's department. The new wing includes an eight-story atrium partly below ground, which is as deep as the Goodhue library is broad. The wing is dedicated to Bradley.

Norman Pfeiffer wanted to have some kind of peaked roof over the atrium. There were many heated debates until Merry Norris, president of the Cultural Affairs Commission, stepped in and the atrium got flattened down so that it does not compete with the fabulous library feature, its tower.

A plaque, with text written by John Welborne, chairman of the Citizens Task Force for the Central Library Development, is located at the west entrance to the library and reads in part:

This plaque commemorates the illumination of the Central Library pyramid and light of learning torch by the Los Angeles Conservancy on November 14, 2003, in recognition of the twenty-fifth anniversary of the founding of the Conservancy, whose first cause was the preservation of the Central library.

This plaque was placed by the Los Angeles chapter of the American Institute of Architects, whose 1978 report advocated the building's preservation and restoration.

The ALOUD podcasts, part of the award-winning speaker series presented by the Library Foundation of Los Angeles, reinforce the concept that the library is very much a social and cultural hub of the city. ALOUD is described as the Library Foundation literary series of conversations, readings, and performances, where Los Angeles engages with today's top writers, thinkers, and performers to listen, learn and exchange ideas.

As Linda Dishman, former head of the LA Conservancy, told me, "Libraries are important because it is the basis of democracy that people come together and can learn, and it is free. We have reaffirmed our commitment to democracy and the inspiration you feel when you read the quotes in the library. It is a great testament to the commitment of people to understand the need for preservation."

The 550 South Hope Tower, built where the Church of the Open Door had stood for seventy years, recognizes the previous occupant of the site by a "yellow brick road" in the building lobby leading through an open door to a room with a beautiful gold dome and video equipment showing the history of the church. The 550 South Hope Tower, designed by Kohn Pedersen Fox with Landon Wilson as the associate architect, was completed in 1991. It is today the Los Angeles headquarters of the accounting firm KPMG.

When the church relocated to Glendora in 1985, televangelist Gene Scott purchased the Hope Street building for $23 million in January 1986 through his Wescott Christian Center. The Church of the Open Door building, known for its two fourteen-foot-high "Jesus Saves" neon signs, was renamed Los Angeles University Cathedral. But Scott soon stopped

550 South Hope/KPMG Center. Central Library on the left and California Club on the right

Church of the Open Door/Biola University building under construction, 1912. Photo: LA Public Library

payments, and the Church of the Open Door foreclosed on him. That building was damaged by the 1987 Whittier Narrows earthquake, and Scott moved his congregation in 1990 into the United Artists' former flagship theater on South Broadway in downtown Los Angeles, which was owned by Bruce Corwin, president of the Miracle on Broadway business group and chair of Metropolitan Theaters. I was introduced to Corwin by Bradley, and we developed a lasting friendship. Bruce was a resolute civic leader, philanthropist, and a loyal and active Democrat. He was courteous, affable and with a smile on his face when he greeted someone.

After foreclosure on Scott, the Church of the Open Door sold the downtown building to a developer, and it was demolished. One of the two "Jesus Saves" signs was moved in 2011 by Scott's widow, preacher Melissa Scott, to a church in Glendale, where she served as pastor. The other sign sits atop the Ace Hotel at Ninth Street and Broadway in downtown Los Angeles.

I met Scott through Fran Savitch, a close advisor and confidant of Bradley, who was a friend of Scott's, an avid philatelist. When in one of my conversations with Fran I mentioned that when I was teenager, I used to collect stamps, she arranged a visit to Scott's mansion, where he showed us his beautiful, exquisite stamp collection.

PROPOSING THE SALE OF THE HISTORIC LIBRARY

Fountains west of Library. Photo: Shirley Bleviss, courtesy of Angels Walk LA

In the summer of 1993, Mayor Richard Riordan proposed the sale of part of the Los Angeles historic Central Library to a subsidiary of tobacco giant Philip Morris. Opponents felt the deal would wipe out much of the city's low-cost housing funding. Under the proposal the city would lease back the building for $5 million annually for twenty years. That drew strong opposition, because the $5 million would come from revenues of the Bunker Hill Redevelopment Project.

Riordan hoped to raise $71 million by selling the Central Library. The mayor planned to use $14 million from the sale to help close a $33 million deficit in the city's budget and $12 million to buy US government securities which would generate $49 million in twenty years for the repurchase of the library. The City Council and mayor would decide how to spend the remaining $45 million.

Los Angeles Councilwoman Rita Walters cited the inconsistency of the city dealing with a cigarette maker. She told the *Los Angeles Times,* "The City Council has just enacted an anti-smoking law, and Philip Morris spent the largest amount of money to defeat our effort...and now we're going to sell them our library?" On September 3, 1993, the council voted against the deal. But on September 7, the council, after intense lobbying by Riordan, revived the proposal to sell part of the library. Council member Zev Yaroslavsky said to the *Los Angeles Times*, "I don't think it's anymore just a housing issue. I think it's a perception issue about selling a public asset." Despite Riordan's pressure, the council on September 10,1993, again rejected the sale by a vote eleven to one, with Councilman Hal Bernson casting the lone vote in favor of the sale.

On May 1, 2001, the City Council renamed the Los Angeles Central Library from Rufus von KleinSmid, former University of Southern California president, and former member of the Board of Library Commissioner, to Richard R. Riordan Central Library.

VIGNETTE

Maguire Thomas Partners owned the library`s west lawn property and it wanted to construct a retail center. John Welborne, member of the West Lawn Coalition and Citizens Task Force for Central Library Development and his group said, "No, it has got to be a lawn. "There was a meeting attended by Welborne; Nelson Rising, senior partner of MTP; David Vena an attorney with Latham & Watkins, which represented Maguire Thomas Partners; and an environmental attorney from Rogers & Wells representing Friends of the East and West Lawns which wanted to *save the east and west two lawns. Welborne proposed a compromise to give up the east Lawn but save the west lawn. Jeff Skornick of the CRA agreed that the West Lawn Coalition could oversee the design. Larry Halprin of San Francisco hired local landscape architect Campbell & Campbell to design the west lawn, working with Welborne. The compromise reached with Maguire Thomas Partners included a three- thousand-square-foot restaurant, where celebrity chef Joachim Splichal opened Cafe Pinot. The restaurant is now closed. Halprin enlisted the support of Councilman Joel Wachs for three rectangular fountains,"Clear," "Lucid," and "Bright," leading into the west entrance of the library that took a large area from the lawn, but Welborne thought it was not a fight in which he was willing to engage.*

THE GRAND CENTRAL MARKET

Grand Central Market. Photo: Shirley Bleviss Courtesy of Angels Walk LA

The Grand Central Market, the oldest public market in Los Angeles, is in the Homer Laughlin Building between Broadway and Hill Streets at the base of the historic funicular Angels Flight. In 1917, the Market replaced the original department store at the site. The Grand Central Market today features international cuisine choices, with vendors offering a large variety of seasonal fruits and vegetables and gourmet products, including numerous cheeses and meats and bread baked on the premises. The 30,000 square-foot food hall is a popular destination for locals and tourists, with eclectic food posts, public programming, and events.

The Grand Central Market exists today due to the financial support of the Los Angeles County Metropolitan Transportation Authority. Without it, a Los Angeles landmark would have gone bankrupt in the early 1990s. In June 1990, the Community Redevelopment Agency (CRA) and developer Ira Yellin agreed to recapture and revitalize a cornerstone of the Historical Core area of the Central Business District Redevelopment Project (CBDRP) through the preservation, renovation, modification, and improvement of the Project known as Grand Central Square (GCS), which included the Grand Central Market as a nexus of what would be the city's monumental impending renaissance as a cultural destination that could attract political and economic capital back from the suburbs, most notably the Westside.

In March 1992, the project developer informed the CRA of his inability to obtain conventional bank funding for the Project, and since private investors typically did not find such prospects opportunistic enough the CRA proposed a comprehensive privately sourced construction loan commitment to be secured via a recapitalization structure composed of "credit rated" taxable bonds for the commercial component and tax-exempt bonds for the residential component. However, the public finance (bond) market at the time had been unwilling to accept real estate as collateral. Therefore, a more traditional, public tax revenue-based credit pledge was required for an acceptable rating and successful marketing of the Bonds.

Another speedbump in the process came in the form of a "cap" on annual expenditures due to CBDRP's tax increment parameters that restricted CRA's ability to assume debt service payment obligation on all Bonds. So, in 1992, CRA approached MTA to become the 'direct pay obligor' to pledge Proposition A sales taxes based on the California statutes which authorize the CRA to enter into agreements with public or private entities to finance projects adjacent to rail facilities. Gerry Hertzberg, MTA Board Alternate for County Supervisor Gloria Molina at the time, addressed the Board expressing his opposition to the contemplated $41 million guaranty of public funds for a private development that had already received $20 million from direct or indirect funding.

Keyser Marston Associates Inc. (KMA) had done the economic analysis for the project. According to a report dated May 19, 1993, and submitted to the Board, Calvin E. Hollis stated: "KMA has performed extensive financial analysis of the project including market analysis of the residential components of the project. The analysis included a thorough review of the project's operating history and projected operating performance. Existing market conditions were evaluated and rent levels were determined. Existing leases were examined, and terms verified. There is a high degree of likelihood that the MTA will be fully and timely reimbursed of all debt service payments it will make on the bonds."

In September 1993, Metro agreed to cover the debt service on $31.1 million in bonds issued for the GSC project by the CRA. The MTA's direct, semiannual payment of debt service would be reimbursed by the Trustee from the Project Net Operating Revenue (NOR).

Unfortunately, the project could not generate revenue to meet the debt obligations. MTA, who held the first trust deed on the project, could foreclose or make other financial arrangements. MTA did not want to go into the real estate business; therefore, the deal was restructured. The Board voted to forgive a substantial portion of the debt. County Supervisor and MTA Board Director Molina voted against the debt forgiveness. The MTA Board at an August 2016 closed session authorized staff to pay off the bonds. In January 2017, the MTA Board was notified that staff finalized the process of paying off the outstanding $16.8 million of principal issued for the GSC project. Once the bonds had been defeated, Metro no longer needed to set aside approximately $2.2 million of Proposition A revenues annually through FY 2027 to pay the principal and interest of the bonds.

ANGELS FLIGHT

Los Angeles Mayor Tom Bradley had said that Metro Rail had nine lives. One might say Angels Flight also had nine lives. It has withstood political forces, developers' failures, accidents, and funding shortfalls to name a few challenges. But this historic and iconic landmark survived because of the Los Angeles Community Redevelopment Agency, the Los Angeles

Angels Flight (!935), view looking west toward the Third Street Tunnel with Angels Flight to its left. Photo: Courtesy of Water & Power, Inc..

Angels Flight after reopening. Photo: wikimedia

County Transportation Commission, and the efforts of individuals such as the "Father of the Funicular" John Welborne, "Mr. Downtown" Hal Bastian, Mayor Eric Garcetti's transportation deputy Borja Leon, CRA Commissioner Dennis R. Luna, and CRA Urban Planner Yukio Kawaratani.

The beloved Angels Flight, dubbed "the world's shortest railway," was built in 1901 as the Los Angeles Incline Railway. It began at Hill and Third streets and ran for two blocks, along the side of the Third Street Tunnel, uphill to its Olive Street terminus. It consisted of two sixteen-seat funicular cars, named Olivet and Sinai, built in a Beaux-Arts architectural style. The track was 315 feet long on a 33 percent slope. It carried passengers between the affluent Bunker Hill residential district and the commercial businesses below. Originally, it served the rich who lived in Victorian mansions, and then later, from 1920s to the1950s, the less fortunate living in mansions that had been converted to flats and flophouses. It was closed and dismantled in 1969, when Bunker Hill was cleared for redevelopment. The parts were stored in an outdoor storage yard in Gardena. During its eighty-eight-year run, Angels Flight carried more than 100 million riders up or down the hill. The fare originally was a penny and rose to a nickel.

At the time of the closure, the city promised to restore and reopen the funicular within two years. It was later postponed until 1975, then until 1981 and then indefinitely.

Kawaratani in his book *Reluctant Samurai*, explains what happened during the redevelopment of Bunker Hill. "In 1975, word came down from City Hall to permit a major elderly housing development on two whole Bunker Hill city blocks along the steep easterly edge of the project. The Retirement Housing Foundation had the support of both the City and Housing and Urban Development (HUD) to construct over 1,000 apartment units for seniors on the blocks bounded by Olive and Hill Streets to the west and east and Second and Fourth Streets to the north and south." It was clearly a political decision not based on good urban planning. Kawaratani voiced his concerns not only because CRA was planning the development on top of Bunker Hill to be the office center of the region with a hotel, apartments and retail stores and cultural uses, but equally important, what was going to happen to Angels Flight, which the city was obligated to put back?

Angels Flight would serve as a connection between the top of the hill and the older commercial retail and office districts to the east on Broadway and Spring Streets. This required the reinstallation of the funicular in the Third Street right-of-way in the middle of the proposed development site at the base of the hill. Kawaratani produced a solution. "What might work is if CRA agreed to locate Angels Flight halfway down the block between Third and Fourth streets. It would work slope and grade-wise. The project would then cover 1 ½ blocks instead of two blocks, but you would still have about 80 percent of the originally allotted land by including the land over the Third Street tunnel." The Retirement Housing Foundation and the powers that be initially had qualms, but in the interest of being "good neighbors in the downtown community," all parties eventually agreed to Kawaratani's proposal. The senior housing complex is the Angelus Plaza.

In the 1980s, the future of Angels Flight became tied to California Plaza, and eleven-acre, $1.2 billion redevelopment project atop Bunker Hill spanning Olive Street between Third and Fourth streets. The developer was Bunker Hill Associates, a partnership of Cadillac Fairview, Nathan Shapell, and Jona Goldrich. It was to include three high-rise office buildings, restaurants, retail shops, two apartment buildings, the Museum of Contemporary Art, the Colburn performing arts school, a hotel, and a courtyard with an elaborate fountain. The first phase, a 42-story tower, was completed in 1985. The second phase, a fifty-two-story skyscraper, was finished in 1992. The Angels Flight restoration was eventually pushed back to the third phase.

By the early 1990s, however, the office market had collapsed, and there was no way the third phase of California Plaza would be built in the foreseeable future. Welborne and Luna directed their sights to obtaining funding from the CRA. In September 1991, CRA commissioners approved a plan to resurrect the Angels Flight Railway.

In October 1991, Angels Flight components were brought back downtown and set at Fourth and Hill. CRA Commissioner Luna and Welborne, the faithful steward, working with the CRA, the city's Cultural Affairs Department and the Los Angeles Conservancy focused in 1991 on the CRA plan for rebuilding Angels Flight. Welborne said that in 1992 and 1993, "the CRA issued contracts for consultants and contractors to restore and rehabilitate the Angels Flight buildings and the two historic rail cars, Olivet and Sinai."

In April 1992, I was quoted in the Downtown News as saying, "There are compelling arguments for reconstructing Angels Flight now, and [the Los Angeles County Transportation Commission] should be a partner in this. Angels Flight would connect Bunker Hill to the heavily used bus lines in the historic core and the bus distribution of Metrolink passengers from Union Station. The restoration of Angels Flight will provide, in addition to transportation service, economic and cultural benefits to our city, and at the same time would promote tourism Downtown."

In early 1993, the City Council approved $4 million for the restoration of the railway, using Bunker Hill redevelopment funds. Because the funding was short $800,000, I secured the remainder from the County Transportation Commission. In 1994, the City Council approved an additional $500,000 to cover cost overruns.

In February 1995, the city hired Pueblo Contracting Services of San Fernando as the general contractor. Pueblo was a partnership between Keller Construction, a large contractor, and the smaller, little-known Trooper Enterprises. Work began in earnest in March. By the time it was finished, about 90 percent of the railways' original material had been retained.

The CRA had intended the railway to be reopened by California Plaza's developer, but when Bunker Hill Associates terminated its development rights, there was no private operator to take over Angels Flight. That led Welborne and his law firm in 1995 to create the nonprofit Angeles Flight Railway Foundation, which became the railway's seventh operator. In February 1996, Angels Flight reopened in its new location, half a block south of the original. At 208 feet, it was a little shorter than the original funicular. Its lower station was across Hill Street from Grand Central Market. The restored Angels Flight was an immediate hit. On opening day, Angelenos stood in line for as long as an hour to ride Sinai or Olivet. The fare was a quarter.

Tragedy struck Angels Flight on February 1, 2001. As Sinai was approaching the upper station, it broke loose, raced down hill, and crashed into Olivet at the bottom, killing one passenger and injuring seven others. Angels Flight was shut down and remained closed for nine years of investigations, litigation and efforts to remove and dispose of all the badly designed equipment from the CRA's reconstruction.

The Angels Flight Railway Foundation's private fundraising campaign commenced and was completed around 2007, when the design and manufacturing of the new equipment got underway. Welborne raised $4.5 million and secured a grant of almost $1 million from the California Cultural and Historical Endowment, whose membership included historian and author Kevin Starr.

After newly developed safety measures were put in place, following testing and California Public Utilities Commission authorization, Angels Flight reopened in March 2010. Another brief closure took place in June 2011, when the PUC ruled that the trains' fifteen-year-old wheels needed replacing. It resumed operation in July 2011. Two years later, in September 2013, yet another accident occurred when the twin cars slipped off the track. No one was hurt, but the PUC required that a stairway be built adjacent to the funicular for emergency evacuation. The cost of that improvement was beyond the foundation's financial abilities. Meanwhile, Bastian raised funds to pay $6,000 monthly for public liability and insurance, otherwise the foundation would have defaulted and lost the ground lease.

Business and downtown interest groups started to lobby the Los Angeles Metropolitan Transportation Authority board members requesting that Metro intervene and assume the operations of the system. (Metro had replaced the County Transportation Commission in 1993). In 2015, the executive director of the nearby REDCAT arts center described the railroad as an important "economic link." There was pressure for the city to fund and reopen Angels Flight. In October 2015, Garcetti introduced a motion at Metro to direct the Metro's chief executive officer to produce the following:

A. A historical summary of operations for Angels Flight, including past closures and safety related issues;
B. A summary of state and federal safety findings pertaining to Angels Flight, and;
C. Recommendations for resuming operations.

Meanwhile, another problem, financial this time, confronted the foundation. As a result of dissolution of community redevelopment agencies statewide, Los Angeles`s agency was forced to sell land it owned, including Angels Flight. Jeffrey Fish of JMF Development submitted bids for the land under the Colburn School, the Omni Los Angeles hotel, and Angels Flight in 2016. Hal Bastian, president of the nonprofit Angels Flight Railway Foundation, discounted JMF's bid because the Foundation had a lease through 2082 that had been prepaid. Besides, considering Angels Flight was designated as a historic-cultural monument, there were limited development opportunities on the site, therefore no income and only obligations such as taxes and potential liabilities. In addition, the foundation had the right to match or beat a land bid per the lease. And that's what it did. The foundation raised $50,000 instead of the dollar that was always expected to be the payment and took control of the land, an unnecessary expense.

Leon, Garcetti's deputy for transportation, thought that a public-private partnership could jump-start Angels Flight again. The idea was for the city and Metro to collaborate with a transportation developer to design, repair, operate and maintain the system for thirty years. The deal would be structured in such a way that the funicular would be operated and maintained to the highest standards, or the developer would not be paid. Leon hired Geoff Yarema, a partner in the law firm Nossaman who specialized in public infrastructure and who had worked on the Alameda Corridor. Yarema came up with a structure that was presented to a few stakeholders, including Welborne, "the Father of the Funicular" and chair of the Angels Flight Railway Foundation, and Bastian, member of the foundation. They were very skeptical at the beginning. Welborne had such a personal relationship with Angels Flight that he second-guessed many of the ideas, but he gradually started to open up.

The foundation negotiated the deal with a team led by ACS Infrastructure that included Dragados USA of New York, and Sener Engineering & Systems of Spain. Once the parameters and requirements of the public-private partnership were accepted, the foundation and the ACS team signed a thirty-year agreement on March 1, 2017, to put Angels Flight back in service. The ACS team would be the investors and operators of the funicular, would have the rights to lease the property to movie studios and other interested parties, and agreed to build the adjacent stairway. The private partners formed the Angels Flight Development Corporation to operate the funicular, and the Angels Flight Railway Foundation maintained ownership. Metro's involvement was limited to studying and assessing the funicular's condition and providing recommendations on how to resume operations.

On August 31, 2017, Labor Day weekend, Garcetti officially reopened Angels Flight to the public. "This is a railway that always had a little engine that could," the mayor said. "It is one of the last relics of Victorian Los Angeles, an iconic LA landmark and it's there with the Griffith Park Observatory and the Hollywood Sign." The reopened railway is an innovative public-private partnership."

In addition to being a tourist attraction, the funicular has served as a transit connection between the Pershing Square Metro station and the top of Bunker Hill and its many amenities, including Walt Disney Concert Hall, the Broad contemporary art museum, the Colburn School, and the Cathedral of Our Lady of the Angels. The fare is one dollar for one-way ride or fifty cents for Metro TAP Card holders, a discount that is subsidized by Metro.

Angels Flight has appeared in many television shows and films, most recently the Oscar-winning movie La La Land.

VIGNETTE

John Welborne was appointed in 1978 by Mayor Tom Bradley and Councilman John Ferraro to the Los Angeles 200 Committee, also known as the Los Angeles Bicentennial Committee, to help plan the 1981 celebration of the bicentennial of the city's founding in 1781. It was called Los Angeles 200 Committee to distinguish it from the Bicentennial Committee of 1976.

At the recommendation of Bradley, Jane Pisano, a college professor, and former White House fellow, was hired as executive director. The forty -four-member committee was composed of community leaders and influential businessmen, including Robert R. Dockson, chief executive officer of California Federal Savings and Loan, architect Albert C. Martin, and James Green, an attorney with O'Melveny & Myers.

Among the committee's fundraisers was a luncheon downtown attended by many corporate executives at $5,000 per person. Since the committee could not go back to the same people, new fundraising avenues had to be explored. Young Welborne had a great idea to get several people to contribute $1,000 or more: Put the names of prominent people on a letterhead and send out a letter to a lot of people asking for donations. It also would say that anyone who gave $1,000 or more would have their names placed on a donor wall. The fundraiser was called the Patron Participation Project for the Los Angeles Bicentennial. Welborne had to find an appropriate wall. After exploring places such as the south lawn of City Hall; Fort Moore Pioneer Memorial at 501 North Hill Street, the largest bas relief military monument in the United States; and Pershing Square, he decided on the top of Angels Flight.

The 1980 fundraising letter brought in enough money for a yearlong bicentennial celebration. The committee even had leftover funds, which were distributed to charities. John Follis, an environmental graphic design pioneer, designed the Los Angeles Bicentennial logo and monument. It is on the lower wall of the Museum of Contemporary Art, facing into California Plaza, and was unveiled by Bradley on September 4, 1991.

Welborne knew that, although there was a requirement in the development agreement for California Plaza to rebuild Angels Flight, Bunker Hill Associates could not fulfill that requirement because of financial setbacks. Meanwhile, the Los Angeles 200 Committee had made a commitment that had to be fulfilled. Therefore, Welborne worked with the Los Angeles Conservancy, the city's Cultural Affairs Department, attorney and CRA Board member Dennis Luna, and a few others to rebuild Angels Flight.

AMBASSADOR HOTEL

When the Robert F. Kennedy Community Schools opened in 2010 at the once-celebrated Ambassador Hotel site on Wilshire Blvd., it marked the inauguration of the nation's most expensive public school. The price tag, according to a report in the AP/HuffPost, was $578 million.

Opened in 1921, the Hotel was where six Oscar shows were held, where the lavish Coconut Grove dazzled, and where the stars performed, including Frank Sinatra, Bing Crosby, Harry Belafonte, Dean Martin, Judy Garland, Barbra Streisand, and Nat King Cole. Every US president from Herbert Hoover to Richard Nixon had stayed there. Sadly, on June 5, 1968, Senator Robert F. Kennedy, winner of the California Democratic presidential primary election, was assassinated in the pantry area of the hotel's main kitchen.

In addition to my interest in preserving historical sites and seeking renewed purposes for their continued life—and the Ambassador Hotel met those objectives—for me it held a personal attraction. In 1967 I met my wife, Sylvia, at a dance in the Embassy Ballroom sponsored by the UCLA Alumni.

The Ambassador began to lose appeal as the city expanded westward and people chose to stay in hotels in Beverly Hills. The period following Kennedy's assassination coincided with the demise of the hotel and the decline of the surrounding neighborhood. The Sheraton Townhouse closed in 1993, as well as the iconic Bullocks Wilshire Department Store. The Ambassador fell into disrepair and closed to guests in 1989, remaining open for filming and hosting private events. Then it became available for purchase.

With announced plans to tear down the Ambassador to build a 124-story building—the tallest west of Chicago—Donald Trump's syndicate bought it for $64 million. But the Board of Education had its eye on the 23.5-acre property for a desperately needed high school in the densely populated area. The school board countered with a 7-0 vote to take the property from Trump via eminent domain, according to Doug Smith, senior writer for the *Los Angeles Times.*

The Los Angeles Unified School District was in desperate need of local schools, having bused some 3,800 students out of the overcrowded neighborhoods around the hotel to schools out of the area.

I knew, of course, that the process to take the land through eminent domain, under more normal circumstances, would require negotiations between appraisers of the school district and Trump's syndicate. The price had to be settled. With Trump, things were different. He initiated a ferocious lobbying effort to block a $50 million state allocation to help the district buy the property.

Barbara Res, executive vice president for Trump Wilshire Associates, accused the school board of "fiscal irresponsibility" for choosing to build a school on "some of the world's most expensive property." Smith quoted Res in the LA Times that the $73 million offered by the school board for 17 acres of the site was far below the developer's estimate of its value—up to $200 million.

Certainly, Trump was playing his favorite game, hardball negotiating by lobbyists, consultants and attorneys and the possible involvement of the courts. Res said the school's response regarding the purchase "will be embroiled for years in litigation it cannot win." But somewhere along the way, Trump blinked, the LA Times concluded. In January 1991, he and his partners decided to take the nearly $48-million deposit the school board offered as part of its eminent domain condemnation suit. By doing this, Trump Wilshire Associates in effect conceded the district's right to take the property.

In the meantime, Linda Dishman, president and CEO of the Los Angeles Conservancy, sought to protect the Ambassador historic building, believing it would be torn down for speculation, she told me. She wanted a "win-win" situation, whereby the hotel would become a state-of-the-art educational facility while keeping the historic building.

Beginning in 2001, the Conservancy and a talented pro bono team of top professional preservation architects and engineers, led by Conservancy Board members, architect Barry Milofsky and structural engineer Nabih Youssef, created a workable plan that would have allowed LA's kids to go to school in an inspiring historic setting.

The Conservancy worked with the school district for a few years in search of a solution, Dishman confided to me. "But the leadership at the top was not interested in that." So, the group turned to the Environmental Impact Report (EIR) process and filed a lawsuit to challenge it. "We were forced to file this lawsuit," Roland Wiley from the Conservancy told me. "LAUSD believed that saving parts of the Ambassador Hotel, and creating a fake version of the real thing, equals preservation. It does not. The school board was not looking at alternatives," Dishman also told me. "And we challenged its engineering reports and a variety of things." Such challenges are difficult, and I asked Dishman what the Conservancy's plans were.

"We potentially had merit, the judge found," she replied. "But this came down to a difference of opinion between experts." She pointed out that the California Environmental Quality Act (CEQA) states if there is disagreement between experts, it doesn't mean the EIR is vulnerable. "So, we lost in court." Rather than appeal, the Conservancy made a deal. In exchange for a $4.9-million contribution to a nonprofit organization aimed at conserving historic school buildings in Los Angeles, it agreed to drop all legal battles to save the Ambassador." We will always believe that the Ambassador Hotel represents a tragic missed opportunity," said Dishman. "But having fought the good fight and lost, we decided to create something lasting."

The school board turned to Dan Rosenfeld and Ira Yellin of Urban Partners, leading real estate professionals, to evaluate the Ambassador Hotel and determine if it could be preserved and converted into a school. The final cost estimate in September 2004 was $412 million to reuse the hotel, compared with $303 million to demolish and replace it. After testimony from civil rights leader Dolores Huerta and architectural photographer Julius Shulman among many others, the Board of Education turned down the adaptive reuse plan and voted 4-3 to demolish all the hotel. Ken Bernstein, director of preservation for the Los Angeles Conservancy said, "It`s a very sad day for Los Angeles." "We ultimately saved the legendary Coconut Grove, the Embassy Ballroom, the former coffee shop, and the pylon sign on Wilshire," Rosenfeld told me.

The Coconut Grove is now a 582-seat theatre. The coffee shop, designed by the Los Angeles best-known African American architect Paul R. Williams, serves as a teacher's lounge. The Embassy Ballroom, the site of Robert F. Kennedy`s 1968 primary victory speech was reconstructed as the library for secondary students The library was named in honor of Paul Schrade, who was instrumental in building the Robert F. Kennedy Community Schools. "The corridor where Senator Kennedy was shot was cut into pieces and stored somewhere," he continued. "It was a pretty meager compromise." Rosenfeld added a noteworthy account regarding the demolition of the hotel. Ethel Kennedy, the senator's widow, "wanted the hotel torn down," he told me.

I had some brief knowledge of that but asked for more clarification. "She had some say on the matter," Rosenfeld explained. Mrs. Kennedy knew Roy Romer, the superintendent of the LAUSD who the Democratic governor of Colorado from was 1987 to 1999. "And the Conservancy stood down because the National Trust for Historic Preservation was quietly negotiating to acquire the Kennedy family compound in Hyannis Port, Massachusetts."

Much later, I learned that the son of Sen. Kennedy, Matthew Maxwell, had said he believed the school district should demolish the Ambassador Hotel to build schools without preserving any of it as a monument. He had released a letter signed by himself, six of his siblings and his mother, Ethel Kennedy, calling on the school district to clear the site for an expeditious building of schools in the Latino neighborhood.

Yet, the Conservancy's Dishman, which fought to preserve most of the hotel, measured the Kennedy family's position and said it should not have carried much weight, given all the other historic events and significant people who had been a part of the hotel.

She had told the *Los Angeles Times* that, "While we are certainly very respectful of the Kennedy family and their association with the hotel, the historic significance of the hotel is much more than just the assassination." She noted that the sites of John F. Kennedy's and Martin Luther King Jr.'s assassinations have been preserved.

The RFK Community Schools opened for the 2011-12 school year with a Kinder through twelfth grade campus comprised of six autonomous Pilot Schools. According to its own write up, it offers a rigorous and personalized instructional program that embodies the social justice legacy of Sen. Kennedy.

Architecturally, according to Sam Lubell of *The Architect's Newspaper*, "the overall design is not really rooted in anything except maybe the city's obsession with loosely recreating the past." He also said, "If anything it's a painful reminder of what was there before; an authentic piece of LA history that's been replaced by a loose nod to it. Much of its neighborhood, which was once one of Hollywood's most electric areas, has the same feeling."

The LAUSD used a model that digested birth rates, in-migration, out-migration, dropouts and other factors, and projected the need for classroom seats, and therefore schools, into the future. Because it often took a decade to build a new school, these projections were needed years before future students were even born. And the projections were inevitably wrong. In the years since the Robert F. Kennedy Schools were opened on the Ambassador Hotel site, LAUSD enrollment has consistently and significantly declined. The enrollment predictions that caused the site to be re-purposed turned out to be wrong. The school, nice as it is, was probably not needed. Many of the schools that were rushed into service in the early part of this century are no longer full, some are even closed, like Selma Avenue Elementary and Trinity Street Elementary. Poor projections coupled with dwindling student populations, decreasing birth rates and families moving away because of rising cost of living, particularly housing, have resulted in student enrollment dropping from 737,000 to 397,623 over the last twenty years. Officials predict that enrollment will continue to drop by another twenty-eight percent by the 2030-31 academic year.

Perhaps the Ambassador Hotel did not need to die.

VIGNETTE, as told by Dan Rosenfeld

I received a call from the leaders of the school district's construction team, asking me to join them for a meal. They were all ex-Navy Seabees, brought in to bring discipline and results to the massive school construction campaign. I sat down between these admirals, with their unique, often charming, immensely confident mannerisms, and they informed me that this was my "alignment dinner," that I was there to be "aligned" with their plans for the Ambassador Hotel. They wanted it torn down, no ifs, ands, or buts. Then, the nails started to pound into the "coffin," hundreds of them. There was a new School Board member, Jose Huizar. Together with his very clever staff, Huizar organized a series of public hearings. The assembly halls were filled with earnest, clean-cut young students, all elementary school kids and mostly children of immigrants. They demanded a school. "Name it after Robert Kennedy" they said.

The Los Angeles Unified School District School Board voted to demolish the Ambassador Hotel.

CHAPTER TWELVE

A NEW DOWNTOWN LOS ANGELES

Uptown is for people who have already done something.
Downtown is where they are doing something now.

—ANDY WARHOL

BUNKER HILL

Unrealized vision of Bunker Hill
Photo: Courtesy of Barton Myers.

An Unrealized Grand Vision | In 1979, the Community Redevelopment Agency held a national competition to select a developer for eleven acres owned by the city on the top of Bunker Hill. It was intended to be the business center of the region. Developer Maguire Thomas Partners asked Harvey Perloff, dean of Architecture and Urban Planning at the University of California, Los Angeles to assemble a team of multiple world-class architects for the competition. Perloff had served as an advisor to President John Kennedy on Latin America and was one of the top people by reputation in the urban planning world.

Their concept was that different architects creating different buildings would produce a richer, as well as a more diverse, and perhaps more locally embedded, design. Perloff did that perfectly. He enlisted Barton Myers as a master architect, Ricardo Legorreta, Bob Kennard, Frank Gehry, Charles Moore, Hardy Holzman Pfeiffer, Sussman Prejza, Edgardo Contini, Lawrence Halprin, Cesar Pelli and Carlos Diniz. It was like a "who's who" of architects.

Cadillac Fairview decided to enter the competition. According to Dan Rosenfeld, who had just started to work for CF, he was given the task of suggesting architects. He started to call firms that he knew. Every firm that he called, it seemed, had already signed up with somebody, and reported back that there must be 20 bidders going after this project. Only later that they realize that many of these architects were all together on the same Maguire Thomas Partners team.

There were three other bidders, Cabot, Cabot and Forbes, Metropolitan Structures, and Trizec with Olympia York. All of these were very big players in North American real estate. Maguire Thomas Partners was local and smaller, but certainly better known in Los Angeles.

The Maguire Thomas Partners proposal was stunning. It is a historical memorialization of the state of the architectural profession at that time. It is very compelling as a complex urban vision, with different buildings by different architects.

Yukio Kawaratani's book, *Reluctant Samurai*, states: "Maguire/Thomas came up with many innovative site planning and architectural design schemes for each parcel but made the major mistake of coming alone as the developer. They had been negotiating with some major insurance companies that had the land development experience and financial resources to strengthen the team, but Maguire/Thomas submitted a proposal relying primarily on the attractiveness of their design." Maguire/Thomas's development proposal included housing, shops, hotels, parks, and offices. Myers designed two residential towers, both containing outdoor space for the residents. The plan integrated the new development with the older neighborhood to the east and with the newer areas of the downtown core.

When surreptitiously CF found out that the finance section of the Maguire/Thomas proposal essentially said that Maguire Thomas Partners was prepared to build the buildings only when they got tenants, the Chairman of CF, Eph Diamond, who came from Toronto, got up in front of the CRA evaluation and selection panel, and said, "We will build our first building with or without a tenant. If it requires a hundred-million-dollar check, we will write it." That was a material factor in the ultimate selection of CF.

The CRA narrowed the field from five to two finalists: the CF team and Maguire Thomas Partners. Initially, the CF team was originally 50 percent CF and 50 percent Nathan Shapell.

CF had experience in doing very large-scale transformative urban projects, like the Eaton Centre in Toronto, Pacific Centre in Vancouver, and other major urban projects of this scale, but recognized that they didn't have the local reputation that would probably be essential in this competition. They invited Nathan Shapell to join them. The reason was that Shapell and CF a couple of years earlier had made a bid on the Irvine Ranch, which was being auctioned off. They came in second to Alfred Taubman of Michigan, but they knew each other at that point, so CF invited Shapell to join them in pursuing the Bunker Hill development.

According to Rosenfeld, Shapell said, "I would like to give half of my interest to my friend, Jona Goldrich." The two of them had worked together in the past on Bunker Hill. They had developed the Promenade Condominiums, with Kamnitzer Cotton, Architects. In the late 1980s, Goldrich developed the Promenade Apartments with Herb Nadel, Architects. They had invested in Bunker Hill when no one else would. They had built housing downtown, and they had put, if you will, their money where their mouth was. They had a track record with the CRA. Goldrich also, had very good political connections with Mayor Tom Bradley, with Councilman Gilbert W. Lindsay, the self-proclaimed "Emperor of the Great 9th District," and with the CRA Board.CF hired Arthur Erickson, A Canadian architect, whom CF knew from Vancouver, as the lead designer. Gruen and Kamnitzer Cotton Vreeland joined the team.

The proposal was due on Leap Day, February 29, 1980, at 5 p.m. The decision was made on or about Bastille Day, July 14, 1980. Marilyn Hudson was the Chair. It was a fascinating moment in Los Angeles history. One team, in a very real sense, represented the old establishment. It was Robert F. Maguire III, John Clydesdale Cushman III from Hancock Park and Pasadena, old money, largely white and Anglo-Saxon, against the CF Shapell-Goldrich team, which was West Side, immigrant, mostly Polish Jewish, and much more recent arrivals. So, you had the old money against the new money, and the decision-makers were mostly Black. They included Tom Bradley, Gil Lindsay, and Marilyn Hudson.

Ed Helfeld recommended Maguire Thomas Partners, but the majority of the CRA Board voted for Cadillac Fairview.Helfeld was disappointed but most of his own staff, including Kawaratani, who was in charge of the Bunker Hill urban plan, did not support him in his recommendation. The vote was 5 to 2 in the end. CF's proposal included three tall office towers, a hotel, two apartment buildings, a museum, the rebuilding Angels Flight, and a performance plaza.

Ultimately, to make those buildings succeed, one needed to relocate tenants and one was going to have to move major tenants like Latham & Watkins and Arthur Anderson to Bunker Hill. One was not going to get three million feet of new office tenants in Los Angeles, but probably was going to have to buy somebody out of their leases in other buildings. Ironically, Maguire Thomas Partners got those tenants for Library Square and the Gas Company Tower. After CF won the competition, the market downtown collapsed. CF won the competition, but Maguire Thomas Partners got the good tenants.

The Museum of Contemporary Art became a development requirement. Bunker Hill Associates funded and developed it as a gift to the city of about 26 million dollars. Angels Flight was committed to restoration. Bella Lewitzky was unable to raise their share of the money, so the dance gallery, which was part of the CF proposal, never got built.

Further, near the end of the Carter administration, it was a period of high inflation, when interest rates were 18 percent. According to Rosenfeld, ultimately the CF deal was negotiated with the CRA and taken to the CF Board of Directors. CF was a public company based in Toronto. It was presented to the Board that CF was going to build a million square foot spec office building in Phase I for over \$200 million and give the city a \$26 million art museum and other public benefits, all with no tenants, and the probability of borrowing money at 18 to 20 percent, floating at that.

The CF Board said, "No." They said, "We want a fixed rate mortgage, we want a take-out, we want to know how you're gonna get out of this when construction is finished." The only CF loan could get was through Metropolitan Life, one of the losing bidders in the early rounds of the competition. They offered a 14 percent permanent mortgage as well as construction financing. They also wanted 50 percent of the deal and control over management decisions. That deal went to the CF Board. Marty Seaton, went to the board as an executive vice president and said, "If we don't perform for the City of Los Angeles, we will never do business there again. We need to accept this deal and establish ourselves." The board was persuaded and approved the deal on that basis.

CF and its partners started designing and constructing the buildings. Nelson Rising, the partner of Maguire Thomas Partners, a very good friend of mine and political mentor, told me that the CRA assisted Maguire Thomas Partners in acquiring the Engstrom Apartments across Fifth Street from the Central Library, and transferring air rights from the library to build two tall buildings. First, there was the Gas Company Building and then the Library Tower, in direct competition with California Plaza. Rising was savvy, very well-respected, local, had better connections, had John Cushman, and was faster. All of CF leases had to go to Met Life in New York, they were very slow and difficult to respond. Big tenants, such as Lathan & Watkins, Arthur Andersen, and the Gas Company, the "anchors," signed with Maguire Thomas Partners. As a result, Cal Plaza had a very hard time leasing.

The original CF proposal had strong modernist architectural integrity. It featured three glass towers that worked together in combination, like the buildings at Rockefeller Center. They were tall, slender, glass towers. They were called "icicles." The towers were striated and articulated to accentuate their verticality. The late 1970s was the era of the "Silver Architects," such as Cesar Pelli and others who did glass buildings in Los Angeles that had a beauty to them and gained international recognition. To that extent, the Cal Plaza towers were very authentically "LA."

Again, according to Rosenfeld, once Met Structůres came in, cost pressures to simplify the building affected their design. Erickson, meanwhile, according to Kawaratani, being from outside of the country was not readily accessible. He opened a local branch office, but his staff were always waiting for him to fly into town for meetings and to make design decisions. "They joked that the project plans and drawings had to be reduced to a small size because Erickson primarily worked on them on his lap while flying."

Then, it was reported that Arthur Erickson began to have all kinds of problems, personally and professionally, and his firm deteriorated as his personal attention went away. Supposedly, he headed for the Canadian border, leaving all kinds of unpaid debts and obligations, and the office really collapsed. The designs of Cal Plaza portions—the buildings bases, the hardscape, and the little structures in the Plaza—are just bad. The second office tower got built, but it was also a money loser. The developer would not construct a major apartment tower on Grand Avenue per the original plan and agreement, forcing the CRA to ground lease the site to the Colburn School of Performing Arts for $1 for ninety-nine years. The third building was never built.

In 2023, there are plans by developers Victor MacFarlane and R. Donahue Peebles to develop that site with a $1.6 billion Angels Landing project. The project is next to the historic Angels Flight funicular.

Barton Myers decried, "Bunker Hill was the largest urban lobotomy in the history of urban renewal. They displaced a huge neighborhood. They knocked 90 feet off the hill to flatten it." It is unfortunate that the city instead of healing the hill with a visionary, innovative complex designed by the Maguire Thomas Partners design team, believed in proposals whereby with time, alliances and partnerships began to water down the dream and the vision became blurry. What could have been was slowly discarded for financial reasons. Was the process to blame? Were the players creative and competitive only when they were bidding? Creating and producing a vision for the ages takes more than money and connections.

The Bunker Hill plan was adopted in 1959. It converted from an urban renewal project to a redevelopment plan in 1970, which in effect paid off all the federal obligations and made it a state-based redevelopment project.

In 1975, a new project was adopted for most of the downtown and central business projects. Mayor Tom Bradley demanded that the revenues of Bunker Hill should be spent on a city-wide basis. So, through the Community Redevelopment Agency (CRA), which by law had to devote a certain amount of money for affordable housing, CRA created two additional funds out of Bunker Hill to do affordable housing for the entire city and use affordable housing as kind of the anchor for rebuilding neighborhoods around the entire city. In addition to its own on-site requirements, Bradley created a Bunker Hill Replacement Housing Trust Fund that was specifically to generate at least one unit somewhere in the City for every unit that had been removed in Bunker Hill. There were approximately 7,300 units that were demolished. Then, a second Housing and Benefit Fund was established to create additional housing and commit funds off Bunker Hill. According to Donald Spivack, Deputy Chief of Operations and Policy of the CRA, "Bradley believed that the center of the City needed to fund improvements in the rest of the city, and a strong city center would generate the revenues that would do that."

Creating a very substantial affordable housing obligation on a city-wide basis was a way of continuing to preserve the Bunker Hill revenues for use within the City of Los Angeles. It was a way to protect redevelopment funds because being a relatively small redevelopment project area, there was only so much that could be spent on Bunker Hill itself. Because Bunker Hill took long time to develop and there was the recognition that Bunker Hill alone was not enough to revitalize downtown, one of the big changes that came out of the Bunker Hill plan was to limit the redevelopment role into downtown to avoid the kind of large-scale clearance that urban renewal had brought to Bunker Hill.

ANECDOTE as told by Dan Rosenfeld

We learned that Maguire's proposal included an endorsement from the newly organized Museum of Contemporary Art, or MOCA. Why should they endorse his proposal, we thought, and not ours? If selected for the project we would work with them just as easily as would Maguire Thomas Partners.

So, I was dispatched—alone, as no one on our team thought we had a chance to meet with MOCA and try to convince them to support both us and Maguire Thomas Partners.

MOCA had been the dream of several prominent art patrons for several years. With support from Mayor Bradley, they convinced the CRA to make their museum a requirement in our competition, and to allow it to be funded by the selected developer as a 1.5 percent of project cost contribution to public art. Given its pedigreed sponsorship, the MOCA endorsement greatly affected the CRA's evaluation of the two remaining proposals. I met with MOCA's founding Chair, Judge William "Bill" Norris, in his courthouse chambers. After some discussion, he offered me a deal: MOCA would endorse our proposal, along with Maguire's, if we would give up Arthur Erickson's Grand Avenue Museum design which was the core of our project. Instead, he wanted us to give MOCA the best plot of land on the site, with 300 feet of Grand Avenue frontage and the right to select their own architect and design their own structure. We, of course, would pay for it all.

Judge Norris's offer would ruin our design. It might also cripple our economics, as the museum would substantially block the public view of our other buildings. I asked if I could borrow a phone – there were no cell phones in those days; I had to step outside and borrow a landline – so I could call Marty and ask him what to do. But Marty didn't pick up. Next, I called Nathan. No answer there. And Jona, but I couldn't reach him either.

I was in a bind. If I said no, we might lose the competition, and I would be blamed. If I said yes, we had a better chance of winning, but I would be blamed for giving in and messing up the deal. Either way, I figured I would be fired. So, I said, yes. That museum cost us $26 million.

CATHEDRAL OF OUR LADY OF THE ANGELS

The Cathedral of Saint Vibiana in downtown Los Angeles was dedicated in 1876. Pope Pius IX chose the Cathedral's name, the Roman martyr Saint Vibiana. Since 2002, the relics of Saint Vibiana have been housed in the mausoleum of the Cathedral of Our Lady of the Angels. The architects W. J. Matthews and Ezra F. Kysor, who also designed the Pico House, modeled the cathedral's façade in the Italian baroque style. Saint Vibiana's Cathedral was designated a Los Angeles Cultural Monument in 1963.

Los Angeles Cathedral. Photo: D. Castor

After the 1994 Northridge Earthquake caused extensive damage to the cathedral, the Archdiocese of Los Angeles decided that the structure needed to be replaced. The archdiocese came to that decision based on a seismic engineering report provided by veteran structural engineer Nabih Youssef, who was also the engineer who designed the seismic retrofit of City Hall. Youssef also did the seismic design for the Los Angeles Memorial Coliseum after the Northridge quake, saving it from demolition. Youssef concluded, however, that the Cathedral would sustain heavy damage, and possibly collapse, should an earthquake the magnitude of Northridge was to occur again.

Ira Yellin, a longtime champion of downtown Los Angeles and the son of an Orthodox rabbi, was invited to participate in the selection of the architect and the site, as a sign of ecumenical progress. His pedigree as a preservationist was held up when the momentum seemed to be toward demolishing the old Saint Vibiana. When Cardinal Roger Mahony began to explore options for a replacement, he asked Monsignor Terrance Fleming, rector of Saint Vibiana`s Cathedral, to assist in finding both a location for a new cathedral and the architect to design it. I was invited as an advisor during the presentations of the proposals and the deliberations of the jury, but as a nonvoting member. The jury included Richard Weinstein, dean of the University of California, Los Angeles School of Architecture; Steve

Lavine, president of California Institute of the Arts; Yellin; Sylvia Lavin, an architecture professor at UCLA; and Robert Harris, former dean of the University of Southern California School of Architecture.

An international architectural competition was held in May 1996. The initial field of fifty was narrowed to fourteen and then to five. The finalists—Santiago Calatrava; Venturi, Scott Brown, & Associates; Frank O. Gehry; Jose Rafael Moneo; and Thom Mayne—met with the Mahony, donors and the jury to discuss budgets and schedules.

Weinstein, chair of the jury, believed that to have a competition on a project that complex would not be wise. He suggested that the way to go "would be to pick a much smaller and something digestible, that it would reveal how the architect would manage the project." O'Malley Miller, legal counsel to the diocese, gave the same advice to Mahony. That was more important than trying to get proposers to design something as complex as the cathedral in a couple of months.

The five finalists were asked to design a shrine near Olvera Street for the statue of 18th century missionary Father Junipero Serra, who established eight of the twenty-one Spanish missions from San Diego to San Francisco. I remember comments from the jury such as that the Venturi- Scott Brown design was "boring" and "conventional." Gehry did a very interesting thing. It looked a lot like the organ that ultimately went into the Walt Disney Concert Hall. None of the candidates had built a cathedral before. Fleming, however, believed Moneo "got the feel of Los Angeles." The jury eliminated Santiago Calatrava and Venturi-Scott Brown. Then Gehry, Mayne and Moneo met with the Mahony, donors and the jury to discuss budgets and schedules.

While the jury was deliberating, Mahony met with twenty to thirty donors. Each person was given three colored cards: red, yellow, and blue. The cardinal then said, "I'd like to go around and have everyone in this room vote among the three proposals. To vote, hold up a colored card." The Moneo proposal was the red card, Mayne yellow, and Gehry blue. Mahony went on to say, "For the record, I'm not espousing any particular direction or outcome." Then he held up a red card. Everyone else in the room followed suit and held up a red card. The selection was unanimous.

Weinstein said, "The cardinal…I think the word is fastidious. He was so able to manage people who knew what he wanted without saying what he wanted, but somehow, it was pretty clear anyway. Who was going to choose? He was going to choose a Catholic architect, who was Spanish or of Spanish extraction, who had a Jesuit education."

Mahony then walked into the jury room late afternoon and said "Well, it's Moneo." I remember there was total silence in the room. First, there was astonishment and disappointment. Then anger. Comments such as "Why did we spend our precious time interviewing, deliberating, and wasting the resources of the competitors, if the cardinal wanted Moneo? He could have selected him from the beginning." People were very upset. They felt they had been used.

In January 1996, the conservancy and Yellin, representing the archdiocese, began a three-day workshop to explore alternatives. The group included architects, engineers, site planners, cost estimators, preservation consultants, historians, liturgical consultants, and clergy.

The alternatives considered were demolition, rehabilitation, incorporation and exploring the possibility of acquiring the entire block surrounding the Saint Vibiana`s site.

A couple of compromises were proposed by Harris, former dean at USC and vice president of the Los Angeles Conservancy. One was to keep a façade or a piece of the older building. Harris suggested that when you combine a new adaptation with pieces of an old building, you can get something special.

They do it all over Europe with confidence. They are not afraid to do modern adjustments and interpretations working within the contexts of older buildings—look at the Louvre with the pyramid in Paris and "The Dancing House" in Prague designed by the Croatian-Czech architect Vlado Milunic in cooperation with Gehry.

However, the two big backers of the cathedral project, the Dan Murphy and the Thomas and Dorothy Leavey Foundations, insisted on a new structure at the same site. Therefore, Mahony decided that the old cathedral had to come down.

Dan Rosenfeld, a private developer, veteran public servant and civic leader—remembers a number of conversations, one in particular where Mahony made the case very eloquently that the cathedral should remain at 2nd and Main streets because that's where the human need was, despite the fact—really because of the fact—that the area had a reputation of some distress. "I want to be where the people are" Mahony was quoted as saying.

The flow of our city has always been north to south. Spring, Broadway, and Main streets. Those are the streets where major activities are. The numbered streets are much less developed. We don't think of 2nd, 3rd, or 4th Streets, but we do think of Spring, Broadway, Los Angeles and Main streets. There was a reason it was called "Main." It is in the middle of the current historic downtown.

Yellin and Miller unsuccessfully advised Mahony not to make an announcement, because the prices of the rest of the block would go up, and they did. Consequently, the cardinal at the end of May 1996 said that he may move the project to the San Fernando Valley or another location if prices of the property adjacent to the Cathedral remain high and if legal battles develop.

The cathedral became the focus of a preservation battle in 1996, when the archdiocese tried to level the building to make room for a new cathedral. The Los Angeles Conservancy's position was that a retrofitted Saint Vibiana's should be incorporated into the structure of the new cathedral complex. Conservancy leaders thought it was a fair compromise.

On Saturday, June 1, 1996, the archdiocese began demolition without a permit. Crews started to knock the cupola off, but they stopped because the conservancy obtained a temporary restraining order literally the day the wrecking ball arrived.

Linda Dishman, executive director of the conservancy explained to me, "The cardinal decided to start demolition of the tower. They had received a notice to abate from the city and took that to mean that was sort of permission to go in and demolish the building. They did not pull a demolition permit. They picked the weekend that preservation leadership was at the state preservation conference in San Jose. I was at this conference and got a call from Larry Gordon, reporter of the *Los Angeles Times*, saying that demolition of the tower will start the next morning because the archdiocese issued a press release that they were going to do that. I flew back the next day to Los Angeles on the 6 a.m. flight. We were able to get a temporary restraining order. We went into court on Monday morning and the conservancy won.

Then, the Los Angeles City Council on a fourteen-to-one vote stripped Saint Vibiana`s of its landmark status. As the conservancy was losing in council, the contractor was pulling the demolition permit. The conservancy went back to court that afternoon before workers could begin demolition.

In a rebuke to the City Council and the archdiocese, Los Angeles County Superior Court Judge Robert H. O'Brien ruled that Saint Vibiana`s Cathedral could not be torn down, even if it was no longer a city landmark. O'Brien added that state law requires an environmental impact study before demolition.

There was a political effort to have the state legislature exclude all of downtown Los Angeles from the California Environmental Quality Act. When that was questioned, the decision was made to seek an exemption for just four blocks around the cathedral. State Senator Tom Hayden, Chair of the Senate Natural Resources Committee, killed the exemption in the committee.

Harris, as member of the conservancy board, said he was assigned to meet with Mahony. "The meetings were difficult. He was, the generous thing to say, he was alarmed about the interest of others. It was his diocese. Who were we? In fact, at some point he told me 'You guys' a kind of terrible thing, it sort of puts everybody in a category, that you guys keep doing this and that. I could not get anywhere."

Then, amid all the chaos, acrimony, recriminations and lawsuits, an angel appeared that provided a solution that made all parties happy. Los Angeles County Supervisor Gloria Molina suggested the county's 5.6-acre parking lot at Temple Street and Grand Avenue as a possible location for the cathedral. Several major donors supported the location because they thought the building would be more prominent and visible. The conservancy could claim victory in saving Saint Vibiana's from demolition.

Los Angeles County could not sell the land directly to the archdiocese, because a public agency must first give another public agency the opportunity to buy it, and if there is no interest, then it can be sold to the private sector. Gerry Hertzberg, the savvy advisor to Molina, came up with the idea for the county to sell the parking lot to the city's Community Redevelopment Agency, which in turn could legally sell it to the archdiocese. Molina and Hertzberg worked with the bureaucracy, and just ninety days later the archdiocese owned the property.

Miller remembers as he walked up the hill to the site on a Saturday with Jose Rafael Moneo. The architect said, "This is where we should build it." And he began to give his reasons. "First of all," pointing at the county buildings across the street, he said, "someday someone will come along and prop them up, and it will frame the cathedral. ...Those buildings (pointing to the ones to the west) and that power station over there, they are obsolete." This is at the apex of the turn where the 101 Freeway comes down from the northwest and curves eastward." So, the Cathedral will be at the apex for millions of people driving every day into downtown from both the east and the west, and the cathedral will be standing there," Moneo said. "This freeway is like the rivers of Europe. The cathedrals were always built near the rivers and people would see them, as they used the rivers for transportation."

Mahony joked that the cross—the big, illuminated cross on the end of the building "would be quite visible from the freeway," a collateral benefit of the selected location. Also on the freeway side is the Donor Wall that commemorates the cathedral's benefactors, the angels who made the complex possible. There are sixteen floating angels forming a continuous band, designed and hand-etched by artists at Judson Studios in Highland Park. Unfortunately, the building itself seems quite walled-in and separated, isolated from the street. It has been described as the "concrete armadillo."

Linda Samuels, professor of urban design at Washington University in Saint Louis, wrote, "The cathedral's traditional public space, the classical urban plaza that foregrounds the entry, is literally walled off from the space of the city, turning its back and locking its doors from the public life of the street. Its largest public component is the etched glass wall facing the 101 Freeway, a billboard for angelic salvation to the captive audience of drivers."

In 1999, developers Tom Gilmore and Jerri Perrone purchased the former cathedral and working with architect Brenda Levin and based on the Adaptive Reuse Ordinance, they restored and retrofitted the structure. Levin, whose major restoration projects include the Bradbury Building, Griffith Observatory, and City Hall—said she and others embarked on a building stabilization effort, particularly of the bell tower of Saint Vibiana's. The state of California provided $4 million for the seismic retrofit and renovation. The Los Angeles Conservancy received federal dollars from US Representative Lucille Roybal-Allard, who made a $1 million grant to the project. Gilmore and Perrone created an event venue called Vibiana. In late 2014, restaurateurs Neal Fraser and Amy Knoll Fraser opened the restaurant Redbird in the former rectory. Vibiana hosts weddings, social and corporate events, nonprofit fundraisers, performing arts, shows, and film shoots.

CIVIC CENTER

A lost opportunity | In the mid-1990s, the City of Los Angeles started the process of creating a master plan for the Civic Center. That was done in conjunction with Los Angeles County through the Civic Center Authority. These two governments were the lead sponsors. The State and Federal governments also participated, as did the Los Angeles Unified School District the Metropolitan Water District and the Los Angeles County Metropolitan Transportation Authority. Consequently, there were five governments participating in and studying land use planning at the Civic Center.

There had not been a comprehensive plan done for the Civic Center in many years. The Civic Center Authority commissioned a group of consultants, an all-star team that included Doug Suisman, urban planner; Bill Fain, Steve Lewis, and Roland Wiley architects and planners; Dan Rosenfeld, Mayor Richard Riordan's Manager of real estate assets; Melendrez Babalas Associates, landscape architects; and Charles Loveman, economic analysis. They proposed the Civic Center Shared Facilities and Enhancement Plan, completed in 1997, commonly known as the Ten-Minute Diamond Plan. Suisman, who had worked with me in designing the Angels Walk among other Metro sponsored projects, determined that a ten-minute walk from City Hall was the pragmatic definition of the Civic Center.

It was not a circle, but a diamond because of the orthogonal grid of the streets. The Civic Center Ten Minute Diamond Plan identified major axes—north, south, east, and west—to connect City Hall with Union Station, the Music Center, the Historic Core and Little Tokyo. One of the revelations of the plan was that the history of Los Angeles has really evolved on a north-south axis along a narrow bench of land between the Los Angeles River flood plain on the east, and the hills—Bunker Hill, what was called Poundcake Hill and Courthouse Hill - on the west. The major streets that define downtown—Hill, Broadway, Spring, Main and Los Angeles - all run north-south and are the dominant streets. The east-west streets—Second, Third, Fourth, and Fifth—are not as significant economically.

The team drew, as a part of this study, what was the "100 percent corner"—the most desirable and valuable street intersection—from the beginning of the City at El Pueblo through the present day. The 100 percent corner literally moved south along Spring and Broadway year by year. In 1890, City Hall was at 3rd Street and was the center of town. By 1940, the corner of 7th and Broadway was the main intersection, the busiest intersection in the city. In later years, the center has moved west over to 7th Street and Figueroa.

The north-south axes that originally defined downtown remained. There was an opportunity at the time that the plan was being developed to acquire the block immediately south of City Hall. That block was owned primarily by Caltrans with a strip along 1st Street that was owned by the city. There was a kosher burrito stand on the site and some bail bond providers. Across the street, on the other side of Main Street, Caltrans owned parts of another block. On one side of Main was the old Caltrans building, 120 South Spring Street, and on the other side was a parking lot. The city owned a strip of land on both blocks along First Street, so it made some sense to do a swap to give Caltrans a full block on which they could build their headquarters building and leave the city with a full block immediately south of City Hall for city purposes. Ron Deaton, the city's chief legislative analyst, and Ed Avila, director of the community redevelopment agency, were very instrumental in the two governments swapping four partial ownerships to create two full blocks, with each government owning one. Caltrans got a full block, and the city then had the full block immediately south of City Hall.

CALTRANS HEADQUARTERS

In A.C. Martin's study of State facilities, they identified the old Caltrans building as an opportunity for replacement. After the Interstate Highway Act was adopted during the Eisenhower Administration in the 1950s, the State built a series of buildings, eventually twelve Caltrans district buildings around the state. All their buildings were finished in about 1955. By the 1990s, those buildings were obsolete. Caltrans could never get an appropriation to replace their buildings, including the one at 120 South Spring Street in Los Angeles. They would get highway appropriations, but not funds for buildings. Seismically, it was unacceptable. But they could never get an appropriation to replace it.

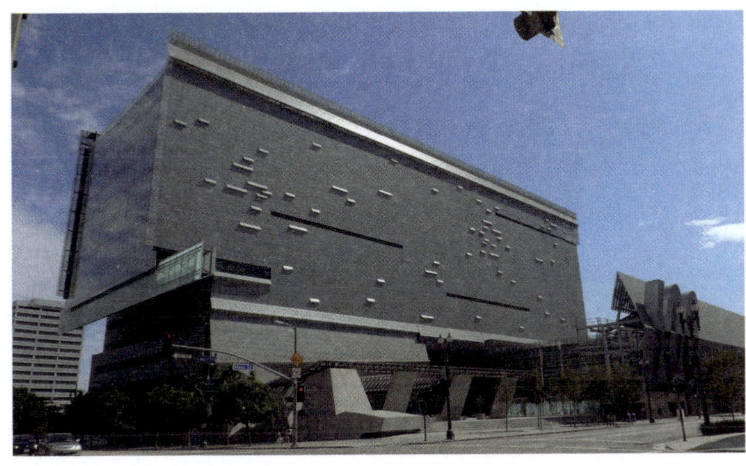

Caltrans Headquarters.
Photo: M. Hogan

There was a meeting with Jerry Epstein and O'Malley Miller, members of the State Building Authority, Jerry Baxter, Caltrans Director District 7, and Dan Rosenfeld. It was agreed that there was a need for a feasibility study. Rosenfeld was working for Jones Lang LaSalle, and he secured from CRA $25,000 for the study. The study compared new construction with rehabilitating the existing building, lease or buy existing buildings. It was estimated the building would require about 400,000 square feet of office space and 400,000 square feet of parking.

There were not many choices for buying or leasing existing contiguous space of that size, so the JLL study concluded that, properly done, building a new building would be economically feasible. On that basis, the State approved an appropriation to replace the existing Los Angeles Caltrans building. Caltrans' preference was to move out to the suburbs. Their operations center is out near Pasadena. However, the team said, "No, you need to be downtown in the Government Center to support the revitalization of the Central Business District."

Once Caltrans had a full block because of the land swap with the city, the decision was made to build the new building at that location. The Caltrans District 7 Headquarters building at 100 South Main Street was one of the State of California's first design-build projects. The members of the team were Clark Construction Co., Thom Mayne, architect, and Urban Partners, developers. The project was built on a $165 million budget and opened in September 2004. It is comprised of a thirteen-story tower with 756,000 square feet of office space and four levels of subterranean parking for 1,142 cars. Mayne, the architect of the project, won the 2005 Pritzker Prize because of its futuristic and environmentally friendly design.

POLICE ADMINISTRATION BUILDING

Selecting a site for the Police Administration building which was effectively a replacement for Parker Center as the headquarters of the LAPD, proved to be a difficult challenge because several of the sites that were originally proposed were rejected for various reasons. The need for a new police headquarters had been identified by the city after the 1994 Northridge

Earthquake. There was a study done by Larry Kosmont on three police space requirements: an administrative building, a support building, and an operations building. The study highlighted the need for a new police headquarters in the range of 400,000 square feet. So, the search began for an appropriate location to place that building.

A number of studies were prepared as to whether that facility could be accommodated on the same block where Parker Center was located. There was land around Parker Center. Inconveniently, Parker Center was somewhat in the middle of the block, but on all four corners there was additional land. One corner was eventually given over to an emergency operations center. Another corner became a detention facility, a jail. The third corner now has an underground parking garage. As a result, the block was chopped up and used for several police-related uses. However, at the time of the Kosmont study there was still land available on the remainder of the site, and plans were drawn to build additional police facilities around the existing Parker Center building.

In another twist in the Parker Center saga, in June 2004, during the James Hahn administration, the City Council voted to buy the Transamerica Building at 1149 South Broadway and relocate LAPD personnel housed in the Parker Center to the site until a new headquarters was constructed. Earvin "Magic" Johnson had bought the Transamerica Complex in May 2003 for $100 million dollars. The complex included the eleven-story prospective building, a second eleven-story office tower, the thirty-two-story Transamerica Center Tower, three parking structures and five and a half acres of adjacent land. The city paid $50.7 million for the eleven-story building and spent an additional $30 million to renovate it. The Public Works Department moved from downtown to the 1149 South Broadway Building, and they have tried ever since to move back near City Hall.

The search for a location for the Police Administration Building evolved in its own trajectory. Location after location was turned down. There was generally a feeling that it probably should go further to the south or east, toward Little Tokyo. The city owned several blocks in that direction. One is at First and Alameda streets called the Mangrove Estates property, adjacent to a Metro station. The City Council moved in August 2006 to exclude First and Alameda as a potential site for a new police headquarters because of opposition from the Little Tokyo community. A site by the Geffen/ MOCA and the Japanese American National Museum was also an option, but it was considered too sensitive historically, with its proximity to the Little Tokyo communities.

Little Tokyo had always been a respected and politically active neighborhood. City Councilmember Jan Perry and others cultivated relationships there carefully, so it was decided not to confront them over this. According to Perry, she and Deaton drove around the neighborhood on a Sunday afternoon looking for sites. "Well, what about that site?" They were pointing at the Civic Square property, the potential great public space in the Los Angeles Civic Center Master Plan. They decided to locate the Police Administration Building there. There was really nobody except a few parks advocates that would have included Adele Yellin and Dan Rosenfeld who stood up for the Civic Square.

The design of the Police Administration Building was influenced by the First Street Master Plan created by the team of Suisman-Campbell-Rios. It made the front and back plaza spaces much more public, and accessible. According to Greg Fisher, deputy of Los Angeles Councilwoman Jan Perry, many people bought units in the Higgins building under the belief that the site would be a park. Part of the reason there is a set-back at the rear of the building is to let the Higgins building not end up with a wall right across the street from it.

The First Street project envisioned a walkable corridor filled with pedestrian activity benefitting current and future developments along the two-mile stretch from Grand Avenue to Boyle Heights. The plan originally terminated at City Hall, but as an advisor to the team, I conveyed to the sponsor, Project Restore, and the designers that Supervisor Gloria Molina wished that the Walt Disney Concert Hall connect with the Mariachi Plaza both symbolically and physically.

LOST OPPORTUNITY

Architecturally, it appears that the main entrance to City Hall is on the Spring Street side, facing up the hill. That's the grand entrance. In practice, over the years, however, most of the ceremonial events that have taken place there have been on the south side, the First Street side, on steps that face south into a small park. That's where Presidents speak, and where Laker rallies are held, and, if there is a major gathering, it has been in that garden on the south side. The idea of creating a Civic Square in the Civic Center, facing City Hall on this side, seemed just serendipitously possible, because the city now owned the block immediately south of City Hall. Note that the Main Street entrance to City Hall, the one that is primarily used today, always seemed to be a secondary entrance.

In the Ten-Minute Diamond Plan, each of the axes from City Hall—north, south, east, and west—provided an opportunity to create a major axial statement. Going up the hill to the west is the Gloria Molina Grand Park. To the north, toward Union Station, I have tried unsuccessfully, first with the *Steel Cloud* and then with Mayne's 101 Bridge to bridge the 101 Freeway with an eventual connection to El Pueblo and Union Station. To the south, toward Little Tokyo, a Japanese American War Memorial was placed on the axis with City Hall. Although Parker Center and the City Hall South building stand in the way, there is the potential for creating an axis in that direction toward Little Tokyo.

But the strongest axis, potentially, was to the south toward the historic core, using the block that had been assembled from Caltrans called the Civic Square. Therefore, in the strategy, which was adopted by the City Council as a guiding document, the Civic Square was identified for that entire block.

To the east, there is now the new Caltrans building, a modern monument, and to the south is the Higgins building, one of the oldest concrete frame historic structures in the city. The Civic Square block was flat, and directly faced City Hall. It would have provided a sort of cauldron or forum for democracy, where people could gather for events. As such, the site was a natural place to create something that Los Angeles does not have, which is a civic square by City Hall.

Interestingly, there was some opposition. The *Los Angeles Times* said, "We don't want it there." Rosenfeld met with their senior leadership, and they said, "We're afraid of demonstrations outside our window." But, despite their opposition, the Civic Square survived in the plan.

There were a series of designs done, some formal and a whole series of ad-hoc ideas. Things started to pop up on the internet. One group called the "Hub" started a series of private design competitions. What should this civic square look like? It had the potential to become a wonderfully powerful autobiographical opportunity for Los Angeles, to create a square, like Trafalgar Square, Red Square, Tiananmen Square, and Union Square in San Francisco, to have a great civic space.

We don't get a chance very often to create a grand civic space. What really defines democracy goes back to Greece, not to a building, but to a public space. Next to Agora, the mercantile complex in Athens, was the Pnyx, which was the public space at the base of the Acropolis, since only priests went up on the Acropolis. It was an open space for public gatherings, an open space for ideas, making the hill an important site in the creation of democracy. It's where Pericles and the city leaders met. The Roman Senate also met, in later years, in an open space. Great demonstrations happen in cities in great public spaces. You can argue that the real architecture of democracy is not buildings but open spaces for the people to meet. The Vikings did it, as they kept democracy alive. Here we had a chance to create a great civic square for Los Angeles.

The public plaza was to be the house of one of Robert Smithson's last earthwork designs, Palm Spiral, a 150-foot-diameter grove of seventy-two native California fan palms. When the plan was canceled Thom Mayne exclaimed in frustration, "Of all things, you want a police headquarters as the symbol of your city."

DEMOLITION OF PARKER CENTER

According to Rosenfeld, it would have been less expensive saving the Parker Center than replacing it, had the options been objectively compared. The Conservancy was very unhappy that the building was demolished.

The decision to demolish Parker Center was made internally by the Chief Administrative Office. The Bureau of Engineering hired the firm IDI to create a case for tearing down the building. There was an outcry. Civic leaders David Abel and Wayne Ratkovich and others spoke up and said, "If you're going to start fiddling with individual buildings in the Civic Center, maybe it's time to update the Civic Center Master Plan. It has been fifteen years. Let's do a complete update of the master plan." Somewhat reluctantly, the City Council agreed to do that.

The master planning team selected by BOE explicitly excluded all the designers who had worked on the original plan—Suisman, Bill Fain, Rosenfeld, and RAW architecture. BOE did not want anybody who had had any history in the Civic Center. The discussions were closed. There were no public hearings. Their draft reports were prepared in secrecy. The community outreach consisted of inviting the directors of the Business Improvement Districts downtown, a handful of them for staged testimony, and that was the only public input. Fifteen years earlier, there had been multiple public hearings, including in City Council

Chambers, on the Ten-Minute Diamond Plan, which had been in the newspapers and had been a very public process.

The new plan recommended to tear down Parker Center, often nicknamed "The Glass House" and build a twenty-seven-story building for the BOE and other city offices. Parker Center designed by Welton Becket and J. E. Stanton, associate architect, was completed in 1955. Its minimalist, midcentury modern façade has appeared in many films and TV shows. Becket had designed numerous landmarks, including the Capitol Records, Santa Monica Civic Auditorium, the Cinerama Dome in Hollywood, the Theme building at LAX, the Music Center, and many others.

The Cultural Heritage Commission gave Parker Center Historic Cultural Monument status. However, a City Council Committee rejected the CHC's recommendation. City Councilmember Jose Huizar backed the demolition because he was sensitive to the feelings of the residents and businesses of Little Tokyo. It was a symbol of their displacement to internment camps during World War II, when the land was taken from them. Also, alleged racism and abuse at LAPD under Chief William Parker was an issue. The full City Council voted at the end of March 2017 to demolish Parker Center.

The *Los Angeles Times* reported at that time that the cost to demolish and build a new tower would cost $480 million. However, the city's final environmental impact report released in November 2016 had the cost ballooning to $536.4 million. This disparity, and other estimates Steve Lopez of the *Los Angeles Times* referred to in an article in January 2007, gave credence to the Conservancy's argument that BOE's estimates are "inaccurate and biased." Erroneous cost estimates by the BOE forced the decision makers to make the wrong choices. The Conservancy questioned all along the city's cost estimates and design assumptions. Their position was that it was possible to preserve and modernize Parker Center and construct a new adjacent tower.

The *Los Angeles Times* in an editorial wrote, "Yet demolishing the building is hardly the only way to provide a better gateway to Little Tokyo and reduce the sense of physical isolation. It's unfortunate that city officials can't seem to envision a middle ground that saves this important piece of LA's history without snubbing Little Tokyo."

Political hacks, crooked politicians, incompetent bureaucrats, unimaginative planners and narrow, selfish interests deprived our city of preserving a significant historical and architectural landmark and at the same time Los Angeles having its own Pnyx. The Parker Center was permanently closed in January 2013. In 2014, the Bureau of Engineering recommended a twenty-seven-story tower in its place, a recommendation that was subsequently canceled. The Parker Center was demolished in 2018, and the site is still vacant.

LA LIVE

Downtown Los Angeles was at a major crossroads in the summer of 2005. While the Adaptive Reuse Ordinance (ARO) adopted in 1999 had triggered the conversion of many long-vacant and underutilized buildings in the downtown historic district to residential use, their supply was limited. Furthermore, the viability of new construction was still very much in question.

How, then, is a live-work-play environment forged in a location where people worked, then rushed home in the evenings? Where were the basic amenities, the grocery and drug stores, movie theaters, restaurant, and general retail? More economic diversification was needed, but commercial developers were not going to build such uses until there were more residential dwellers.

Anschutz Entertainment Group (AEG) a stakeholder at the Staples Center, offered to break the logjam. It proposed the LA Live development. Extraordinarily successful Staples (now called Crypto.com Arena), home venue to the Los Angeles Clippers, Los Angeles Lakers, and the Los Angeles Kings, did not have nearby restaurants and clubs. Fans headed home after the final buzzer. Next door, the expanded Convention Center, had become primarily a venue for shows for boats, cars, gifts, and home improvement. Again, with a few nearby hotels and virtually no retail shopping, dining, and entertainment opportunities, it was perceived as a "white elephant" unable to attract big groups of out-of-town conventioneers who would spend large amounts of money over a short period of time.

Plans for LA Live were exciting, on paper. Progress and implementation were at a standstill. Fearing that a new, big hotel on the other side of town would damage his business, Peter Zen, owner of the postmodern Bonaventure Hotel, threatened a lawsuit and a referendum to stop the project.

At the time other fervid issues preoccupied City Hall: San Fernando Valley fought for secession from Los Angeles, and the city was consumed by the tough rematch for leadership between incumbent Mayor James Hahn and City Councilman Antonio Villaraigosa, former Speaker of the California State Assembly. When Villaraigosa defeated Hahn in a rare upset, political and business leaders in Hahn's camp approached the incoming mayor, reputed to be a hot-shot negotiator, and said: "OK, Mr. New Mayor, show us what you can do to get LA Live off the ground."

Villaraigosa jumped right in. It was a strenuous undertaking. The Bonaventure owner was convinced that he would suffer losses, but the mayor was not persuaded. Conversely, LA Live would be a new spark plug for downtown and all hotels and businesses would prosper. But Villaraigosa did agree to support Zen's request to convert one-third of his hotel's rooms to condominiums and apartments. It was a compromise that fueled deep concerns among union leaders who feared such conversion would result in fewer jobs for housekeepers, security guards, and custodians.

I clearly recollect the anxiety of the time. True to his reputation, Villaraigosa met with all disputing parties at City Hall with the union leaders and hotel owners taken to different rooms at either end of the mayor's suite of offices on the third floor. AEG was in an office on the thirteenth City Hall floor. Staff people were assigned to each location to clarify and resolve issues. The mayor shuttled between the three offices seeking common ground and encouraging compromise. No one was to leave the building until an agreement was reached.

According to Robert Ovrom, deputy mayor for economic development, during the prolonged negotiations the City Hall elevators broke down with the AEG point person on the thirteenth floor, hanging on crutches because of a recent knee surgery, jesting that this happened because of Villaraigosa's directive: no deal, no leaving. Wrong, of course, about the cause of the elevator problems, but right about Villaraigosa's determination to broker a settlement.

A settlement was reached in October 2005, with Bonaventure agreeing to drop challenges and the mayor concurring to support conversion of one-third of the hotel rooms to condominiums—if that ever became necessary due to the loss of business. The mayor also convinced union leaders not to oppose the agreement, stating that the loss of hotel rooms was unlikely and that he would continue to support more union hotels in Los Angeles.

The city also would provide a $270 million financing package for AEG Entertainment, with Tim Leiweke, then CEO and president of AEG, stating the success of the LA Live complex would rest with the hotel's construction. Maria Elena Durazo, business manager of UNITE NOW, which represented hotel workers, called the agreement important since her members were guaranteed job security.

AEG went to work immediately. The public-private partnership between AEG's exceptional management team and Villaraigosa's administration continued into construction. What was once a vacant parking lot, LA Live's initial phase was opened for business before the end of the mayor's first term. Experts said it was fast for such a large project by any city standard, with newfound lightning speed for the City of Los Angeles. Villaraigosa kept a tight rein on the project throughout its development, from negotiating the original agreement to overseeing all involved city departments to achieve a seamless partnership and a successful completion. Ovrom remembered Villaraigosa telling all city general managers: "Get it done, or your successors will."

LA Live turned out to be everything everyone hoped it would be: the first phase included the 7,100-seat Microsoft Theatre, renamed Peacock Theatre in 2023 and Xbox Plaza (formerly Microsoft Square), a 40,000 sq. ft. open air space featuring six seventy-five-foot-towers with LED and static signage with 1,500 parking spaces; the second phase saw completion of the ESPN studios and ESPN Zone restaurant/arcade complex, restaurants, Grammy Museum, Club Nokia, Lucky Strike bowling alley, and The Conga Room; the third phase, completed in 2009, included a fifty-four-story Ritz-Carlton/JW Marriott hotel and the fourteen-screen West Coast flagship theatre multiplex operated by Regal Entertainment Group. There were also over twenty-five restaurants and clubs, and other professional offices.

I remember a conversation I had with Greg Fisher, the deputy for Councilmember Jan Perry and downtown historian regarding events leading to the LA Live project. The area selected had ample space and, in fact, a huge outdoor event was held in concert with the Obama inauguration. A jumbotron—a video display using large-screen television technology—was erected and people stood all the way back to the Staple Center to watch the inaugural. It was a brilliant idea. Two visionary people, Fisher insisted, turned downtown around: Tom Gilmore, the Old Bank District transformative program, and Tim Leiweke, AEG's president. For me, if one project of catalytic importance had to be picked out of the numerous important projects of recent years, it would be LA Live.

I cannot overstate the importance of LA Live to downtown Los Angeles. Many important factors have contributed to the phenomenal rebirth of downtown, including the Adaptive Reuse Ordinance, Staples (Crypto.com), Disney Concert Hall, Our Lady of the Angeles

Cathedral, mass transit, and the Broad Museum. But everyone will agree that if they had to pick just one catalytic project that was the most important, it would be LA Live.

The reason is unambiguously obvious. After LA Live, thousands of new residential units and hundreds of hotel rooms have been built or are under construction. Further, hotel occupancy and revenues have reached record highs throughout Downtown, including at the hotel that once opposed LA Live (and which never converted any hotel rooms to residential uses). The Convention Center has experienced repeated successes, and retail development has been flourishing for the first time in decades. It is not coincidental that most of the residential and commercial development has occurred in the South Park neighborhood surrounding LA Live, once considered a blighted area.

I have heard cynics say that LA Live might still have developed without Villaraigosa, forgetting that the Great Recession was already on the horizon and suddenly fell between 2007 and 2009 where the medium family income dropped by more than 5 and 6 percent by 2010. Over nineteen months, billions of wealth were lost, jobs were destroyed, and homes were lost.

Also, Villaraigosa accomplished a great deal more. Many of the projects seen today under construction were conceived during his administration. It would be fair to state that had Phil Anschutz did not pursue LA Live at a time when other developers folded and walked away from their projects, and if Villaraigosa had not hammered out the compromise to move forward quickly, and if a mere six months had elapsed before the project's start, LA Live could have been delayed by an additional five years.

LA Live and Staples Center were central to Los Angeles's bid for the 2028 Olympics. The JW Marriott-Ritz Carlton hotel complex will serve as headquarters for the International Olympic Committee.

The sports world raves about the LA Live complex and Staples Center. After the NBA All-Start Weekend in 2018, Commissioner Adam Silver said that if team owners cannot have the annual showcase in their own cities, they want to have it in Los Angeles. All in all, when I reconsider the complexity of events and weigh myriad details encompassing LA Live and the imposing downtown development, I come to one conclusion: What made it all happen? Leadership.

LA PLAZA DE CULTURA Y ARTES

La Plaza de Cultura y Artes is a Mexican American Museum and cultural center in Los Angeles that opened in April 2011. It is located near Olvera Street next to La Iglesia de Nuestra Senora Reina de Los Angeles, La Placita. It consists of two buildings owned by Los Angeles County, the Vickrey-Brunswig Building (1888) and the Plaza House (1883).

Los Angeles County Supervisor Gloria Molina is the person most responsible for the project's vision and implementation. The construction cost of $54 million was funded partially by Supervisor Molina's County discretionary funds. It was designed by Chu+Gooding Architects and involved the renovation of the shell and core of the two buildings. Dan Mendoza was hired as the construction manager.

As a volunteer, I reviewed the construction drawings for constructability and provided assistance to Mendoza during construction. The renovation seismically reinforced the buildings and connected them internally, restoring the facades under the Conservancy guidelines because the Conservancy holds an easement protecting the exterior of the buildings. Unfortunately, the Environmental Impact Report had missed that there was an old cemetery under the property. During excavations, one hundred human remains of possible Native American origin and settlers were found and removed. Construction was halted in January 2011, resulting in additional costs and delays.

The museum, which is owned by the Los Angeles County, provides exhibitions, cultural and educational programs to share the history and traditions of Mexicans, Mexican Americans, and Latinos in Southern California. A nonprofit foundation runs the Plaza de Cultura y Artes, and part of its operation is funded by LA Plaza Village, a mixed-use project consisting of 341 apartments with shops and community facilities adjacent to the Museum. Because of Supervisor Gloria Molina's vision and guidance, the Los Angeles County leased

La Plaza de Cultura y Artes.

Paseo from La Placita Church to Fort Moore.

La Plaza Village and Paseo from La Placita Church to Fort Moore: photographer Greg Keatins. Photo: courtesy of Johnson Fain

Fort Moore Pioneer Memorial.

to the foundation the site that had two public parking lots for a dollar, and in turn the foundation sublets it to the developer, Trammell Crow. The County receives property taxes from the development. The architect of the complex was Johnson Fain.

I was familiar with the area, having spearheaded the Gateway Center and MTA Headquarters at Union Station, and in the 1990s, I had suggested to Supervisor Molina that a pedestrian path, a paseo, be developed on the county land leading from La Placita to Fort Moore, to be used for holiday processions from La Placita to the Cathedral. The Supervisor found the idea intriguing. She walked up to Fort Moore, on Hill Street, gazed down towards Placita, Olvera Street and Union Station, and became very interested.

Suisman Urban Design was commissioned by Ed Avila of Project Restore to provide a master plan for the LA Plaza de Cultura y Artes site. It included the paseo between two residential complexes that later became LA Plaza Village. The work included an in-depth historical analysis of the entire historic district. Suisman, author of 'Los Angeles Boulevard' wrote, "For many of us, the belief in the importance of the work we do in the public realm derives not just from ego and self-interest, but from a genuine commitment to making spaces where public life can unfold and flourish." Supervisor Molina assigned the implementation of the paseo to her transportation deputy, Nicole Englund, who was successful in obtaining a grant for its construction and guided the project through the bureaucracy.

At the same time, Molina set in motion the rehabilitation of Fort Moore Pioneer Memorial at 501 North Hill Street, Los Angeles. In 2014, the County Board of Supervisors approved $4.1 million to restore the monument. In December 2019 water started to flow at the Forte Moore waterfalls, a sight not seen since 1977. The monument that was dedicated in 1958 commemorates the Mormon Battalion and the New York Volunteer American military forces that first raised the United States flag in the recently acquired California territory on July 4, 1847. The terra-cotta relief memorial wall depicts the flag raising. It contains three images that represent Spanish ranchos, prairie schooners and industrial innovations. Repairs included redoing the work behind the 80-foot waterfall, replacing the waterfall pools and the kilning of close to 300,000 tiles. The modernist LA Plaza Village opposite the monument provides a new sense of place. The landscaped historic paseo connecting La Placita Church with Fort Moore opened in 2019. The artists involved were Judithe Hernandez, Jose Lozano, Miguel Angele Reyes, and Barbara Carrasco.

US Representative Esteban E. Torres was the founding chairman of La Plaza de Cultura y Artes (2002–15).

MOCA (Museum of Contemporary Art. Photo: istock

THE MUSEUM OF CONTEMPORARY ART

During a 1979 fundraiser at the Beverly Hills Hotel, the conversation at the table of Mayor Tom Bradley somehow had shifted from politics to art. And, more specifically, why establishing a contemporary art museum in Los Angeles was essential for the city. An adamant advocate was Marcia Simon Weisman, sister of the industrialist, collector, and philanthropist Norton Simon. Los Angeles Councilman Joel Wachs was an enthusiastic backer. Subsequently, within a few weeks, the Los Angeles mayor had organized a Museum Advisory Committee led by federal appeals court judge William A. Norris. Immediate and challenging objectives in creating a new museum from scratch were many, namely: securing funds, recruiting trustees and directors, building a gallery, and filling it with an art collection. The vice chair was given to the determined Weisman who quickly amassed pledges of support from nearly forty artists, politicians, and art patrons. The fledgling Museum of Contemporary Art (MOCA), which showcases the art of our time, began to take shape. Please note that in the Promoting Arts chapter, insightful factors and dynamics on MOCA and the other distinctive Los Angeles museums are presented.

MOCA needed to immediately provide an authentic charisma, so Weisman and five other key local collectors agreed to pledge parts of their collections, worth up to $6 million to the museum. The city's most prominent philanthropists and collectors were assembled to sit on the Board of Trustees and a goal to raise $10 million in the first year was set. Weisman's handiwork brought in $1 million contributions each from Eli Broad, Max Palevsky, and Atlantic Richfield Co. Broad became MOCA's founding chair, and Palevsky chaired the architectural search committee. At the start, MOCA operated out of an office on Boyd Street. Aside from its list of celebrated patrons, many young donors connected with the museum, some supporting the arts for the first time, joining as founders at the $10,000 minimum.

In 1979, the Los Angeles Community Redevelopment Agency held a national competition to select a developer for eleven acres owned by the city atop Bunker Hill. It was intended to be the business center of the region. Cadillac Fairview partnered with Nathan Shapell and Jona Goldrich as Bunker Hill Associates. Cadillac Fairview invests in and manages commercial real estate, in Canada and the United States. Bunker Hill Associates entered the competition and won. Its proposal included three tall office towers, a hotel, two apartment buildings, a museum, the rebuilding of Angels Flight, and a performance plaza. In addition to private donations, funds for MOCA came from a 1.5 percent fee on Bunker Hill development projects required to fund public art.

Yet, delivering a permanent home for MOCA became a challenging consignment testing nerves and personalities. Fred Nicholas, an attorney, and collector and well-known in the arts, told me that an exasperated Palevsky called him seeking assistance. "Fred, I'm dealing with a Japanese artist who doesn't speak English and I'm having a terrible time," Palevsky told Nicholas. "Can you help me?"

Palevsky, computer technology pioneer, venture capitalist, art collector, and philanthropist—had picked the award-winning Japanese architect Arata Isozaki to design MOCA. "Palevsky had given a million dollars, and the request he made for that gift was that he would be in charge of the architect," Nicholas told me. "And he was." However, unable to communicate with Isozaki, Palevsky became frustrated and turned to Nicholas. "I went downtown to his office, met Isozaki and liked him very much," Nicholas said, "even though he spoke three words in English." Isozaki needed an American architect who knew how to do things in the United States since he had never worked outside of Japan.

Nicholas described how he subtly handled the delicate issue that had arisen and threatened the building of MOCA's home. First, he called Victor Gruen, an architect known as a pioneer in the design of shopping malls in the United States, and Herman Guttman, who ran Gruen's offices in Los Angeles. Guttman met Isozaki and provided an office for him to work on MOCA.

But Palevsky wouldn't have it. He hired his own architect, Coy Howard of Venice, California, to work on a plan for MOCA. "It got very testy," Nicholas said. Palevsky told Nicholas to take charge of the architect and "insisted that the work of his architect be adopted by MOCA and used, and Isozaki be thrown out." When Isozaki unveiled designs for the museum at a March 1982 news conference, the reaction was underwhelming. *Los Angeles Times* architecture and design critic John Dreyfuss deemed the plan "forgettable and architecturally mediocre." But it quickly became clear that Isozaki didn't care for it either, preferring three designs he just happened to bring along with the selected scheme. Pressed by reporters, he acknowledged that the "final" design was crafted only because Palevsky's committee had insisted on it. He also confided that he was considering resigning.

Just to be clear, I queried Nicholas: "Did not Palevsky select Isozaki to start with?"

"Yes, but he was influenced in the decision by Sam Francis, the American painter and printmaker who had worked in Japan and knew Isozaki. Palevsky went to Japan, saw his work, loved it, and hired him," he replied

"How was it resolved?" I asked.

"We had a meeting with the board of MOCA with Broad the chairman," Nicholas said.

Always contrary, Palevsky asked the board to vote, and it did, twenty-five to one in favor of Isozaki, with Broad not voting. "Palevsky left the museum and filed a lawsuit against the museum to recover his $1 million. A year of vicious litigation ensued," Nicholas told me.

I asked Bill Fain, an urban planner and architect, who held a long list of professional honors, to offer corroboration on MOCA's stormy building controversy for me. At the time, Fain was president of the Architecture and Design Support Committee of MOCA. He remembered being there when Isozaki presented his original concepts to the board. "I don't know how many other architects were there, but Joseph Giovannini, architectural designer and critic, had just seen Isozaki who was about ready to quit." Fain vividly remembered the moment, and he described it to me. "Joseph was just beside himself; he was shell-shocked. He came to us saying, "God, Isozaki is going to resign!" "What caused this abrupt outcome?" I asked Fain. "Palevsky had interrupted Isozaki during the presentation, saying: 'No this is not what we want,' and he brought in Coy Howard, his own architect working on a stealth scheme," Fain said.

The board voted for Isozaki's concept and Palevsky resigned, turning to the courts to seek withdrawal of his donation.

In December 1986, litigation between MOCA and Palevsky was resolved. The *Los Angeles Times* reported that a press release said the case was settled for "an amount exceeding the sum ($500,000) paid to the museum" by Palevsky but less than the total $1 million he pledged. Nicholas became head of architecture. Nicholas said he then went to Japan, met with Isozaki's staff, and brought some to Los Angeles to work on the project with the Gruen office. Palevsky didn't speak with Nicholas for about 15 years. However, one day they met on the street and Palevsky apologized for "losing his cool" over the architect selection. "I want to be friends again," he added.

Isozaki completed the MOCA designs in 1986 with Los Angeles popular culture and classical architecture in mind. To contrast with the extreme heights of the glass-and-steel high-rise towers of Bunker Hill, Isozaki designed a sunken, red sandstone-clad structure. The entrance is marked by an arch leading to a subterranean terraced courtyard. Under and around the courtyard are the public galleries. Only four of its seven levels are above street level. The museum was planned and built concurrently with the 1 California Plaza Office Building at 300 South Grand Avenue, designed by Arthur Erickson Architects and Gruen as associate architect. Gruen was associate architect also for MOCA.

Spanish architect Josep M. Montaner, writing in New Museums, described the whole geometric composition of the building which is based on the golden section as the Western method of planning shapes and subdivided the spaces, and on the Asian theory of ying and yang, positive-negative. The rooms in the extremes of the building have expressive skylights in volumetrically pure shapes: various pyramids and a series of linear skylights.

The *Los Angeles Times* wrote that Isozaki is "an architect of worldwide renown — he has more than 100 built works internationally, including his acclaimed design for the Museum of Contemporary Art on Grand Avenue in Los Angeles." In 2019, Isozaki won the Pritzker

Prize, an international award given annually to recognize the contributions of a living architect—often called the Nobel Prize of architecture.

Nicholas told me that it was because of MOCA that Los Angeles became an important art center, and he credited Mayor Bradley and Marcia Weisman for making it happen.

My thoughts meandered to additional actions that also affected MOCA, strategies that produced worthy results.

Jerry Brown had been the most consequential governor in the last fifty years. He was wise, effective, independent with absolute integrity and backbone, characteristics unfortunately lacking in many of our present leaders. In 2011, Brown, facing a serious budget shortfall in the state, proposed eliminating the 400-plus Community Redevelopment Agencies across California. Brown argued that CRAs had veered from their original goals and directives to invest in blighted communities, and to finance the preservation and development of affordable housing in many communities. He also believed that there was up to $8 billion in uncommitted redevelopment funds – much of it in "hoarded" housing money – that could be redirected to solve a portion of the state's budget shortfall. He also argued that, in some places, CRAs financed projects that included billionaires' museum parking garages and hotels, which he thought were not priorities (although many cities cited such investments as anchors to create jobs, attract tourists and visitors, and support local economies).

The state Legislature respondent by passing Assembly Bill ABx 1 26 which Brown signed in Los Angeles. The CRAs and cities sued, but the state Supreme Court upheld the bill, which went into effect February 1, 2012.

ABx 1 26 also created Successor Agencies responsible for dissolving the CRAs, closing out their then on-going contracts and projects, paying down outstanding debt, disposing former agency assets, and returning uncommitted funds to the state. Each Successor Agency would have an Oversight Board to review its actions. The Successor Agency would be a CRA's sponsoring community unless it decided not to serve in that capacity. In that case, the state or another taxing entity could be the Successor Agency.

In Los Angeles, Mayor Antonio Villaraigosa and the City Council were unwilling to assume the risks of unwinding their CRA. The state stepped in, and Brown appointed a three-member designated local authority. The appointees were attorney and now City Councilmember Timothy McCosker, Nelson Rising, a real estate investor; and Mee Semcken, a government relations consultant.

There was also an Oversight Board for all Successor Agencies in Los Angeles County. It was composed of seven members appointed by the local taxing authorities. Dan Rosenfeld was a member of the board.

Attorney O'Malley Miller represented MOCA for many years. When Los Angeles's CRA was ordered to close, Miller knew that the agency had to sell the fee simple estate underlying the museum, and he suggested to MOCA board members that they ought to acquire it. The Successor Agency thought it was a good idea as well. Then it had to be approved by the Oversight Board. Miller suggested to the Oversight Board that each of the cultural institutions—MOCA, Angels Flight, and Colburn School—ought to have an option to purchase their fee at fair market value. Rosenfeld introduced a motion accordingly, and it passed unanimously.

The decision came down to the Successor Agency, which authorized the sale of the land to MOCA at fair market value.

After vigorous negotiations with the Successor Agency, Miller suggested to the MOCA board that, since it could add millions of dollars to its balance sheet by virtue of owning the fee, it should pay the Successor Agency's price, because it would be like purchasing an endowment worth millions of dollars at a huge discount, taking advantage of the ninety-nine-year lease for one dollar a year with CRA.

MOCA's value to today's art, and to Los Angeles, is enormous. It is the only artist-founded museum in the city, and it is dedicated to collecting and exhibiting contemporary art. It has the most compelling collection of contemporary art in the world, consisting of roughly seven thousand objects. MOCA has already written a diverse history of ground-breaking and historically significant exhibitions.

STATE OFFICE FACILITIES IN DOWNTOWN LOS ANGELES

RONALD REAGAN STATE BUILDING

On July 30, 1982, the State of California created the Los Angeles State Building Authority, a Joint Powers Authority to oversee the development of California State office facilities in downtown Los Angeles. The Authority was comprised of three members, two appointed by the governor and one by the Los Angeles Community Redevelopment Agency (CRA). The governor's appointees were Jerry B. Epstein and A. Redmond "Rusty" Doms. (I got to know both Epstein and Doms when I served with them in overseeing the construction of the LACO + USC Medical Center in 2002). The CRA appointee was John A. Perez then a CRA commissioner, who was replaced by Donald R. Spivack, deputy director of policy and operations, as alternate on April 5, 2007, when Perez was elected to the California State Assembly.

Jim Wood, chairman of CRA, was very instrumental in creating the program to develop the State Building, which eventually became the Ronald Reagan Building. The State Building originally had been on First Street. That building had to be closed down after the 1971 earthquake, and all employees were dispersed in surrounding facilities.

The Authority would be responsible for assembling the site, designing, and constructing the building, and leasing the building to the State. The State issued lease revenue bonds to finance the construction of both the Ronald Reagan and Junipero Serra buildings. The State would pay off the bonds in lieu of rent. On a parallel track, CRA bought the land across the street for a parking garage. CRA issued a Request for Proposals (RFP) to all of the major parking operators Downtown and received a response from the three major parking operators at the time, Eleanor Silberman and L&R group, who formed a consortium to build a parking structure. CRA required the garage to be built before the office building, and to be expanded by 25–30 percent in terms of its capacity as a way of providing parking for the surrounding areas of Broadway Street.

There was also a second garage built on Main Street. Consequently, two garages were built to serve the under-parked portions of downtown. That was one of the conditions to get the State Building to commit. According to Spivack he got the call from Wood saying he had good news and bad news. He said, "The good news is the Governor (Deukmejian) approved the State Building to go up. The bad news is he named it (Ronald Reagan State Building)." There was resistance to bring employees to the new building from some of the other offices, because of safety concerns, but CRA was able to document that crime was actually worse in the neighborhoods where they had moved from than it was around the new building. Because there were very few places to eat at the time when it first opened, it did spur a number of restaurants opening up. The Reagan Building employees would wander out into the neighborhood to find places to eat, and the CRA people wandered into the State Building to eat at that building's cafeteria.

The Ronald Reagan State Building at 300 South Spring Street is sixteen stories high, 780,000 square feet, and it is largely occupied by Courts, the Los Angeles Offices of the Governor and Lieutenant Governor, the California Highway Patrol, the Department of Insurance, and General Services, among others. It opened in 1990.

JUNIPERO SERRA STATE OFFICE BUILDING

Dan Rosenfeld was appointed by Governor Wilson as deputy director of real estate services and building portfolio of the State of California. This was at a time when the state was in a serious recession, with high unemployment in architecture, construction, and other building fields. The State is the second biggest landlord in California after the federal government. The State spent at that time in excess of more than $500 million dollars a year on leases, and a billion dollars a year on new construction. The state had never done an inventory of its properties. According to Rosenfeld, the state's inventory consisted of a file of Thomas Brothers maps into which someone had placed little pins. The state owned 5,000 acres on Mount Shasta, and there was a pin. Rosenfeld was joined by John Salmon, who had been with Santa Fe Southern Pacific Railroad. Rosenfeld and Salmon understood that the state was not for maximum economic gain or shareholder value. Real estate represents approximately 3 percent of the State's operating budget, but it was 90 percent of its balance sheet. Governments tend to think year-to-year in terms of budget but don't think of assets.

Junipero Serra State Office Building

Through an executive order, Rosenfeld and Salmon published, and the governor signed and endorsed, an Asset Management Mission. "The purpose of the management of the State's diverse portfolio of real estate and buildings was to ensure optimal utilization by the public, and maximum value from the excess" read part of the Mission statement. Then the team came up with a five-step program to implement that mission, which also became an Executive Order. The steps were inventory, plan, consolidate, finance, and manage. First, they did an inventory and discovered that the State had 2,305 leases. It was leasing to meet almost all of its new office requirements, simply because it was easier. To receive an appropriation to build a new building took ten years.

First, one had to go through the Legislature for planning funds, then back for design money, then go for construction funds, and so on. Therefore, the path of least resistance was to lease. There was a consolidation requirement for plus or minus a million feet of new buildings in Los Angeles. By consolidating, the state would need a lot less space, and could finance it by issuing tax-exempt bonds, could deliver it at a lower occupancy cost, over time, than if it continued to lease, and it would be more efficient. A new State office building study for Los Angeles was commissioned. How should the state procure those million feet? And where?

The Authority had led the effort to build the Ronald Reagan Building and was determined to build a second, similar building next to it. The Authority had even identified a site on Main Street. There was a rumor it would be the "Nancy" Building because it would be the second Reagan building downtown.

According to Rosenfeld, he was invited to the Hillcrest Country Club by Jerry Epstein who said, "Your job is to help us build." Rosenfeld subsequently went to CRA Executive Director Ed Avila, and told him, "You know, Ed, the State needs about a million feet of space Downtown. Where do you think we should go? Where would it be the most helpful?" Ed pointed out the window of his office in the Banco Popular Building, and said, "Do you see that wreck?" It was the old Broadway Department Store at Fourth and Broadway that he was pointing at, covered with graffiti, and filthy, grungy, with broken windows, and it got worse when you went inside. Avila said, "The most useful thing you could do would be to restore that building."

The building had been the Broadway Department Store, the flagship store of Arthur T. Letts Jr., an English immigrant and a visionary retailer who founded the Broadway chain of department stores. He transformed a small, bankrupt dry goods store in downtown into the Broadway Department Store, later adding the Bullock's Department Store. The building was Beaux Arts with restrained Italian Renaissance Revival ornamentation designed by John Parkinson and Edwin Bergstrom. Arthur Letts revolutionized retailing. He made shopping into an enjoyable, day-long experience. He created an environment where mostly women could go for the day, wander around, and try on clothes. There was a cafeteria, a writing lounge where you could write gift cards, and private little rooms where you could unlace your shoes and relax. There were interior landscapes and skylights. Letts made shopping into an enjoyable experience at the Broadway. The abandoned building at Fourth and Broadway was purchased by Roger Luby, the son-in-law of actor John Wayne. Luby had lost the building to the Savings and Loan (S&L), and they in turn had lost it to the Resolution Trust Corporation (RTC) when the S&L industry melted down.

Rosenfeld decided to buy it, and to convert it into the next State Office Building. He had support for this from AC Martin, the planner, and from Ed Avila. But he needed higher level support in the State administration, from Joanne Kozberg, the Governor's Secretary of State and Consumer Services. Joanne was a staunch conservative Republican. "She liked the idea of a gleaming new "Nancy Building," and she loathed the suggestion that the Luby wreck be rehabilitated," according to Rosenfeld.

Rosenfeld told her, "Joanne, we need to talk to the city about what the state is doing, and what our choices are. We really should start with Richard Alatorre. He's the Councilmember for Broadway. Let's go in and talk with Richard and just tell him we're at a point now where we have sort of narrowed down our choices." Rosenfeld had done the financial runs, estimating the costs of historic building adaptive reuse, new construction, redevelopment, initial costs, operating costs, and present values, over different lifecycles.

Rosenfeld and Kozberg walked into Alatorre's office and, according to Rosenberg, "Joanne is in this red Republican business dress with gold jewelry, earrings, and a bracelet, and Alatorre is sitting there. We sit down, Alatorre puts his shoes up on his desk, looks at her, and he says, 'I understand you're looking at some of the historic buildings downtown.' And Joanne says something like, 'Yeah, don't you think that's a horrible idea?' And Alatorre says, (and I quote), 'I think it's fucking awesome.' And she goes, 'What?' And he says, 'Not only that, but I can help you get it approved.'" Rosenfeld continues "Alatorre had a speaker phone on his desk. He immediately punches a button, and he gets Willie Brown, the Speaker of the California State Assembly on the Assembly floor in Sacramento, and he says, 'Willie?' This is all on the speakerphone for Joanne to hear. And the Speaker says, 'Richard, yes.' And Richard says, 'Willie, we've got this great idea for downtown LA. We want the State to buy these historic buildings and move their tenants into them to revitalize our city.' And the Speaker says, 'Consider it done. I will sponsor the legislation.' Click. And Joanne is just sitting there."

CRA paid $1.7 million dollars delinquent taxes to the County, got the title to the building, and turned it over to the State. The State renovated the building. The renovation cost was roughly at that point the same as the cost of new construction and the land cost was substantially lower by taking the building. The extra benefit was that they were able to avoid having to duplicate certain facilities, one of the whole concepts of the Ten Diamond. The Reagan has an auditorium, and the new building, the Junipero Serra Building, has an all-purpose room. The Reagan Building has a cafeteria. The Junipero Serra has a little coffee shop. For the most part, they both use the Broadway Spring Center for their parking, which is relatively equidistant between the two buildings.

There were facilities that they did not have to duplicate in the Junipero Serra building.

The State calculated savings of 22 percent on the cost of the building, because they did not have to build another auditorium and another cafeteria.

The Junipero Serra Building, at 320 W. Fourth Street, is ten stories tall. The 519,000-square-foot structure houses Rehabilitation, Real Estate, Motor Vehicles, and the Public Utilities Commission Departments, among other tenants. It opened in 1998.The Caltrans building followed at Main and First Streets, a third significant State investment within the Ten Minute

Diamond. The State of California invested close to a half billion dollars Downtown between the two State Buildings and the Caltrans building.

In 2009, Governor Arnold Schwarzenegger decided to sell seventeen State-owned properties, including the Ronald Reagan Building and the Junipero Serra Building in order to bridge an estimated $21 billion State budget deficit. Jerry Epstein and "Rusty" Doms vehemently objected, and as result they were fired by the Governor. They had questioned whether the Administration's plan was in the best long-term interests of California taxpayers. As builders and businessmen, Epstein and Doms understood that public service agencies are typically long-term occupants and heavy users of real estate, so the conventional wisdom has been that it is almost always in the best interest of governmental entities to own their own real estate. For starters, government entities can secure cheaper and more flexible financing and spread their acquisition and improvement costs over decades, thereby mitigating the swings of real estate and capital markets cycles. Moreover, while government entities are entrusted to be prudent stewards of capital, they are rarely obligated to manage real estate operations with a mission to generate free net cash flows or recapitalization events to reward itself, its investors, or even its citizenry. Lastly, many governments have the flexibility to reduce, increase, or repurpose use without the degree of legal, logistical, and financial burdens if they were committed to a lease with a profit-motivated property owner.

STAPLES (Crypto.com) ARENA

An Aspiration Becoming a Spectacular Reality | Long before the first game was played at the magnificent Staples Center, now called Crypto.com Arena, a high-caliber struggle over its fate had taken place with superstar competitors and probable sudden death

Staples Center.
Photo: M. Mauno

finales—struggles so intense the sports arena almost did not happen. As a matter of fact, it took a sundry of midwives—politicians, real estate investors, attorneys, builders, planners, even a cardinal—to give it birth. Staples not only happened, but it also set the stage for the development of downtown Los Angeles. The iconic sports arena, opened with a concert by Bruce Springsteen on October 17, 1999, belonged to Anschutz Entertainment Group, the global sporting and music entertainment organization and owner of sports teams and events.

I recall its risky and shaky formative history and was familiar with key players involved in the multipurpose arena project, and how the lengthy and chaotic negotiations finally turned positive, leading to its development. It all began a year after the owners of the Los Angeles Kings, Ed Roski, Jr. and Philip Anschutz, who had purchased the hockey team in 1995 for $113.5 million, began looking for a new home for the Kings in downtown Los Angeles. Since the team's creation with the 1967 National Hockey League expansion the Kings had played their home games at the Great Western Forum in Inglewood.

Jerry Buss, then owner of the Los Angeles Lakers, was simultaneously seeking a move out of the Forum. Interestingly, Buss, an owner of the Los Angeles Strings in World Team Tennis, had purchased the Lakers along with the Kings, the Forum, and 13,000-acre ranch in Sierra Nevada—all for $67.5 million from Jack Kent Cooke in 1979. Buss later sold his controlling interest in the ice hockey team to coin collector Bruce McNall.

The Forum, built in 1967, had no luxury boxes or other corporate suites that are generally sold for the season for a great deal of money, nor room for restaurants and retail stores that accessorize modern arenas. But finding a suitable location for a sport arena was not easy—until Steve Soboroff came on board. He is now recognized as the driving force behind Staples Center.

Soboroff, Mayor Richard Riordan's senior advisor, was himself a politician, businessman and philanthropist, later serving as president of the Board of the Los Angeles Police Commissioners, president of the Board of the Los Angeles Recreation and Parks Commissioners, and a member of the Board of the Los Angeles Harbor Commissioners. He had also successfully guided the creation of the Alameda Corridor, a cargo-only rail route between the port and downtown that proved to be a formidable project. Soboroff was surveying properties from a helicopter, a regular ploy for him, when he spotted an area next to the Convention Center and imagined a grand spectacle.

"My business was finding locations for retail stores and people were visiting me all the time to look at places," he told me. Rather than drive around for three or four days, he could do it via helicopter in one day. Most of his clients were corporate executives who had expected the searches to take four days. He got the job done in one day, the clients eagerly took their per diems and spent the rest of the time partying, he humorously explained. One day, Riordan told him that he wanted to create a group to bring professional football back to Los Angeles—the Rams and Raiders both left after the 1994 season—and named him and Fred Rosen, an attorney and chief executive officer of Ticketmaster, to head up a committee called Football LA.

"I felt like a duck out of water," Soboroff charismatically explained to me. "Everybody on the committee knew more than me." He recalled a committee meeting at the Four Seasons Hotel in Beverly Hills when someone stood up and said of the National Football League's franchise fee: "It's $300 million. Let's just put together a group and buy it ourselves," The speaker then said, "I'm in for $15 million," and others began raising their hands. Some $190 million was raised. It was a giddying experience for Soboroff, and he related to me the deflating outcome. "Oh, my God. We got great community people with everyone going in for $15 million at a pop," he first thought. But when he went to the hotel valet for his car, he was struck by what he witnessed. "Of the fifteen people at the meeting, twelve had parked across the street to avoid paying the three-dollar valet charge." "This doesn't work. These are a bunch of bullshitters," he concluded.

When Roger Goodell, who later became the National Football League commissioner, was helping select a stadium in Los Angeles for the league, Soboroff rented a helicopter, and they flew over Dodger Stadium and then over the Convention Center. Soboroff explained to me that Riordan had earlier shared with him the annual report of the Convention Center, stating, "They had built the new wing for half a billion dollars, costing $55 million a year out of the general fund. It was horrible." Conventions were not going to the Convention Center. Trade shows were the main users of the site. "Nick," he said, "if you were picking a location for your convention that had 10,000 people, other than Las Vegas you would go to San Francisco, San Diego or Phoenix, because if you were looking down from a helicopter on this area you would see drug dens and just crap."

THE ASPIRATION, AND THE GOAL

That morning Soboroff had read a newspaper report about the Los Angeles Kings being sold to Anschutz, "my buddy," he noted. There's land down there near the Convention Center, which can fit an arena, he determined. He took photographs from the helicopter.

I knew about Anschutz from my days on the Los Angeles County Transportation Commission board where attorney George Mihlsten was negotiating on his behalf to lease a path for the installation of fiber optics along the rights-of-way, owned by the Los Angeles County Transportation Commission. I remember commission staff had negotiated a price that seemed ridiculously low. I pulled the item off the agenda and sent it back for renegotiation. The end result was that Anschutz paid many times higher fees for the leases.

Soboroff had worked with Anschutz on the Alameda Corridor project. "I called up Anschutz and said I have an idea," Soboroff shared with me. "Let me see if I can get the city to get you the land on the corner of the 110 and 10 freeways, one of the great sites in America. Let's not screw around here."

Anschutz told him that he didn't know real estate and that they must talk with Roski, his fifty-fifty partner. Soboroff then called a hesitant Roski who informed him of a potential deal with the Forum in Inglewood and said that progress was being made. Mihlsten had once informed me that Roski had acquired the Cornfield site half a mile north of Union Station and didn't know what to do with it. "He thought it would be a great place to put an arena." After he put some plans together, he began to talk to the Kings and the Lakers but wasn't getting much traction.

The thirty-two-acre cornfield stirred controversy because some people thought it should be used for a park, while developers thought it should be used for an industrial park, Mihlsten said. Ultimately, a deal was struck to sell the site to the state park system.

"Give me a chance, Eddie," Soboroff pleaded with Roski. As a result, a meeting was scheduled to be held at the architecture firm, Gruen Associates. In the interim he had asked Mike Enomoto, who worked at Gruen, to find the latest photos of arenas and superimpose them on the Convention Center site. When Roski walked into the meeting room the walls were filled with pictures. To make the deal more attractive, Soboroff offered land around the proposed arena. Well, he deduced, they can't develop anything around the Forum. A hotel, he knew, was what they would want, possibly movie theaters and stores, a city walk, and business activities that would help downtown.

Roski loved it. Soboroff then turned to John Ferraro, the City Council president, and some council members, who embraced the concept, but Soboroff's involvement with professional football triggered concerns. Considering the sports arena to be a political springboard for himself, Soboroff promptly quit his football assignment. Support also came from Keith Comrie, chief administrative officer for the city, and John Molloy, administrator of Los Angeles's Community Redevelopment Agency.

I recall Molloy's comments clearly when he insisted that the Convention Center needed an adjacent hotel to make it a real player in the highly competitive business of attracting major conventions. He underscored that unless developers build the arena and follow through with a 1,500- to 1,800-room hotel within a few years, taxpayers would probably wind up helping build a hotel there as well. "Not only did they want it," he revealed to me. "They knew how to make it happen."

Soboroff then met with Ron Deaton, chief legislative analyst for the City Council, the influential official sometimes referred to as the sixteenth council member. "I was a flunky for the mayor then, a young guy," he continued while relating his early steps. Deaton listened to Soboroff, then said, "Steve, this is a great thing, and you can make it happen, and you can make it happen with me, and you can make it happen without me. Usually, when I am not involved things don't happen at the City Council, but it's your choice." Soboroff got the message. "I said, 'Yes sir, Mr. Deaton, you just tell me.'" Masking his irritation, Soboroff deciphered for me what Deaton was really saying. "There is no fucking way this is going to happen unless you put it through the system, and I know how the system works."

Echoing a timeworn saying, that no good deed goes unpunished, he said he came to the realization that Staples was more important to the city of Los Angeles than he was. "I wanted to be mayor, but if nobody knew that I was involved in the project" it wouldn't benefit his career goal. Conscious of that, he began to behave accordingly, meaning that he would fight back. If a secret meeting was going on, he would tip off the media "because the media drives the political." On television, he would deride opponents. "John (Ferraro) would be so mad at me, but he loved me. I just said I'm going to fall on my sword for this deal." It was clear to Soboroff that the deal had to be made simpler, which is much harder than to make it complicated. "Complicated things," he said, "aren't allowed to happen because bureaucrats hurt their careers. It's easier to reject them."

Rita Walters, who in 1991 became the first African American woman elected to the City Council and whose district included the Convention Center, never liked him, Soboroff admitted. He said that Rita reminded him of his aunt. "Nothing I do is ever enough for her." And there were members of the council who considered "that the venue was for rich people, only for the elitist, that it cost a fortune to go to a Laker game."

The owner of the Los Angeles Clippers, Donald Sterling, had been talking with Walt Disney Company and its chief executive, Michael Eisner, about building a sports arena in Anaheim, and Anschutz didn't want to have anything to do with him, Soboroff told me. So, he personally went to Sterling's office in Beverly Hills, the top floor of a building with the other floors purposely kept empty since Sterling said he didn't want tenants because they were noisy. "The truth is," Soboroff confided to me, "any rent would go to another landlord who Sterling was trying to drive out." Eisner wanted the Clippers in Anaheim and had promised that a helicopter would take Sterling from his home in Malibu to the Clippers games. This was appealing to him.

"I know what you are saying," Soboroff responded. "But you are not going to move there. You've got hives all over the side of your neck and people like you don't make decisions when their body is telling them to do something else." Anschutz eventually met with Sterling and the Clippers and signed a deal to move the team to the sports arena next to the convention center. Council members liked the idea because the Clippers ticket prices were affordable for many people.

MOTIVATING A DOWNTOWN RESURGENCE

Soboroff's plan could spark a downtown renaissance, an idea that appealed to the business sense of Ed Roski Jr., who ran Majestic Realty Company, which his father founded, and turned it into the largest industrial developer in Southern California. With his partner Anschutz in Denver, Roski was the local guy with real estate expertise. The indication that a new downtown sports venue might revitalize the area appealed to Ferraro, who told the *Los Angeles Times* "We needed something to spark that area, and this was a great opportunity." Whenever the project hit snags, and there were many and often, he sprang into action, smoothing over rough spots with memos and telephone calls. It was Ferraro who assembled a team of administrators from various city agencies to wrestle with the countless legal and financial elements involved with an agreement. Roski agreed the deal was complex and Ferraro kept it moving forward, and resolved issues as they arose.

There were also human consequences to deal with in creating the sports arena in downtown's South Park area. More than 250 residents, mostly Latino immigrants, and their children, were forced out and relocated into government-subsidized housing complexes with most receiving assistance to help pay their higher rents for a time.

The city had offered to issue $58 million in municipal bonds as a loan and the developers wanted to repay the debt with tax dollars generated by the arena. Council member Joel Wachs wanted the city to keep the tax revenue and be repaid from somewhere else. *Los*

Angeles Times reporters David Wharton and Robyn Norwood wrote in October 1999, that Wachs was angered by the hush-hush negotiations. So, he took one of the biggest risks of his political career: He threatened a ballot initiative requiring voter approval of any public funding for professional sports facilities.

Dave Farrar, who had served as chair of the City of Los Angeles's Community Redevelopment Agency and was later the attorney for the city on development of the sports arena, spoke with me about the controversy surrounding the North Hall of the Convention Center which had to be torn down to make room. "This hall was the largest money-maker in the center because small conventions could be held there all the time."

Farrar told me he wondered why the site just north of the Convention Center couldn't be used. After all, it was in a Community Redevelopment Agency area and was destined for development anyway. I remembered that this site was also included in the project, but the arena was still on the North Hall site.

I asked Farrar if he met with Wachs regarding Staples. He said that the councilman was the only one asking the right questions. However, seeing the dynamics, the relationships between the developer and the members of the City Council, he said. "It was clear in our analysis that the developer already had the support of everyone on the City Council except for Joel Wachs because no one else asked any questions. Everybody else was Rah-rah-rah, let's do it."

He explained to me there were a couple of good reasons for that. "Downtown was in a significant economic downturn and the site was terribly blighted with hostess dancing and two-hour motels." Like Chinatown, he said, city officials wanted to clean up the area. He used to have breakfast across the street from a car wash there and could witness the bad uses taking place. "We signed the sports arena deal on a Wednesday, and when I went to have breakfast on Friday the bulldozers were already taking the place down." The power of sports is immense, he said, noting that about half the people who buy a newspaper read the sports pages and ignore the rest. "The *Los Angeles Times*, like every other newspaper, needed to have a lot of energy around sports. Anybody that didn't think we ought to take down the Convention Center and build a sports arena basically was an enemy of the *Los Angeles Times*," Farrar said.

It was Wachs's position that the agreement as was worked out was not an economically justifiable investment for the city. There was uncertainty as to whether the taxes would cover the city's debt payment, thereby requiring the city to supplement the payment with money from the General Fund. Further, the city would not receive any compensation for the properties, estimated at almost $5 million, that would be transferred to the developer. Because Wachs was eyeing a run for mayor, his position made him popular as a public speaker. He struck a chord of resentment against "billionaire owners and gazillionaire players"—a memorable phrase he used so effectively in a series of public debates.

Wachs had also used some of the convention center's biggest customers to expand his attack on the sports arena by writing letters in opposition. Riordan's aide Steven Sugerman scrambled to contact the letter-writers and told them their issues could be worked out. Further, Dick Walsh, the convention center's director who opposed the sports arena, was criticized for writing letters to clients warning them of potential inconveniences that could be created by arena construction. After it was disclosed that he was moonlighting for a competing agency in Hawaii, he resigned.

I recall how intense the political heat had become, and how it was feared that if the sports arena developers abandoned the deal, Wachs would have been labelled as the man who killed the arena and prevented downtown growth spurt.

The public commentary against him was also intense. A 1997 Los Angeles Daily News editorial, "Joel Wachs, Anarchist?" alleged that he was "bordering on political terrorism" by seeking an initiative that could hold the arena project hostage.

Finally, after nine months of negotiations, a more favorable financial deal for the city was crafted, decreasing its contributions, and increasing its revenues and benefits, along with a guarantee from the developers that the city would receive enough revenue to meet its yearly debt service—an agreement unmatched by other sports facility financial deals. Throughout the entire process Soboroff, as deputy mayor, represented Riordan who had a conflict of interest because he owned The Original Pantry Café restaurant a few blocks from the proposed arena site. Deaton headed up the negotiations for the city.

Most interesting was how the City Council was persuaded to approve the project. I knew that AEG executive officer Tim Leiweke had sought and obtained Cardinal Mahony's help.

CALLING UP THE CARDINAL

Indeed, Leiweke asked Mahony to help persuade City Council to approve the project, and the cardinal quickly responded, rebuking Wachs for voicing his opposition to the agreement between the city and AEG. In a 1997 article in the *Los Angeles Times*, reporter Ted Rohrlich, wrote that Mahony was mystified by Wachs' exaggerated hostility and opposition to a new downtown sports arena, which would help create "a mosaic of new life and energy in our city." The cardinal promised to work against the councilman's possible initiative. In a letter to Wachs he wrote that direct democracy can be a foolish way to make public policy and that council members, as elected representatives, should decide the issue. A large majority of the council appeared to back public subsidies for the arena.

I was intrigued, of course, when Mahony was determined to link his efforts to build a cathedral downtown to the sports arena project, saying that an imaginative and energetic city needed revival of properties and creation of a concert halls and the sports arena. And more so when he insisted that Wachs did not propose an initiative before hundreds of millions of dollars in public funds were allocated to make City Hall seismically safe. In speaking with Farrar, he described Mahony's efforts with some perplexity.

Greg Nelson, deputy to Wachs, said the councilmember was baffled by AEG (known then as the Sports Arena Company). "They were going to ask for a subsidy from the general fund, aside from getting money from the Community Redevelopment Agency, aside from using the agency's power of condemnation to get property, aside from tax breaks and debt tax forgiveness. Wachs's first reaction was: 'Why do the richest people in the world need the public money?'" Convinced they didn't need the city's money, the tough questioning period began, Nelson said. "The more questions we asked the more we realized we weren't getting good answers."

Roski came in to speak with Wachs, Nelson told me. In frustration he asked Wachs whether the city was willing to "share in our loss?" "If we can share in your profits," was Wachs' response. Nelson told me they believed the threat the Lakers and Kings would stay in Inglewood was empty, or that they would move elsewhere. Profits were made from naming rights and advertising. Exposure was key and that's what a downtown move would give them.

Wachs had contrived a strategy. He brought together three of his best attorney friends and kept them anonymous since their law firms couldn't know what they were doing. They began drafting a charter amendment to prohibit the city from giving any general fund money to professional sports teams.

"We started waving that around and threatened to put it on the ballot," Nelson said. It was a bluff. And it apparently worked. AEG thought the initiative would pass, Nelson told me, so it basically folded.

However, Wachs was the target of numerous threats from the business community, organized labor, construction, and trades groups. Even Cardinal Mahony. "I remember the day I walked into Joel's office to find the Cardinal in the waiting room. I about pooped in my pants," Nelson said.

"Look, I don't blame you for being angry with me," Wachs told Mahony. "I'm not against the Lakers or the Kings being here. I'm not against the arena being there. I'm against having city money used to build it." Wachs said the cardinal was being used. "Those business developers have come to you as fellow downtown developer and asked for your help. They are misleading you. So, you're in the clear. I'm not mad at you." He also pointed out that Mahony was building a cathedral without city support, so AEG should do the same.

Nelson also told me that they didn't know at the time that the Clippers were also coming to the sports arena. And, of course, much later, LA Live and other developments created additional revenue.

An AEG top executive later told Wachs that he was right, Nelson told me. "We didn't need your money, but your colleagues were so anxious to give us the money, we're not going to turn it down."

Wachs responded candidly. He said he understood they were businesspeople and would not turn down free money. "I'm mad at my colleagues for being so willing to give it to you."

I wanted to pursue a connected issue with Nelson, specifically relating to the way property was bought and sold in the sport arena deal. "They got the property for around $10 per foot," I said. Nelson agreed. "Then they flipped it, selling it at outrageous multiples of the purchase price." "There may be a lawsuit there if someone wanted to pursue it," Nelson admitted.

FROM TOP GUN TO HIGH PROFILE PROJECTS

John Semcken, a graduate of the US Naval Academy and the prestigious Navy Fighter Weapons School's "Top Gun" program, joined Majestic Realty Co. in January 1996 as vice president and managed some of the company's largest, highest profile development projects, including the Staples Center.

During the early period of the sports arena odyssey, Leiweke, who was hired to run Staples Center, and G. Kevin Conwick, an attorney who advised Anschutz on sports deals, apprised Semcken that they were in "big trouble." Bill Boyarsky, of the *Los Angeles Times*, working closely with Wachs, wanted to see the Lakers lease to determine what would happen if the team walked. Boyarsky had earlier bashed the Lakers over the use of public money and not for being honest, Semcken told me. "The Lakers wouldn't let us show the lease, it was confidential, and we were getting destroyed," Semcken told me. Six weeks later, Lakers owner Jerry Buss agreed to redact everything, and they showed the lease. "It created a hero out of Wachs. After that we had the meeting with the cardinal." After nine months of arduous negotiations the final day had arrived. Semcken told me that "we had decided no public money—zero—would be applied." I was puzzled. What did he mean by 'public money?'

He said the Community Redevelopment Agency had a $12 million surplus and that wasn't Los Angeles's money because redevelopment money is the State of California's money. "So, the $60 million that we were going to need to acquire the land, $12 million of it was redevelopment dollars, but there was no city money. The other $48 million we had to pay for."

"There was no general fund money?" I pressed. "Zero!" But certainly, state money is public money, although that was not what Semcken implied.

All the conferees considered the document complete. "Ah, we have one thing that's gotta come out of the document," Semcken said."No, John," Conwick replied, "we're done."Semcken was insistent. "We have one very important thing that's gotta come out of this document. We are now paying for all this land ourselves. Before, we had a reversionary interest in the land. If we don't build the hotel the city gets the land back, OK, but they are not paying for the land anymore." "I don't care about the reversionary interest," Wachs said. Knowing that this was the only leverage the city had to force them to build the hotel, Deaton stared at Semcken and called him a son of a bitch. "So, Deaton agreed?" I queried. "He just didn't have a choice."

Semcken fondly remembered that Councilmembers Ferraro and Mark Ridley-Thomas were constantly fighting for the project, with Walters opposing it. Then there was Councilmember Nate Holden. Semcken said they had met with him at least fifteen times and each time he "put out his hand and said, 'you got my vote.'" But every time he voted, "he voted against us." How well I remembered Holden at the RTD. Nate always agreed, and then voted "No."

Renovating the Los Angeles Memorial Coliseum for the National Football League was foremost on the mind of Ridley-Thomas, Semcken said. After Staples Center, he said, Roski spent $6 million to come in second on the expansion franchise.

"We always had an honest desire to go to Inglewood," he related to me, "because that may have been our only choice. We negotiated with both sides. The Anschutz guys preferred

Inglewood because it was easier, Roski and me preferred downtown because it was better." He concluded that football can't be played downtown because it requires tailgating. "People get there at 8 in the morning and tailgate all morning and all night. You need exceptionally large, dedicated parking spaces."

But Staples Center came alive. After an implausible start, stormy public debates, myriad acts motivated by political intrusions and developer interests, the blessings of a Cardinal and the skepticisms of detractors, a world-class sports and entertainment venue became real, hosting four professional sports franchises, and holding more than 250 events and more than four million guests annually.

Located at the spectacular LA Live complex downtown, Staples Center added to Los Angeles's international fame and its position as a prominent world-class city.

WALT DISNEY CONCERT HALL

Widely advertised as "the happiest place on earth," Disneyland has long claimed magical characteristics. Therefore, when the concept of the Walt Disney Concert Hall was officially announced it was natural to assume that it would have the same legendary Disney enchantment. But on the way to becoming Los Angeles's symphonic masterpiece the project limped badly and almost crashed, victimized by disturbing funding shortages, bickering, and protracted construction holdups.

For years, the prospect of never hearing a note reverberate on its walls had become real and disheartening. A disharmony had ensued that stigmatized the project and its stewards, and a bitterness surfaced that was widely viewed as a dark omen for the concert hall.

On May 12, 1987, Lillian Disney, Walt's widow, donated $50 million to the Music Center to construct a new home for the Los Angeles Philharmonic—one of the largest single cash donations to support the arts. Her conditions were firm, among them being its location on a Los Angeles County-owned parking lot across 1st Street from the Dorothy Chandler Pavilion at the Los Angeles Music Center, and of course, it being named after her late husband. Her offer was subject to approval of Los Angeles County, the Music Center, and the Philharmonic Association within thirty days. Required also was a county agreement to build an underground parking garage on the 3.6-acre site with groundbreaking in five years, by December 31,1992, or the gift would be rescinded. Lillian Disney also insisted that any adjoining development be designed by the same architect who designed the hall.

Attorney F. Daniel Frost was then chairman and chief executive officer of the Music Center, but it was his wife, Camilla, a member of the influential Chandler family that owned the *Los Angeles Times*, who immediately recommended Frederick Nicholas to chair the Walt Disney Concert Hall Committee. She had voiced her staunch support noting that Nicholas was an old hand in dealing with civic complexities, had built the Museum of Contemporary Art and was also MOCA's chairman.

I had known Nicholas since the mid-1970s, and had always respected and admired the quality and elegance of his work, combining his legal career with major real estate

Walt Disney Concert Hall. Photo: wikimedia

engagements. Indeed, for me, he was a notable builder of institutions for the arts in our city. Besides his role in the building of MOCA, the Geffen Contemporary, and the Walt Disney Concert Hall (for which he was called "Mr. Los Angeles Downtown Culture"), Nicholas practiced real estate law for more than fifty years and was involved in founding Public Counsel, the largest pro bono law firm in the world; developing numerous shopping centers and office tower complexes around the country; and major activism in Democratic politics. Over lunch he explained to me that when the offer came, he was not sure he could take on the added responsibility, but his wife insisted.

"Well, let me talk to Mrs. Disney," he finally said, and described for me the reason; he wanted to "get her feelings about what she wanted and whether or not I can do the job." Nicholas was driven to her house in Carolwood Estates in Holmby Hills and had an hour-long meeting. The meeting was crucial, he told me, because he was seeking answers on significant subjects, first being his desire to know if she wanted a world-class architect. "If not, I'm not interested in the project." "You were not interested in building a box," I surmised. "Yeah, a box it cannot be. It had to be world-class." "That's what I want: a world-class project," Lillian Disney said, according to Nicholas' recollection of their meeting. "I want lots of flowers, a beautiful garden."

The conversation continued, embracing other fundamental issues, before Nicholas became unusually assertive. "I want to resolve another issue with you." "What's that?" she asked. "I'm Jewish, and I want to know if that's a problem for you." "Why would you ask me a question like that?" she wondered.

"Because your husband, Walt Disney, had a reputation of being anti-Semitic." Her response was genuine and straightforward. "That is the most ridiculous thing I've ever heard. Of course, I have no objection."

With a simple nod and an emphatic "Fine!" Nicholas accepted the role and began to plan his work.

"My great contribution would be how I organized. I knew there would be many people involved," he clarified for me. "I structured different groups, and appointed special subcommittees to cover the building, fundraising, the arts, and the architecture."

Nicholas formed a committee in charge of the design and construction, the Walt Disney Concert Hall (WDCH) Committee, dubbed "the Nicholas Committee." Members of the committee were Nicholas, Disney family attorney Ronald Gother, and Robert Wilson of the Disney Foundation. In addition, he organized the architectural subcommittee for the selection of the architect and a subcommittee comprised of Robert Maguire and James Thomas for the selection of the general contractor and construction manager.

Nicholas deemed the architectural subcommittee the most crucial. To keep politics at a distance, he did not include representatives from the city and county. Culture, excitement, and creativity were his guiding factors, and he appointed John Walsh, director of the J. Paul Getty Museum; Earl A. "Rusty" Powell III, director of the Los Angeles County Museum of Art; Richard S. Weinstein, dean of the UCLA Graduate School of Architecture and Urban Planning; Robert S. Harris, dean of the USC School of Architecture; and Richard Koshalek, director of MOCA, to chair the committee. Along with Nicholas, the five-member group seemed primed for the challenge. Nicholas also appointed music consultants: conductors Andre Previn, Simon Rattle, Pierre Boulez, and Zubin Mehta, and violinists Isaac Stern and Itzhak Perlman.

SNAGS EVEN BEFORE THE START

However, the gift and Lillian Disney's desire to build the foremost concert hall in the world had a rocky start. Charles Champlin, the *Los Angeles Times* art critic, on May 24, 1987, wrote: "The irony of Mrs. Disney's offering is that it really is a challenge. It is a blessing, but it carries undisguised worries and philosophical questions along with its promise for the cultural life of Southern California." Basically, Champlin believed that the gift precipitated some sharp specific questions and at least one mournful overall observation. "The general observation is that it has always been easier for public institutions to attract big money for buildings than for day-to-day and year-to-year operations." On the same day, the *Los Angeles Times* published another view of the Disney endowment from theater critic Dan Sullivan: "Are we creating mausoleums filled with starving artists?" He wrote that buildings were made to "keep the rain off the artists." He put it bluntly: millions for the roof, pennies for the fiddler. "If only Mrs. Disney had offered the Music Center a $50-million gift, free and clear, to be used in whatever way would do its artists the most good!" he added.

Nicholas was in the eye of a brewing storm, and I wanted to know what moves he undertook to supercharge the beginning of his complicated assignment. To build a concert hall befitting the Los Angeles Philharmonic, Nicholas felt it had to connect with the Music Center and relate to the orchestra and the audience, and to the city's urban environment. Therefore, definitive work had to be undertaken, beginning with a research tour.

In November 1987, Nicholas organized a tour of Europe's concert halls to gauge the vitality and artistry of each one, and to evaluate the acoustics. He picked relevant and suitable companions: Koshalek, Ernest Fleischmann, executive director of the Los Angeles Philharmonic; Ronald Gother, the Disney family attorney, Joanne C. Kozberg, chair of the California Arts Council; Stanley Beyer and Royce Diener of the Los Angeles Philharmonic Association's board; architect Donna Vaccarino; cellist Barry Gold; and trombonist Byron Peebles. Returning to Los Angeles, he had Vaccarino draft the building program with the help of Fleischmann.

Staying organized and compelled, Nicholas then approached the Music Center's key players to communicate his vision. He imagined a concert hall that would charm and capture attention and be a major focal point for the city, as was the case with the Sydney Opera House. Much later, Koshalek, along with Dana Hutt, in their concert hall review ("The Impossible Becomes Possible"), wrote the Music Center's old guard resisted Nicholas' vision. One trustee even suggested that the Dorothy Chandler Pavilion drawings be pulled out of the cabinet, that the same architect be hired, the mechanical, lighting, and sound systems be upgraded, "and then build the same damn building across the street."

A RIGOROUS ARCHITECT SELECTION PROCESS

Nicholas would not be discouraged and moved forward calling for a broad competition for the architect. It was a demanding task. He reminisced for me that "the architectural subcommittee picked one hundred architects and through meetings finally ended up with thirty-six." The thirty-six were asked to submit their qualifications.

At a subsequent meeting with Lillian Disney at her home, the subcommittee reduced the list to six: Gottfried Böhm of Cologne, Germany; Henry N. Cobb of New York; Frank Gehry of Venice, California; Hans Hollein of Vienna, Austria; Renzo Piano of Genoa, Italy; and James Stirling of London, England. As had been agreed earlier by the WDCH committee and the architecture subcommittee, one candidate by each group would be dropped, and they were: Piano, who had designed the Georges Pompidou Center in Paris, and Cobb, who had designed the Library Tower in Los Angeles (now US Bank Tower). Of the final four contenders, three had already won the prestigious Pritzker Architecture Prize (equivalent to the Nobel Prize for living architects). Gehry later won it in 1989.

The competition had three main focuses: a conceptual link to the Music Center; designing of the building to its optimum potential and preliminary planning analysis of adjacent lots for commercial and retail space; and acoustics. I was cognizant of the selection process and was provided with the meeting notes taken by subcommittee member Robert Harris. He noted that Böhm was "exaggerated, extravagant, impractical, and seemingly disconnected from both the central purpose of this project and from the nature of Los Angeles." Regarding Stirling, he noted his work became fragmented, and unconvincing. Of Hollein, Harris said his performance was disappointing both urbanistically and programmatically. "He brought to our attention the opportunity for a sculptural, inventive, animated place, but he is not the person to provide it." Gehry was a happy narrative for Harris. His proposal included a particular quality that Harris encouraged in all architecture, "the kind of surprise that over-realizes our expectations. His design is not only clear but somewhat familiar," he noted. "I didn't know Walt Disney, of course, and I can't say that he would approve. But I grew up with his films and I know his fans will understand the connection." Weinstein told me they also had consultants who independently evaluated the cost, acoustics, and the functional issues of each concert hall design. Therefore, "the jury, in addition to its own expertise, also had very distinguished consultants answering questions just to the jury."

Finally, on December 5, 1988, after exhaustive deliberations, the Walt Disney Concert Hall Committee gathered to hear the recommendations of the subcommittee. Lillian Disney was also present, wearing her "lucky red dress." Four of the five subcommittee members nominated Frank Gehry for the project. Each of the five subcommittee members explained the reason for the selection. Weinstein was picked to begin the discussion because he was openly passionate about the most innovative architecture, and Walsh was the closer because he had a calm and confident manner. A ranking of the architects was provided, placing Böhm at the bottom, with Weinstein finding his proposal "preposterous, sort of romantic, Wagnerian excess to be really a way of showing contempt for Los Angeles." Stirling had disappointed members with his tiered interlocking balconies design, and when asked to redesign, to improve sight lines, he refused. Weinstein was disturbed by "his kind of belligerence," and Walsh said his project could "be anywhere, Detroit or Dusseldorf." Hollein provided four alternative schemes, and a fifth later which was disqualified by the rules. He intended to show exuberance and splendor with literal allusions to Disney, aiming to connect with populist culture. It was "beyond tastelessness," Weinstein later noted. Walsh said that the relation to the Music Center was tenuous.

In the intervening period I was familiar with the Music Center leadership and knew they had openly feared Gehry because he was known to use corrugated steel, chain-link fencing, unpainted plywood, and other everyday materials in his work. Ten months before Gehry's selection, *Los Angeles Times* design critic Sam Hall Kaplan, wrote an article under the headline "Gehry's work in the real world." In it, he said, "Perhaps the most dramatic example of this phase of Gehry's career was the design of his own house in Santa Monica.

Here, in 1977, he took a modest pink, nondescript, two-story house, exposed portions of the framework and wrapped it all in an expanded shell of odd-angled metal, plywood, glass, and chain link." Kaplan added that though remodeling was completed years ago, the unfinished, raw materials make the house appear that "it is still under construction, or deconstruction, an effect the architect says he wanted to achieve."

But for the subcommittee the decisive winner remained Gehry because he presented an original architectural statement, a "living room" for the city, with openness and space and a lush garden. The question that remained was how to sell Gehry to the Walt Disney Concert Hall Committee. A diplomatic Walsh took the lead: "For you," he told the members, "Like a lot of people, his trademark may be chain link and plywood, cheap materials, and a kind of bohemian thumb-your-nose attitude. And you may also think of him as on the fringe, artistically." Yet his biggest clients saw him differently, he added, a man with lots of pride in being reliable, "down-to-earth, businesslike builder of buildings that work."

Nicholas expressed his anxiety during the five to six days it took the committee to reach a decision. He admitted to me that he played the key role in Gehry's selection. He then met with the Disney family and the Music Center Concert Hall Committee seeking its approval. Nineteen months after Lillian Disney's donation, on December 12, 1988, Gehry was announced as the architect for the Walt Disney Concert Hall. It has been written that Gehry was selected only after the committee members threatened to go public if their decision wasn't honored.

"This is the biggest thing in my life, and something I have dreamed of," Gehry said at a news conference in the Dorothy Chandler Pavilion. The Toronto native who came to Los Angeles as a teenager said he was told of his selection less than an hour before the news conference and had to rush downtown with Berta, his wife, according to the *Los Angeles Times.*

Lillian Disney, who had the right to veto any choice the committee made, said she had chosen Gehry the day before in a phone call from her home, Nicholas explained to me.

Gehry told *Los Angeles Times* reporter Leon Whiteson that awarding a local guy a major public project like the Walt Disney Concert Hall "It is a sign of LA's increasing cultural confidence, its willingness to trust the hometown boy. Frankly, this event is more than a little miraculous."

It was understood during the selection process that the subcommittee was recommending the architect, not the project, knowing that the design process would lead to considerable changes. The first factor, however, was the acoustics. A research tour in Japan resulted in high praises for the Suntory Hall in Tokyo, a concert venue considered one of the finest in the world, especially gratifying with its clear, warm sound. Gehry flew to Tokyo to meet and hire Minoru Nagata, a pioneer in architectural acoustics and designer of more than sixty halls and theaters, including Suntory Hall. Nagata's assistant, Yasuhisa Toyota later became the chief concert hall acoustician when Nagata retired. The design of the hall and the acoustics advanced together. Because of Toyota's superb acoustics design, it is one of the greatest concert halls in the world.

Gehry, the designated architect, would produce the conceptual designs, and an executive architect would then translate them into working drawings that would meet building code specifications. In February 1989, the Walt Disney Concert Hall Committee agreed with the selection of Daniel Dworsky to be that person. The Gehry staff of thirty was not trusted to do the construction drawings for a job of this size. As a result, Gehry had picked Dworsky, an old friend.

O'Malley Miller, an attorney with a noteworthy history of representing business enterprises and institutions in developing their closely held real property assets, and a civic leader, was retained in June 1992 to represent both the Walt Disney Concert Hall and Music Center. When Lillian Disney announced her gift of $50 million in 1987 to build the hall, there was a five-year string on the gift. Groundbreaking had to be held before five years were up. It was now December 1992, and the time fast approaching when the gift string could be yanked.

Miller indicated to me how a symbolic groundbreaking was staged on December 10, 1992. A dump truck full of dirt was brought to the top of the parking structure and dropped its load there. Shovels in hand, Gehry posed for photographers before the dirt pile with Lillian Disney's daughters, Diane Disney Miller and Sharon Disney Lund, Nicholas, Fleischmann, and Los Angeles County supervisors Deane Dana and Edmund Edelman, among others.

THE FINGER-POINTING BEGINS

Two years later, Dworsky's firm allegedly failed to produce workable drawings.

I was the electrical engineer for a number of Dworsky projects and had worked closely with Robert Rosenberg, the firm's project manager for the Walt Disney Concert Hall. Rosenberg was a very competent architect and manager who had worked successfully on a few projects with Los Angeles County. Most of the projects of which he was in charge were built on time and under budget.

I had a long conversation with Rosenberg about the Concert Hall, the design challenges, engineering decisions that had to be made quickly, considering the project was designed on a "fast track" schedule, the strong personalities involved, the conflicts and tensions between Dworsky's and Gehry's offices. My understanding is that it was a very complicated project with a limited budget and unreasonable expectations.

Rosenberg explained to me that, at the schematic phase of the design, the construction cost was estimated to be approximately $100 million, and there was about $90 million available from the Disney family, including the investment income, minus fees for architects and other consultants. Fred Nicholas authorized the architects to proceed with the design development and construction documents phase because the project was on a fast track and the county was building the underground garage while Gehry was designing the hall. The original design had the building clad with granite, a stunningly inappropriate design choice for a structure subject to earthquakes, but the choice of stone was challenged only after the building's steel frame was developed. In a cost-saving move the stone exterior was replaced with a less-costly stainless-steel skin.

We knew that Gehry worked with models using scraps of paper—anything lying around. He was illiterate with computers, he claimed, but Jim Glymph, a partner of his and project manager, was very learned. And because computers allow the architect to make accurate, descriptive drawings of complicated forms, he dispatched Glymph to the Dassault Systèmes in France to learn CATIA (Computer-Aided Three-Dimensional Interactive Application). Now he would be empowered to build beyond the limits of traditional project delivery methods with a range of 3D modeling solutions that spanned all design and engineering phases. Glymph sent a crew to Italy, and they were able to program the cutting machine to the CATIA system. The cost for all stone based on the design development drawings was $12 million, which was considered a bargain, and it was bought. Supporting the stone in these shapes was a herculean task. George Smith from New York, an expert for this type of design, produced the stone support drawings. When 70 percent to 80 percent of the construction documents were complete, most of the steel for the project was bought. At this point, a GMax was requested. (GMax contract means a cost-plus agreement with a cap on the owner's total liability for the costs of construction of the project).

It is important to note that the construction manager for the project was Fred Stegeman of Stegeman & Kastner, one of the best in the industry.

The GMax for the project using granite for the exterior was $132 million. However, after all the fees for the architects, engineers, specialists, CATIA programmers, etc., were paid, only $60 million was left for construction. Richard S. Volpert, the outside attorney representing Los Angeles County, demanded that 95 percent of the $132 million GMax be on hand before any steel was erected.

George Hines was brought in for value engineering, but Hines's estimate also supported the $132 million GMax. The county was adamant that it was not going to spend an additional $60 million to $70 million for the concert hall after spending $110 million to build the parking structure, regardless how good the project was for Los Angeles. The parking structure was financed with construction bonds to be paid with parking revenues from the concert hall patrons. It was, therefore, important that the Concert Hall open shortly after the completion of the garage, one of the reasons the fast-track design was chosen.

If the cost of the original design had been $60 million, there would have been funds to build the hall. But the design was never a $60 million structure. It started out at $100 million then went to $132million when the final drawings were produced. The final construction cost of $284 million proves the fact that no one should have been blamed, neither Dworsky nor Nicholas.

That's when the finger pointing started. At the time, Gehry was quoted in the *Los Angeles Times* as saying: "We had the wrong executive architect doing the drawings. I helped pick him, I'm partly responsible. It brought us to a stop." Gehry told Prospect Magazine in London, that the project had turned into his ultimate nightmare: dealing with a multiheaded client with whom he could not form a creative partnership or assert his authority. Dworsky was quoted in the same Times article: "Knowledgeable people were supportive of us. They were saying it's a very complex and unusual design, and they can understand the difficulties in trying to achieve this within a limited budget and a limited schedule. It was unfortunate that Frank came out with his criticism, but he was the center of the storm, having designed the building, and he was just trying to lessen the blame on himself."

Regarding this controversy, Fred Nicholas said to me, "There were no problems with the Dworsky drawings. They were not bad drawings. Simply the contractors could not understand them." The contractors could not understand the drawings because no one had ever tried to build a building with this level of complexity. This project was cutting edge in so many ways that the contractors did not know how they would need to approach the construction, nor how to fairly price their efforts required to build the project.

But delays upon delays had piled up, among them being the opposition of environmental groups that blamed county officials for failing to consider how much the project would affect traffic and water use. The complaint was rejected in 1991. The groups appealed, but the appeal was denied. The Los Angeles County Board of Supervisors finally approved a final environmental impact report for the development, clearly determining the benefits outweighed potential adverse impact on transportation and water supply.

By 1994, financial crises, Los Angeles riots, the Northridge Earthquake, and disputes within committees meant that Disney Concert Hall was no more than a grand idea on top of an underground parking that had already cost the county $110 million. The construction of the garage began in 1992 and was completed in 1996. Los Angeles County stopped the design of the Concert Hall in November 1994.

I remember having lunch once a month with Gehry in a restaurant around the corner from his office on Cloverfield Boulevard in Santa Monica. He would be despondent, discouraged, feeling helpless, and bemoaning that the only Los Angeles project of significance that he had designed was stopped. He blamed Dworsky and Nicholas. I had a relationship with Gehry because I was the electrical engineer designing the electrical systems for some of his buildings. In addition, I was at that time a big booster of downtown Los Angeles, promoting the mass transit system, and I had good relationships with Mayor Bradley and the county supervisors, so conceivably I could be of assistance.

THE HIATUS AND BILBAO

Gehry went to Bilbao, Spain, where he was designing the Guggenheim Museum, Nicholas said. When I inquired why, he said, "Because he didn't have anybody telling him what to do. He just did it."

So, in the middle of the Disney project, he went to Bilbao? I sought a more defining response.

"Gehry had the problem of never accepting responsibility. He blamed everybody for everything and that was one of the problems I had working with him," he said. In Bilbao he did the working drawings and did the whole work himself. Nicholas spoke slowly, baring underlying thoughts about the Disney project, now placed on hold. "Nobody had to interpret them."

"There were a lot of reasons why the concert hall didn't work under my tutelage," Nicholas told me. "It was the rush to blame somebody, so they blamed Dworsky, and they blamed me." He also told me that Lillian Disney and her daughter Diane had love and affection for Gehry, and he felt protected, so that everyone else was blamed. "As a result, it became a very difficult experience for me."

Gehry's Guggenheim Museum Bilbao, a place of modern and contemporary art, was inaugurated on October 18, 1997. It has since been called one of the most admired works of contemporary architecture, widely hailed as a "signal moment in architectural culture." When Gehry was selected as the architect he was encouraged to design something daring and innovative. Its budget was $100 million, and Gehry brought it under budget and on time.

RIORDAN COMES TO THE RESCUE

O'Malley Miller remembered he bumped into Bill Ouchi, a professor of business management at UCLA and Los Angeles Mayor Richard Riordan's chief of staff, at the California Club in 1996.The concert hall is never going to get started up again unless the mayor throws his effort behind it, Miller told Ouchi. As a result, Riordan, who took office in 1993 after Bradley decided not to seek a sixth term, had Miller in his office the next day. After a background recap, Riordan said "We can't let this go." Then the mayor reached out to Supervisor Zev Yaroslavsky, businessman and philanthropist Eli Broad and Music Center chairperson Andrea Van de Kamp. In the spring of 1997, Riordan and Broad launched a fundraising campaign, "Heart of the City—Los Angeles, City of the 21st Century."

Van de Kamp's ability to raise funds was well known. She had immense energy and enthusiasm, with good connections in the political, cultural, and educational world, and she was the one who spearheaded the drive to raise an endowment for the Museum of Contemporary Art and served on the board of the Los Angeles County Museum of Art. She was known for her ability to get along with people and her perpetual cheerfulness, and her husband, John Van de Kamp, a Democrat, who unsuccessfully ran for governor of California in 1990, said she was "a naturally ebullient person."

When she became chair of the Music Center in July 1996, she flew to Bilbao to see Gehry's work. "It was an epiphany for me," she told Mike Boehm of the *Los Angeles Times* in 2003. "I thought it was drop-dead beautiful." Her desire to build the concert hall intensified, agreeing that funding was one of the reasons for the holdup, but she also blamed the tussle between opera and dance interests and the lack of results by the county bureaucracy.

Riordan said that Sally Reed, Los Angeles County chief administrative officer, was expected to recommend that the entire project be scuttled. Money the county spent on the underground parking garage for the concert hall was to be paid off by concert hall parking fees. Delays in the project completion caused many financial problems for the county.

Writing in the New Yorker in November 2010, Connie Bruck said that when Riordan asked his good friend Broad to take over the project, he eagerly agreed. "Fred Nicholas, Broad's old antagonist at MOCA, had been the head of the Disney Hall committee since the project's inception; Broad quickly pushed him out." However, Broad and Gehry had their own bitter history. In the early 1990s, Broad pursued Gehry to design a house for him, and Gehry finally accepted. Two years into the project, Broad decided that Gehry was taking too long and hired Langdon & Wilson, Architects to carry out the design drawings.

Regarding the concert hall, Nicholas confided to me that Broad told Gehry he wanted to appropriate his design and have it done as a design-build project, then Riordan and Broad would hire contractors to build it. "Frank had apoplexy," according to Robert Maguire, the prolific developer who shaped Los Angeles's skyline and who also had hired Gehry to design four office buildings on a site near Los Angeles International Airport. In the New Yorker, Bruck also said that several people recalled a tense meeting at which Gehry told Broad that he did not want him in his studio—did not want to have to see his face. Maguire also urged Broad and Riordan not to bastardize Gehry's plan.

O'Malley Miller told me that of Lillian Disney's two daughters, both of whom were donors, Diane was the moving force. Richard Weinstein told me about Riordan's and Broad's attempt to see Diane Disney Miller and to apprise her of their design-build plan. "They wanted to fly to Napa Valley, her home, and talk to her," Weinstein said. After all, the mayor of Los Angeles's visits were always well-received, it was presumed. But Diane was furious that her lawyer had given them her phone number, according to Weinstein. There was a strict arrangement that nothing like this was possible. O'Malley Miller had also told me that Diane had insisted that Gehry must do the construction documents because Gehry felt others would dumb down his design.

Overruled by Lillian Disney's daughter, Broad told the New Yorker that "Frank won." Diane then decided to play a more prominent role and became co-chair of a new oversight committee for the building.

The moribund project was resurrected by Broad, who enticed more funding from corporations, foundations, and private donors. Broad was impressed with Gehry's work in Bilbao. But his attempt to control the construction drawings raised the concern of Diane Miller Disney.

On August 7, 1997, she told Joseph Giovannini of the *New York Times* that she felt a responsibility to Gehry. "All of a sudden, I'm hearing Gehry-bashing," Dianne Disney Miller is quoted as saying. "The project has not been good for him—it's made victims of the people whose lives should have been enhanced by it. In all honesty, I can't blame Frank for anything that went wrong on this project, and I can't find any verification that Frank changes things constantly and never finishes." Her commitment had also personal reasons, as per her comments to Giovannini. "When mother made the bequest, my greatest fear was that if it wasn't done right, if it wasn't exciting, if it didn't have great acoustics, it would not reflect well on Dad. But I think Frank did very well. This building will be wonderful if it's done right. If not, I'll take Dad's name off."

Koshalek was moved. He said "that Diane, at a crucial moment, has come forward with great strength and the right decisions. She deserves our applause for her leadership." Impressive, indeed, was Diane's assertiveness. "We promised Los Angeles a Frank Gehry building, and that's what we intend to deliver. I would feel ashamed and embarrassed to shortchange the city," she told the *New York Times*.

The Walt Disney Company was being openly criticized for failing to step to the plate and in December 1997 it announced a "challenge gift" of $25 million toward construction—almost ten years after Lillian Disney's $50 million gift. Patricia and Roy E. Disney, Walt's brother, contributed $5 million, the first of the matching gifts for the Disney Company challenge. In announcing the Walt Disney Company gift, Michael D. Eisner, the company's chairman and chief executive, said at a news conference that it was conditioned on the project's ability to raise matching funds. Eisner's announcement virtually ensured that the concert hall would be built by bringing the fundraising total to $168.38 million—80 percent of the approximately $200 million needed to complete the $255-million hall, according to a *Los Angeles Times* article by Diane Haithman. Aside from securing the concert hall's future, it also appeared to mark a healing of the perceived rift between two branches of the Disney family, Haithman wrote.

The Walt Disney Company donation went toward building the Roy & Edna Disney/Cal Arts Theater (REDCAT) at the southwest corner of the concert hall.

In fact, the fundraising had stalled in 1990 because of a feud between the families of the two brothers, Roy and Walt Disney. O'Malley Miller described for me how Roy's family, together with the Bass Brothers Enterprises, Goldman Sachs, and Richard Raintree, an investor and chief investment advisor to the Bass family and former Goldman Sachs employee, had teamed up to take control of the Walt Disney Company. "They brought in Michael Eisner and Frank Wells and their teams," he told me, "And turned the then second tier studio into an incredible powerhouse making the Walt Disney family fabulously wealthy in the bargain."

Why, I pressed, didn't folks in the entertainment industry contribute to the concert hall. "If the Walt Disney Company wasn't giving money, why should anybody else?" Miller said. "The one exception was Lew Wasserman who made a gift of his own money because, he said, 'people around this town forget that Walt Disney created this business.' They also said, I added, that if it is there with Disney's name, "where do we fit?" Eisner was awfully slow the first time around to give money because of that.

A new groundbreaking for the concert hall was held on December 8, 1999.

Gehry designed a flower-shaped fountain called "A Rose for Lilly," a centerpiece in the public gardens in honor of Lillian Disney. The fountain is made from the pieces of more than two hundred Royal Delft porcelain vases, a favorite of Lillian's. Lillian Disney died in 1997—thirty-one years to the day after the death of her husband on December 15, 1966. The Walt Disney Concert Hall opened October 23, 2003, and has received wide acclaim for its excellent acoustics and its distinctive architecture with more than six thousand panels creating a curving stainless steel skin resembling silver sails. It plays off the bowed cornice in the nearby Dorothy Chandler Pavilion, forging a link between the old and the new.

It has been dubbed a dazzling landmark, with its state-of-the art acoustics and its undulating mass of shiny metal, appearing as a ship at full sail, heading for the horizon. It seats 2,265 people and serves as the home of the Los Angeles Philharmonic Orchestra and the Los Angeles Master Chorale. The LA Phil has had talented conductors since the opening of the Dorothy Chandler Pavilion on December 6, 1964, including conductor emeritus Zubin Mehta, Carlo Maria Giulini, Andre Previn and Esa-Pekka Salonen. Salonen, the first-ever conductor laureate, directed the orchestra at the Walt Disney Concert Hall opening ceremonies. He was succeeded in 2009 by the Gustavo Dudamel, a talented Venezuelan conductor and violinist who is scheduled to become director of the New York Philharmonic in 2026.

I often reflect on the innumerable accolades for the Walt Disney Concert Hall while concurrently recalling its fits and starts, the intense and impassioned individuals involved, the enormous $284 million cost, and the final extraordinary work of public architecture that intuitively links us to our city—and recall what Aristotle once said: "Probable impossibilities are to be preferred to improbable possibilities."

Metropolitan Watr District Headquarters. Photo: G. Hauser

METROPOLITAN WATER DISTRICT HEADQUARTERS

For two years the Metropolitan Water District (MWD) of Southern California—a cooperative of fourteen cities, eleven municipal water districts, and one county water authority that provides water to 19 million people—searched for a new home. At stake were over $100 million to be allocated for a new building. And the suitors were many, and for different reasons.

To verify the facts I knew, I spoke with David Farrar, the attorney who shepherded the search for the headquarters location. Farrar had also been the outside counsel for the Southern California Rapid Transit District (RTD) when it developed its headquarters at Union Station. My determination was to discern if politics and special interests were kept visibly accountable. In addition to Farrar the search team included attorney Amy Freilich, a skilled negotiator, experienced in public-private partnerships.

For investors and major real estate players, this became the big game in town and numerous locations and strategies were relentlessly advocated, considering the office market had collapsed in the early 1990s. Some had powerful backing. "At the time, every decision was vital, and big, and so many people were involved, and the strain put on people would have Profile of Courage pressure," Farrar told me. "So tremendous was the pressure that it's a story like the Barbarians at the Gates."

"Games were being played here" Farrar said. A Request for Proposal (RFP) was issued, essentially using the same process as the RTD. "We started out with ten possible sites, narrowed it down to five, then to three, which we considered the finalists," Farrar recounted.

Among the sites considered were the Transamerica Tower downtown, the *Los Angeles Times* Building, represented by John Cushman, Cal Plaza, in the Bunker Hill District, a site at Union Station, and MWD property in the city of La Verne. The advisor working on the project was Larry Kosmont, the economic consultant for MWD. Farrar said tensions over which location to be selected surfaced early.

In September 1993, John Killefer, chairman of the MWD site selection committee, quit the board where he served for 20 years after committee members rejected his proposal to go to the Transamerica building. "Well, I can tell that my advice and counsel are no longer important here," Farrar remembered Killefer saying. Behind the scenes, deliberation over the building location grew more intense.

"A congressman who represented the City of La Verne was upset that MWD would build downtown and not on land they already owned," Farrar related to me. A two-story building in La Verne would cost far less than a twelve-story tower downtown. Asked by the general counsel Greg Taylor to draft a letter in response, Farrar wrote that the congressman's scenario would work only if all employees were required to wear roller skates. The building would cover a footprint of about five football fields.

"That paragraph was taken out of the final letter sent," he added.

California Plaza is a business office and commercial complex in the Bunker Hill District, downtown. It consists of two skyscrapers, Cal Plaza One, Cal Plaza Two and Cal Plaza Three, a vacant lot. Cal Plaza Three, ranked high with board members, was envisioned as the site where MWD could build its headquarters, according to Farrar. The CRA owned the land and would lease the ground to MWD. The delegation on the MWD from Los Angeles wanted the headquarters to be located in the city. Acquiring the Transamerica Tower, or going to be in Cal Plaza Three, or renovating the historic *Los Angeles Times* building were prime considerations, as was the Union Station site. "One party who favored the Transamerica building filed a protest to the selection of Cal Plaza Three site, holding up the decision for two months," Farrar informed me. The decision eventually was revisited. Over concerns about rehabilitating the Times Mirror Square, in a closed meeting, the MWD board of directors eliminated the offer from the Times Mirror Co.

With the board leaning toward Cal Plaza Three, Ted Tanner, an officer of Catellus Development Corp. promoting the Union Station site, graciously accepted the decision and said that if things didn't work out, his group was still there. Other developers who lost in the selection process accused the board of "stupidity and wrongdoing," according to Farrar.

MWD had been renting interim space at Cal Plaza Two for five years. Robert Maguire, the developer of prominent high rises that changed the city's skyline, had proposed to joint-develop with the agency although he didn't own the building. Metropolitan Life did and a deal was in the works.

On December 14, 1993, the MWD board voted to start formal negotiations with Catellus Development Corp. which proposed a twelve-story building south of the transit center at Union Station.

On April 12, 1994, prior to the full board meeting, Mayor Richard Riordan called the head of the MWD, John R. Wodraska, advocating that MWD abandon the RFP process and stay in Cal Plaza Two and work a deal with Robert Maguire. In addition to Riordan, the speaker phone conversation had many listeners, according to Farrar, including himself, Maguire, Greg Taylor, executive assistant to the general manager and the chair of the board John V. Foley. Riordan wanted to instruct the delegation representing Los Angeles not to support relocation to Union Station, one of the prime sites under consideration.

Bill Luddy, former chair of the Los Angeles Planning Commission serving on the MWD board, was in the chairman's office during the entire time, and finally spoke up: "Well, mayor, we've talked it over and I've been instructed to tell you that we've gone through a process and have selected the Union Station site to build our headquarters. If this is not approved today, then the MWD will not have its headquarters in the city of Los Angeles. We are moving to La Verne." The menacing silence finally ended when Riordan said, "Okay, thank you," and the line went dead.

As a result of differences, regional groups cropped up on the MWD board and fights arose from the San Diego contingency, and then Riverside, and even Orange County. downtown Los Angeles was not on their list of favorite places. Politically, just as in the case of other regional agencies, the yearning was to lessen the political power base of Los Angeles.

According to Kosmont, Cal Plaza Two was a very strong contender because it was built, located downtown, and half of the building could be purchased. However, Union Station was attractive, Kosmont told me, pointing out that RTD had already made the decision to go there. Further, with so many agencies involved, whether one is in San Diego or Riverside, traveling to Union Station with rail became a practical choice. I asked Kosmont if he remembered the Riordan telephone call. "I remember pressure from the mayor," he replied, "first to be downtown, and then at Cal Plaza Two."

MWD expended more than $100 million for its headquarters, which opened in 1998. Its development agreement was signed with Union Station Partners to build its headquarters next to Union Station within a twenty-nine-month period. The partnership was comprised of Charles Pankow Builders, Ltd. and Catellus-Union Station, Inc.

The twelve-story office tower and its 768 subterranean parking capacity, motor pool and fleet maintenance facility, also has a suspended courtyard and plaza. The building also features a two-story rotunda, skylight, public galleries, a large cafeteria and dining facilities and an extensive boardroom.

The MWD headquarters has been described as a nondescript institutional building of the last era design. It is of the same square footage and constructed at the same cost as the headquarters of the RTD, the predecessor of Metro, but the appearance and quality are very different.

There are reasons for these failures. While the RTD building was constructed under the supervision of the Union Station Gateway board, a six-member entity representing the full RTD board and charged with the sole purpose to build the building on time and on budget, the MWD building was supervised theoretically by the 38-member board of directors. In addition, while the MWD building was in the planning and design stage, the RTD headquarters was under construction and criticized for its opulence, nicknamed as "Taj Mahal." That criticism was of course totally erroneous and not based on solid facts. As a result, the MWD designers and board members got shy and timid during the design of the building. They were afraid of what the *Los Angeles Times* might write.

It was related to me by a MWD official, the agency was excited about the headquarters site because it was at a central location with excellent transit for employees, and it had great visibility along the 101 Freeway near the interchange with I-5. This was viewed as an opportunity for MWD to increase its visibility, along with its critical mission. However, when it came time to decide on signage, the powers-that-be worried that a distinctive and/or bold statement would not draw the positive attention that they originally valued, but instead would create negative perception of the cost of the new headquarters. Design, signage, and lighting were downplayed to draw less attention to the building rather than create a positive image, as originally intended.

Another difference between the two headquarters is the fact the Metro building is classified as "essential facility," whereas the MWD building is not. In May 2014, after a structural analysis found the MWD headquarters would experience significant damage after a major earthquake, the board authorized a plan to spend $20-$25 million to strengthen the twelve-story high rise. Thc upgrade, however, still would not bring the building up to code requirements for an "essential facility," which would ensure that the building remains in operation after a major earthquake. MWD would need to spend more than $90 million to make the building an "essential facility." The MWD headquarters was constructed by the same team that built the RTD headquarters, also a "design-build" structure. Catellus was the developer and Pankow was the general contractor. There were different architects. The RTD building was designed by McLarand, Vasquez & Partners, Inc. and the MWD by Gensler.

ONE SANTE FE

Catalyst in Art District's Renaissance | On a visit to SCI- Arc, School of Architecture to attend a lecture in the mid-2000s, I noticed a small parking lot across the street adjacent to the rail yards. From the street the site looked like nothing but infrastructure, and in fact many people did not know it was there, despite the fact that until 1939, when Union Station was inaugurated, it was the site of Le Grande Station, the main passenger terminal for the Atchison, Topeka and Santa Fe railways. I contacted the joint development staff of the Los Angeles County Metropolitan Transportation Authority (Metro) and pointed out to them that there was an opportunity for development on this small lot. Metro staff indicated it was not in their radar, but they would consider it and get back to me.

A few months later, the Metro Board authorized discussions for a possible development of the site without big hopes, as the subject site, the project that would become One Santa Fe, had many constraints. At that time, few foresaw the transformation that was poised to take place in the area known as the Arts District, east of the Los Angeles downtown core. Few developers considered the neighborhood for investment. Artists leased empty warehouses inexpensively.

In 1981, the City of Los Angeles passed an Artist in Residence (AIR) ordinance, which allowed the residential use of formerly industrial and commercially zoned buildings. Artists

One Santa Fe, before and after. Photo: Shervin Khazra

had used such spaces as living quarters illegally, and the new law sought to bring this practice into legality and regulation.

Bordering a Metro maintenance rail yard and the concrete channel of the Los Angeles River, the potential site was an unremarkable combination of asphalt parking lots, a wide, empty, gravel-strewn shoulder of Santa Fe Avenue, and large-scale infrastructure, including unsightly high voltage power lines. The main signs of life were the periodic Red Line cars moving behind the razor wire perimeter of the rail yard, and a steady parade of eighteen-wheel trucks making their way towards the highways. Much of what characterizes the neighborhood now existed then: rail right-of-way, the First and Fourth Street bridges, and buildings that had continued to serve industry and shipping.

Of particular note was the century-old freight depot building that the Southern California Institute of Architecture (SCI-Arc) had begun to take over as its home. SCI-Arc's building, preposterously long and thin, was similar to the other notable forms in the area that had gotten their exaggerated shapes from the pragmatic needs of transporting goods and people. Other than SCI-Arc, there were no other buildings of consequence in the area, with the exception of the Church & State Restaurant and the Wurstkuche: The Sausage Kings of LA.

I reflected on who of all the architects I had worked with could design a building to relate to the Los Angeles River, rail tracks, SCI-Arc, and above all to the "edginess of the area?" I had met Michael Maltzan in the mid-1980s, when Maltzan was a member of the team in Frank O. Gehry's office designing the Walt Disney Concert Hall, and I knew that Maltzan was the right architect. And, indeed, Maltzan designed a unique building that embraced the historic First Street Bridge, considered the future expansion of the subway going east from downtown Los Angeles, and a connection of the Los Angeles River to the Arts District.

The project, named ONE SANTA FE, is a mixed-use complex of residential, retail, commercial and open spaces within the industrial Arts District. Extending from First Street south towards Fourth Street along Santa Fe Avenue, the building's length of more than a quarter mile, stood on its end, it would join the supertalls of the world, echoes the strong, linear forms of the river, adjacent rail lines, and the former rail freight depot building that now houses SCI-Arc. At its northernmost end, the project links directly to the First Street Bridge, which carries pedestrian sidewalks, vehicular traffic, and the Los Angeles Metro Gold Line.

As the project's linear form moves south, it begins to shift, delaminating to create views and ground-level connections across the width of the site to the railways, the Los Angeles River, and the potential future Metro station. Just south of Third Street, the building lifts to create a "bridge" over a new ground level parking area and an expansive public courtyard active by twenty-five unique specialty boutiques, restaurants, bars, coffee, ice cream shops and a neighborhood market. This "infrastructural" form also became a primary driver shaping the unique "city scaled" building of One Santa Fe.

As the building was going up, it was commended and criticized for its scale. It's been referred to as a "battleship," a "cruise ship," the "Death Star." It is nicknamed the "Empire State Building on its side." It is a project that tries to use architecture to project how the city might continue to emerge. Since the Los Angeles River is being developed as an amenity, One Santa Fe incorporates moments in the building where a series of bridges might spring off and tether to the river. They could become community gardens, not owned by people in the building, but by the community.

Christopher Hawthorne, former architecture critic for the *Los Angeles Times* wrote, "Every once in a while, a piece of architecture comes along that is emblematic of a moment in a city's architectural and urban development. One Santa Fe in the arts district by Michael Maltzan Architecture, is that kind of building. It is a fractal of contemporary Los Angeles architecture, the fragment that both contains and helps explain the whole. One Santa Fe is not a flashy or gymnastic piece of architecture. What gives the project its unusual symbolic power is that it takes the generic stuff of a typical LA apartment building and expands it dramatically to urban scale… The design takes banality and stretches it like taffy in the direction of monumentality. It makes the famous linear campus of SCI-Arc directly across the street to the west, look stubby.

This is the project in a nutshell: It doesn't want to be run-of-the-mill transit -oriented development, reacting to planning moves already made. It wants to anticipate and even accelerate change." Hawthorne continues, "As Maltzan understands, what Los Angeles needs most from its leading architects at the moment is not brilliance at the level of the curve or even the room but the ability to think and operate at a macro level-to achieve with individual buildings what urban planners have largely failed to do in Los Angeles, which is to make density not anxiety-producing (or necessarily vertical, for that matter) but forward -looking and charismatic."

Since One Santa Fe opened in 2014, the Arts District has gone through a dramatic change. In honoring the One Santa Fe with the 'Distinction Award,' the Downtown News wrote, "The Arts District changed forever when One Santa Fe opened." The Arts District has become the hotbed of residential development. There is a surge in new retail and creative office space. The Institute of Contemporary Art, Los Angeles, moved into the area. Formerly known as the Santa Monica Museum of Art, it exhibits the work of local, national, and international artists. Hauser & Wirth Los Angeles, the gallery complex with museum caliber exhibits, opened in 2015 on Third Street and Santa Fe. The A+D Museum, focused on architecture and design, has also come in.

Los Angeles continues to be under tremendous urban pressures, which include density, transportation, mixed use, and affordability. Increasingly, younger generations living in the city are also looking toward a more urban lifestyle in Los Angeles, as opposed to their parents' suburbs. The Arts District had the potential space and proximity to support a new kind of development focusing on this future.

One Santa Fe was envisioned as a new, and unique Los Angeles development model in this context. It is both a singular building and works simultaneously at the scale or urban design. It creates a true mixed-use community that both reaches out to, and folds in, the varied landscape of industry, infrastructure, and urban space around it. While One Santa Fe is home to many residents, its other retail, commercial, and office space programs serve the growing community around it. Its various open public spaces are a part of daily pedestrian life that now seems inevitable, but only years ago was unimaginable.

The catalytic presence of One Santa Fe is one factor in the rapid transformation of the Arts District. The area continues to evolve and grow exponentially. Its identity and presence is felt throughout the city, but also nationally and internationally through the media. The speed of these changes has created widespread excitement about what is possible in an evolving vision of contemporary Los Angeles urbanism. It has also sparked a spirited debate about development in Los Angeles.

The urban pressures that have led to the development of the Arts District (and now other areas in the Los Angeles region) are not abating, and a larger civic conversation around the future of this urban metropolis is in its earliest forms. One Santa Fe and other projects in the Arts District have become models for that conversation and debate to take place. Far from idle speculation, they provide new, visionary, and working examples around which to evaluate and continue to propose creative Los Angeles forms for urbanism for the contemporary city.

Michael Maltzan said, "The skyline is often our first association with cities since it's supposed to be the most iconic and creative representation of what a city is. But increasingly, architects, developers and citizens are becoming alert to the fact that programmatic typologies like housing are just as important, if not more important., to invest with inventiveness." Maltzan continues, "The representation of the city needs to include the work of making visible the city's different populations and their ways of being in the city, expressing the continual emergence of the city in subtler ways. The individual unit has long been the main object study in housing—how it functions, how you live in it, how multiple units come together. But we shouldn't forget that the accumulation of all those individual units, all those individual lives, not only builds community, but also renders a very powerful representation of the city itself."

In 2014 One Santa Fe received from the Los Angeles Business Council the "Award of Excellence honoring outstanding architecture and design projects that significantly enhance the Los Angeles community's urban environment."

One Santa Fe also receive the American Institute of Architects, Los Angeles Chapter's "2015 AIA/LA Design Honor Award" for excellence in architectural design.

JAMES M. WOOD

A Civic Leader | James Wood was a friend of mine. We worked closely during the Mayor Tom Bradley Administration, he, as chairman of the Community Redevelopment Agency and I, as president of the City of Los Angeles Board of Zoning Appeals. Jim was a member of the Communications Workers of America, a protégé of Bill Robertson, Executive Secretary-Treasurer of the Los Angeles County Federation of Labor, AFL-CIO, whom Jim succeeded. Robertson was a big booster of Metro Rail, and he testified with me on several occasions before Congressional Committees.

Jim's legacy includes the beginning of the Downtown skyline, the Central Library, the Museum of Contemporary Art, and thousands of units of low-income housing. He was compassionate and cared for the underprivileged and those in need. His mission was to help people. Jim had a very strong personality, but he was very focused on carrying out his mission Downtown, with two or three primary goals. One, fix the Skid Row. He was the one person who readily spearheaded an approach to Skid Row which was different than almost any other urban center project. Almost every city that had a skid row area wanted to scrap it. When we got to Skid Row, he said, "That's not humane. We have an obligation to the people who live in this community." He spearheaded first setting up in the plan a program to rehabilitate or replace as much of the housing as soon as possible and introduce other amenities. He was instrumental in acquiring land in Skid Row to build a public park, the San Julian Park at San Julian Street and Fifth Street. He also fixed up the school that was serving the area and created two subsidiary organizations, one for economic development and one for housing development, the Skid Row Development Corporation, and the Single Room Occupancy (SRO) Housing Corporation.

James M. Wood with Los Angeles Mayor Tom Bradley.

The Skid Row Development Corporation merged with Volunteers of America and was essentially phasing out its operations because it was largely dependent on Federal funding that no longer exists. SRO Housing Corporation continues to be the largest owner and operator of Skid Row hotels and single room occupancy hotels in Los Angeles, and one of the largest in the country. The total investment between funding that came from Bunker Hill and money that came out of the Central Business District was close to $100 million in total investment in the Skid Row area. It created several thousand units of decent housing, and that really is his legacy. To honor Jim's efforts, SRO Housing built in 2002 a community center at Fifth Street and San Julian, the James M. Wood Center.

Jim is also credited with three more programs. One, Skid Row had to be cleaned up and made a safe place for people who have no other alternative for a place to live. Two, he agreed with Mayor Bradley that a strong Downtown funds the rest of the City. Three, the city should not be built on the backs of labor without labor being fully compensated. He was a strong proponent of expanding the prevailing wage and other similar requirements to make sure that people who worked on CRA funded projects received decent wages. He believed that a large part of poverty and poor housing was really a result of people having insufficient income. By solving the income problem, one could largely solve other problems, including housing and education.

Jim Wood led the efforts to revitalize Downtown with the generation of revenues that were used in other neighborhoods. A downtown Los Angeles boulevard (a portion of Ninth Street) was named in his honor as the "James M. Wood Boulevard." Sue Laris, Publisher of the Los Angeles Downtown News, wrote the following in favor of the street name change: "He deserves it, and the name Wood Blvd. would serve as an omnipresent reminder of community dedication, commitment to ideals, vision, willingness to overcome obstacles, the symbiotic relationship that ought to exist between business and labor, bridges that can be built between forces that think they are at odds and any manner of other good qualities we want ourselves and our children to be reminded of on a regular basis."

CHAPTER THIRTEEN

INITIATIVES THAT AFFECTED OUR LIVES

Do not go where the path may lead, go instead where there is no path and leave a trail.

—RALPH WALDO EMERSON

TRANSIT ORIENTED DEVELOPMENT

During my presidency on the Southern California Rapid Transit District Board of Directors, I worked with Gary Spivack, assistant general manager for operations, to develop Joint Development policies and procedures. Excess land used in conjunction with the construction of the Metro Rail system was a new concept at that time in Los Angeles.

Joint development (Transit Villages):

a. Involves a partnership between a public agency and a private sector entity to develop infrastructure assets.
b. Generates long-term revenue for the transportation system.
c. Often revitalizes blighted areas.
d. Increases transit ridership.
e. Increases public safety.

The Joint Development Policies include, but are not limited to:

- Encouraging transit compatible land-use plans.
- Providing comprehensive urban design, planning, and development activities.
- Establishing procedures for the selection of private sector partners except in instances of joint ventures entered into with adjacent property owners at the transit agency's discretion.
- Ensuring the involvement of disadvantaged, minority and women-owned business enterprises in project planning, design, financing, equity participation, construction, and operation.
- Negotiating joint development transactions which create a long-term source of revenue to the agency for the development, operation, and maintenance of the transit system.
- Ensuring that investment of real property and financial resources are carefully considered with respect to investment risk, financial return, and asset security for the agency.

In their book *Transit Villages in the 21st Century*, Michael Bernick and Robert Cervero wrote, "The sustainable metropolis of the future, rail backers contend, will be transit-oriented metropolis. Nick Patsaouras has for years been one of the chief purveyors of this viewpoint... Patsaouras spent much of the 1980s flying back and forth to Washington, DC, lobbying for funds to build Los Angeles's rail network. Once federal funding was secured, he turned his attention to heading Los Angeles's transit village movement. In 1993, he even ran for mayor of Los Angeles, primarily on a transit-land use platform. 'Linking land use and transportation decisions creates the opportunity to accommodate regional and local growth in transit station areas, where future development can be well-served by the regional transportation system, with minimum impact on existing residential neighborhoods.' Patsaouras wrote in the Planning Report in June of 1993." In another section of the book, Bernick and Cervero wrote, "In California, we are reminded of Sunne McPeak's perseverance in transforming Pleasant Hill from bedroom community into transit village, Rod Diridon's vision of the Silicon Valley and surroundings being populated by trandominiums, and Nick Patsaouras staking his political future by relentlessly pursuing transit-oriented development in the land of 'auto-mobililty,' Los Angeles."

The first joint development project along the rail system was at the Seventh Street Metro Center Station, the Home Savings Tower. It was a partnership between RTD and Home Savings. Home Savings paid for the construction of the station box after difficult and extensive negotiations led by me, RTD General Manager John Dyer, and Home Savings representative Steve Gavin. Gavin, a friend of mine, was a civic leader and member of the Committee of the twenty-five. Unfortunately, there were no joint development projects until the mid-1990s, apart from the RTD headquarters at Union Station.

In the first phase of the Red Line, there was no planning or consideration for joint development opportunities. In 1983, I was a member of the panel for the selection of consultants, planners, architects, and engineers for the first phase of the Red Line. I clearly remember comments during the interviews, such as "We have planned and designed similar projects in Atlanta, Washington, DC, etc. We are experts. We have the best and most experienced designers and planners." Although I had technical knowledge as an electrical engineer in the construction industry, I was not an expert on subway systems, and therefore trusted the so called "experts." Today, anyone can witness these failures.

The Civic Center Station at 1st and Hill streets has a nondescript entrance. The Fourth and Hill streets Station is just a stair adjacent to a hot dog stand and a parking lot. It is close to Grand Central Market, the Bradbury Building, Bunker Hill and Angels Flight, architectural jewels of the city. Pershing Square Station is limited to stairs and an escalator facing the back of a 1920s brick building, instead of facing the historic Biltmore Los Angeles hotel and Pershing Square Park.

There has not been a development at Westlake/McArthur Park Station, although there have been repeated efforts, because the "experts" designed the tunnel to run diagonally thru the property, making it economically unfeasible to build structurally anything above it. Engineers and planners were ignoring long-term development prospects. The Metro Rail design was viewed in very simplistic terms, a way to spend billions of dollars to move people from

Fourth and Hill streets Metro Station.

Pershing Square Metro Station.

Point A to Point B, as Supervisor Edmund Edelman admonished me in one of the Los Angeles County Transportation Commission meetings," Nick our task here is to design a system to transport people, and not city building."

Neil Peterson, the transportation commission's executive director, in an interview with Los Angeles Business Journal, admitted, "We obviously want to get maximum utilization of those sites and we are working hard as we can. We are behind the eight ball." Jack Keyser, Chief Economist for the Los Angeles Economic Development, commented to the Business Journal. "I think they were blowing some big deals because it makes sense for some high-density mixed-use development around Metro Rail stations. Land is scarce and you'll find new mass transit attracts development sooner or later. You have to take advantage of it." The Business Journal in April 1991 ran a story with the headline, "Wrangling delays Metro stations projects." The transportation commission had the lead role in working with private developers to build projects around the stations that would be part of the Metro Rail second phase. I was very vociferous that there had not been communication among the agencies. As a result, there had been conflicting goals and haphazard planning. Los Angeles Community Redevelopment Agency Board member Norm Emerson told the Los Angeles Business Journal, "The Planning Department has not done Metro Rail specific plans, CRA has attempted to plan on a station-by-station basis, and the Rail Construction Corporation, the subsidiary of LACTC overseeing the planning and construction of the second phase of the subway wants to build it as cheap as possible." Judy Weiss, the transportation commission' deputy executive director, acknowledged the problems. "Some of the commissioners, especially Patsaouras, are concerned that we don't lose the opportunity and I share that." Los Angeles Planning Director Melanie Fallon said to the Los Angeles Business Journal, "The City and LACTC are working on details to fund a $1 million study for specific plans and environmental studies around the stations. But so far, the effort has been hampered by the City's budget crunch."

Having observed the failures of the planning around the stations of the first phase of the Red Line, as a member of the transportation commission, I took immediate action. In reviewing the completed drawings designed by the same "experts" for the second phase of the Red Line, and ready to go out to bid, I discovered the same mistakes. I met right away with Peterson, and I demanded that the drawings should not be sent out to bid. Peterson initially resisted because of the costs of the existing design and the delays, but he eventually relented.

In December of 1992, the transportation commission authorized funding in an amount not-to-exceed $36.9 million to design, construct, and secure real estate for Metro Red Line Segment Two. The Design Transit Enhancements were for the Vermont/Beverly; Vermont/Santa Monica; Vermont/Sunset, Hollywood/Western; Hollywood/Vine and Wilshire/Vermont stations. I requested that an urban planner be hired for each of the stations to develop a master plan working with the transportation commission engineers, the city Planning Department and CRA.

At the Wilshire/Vermont Station, in the heart of Koreatown, there was a Bank of America branch. A developer had acquired the property, and he was planning to build the same high-rise office building that was at the southeast corner of Ventura and Sepulveda boulevards in Encino. The entrance to the station was adjacent to the dock area. I sarcastically commented "We will have to hire guides to show the riders the entrance to the station." Moreover, I pointed out that the same office building that may fit in the Valley does not belong in Koreatown.

I recommended that the agency and the developer split the costs to produce a master plan. Once the developer refused, the agency initiated eminent domain proceedings and hired Gruen Associates to do the master plan. At that time a transit agency could use eminent domain only for transit uses and not for development purposes. I was often quoted in the press discussing joint development opportunities and therefore I was deposed as a Board Member in a lawsuit against the transportation commission. The agency was using a capable attorney, Jed Springer, for eminent domain issues. He was successful in that, instead of the

Wilshire/Vermont Complex. Photo: courtesy of Metro

approximately fifteen million dollars the agency had offered to the developer before the trial, the court decided on eleven million dollars.

Springer recounted some of the events. “There was a substantial challenge to the right to take on that property because Joel Sandberg, RTD engineer, testified at a deposition from his notes, that I had been in a meeting with him, and I wanted to have the whole property be acquired so that LACTC could do a master plan and build an appropriate development there. Nothing would really budge me from that. Other people who had attended the same meeting did not have the same recollection. However, they remembered that I had concern over the entrance because it was hidden. It was dangerous because it was right next to one of the alley entrances to the building's loading dock and trash area.” Springer continued: “There was no CEQA [California Environmental Quality Act] clearance for the development on the property. There was only CEQA clearance for the construction of the subway, so I could not use it. If I had said the purpose of the eminent domain is to build a big project, I would have failed. However, I was allowed to argue that a public agency has a right to design a facility so that it is not just merely adequate for its purpose but has a proper site for its features so that people can orient to it, learn it's there, and use it properly, and also so that it is intrinsically useful for transportation. The judge ultimately did uphold the acquisition.” Attorney S, who represented Bank of America, was member of a law firm that represented property owners on eminent domain cases. Developer M was represented by Attorney G. The attorneys' and developer's names are being withheld to avoid embarrassing them.

The transportation commission had offered fifteen million dollars for the property. There was an option agreement under which Developer M would pay Bank of America eight million dollars. That contract was entered into before the transportation commission had its project approved, so that was a valid market transaction. By the time the commission condemned the property, Developer M had invested four million dollars in planning, architecture, and engineering, although he used the same design as the Encino, California project, a mirror image of the building proposed at Wilshire and Vermont. Springer served a subpoena on Developer M and got all canceled checks but did lie about one thing. Developer M had said he was going to sell the property for an astronomical sum of money, and he had a piece of paper signed by a certain person. Springer decided to investigate it. He got the person's name and hired a private investigator to find out who that person was and where he lived. That purported buyer was living in a shack on the roof of a building in Beverly Hills. So, the process server served him up there. That person was deposed, and it was determined that he had no money, and of course it was not a real offer.

Springer asked what his experience in real estate development was and interestingly, other than a building in Iran, he had no experience in the United States. He had never developed any property, and he had never bought any property in the United States. It was obviously a flaky offer, and so they were not able to use that “offer” in evidence. In the end the judge awarded them eleven million dollars.

Springer recounted to me an anecdote. “The case is over and about a year later, I walk into Department Four of the courts and I looked down at the clerk's desk and I'm checking in just for my hearing. I was just chit-chatting with the clerk, and I see this pleading that says Developer M vs Attorney G, who was the attorney for the Wilshire/Vermont case. I said, 'What's that?' The clerk says, 'It's a public document, you can read it.' It was a complaint for malpractice by Developer M against Attorney G for having botched their case against LACTC."

Presently on the site there is a striking mixed-use project with 449 apartments and numerous shops for locals and commuters. There is also a lively public plaza and a Los Angeles Unified School District middle school campus. It has transformed the area devastated after the 1992 riots into a bustling urban hub. (See the section Linking schools to the subway system.) It was developed by Urban Partners.

At Western Avenue and Hollywood Boulevard there was a hamburger stand, an adult bookstore and a motel, and the Hollywood/Western Station was limited by this small piece of land. After a master plan, the agency was able to purchase land south of Hollywood Boulevard for about five hundred thousand dollars, a steal because the real estate market was depressed in the early 1990s and Hollywood was a blighted, undesirable area. Presently a mixed-use project stands there with 120 affordable units and ground floor retail. It was developed by McCormack Baron Salazar.

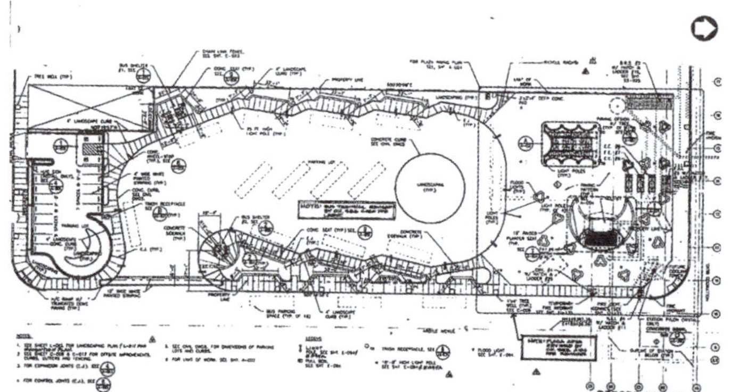

Original plan for the Hollywood and Vine Station. Photo: courtesy of Metro

Hollywood and Vine Complex, W Hotel, Condos and Retail. Photo: courtesy of Metro

The Hollywood/Vine Station, at the world-famous intersection, was limited to a stairway coming up and facing south, not towards the famous Pantages Theatre. It was surrounded by parking lots and blighted buildings. The theater's founder, Alexander Pantages was a Greek American vaudeville impresario and early motion picture producer who built several theaters across the United States and Canada. A master plan for the area bounded by Hollywood Boulevard, Selma Avenue, Vine Street, and Argyle Avenue was developed by a University of California Los Angeles team of architects and planners. Additional property was purchased or acquired through eminent domain procedures from the Nederlander Organization, which owns the Pantages Theatre.

Presently the 300-room W Hotel and 143 condominiums stand over the entrance to the Metro station. Apartments and offices are on Vine Street and the Eastown luxury apartment complex is on Hollywood Boulevard. The project was certainly the catalyst of Hollywood's Renaissance. It was developed by Legacy Partners, Gatehouse Capital Corp. & HEI Hospitality.

At the Hollywood/Highland Station, the entrance was hidden, and I insisted on a more visible location. Meetings took place in Councilwoman Jackie Goldberg's office among the City Council office, the developer and me. I was obstinate in my demand to the point that Goldberg took me aside and told me, "Don't be so tough because the developer may walk away." In the end, the developer, TrizecHahn, which was not going to walk away from such a terrific opportunity, agreed with the transportation commission architect's plan.

There is, finally, acceptance that building around transit stations will help solve our housing crisis. Los Angeles is in the process of updating the City's thirty-five community plans and to rezone land around transit stations.

In 2016, the City of Los Angeles enacted a Transit Oriented Communities incentive program that encourages developers to build taller, denser projects, and with less parking near transit stops if the developer includes affordable housing.

LINKING SCHOOLS TO THE SUBWAY SYSTEM

I was aware that the Los Angeles Unified School District had difficulty in finding land for overcrowded inner city schools. This predicament brought me memories from my high school days when, because of lack of classrooms, the classes had to be split between morning and afternoon hours.

I wondered whether some of the land at the Wilshire/Vermont Station could be used for a school. I was instrumental in MTA acquiring a whole square block of land bordered by Wilshire Boulevard, Vermont Avenue, Sixth Street, and Shato Place for development. I knew that a similar opportunity existed adjacent to North Hollywood station. I called the president of the Los Angeles Unified School District Board of Trustees, Caprice Young, whom I knew when she was financial officer for the transportation commission. We met for breakfast at the Original Pantry Café in downtown Los Angeles. Young loved the idea that schools could be next to rail stations and promised she would follow up with her staff and the other board

Wilshire/Vermont Middle School. Photo: courtesy of Metro

members. However, when she asked an MTA board member to do a joint development with a school, the response was, "Go do your own damn eminent domain!"

Nicolai Ouroussoff, architectural critic for the *Los Angeles Times*, wrote a March of 2001 article with the title, "Next Stop: A truly Connected Community." In the article, Ouroussoff wrote "It has become commonplace for writers to depict Los Angeles's future as a dismal, 'Blade Runner'-like dystopia of ethnic friction and corporate greed. In truth, the greatest threat to the city's future may be the dull minds of its urban thinkers. But a recent proposal to build new schools near two existing Red Line subway stops—one at Vermont Avenue and Wilshire Boulevard, the other on Lankershim Boulevard in North Hollywood—hints at what the city's future might look like if our civic leaders were infected with a sudden dose of creative imagination.

"Conceived by Nick Patsaouras, the plan is intended as a practical—if partial—solution to two seemingly unrelated problems: The LAUSD's desperate search for sites to accommodate the approximately 85 schools it plans to build in the next five years; and the MTA's indecision about what to do with large parcels of undeveloped land surrounding many of its subway portals. But why stop there? It's an encouraging start, as far as it goes. Imagine, for a moment, a much broader urban scheme—one that would link a whole network of new schools to a citywide subway system. The result would be a radical reworking of the civic infrastructure. Knowledge, in effect, would become our new connective tissue.

"What makes the idea compelling is its connection to the city's broader social infrastructure. By linking each school to the subway system, the scheme treats education as a fluid component of everyday life. It evokes both Bill Gates' vision of an Information Age, accessible to all, and the old socialist dream of a 'school without walls.' The subway becomes a mechanized school corridor, the subway cars mobile study halls. Los Angeles, meanwhile, is at crossroads—a moment when its cultural and social infrastructure need to be aggressively reexamined. Congested neighborhoods, overburdened freeways and continuing sprawl are slowly tearing apart the urban fabric. Those distances are not only physical, but they are also psychological. They contribute to a deepening sense of alienation. Such notions could be the basis for a larger public dialogue about the city's future."

The schools were built through persistence, perseverance, and creativity. The school at Wilshire / Vermont Station, established in 2009, is a middle school named Young Oak Kim Academy, with grades six through eight. The school in North Hollywood, established in 2006, is East Valley High School.

An extensive study and panel discussion of "Red Line School District" is included in the LANow volume two, "Shaping a New Vision for downtown Los Angeles." The LA Now project is a collaboration between Art Center, UCLA, and CalArts.

GREENWAYS

Leave the road, take the trails.

—PYTHAGORAS

A Transportation System with Green Spaces | Changing the transportation paradigm went beyond improving pedestrian connections to the returning rail system in Los Angeles County. (See Angels Walk.) This new awareness of transportation alternatives included heightened interests in other non-auto or "non-motorized" methods of transportation in the region. Several independent but crucial elements were gaining political and environmental followings that challenged the disproportionate policy focus on the automobile. Newer immigrants from places not dominated by the automobile questioned the over-reliance on the auto-centric built form and transportation method. Rising concern for the environment, especially air quality, and the different values of newer generations and populations

Announcing first Greenway along Burbank/Chandler rail right-of-way. With Councilmember M. Braude and Supervisor M. Antonovich. Photo: courtesy of Metro

demanded a shift in focus on what transportation in Los Angeles would look like. The new conversations and ideas often trickled up from the local community and often overlapped with the new rail and new focus on the quality of the transportation experience. Metro's public outreach for the rail system designs and acceptance became a public forum for the way to present different transportation options.

I remember fondly the railroad tracks within three hundred feet of where I was born and raised in Athens. My friends and I would walk on the rails or race along the tracks. Every day we would play soccer at a field next to the tracks and, sadly, sometimes we would lose the ball in the racing train.

So, in the late 1980s, when I read articles on greenways, it brought sweet memories and inspired me to add greenways and bike paths into the development of Los Angeles County's rail corridors. The articles described the rising interests in combining greenbelts and parkways as part of urban and suburban changes. The merged elements created the conceptual Greenway that I began to promote within the Southern California Rapid Transit District and the Los Angeles County Transportation Commission. I worked diligently on getting additional support from other members of the two agencies' boards with similar interests.

I announced one of the first efforts to develop a greenway/bikeway along rail rights-of-way in the County in May 1990, while standing in the middle of a dusty rail yard, joined by county Supervisor Michael Antonovich and Los Angeles City Councilman Marvin Braude. We jointly advocated for a fifteen-mile Rails to Trails greenway along the right-of-way between North Hollywood and Canoga Park.

Greenways, especially in Los Angeles, are generically linear corridors that incorporate improved or unimproved "trails" within other regional uses such as the beaches, riverbeds, drainage areas, railroad rights-of-way, or utility corridors. They tended to rely on service roads, pedestrian paths and/or moderate modifications to existing conditions connecting non-motorized access to people, places, and destinations.

The transportation commission was in the process of purchasing the rights-of-way from the Southern Pacific and Santa Fe railroads to expand the Metro Rail and Metrolink systems. I believed that the concept could be applied to other railroad rights-of -way in other parts of the county. Although the initial concept had limited success in bringing attention to the development of expanded bikeways, momentum for these options had started and was also a motivator for other Metro non-motorized transportation improvements.

Greenways and bikeways became integrated into Metro's countywide Transportation Improvement Plans by the mid-1990s as RTD and the transportation commission merged into the Los Angeles County Metropolitan Transportation Authority. As with many of the "new" transportation modes that were evolving in the region, there was often more advocacy and creativity than credibility or funding. Every new advance in transportation technology faced a wall of skeptics, rules, and regulations antagonistic to change. But the effort did plant a seed that has continued to expand Greenway and Bikeway improvements throughout Los Angeles County.

Metro, including its preceding organizations, had a nascent bicycle and pedestrian program in the early 1990s. Both were considered as incidental to the larger regional transportation program and were largely treated as mitigations for, but seldom essential to, the larger regional transportation projects. As of the early 1990s, Metro had set aside three million dollars through its countywide bi-annual Call for Projects program that could be awarded to bicycle and pedestrian projects within the eighty-eight jurisdictions in Los Angeles County. The Metro process was competitive and for the most part received nominal applications for what were largely seen as recreational trails. The state of California, through its Department of Transportation, or Caltrans, had also set aside an additional funding source for pedestrian and bicycle improvements under the Transportation Development Act which minimally provided resources to support connections to transit facilities. Its greatest value was in supporting local traffic engineers' reluctant inclusion of pedestrian and bicycle improvements because the additional funds could be used only for the bicycle and pedestrian elements of street improvements. The additional funds allowed inclusion of the improvements without adding unfunded components to the traffic projects. As with the pedestrian improvements tied to the new rail station environments, the greenways and bikeways movement gained momentum, as the non-auto transportation improvements increased in size and usefulness.

Most public advocates for change were overwhelmingly "on the fringe" of the Los Angeles transportation world. Mayor Tom Bradley and I successfully secured the transportation commission's approval for an urban greenway demonstration project along the Metro Blue Line right-of-way next to the 103rd Street Station in Watts in October 1991. Further, the commission allocated ninety thousand dollars in fiscal year 1991–92 Proposition A Rail Program Development funds to design and construct the project.

The actual construction of the improvements was also dependent on financial commitments from the Los Angeles Community Redevelopment Agency and completion of a State Environmental Enhancement and Mitigation Program grant application by the City of Compton. The Enhancement and Mitigation Program was required to help fully maintain the physical improvements once completed.

On my motion in December 1992, the transportation commission voted to:

1. Adopt a policy to incorporate appropriate urban design/greenway/bikeway elements as interim or adjunct design features of future transportation projects on transportation commission-owned rights-of-way...The projects will provide landscaping and bicycle and pedestrian access within a quarter mile of commission-owned rights-of-way. To accomplish this, it will be necessary to authorize staff to incorporate into each rail project already underway and each candidate rail project a separate budgetary line item of up to 1 percent of project cost for greenway/bikeway/urban design enhancements.
2. Authorize staff to issue three Request for Proposals for feasibility studies and conceptual designs of greenway/bikeway/urban design projects for the Alla Branch, West Santa Ana Branch and Azusa Spur.

At the same meeting, the transportation commission approved the Northeast San Fernando Valley Greenway's application for State funds from fiscal year 1993–94 under the Environmental Enhancement and Mitigation Program. In February 1993 Metro issued a white paper on "Urban Greenways Program."

In December 1995, Metro adopted the 8.4 miles long West Santa Ana Branch Railroad right-of-way feasibility study and comprehensive plan.

Recreational bikeways were not new to Los Angeles County, having existed since the early 1900s. Two of note were the Horace Dobbins Bikeway between Pasadena and downtown Los Angeles and the Strand along the beach in Santa Monica/Venice. Horace Dobbins, while he was the mayor of Pasadena in the late 1890s, proposed a nine-mile elevated toll bikeway along Arroyo Seco Parkway. The project came to a halt once the early automobiles demonstrated their utility. The lumber acquired to build the first portions of the elevated bikeway had become so valuable that the sections already built were torn down and the lumber sold at a profit. What remains of the concept is an at-grade, two-and-a-half-mile Arroyo Seco concrete bikeway along the Arroyo Seco Parkway drainage area located primarily along the original bikeway right-of-way.

The more successful bikeway effort started along the beaches in the early 1900s when wood planking was laid on the sand parallel to the shoreline in Venice, Manhattan, Hermosa, and Santa Monica along the Santa Monica Bay. At best, the efforts began as fragmented pathways that haphazardly connected to other fragments of walkways that aided access along the beach. Over time, the wooden and temporary segments were replaced with asphalt and concrete. Multiple beach cities, the Los Angeles County Department of Beaches and Harbors, the state of California, and some private owners worked to complete a cohesive continuous twenty-two-mile path from Will Rogers State Beach to Torrance County Beach. Segments were developed separately and had various names over the years including: the Beach Bike Path, the Coastal Bike Trail, The Strand, or the South Bay Bicycle Trail. Eventually, the combined and connected segments were dedicated in 2006 by state Sen. Sheila Kuehl as the Marvin Braude Bike Trail for the long-time Los Angeles City Council member after his death in 2005. Braude was known as a champion of bike paths and advocated for protecting the open space and trails of the Santa Monica Mountains.

The combined twenty-two-mile plus paved trail is one of the nation's more successful bikeways/linear parks with an estimated ten thousand daily users during good weather and one hundred thousand-plus users during peak summer weekends. The crowded trails on summer weekends have made bicycling difficult as the slower moving strollers, roller skaters, pedestrians, and street performers limit bicycle movements and speeds on the path. The focus is not on the success of the beach path, but the obvious lack of similar linear parks and similar successes in other parts of the county and how the rail and transit programs integrated active transportation improvements as part of regional transportation capital improvements. Not every community had a world class beach to work with, and not everyone in Los Angeles could afford to live near or access the beach.

In 1996, a promising fifty-one-mile greenway was proposed along the Los Angeles River through the San Fernando Valley to Long Beach and the Pacific Ocean. It would pass through thirteen cities and numerous jurisdictions. In 2005, the Los Angeles City Council approved the city's thirty-two-mile section of the greenway. The greenway moved forward slowly because of multiple jurisdictions along the fifty-one-mile path, long environmental reviews, the need to cobble together multiple funding sources and the awarding of construction contract for fragmented sections.

The city and county, in cooperation with the US Army Corps of Engineers, had by 2017 completed hike-and-bike trails along twelve miles of the thirty-two miles of the LA River through Los Angeles. In May 2017, county Supervisor Kathryn Barger announced an initiative to transform flood control channels, washes, and creeks in the San Gabriel Valley into bikeable and pedestrian-friendly networks. In June 2017, county Supervisor Zev Yaroslavsky dedicated a half-mile greenway that provided a missing link for a four-mile walk on the north bank of the Los Angeles River in Studio City.

Cyclists in Los Angeles historically had minimal opportunity to voice their support for new infrastructure and facilities and were for the most considered transportation "outliers." In the early 1990s, the cycling demographics split between the predominately affluent males ages eighteen to forty-five who rode for health and environmental reasons, and the poorer new generation immigrants who rode because of financial and practical necessity. Seventy-five percent of riders were male in the 1990s. The predominance of male riders was largely associated with the perception that trails and bicycling were inherently unsafe in Los Angeles County.

Finding political advocates for such a disparate group of users willing to chase scarce transportation dollars would not be easy. More so, when regional bicycle trips seldom exceeded 1 percent of the region's travel, despite the enthusiasm from avid bicyclists such as actor Ed Begley, Jr., who, despite a prolific career that includes hundreds of films, television shows, and stage performances that have earned him Primetime Emmy and Golden Globe award nominations, has also been an environmental activist all his adult life. I have known Begley for many years and have admired his dedication to environmental issues. In April 1990, when I was on the RTD, Begley was chairman for the American Public Transportation Association National Event, Transit Appreciation Day.

"I very happily declare myself a lifelong bike rider. I rode a bike to and from school as a young man, as well as using it to generate income with my paper route. After the first Earth Day in 1970, I renewed my love of bike riding, and along with my bus pass, my bicycle got me around for the many years that I did not have a car. I quickly realized that the bicycle is the most energy efficient form of ground transportation man has ever known. There is no other form of transportation that can get you 40 miles on a bowl of rice and an ear of corn. But a bicycle can do just that. With a modest amount of food as your fuel source, you can travel a great distance on a bicycle." —ED BEGEY, JR.

I relentlessly continued to empower Metro pedestrian and bicycle planning staff to think outside the box—sometimes way outside the box. My interests and advocacy gave license to other professionals who advocated for improved non-motorized infrastructure and, once again, given the license to create something new, the opportunity and support was exploited Once Metro transportation staff realized they had political support for such improvements, they began presenting the transportation case for improved bicycling infrastructure. In perspective, bicycle travel increased from 0.6 percent in 1990 to 1 percent of regional household trips by 2020, a 65 percent increase from 1990 to 2020. The increase reflects the continuous addition of bicycle infrastructure during the same period and the increased perception of safety along more prominent greenways near transit corridors.

The first step was to recognize bicycling as a legitimate means of regional transportation worthy of investment. The Metro Board had already passed several motions by 1995 to "conceptualize" greenways in various areas of the county, most along rail rights-of-way owned by Metro or along existing flood control channels and river shed areas. Most previously segmented bicycle/greenway improvements were perceived as local concerns fitting under parks and recreation improvements. Metro's transportation interests and Board actions shifted the transportation paradigm.

Most of the household trips in Los Angeles were less than five miles and could complement bicycle use. A significant percentage of bicyclists were from poorer households without the means to buy a car, and especially going to destinations poorly served by transit. In short, a large percentage of bicyclists relied on the bicycle infrastructure to get to work and increasing bicycling could be one method to reduce regional traffic and demand. The problem was that the majority of bicycle supporting infrastructure was in more affluent areas and often identified as recreational amenities.

The second concern was the fragmentation of bicycle improvements. Before multiple beach bike paths were coalesced into the greater twenty-two-mile Marvin Braude Bike Trail, there were no other extended bike "roads" in the Los Angeles area adjacent to denser populations. There were some paved trails, including service roads and park improvements along the area's flood control channels, rivers, and reservoirs—again largely presumed to be recreational. The third essential issue arose from an increasing acknowledgement of the value of "active transportation" and the beneficial health outcomes from a successful program. Documenting the poor health consequences and outcomes resulting from poor urban and suburban environments was thought to be a difficult task.

During the late 1990s Metro's planning staff began to incorporate findings on active transportation's effects on health and increasing non-motorized access to transit. Metro had the means and funding to help build street and pedestrian improvements near transit, but still needed to convince others in the transportation world that such investments were worthy. One clear voice on health and transportation came from University of California, Los Angeles, professor Dr. Richard Jackson of the UCLA Fielding School of Public Health.

Metro staff worked with the UCLA/Fielding School of Public Health, the Community Redevelopment Agency, and, eventually, the Los Angeles County of Department of Public Health to move the study of built environments on public health to actual changes to the built environment. These groups had documented that need. Metro had the money to fund the improvements.

Independent of Metro's interest, Jackson was in the process of detailing the health effects of the quality and design of a child's physical environment. His advocacy identified how the built environment can cause or prevent illness, disability, and injury; therefore, a high-quality environment is essential for children to achieve optimal health and development. Although pediatricians are accustomed to thinking about health hazards from toxic exposures, much less attention has been given to the potential for adverse effects from poor built environments, such as poor-quality housing and haphazard land use, poor transportation, and poor community planning. Children had become more and more isolated from natural environments when compared with the time they spent indoors and in poorly laid out hardscape neighborhoods. The Metro board and my advocacy for greenways as an improvement to the community and improved access to transit could also show a documentable improvement to public health.

Jackson's later work along with the studies from the Los Angeles County Department of Public health opined that each hour spent in a car per day is associated with a 6 percent increase in the risk of obesity, while any additional kilometer walked per day is associated with a 5 percent decrease in risk of obesity. People who use public transit are two to four times more likely to achieve daily physical activity recommendations as compared with sedentary drivers (or passengers). Simply using transit (and the related walking required) was healthier than spending time in traffic.

Lost time in traffic could otherwise be spent engaging in activities such as exercising, socializing, cooking, and volunteering, thus promoting social capital, and providing a range of health benefits. Jackson's studies recognized that more than 30 percent of the population does not drive, either because of age, income, or disability, and highlighted that the region was developed for automobiles rather than pedestrians. His work recognized that investments in subway, bus, and light rail connecting pedestrian and bicycle access have begun to turn this around. For the Metro, simply getting more people to walk, use transit and drive less was a great regional transportation goal. For Jackson it was a means to add years to the average life span.

The partnership of health researchers and Metro's expanding infrastructure led to tangible increases in more physically active modes of transportation. One tangible result was that bicycle travel increased from 0.6 percent in 1990 to 1 percent of regional household trips by 2020, a 65 percent increase. The increase reflects the continuous addition of bicycle infrastructure during the same period and the increased perception of safety along more prominent greenways near transit corridors.

My advocacy did not end with greenways. I had separately and actively advocated and participated in the Transit Oriented Developments that further extended the thoughtful built environment into the transportation system thinking. Jackson highlighted in his later research that there are positive signs for future sustainable development in the region, including pockets of "smart growth," and commitments to create enhanced bicycle infrastructure in the region that supported a healthier built form. Jackson's later research highlights the contributions the expanding transit system had to providing additional options for increasing active populations.

This outcome cannot be overstated. Other researchers along with UCLA Fielding School of Public Health findings confirmed that increasing park acreage has the potential to increase life expectancy for Los Angeles County residents in areas that have less tree cover or lower vegetation levels than the County median. One clear finding was that Los Angeles County census tracts with less tree cover were typically "park poor," disproportionately low income, and primarily home to people of color. Further, real estate valuation consistently recognizes that the presence of park amenities, trails, and bikeways translates to higher real estate values. This continued a cycle in which health benefitting amenities increase home values and then economic forces push the relocation of poorer populations to areas of lesser quality environmental amenities. The outcome is decreased life expectancy within those relocated populations.

Studies have shown that exposure to green spaces can fight depression, reduce attention-deficit/hyperactivity disorder symptoms in children, and improve cognitive development and brain function-- (UCLA Fielding School of Public Health) (https://healthyclimatesolutions.org/2020/11/20/parks-and-green-spaces-improve-community-health-and-reduce-health-inequalities/)

A study by the Los Angeles County Department of Public Health found that areas with less park space per capita have higher rates of premature mortality from cardiovascular disease and diabetes, and higher prevalence of eating- and physical activity-related chronic illness among children. And, as shown by recent UCLA research, access to parks and green spaces may even increase life expectancy. (https://preventioninstitute.org/sites/default/files/uploads/PI_Park_Equity_Policy_Brief.pdf)

The leading cause of death in Los Angeles County in 2019 was coronary heart disease, accounting for 11,075 (17.2 percent) of the 64,517 total deaths among county residents. (http://publichealth.lacounty.gov/epi/docs/2019 Mortality_Report_FINAL_052022.pdf)

The mortality rate for coronary heart disease in Los Angeles County decreased 29 percent from 2010 to 2019. There are lots of other factors that may have contributed to this decrease, but one that stands out is the changing built form along the major transit corridors and a greater advocacy for recognizing health consequences inherit in our lifestyle. Even among the same neighborhood populations, those who used transit (and walked) were two to four times less likely to suffer coronary heart disease or diabetes.

This outcome becomes more apparent when comparing the health disparities between communities. The South Los Angeles Health Equity Scorecard was the result of the efforts of the Community Health Councils formed in 1992 and the Coalition of Health and Justice founded in 2004 with a mission to improve health, health education and improving health access. The Scorecard explored the relative availability of Physical Activity Options between different neighborhoods based on eighteen categories. What stood out in the study was the stark contrast between the physical environment resources between South Los Angeles and the overall Los Angeles County, with an even greater contrast with wealthier households in West Los Angeles.

Coronary heart disease mortality was the highest among Black men (205 deaths per 100,000) and the lowest was among Asian females (forty-nine deaths per 100,000) in 2019. The Scorecard was designed to help recognize negative outcomes from entrenched policies that hindered the revitalization of South Los Angeles and highlighted the lack of infrastructure supporting active transportation. This measure also takes unwalkable or

CATEGORY	SOUTH LA	WEST LA	DISPARITY (Percentage points)
Healthcare Environment Resources	-43%	+72%	115
Healthcare Facilities	-28%	59%	87
Healthcare Workforce	-76%	182%	258
Healthcare Financing	-65%	22%	87
Healthcare Coverage	-30%	38%	68
Primary & Preventive Care Access	-34%	27%	61
Primary & Preventive Care Utilization	-24%	103%	127
Physical Environment Resources	-43%	+42%	85
Nutrition	-106%	101%	207
Physical Activity Options	-55%	24%	79
Public Safety	-17%	7%	24
Housing	-40%	16%	56
Schools	-43%	63%	106
Air & Land	5%	39%	34

(Park, Annie & Watson, Nancy & Galloway-Gilliam, Lark. (2016). South LA Health Equity Scorecard. 10.13140/RG.2.1.1654.8887).

Disparities in Healthcare and Physical Environment Resources: South LA and West LA Compared to LA County. Source: Park, Annie & Watson, Nancy & Galloway-Gilliam, Lark (2016).

inaccessible areas into consideration when assessing the relationship between built form and health problems.

The Scorecard showed a disparity of 79 percentage points in availability of Physical Activity Options between South Los Angeles and West Los Angeles. The willingness of non-automobile travelers—distance walkers, bicyclists, transit riders, and the general public—is greatly diminished without the supporting greenway/park amenities (Journal of Internal Medicine in 2007; American Journal of Preventive Medicine in 2006, 2008). When the physical environment encouraged walking, bicycling or other non-motorized alternatives, more physical activity followed. These factors in built form may play a role in the disparities in health outcomes between South Los Angeles and other areas of Los Angeles.

The Scorecard was developed at the same time Metro was building the Expo Line Greenway in South Los Angeles parallel to or connecting with the new Expo Light Rail Line. The Expo Greenway would ultimately connect to the Marvin Braude Bike Trail along the Beach and provide significant access to the coastal recreation amenities. Inequality in the health of South Los Angeles had become a condition that went beyond the limits of any specific city policy and necessitated collaboration and cooperation at all levels of government and across multiple jurisdictions.

One of the ways to address this environmental disparity is if the census tracts in Los Angeles County with park deficits and low tree canopy levels had an increase in park acreage up to the median for Los Angeles County tracts (about fifty-four acres within a two-mile radius of each census tract). The assumption is that Los Angeles County would probably see considerable life expectancy gains for each resident living in those improved tracts. Approximately fifty-four acres of greenway space is added to the adjacent communities for every seven miles of greenway developed. Although this was not the reason for advocating for greenways, there was an intrinsic belief from me and other political leaders that improving the quality of the environment would also improve the quality of life. The studies confirmed that the park and greenway additions added much higher levels of benefits than expected. Most new light rail lines and the Bus Rapid Transit corridors with greenways or improved bikeways developed since the 1990s traveled through or remarkably close to a majority of the City of Los Angeles's lower income census tracts.

The Tree People organization under the leadership of Andy Lipkis partnered with the county transportation commission to provide equipment and funds to schools as part of the Greenways Program. The program included planting tree seeds for an on-campus nursery. The trees grown at the schools were used to beautify transportation rights-of-way in low-income areas.

"Physical activity is the closest thing we have to a wonder drug. Being active is one of the most important things people of all ages, sizes, and shapes can do to improve their health." - Dr. Thomas Frieden Director of the Centers for Disease Control and Prevention.

Nothing in the process happened very fast, but it did happen. Metro ultimately built, or partnered in, the building of some forty miles of greenways or traffic separated Class 1 bikeways throughout Los Angeles County since my initial efforts to create greenways in 1990. Combining different segments of the coastal bikeway into the twenty-two mile Marvin Braude Bike Trail, advocating for a "rails to trails" policy and masterplans, laying out the fifty-one mile Los Angeles River Bikeway, and ultimately building out greenway/bikeways along Metro's Expo, Orange and Blue line rights-of-ways integrated into other county areas were initiated by the forward thinking and political advocacy of a few "dreamers" willing to step outside the accepted practices of the past. Metro frequently contributed funding for many more miles that were built in the water shed and river channel areas of the county as well. This is separate from the approximately five hundred miles of bike routes or striped bike lanes throughout the county that have been added during the same period.

One clear outcome from the greenway efforts has been the measurable improvement to the quality of life and health of multiple communities that historically suffered from poor urban form. The improvements mentioned here are just a start, and a slow one at that, but a far cry from the conditions that existed in the early 1990s.

William Fain of Johnson Fain, an architecture, planning and interior design firm, developed in the early 1990s a plan detailing existing parks and the overall structure of the city, both current and planned. He mapped multi-family housing, transit rights-of-way and the stations and routes of the subway, light rail and commuter rail lines. The plan revealed a grid of open space formed by unused rights-of-way, existing and proposed transit lines, natural washes, and flood control areas. "Soon mass transit will occupy many of these areas, but there is a larger potential for what has come to be called greenway," Fain said. Fain and his team have sketched a city tied together not just by freeways but also by stands of eucalyptus trees and hedge rows that conjure up images of early Los Angeles, of arroyos, farms and orchards. These greenways connecting a vast and undifferentiated landscape are "a chance to reinvent the city," Fain said. "There would be a chance to work together, to create a true garden -city based on a new kind of social contract, an agreement to use the city together," he added.

In 2010, seventy-four miles of bike lanes were completed in Los Angeles. In March 2011, the Los Angeles City Council approved the 1,680-mile bicycle master plan. A 2011, LA County Bike Coalition Survey found that bicycle ridership doubled where bike lanes were built. In 2012, the League of American Bicyclists for the first time put Los Angeles on its list of Bike Friendly Communities.

Mayor Garcetti launched LA's Green New Deal in 2019 calling for reducing the number of miles we travel in cars by 40 percent per person by 2035. That goal will be accomplished in part by supporting walking, biking, and transit-oriented development.

In August of 2023, Metro provided sixty million dollars for the design and construction of approximately thirteen miles of new twelve-foot-wide bikeway and greenway along the Los Angeles River in the San Fernando Valley that fill in gaps in the Valley River bikeway, between Vanalden Avenue to the west and Forest Lawn Drive/Zoo Drive to the east. The improvements will also include pedestrian walking paths, decorative fencing and gates, roadway crossing, pet waste stations, drinking fountains, lighting, operational and directional signage, site furnishings, educational interpretive elements, landscaping and irrigation.

CicLAvia

Adonia Lugo, a UC Irvine doctoral student, had developed the name CicLAvia and the concept for a Los Angeles event based on the Ciclovias of Bogota, Columbia. Her CicLAvia partner Aaron Paley, a street festival planner, made a presentation in 2009 to David Freeman, general manager of Los Angeles Department of Water and Power and Romel Pascual, Los Angeles deputy mayor for energy and environment. There was interest, but unsurprisingly no rush to implement the program.

On July 17, 2010, Mayor Antonio Villaraigosa and his police bodyguard were riding their bicycles in the bike lane of Venice Boulevard, when a taxicab pulled in front of the mayor forcing him to hit the brakes, fall and break his elbow. A couple of days later, according to Borja Leon, deputy for transportation, the mayor told his staff, "Let's use this as a teachable moment."

After Villaraigosa saw a Ciclovia event in Mexico City, and because of his accident, the first CicLAvia event was held Sunday, October 10, 2010. A stretch of streets from East Hollywood through downtown Los Angeles into Boyle Heights was temporarily closed to motor vehicles, and opened for people to bike, skate, run, stroll or ride a scooter. More than one hundred thousand people turned out. Villaraigosa participated in every CicLAvia during his administration. Mayor Eric Garcetti continued the tradition.

EXPOSITION (E) LINE

The San Fernando Valley has a busway, and the Westside of Los Angeles has a light rail line. One should ask, why?

In the Valley there was no consensus, the political leaders were fighting one another. Los Angeles County Supervisor Michael Antonovich was championing a monorail along the 101 Freeway while all the other politicians were ganging up against him. My proposal of a subway along Ventura Boulevard was dismissed out of hand. Homeowner groups had different opinions. The Orthodox Jewish community was against anything along the Southern Pacific Railroad Burbank branch and Chandler Boulevard right-of-way, and the politicians couldn't make up their minds, introducing contradicting legislation to be pulled back later. The Expo Line also had opposition, but a well-organized group, Friends 4 Expo Transit, with dedicated leaders such as Darrell Clarke, was able to overcome the objections of homeowners' groups and politicians.

In September 1989, there was a community meeting at the Saint Timothy Church auditorium with the Los Angeles County Transportation Commission Executive Director Neil Peterson present. The forum was sponsored by the Cheviot Hills Homeowners Association and other groups vehemently opposed to a Westside light-rail line. According to Peterson, Los Angeles City Councilman Zev Yaroslavsky told him, "You have unleashed in this area a political monster." Yaroslavsky was referring to Peterson's negotiations to purchase from billionaire businessperson Philip Anschutz 76.5 miles of the Southern Pacific Railroad rights-of-ways that included the Exposition Boulevard right-of-way.

University of California, Los Angeles, Professor Martin Wachs joined Yaroslavsky, Councilman Nate Holden and Sara Berman, president of the West of Westwood homeowners Association, in opposing a light rail and supporting a busway. In an interview with the Planning Report, Yaroslavsky said, "The Exposition Boulevard corridor does not meet the West Los Angeles community's need for transit services. Therefore, the right-of-way should not be purchased in a way that requires its use for rail. Surface light rail in residential areas is not environmentally sound. Surface light rail disrupts cross traffic; the cost of mitigation is enormous and would quickly erode the savings advantage of a surface line."

Jon Wiener, a historian and writer, was quoted in the Los Angeles Reader as saying, "There is another word for their position. I'd call it racism. They're preoccupied with the possibility that non-white kids will get off the train in their neighborhood and lower their property values."

I heard the same concerns voiced when the Red Line was planned. Yaroslavsky told the *Los Angeles Times*, "It was a preposterous notion to envision commuters flocking through already congested single family residential areas to leave their cars in giant park-and-ride lots near the proposed rail line."

But even the busway could not get traction. On March 7, 1991, I proposed an electrified busway. The cost was estimated at $250 million, plus $50 million for the electrification of the buses. County Supervisor Kenneth Hahn joined me in support of a busway, saying, "An electrified busway from Santa Monica via Exposition Boulevard will not only ease traffic congestion but will improve the air quality." My plan also called for greenbelts. The bus system would begin in the City of Santa Monica at Pacific Street and travel east on Venice Boulevard. From Robertson Boulevard to Figueroa Street, the line would cut back onto the right-of-way to Exposition, where a station would link the busway with the Harbor Transitway and the Metro Blue Line. The busway would bypass the Rancho Park neighborhood that had opposed the light rail, and the strip of land through Rancho Park would be converted to a jogging and bicycle path and greenbelt.

Expo Busway Proposal: with Alan Pegg, Gary Spivack, Art Leahy, and Albert Perdon. Photo: courtesy of Metro

The benefit of a busway would be that one could operate local service or a variety of express lines that fan out to serve surrounding communities such as Century City, the University of California, Westwood, Santa Monica, and Los Angeles International Airport. The buses would get power from overhead electrical cables like those that once energized the old "Red Car" line. The project could be completed in three years.

When the 1994 Northridge quake took out sections of the 10 Freeway, the busway that I proposed was seriously considered. However, California Gov. Pete Wilson suspended all the California Department of Transportation red tape, rules, and regulations for the freeway repairs. In addition, the state offered a bonus to the contractor if it finished the project early. The freeway was repaired and open to vehicles at full capacity within three months.

Friends 4 Expo Transit was formed around 1989 to ensure that Expo had a light rail rather than a busway. The group was co-chaired by Darrell Clarke. The group was formed to counter the Cheviot Hills and Rancho Park opposition to light rail. The activity around Expo went dormant for a few years due to budget woes at the transportation commission. However, they organized a grass roots campaign to inform the public of the benefits of light rail. They held community forums, prepared graphs, economic analyses and ridership projections.

Meanwhile, the transportation commission bought the Exposition Boulevard right-of-way, and in 1998 the bus rapid transit idea was getting positive response from the Los Angeles County Metropolitan Transportation Authority. In fact, during an MTA meeting in 2000, Jaime de la Vega, an appointee of Los Angeles Mayor Richard Riordan, moved that bus rapid transit be the only alternative. Director John Fasana amended the motion to include light rail. The *Los Angeles Times* quoted Yaroslavsky as saying at the MTA meeting, "Why punish ourselves on a route that has so many problems." The board voted eleven to one to study Yaroslavsky's proposed alternative along Venice Boulevard.

The task then before the Friends 4 Expo Transit was to kill the busway option. Fortuitously, Santa Monica City Councilmember Pam O' Connor, a staunch supporter of light rail, won a seat on the MTA board and was successful in convincing the MTA Board to approve a light rail line.

Politics and the poor economy put the brakes once again to the Expo Line. In 2004, state legislation created the Exposition Metro Line Construction Authority to build the project. The environmental review was finished in 2005. On September 29, 2006, with funds secured for the first phase of the project from downtown Los Angeles to Culver City, a groundbreaking took place.

The main reason the Westside got a light rail, and the Valley got a busway was the advocacy of the dedicated, committed and organized group, Friends 4 Expo Transit which neutralized the unreasonable opposition of Cheviot Hills and Rancho Park. Friends 4 Expo Transit did not "stop the project but helped to build it." In addition, there was strong political leadership, such as state Sen. Diane Watson, Santa Monica Councilmember O'Connor, and Los Angeles Mayor Antonio Villaraigosa, who worked smartly and diligently to secure funding and shepherd the project through the halls of power and checkmate the political opposition.

ORANGE (G) LINE

The San Fernando Valley was included in the thirteen-corridor map the Los Angeles County Transportation Commission had approved to gain county-wide support for Los Angeles County Supervisor Kenneth Hahn's Proposition A, the half-cent sales tax approved by the voters on November 4,1980.

The commission had purchased the rights-of-way along the former Southern Pacific Railroad Burbank-branch and Chandler Boulevard in 1990 with the intent of building a light rail line. In the early 1990s, the Los Angeles County Metropolitan Transportation Authority (the successor of the transportation commission) had designated the San Fernando Valley East-West corridor as one of the six high-priority transit corridors. While other parts of the county got their subway or light rail lines, the Burbank-Chandler line, known as the Orange Line, did not open until 2005. It has been viewed as "a busway built on a rail bed, the last and cheapest option." Again, the Valley was left holding the short end of the stick!

The Blue Line broke ground in 1985 and opened in 1990. The first leg of the Red Line broke ground in 1986, opened in 1993, and was completed in 2000. The Green Line opened in 1995. The Gold line to Pasadena opened in 2003. The Orange Line opened in 2005.

There were endless debates, hearings, transportation commission meetings, Los Angeles City Council votes, vocal self- proclaimed community leaders supporting or opposing one option or another, demagogues, and politicians testing the political winds and changing their votes many times over. After \$2.5million in studies, officials still by 1991 could not agree on where the line should go; which areas and people should be served; whether the system should be above ground, underground, or even in the Los Angeles River channel; or whether the systems should have wheels, hang from elevated rails, or float on a magnetic field.

As a result, money dried up and, with Los Angeles County Supervisor Zev Yaroslavsky's Proposition A in 1998 to cut off funding for a potential subway line in the corridor and state Senator Alan Robbins's Senate Bill 211 that prohibited light rail, the Valley got a busway that cost \$400 million. It was viewed as a Band Aid because the San Fernando Valley was promised the line would be converted to light rail, a promise that has been projected to be fulfilled in 2050! True, the line fell victim to conflicting plans and agenda, but the question that should have been asked from the beginning by the planners and decision makers: Why is the San Fernando Valley Transit Line limited to the Southern Pacific Railroad right-of-way? Just because the transportation commission purchased the rights-of-way throughout Los

Angeles County from the railroads, and the Burbank- Chandler right-of-way was included in the package.

The right-of-way goes through predominantly residential areas and naturally one would expect fierce opposition from the homeowners. The premise that the right-of-way exists, therefore, we should build a transit line there, is not valid. It could be used instead for a linear park / promenade, like the High Line in New York's hybrid public space, where visitors experience nature, art, and design. The High Line is a public park built on an abandoned freight rail line. Based on residential and commercial density, the ideal routes for a transit line in the San Fernando Valley are along the 101 Freeway and Ventura Boulevard. Anyone traveling along those routes any time of the day, any day of the week will attest that the traffic is a nightmare.

The local Orthodox Jewish community resisted an above-ground line along the Burbank-Chandler right-of-way because Shabbat prohibits driving from sundown Friday through Saturday, and therefore those going to the synagogue must walk and would be exposed to danger by crossing the line on foot. In response, Robbins, a political opportunist, introduced SB-211 in 1991 that prohibited "any form of rail transit other than deep bore subway located at least twenty-five feet below ground." It was signed by California Governor Pete Wilson in June 1991.

Instead of joining forces to lobby the federal and state government for funding, the Valley's political leaders, business community and homeowners' groups spent years fighting among themselves. In fact, in October 1994, Councilman Yaroslavsky had successfully introduced a motion to seek federal funding to be matched with the $600 million to $800 million available from the half-cent sales tax funds from Proposition A for a subway.

I had written an op-ed article in the Los Angeles Daily News on January 29, 1990, "Ventura Boulevard subway is the only cost-effective choice," outlining the benefits of a Ventura Boulevard subway including higher ridership, cost effectiveness, and multimillion-joint developments with mixed-income housing, as has been done along the Red Line, generating funding resources to operate the system.

In January 1987, the transportation commission's staff had narrowed the light-rail routes to three: one along Chandler Boulevard, which had been opposed by area homeowners; the second along Victory Boulevard that would be elevated east of the San Diego Freeway and at street level west of the freeway; and the third from the southern end of Burbank-Glendale-Pasadena Airport across the Valley diagonally to Chatsworth. The commission's Rapid Transit Committee considered four others, along Sherman Way, Ventura Boulevard, the 101 Freeway, and the Los Angeles River flood control channel. Senator Robbins and state Assemblyman Tom Bane in August 1987, assured a crowd at St. Charles Catholic Church in North Hollywood that "the Legislature will promptly pass their bill incorporating a trolley moratorium."

On February 28, 1988, the transportation commission approved the environmental impact report for an east-west rail transit line crossing the Valley. The commissioners selected a combination subway-aerial alignment on the Southern Pacific Burbank Branch as the preferred alternative.

In a presentation to Antonovich in February 1988, the TGI group, a subsidiary of the Canadian business jet maker Bombardier Inc., stated, "The physical characteristics of the TGI monorail allow it to productively use freeway and aerial rights of way, thereby minimizing the impacts to the Valley sensitive residential neighborhoods. The conceptual construction cost estimate for the entire twenty-six-mile line from downtown to Canoga Park is $715 million, excluding right-of way acquisition." As a result, the Supervisor was successful in persuading the transportation commission to authorize a complete preliminary engineering to establish budget, timing, and real estate issues. I had taken Mayor Richard Riordan, Supervisor Antonovich, and Antonovich's assistant transportation deputy, Habib Balian, to architect Frank Gehry's office to view designs of the aerial stations to address and alleviate aesthetic concerns.

On August 26, 1988, Yaroslavsky who was then on the Los Angeles City Council, and fellow member Michael Woo proposed that the Council go on record declaring that, "all rail transit construction in residential areas in the San Fernando Valley shall be in subway configuration, and this action should not be construed as an endorsement of at grade or elevated technology along residentially zoned portions of any of proposed routes."

In 1990, Los Angeles County Supervisor Michael Antonovich had proposed that a monorail be built along the median of the 101 Freeway. He placed an advisory ballot measure on the June election ballot. Forty-eight percent of voters supported a monorail, 21 percent favored light rail, 10 percent were for a subway, and 20 percent wanted no rail. Contrary to expectations, there were many precincts along the freeway where voters were supportive of a freeway alignment.

In February 1990, a transportation commission transit committee endorsed an extension of the Metro Rail subway, rejected a light rail line, and left open the question of whether a monorail should be built along the 101 Freeway. Christine Reed, a transportation commission member, said, "I don't see any other need to fool around with the other alternatives," voicing her support of the subway "as much as I like light rail, it does not appear to be an alternative worth pursuing in the Valley."

Jackie Bacharach, another transportation commission member, said, "If we are going to put a subway in the Valley, where are we going to put it? We've never looked thoroughly at all subway alternatives." Another decision maker in addition to Antonovich had decoupled the Southern Pacific Railroad right-of-way and where a transit line belongs based on its merits.

In the 1993 mayoral race, Los Angeles City Councilman Michael Woo was in favor of the Burbank-Chandler subway line, while his chief rival, Richard Riordan, was in favor of the elevated line along the 101 Freeway. Riordan said, "I am in favor of the monorail line because studies indicate it will save $700 million. Unless other studies contradict that, monorail makes the most fiscal sense."

In 1993, MTA had received bids for design-build-maintain-operate Valley Lines, one on the 101 Freeway and one on the Burbank / Chandler route. The private sector had invested several hundred thousand dollars and secured financing, but at his first meeting as MTA Chief Executive Officer, Frank White closed the boxes containing the bids and they were never opened to see what the bids were. There were eight bids for both lines.

In June 1994, Councilman Yaroslavsky and County Supervisor Edmund Edelman advocated a plan to build a mostly underground rail line that would begin at the Metro Rail terminus in North Hollywood and parallel Burbank and Chandler Boulevards to Woodland Hills. However, this was a very expensive plan because it meant that the subway extension could not both stop at Chandler and make an immediate westward bend to the Southern Pacific right-of-way based on the minimum turning radius. The resulting subway loop required to get back to the right-of-way would have a subway section under houses. The cost of this loop was close to $300 million.

On October 26, 1994, the MTA on Riordan`s motion, voted to approve a subway option from Universal City to Canoga Park along Burbank and Chandler boulevards on Riordan's motion. The vote was eight to five, with Riordan and his appointees in the majority. Riordan's motion stated that the MTA board initiate a Major Investment Study, Draft Environmental Impact Statement, and Supplemental Environmental Impact Report for the Southern Pacific Railroad Burbank Branch alignment from North Hollywood to the San Diego Freeway. It included reviews of non-deep bore subway construction, open air or skylight subway station design. The night before the vote, according to Habib Balian, then Antonovich's assistant transportation deputy, Riordan, accompanied by his then chief of staff, William Ouchi, had gone to Antonovich's office and told him he was withdrawing his support. (The mayor controls four votes on the MTA Board).

Thus, Antonovich's light rail along the 101 Freeway from Union Station to Canoga Park was killed. Riordan had changed his mind because Yaroslavsky had successfully introduced a motion opposing the light rail line and listening to the NIMBY voices such as those of Jerry Silver, president of Homeowners of Encino, Tarzana Property Owners Association and Encino Property Owners Association, and others with concerns such as, "appearance, noise, station congestion, potential earthquake." Jerry Silver told me, "We don't want the train riders to look into our backyards."

At that board meeting, according to Rosa Kortizija-Fuquay, transportation deputy for county Supervisor Antonovich, "MTA staff reported an elevated structure was feasible for all technologies (monorail, conventional heavy rail, conventional light rail technology, and automated guideway technology. According to the report, surface (at grade) rail was determined feasible." The extensive preliminary engineering determined there was sufficient real estate along the freeway for an at grade rail system with very few land acquisitions in Sherman Oaks and Van Nuys.

In December 1995, Riordan again changed his position in favor of above ground rail because of a sink hole in Hollywood and his concern of cost overruns.

On January 22, 1997, the MTA board voted to apply to the federal government for $58 million to design a route across the Valley. It also accepted a commitment of $200 million in citywide subway construction funds from Los Angeles in exchange for the promise to begin designing some type of Valley route by 2000.

In 1999, Mayor Riordan, county Supervisors Yaroslavsky and Yvonne Braithwaite-Burke, state Assemblyman Robert Hertzberg, and others went to Curitiba, Brazil, to see that city's busway. And there had been another trip to Curitiba by staff members before the mayor's trip. Instead, they all should have walked to one of the most successful busways in the nation, the El Monte Busway linking downtown Los Angeles and El Monte that opened in1974. Riordan, according to his Deputy Mayor Jaime de la Vega, had changed his mind for the third time and now was pushing busway, before the Curitiba trip, whereas Yaroslavsky was opposed.

In June 2001, MTA held two public hearings in the Valley to receive comments on the dedicated busway from North Hollywood to Warner Center. It would run through incredibly quiet residential neighborhoods in Tarzana, Encino, Sherman Oaks, Van Nuys, Valley Glen and North Hollywood. The opponents said the use of the old railroad right-of-way would create a "freeway for buses." "The MTA gives us a Band-Aid when what we need is a tourniquet. We need a subway," one man said. Rabbis, including Aron Tendler of Shaarey Zedek and Avrohom Stulberger of Valley Torah High School, appeared before the MTA Board of Directors. "How could consideration be given to a plan that would split a community?" Stulberger asked. "It's unthinkable to me."

On July 26, 2001, the MTA board approved a fourteen-mile busway between Woodland Hills and North Hollywood. The vote was eight to three. Assembly Speaker Hertzberg and county Supervisor Yaroslavsky warned that the MTA would have to use or lose $145 million in state funds allocated for the project.

On July 10, 2014, California Governor Jerry Brown signed Assembly Bill 517 which allowed MTA to convert Metro Orange Line to light-rail. Brown's signature reversed Robbins 1991 law that banned above-ground rail through North Hollywood and Van Nuys.

The Valley Industry & Commerce Association has said that the Orange Line is overcrowded and inefficient and conversion to light rail is the best option. However, Metro spokesperson Marc Littman said, "An Orange Line project is not included in MTA's list of short-term priorities. There is no additional funding identified in Measure R, the half-cent sales tax for transportation passed by Los Angeles voters in 2008."

Alas, years later, the light-rail is still a pipe dream. Metro has promised that the busway will be converted to light rail with Measure M funds in 2050. In 2024, Metro was negotiating with a contractor for Orange Line "improvements" at an estimated cost of $500 million, which means that, after spending a staggering $1 billion of taxpayers' money, the Valley will have a busway for the foreseeable future!

BENEFIT ASSESSMENT DISTRICTS

During my negotiations with the federal government to secure funding for the Los Angeles Metro Rail system, David Stockman, Budget Director under President Reagan, demanded that the private sector participate in the funding and have "skin in the game." To gain support in Congress, the Southern California Rapid Transit District established "Benefit Assessment Districts." A Benefit Assessment is a fee on properties in a specified area that is used to pay for part of the costs of specific capital improvements made within and specifically benefiting the area. Benefit assessment districts have been used in California and throughout the

United States to finance such public improvements as street lighting, sewer systems, parking structures and flood control facilities.

California State Senator Diane Watson introduced Bill SB 1238, which allowed the SCRTD to create Benefit Assessment Districts. After a public hearing held by the SCRTD Board of Directors on January 24, 1985, the Board approved on February 14, 1985, a resolution to proceed with the establishment of benefit assessment districts for the Central Business District and the Wilshire/Alvarado areas. The resolution was transmitted to the Los Angeles City Council, which held a public hearing on May 28, 1985. The City Council amended and approved the resolution on May 31, 1985, and returned it to the SCRTD Board on the same day. On July 11, 1985, the SCRTD adopted a resolution creating the two special benefit assessment districts for the first phase (MOS-1) of its rail project, which would provide $130.3 million funding for the first phase MOS-1.

The legislation spelled out that the revenue generated by benefit assessment districts would only be used for the construction of Metro Rail stations and not to subsidize operations. As President of the SCRTD Board, I led those efforts, because this unprecedented support by the private sector for a modern rail project was the key to securing Federal funding for the initial segment of the project.

During a visit to Los Angeles, US Transportation Secretary Elizabeth Dole commended the Los Angeles community for its efforts to create private-sector funding mechanisms to build Metro Rail. Other cities such as Houston, had made the mistake of going to Washington before they had that support. Houston had to withdraw its request after the public turned down its assessment.

Developer Wayne Ratkovich chaired a citizens committee that helped SCRTD develop the benefit assessment districts.

One benefit assessment district was established for the Central Business District (CBD) and one for the Westlake/MacArthur Park area. Walking distances from the transit station of one-half a mile for the CBD and one-third a mile for the Westlake/McArthur Park area were the primary determinants of benefit assessment district boundaries. All residential properties in the benefit assessment districts except hotels and motels were exempted, as well as parcels owned and occupied by non-profit organizations and public land in public use under a compromise worked out among me, Councilwoman Russell, who was President of the Los Angeles City Council, Councilman Yaroslavsky, and John Dyer, who was General Manager of SCRTD. The negotiations over a ten-day period were "intense," according to Yaroslavsky.

Initially, SCRTD officials had contented it could be unconstitutional to write legislation imposing the charge just on commercial property. However, the lawyers worked out language acceptable to both parties. The compromise also assured the City Council would have the right to approve the boundaries of the assessment districts and the size of the assessments against property owners.

Some City Council members, especially Zev Yaroslavsky, had voiced fears that assessments on residential properties would result in rent increases. SCRTD levied a 1986 assessment of thirty cents per each assessable square foot of property." According to Gary Spivack, "Following this assessment, the SCRTD deferred collection of further monies until the start of the first phase of rail operations. In October 1988, the SCRTD began establishing five new benefit assessment districts for phase II of the project. Still, there were judicial battles the SCRTD had to deal with. Several property owners led by the Atchison, Topeka and Santa Fe Railway Co. filed suit in the Superior Court in 1987, contending that the taxes were being unfairly levied only on commercial property. But the Superior Court found in favor of SCRTD.

In 1990, the State Court of Appeal invalidated the SCRTD plan to have commercial property owners pay part of the construction costs for the first leg of the Metro Rail. They ruled that the SCRTD had no authority to exclude residential property from the districts. The panel also found that the sole means by which property owners could protest this taxation was by a referendum election process that did not follow constitutional one-person, one-vote guarantees. "As a result, the statutory scheme in its entirety must fall as unconstitutional," Justice Lynn D. Compton wrote in a unanimous three-judge panel.

In 1992 the State Supreme Court affirmed the constitutionality of Benefit Assessment Districts. The case was appealed to and refused to be heard by the US Supreme Court, letting stand the decision of the State Supreme Court that assessment districts are legal.

According to Jed Springer, outside counsel of SCRTD, "There was a benefit assessment district in the first phase of the Red Line (MOS-1) that included the Home Savings Tower at 7th St and Figueroa St. The Home Savings executives, including Chair Chuck Reed, were absolutely astounded that the benefit assessment was going to be applied on all floors. They were threatening to pull out of the project. It was one of my first cases defending the benefit assessment district." Jed continued, "When we were first introduced into the program, there were over 1,000 cases pending, challenging its legality. The County Counsel office was defending it initially, and then they hired the law firm of Jones Day."

I remember Jones Day was doing a lot of construction litigation for SCRTD, but they were losing half of their cases because they could not prove benefit. Jed had a statistical background, and he researched to determine why they were losing them. According to Jed, "There was a study done by Economic Research Associates that attempted to draw correlation between value impacts and location of Metro Rail stations. The report showed a negative correlation." Jed added, " I determined when you have a statistical study you have to look at the data to understand what is driving that conclusion." It turned out that there were two properties driving that conclusion. They were the Union Oil Company building on the west side of the Harbor Freeway. Someone had paid such an enormous amount for the property, and the way that had been accounted for in their correlation resulted in an erroneous conclusion. Once that sale was taken out, the results showed a magnificent correlation. Jed won every single one of SCRTD`s benefit assessment cases.

The benefit assessment district for the first phase of the subway MOS-1 was successful, but the second phase MOS-2 and the third phase MOS-3 failed. According to Springer, "the linchpin was Universal Studios," because as we shall see in another chapter, MTA Board succumbed to political pressures and exempted the Studios from the benefit assessment taxes.

VIGNETTE

The SCRTD Board of directors was on stand- by at the district`s headquarters at 425 South Main Street on May 31, 1985, waiting for Los Angeles City Council approval of the establishment of the benefit assessment districts because the County Assessor had to certify it by the next day. Otherwise, it would be a moot point. The funding provided by the benefit assessment districts was the linchpin of the federal funding agreement, and failure to certify it could jeopardize the subway funding.

As explained to me by Fran Savitch, Tom Bradley`s senior advisor and confidant, Councilman David Cunningham Jr. left in the middle of the Council deliberations to attend a fundraiser. Savitch ran down into the garage and brought Cunningham back to cast the eighth critical vote.

RAIL CONSTRUCTION CORPORATION

Precursor of LAMTA | In 1976, the California State Legislature enacted Assembly Bill 31246, by Assemblyman Walter Ingalls, which created the Los Angeles County Transportation Commission to oversee public transit and highway policy in the nation's largest county. Ingalls disliked the Southern California Rapid Transit District. the regional bus operator, considering it "incompetent and leaderless." The law required the new commission to approve all plans and funding with respect to transit capital development and transit operations. It was a recipe for disaster. Overlapping bureaucracy and duplication, feuds over jurisdictional authority between the commission and the RTD, turf wars, bickering, threats and blackmailing over funding for bus operations and poor coordination between the two agencies, political and bureaucratic gridlock, employees jockeying for position.

By 1985, the commission was working with Caltrans to accommodate a future light rail line, The Green Line, into the median of the 105 Freeway that Caltrans was building at that time. Ed McSpedon, a Civil Engineer from New York with extensive rail transit planning, design, and construction experience had been hired by LACTC to lead this effort. By 1986, the RTD had advanced engineering work and was finalizing Federal Construction Funding for the Downtown segment of a new underground subway project that would eventually run from Union Station to North Hollywood.

Also, in 1986 LACTC started construction of what was to become the first modern rail transit line in Los Angeles, the twenty-two-mile Blue Line connecting downtown Los Angeles with Downtown Long Beach. The Blue Line was being built using LA County Proposition A sales tax funds. In June 1986, after a national candidate search by a panel that included outside public works professionals, McSpedon was chosen to lead the Engineering and Construction of the Blue Line in addition to his Green Line duties. A target operational date for the Blue Line had been set for July 1990, a goal that was successfully achieved on July 14, 1990.

The Red Line and the Blue Line were to connect at a two-level underground passenger transfer station in the heart of downtown Los Angeles. The Blue Line would also connect with the future Green Line via a passenger transfer station at Wilmington Avenue and Imperial Highway.

Having different agencies leading the development of separate rail transit projects (which were legs of what was planned to become an integrated regional "rail transit system") presented numerous challenges at the staff level but these were worked out professionally under McSpedon' s leadership at LACTC and William Rhine's leadership at RTD. Their joint philosophy was to ensure the most efficient construction approach to these projects and to ensure their maximum interoperability. There were many positive results achieved, including agreeing to have RTD lead the design and construction of the Downtown transfer station construction at Seventh and Flower Streets with LACTC in a supporting role. Eliminating duplicate Operations Control Centers and consolidating these functions into a single facility at Wilmington and Imperial. Employing common passenger signage standards throughout the rail lines and using a common proof of payment fare collection system during the initial years of subway operation, while at the same time incorporating provisions for a future Barrier System on the subway once ridership levels reached the point where proof of payment system enforcement could no longer be effective.

The most difficult issues, however, were at the board levels where disagreements over control and micro-managing ran rampant, with some senior staff complaining that certain board members were meddling even in personnel and contracting decisions. In 1989, I discussed with Neil Peterson, executive director of the LACTC, ways and methods to improve the problematic situation. I consulted with David Kelsey, assistant Los Angeles County Counsel, who was also acting as the LACTC counsel, and he suggested a Public Benefit Corporation model. Kelsey had seen this type of governance model successfully used in the past. It would be called the Rail Construction Corporation.

The basic idea was to assemble an RCC board made up of individuals with experience and knowledge in the delivery of public works projects, instead of politicians. Three board positions would be nominated by RTD, three by LACTC, with Mayor Tom Bradley appointing a seventh member. For the plan to go into effect, both the LACTC and the RTD would have to give up control over the design and construction of the rail system. The LACTC was amenable to the proposal, but the RTD Board rejected it by a vote of 6-5, asking for further negotiations. The LACTC's Transit Committee immediately recommended that the commission take the second leg of the subway out of the hands of the RTD entirely. My reaction was, "We have reached the bottom. This is the lowest. The lines have been drawn and I'm sure the RTD is now out in the cold. It's stupid." After some behind- the scenes negotiating, I proposed a compromise to settle the issue. The Patsaouras Compromise proposed that the rail construction firm's board have a neutral seventh, tie-breaking member, so that neither agency could dominate its actions. The six board members appointed, three each by RTD and LACTC, would be allowed to choose their seventh independent voting member. The compromise was rejected twice by the RTD board, six to five. Board President Swanson and her supporters added amendments to my proposal. The amendments were approved by a bare board majority of the RTD board but proved unacceptable to the commission. I then worked feverishly to revive my compromise. I visited and was successful in convincing RTD

Director Kenneth R. Thomas, publisher of The Sentinel, to reconsider his position.

I wanted a special RTD board meeting before the holidays. However, Swanson refused to place the item on the agenda. I felt frustrated and helpless. Fortunately, I was approached by the capable board secretary, Helen Bolen, who advised me that if the majority of the board signs a request that an item be placed on the agenda, it automatically is part of the agenda. (A piece of advice that became useful when I faced the same predicament when I served on the LADWP board a few years later.) It was the weekend before Christmas, and I had to collect the signatures. I went to Burbank Airport to pick up my daughter Tanya, who was coming home from UC Berkley for Christmas vacation, and told her, "I need you to drive me to a few places around the county, because I have a cold and I don't feel well." I collected the five signatures, and the item was placed on the agenda. The vote in December 1989 was six to four in favor of my compromise. The agreement turned all Metro Rail design and construction to a new third agency, the Rail Construction Corporation. "This is not a peace offering. . .it's an abomination," Swanson said of the compromise.

Under the terms of the agreement, the RTD not only had three seats on the RCC board but also continued to have an important role in building the subway as its future operator. Most members of RTD's former Metro Rail staff would continue to work on design and construction of the project's next phases, as RCC employees. Ed McSpedon was selected to lead the RCC. The six appointed RCC board members agreed to add Judith Hopkinson, a highly respected real estate developer, as the seventh member of their board and the board-appointed David Anderson, retired GTC Telecom chief executive officer and former chairman of the Los Angeles Chamber of Commerce, as RCC's first chairman.

With the approval of the RCC board, McSpedon developed and implemented a plan to consolidate the many groups of engineering companies that were involved in the design and construction of the rail system into a much more streamlined and manageable structure. McSpedon had hired Charles Stark from the New York Metropolitan Transit Authority as the new project manager for the downtown subway, and together they set about clearing up many unresolved construction disputes with contractors, picking up the pace of subway construction, and seeking ways to accelerate the production of the new subway cars, which had fallen behind schedule in Italy.

In an out-of-the-box idea, the RCC decided, with the approval of the Federal Transit Administration, to immediately lease four subway cars from the new Miami Transit System, which had surplus new rail cars at that time. The Miami cars would be used to test the Los Angeles Subway and to buy time to complete production of the Los Angeles new Breda Cars in Italy. This also provided time to send the Los Angeles cars to the US Department of Transportation Test Center in Pueblo, Colorado, to make sure they were ready for trouble free revenue service when they finally arrived in Los Angeles.

Despite some positive staff level results from the organizational changes, however, board level conflicts between the agencies were not fully resolved, even with the Patsaouras compromise. It took legislative action in the form of AB 152 introduced by California State Assemblyman Richard Katz to finally merge the LACTC and RTD into the Los Angeles Metropolitan Transportation Authority effective February 1, 1993. In 1994, the Metro board disbanded the RCC, thereby giving a single group of politicians direct control of Los Angeles Rail Transit planning, design, construction and operations.

TRANSIT INDUSTRY JOBS CREATION INITIATIVE

As president of the Southern California Rapid Transit District Board of Directors and member of the Los Angeles County Transportation Commission, I proposed in May 1991 to redirect laid-off aerospace and defense employees into local manufacturing of buses, light rail, commuter rail, and subway cars and parts instead of purchasing equipment from abroad.

To underscore the crisis in the Southland's defense industry, I outlined my proposal at a news conference in front of the Rockwell International plant in Downey, which had laid off about three thousand workers during the previous two years. The news conference was attended by union leaders including AFL-CIO president Bill Robertson and Neil Peterson, executive director of the transportation commission. I pointed out that, "It means the production of six thousand buses, three hundred rail cars and related equipment, as well as the development of new technology for fare (toll) collection, street signal controls in smart corridors, telecommunications, and information dissemination." Peterson said, "We need to initiate the momentum to keep local tax dollars here in Southern California and provide much-needed jobs to those who have been left out as result of the defense and aerospace closures."

Bruce Lee, director of the United Auto Workers, Region 6, stated, "Patsaouras' program was the only viable plan on the table that promises to save the talent and experience of tens of thousands of skilled workers from vanishing forever while giving the Southern California economy a massive boost for years to come…The foresight of Nick Patsaouras in developing the Jobs Creation Initiative deserves the tribute of the entire state." Bill Duplissea, special assistant to the state's secretary of business, housing and transportation, in a phone interview with the *Los Angeles Business Journal*, said, "This a phenomenal idea. California has everything it needs to be a center of transportation and cutting-edge technology."

Flanked by union leaders and LACTC Executive Director Neil Peterson, announcing my transit industry initiative to produce buses, rail cars and other equipment, thus creating jobs and boosting the local economy. Photo: courtesy of Metro

I explained the benefits to the community:

1) We will retain jobs locally using our tax dollars to pay our citizens.
2) Tax proceeds from the purchases will accrue to the region.

3) The cost of these systems will decrease, stretching our scarce resources.
4) The creation of job retraining and employment opportunities in Southern California.

Other elements of the proposal included:

- Urging the federal government to establish a "re-utilization tax credit" for defense manufacturing plants that convert to facilities involved with public works projects. Those companies must promise to use local labor pools.
- Creating a local, state, and federal partnership to help US companies become more competitive in the transit arena and understand why foreign-owned firms land so many transportation contracts.
- Developing management training programs at local universities and colleges to instruct workers in transportation issues such as maintenance and repair.

Jack Keyser of the Los Angeles County Economic Development Corporation, commented, "Long term, it will be the maintenance that could make Southern California a center for transportation work." Palmdale, traditionally a hub of weapons production, was suggested as a location to set up transportation building facilities by either startup firms or aerospace companies moving into commercial work. The Los Angeles County Metropolitan Transportation Authority's Blue Line cars are Japanese, and Metro Rail Red Line cars and equipment came from Canada, Germany, and Japan.

Initially, my local industrial policy was met with skepticism. Los Angeles County Supervisor Edmund D. Edelman and Long Beach City Councilman Ray Grabinski, both members of the transportation commission, emphasized that the commission's first duty was to provide transportation. However, the Sumitomo debacle made my proposal a top priority for the commission. (See Sumitomo debacle section) But even the skeptics admitted that some kind of local jobs development program was worth trying. Peterson opened discussions with leading aerospace companies regarding the transportation industry's needs.

The commission released a ninety-one-page directory of every locally available product and service a rail car manufacturer might use, cross referenced by products and by businesses owned by women and minorities. It also commissioned a wide-ranging study that included the effects of building or assembling buses and commuter rail cars locally. As a result of a motion I made, the commission investigated leasing excess fiber optics capacity on its rail rights-of-way and strategies to develop transportation education and training with local universities and institutions. I also suggested that the commission consider an industrial offset program that would encourage foreign manufacturers to help local businesses obtain offset credit from the government of that manufacturer. The plan would encourage foreign companies to use local employers in the design, manufacture, and maintenance of equipment, or to make direct investments in them.

If such a plan had been in place when the Japan-built Blue Line rail cars were bought, local aerospace companies that were buying products from Japan could have received credits from Japan for part of the $70 million cost of the rail cars. The prospect of an industrial offset program had already had an effect. Sumitomo Corporation of America had voluntarily offered to establish a local assembly of rail cars in its $121 million bid to make Green Line rail cars.

In November 2014, Los Angeles Mayor Eric Garcetti announced an agreement between the rail-car manufacturer Kinkisharyo and the electrical workers union and community groups. The company won a $900-million contract from Metro in 2012 based in part on its promise to employ more people and build cars here, but two manufacturing sites it proposed in Palmdale drew environmental challenges by organized labor and its allies. Kinkisharyo threatened to move the manufacturing operation to another state. After a series of very difficult negotiations facilitated by Borja Leon, Garcetti's deputy for transportation, Kinkisharyo representatives, Marvin Kropke of the International Brotherhood of Electric Workers Local 11, Madeline Janis of Los Angeles Alliance for a New Economy, and Maria Elena Durazo of the Los Angeles County Federation of Labor, an agreement was reached under which Kinkisharyo would expand its rail assembly and testing operations at its existing site in Palmdale. It included manufacturing tasks, which created 250 new jobs, skills training, and assistance for disadvantaged Los Angeles County workers. With Kinkisharyo and BYD, manufacturers of rail cars and electric buses in Palmdale and Lancaster, the Antelope Valley is becoming an epicenter of transportation manufacturing.

The one trillion-dollar bipartisan infrastructure bill signed by President Joe Biden in 2021 includes close to two billion dollars for the transition to zero emission vehicles. The MTA plans to phase out two thousand compressed-natural gas buses by 2030 and replace them with zero-emission buses and will cover the purchase of 182 rail cars for Metro's Regional Connector and the Purple Line. In December 2022, the MTA Board of Directors approved a policy requiring any company bidding for a manufacturing contract worth more than fifty million dollars to include hiring, pay and training commitments. The policy requires bus and rail manufacturers to provide workforce training or apprenticeships, requirements that had been included in my Jobs Creation Initiative.

BLUE (A) LINE ALIGNMENT DECISIONS

Downtown Los Angeles Alignment | When the Los Angeles County Transportation Commission was first laying out the Los Angeles to Long Beach line, the A (Blue) Line, the intent was to create a connection between the two cities in the least expensive manner. Thus, in downtown Los Angeles, the line was proposed to enter the Central City along Alameda Street at street grade and terminate in front of Union Station. The City of Los Angeles objected that this was remote from and disconnected from the core of downtown Los Angeles. Subsequent proposals to route the light rail on the surface along Broadway Avenue were rejected as untenable given other traffic volumes along that street. A third proposed alignment would have followed the aerial configuration of the never built Downtown People Mover, along Figueroa Street from south of the Convention Center, across Bunker Hill via Fourth and Fifth streets, then along Hill Street and the US-101 Freeway to Union Station. The city noted that the aerial alignment of the People Mover had raised objections including

Opening day of the Blue Line. With Los Angeles County Supervisor Ed Edelman. July 14, 1990. Photo: courtesy of Metro

unsightliness and impact on historic buildings, both visual and physical, and that a good portion of its potential walk-to-station area was in fact occupied by the Harbor Freeway and thus would not generate ridership.

The city and the Community Redevelopment Agency proposed alignment on Flower Street instead. The Long Beach line, in this configuration, would be routed across the south end of downtown at grade in the median of Washington Boulevard, turning north at Flower Street and entering a tunnel north of the Pico Station (to minimize traffic interference). This alignment would put the line into the heart of the redeveloping Downtown Financial District and the then-emerging South Park residential district, allow a connection to the Union Station to North Hollywood B (Red) line at Seventh Street, and place the line within walking distance of much of Bunker Hill. The city and CRA offered to split the incremental cost, arguing that additional transit-oriented core development induced by the transit investment would eventually pay back that added cost through the increased property and other taxes. With City Council approval, this alignment was accepted and built. That decision has made possible the Regional Connector, linking the subsequently added Santa Monica (E) and Azusa to East Los Angeles (L) lines into an integrated regional network.

Key players included Calvin Hamilton, director of Los Angeles City Planning; Don Howery, general manager of the Los Angeles Department of Transportation; and Ed Helfeld, administrator of the Los Angeles Community Redevelopment Agency.

Downtown Long Beach Alignment | The downtown Long Beach segment of the project was planned to run down the center of Long Beach Boulevard, and to terminate at First Street. From there trains were to reverse direction and head back to Los Angeles.

Long after construction had started on the northern parts of the project, activist citizens, business owners and elected officials in Long Beach began to object to the construction impacts that the project would have on the many automobile dealerships that operated along Long Beach Boulevard. The auto dealers' position was that nobody would come to buy a car by train and the construction of the rail line would disrupt their businesses and send customers elsewhere. Throughout construction the auto dealers continued to demand extraordinary concessions and mitigation measures.* The City of Long Beach supported the project but objected to the alignment. After completing a study of options, the city came back with a proposal to change the alignment on lower Long Beach Boulevard from a double track with a stub-end terminal to a single-track loop that would travel west on First Street to serve the city's growing Pine Avenue entertainment district and then reconnect with the double track line on Long Beach Boulevard at Eighth Street. The city also wanted to use some of its Proposition A local return funds to enhance the aesthetics of its downtown Long Beach stations. Specifically, the city wanted those stations to reflect an "Art Moderne" architectural style. After much back and forth, the single track "Long Beach Loop" alignment and the new station designs were agreed upon and incorporated into the project.

Key players in the Long Beach Alignment decisions included Long Beach Mayor Ernie Kell, Long Beach City Engineer Ray Holland, and North Long Beach business owner and activist, Ray Grabinski.**

NOTES:

*Ironically, the Auto Dealers soon left Long Beach Boulevard for the new Long Beach Auto Center in the Signal Hill area of the city.

** Ray Grabinski was eventually elected to the Long Beach City Council. He served as the city's representative on the LACTC Board and then on the LAMTA Board, including a term as its chairman.

MEASURE R

Kevin Starr in his book *Coast of Dreams* wrote in 2004, "Like a half-built medieval cathedral interrupted by plague, famine, or war, the fixed rail system in operation by 2002 only fragmentarily expressed the vision that had so exhilarated Nick Patsaouras and an entire generation of advocates. Yet medieval cathedrals, even when interrupted, had a way of getting finished. For those who still kept the faith, fixed rail remained a certainty for some future time in the drawing millennium." Antonio Villaraigosa "kept the faith," and when he campaigned for mayor of Los Angeles in 2005, he led the efforts to jump-start the stalled fixed rail system.

Villaraigosa's clarion "subway to the sea" distinguished him as a bold, visionary leader. The subway to the sea became the metaphor for the whole transportation system. Villaraigosa had asked me to prepare a map showing in color an extension of the subway to Santa Monica and light rail lines throughout Los Angeles County. The ever exuberant but also knowledgeable Villaraigosa insisted that I include the Lincoln Boulevard Transit Corridor that I had omitted because I had considered that it was not feasible at the time. Dan Turner, *Los Angeles Times* editor covering among other subjects transportation, called me to discuss the map, and he made the comment, "The map looks like a Vincent van Gogh drawing." In his inaugural address Mayor Villaraigosa urged Angelenos to "dream with me." Villaraigosa worked feverishly to rescind the ill-conceived Henry Waxman legislation that banned the use of federal funds for a subway under Wilshire Boulevard.

In October 2005, Villaraigosa announced an expert safety panel, the "Tunnel Advisory Panel," to evaluate subway tunnel safety. Congressman Henry Waxman was skeptical but was allowed to appoint two members in a five-member committee. Dr. Z. Eisenstein led the panel. The five-member expert panel concluded unanimously that tunneling could be done safely if proper procedures were followed and appropriate technologies were used.

In December 2005, Congressman Henry Waxman, in a reversal, introduced legislation that would lift the two-decade prohibition against tunneling. The House voted unanimously in February 2007 to lift the ban on tunneling under Wilshire Boulevard. On December 26, 2007, President George W. Bush signed the bill into law.

Villaraigosa had made the "subway to the sea" one of his top priorities once he was seated as member of the Metro Board of Directors. He had mustered seven votes to start planning and environmental work for the subway in July 2005. However, because of rivalries within the board, he could not get the eighth vote even from board members whose constituencies would benefit from a subway along Wilshire Boulevard. That delayed the extension of the subway to the west side by two years. During his first three years in office, the *Los Angeles Times* kept writing: where is the money for the subway to the sea? Villaraigosa, however, determined to find the money, looked to the State.

In 2006 Governor Arnold Schwarzenegger was sponsoring Proposition 1B to go on the November ballot. There was neither a transit category nor transit money in the bill, but Villaraigosa convinced the governor to include in the bill seed money for the Wilshire subway. The mayor actually succeeded in getting one billion dollars from the state in 2006, but none of it went to the Wilshire subway and instead the money went to other projects. It turned out Metro had to use all that money to cover cost overruns and budget deficits for the Expo, Crenshaw, and Orange transit lines. For example, the engineer's estimate for the Expo line was $640 million. But the bid came in at $800 million. Steve Hymon, Metro blogger and former *Los Angeles Times* reporter, observed that Villaraigosa had to fight for Measure R twice, in 2008 to get it through, and then again in 2009 to make sure that the Long-Range Transportation Plan conformed with Measure R.

THE STRATEGY

Villaraigosa and his staff looked at gasoline tax, vehicle license tax, congestion pricing and sales tax to raise revenue for extension of the rail system. However, the polling showed the only tax the public would support was sales tax.

Denny Zane, a former mayor of the City of Santa Monica, created "Move LA" in 2007 to bring business, labor, and environmental leaders and organizations together with the goal of raising new funding and grassroots support for Los Angeles County's transit system. Zane, a dedicated public servant committed to environmental and transportation issues in the region, was joined in his "Move LA" efforts by other long time transportation advocates such as Marlene Grossman and Gloria Ohland.

Zane had been close to Villaraigosa from work they had done together while Villaraigosa was Speaker of the California State Assembly in the early 1990s. While Zane was the executive director of the Coalition for Clean Air, they had worked together to create the

Carl Moyer Program which still provides significant funding for clean alternatives to diesel engines. After Villaraigosa's election as Los Angeles mayor, Zane saw an opportunity to move a transit agenda forward, and he went to work right away to organize support and fundraising for ballot Measure R, which called for a half-cent sales tax increase that would generate close to $40 billion over thirty years for transit, highway, and street projects. Measure R had a 30-year sunset clause. Zane's work as executive director of the Coalition for Clean Air gave him entre to the environmental community and working on living wage strategies in Santa Monica gave him entre to labor. Those credentials gave him the incentive to try to get the business-labor-environmental coalition together in order to promote transit solutions.

Zane, civic leader Dan Rosenfeld, and environmentalist Terry O'Day called a meeting in Rosenfeld's office at the Bradbury Building. Rosenfeld was the Chair of the Environmental and the Land Use Committee of the Los Angeles Chamber of Commerce. They invited thirty-five organizations, including environmental, labor and business, non-profits, and community groups. Thirty-four organizations showed up, indicating the appetite for transit progress at the time. The goal of the meeting was to strategize how to raise funding and grassroots support to expand the transit system in the region. They agreed that the only way was to go to the voters. By the time they were ready for a second meeting, they needed the conference facilities at the Cathedral to accommodate the crowd in January 2008.

Out of that conference, the essential course became clear: seek authorization from the State Legislature for a sales tax measure in Los Angeles County for transit investments, conduct the necessary polling, build the necessary coalition, and raise enough money. There were about 350 people attending and participating in the conference, including Supervisor Yaroslavsky, Mayor Villaraigosa, Maria Elena Durazo, secretary-treasurer AFL-CIO, David Fleming from the LA Chamber and Metro Board member, and Mike Feuer, who was the chairman of the California Assembly Subcommittee on Transportation, the appropriate person to introduce the legislation.

Mike Feuer, after the conference, went to Sacramento and reintroduced Senator Kevin Murray's old bill, which had been approved before, but only for six years, and that was never acted on. Feuer smartly modified that bill and submitted it this time. As it turns out, the new chair of the Metro Board was Pam O'Connor, Councilwoman in Santa Monica and a friend of Zane. It was a serendipitous moment. O'Connor made a motion to start the process. However, there were a lot of twists and turns around this. Metro Board member Richard Katz, Deputy Mayor for Transportation Jaime de la Vega and Mayor Villaraigosa were working with the Council of Governments in regional communities to enlist their support.

They were all trying to get the *Los Angeles Times* and the *Daily News* endorsements, how to keep the Auto Club from opposing the measure, and how to mobilize labor. Zane solicited and received a contribution from Santa Monica College, who wanted to have an Exposition Light Rail station close to the college. They contributed $25,000 to do a poll by Paul Goodwin. The poll showed 69 percent "yes" for a sales tax county-wide. Metro did a poll by John Fairbank that showed 71 percent. Yes. Villaraigosa did another poll with Diane Feldman that showed 66 percent Yes. This was now giving people enough confidence that it could really happen,

In the legislature, Feuer did a masterful job of holding the line because there were several Los Angeles based members who wanted their special projects in the measure. But Feuer knew that if he opened the door, he would have to open it up for all kinds of pet projects. So, the drama came down to the last 20 minutes when it could legally be acted upon. Feuer was saying, "Nope, it's up or down on this," and finally the recalcitrants agreed and fell in line. Then it went to the Metro Board on July 24, 2008, and the Metro Board voted Yes 9–3. Supervisors Michael Antonovich and Councilman of Duarte John Fasana voted No. Supervisor Don Knabe was absent and Gloria Molina abstained.

Metro submitted a request to the county Board of Supervisors to consolidate the measure with the county election. When the measure came before the supervisors, Michael Antonovich, Don Knabe and Gloria Molina voted, No! Panic set in. However, a week later, after intensive lobbying, Knabe changed his vote to Yes, and the measure moved forward. By the time Governor Arnold Schwarzenegger signed the bill, there were only a couple of months left to raise the money needed to move forward with the Measure R campaign.

Supervisor Yaroslavsky solicited and received $900,000 from the LA County Museum of Art Foundation. Villaraigosa raised about $3 million. He brought his team, Ace Smith and Sean Clegg, to run the campaign. The election was in November 2008. Unfortunately, and remarkably, in September the economic crash happened and financial institutions all around the country went bankrupt. President Bush and Presidential candidates John McCain and Barack Obama were on TV, all talking about what they would do to protect the nation's economy. The belief was that Measure R would fail considering the events unfolding.

However, Mayor Villaraigosa kept the faith. He was the hero and the inspiration of the campaign, and he raised the money needed to win, campaigned vigorously, and led the charge, with a lot to lose. He made the decision not to appear in the media personally, even though he was up for re-election shortly afterward. He was wise to recognize that the measure should not be identified with any politician.

On election night, November 4, 2008, 67.39 percent of the county voters voted yes (66.6 percent was required. The voters approved a half-cent sales tax increase (from 8.25 percent to 8.75 percent) that would be in effect for thirty years and generate $40 billion dollars. The fact that Obama was on the ballot helped a lot with votes from minorities and liberals, who usually are inclined to support a tax.

Villaraigosa fulfilled Kevin Starr's prophecy that the fixed rail in LA would get finished. Villaraigosa accomplished this with help from Deputy Mayor for transportation Jaime de la Vega, his appointee to the Metro Board Richard Katz, County Supervisor Zev Yaroslavsky, and most importantly, from Denny Zane and his Move LA Coalition, who proved to be a powerful force in helping get Measure R on the 2008 ballot and winning its passage. As a result, the city was able to continue to build its transportation system.

MEASURE J

The realization that there would be many years, even decades, before Measure R could deliver on its promise prompted Metro, Denny Zane, and community leaders to envision what it would take to accelerate these investments.

Metro supported Connecticut Senator Chris Dodd's legislation to create a National Infrastructure Development Bank. It was envisioned the bank would provide access to federal dollars secured by Measure R revenue to enable acceleration of transit investments so that Metro could build the thirty-year Measure R plan in just ten years. President Obama endorsed the National Infrastructure Development Bank, but it fell aside during the struggle to create the president's signature Affordable Care Act.

Jaime De La Vega, Villaraigosa's transportation deputy, and Richard Katz, Metro board member, designed a second ballot measure for November 2012 that would extend Measure R's term from thirty years to sixty years, Measure J and the "30/10 Plan." The additional revenue Measure J would provide in the second thirty years, it was argued, would allow Metro to secure greater and more favorable bond and federal financing and enable the acceleration of the Measure R`s 30-year program such that it might be built in 10 years.

However, Measure J failed on November 6, 2012, to reach the required two-thirds vote, though it won a supermajority of 66.11 percent with a relatively low turnout election and limited campaign funds. It can be argued that if the Gold Line (L Line) in San Gabriel Valley had been included in Measure J, the voters might have approved it. Measure J demonstrated that LA County voters had a real appetite for investment in transportation progress and were not afraid of taxing themselves to pay for it.

Possibly, the loss of Measure J was fortuitous. Measure J made Measure M possible - another half-cent sales tax for November 2016. Measure M proposed to not only accelerate Measure R projects but also to add more projects around the county to ensure all the county's communities would benefit. Measure M had no sunset and amended Measure R to eliminate its thirty-year sunset.

Both measures would be operative until L. County voters might elect to end them. Together, they could provide, along with Propositions A and C, a permanent funding for investments in Los Angeles County`s transportation modernization.

MEASURE M

Mayor Eric Garcetti, elected in 2013, started to put together a plan for a new Metro countywide ballot measure in his second month in office. It would be similar to Measure R, which was approved by the voters during Mayor Antonio Villaraigosa's administration in 2008.

Garcetti's vision was big, thinking regionally, emphasizing the importance of working with every mayor in Los Angeles County. He wanted to be seen as a consensus and coalition builder. He delegated the project to his capable and savvy deputy for transportation,

Mayor Eric Garcetti's rail plan for the 2028 Summer Olympics in Los Angeles. Courtesy of Jake Berman of 53 Studio

Borja Leon. Garcetti convened a meeting in City Hall with the majority of the mayors of the eighty-eight cities in Los Angeles County. Borja made a presentation on the state of transportation and infrastructure in Los Angeles County. Garcetti asked the mayors if they would be supportive of another transportation ballot measure that would further fund Metro's rail, bus, and highway programs. Almost all the mayors raised their hands in support of another ballot measure. The next step was to do a countywide poll to determine if the voters would support such a measure. The services of Garcetti's pollster Fred Yang and chief strategist Bill Carrick were enlisted. In the fall of 2013, a poll was conducted, and the measure received decent support.

During that time, Metro was conducting an outreach effort to all the subregions in the county to identify all transportation related priorities. The effort was helpful to understand the different projects that were important at different parts of the county. This effort started after Measure J failed to be approved in 2012. Measure J would have extended the existing one-half cent sales tax for additional years. Because of the failure of Measure J, several Metro board members were reluctant to support a new measure. Los Angeles County Supervisor and Metro board member Michael Antonovich argued that Measure J favored the acceleration of projects within the City of Los Angeles. This time, however, Antonovich initiated the meetings with the cities trying to get their buy-in by asking them to give Metro a list of possible projects, what Metro called the "Mobility Matrix."

According to Denny Zane, founder of "Move LA," there were two processes in the development of Measure M. One was the official Metro-run geographic Council of Governments (COG) process. Under the leadership of CEO, Phil Washington, Metro embarked on an educational campaign, as it could not legally spend funds for a political campaign. Metro spent two years working with cities to develop a list of projects that could deliver the greatest value, while also ensuring that every corner of Los Angeles County would get a priority project built. The other was an informal process whereby Denny Zane's "Move LA" and its supporters were visiting constituency groups all around the county to energize them. Zane expanded the coalition of support to include seniors, persons with disabilities, students, bicycle, pedestrian, environmental justice, and smart growth advocates.

One of the key organizing strategies was to engage Mayor Eric Garcetti. He was bold, energetic, effective, and smart. He did a magnificent job as the leader of the campaign, raising sufficient funds, being the voice of the campaign, and framing it in positive ways. In 2014, Garcetti visited every region in the county to meet with elected officials and stakeholders. He cajoled, persuaded, and promised to deliver for every region of the county, not just the City of Los Angeles. He applied a "bottoms-up "approach that meant projects would be proposed to Metro from each city and then ranked based on a number of factors.

Zane focused in addressing the concerns and issues of different groups. For example, he pointed out to the bike coalition that it was not wise to have an 8–10 percent carved out for bike programs because that would become a target for other constituencies who would also want big projects, either it be labor or business. Zane stressed that bike and pedestrian interests were better served if they were integrated into the transit and road systems. The big challenge was that some of the COGs were upset because of the schedule of projects, not because of the projects themselves. For example, the Gateway COG was initially opposed, however it changed to neutral. The ultimate YES vote in that region was among the highest in the county. This change of position was the result of Garcetti visiting the Gateway COG and making a strong case. Through the efforts of Leon, County Supervisor Don Knabe stayed neutral this time, in contrast to his opposing Measure R in 2008.

Leon also convened a meeting with Congressional Democratic Whip Linda Sanchez representing Norwalk in the Congress member's office attended by Knabe and several Councilmembers from the region whereby suggestions were discussed on accelerating the I-5 project. The appropriate language was included in Measure M to appease that part of the county.

Measure M was on the November 2016 ballot, adding another half-cent sales tax without sunset and extending Measure R without sunset as well. Mayor Garcetti and Metro board member Councilman John Fasana of the City of Duarte led voters to a victory at 71.15 percent in support of Measure M. Measure M and an extended Measure R would raise $120 billion on top of the first Measure R's estimated $40 billion for a total of almost $160 billion by 2057—and continue beyond that date.

Garcetti accomplished this with help from Supervisor Antonovich, Phil Washington, fundraiser Rick Jacobs with Denny Zane's assistance and mine, transportation deputy Borja Leon, and campaign manager Bill Carrick.

Mayor Garcetti characterized Denny Zane of "Move LA" as the grandfather of Measure M and Measure R.

LESSON LEARNED

Measure M was not on the ballot alone, Prop A for County Parks, Measures HHH and H for the homeless, the Community College District bond was all on the ballot at the same time, and all those measures got more than 70 percent YES. The lesson learned is that the voter attitude had not changed, but the voters had changed. There was a new demographic in Los Angeles County – Latino voters, Asian voters, younger millennial voters, who were far less tax wary and more public investment oriented than the Howard Jarvis demographic.

VIGNETTE

According to Bill Carrick, Measure M is one of the biggest challenges he ever faced in a campaign. Why? To pass, it required a two-thirds Yes vote from the voters in the largest and most diverse County in America to tax themselves.

Carrick noted that, from past elections, one could tell that many communities in Los Angeles County were skeptical about a big transportation measure. The communities that were in Los Angeles County but not Los Angeles City were harder to get to vote yes. In addition, working class voters, Latinos, and younger voters were also skeptical. One key decision was to do focus groups in communities all over LA County. He told me they did twenty nights of focus groups in different communities, which outside of a Presidential campaign, is an extremely large research project. Combined with their polling, the campaign learned several important things from these focus groups. Voters wanted to know what specifically Measure M would do for them. It was clear that the campaign had to make sure votes understood that Measure M would impact their lives positively. Voters also needed to understand that this was not just one project but multiple projects all over Los Angeles County. This research led to critical strategic decisions. They needed to start the campaign early and dominate paid advertising. They started full blown advertising by Labor Day and stayed on the air through the election. The messaging was a combination of describing larger projects that impacted the entire County and specific targeting of Community projects to individual communities, such as Antelope Valley, Palos Verdes Peninsula, Gateway Cities, San Fernando Valley, San Gabriel Valley, Malibu, and Agoura Hills.

Digital ads were the prime vehicle for this targeting along with direct mail. The campaign also did a large Spanish language ad campaign for the last two months of the campaign. Latino voters were a big target group for the campaign. The last ad featured Mayor Eric Garcetti driving in traffic asking for a Yes on Measure M vote. It was a great wrap up. Finally, in the research the campaign discovered that voters did not care about or want a "sunset" provision on Measure M. The "sunset" provision would have put a time limit on Measure M. Without the "sunset" limit, LA County could fix its transportation problems.

GREEN (C) LINE CONNECTION TO LAX

The original plan for the Metro Greenline was for it to be an express bus service that would operate in exclusive bus lanes in the center of the I-105 Freeway. This bus operation could be upgraded to rail in the future if money were available. With the passage and validation of Proposition A, the LACTC voted to skip the bus lane concept and to build light rail as part of the original construction of the I-105.

The Green Line plan included an extension west from a station at Aviation Boulevard into El Segundo and Redondo Beach where the Los Angeles Transportation Commission built a rail car storage and light maintenance facility. Periodic Heavy Maintenance functions (wheel truing, painting, etc.) for the Green Line rail cars would be conducted at a Heavy Maintenance facility to be built in Long Beach as part of the Blue Line. A "non-revenue connector track" would be built as part of the Green Line / I-105 project at the Imperial Highway Station. This would allow Green Line rail cars to travel onto the Blue Line to Long Beach for Heavy Maintenance and it would also allow specialized maintenance vehicles housed in Long Beach to service the Green Line.

Another part of the original plan was for the Green Line to connect with LAX in the future. A "WYE" rail interchange was built just west of the Aviation Boulevard Station to allow trains to travel to and from LAX east to Norwalk or west to Redondo Beach in the Future. In order to get to LAX, the Green Line would travel north along the west side of Aviation Boulevard on an elevated guideway and then across Century Boulevard and to an elevated station in Lot C at the site of SCRTD's 96th Street Bus Terminal. There, passengers could make an "across platform transfer" from the Green Line onto a new airport people mover to be built by LAWA. Until the new LAX People Mover was operational, Green Line Passengers could reach their terminals by transferring to airport shuttle buses at the 96th Street station.

MYTHS AND TRUTH

Several views and opinions have been expressed over the years, such as why the Green Line did not go to LAX.

Some claimed that there was a turf war between Neil Peterson the CEO of the LACTC and the Executive Director of LAWA, Cliff Moore. Others claimed that Moore did not want to lose parking fees income. FAA was blamed because of their concern of signal interference (an issue could had been resolved with trains going underground at the airport) And finally, a view was expressed to me during an interview with a senior LACTC board member who told me "...it was designed ready to roll, and then that funding was pulled. The agency pulled the funding from there to put it toward the Red Line."

According to Ed McSpedon, the LACTC project manager, the EIS and the design for the Green Line-LAX connector were completed and approved by the FAA and LAWA. The contract for the construction was awarded and work began to build the guideway foundations along the West side of Aviation Boulevard heading north toward the airport. The LACTC included "priced options" for the signal and power systems on the LAX Connector within the main Green Line Contracts. McSpedon's point of contact at LAWA was senior civil engineer Bob Millard. McSpedon recollects" Bob was the first person to tell me that LAWA Executive Director Cliff Moore was furious that LACTC was starting construction of the LAX connection and that he had called Mayor Bradley demanding that the work be stopped." The understanding was that the real issue was that LAWA was way behind in their planning for their future airport expansion and that they were not ready to commit to having a people mover connection in Lot C on 96th Street. It seemed that Moore had somehow been caught by surprise by the pace of the construction. McSpedon discussed this with Neil Peterson, and it was clear that Mayor Bradley wanted us to stop construction of the connector. It also seemed that someone had convinced the FAA to reconsider their prior approvals and they were now expressing concerns about the possible distraction to pilots by elevated trains crossing the approach path to the airport. "The connection to the airport had to be right and it could only be right with the support of LAWA and of the mayor's office. So, when Peterson asked me what I thought we should do, I told him that we should terminate our on-going construction contracts and work with LAWA on a new plan that they would support," McSpedon explained to me.

The fact that Los Angeles does not have a rail connection to LAX has always been used to disparage LACTC as being incompetent. However, whenever someone asked why we never built a rail connection to LAX the answer is: "We fully intended to, and we had started construction of a connection in the early 1990s but the airport stopped it because they were not far enough along in their expansion plans to determine how and where they wanted a rail connection," McSpedon told me.

THE LOS ANGELES RIVER

Water is the driving force of all nature.

—Leonardo da Vinci

If we go back over the last twenty-five years, the Los Angeles River has gone from obscurity to celebrity. Few knew the river was there, let alone cared about it. But now there is probably more going on and more players involved than at any time in the past.

The Los Angeles River, known as West River by the Tongva and the Porciuncula River by the Spanish, has its headwaters in the Simi Hills and Santa Susana Mountains and flows approximately fifty-one miles from Canoga Park through the San Fernando Valley and downtown Los Angeles to Long Beach, where it drains into San Pedro Bay. The river was once free flowing, but because of frequent floods, it now flows on a fixed course through a concrete channel built after a series of devastating floods in the early 20th century.

Lewis MacAdams one of the founders of Friends of the Los Angeles River (FoLAR) remembered, "I was walking back to the bus stop one night to go to Venice from Downtown

LA River.

and I saw the LA River for the first time in 1985." Lewis had served in the Bolinas Public Utility District in northern California, he had a longtime interest in water issues and the neglected river impressed him. "I knew right there and then I would be involved." Lewis MacAdams, sculptor Pat Patterson, gallery owner Roger Wong, and architect Fred Fisher took a pair of wire cutters to the fence separating the river from the city and declared the river open to the public in 1986, and with that Friends of the Los Angeles River (FoLAR) and the River Movement were born.

FoLAR was established as a nonprofit organization in 1986. Today it is well known, and there are numerous factions competing for attention. The river is the ecological backbone of our community. It drains the entire basin, and it is physiologically the one feature that unites us all.

Excoriated because of the damage it caused in several floods in the early part of the 20th century led to its entombment. And that is the word that's often used in a concrete channel, entombment, for much of its course, and it languished there. The river really was not a major feature in the discussions of what makes Los Angeles what it is. We owe a lot of our awareness and interest in the river to Lewis MacAdams, a smart, creative individual, a journalist, poet, and sort of a self-styled iconoclast as well.

Lewis recounted to me: "I had a soiree-type of event at our house, and Gary Snyder, who is a very great poet, an American poet, came down. He was doing a reading at the LA. Theatre Center, but that afternoon he did a reading at my house for whoever I could get to show up, maybe thirty people, and he read poems about rivers. We got enough money out of that to get stationery and bumper stickers, of course, it is LA.

"That night, Gary gave this reading, and he said as he was talking in between poems, 'This afternoon I went to the first meeting of Friends of the Los Angeles River,' and everybody in the audience laughed, and Gary said, 'Don't laugh.' It's like the first public statement mentioning the Friends of the Los Angeles River." So, I just kept it going, and it was basically just me in the first two or three years.

Then, in October 1989, Assemblyman Richard Katz decided that he was going to put a freeway in the LA River. I was working directing videotapes for a foundation called the Lannan Foundation. I was working in West Hollywood in a studio, and I got a phone call from a reporter from the *Los Angeles Times*, and he said, 'Richard Katz, the State Assemblyman, has just held a press conference and he wants to build a freeway in the LA River. What do you think?' and I just said, 'Over our dead bodies.' The next morning, sure enough, it had the picture of Richard with his little sign of it in front of this imaginary LA River freeway. I was quoted as saying, "Over our dead bodies."

We started getting phone calls, "What's Friends of the Los Angeles River?" It really was the turning point. I called it a forty-year artwork to bring the river back to life because I never felt like I was an environmentalist per se. I just didn't see myself that way. I always saw myself as an artist and a poet, and I wrote poems about the river. I saw the whole thing as a kind of performance art piece. I called it a forty-year artwork to bring the river back to life, which was useful because then people would say, "What does that mean, a forty-year artwork?" And then I would have my toe in the door, and I could go from there. I became a kind of salesman. "Richard Katz was one of the best friends the Los Angeles River ever had."

"Everything we did was to bring people down to the river, and we had to bring people down almost one by one. 20th Century Fox gave us this giant fiberglass canoe that had been used in the remake of Last of the Mohicans with Daniel Day-Lewis, and we would take politicians, journalists, anybody that was connected or had influence, on little five-minute canoe trips in the LA River because you couldn't go any further than that in this canoe. Among them were Secretary of HUD Henry Cisneros, *Los Angeles Times* journalist Bill Boyarsky, and City Councilman Tom LaBonge. Tom convinced Mayor Tom Bradley to take a little LA Riverwalk. We've since learned you can take kayaks and go all the way to Long Beach."

Lewis emerged as a river spokesperson, and he managed that role very well. Parenthetically, that caused some problems. Lewis guarded his reputation as the guerrilla poet so carefully that FoLAR was never able to expand as a nonprofit environmental organization the way some of its peers did. For example, the way Tree People or Heal the Bay became region wide causes with substantial fundraising and large organizations. FoLAR kept its grassroots. Lewis was always its spokesperson, but he certainly raised consciousness of the river. There is a park named after him, and I think history appropriately will memorialize him as the initiator of what has happened in the last twenty-five years.

It is because of Lewis the river has been elevated in people's minds. There were only thirty people at the "Great LA River Clean-up" in 1990. The "Great LA River Clean-up" is now an annual event attracting over 10,000 volunteers. It is one of the most significant environmental stewardship events, and it is now the country's largest river clean up. At his retirement speech, Lewis said, "The LA River speaks to me. And she has been a vigorous muse for more than thirty years." When Lewis retired, there was a list of 40,000 supporters of FoLAR.

THE GENESIS OF TWO GREAT PARKS

Two big lawsuits were the turning point for the river: the Chinatown Cornfield Railyard and the Taylor Yards, two large, railroad-owned properties that were planned for industrial development. There were major industrial developers who wanted to build facilities there. There was clearly a market to support industrial development. The powers that be included Mayor Riordan, who supported such a development.

FoLAR, with no corporate presence, organized itself to protest these two projects. Dan Rosenfeld, a veteran public servant, recounted to me, "There was a meeting in the Valley in the garage of Melanie Winter, who was serving as the executive director of FoLAR under Lewis. They were partners in managing the organization for a long time until they had a falling out and went different ways. The FoLAR meetings at that time were difficult. We would spend hours debating some arcane issues in Long Beach. People came without a real focus on what they were trying to do." However, two big industrial proposals galvanized attention. They were both about forty acres and were the heart of the river, adjacent properties in downtown Los Angeles.

FoLAR divided its membership into two teams. One team under Lewis would fight the Cornfield project. Lewis told me that, "Councilman LaBonge turned me onto Cornfield." The other under Winter was going to take on Taylor Yards. Lewis's team which included Chi Mui, a Chinatown activist, worked with the Shaolin Temple and others in Chinatown to build community support for challenging the project at the Cornfields, which was being sponsored by Ed Roski's Majestic Realty. Roski, with the support of Mayor Riordan, Councilman Mike Hernandez and other influential individuals was planning on building warehouses there, but FoLAR's suit stopped him. At Taylor Yards, Winter's team enlisted community support. The most consequential member was the Anahuak Youth Soccer Club, little kids from the neighborhood. They became poster children, quite literally. They were in the photographs. It was never Lewis or Melanie or the board of directors of FoLAR. The issue was these little kids who wanted to play soccer there. They were challenging a project proposed by Lennar, a big national developer.

To Majestic's and Lennar's defense, these were projects that the city encouraged. The city wanted to keep its industrial base and wanted to keep manufacturing jobs. Many of those jobs historically had been downtown. One could make an argument that building additional industrial space in the historic industrial areas along the river was consistent with the city's economic goals. The problem was that it was along the river, and two public virtues were in conflict.

Community support was built. There were press conferences. Some of the *Los Angeles Times* writers began to cover the opposition to these projects. However, the projects were steaming through, until something happened.

The attorneys representing the communities, two very well-known environmental attorneys Chatten-Brown & Carstens learned that the Majestic Project relied on a $12 million pledge of financial support from the Department of Housing and Urban Development for an $80 million warehouse complex. HUD was supportive of the project because of job creation and urban development. They challenged the project on environmental grounds.

Robert Garcia of the Center for Law in the Public Interest challenged the project under Title VI of the Civil Rights Act.On a personal level the plaintiffs 'attorneys had a relationship with Robert F. Kennedy Jr., a senior attorney for the Natural Resources Defense Council in New York, who intervened in Washington, DC on behalf of the alliance. In September, HUD Secretary Andrew Cuomo announced that the $12 million HUD funding was canceled. Without federal funding the project was stopped.

Discussions started with Majestic and then with Lennar about an exit strategy. Attorney George Mihlsten with Latham & Watkins was involved as well. There was an agreement reached where the properties could be purchased from Majestic and Lennar. At that point, Melanie Winter went to Sacramento to talk with Speaker of the Assembly Antonio Villaraigosa. Villaraigosa was able to secure the funding that enabled the State to buy the properties from Majestic and Lennar. Those two properties, which became the Los Angeles State Historic Park, a thirty-two-acre park and the Rio de Los Angeles State Park, a forty-acre park, are the real cornerstones of the river reclamation effort. Majestic settled in April 2001.

Dan Rosenfeld, when he was a partner with Urban Partners, was approached as to whether they would be interested in buying the property at the eastern terminus of the Broadway Bridge, right on the river facing back to the skyline of downtown, to develop housing. It was owned by Swiss Dairy. Rosenfeld asked whether the owners of Swiss Dairy would wait until Urban Partners raised the money to buy the land for a park. With funding secured by the Trust for Public Land, the City and others, the property was purchased, and is now called the Albion Riverside Park. Bette Davis Park, what became Lewis MacAdams Park, along with projects in the Valley such as landscaping, greenways, and bike paths along the river created a mosaic being filled in slowly, piece by piece.

CITY OF LOS ANGELES RIVER REVITALIZATION MASTER PLAN

Another milestone happened in about 2005, when the City of Los Angeles Public Works Department commissioned a master plan for the river (https://boe.lacity.org/lariverrmp). The prime consultant was TetraTech. The team for the study included Mia Lehrer, Urban Partners, and two firms from Denver, one called Civitas Inc. run by Mark Johnson and the other a landscape firm run by Bill Wenk. These were people who understood river restoration projects. They had worked on the South Platte River in Denver, the Guadalupe River in San Jose, the San Diego River, and others. That plan had a lot of very good features that identified dozens of sites that provided prime opportunities for public use.

Rosenfeld worked on the economic impact and governance to study the potential for River development. It began to address what later became one of the most difficult questions: what is the right economic course for the river? One could easily build expensive high-rise condominiums along the river, and a few very wealthy people would have a beautiful view. Or one could do all kinds of alternatives, including trying to preserve lower-income neighborhoods like Elysian Valley (commonly known as Frogtown), Glassell Park, and Lincoln Heights which are river-adjacent and not nearly so affluent. That dichotomy of

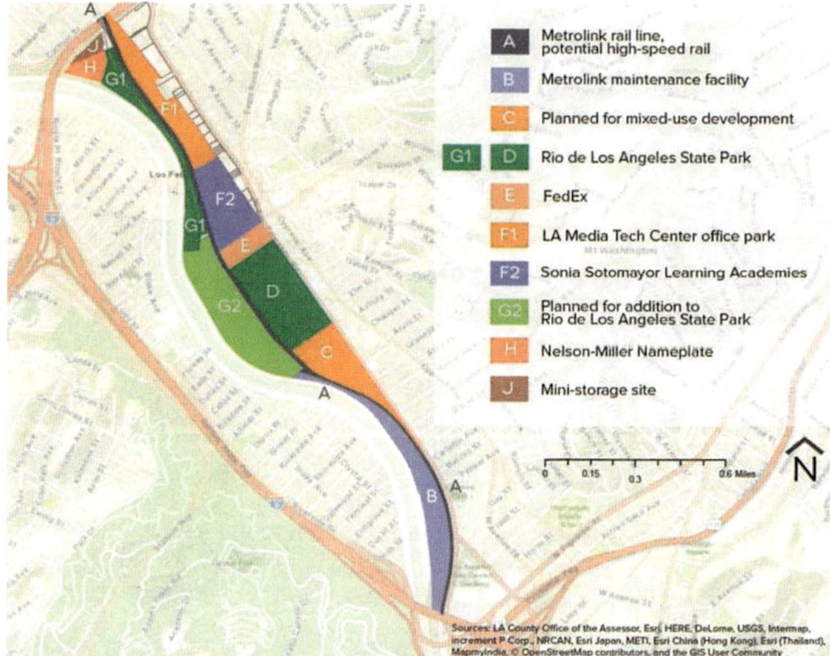

Taylor Yards.

the gentrification question began to come up in that study. The study was approved and had a chapter on governance that Mark Johnson wrote. It recommended the creation of three organizations.

One existed: FoLAR, a non-profit, unifying force on the river, educating, empowering and mobilizing thousands of Angelenos each year through the annual "Great LA River Clean Up" and school and community programs. Volunteers also take part in habitat restorations, nature walks, and river education activities. In 2022, volunteers removed 50,000 pounds of trash from the river. FoLAR put out the first study of fish and fishing in the Los Angeles River. It did the first water quality and monitoring reports of the LA River, and the first study of birds of the LA River. Thousands of children come to the river every year to look at birds and fish and learn how to monitor water quality.

The second was a joint powers authority of the various governments that had jurisdiction. This was identified early on as an issue because the US Army Corps of Engineers oversees the drainage system of the Los Angeles Basin. The LA County Department of Flood Control manages the systems that operate the water flow through the river. The City of Los Angeles has jurisdiction over the land, on the banks of the river, but really has no ownership per se on the riverbed itself. So, there were three governments whose policies were being pursued independently, and the recommendation was there a joint powers authority.

One of the issues that bubbled up is that the County wanted to take over more of the federal role and really become the river masters. Meanwhile, the LA City Public Works Department says everything that really affects people is outside the channel and they need to be at the table. But Public Works has nothing to do with the river itself. It is a Federal-County flood control channel. Parenthetically, the environmental community has always objected to the word "flood control," because one cannot control floods any more than one can control volcanoes or earthquakes. They say it should be the Watershed Management Department. Unfortunately, the intergovernmental cooperation leg of this tripod has never been resolved.

The third piece was born with noble intentions, and that was to create a private non-profit economic development corporation to work along the river.

There are examples around the country, and the one that was noted most frequently was in Pennsylvania Avenue in Washington DC, which had become quite run-down. The Federal government and the governments of the District of Columbia and two states got together and, block by block, have done an admirable job of improving Pennsylvania Avenue.

The "River LA," a nonprofit organization was established in 2009 by the City of Los Angeles to coordinate river policy as part of the Los Angeles River Revitalization Master Plan.

In 2014, the Army Corps of Engineers announced the selection of Alternative 20, the most comprehensive alternative in their Ecosystem Restoration Feasibility Study. That was then estimated to cost $1.3 billion. The share of the cost to the city according to Mayor Garcetti was $500 million. The Corps of Engineers designated along with the Everglades restoration, the LA River as one of their highest environmental priorities.

In March 2017, the City of Los Angeles bought the land known as the G2 parcel part of the 250-acre Taylor Yard complex for $60 million to develop a combination of park space, walking trails, wetlands, wildlife habitat, river access, public recreation, and other amenities. Parcel G2 is a forty-two-acre parcel located on the river's east bank in the Cypress Park neighborhood, and it is the last remnant of the Union Pacific Railroad's former Taylor Yard. The rest of the land has been developed into a park, space, a public school and a transit village. The State provided an additional $25 million to fund the acquisition.

Mayor Eric Garcetti described G2 as the "crown jewel" of a broader ongoing initiative to restore eleven miles of the LA River. The park is expected to be completed by 2028 in time for the 2028 Summer Olympic Games. It is a portion of the Los Angeles River Revitalization Master Plan (https://boe.lacity.org/lariverrmp), and it is expected to connect the surrounding Rio de Los Angeles State Park and the State-owned G1, "Bowtie" parcel, which together would form 100 acres of open space along the LA River. "Bowtie" is an eighteen-acre parcel used today for public art programming and numerous pop-up events, in collaboration with the local nonprofit, Clockshop.

According to Deborah Weintraub, City of Los Angeles Chief Deputy City Engineer, in January 2022, Congress gave the Los Angeles River Ecosystem Restoration Project $28 million in new federal funding under the Infrastructure Investments and Jobs Act. The community-embraced projects would restore hundreds of acres of habitat along the river, add trails to connect people with nature and the river, and support equity, environmental justice, and climate resilience for underserved communities that are adjacent to the river.

To tap into those Federal funds, the city and corps, need to sign a Project Partnership Agreement, projected to occur in the fall of 2023, following Council and Mayoral approval.

The Bureau of Engineering (BOE) is proceeding with design at Reach 6—the Taylor Yard G2 site. The Corps is working on the design at Reach 1, Pollywog Park. Also, BOE is working with the Corps on technical analyses including a full rebase lining of the area's hydrology and hydraulics to inform the design of the restoration features. Of the total estimated cost for Alternative 20, the city is responsible for 72 percent and the Corps for 28 percent, per the approval of a Locally Preferred Plan.

However, the cost of the G2 parcel revitalization grew from $252 million in 2016 to $1.06 billion in 2022, roughly equivalent to the estimated cost of the full restoration program when it was announced in 2014.

RIVER LA CORP.

Under the leadership of Chief Executive Officer Kate Moulene, River LA has built public-private partnerships to support several projects that have ranged from a private conference with U.N. Secretary Ban Ki-moon to over forty NGO's and as many corporations.

River LA-led extensive community engagement and outreach process in partnership with local leaders, NGO's and people living along the river to support the Los Angeles River Revitalization Master Plan (LARMP), planned by architect Frank Gehry and urban planner and landscape architect Laurie Olin.

I am gratified that the greenway concept that I unveiled in 1990 has become a reality, with many projects around the County already built, and this mega greenway that River LA launched in 2020 to advocate for connecting all fity-one miles of the LA River Bike Path is in progress.

Collaborating with other community partners, River LA hosted community one-on-ones, policy brown bag lunches with stakeholders, and community activations. Once the fifty-one miles of the LA River are connected, the LA River will be one of the longest urban recreational arteries in the country.

River LA helped to create The River Index—a reference document used to tell the story of the Los Angeles River and the communities it impacts. The index has been broken into nine sections and views the river through the lens of people, water, and nature. The information from the index is now integrated into the new Los Angeles 2022 Master Plan.

River LA was selected to lead the Outdoor Equity Grants Program (OEP) for the city of Compton. The OEP was funded by the California Department of Parks and Recreation with the goal of increasing the ability of residents in low-income urban and rural communities to participate in outdoor experiences at state parks and other public lands. River LA's role is to empower over two thousand youth and families through outdoor leadership education, career pathways, environmental justice engagement, and access to nature.

LOS ANGELES COUNTY'S LA RIVER MASTER PLAN

The development of the LA River Master Plan by the Los Angeles County Department of Public Works (LACODPW) started on Supervisor Gloria Molina's initiative, an early supporter of revitalizing the river.

In March 2018, "River LA" engaged architect Frank Gehry and Partners for the Master Plan project. Others working on the Master Plan included Geosyntec and Laurie Olin, urban planner and landscape architect. The new master plan was unanimously adopted by the County Board of Supervisors in 2022, which has been in the works for more than five years (https://lariver masterplan.org). Los Angeles County has no jurisdiction over the riverfront, and therefore it has no authority to implement the plan. It serves mainly as a blueprint of what is possible along the river.

Every river advocate thinks that safety is a paramount issue. The river cannot hurt people and destroy property. The County takes that role very seriously, as does the Corps of Engineers. Nobody is going to be allowed to do anything on the river that is seen as jeopardizing safety. And safety is becoming a bigger problem because, as the climate changes, and storm events become more predictable and perhaps more severe and more of the basin gets paved, the amount of water that rushes into the river increases and becomes faster and faster.

So, there is another issue on the table today, the vulnerability of the lower regions of the river to flooding. There are maps of FEMA that show serious flood danger in places like Rancho Dominguez on the Lower River. And if the river were to top its banks, people on the roofs could be waving at helicopters, like with Hurricane Katrina. There would be a real catastrophe in a very vulnerable neighborhood.

The Gehry Plan started with the safety premise, and there were a series of public hearings. Many people were shocked at the results because the most visible recommendation was that certain portions of the river should be covered with concrete, so that buildings could be built on top of them.

The first one proposed was in South Gate. It was called a platform park, with a deck over about a mile of the river, basically covering it. It was presented to the community as an opportunity to have soccer fields, which was very disingenuous. The community said, wow, we would love to have soccer fields. Former Speaker Rendon, who represented that area, was a proponent of these platform parks. Two environmental groups sued Los Angeles County over a Los Angeles River plan to create platform parks designed by Gehry. LA Waterkeeper and the Center for Biological Diversity filed the lawsuit accusing officials of violating state environmental laws when they approved the Los Angeles River Master Plan.

The FoLAR side just went apoplectic, "After all these years, we are trying to rediscover and rehabilitate the river, and Gehry wants to bury it?" Lewis called me one day to vent his anger.

An advisory group faced a quandary: do we support or oppose this plan? They disagreed with most of the recommendations of the plan and, as result, LA Waterkeeper, the Center for Biological Diversity, FoLAR, East Yard Communities for Environmental Justice, Heal the Bay, and the Nature Conservancy withdrew support for the project before the master plan vote by the LA County Board of Supervisors in June 2022.

THE RIVER PROJECT

Melanie Winter continued to work in 2023 as director of "The River Project," founded in 2000. She advocates for floodplain buyback and giving it a natural ability to meander. That is a very expensive long-term proposition. But that is her goal. She has received several grants to do projects, and she has done them very well. One on Tujunga Wash in the Valley and some parts of the River in Studio City.

Winter received a grant from the Santa Monica Mountains Conservancy to do a study of the Sepulveda Basin. The Sepulveda Basin is probably the most natural, biggest source of opportunity on the Los Angeles River. And it is entirely publicly owned. Therefore, the opportunity to do something there is probably greater than anywhere else on the river. It is owned by the US Army Corps of Engineers and leased to the City of LA Department of Recreation and Parks.

Winter did a brilliant plan, which came out in 2022, proposing restoring certain parts of the river. The Sepulveda Basin is like a tropical country, with the river wandering through vegetation and giving people the ability to canoe, fish, and kayak. There are hundreds of acres of park space for various uses. Part of the Basin is a nature preserve. There are three golf courses, an eighty-acre sports field, an archery range, playgrounds, bike paths, hiking trails, tennis courts, a velodrome, cricket grounds, a model aircraft field, and a dog park.

Winter produced a plan which really brings back a lot of the beauty and character of the Sepulveda Basin, which has half a dozen tributary streams, including Haskell Creek, Woodley Creek, Bull Creek, and Encino Creek. Very few people even know these facilities exist running across the Valley, and they all meet in the Sepulveda Basin.

PIECES OF THE MOSAIC ALONG THE RIVER

The North Atwater Bridge received unanimous approval from Los Angeles City Council members on May 26, 2017, to allocate the funds needed to move the Atwater Bridge project forward into construction. It is a public-private infrastructure project funded by the city and private donations through the efforts led by River LA. The La Kretz Bridge is the second bridge to cross the LA River in the 21st century. It is a cable-stayed steel pedestrian, equestrian and cyclist bridge connecting Griffith Park and Atwater Village.

In 2019 the State of California funded the construction of the Alondra Gateway Park in Compton and the Southeast LA (SELA) Cultural Center, projects in the Lower LA River Revitalization Plan. The half-acre property will have space for picnics, seating areas and exercise equipment. The SELA Cultural Center will include a performance hall, a music education space, recording studios, a dance theater, a café, and galleries.

The "Rumblefish" Taylor Yard Bikeway and Pedestrian Bridge connecting Taylor Yard with Elysian Valley on the west of the Los Angeles River was completed in 2020 with $20.8 million provided by the Los Angeles Metropolitan Transportation Authority.

In early 2020, the City and MRCA signed a letter of intent with the California Department of Parks and Recreation (State Parks) to create the "100-Acre Partnership at Taylor Yard." This partnership includes Parcel G2, Parcel G1," Bowtie Parcel" an eighteen-acre property, MRCA's twelve-and-a-half-acre easement on Parcel G2 that was purchased from the City in 2019 and the "Rio de Los Angeles State Park." The partnership's goals and objectives are to plan the continuous open space along the river collaboratively.

The Paseo del Rio project that spans one mile along the east side of the river was the first project of the "100-acre Partnership."

A number of restoration efforts are being undertaken for various segments of the river by the City of LA, the Los Angeles River Revitalization Master Plan, completed in 2007, the Lower LA River Revitalization Plan, completed in 2018, and the County's Plan Master Plan approved by the Los Angeles County Board of Supervisors in 2022, addresses the full fifty-one-mile corridor between the San Fernando Valley and San Pedro Bay.

ENHANCED INFRASTRUCTURE FINANCING DISTRICTS

Tax increment financing (TIF) has historically been used by redevelopment agencies to raise funding for infrastructure improvements, housing, and other projects in redevelopment areas. However, Governor Jerry Brown dissolved redevelopment agencies. In 2014 with Senate Bill (SB) 628 the State replaced the existing Infrastructure Financing Districts with Enhanced Infrastructure Financing Districts.

A study prepared in 2014 by the LA River Team Planning Studio and USC Price School of Public Policy outlined funding streams using the Enhanced Infrastructure Financing District (EIFD) for the LA River Revitalization. Professor Mark Pisano, co-author, has been a great promoter of EIFDs.

In 2016, Los Angeles City Councilman Mitch O'Farrell proposed the EIFD as a funding mechanism to generate $50 million annually to revitalize the Los Angeles River. It would finance affordable housing, bridges, and bikeways.

A report issued by the Economic and Workforce Development Department (EWDD) in 2017 recommended the establishment of nine EIFDs along thirty-two miles of the river. Unfortunately, as has always been the case in City Hall, creative and innovative ideas are "filed." Meanwhile many agencies up and down the State are using the EIFDs with great success. Larry Kosmont Companies have mapped out this progress.

LEWIS MacADAMS' LONG TERM VISION

I met Lewis MacAdams in 1992 when he was writing my profile for the *LA Weekly* over a few weeks. We developed a friendship over the years. I sensed so because we were both dreamers of big projects. He used to remind me of Daniel Burnham's quote, "Make no small plans. They have no magic to stir men's blood." Burnham was the visionary 19th-century Chicago architect who laid out the city after its great fire. Chicago's lakeshore is today one of America's recreationally colorful downtown districts.

Because I was on the Board of SCRTD and then LAMTA, he tried to interest me in supporting his grand vision, undergrounding the railroad tracks at the east and west banks of the river. There are 4.5 miles of railroad tracks between Arroyo Seco and the city limits, isolating the central city from its river. On the east bank are the tracks of the Union Pacific railroad. This service, the "Piggyback Rail Yard" technically referred to as the Los Angeles Transportation Center, covers two miles of riverfront.

In 2009, FoLAR approached four landscape architecture and architecture firms to work pro-bono developing the Piggyback Yard Masterplan. These four firms were comprised of Michael Maltzan Architecture, Mia Lehrer + Associates, Perkins + Will, and Chee Salette Architecture.

The proposed plan envisions redevelopment of 125 acres of land and approximately twenty-five acres of the riverbed to generate a strengthened connection of the community and its local ecologies. On the property the plan proposes to develop areas of educational, cultural, commercial, health care, and minor industrial buildings. On the west are the tracks for Amtrak and Metrolink.

Lewis's dream was to consolidate the tracks on the west side of the river, and then run them underground into Union Station. His vision was once the tracks were buried, the city could create riverfront parks on both the east and west banks. Lewis pointed out to me that New York built Park Avenue on top of the New York Central tracks, eventually developed into midtown Manhattan. The Millennium Park in Chicago was built on top of the Illinois Central railroad tracks. To accomplish this plan, Los Angeles needs a mayor who is a "dreamer" with a bold vision and strong personality to assemble planners, architects, engineering, and landscape architects, allow them to think big and most importantly give them cover from the press and naysayers. It will be a "once in a century" urban waterside project that will stimulate and energize Angelenos and lead us out of the funk.

The river remains the spiritual bloodstream and the economic and social heart of our community. It is why we are here (and not somewhere else nearby), and it holds many opportunities for guiding our future. On a technical level, we must learn to manage our storm water more wisely, not just to protect lives and property, but to provide a real source of usable water as others run dry. On social and recreational dimensions, the river provides venues for health, recreation, social, and commercial activities that we all enjoy. And, on a higher plane, the river is a magnet that will draw this metropolis back together. After decades of centrifugal sprawl, people are coming back to the river, back to where Los Angeles started. It is forming a new sense of community, the root terms of which are, of course, "common" and "unity." The river brings us together.

CHAPTER FOURTEEN

FINDING BEAUTY AND CREATING IT

Whenever you are creating beauty around you,
you are restoring your own soul.
—ALICE WALKER

STEEL CLOUD

In 1987, Los Angeles mayor Tom Bradley appointed me as chairman of a blue-ribbon committee to find a location and come up with a design symbolic of a "monument to welcome immigrants to America's shore," sort of like the Statue of Liberty. The monument was perceived then to be a static structure or a sculpture, maybe a statue that would complement a park, rise over Los Angeles Harbor, or be placed atop a hill overlooking Los Angeles International Airport.

However, the Committee concluded that Los Angeles did not need a static edifice, a monument in the conventional sense that would fit in cities such a Rome, Paris, or Athens. The committee decided to propose instead a living, utilitarian reminder of our diverse cultural heritage—a continuous, evolving source of learning and appreciation of our collective

Steel Cloud.

national identity, a landmark that would be a rallying point for the community, a public space that would bring people together in a renewed spirit of pride and cooperation, a symbol that would reflect all the values and institutions related to America's traditional hospitality toward immigrants, refugees, visitors, and international events.

Once the general concept of the project was developed, the next step was to find an appropriate location. A number of criteria were set forth: accessibility, visibility, readily available, and minimum environmental impact, expansion potential, appropriate size, proximity to other strategic areas, and local community benefits. Because Union Station would be the transportation hub of Los Angeles County with the completion of Metro Rail and light rail lines, placing the project there would make it easily accessible. It was determined that Union Station met the other criteria and had some unique features. It is near the Civic Center, one of the largest concentrations of government offices outside Washington, DC. Three ethnic districts are within walking distance: Chinatown, El Pueblo de Los Angeles Historical Monument (Olvera Street), and Little Tokyo. If we were to connect these three ethnic islands, we could designate that area as our "monument."

Inexpensive ideas, such as banners, posters, the painting of existing streets and alleys through these areas, awning designs, landscaping, fountains, play zones and performance spaces would actually and symbolically link the ethnic roots of Los Angeles (see Angeles Walk). The plan also called for developing the public space between the Music Center and City Hall. (Thanks to Los Angeles County Supervisor Gloria Molina's vision, foresight, persistence, and perseverance, the "Gloria Molina Grand Park" was later built as part of the Grand Avenue Complex developed by the Related Companies of New York.)

There is, however, a physical obstacle to the "connector" scheme. A river of automobiles separates Little Tokyo from Olvera Street and Chinatown. This river is the 101 Freeway, a psychological and physical barrier between the north and south sections of our city. If we were to build a bridge over the freeway, the connection would be complete. A big challenge, but what a fantastic opportunity it would be to build a public space on top of the freeway. And so, the "West Coast Gateway" was born—the crown jewel of the "monument."

The Committee organized an international design competition in April 1988 with an international jury of thirteen notable architects, writers, poets, visual artists, and authors from seven countries. The jury included author/futurist Ray Bradbury; Jon Jerde, the architect of Universal CityWalk Hollywood; Sverre Fehn, a Norwegian architect who won the Pritzker Architecture Prize in 1997; actor George Takei; British architect Colin St John "Sandy" Wilson; and Los Angeles architect Michael Rotondi.

The committee received 150 responses from all around the world. These were narrowed to five semifinalists: Neil Denari and Alex Kobayashi of Los Angeles; Vilen Künnapu, Ain Padrik and Andres Siim of Estonia; Irmfried Windbichler of Austria; Dagar Richter and Shayne O'Neil of Cambridge, of Massachusetts; and Studio Asymptote, led by Hani Rashid and Lise Anne Couture, of New York.

The winner was the team of Hani Rashid, a native of Egypt, and Lise Anne Couture a native of Montreal, of Studio Asymptote, who had proposed a structure titled *Steel Cloud*. It was announced on December 5, 1988. The winning design called for a four block long,

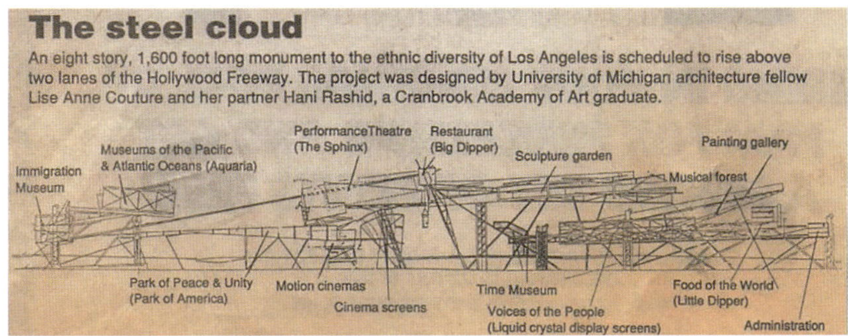

Steel Cloud diagram.

eight story high superstructure to rise on piers from the median strip of the 101 Freeway. According to English magazine Blueprints, "Contrary to the sedentary nature of a building structure, *Steel Cloud* appears to be moving in continuous layers of jet like movements in the style of works by the Italian Futurists. Though inspired by the clouds above LA and the round the clock activity within LA, *Steel Cloud* is very much in touch with reality and the ground it will spring from when built."

The proposal for the *Steel Cloud* complex included museums, libraries, restaurants, aquaria representing the Pacific and Atlantic Oceans, liquid crystal display screens, movie screens, a theater, a sculpture garden, a painting gallery, a Park of Unity, and a "musical forest" of synthesizers which would transform the surrounding city sounds into music.

A ceremony unveiling the design at El Pueblo de Los Angeles Historical Monument was held February 12,1989, with television and radio broadcaster and event emcee Mario Machado noting, "The stage was decorated with balloons colored white, black, brown, yellow, and red, symbolizing the city's ethnic diversity." Mayor Bradley called the Gateway project, "An exciting concept that will pay tribute to the contributions of immigrants who have helped shape Los Angeles." And Bradbury said, "These proofs of our immigrant past stand a few hundred yards or a few blocks apart. Yet, they might as well be separated by tens of miles for all the mixing between these towns within a city. Rarely do the inhabitants of the three or four communities stroll from one to the other. Rarely do tourists, abandoning their cars, ricochet happily from one immigrant duchy to the next. All this must change."

The jury's comments included the following:

- "The project is the realization of a current avant-garde exploration in architecture. In the view of this selection jury, it provides the first occasion upon which that exploration has produced the appropriate solution to a major public occasion."
- "The architecture, in which the underside of the structures is as important as the facades and roof, not only relates well to the movement of cars in the freeway, but also produces forms that encapsulate and give form to the qualities of movement, energy and innovation for which Los Angeles is uniquely celebrated."
- "The sheer boldness of this project is sustained under close inspection, not only by the integrity of its strategic decisions, but also through the poetic force of the images, metaphors and sensual experiences that it offers to the visitor."

Tatlin Tower. wikimedia.

The geometric elements of the design have been likened to the "deconstructivism" movement in contemporary architecture, though *LA Weekly* art and design critic Peter Frank noted that they really are closer to the "constructivist" designs of the early part of the century such as the Monument to the Third International, designed by Russian architect Vladimir Tatlin in 1920 but never built.

Creating a city monument is a tricky venture because you are committing to iron and stone a reflection of the city's self. Not everyone is going to like the selection. Many will call for a safe monument; something tall and simple that tourists will flock to and take pictures of; a monument that can withstand a myriad of interpretations. New York's Empire State Building, Chicago's Willis Tower (formerly Sears Tower), and San Francisco's Transamerica Pyramid all became monuments of their cities because of the attention, both positive and negative, that they attracted, though none was built with the intention of being a monument.

Rashid said, "We didn't set out to design a monument. We set out to design a gateway, a building that would be a response to these people journeying from all over the world to live in LA. A kind of beacon, with space for programs, galleries, video screens, and museums, which would ultimately become monument only by virtue of the people using it and inhabiting it. The designation of a monument would come onto it afterward." Couture said, "We wanted to capture the notion of the horizontal on the horizon, a projection of desire and dreams, the idea that the sky is the limit, instead of a more traditional tower some sort of icon that would be an isolated dinosaur."

The Disney Concert Hall was also admired by the professionals but hated by the public. *Los Angeles Times* reporter Dianne Haithman wrote, "When photographs of Gehry's models were published on the front page, the newspaper was deluged with scathing letters."

Although the public reaction to the *Steel Cloud* was mostly negative and nasty, support in the art and architecture world continued to grow. The ran a story covering the debate as much as the project itself. The *New York Times* covered the *Steel Cloud*. The *San Francisco Examiner* carried a story by Kevin Starr. *The Detroit News*, *Insight Magazine*, and *Blueprints of England*, and other news media also ran articles. The project was placed under international scrutiny.

Sam Kaplan, *Los Angeles Times* architectural critic at that time, made a sarcastic remark to the jurors, "Well, now that you had your free trip to LA and a fancy dinner, what are you going to show us?" This is the same critic who was quoted in reviewing the design of Frank

Gehry's own house in Santa Monica as saying, "I wouldn't take my dog to piss in the front yard of this house." Los Angeles City Councilwoman Gloria Molina when presented with a picture of the two-foot model said, "It looks like a freeway that just blew up," and that "It is stressful just to look at it."

Jury member Michael Rotondi said, "Ultimately, it has to do with how to reclaim parts of the city that tend to be left unused. This makes the site over the freeway an asset rather than a liability. Freeways are thought of as a problem, but this incorporates, uses the freeway...The eight non-Angelenos of the thirteen-member international jury thought Los Angeles would be more eager than most cities to accept innovation. This was the first time I had conversations about Los Angeles with outsiders that discussed LA like other great cities. They did not use LA, Disneyland, and palm trees in the same sentence."

New Perspectives Journal editor Nathan Gardels asked, "If the aesthetic of LA is so impoverished, why reproduce it?" The *Los Angeles Herald Examiner* unleased a vicious campaign against the *Steel Cloud* with a page 1 invitation to residents to write their opinions of it. Gordon Dillow, the newspaper's columnist, likened it to, "a bad accident on the southbound 101 Freeway." Other critics said the *Steel Cloud* looked like a "praying mantis," or a "horizontal oil rig."

However, in the Chinatown and Mexican American neighborhoods that adjoin the site, residents were pleased by the '*Steel Cloud*,' with comments such as, "It looks like the skeleton of an airplane." And "It's something new, very modern, we need something like that in LA."

Kevin Starr, in an article in the *San Francisco Examiner* in August of 1989 with the headline "An Urban Dream" wrote, "It is hard to describe this structure without seeing the model. It's a unique proposal that bridges art, architecture, and technology. Like all visionary proposals, the *Steel Cloud* stimulates us to think about the future, and to dream of the cities that might be. In extending our range of vision, we keep alive hopes that have accounted for the best aspects of our existing cities."

Joseph Giovannini, in an article in *Metropolitan Home* in August 1989 with the headline "Key to the City: A healing Arch" wrote, "Surprisingly, the judges chose more than a striking design. The winning proposal may, if built, have the charisma and critical mass to center the city-like planting an Eiffel Tower downtown. It is the kind of monument that imprints the mind's eye because of its originality. It looks like no other. Freeways are the life blood of LA, but they are also its scars. The proposed Gateway sutures the area together by turning the void over the freeway into both a compelling object and walkable, sittable urban space densely programmed with activities. On one level, the Gateway resonates as a monumental interpretation in steel of 20th century culture. On another, it is simply the stuff of which exhilarating weekend afternoons are made. The West Coast Gateway could be LA's Sunday in the park."

Christopher Knight, *Herald Examiner* art critic in 1988 and now with the *Los Angeles Times,* wrote an article with the headline Brilliant or Barbaric? "Not all Angelenos despise the controversial Gateway...I like the West Coast Gateway proposal a lot. Let me repeat that, just to erase any possible ambiguity. After all, this is a proposal whose recent unveiling immediately generated knee-jerk condemnation and ridicule on a scale and with a uniformity worthy of a Busby Berkley chorus line. So, it's important to be plain-spoken: I like the

West Coast Gateway proposal a lot. The structure's designation as 'a monument' coupled with surprisingly uninformative reporting in the press, has led a lot of people to believe the *Steel Cloud* is a gigantic sculpture. It is not. It is a building-or, rather, a cluster of them interconnected by the larger superstructure. I find this proposal to be a brilliant evocation of the spirit and history of this city. I write this as an ordinary citizen, a resident of the metropolis for whom this amazing structure has been designed, and to whose dreams and memories it so remarkably-and with such emphatic generosity-addresses itself. *Steel Cloud* has a masterful legendary ancestor: Vladimir Tatlin's unbuilt Monument to the Third International, designed by the thirty-five-year-old visionary for the center of Moscow in 1920 as a symbol for the popular revolution. Tatlin's radical plan called for a spiraling tower of glass and iron, tilted on the axis of the earth and twice as tall as the Empire State Building. Huge geometric forms were buildings meant to house conference centers, legislative offices, and a propaganda center. But *Steel Cloud* is radically different from its Russian ancestor, and in ways that are peculiar to the democratic European dream that built America and culminated in that most American of cities, LA. This colossus is horizontal not vertical. The recollection of a construction site permanently in progress replaces a more finished look (what better style for this always rebuilding city?) The whole is not a singularly centered structure around which all else revolves, but a meandering aggregate of interdependent parts that could expand endlessly in other words, it is suburban, not urban. Perhaps the most important difference is that its buoyant, catapulting forms house museums, theaters, libraries, and parks. Functions of government and propaganda, central to Tatlin's tower, have been replaced by history, art, and nature. Tatlin's planned tower is now universally regarded as a work of a genius. Likewise, no design I know of, past or present, more brilliantly or provocatively evokes the history and the image of LA than Lise Anne Couture and Hani Rashid's amazing *Steel Cloud.*"

The Los Angeles Cultural Affairs Commission conducted an early review that was more supportive than the general public. Commission President Merry Norris was fascinated by its boldness. Commissioner David Simon commented, "The project is very exciting and worthy of strong support by this Commission. The project will be attacked from all angles. It may have to be built and people live with it for a while before they get comfortable with it."

I worked with state Sen. Art Torres to secure the air rights for the project. Senate Bill 1127 read, "Caltrans shall reserve and designate all rights to the airspace immediately above Route 101...extending from Broadway on the west to Alameda St on the east in the City of Los Angeles, for lease for the purpose of development of a cultural center as proposed by the entity known as West Coast Gateway."

The *Steel Cloud* has been exhibited and has been the subject of lectures and articles around the world. The concept of "capping" the freeway has been considered elsewhere: Hollywood Central Park is a proposed forty-four-acre site atop the 101 Freeway between Santa Monica Boulevard and Bronson Avenue. Park 101was proposed in 2008 above the "Big Trench" section of the 101 Freeway downtown. Cap parks have also been proposed in Santa Monica at two locations along the 10 Freeway: between 14th and 17th streets and between Ocean Avenue and 4th Street.

In 2023, City of Pasadena officials were studying a plan that identifies the future land uses, scale of development, and infrastructure needs for the 710 Freeway "ditch." The roughly forty-acre site once was planned, and later aborted, for the 710 Freeway extension.

Alas, *Steel Cloud* has joined the list of projects referenced in Greg Goldin's and Sam Lubell's book *Never Built Los Angeles*. I explained some of the reasons that *Steel Cloud* did not move ahead. First, the city had entered a recession, the office market had 33 percent vacancy rate and Pacific Rim interests among others were pulling out of downtown, Los Angeles, thus private funding became almost impossible. In the early 1990s, the increasing influx of minority residents was engendering social upheaval rather than an appreciation for diversity. The riots of 1992 certainly did not help.

I also made a few mistakes. On reflection I would have made the scope "doable, believable, and financeable in our lifetime." I felt starting with one block rather than four might have been more palatable to the public and affordable. I also mishandled the media. The proposal was unveiled to the media right after the jury had selected the *Steel Cloud*. It was not under controlled conditions, staged, enlisting supporters to be present and talk of the strengths of the proposals in addition to the jurists. The model was a two-foot rough depiction of the project four blocks long between Broadway Street and Alameda Street. Therefore, it was natural for the average person to view it as a sculpture rather than as a series of buildings. An eternal optimist, I had undertaken, in retrospect, quixotically a gargantuan project that was ahead of its time and at the wrong time. But I always acted guided by Bernard Shaw's quote, often used by Robert Kennedy, "Some men see things as they are and say why? I dream things that never were and say why not?"

In *A Weekly Dose of Architectural Books*, architect and blogger John Hill wrote, "In the competition's unbuilt nature lies its potential. It will become a piece of architectural influence and history, as much as [Giovanni Battista] Piranesi's imaginary views, [Claude Nicolas] Ledoux and [Etienne Louis] Boullee's fantastical projects, Antonio Sant-Elia's futuristic cities, Le Corbusier's League of Nations project and Rem Koolhaas' entry for the Tres Grande Biblioteque in Paris, among others. The power of these projects lies in their strong conceptual clarity and ability to see beyond the present constraints of architectural practice. Recently many architectural competitions have become generators for ideas but when these ideas are confronted with a potential to be built, they remain ideas and are carried through into the architectural continuum.

"The *Steel Cloud* is significant in many respects: its symbolic representation of life at the end of the twentieth century, its forward-thinking architectural vocabulary (almost without precedent) and especially its attempt to mend different parts of the city together by utilizing typically unusable space above a part of the city that has acted as a separator as much as it has a connector."

Steel Cloud appears decades later in publications and exhibitions as an example of disciplinary urbanism grounded in the city's loudest temporal and physical moments of discontent, according to Linda Samuels, an author and associate Professor of Urban Design at Washington University in St. Louis.

PEDESTRIAN BRIDGE OVER THE 101 FREEWAY

While serving on the Board of Directors of the Los Angeles County Metropolitan Transportation Authority in early 1997, I secured $4.5 million from Metro's Transportation Improvement Program "Call for Projects" for a bridge across the 101 Freeway. Metro's Call for Projects program was a competitive process that distributed discretionary capital funds to regionally significant transportation projects.

MTA held an architectural design competition in 1997 for a pedestrian "bridge" over the 101 Freeway to improve the pedestrian connections and environments between Union Station/El Pueblo de Los Angeles Historical Monument and the Civic Center employment center. Reconstruction of the historic walking system between Union Station/Olvera Street and one of the nation's largest government centers had been identified as an essential improvement in the Union Station Capacity Study funded by the Transit Administration.

In the fall of 1993, the Community Redevelopment Agency issued The Downtown Strategic Plan, developed by Stefanos Polyzoides and Elizabeth Moule in cooperation with Andres Duany, Elizabeth Plater-Zyberk, and Robert Harris, that called for decking that section of the 101 Freeway. Also, the designer of the Angels Walk plan, Doug Suisman, developed in cooperation with urban designer William Fain, developer Dan Rosenfeld, and landscape architect Lauren Melendrez the Ten-Minute Diamond vision. As part of that plan, Spring and Los Angeles streets were envisioned as treelined across the 101 freeway. Main Street was envisioned as another Ponte Vecchio. Completion of this pedestrian promenade would encourage commuters and visitors to use the bus or train to travel to Union Station and then take a short and pleasant walk to City Hall and other government offices south of the freeway.

Because Union Station is the hub for Metrolink, Metro Rail, Amtrak, and numerous local bus lines, it would serve a large pool of transit users. The jury included representatives from the City of Los Angeles, Caltrans, the University of Southern California School of Architecture, the Southern California Institute of Architecture, the Los Angeles Museum of Contemporary Art, and the Structural Engineers Association of Southern California. There were four semi-finalists:

1) Morphosis/Aleks Istanbullu John Kaliski and Jenny Holzer artist.
2) Levin Associates/Olin Partnership and Rod Baer artist.
3) Angelli/Graham and BJ Krivanek artist.
4) Siegel Diamond/R. S. Harris and Bruce Odland artist.

The winning team was Morphosis Architects.

Because MTA was the funding source, it could not also be the sponsor of the project, and unfortunately the lead agencies for execution of the project were the Los Angeles Transportation and Public Works departments, and the California Department of Transportation. That arrangement limited my direct leadership of the project and ultimately precipitated its death.

Robin Blair, deputy director of planning and programming at MTA, was the project manager. The selected design called for widening the Main Street overpass and visually weaving together the very pedestrian-oriented Olvera Street/El Pueblo and the Civic Center/City Hall job center. An extraordinary armature would rise from the freeway median. The armature would support a ninety-five-foot "Tri-Action" billboard with flickering LED readouts and changeable signs that speak to the historic and contemporary centers of the city. This portion of the work would initially be programmed with text compositions by Jenny Holzer and later programmed by other artists' work curated by MOCA. The proposal also included the shell of a restaurant that dramatically cantilevered over the freeway, offering patrons spectacular views and a true LA experience.

The design received a prestigious Progressive Architecture 2000 citation award and was featured in the MOCA exhibition *At the End of the Century: 100 Years of Architecture*. It was included in numerous books and exhibitions. Nicolai Ouroussoff, architectural critic of the *Los Angeles Times*, wrote "The Morphosis' design will transform what was once a vision of urban blight into a lively civic forum. To those with healthy memory the design may seem oddly like the *Steel Cloud* designed by Asymptote, although on a much smaller scale. That *Steel Cloud*, despite of its genuine originality, also harked back to a long tradition of urban structures whose muscular forms and structural virtuosity were meant to celebrate notions of progress and mass culture Think of Paris' playful, machine-like Pompidou Center that continues to evoke images of cultural renewal long after its design. The two sides of the ninety-five-foot billboard-like frame would also subtly reflect economic realities of different communities. While the images facing City Hall evoke a slicker ethos-the signage facing north is intentionally lower tech. By placing two opposing aesthetics back-to-back, the design subtly alludes to the friction inherent in bringing the two communities together."

The Morphosis plan rotated the horizontal surface separating the city into vertical surface linking El Pueblo and Union Station with the Civic Center, thus eliminating the expensive freeway cap. I arranged a meeting so that Morphosis co-founder Thom Mayne could present and explain the vision of his design to the new 14th District councilman, Nick Pacheco, and I convinced Mayne to bring the model to City Hall. I remember it was a hot summer day and saw this very tall man along with his staff visibly hot and carrying a huge model. In the Councilman's office, besides Pacheco, were his transportation deputy and a couple of other staff. As Mayne started to articulate his "vision" Pacheco said, "I don't give an f…about your vision. This is garbage." Mayne got up and moved toward Pacheco angrily. I jumped up to calm down Mayne. It was an outright, rude insult to Mayne's professional integrity. As it turned out, Pacheco was a one-term councilman defeated by Antonio Villaraigosa and Mayne went on to win the Pritzker Architecture Prize.

Pacheco ignored Mayne's design and instructed the Bureau of Engineering "to proceed with a number of studies," according to Los Angeles City Engineer Gary Moore. Phase I was a Project Study Report to study decking between Los Angeles Street and North Main Street. This study took three years to complete! Doug Failing, Caltrans District Seven director, proposed to advance the Project Study Report to the Project Approval Environmental Documentation and expand its scope from Alameda Street to North Broadway with an

Gateway to Los Angeles. Artists: Jenna Didier, Oliver Hess (1/24/2024)

approximate construction price tag of $250 million to $300 million, although the source of funds had not yet been identified. Other environmental studies mostly centered around the freeway's on-ramps and off-ramps in this stretch of decking. The Bureau of Engineering wasted about half the $4.5 million in project funding on staff pay and feasibility studies to cap the freeway, which was unrelated to Morphosis' plan. A total of $1 million was spent on the Project Study Report. Another $1 million was wasted on mundane widening of sidewalks on Main and Los Angeles streets. The city bureaucracy ran amok once again!

In the end, with the amount left from the $4.5 million budget, which Mayne said was sufficient to design and construct his project, the Los Angeles Cultural Affairs Department commissioned the Gateway to Los Angeles, which was completed by artists Jenna Didier and Oliver Hess in 2015. Homeless encampments started popping up at the site soon thereafter.

Samuels of Washington University wrote a thesis in 2017 with the title, Resistance at the Trench: Why Efforts to Reinvent the 101 Freeway in Downtown Los Angeles Continue to Fail. It is an excellent analysis and critique of the *Steel Cloud* and Bridge 101. In that publication, she aptly describes the merits of the concept, the challenges, reasons of the failures, press coverage, and how it was received by the public and the architectural and artistic communities.

"The Robert Moses project champion model (which Patsaouras in some ways resembles), tends to use power of the bully pulpit to convince or coerce support, in often positive and sometimes suspect ways…Although the political, economic, and social context may be ripe, a new 101 in downtown would require collective action across agencies and with bottom-up as well as top-down support.

"This is part of the model that worked for the hugely successful High Line and Atlanta Beltline projects, both obsolete rails turned into public space. But the 101-trench site is anything but abandoned; it is a unique, critical case, with an active state freeway operating at peak traffic capacity. A reconceptualization of the 101 as a next-generation architectural/infrastructural hybrid would need to renegotiate the relationship between the car, the driver, the pedestrian, and the newly emerging downtown Los Angeles. A solution that capitalizes on technological smartness and demands, socioenvironmental sustainability by creating symbiotic, adaptable relationships could help guide a twenty-first century vision around the redevelopment of the north end of downtown—and keep it relevant for generations. Projects like these require a sea change in urban values. That sea change in values, in turn, requires new processes and relationships for successful implementation. As the face of downtown changes radically, again, these defining efforts continue."

ANGELS WALK

Walking is man's best medicine.

—HIPPOCRATES

Los Angeles fascinates and intrigues, it embraces an endless mixture of dreams and possibilities, of discovery and enlightenment. But driving through the city only provides an opportunity to look in, not to be inside, to feel its pulse. A multitude of parts exist in this grand metropolis that when grouped together deliver an enduring connection and a rare opportunity to experience closely the City of Angels' history, life, and rhythm. That's what I concluded, remembering a favorite quote by Aristotle: "The whole is greater than the sum of parts." By connecting the dots Los Angeles could flourish anew as a city with a complete story.

I imagined a way in which people could grasp the area's varied history by taking a short walk on specific routes. I envisioned "Angels Walk."

The name itself is derived through an uncanny outcome of viewing a conceptual map of the planned walk from a side position. Doug Suisman, urban planner and architect, thought it resembled the walking man in "walk/don't walk" signs. Angels Walk was the natural outcome, although names like "Yellow Brick Road" were discussed. "If you create a pleasant, interesting environment, people will walk," I told the *Los Angeles Times* in 1995. I believed Downtown would be reborn with walkers shopping and dining out. Through Angels Walk, I felt a bustling round-the-clock metropolis was in the making.

This concept intrigued me over a long period and unfolded in parts. In 1990, when I was President of the Southern Californian Rapid Transit District Board, I authored a Transit Rider Bill of Rights which altered priorities in transportation planning. Providing transportation services to the public is the primary function of transit agencies but offering amenities and a quality environment for the rider was not. So, I fervently pursued changes and got them.

But users of the vast transportation network were often stymied. When they disembarked, they encountered difficulties reaching their ultimate destination because pedestrian considerations were secondary to those of the motor vehicle—which long dominated Los Angeles. In deference to the automobile, the city had altered its physical appearance, including reducing sidewalk widths to make more lanes for more cars. A walkable city, therefore, requires walkable spaces.

I steadfastly pursued safe, easily accessible pedestrian corridors through the existing street system. At the same time, by escalating this concept to a loftier echelon, I envisaged linking the historical and ethnic facets of the city with the planned walks. Furthermore, the program could sensibly integrate the pedestrian component into the transportation system.

A quotation by playwright George Bernard Shaw is a favorite of mine, "The reasonable man adapts himself to the world; the unreasonable man persists in trying to adapt the world to himself—therefore all progress depends on the unreasonable man." The shift away from the auto-priority downtown city began with the unreasonable conviction that the city could do better, and that transit use could and should be desirable. Unreasonable because those who grew up in the auto-priority city saw it as normal. And those dependent on transit had "reasonably" accepted their fate. The unreasonable me had already been collaborating with those that started the herculean effort to bring rail back to Los Angeles and now believed that by sheer will and political arm twisting, they could change the city's-built form to welcome rail's return and improve the transit user's experience.

The RTD's adoption of my emphasis on improving the transit rider quality of life energized the district's planning staff, under the leadership of Robin Blair, Deputy Director of Programming and Planning. With their Community Redevelopment Agency partners, they began to advocate for a more comprehensive pedestrian connection from transit stops to other destinations.

One time when I was visiting Union Station, I was approached by two women with children who asked me for directions to Olvera Street. I pointed across Alameda Street and the ladies, with children in hand, moved ahead, only to return confused. "How the hell do you get there?" they inquired. So, I concluded that Angels Walk's first stroll must start right there, at the Union Station area. It was the perfect starting point for people to understand and gain respect for Los Angeles's past, while creating visions for tomorrow.

The formal Angels Walk LA organization with books and maps developed around 1995 by downtown artist Sandy Bleifer and Deanna Malloy. The first book (Bunker Hill) was completed in 1997. Their involvement began while working on the development of a set of walking improvements between the proposed Little Tokyo light rail station and the activities in Little Tokyo and the adjacent Loft District (1995). They coordinated with Metro's outreach staff and included participation with the Japanese American Cultural and Community Center.

Los Angeles City Councilman Richard Alatorre's field deputy, Bonnie Brody, had gained recognition for her early work on access to transit for persons with disabilities and got involved as the Americans with Disabilities Act began to address greater mobility for persons with disabilities in Los Angeles. Reliant on a wheelchair, Bonnie frequently discussed the limited access in the city for those with mobility restrictions. An attorney and gifted City Hall insider, she ran interference for Angels Walk and successfully helped coordinate the first funding for the program to create the first Angels Walk map. Specifically, funding for the first Angels Walk project came from contributions made by the Convention and Visitors Bureau, the Maguire Thomas Partners, the Community Redevelopment Agency and Metro.

Patt Morrison and Cecilia Rasmussen from the *Los Angeles Times*, and legal historian Robert Wolfe provided in-depth information on some of the potential destinations once they were identified. The design of the walk considered large city walks such as Philadelphia's Freedom Trail and New York's Heritage Trail.

Angels Walk developed from a simple map showing where to go and how to connect to transit to get there. Then came a guidebook, physical plaques and stanchions to inform users of where they are and why the specific place was important. There are now thirteen Angels Walks including Hollywood Boulevard; 180 historic stanchions have been placed within LA neighborhood sidewalks, and over 800,000 guidebooks have been distributed throughout the city. Terms like "the first and last mile," the Federal Transit Administration's adoption of "Planning and Environmental Linkages" and equity in transit systems all trace their origins from improving transit rider quality of life and improving the physical environments near transit.

Angels Walk naissance had a natural starting point.

PATSAOURAS TRANSIT PLAZA

Across the tracks from Union Station is the Los Angeles County Metropolitan Transportation Authority (MTA) Headquarters Building, completed in 1995. It is a bold building, twenty-six stories, elegantly featuring the stylistic influences of Hispanic-Deco and post-modern

Patsaouras Transit Plaza. Photo: Shervin Khazra

Dodger fans boarding buses to Dodgers Stadium at Patsaouras Transit Plaza

architecture with exquisite artwork in its exterior façade and interior lobby, and the central fixture of the Patsaouras Transit Plaza. Seventeen artists and architects over a three-year period produced a structure that exemplifies Los Angeles's purpose and destiny with an artistic vision.

The first Angels Walk was designed to link five Downtown districts to City Hall: Bunker Hill; Music Center and Civic Center; Chinatown; Union Station and El Pueblo; and the Little Tokyo and artist loft section. A short stroll through the Gateway Towers' East Portal Pavilion would bring walkers to the Patsaouras Transit Plaza, which was named in my honor for my devotion to public transit for Los Angeles. As per the historic statement in the Plaza's write up, I, a Greek immigrant, was honored with my bust standing at the north end of the center divider. I had envisioned the MTA headquarters as a "palace for the people." The Plaza is enriched with a circular drive adorned with kinetic patterns that fit the steady motion of buses constantly weaving around it. The roadway is paved in English brick and the center walkway features flowering plants.

UNION STATION

From the Patsaouras Plaza, the route moves to Union Station which had captured the spirit of Los Angeles with its exquisite facility, a blend of Spanish Colonial, Mission Revival, and Art Deco structural design expressing the city's lifestyle. Representing a significant accomplishment, it opened May 3, 1939, with a half million people in attendance, taking six years and $11 million to build. Awaiting visitors were banks of chairs with leather cushions below a fifty-two-foot ornate ceiling and a magnificent Harvey House restaurant. A stanchion on site explains to the visitor the historic significance of Union Station. Titled, "Riding the Rails

Union Station.
Photo: B. Vibber

into History," it says this is a monument to the entwined elements of history and transportation. It was the last of the great train stations built in the nation and a major entry point to Los Angeles.

A soaring clock tower rising one hundred feet above the city made it an instant landmark. Its hall with a long ticket counter fashioned from American Black Walnut, its vast waiting room with 300-foot windows decorated with brass and enormous 3,000-pound chandeliers and hand-painted mission tiles, marked the place where Los Angeles began for millions of travelers. I have long held that art in transit facilities is an unequivocal component for travelers because it offers verve and cheerfulness and creates a significant positive impression. So, I backed a series of programs to create this atmosphere at Union Station. Today rotating collections of unique events, performances and evocative music are standard features showcased at the station, along with cultural programs with a diversity of entertainers and artists.

EL PUEBLO DE LOS ANGELES

From Union Station, the Angels Walk path meanders to the front landscaped area and crosses Alameda Street to El Pueblo de Los Angeles. Here Los Angeles was born. The pueblo, or town, marks the place where, in September of 1781, forty-four settlers of Native American, African, and European heritage journeyed more than one thousand miles from present-day northern Mexico to establish a farming community.

Today this historic and symbolic heart of Los Angeles is a living museum that attracts over two million visitors annually. Celebrated Olvera Street, a block-long tree-shaded Mexican marketplace with old structures, painted stalls and gift shops, restaurants, and street vendors, recreates a romantic past. It opened on Easter Sunday, April 20, 1930, following a

Olvera Street.
Photo: Visitor7

preservation campaign led by Christine Sterling to maintain the customs and trades of early California. Many merchants are descendants of the original vendors. El Pueblo de la Reina de Los Angeles with its plaza area was the center of Los Angeles's community throughout the 19th century. The Avila Adobe, a home built in 1818 for a ranchero family, was named after the head of the household and former mayor of Los Angeles, Francisco Adobe. It is the oldest existing house in Los Angeles. The city's oldest church, known locally as La Placita Church, was dedicated in December 1822 as La Iglesia de Nuestra Senora la Reina de Los Angeles. Today it serves as an active parish, the only building that is still used for its original purpose.

La Plaza de Cultura y Artes is a Mexican American Museum and cultural center in Los Angeles that opened in April of 2011. It is located near Olvera Street next to La Iglesia de Nuestra Senora la Reina de Los Angeles, La Placita. The museum provides exhibitions, cultural and educational programs and shares the history and traditions of Mexicans, Mexican Americans, and Latinos in Southern California. Former Los Angeles County Supervisor Gloria Molina is the person most responsible for the vision and its implementation.

Long before Hollywood, dramatic performances and theatrical activity were held at the Merced Theater from 1871 to 1876. The theater was built in 1870 and is one of the oldest structures erected in Los Angeles for the presentation of dramatic performances. William Abbot, the son of Swiss immigrants, settled in Los Angeles in 1854 and married the woman for whom he would name the theatre, Maria Merced Garcia.

The Garnier Building was built in 1890, by Philippe Garnier, a French settler who arrived in Los Angeles in 1859 at the age of eighteen. The structure was designed primarily for Chinese commercial tenants and is the oldest building in the city exclusively inhabited by Chinese immigrants. It was an important structure in the original Los Angeles Chinatown.

The historic Italian Hall, constructed in 1908 to be a gathering place for Los Angeles's Italian community, is also the location of a controversial mural painted by David Alfaro

Siqueiros who, along with Diego Rivera and Jose Clemente Orozco, helped establish the Mexican mural movement. Painted in 1932 on the second floor of the Italian Hall and named "Tropical America," it exhibits a Mexican peon crucified under an American eagle—a highly politicized critique of American imperialism. A public and official outcry led to the mural being whitewashed. Eighty years after its creation, the mural was re-unveiled to the world. Interestingly, the whitewash helped preserve the artwork.

CHINATOWN

Significant history is relived at the next Angels Walk stop, Chinatown, with its traditional and themed restaurants, shops and art galleries which opened in 1938 after the original Chinatown was torn down to make room for Union Station. Further back, in the 1890s, the earliest Chinatown was located near Olvera Street where the notorious Chinese massacre occurred (1891). The first Chinese arrived in the city in 1850.

The neon flooded Central Plaza with its detailed Chinese artwork and geometric patterns and lanterns, conveys the heritage of the people. It's the neighborhood's vivid core of interest, and the Dragon Gate is known as the Chinatown Gateway Monument. The town's Far East Plaza was an early ethnic shopping mall, among the first in America. The illustrious East Gate, also called the Gate of Maternal Virtues, was commissioned by Attorney You Chung Hong to honor his mother's memory, and all mothers. The West Gate was the first to be built for the 1938 opening and it is made from camphor wood imported from China, now over 150 years old. At the top of the gate an inscription in Chinese characters instructs: "Cooperate to Achieve." Bricks from Philadelphia, millstones from France, murals hanging like traditional scrolls, curios stores and antique shops, importing companies and fortune tellers, all combine to bring a Chinese ambiance, with its notable established restaurants and other Asian eateries.

Chinatown.
Photo: LWYang

Japanese American National Museum.

LITTLE TOKYO HISTORIC DISTRICT

Angels Walk then moves to Little Tokyo which has the largest Japanese American population in North America. At its peak, some 30,000 Japanese Americans lived in the area, and it became—and continues to be—a major cultural point with its shopping district and restaurants. It represents the commercial heart of the community.

It was first settled in 1885 when a former sailor, Hamanosuke "Charles Hama" Shigeta, opened the Kame Restaurant on East First Street, Little Tokyo attracted large numbers of Japanese immigrants, nearly all males coming for work. They concentrated in boarding houses in the East First Street vicinity, turning it into a thriving business and residency location with primary and secondary schools as well as trade schools. Newspapers flourished, led by the Rafu Shimpo, the oldest Japanese newspaper in the US, founded in 1903. There, the Los Angeles Hompa Hongwanji Buddhist Temple serves Southern California as it has since 1905.

The bombing of Pearl Harbor in 1941 by Japan ended Little Tokyo's early prosperity. People of Japanese descent were evacuated from the West Coast and Little Tokyo residents were forced to abandon their homes and businesses. After the war not everyone returned, but Little Tokyo started to experience a revival in the 1970s.

At the same time artists began to move into nearby aging warehouse spaces, forming an obscure creative community in the industrialized area. The artist group, Artcore, helped organize a noontime panel discussion there. Artcore members saw that bringing the art community together with Little Tokyo created exciting opportunities, since art is what makes the city.

Angels Walk then moves through two blocks of the original pre-World War II commercial heart of Little Tokyo with the Japanese Union Church, a 1923 brick building in the Classical Revival style on one end and the Japanese American National Museum on the other. Thirteen buildings, some four stories, house the largest concentration of Nisei (second generation Japanese Americans) in the nation. Nearby is the San Pedro Firm Building, another large Classical Revival style structure initially owned by a group of fifty-four local Japanese flower growers who opened the Southern California Flower Market in 1913. The three-story Far East Building, which dates to 1896 but was remodeled in 1935 in the Art Deco style, houses a hotel and storefront, but was particularly well-known for its Far East Café.

BUNKER HILL

Angels Walk weaves to Los Angeles's historic core, Bunker Hill, the highest point in Los Angeles which has changed over time but continues to be the center of the great metropolis. Historically, it began in 1870 as an upper-class community—LA's first suburb—only to be converted to a working-class area by 1910.

Angels Walk then shifts to a noteworthy landmark, Angels Flight, a historic two-foot-by-six-inch narrow gauge funicular railway in Bunker Hill—called the world's shortest railroad. The first location was along the side of Third Street Tunnel, connecting Hill Street and Olive Street, and operated from 1901 until it closed in 1969 for redevelopment. Accidents over the years suspended service until it reopened on August 31st, 2017, in a new location, one-half block south of the original site, mid-block between 3rd and 4th Streets, with tracks connecting Hill Street and California Plaza.

Grand Central Market.

The walk continues to one of downtown's most photographed icons, the Bradbury Building, located on Third Street and Broadway. Built in 1893, it has a Romanesque exterior and a light-filled Victorian court that rises almost fifty feet with open cage elevators, marble stairs and ornate railings. This architectural landmark was constructed for Los Angeles gold-mining millionaire Lewis L. Bradbury.

Also, the Grand Central Market, a Los Angeles essential spot since 1917, was identified as the "Wonder Market," and said to be "the largest and finest public market on the Pacific Coast." It filled the entire ground floor of the Beaux-Arts-style Homer Laughlin Building, the region's first steel-reinforced, fireproof structure. Dozens of stalls are home to legacy vendors. Often referred to as a microcosm of the historic immigrant communities that have shaped Los Angeles, it is a mosaic of the inspiration and image of the Los Angeles populace. As in all Angels Walks, public transportation is provided to the historic site. Two million people visit the Grand Central Market annually.

The Million Dollar Theater, across the street from the Bradbury building, was built by showman Sid Grauman in 1918 for one million dollars. It was the city's first movie palace; its 2,200-seat auditorium resembles a Spanish colonial cathedral. Grauman was partly responsible for the entertainment district shifting to Hollywood in the mid-1920s when he opened Grauman's Egyptian Theatre and Grauman's Chinese Theatre.

MUSIC CENTER

Angels Walk moves to one of the nation's largest performing arts centers whose history began in April 1955 when Dorothy Chandler, wife of *Los Angeles Times* publisher Norman Chandler, held a fundraising event for a permanent home for the Philharmonic. On December 6, 1964, the Dorothy Chandler Pavilion opened, and Zubin Mehta led the Los Angeles Philharmonic in a program that included violinist Jascha Heifetz and performances of Strauss' Fanfare and Beethoven's Violin Concerto in D Major.

Music Center. Photo: A. Praefcke

The Music Center (officially named the Performing Arts Center of Los Angeles County) is composed of the Dorothy Chandler Pavilion, Ahmanson Theatre, Mark Taper Forum, Roy and Edna Disney/CalArts Theatre, and Walt Disney Concert Hall. The Music Center greets over one million people annually to performances by its four internationally renowned resident companies: Los Angeles Philharmonic, Los Angeles Opera, Los Angeles Master Chorale, and Center Theatre Group, as well as performances by the dance series Glorya Kaufman Presents Dance at The Music Center. The center is home to on-going community events, arts festivals, outdoor concerts, participatory arts activities and workshops, and educational programs.

CIVIC CENTER

The administrative center of the City of Los Angeles and the County of Los Angeles is in the northern part of downtown Los Angeles, bordering Bunker Hill, Little Tokyo, Chinatown, and the Historic Core of the old Downtown and the Music Center. It is a complex of city, county, state, and federal government offices, buildings, and courthouses.

The pedestrian corridors created by Angels Walk link all the historic areas, including downtown and the civic center, and lead to City Hall. On October 4, 1995, I was quoted in the *Los Angeles Times*, "We are around the corner from seeing Los Angeles become a twenty-four-hour city."

Los Angeles's proud jewel, its City Hall, was built in 1928 by three famous architects who eschewed all styles and all eras to create their own hybrid, "Modern American." However, the monumental steps leading to the Spring Street entrance are reminiscent of classical designs, and its iconic tower has a stepped pyramid conforming to the Art Deco style. City Hall rightfully is the city's most widely recognized landmark appearing on all official documents from commendations to business licenses. By law, the building towered for years over the rest of the city through a municipal height ordinance. Wanting to portray Los Angeles as a center for health and resort, fresh air and sunshine, the city denied itself the opportunity to soar skyward. The image of a downtown with tall buildings and narrow canyons at the street level was shunned. The early city beautiful movements incorporated height limits into the charter in 1911 and a municipal ordinance was adopted to ascertain the city had "harmonious lines." It prohibited construction of buildings taller than thirteen stories or 150 feet in height until the late 1950s. City Hall stood tall with its twenty-eight stories, the first building to exceed the height limitations. The building's interior design and decoration associate Los Angeles with great cities of the world while the city's exciting industries of filmmaking, aviation and the automobile are artistically portrayed. Today, with the lifting of the height requirement, a new Downtown skyline has been born, the bold result of world-class contemporary architects.

My pioneering efforts to encourage pedestrian walks and public transportation and to preserve the history of Los Angeles, led to the launching of Angels Walk. I enthusiastically supported Deanna Molloy who founded Angels Walk LA, a non-profit public benefit corporation working with the City of Los Angeles and Metro to expand the self-guided walking trails throughout the historically affluent neighborhoods.

In the fall of 1993, the Community Redevelopment Agency issued a Downtown Strategic Plan prepared by the team of Stefanos Polyzoides and Elizabeth Moule, Duany Plater-Zyberk and Robert Harris. The plan from Chinatown through the El Pueblo Historic Park District, Union Station, Civic Center, Little Tokyo, Bunker Hill, the financial district, South Park, and USC/Exposition Park envisioned a localized revitalization as opposed to big concept development. Robert Harris, USC dean of architecture, said "downtown was an assemblage of patches that require stitching into a quilt," one of the Angels Walk objectives.

Along with Doug Suisman, urban planner and architect, I co-authored an Op-Ed piece for the *Los Angeles Times* titled, "When Angels Walk, They Share the City": "Angels Walk is a network of streets in historic Downtown that should be improved expressly for pedestrians, including those in strollers, wheelchairs and on bikes. The network links Chinatown, Union Station, Olvera Streets, and the Old Plaza on the north, to Little Tokyo, the Cathedral, the historic Core along Broadway and Spring Street, Angels Flight, and Bunker Hill on the south. Angels Walk is not so much about creating great places as connecting the ones we already have. In the shadow of the City Hall's Byzantine splendors, amidst the ghosts of the Mexican, Chinese, French, Japanese, English, Greek, Jewish, Italian, African and other settlers, who have walked those streets for over two hundred years, late 20th-century walking angels can come together, rub shoulders, link arms, and perhaps take wing."

Angels Walk received the "Rose Award" from the Los Angeles Downtown Breakfast Club.

VIGNETTE

The futuristic sidewalk stanchions were designed by Rogerio Carvalheiro pro bono at the request of Ira Yellin. They remain today a blend of Star Wars with the Pan Pacific Golden Age, somehow perfectly fitted to the past and future of the city they serve.

After the stanchions were designed, no City department would pay to have them fabricated and installed. The initial cost was $50,000. Street Services, Planning, and Public Works all declined. In a meeting at the office of then-City Councilmember Rita Walters, Dan Rosenfeld of the Department of General Services spoke up and volunteered to fund the cost of the stanchions out of his department's budget, even though he had no mandate or authority to do so. Everyone in the room, including the Councilmember, said he couldn't do that. But he did.

Angels Walk stanchion.

UNIVERSAL CITYWALK

Lew Wasserman, Hollywood's powerful mogul and patriarch, craved something, but didn't know exactly what. So, Al Dorskind, his vice president at MCA, Inc., visited the offices of William L. Pereira & Associates to speak with the renowned architect. "Lew is interested in the top of the hill, the parking lot at Universal City," he said. "Look, I'd like to have you do some studies," he told Pereira. In turn, Pereira pointed to Bill Fain who was asked to generate some ideas. This was in 1981 when he was "an underling," Fain explained. Basically, he was to conceive a plan for the parking lot which sits next to the amphitheater and the tour entrance.

The bridge above Lankershim Boulevard offers a new front doorway to enter the Universal property. This is the only window for the landlocked area. Fain later became director of urban design and planning and partner of Pereira Johnson Fain Associates in Los Angeles. He worked with Mark Gershen and in one week they generated some core ideas. A week later they began to illustrate them.

Dorskind called again. "Monday morning Lew wants to see you." The meeting was set for 8:00 a.m. In those days computers were unavailable, Fain explained, "so we worked over the weekend, took our drawings, dry-mounted them and put them on larger sheets, and clipped them to hardboards." Pereira and Fain left at 7:00 a.m. for the Black Building, MCA's headquarters at Universal. When they arrived, they met a guard in the lobby who instructed them to take the elevator to the top floor.

"We get in the elevator, and it was crammed with tons of people, and they were all going to the top floor." He was confused, he admitted. He turned to Pereira and said, "What's going on here?" He said that thirty or forty people were already on the top floor. A guard with a "walkie-talkie thing in his ear" told them they must go upstairs, indicating a staircase that leads to the Board room. "We realized that all these people are going upstairs, as well." "Oh, my God! What's going on here?" he reiterated. Inside the Board room they saw a large model of the top of the hill, twenty feet long and ten feet wide. He was baffled, but mindful of how events unfolded in the Black Building. Whenever Wasserman wanted something, everybody ran. This was Hollywood, and it was his. Nevertheless, he looked again at Pereira and again said, "What the hell is going on here?"

"I think we've been set up," Pereira responded. He believed that someone else was going to give a presentation. Obviously, it was not going to be a private discussion with Wasserman. "We had nothing to show. All we had were these four drawings on a clipboard," he repeated. Present were all the vice presidents of MCA and dozens more in the room, and they were all standing. "So, we move along in search of a little corner." At that moment, Wasserman walked in. A confused Fain viewed the entrance and described it as a "parting of the sea." Unexpectedly, Pereira made a quick turn and moved to the middle of the room, extending his hand: "Hello, Lew." "Hi, Bill, what are you doing here?" They grabbed each other's arms. "Well, Dorskind asked me to come."

Pereira called Fain down and introduced him to Wasserman who offered a hand. "It was a spiritless handshake, limp and clammy," as Fain disclosed. "But you know about Wasserman's handshake." When Wasserman was ready, the meeting began. "You were making a presentation?" I asked.

"No, we were sitting in the back, the third row." Talking were the studio tour group people who explained tram problems and issues pertaining to the amphitheater. By 11:30 a.m.—two hours and more into the meeting—Wasserman became visibly upset. Lots of talk, but no one had figured out what he wanted. What was presented to him was a kind of frontier façade that people would see as they parked and walked to the tour entrance. Aspects of that design were shown. "How much is that going to cost?" Wasserman asked. "Two or three million," was the reply.

Wasserman reached over the table and slammed his hand with a loud whack. "Sit down, mister! You're wasting my time." His tone was sharp. He was ready to explode. Stone-cold silence filled the room. A panicky pause ensued. From across the room, Dorskind said: "Lew, Bill Pereira and Bill Fain have something they want to show you." A hesitant Pereira stood, looked at his watch and said, "Oh, Lew, it's ten to twelve."

"It's almost lunchtime," Wasserman responded. "Let's break for lunch and come back." For the moment, the edginess was dissolved. Pereira's sense of timing had a Hollywood panache. In 1942, he shared an Academy Award for Best Special Effects for the action/adventure film "Reap the Wild Wind." Off they went to the commissary. The tour folks sat at the very end of the table "like puppy dogs, their tails between their legs," while he, Pereira and Wasserman were at the other end. Wasserman began to relate stories about Cary Grant and Vivien Leigh when he was an agent for them. After lunch, they returned to the Board room. Fain, using a tripod next to Wasserman, began his presentation using the small drawings he had developed and noticed that Wasserman was getting impatient. All morning Fain had been listening attentively to what was being said and believed that the puzzle could be solved.

"Screw it," he said. "This is what it is." He went to his third chart. "You have a tour line here," he said, pointing to the drawing, "you have a tour entrance there, and you have parking here. You develop a street that goes from the car park to the entrance to the tour. "We call it the 'Carnivorous Flower' in our place. It is based on a project developed in Boston called 'Faneuil Hall.' It was created by Jim Rouse, a pioneering real estate developer. Fain had worked there for three years with the Boston Redevelopment Authority. And he sensed that Wasserman's desire was to capitalize on a walking street.

Wasserman looked at the drawing, got up on his chair, and said, "Yes, that's it!"

Sidney Sheinberg, President and Chief Operating Officer of MCA, Inc., was startled. "Who's Jim Rouse?"

"Oh, he's fantastic," was Wasserman's response, He knew and admired his work.

The next morning Dorskind called again. "That's a home run," he said. "We need to start planning the property." Wasserman envisaged the project having a dramatic effect on his personal wealth. The Universal CityWalk concept was born. Fain said he continued making presentations to Wasserman each month for two-three years, each time starting at ground zero. "Why ground zero?" I asked. "I always started at the beginning because he always went for the bottom line. I never felt comfortable, but I never feared him." I asked if Fain developed a warm working relationship with him. "No," he replied. "It was a respectable relationship. I was able to survive. Whenever we met, I was able to depart as a survivor. Except for the last meeting. I knew that was my last discussion with him."

Universal CityWalk Hollywood became a three-block entertainment, dining, and shopping promenade. It has more than thirty eateries, a nineteen-screen movie theater featuring IMAX, seven-night spots, indoor skydiving and more than thirty stores.

However, two months before it opened, lawsuits over its very name were filed. City Wok, a Chinese restaurant in North Hollywood, alleged trademark infringement, unfair competition, and trademark dilution. Despite the publicity over the case, the judge was not too troubled allowing the name "Universal CityWalk."

Designed by Jon Jerde, CityWalk opened in May 1993 and quickly became a popular drawing space for tourists, eventually evolving into a three-block entertainment, dining, and shopping promenade. Its 2000 expansion of 93,000 square feet under Jerde Associates cost about $1 billion. But what was it, really? Critics had difficulty defining its identity. Amy Wallace, writing for the *Los Angeles Times* on February 29, 1992, said that "folks at MCA have a vision of Los Angeles as they would like it to be. It starts with what they wish it was not." Wallace said that from its inception CityWalk's goal has been to deliver on the unkept promise of Los Angeles. "It is a grand notion, based on the presumption that a city's essence can be distilled, enhanced and artfully packaged, like so much synthetic perfume." Reality has become too much of a hassle, determined the market research of MCA. With a simulated slice of Los Angeles, according to Wallace, CityWalk may encourage the abandonment of the real city.

Jerde, a Los Angeles native, and his colleagues tried to comprehend Los Angeles, to see what makes it what it is. They wanted to design the quintessential city, according to Wallace. Jerde concluded that the city was not a "fixed thing," but a moving target with an elusive psyche. He told the newspaper that CityWalk's biggest challenge was to capture Los Angeles's spirit, not its architecture.

Another *Los Angeles Times* staff writer, David Wharton, wrote in May of 1994, that "CityWalk is an abracadabra solution of Los Angeles's woes." MCA president Lawrence Spungin called it "idealized reality," a controlled complex that sought to act like a new brand town square, according to Wharton. "It offered a tempting placebo at a time when people should be working to revive the real city," wrote Wharton, referring to a Hollywood Boulevard presented with a child-proof cap, a sanitized Venice Beach for a populace grown weary of looking over its shoulder. "Never mind that a thoroughly contrived 'boulevard' seemed Orwellian," he continued. "It smacked of an elitist enclave with it private guards shuttling panhandlers and suspected gang members off premises." Kevin Starr, a USC professor and local historian, was troubled by CityWalk. "This sounds like the end of LA history," he was quoted by the newspaper.

An associate of the Jerde Partnership and the complex's chief project designer, Richard Orne, told the *Los Angeles Times* that "the notion of CityWalk's being a new Los Angeles is an unfortunate bent. "There has been a fearful overreaction—oh my God, this is '1984' and private corporations are going to build fantasy versions of cities and manipulate the population." CityWalk, he said, "has become a lightning rod for a lot of emotional reaction."

Architect, urban planner and author of Los Angeles Boulevard Doug Suisman had a different observation. "When you see people walking around, there is not that look of the dazed, manipulated consumer," he told the *Los Angeles Times*. "People seemed to be relaxed and enjoying the place for what it is."

But the critics persisted. Mike Davis, an urban theorist who concentrated on class separation in Los Angeles, told the newspaper, "They have censored out people, the rank-and-file and the homeless, by giving subtle signals that they aren't wanted." Davis pointed to the giant King Kong over the gate visitor pass, subtly communicating expected behavior. Also, a Los Angeles County Sheriff's Department substation there displays the constant presence of police. Spurgin was quoted saying, "We're not making a demographic selection. We are making sure that people who come here behave in a certain way." Davis's retort was emphatic. "There is a fundamental confusion between safety and people who simply make us uncomfortable because they are poor, or they are young minorities. Old-fashioned American ideals of democracy are being sacrificed."

Despite detractors, CityWalk with its textured and wildly painted buildings, waterfalls and light shows, plethora of antique neon signs, fanciful facades of Melrose, the gritty billboard of the Sunset Strip, and a faux Venice Beach with sand, millions of people approve of it by flocking to the complex every year.

The debate over defining what it really represents and means continues.

CHAPTER FIFTEEN

ASPIRING FOR OFFICE

Aspire not to have more, but to be more.

—OSCAR ROMERO

LOS ANGELES MAYOR'S RACE 1993

In 1993, Mayor Tom Bradley had decided after twenty years in office he was not going to run for reelection. It was the first open election since 1929 and I decided to enter the race. I knew the inner workings of government, I had a vision for Los Angeles, and I was passionate and committed to public service. The nation's second largest city was in a crisis, facing many challenges: economic slowdown worse than in many cities, fears of more rioting as the Rodney King trial was going on, crime, and pessimism that this ethnically diverse city was too difficult to govern. With the Mayoral race taking place after the 1992 Los Angeles riots and in the middle of a recession and an ugly anti-immigrant backlash, fear was in the citizens' minds. And the candidates for Mayor addressed the concerns and fears in different ways.

Los Angeles City Councilman Michael Woo talked about the poor, minorities, and disaffection of the middle class and proposed an Urban Peace Corps and the establishment of a community development bank for small businesses.

Attorney Richard Riordan presented himself as a political outsider with a slogan, "tough enough to turn LA around," and promising to hire three thousand more police officers. Attorney and financier William Wardlaw persuaded Riordan to come out for term limits before he announced his candidacy for mayor to raise his name recognition which stood at the time at 2 percent. Woo and Los Angeles City Councilmember Joel Wachs also came out for term limits.

Larry Berg, Director of the Jesse M. Unruh Institute of Politics at the University of Southern California, said about the term limits discussions going on among some candidates, "This is a play to the polls. The rush to enact term limits illustrates what's happening in politics in too much of America. That is, do what the polls say, not necessarily what is best for government or the public." Riordan spent three hundred thousand dollars to gather 305,225 signatures to place on the April 1993 city ballot a measure limiting the terms of elected city officials. In 1992, Riordan mailed to every registered voter in the city a glossy, colorful pamphlet promoting term limits.

Then City Councilman Zev Yaroslavsky, a foe of term limits, said, "Riordan sent out a number of mailings to voters that promoted the initiative but also featured the businessman's picture." Riordan later acknowledged that "term limits was a very bad idea." Riordan had

Announcing my candidacy for mayor of Los Angeles, Olvera Street. With my daughter Tanya and Sylvia.

never been involved in civic affairs other than serving as an appointed member of the Recreation and Parks Commission.

State Assemblyman Richard Katz had a strong base of support in the voter rich and important San Fernando Valley. He proposed to turn the bed of the Los Angeles River into a roadway for carpools and trucks. Wachs appealed to suburbanites, the Jewish community, gays and the elderly, and he also proposed the breakup of the Los Angeles Unified School District. Former Deputy Mayor Tom Houston tried to ride the anti-immigrant wave, which was viewed as a hypocritical stance, coming from a liberal Democrat.

Former US Ambassador to Mexico Julian Nava suggested posting ten thousand federal troops in the streets, playing to the fears of residents after the 1992 riots. Others in the race were Los Angeles City Councilman Nate Holden, lawyer J. Stanley Sanders, former Deputy Mayor Linda Griego, as well as me, a businessman and electrical engineer.

I had been meeting at architect Frank Gehry's office with planners, architects, and artists to develop a vision for Los Angeles. Besides Gehry, the group included architects Willian Fain, Frank Israel, Doug Suisman, and historian Kevin Starr.

My platform was: A Shared Vision 4 A New LA: Transportation as a Catalyst for Remaking Our City.

My campaign slogan was "A Man with a Plan." The Plan proposed to use "transit levers" to implement the vision, and included:

- Establishing Transit Districts and transit corridors to accommodate growth with construction of retail and affordable housing.
- Developing clean and quiet electric cars and buses, thus enhancing the boulevards as places to live, work, shop, and socialize.
- Bringing public art to the boulevards along transit lines and transit stations.
- Using transit rights-of-ways to build a greenway system, including mountain trails, historic sites, and the Los Angeles River.
- Encouraging adaptive reuse of historic landmarks and old office buildings through revisions of the Building Code.
- Redirecting the aerospace workforce to transit research and development.
- Developing a "set-aside" job training program for all transit contractors and consultants.

Unfortunately, my vision was too esoteric to be explained to the public at large and condensed in thirty-second sound bites. I was years ahead of the times. Transit-oriented development is now part of every planner's and politician's lexicon.

Carol E Schatz, president of the Los Angeles Central City Association, picked up the torch of my 1993 vision and spearheaded the Adaptive Reuse Ordinance which made it easier to renovate old office building and housing. It was adopted by the Los Angeles City Council in June of 1999. Developer Tom Gilmore and his partner Jerri Perrone took advantage of this new law and redeveloped three old buildings, which he dubbed the Old Bank District. The early 20th century commercial buildings were the historic core of downtown Los Angeles. The Old Bank District and Staples Center were two developments that set off the downtown Los Angeles renaissance. Other developers successfully converted a host of vacant office towers into residential units without dedicated on-site parking. Nearly twelve thousand new housing units were created through adaptive reuse of mostly old office buildings since downtown's residential renaissance kicked off in 2000.

When I was interviewed during the mayoral campaign by Frank Clifford at the Picasso Cafeteria in the paper's building for a story in the *Los Angeles Times*, Clifford said, "Nick, you are the Paul Tsongas of the campaign. People will not comprehend your vision, too complicated." He was referring to the Greek American and cerebral US Senator from Massachusetts who ran for President in 1992. I was pigeon-holed as a "policy wonk." Certainly, I was not fainthearted.

"Every man worthy of being called a son of man bears his cross and mounts his Golgotha. Many, indeed most, reach the first or second step, collapse pantingly in the middle of the journey, and do not attain the summit of Golgotha, in other words the summit of their duty: to be crucified, resurrected, and to save their souls. Afraid of crucifixion, they grow fainthearted; they do not know that the cross is the only path to resurrection. There is no other path." —NIKOS KAZANTZAKIS

The early focus of the mayor's race was on issues such as immigration and whether to break up the school district, thinly veiled appeals to racial divisiveness and matters that fall outside the mayor's purview, unlike planning initiatives which were the basis of my plan.

According to the *Los Angeles Times*, "Some outside of Los Angeles have been intrigued by the notion of a candidate with ideas." The San Jose Mercury News devoted much of a front-page story on the mayor's race to me, noting that observers, "say he's the only candidate so far to advance a comprehensive vision for the city." Then Councilman Yaroslavsky said at the time, "More than any other campaign, his is actually tackling issues and taking them seriously." Urban theorist Mike Davis commented on my candidacy, "He is the closest thing this city has to a Fiorello La Guardia." Historian Kevin Starr credited me with, "a unique combination of vision and hardball skills."

Harold Meyerson wrote in the *LA Weekly*, "Nick Patsaouras is already well on his way to becoming LA's master builder-sort of a good guy Robert Moses. He also envisions the creation of green belt parks to run alongside the light rails, and vast public plazas in the European tradition at the major Metrorail stops -along with mixed-use buildings combining restaurants, stores, and affordable housing. He is also a drumbeater for a local industrial policy, creating a new manufacturing sector to meet the needs of LA's new transit systems. Not content to be Moses, Patsaouras wants to be La Guardia, too. Of all the candidates in the field, he comes closest to having La Guardia's tenacity when confronting the inertia that is Los Angeles city government, though some of his ideas will doubtless strike some Angelenos as too 'Eastern' (meaning either too New York or too European)."

Davis, the author of City of Quartz, which he described as a critique of the tendency "to militarize the public spaces of Los Angeles and the failure to invest in public services," said I was the only candidate "committed to expanding public space and avoiding the idea of the fortified city." He called my candidacy, "a party of imagination." In a prescient way, Davis said back in 1992, "Patsaouras's candidacy will transcend the election, even if he does not win his ideas will continue to play an important role."

The April 20, 1993, primary election narrowed the field to two candidates: Riordan and Woo.

Riordan had a simple message tapping into the fears and anxiety of the public after the 1992 riots. He promised he would hire three thousand more police officers, a promise he did not keep. Riordan was known as a terrible debater, but mass mailing and saturation television ads compensated. Woo was an undistinguishable City Council member with no basic foundation. But Woo had coalesced the African American community behind him by calling for Chief of Police Daryl Gates to resign. Ironically, Woo outmaneuvered City Councilman Marvin Braude in calling for Gates' resignation. Braude had drafted a news release asking for Gates's resignation. Woo got wind of it, rushed to his office, wrote a news release, and beat Braude in releasing it to the media. Consequently, with the African American community, which at that time accounted for 12 percent of the city's voters behind Woo, and with the support of the liberals, he was assured a seat in the runoff election.

The *Los Angeles Times* also contributed to the perception that the race was between Riordan and Woo. In early February, the front-page upper fold had a story, "The Mayor's race is between Riordan and Woo," with photographs. A race between the right and the left was easier to cover.

Raphael J. Sonenshein, executive director of the Pat Brown Institute for Public Affairs at the California State University, Los Angeles, told the *New York Times*, "In the short term, the events of last year had exactly the opposite outcome of what people expected: they really strengthened the forces of order." John Mack, regional director of the Urban League, told the same newspaper, "There is a great deal of apprehension and uncertainty about the rhetoric of toughness." Many voters told poll takers they were voting for "the lesser of two evils." In the June 8, 1993, general election, Riordan defeated Woo by 54 to 46 percent.

It was a key transitional moment. Cities across America, including New York, Chicago, and Cleveland, as well as Los Angeles, replaced "breakthrough" liberal Black mayors with white, conservative tough guys. Fear overwhelmed hope.

VIGNETTE

I clearly remember two things while serving on Mayor Richard Riordan's Transition Team in 1993. The first had to do with the appointment of a chief of staff. Riordan and the chief strategist of his mayoral campaign and closest confidant and senior advisor, William "Bill" Wardlaw, were wise and savvy to know that the mayor needed an experienced chief of staff. The chief of staff had to know the corridors and centers of power in City Hall, be knowledgeable enough to navigate through the bureaucracy, and be familiar with the fifteen councilmembers, the fifteen "feudal lords." As inauguration day was getting closer, we did not have problems in appointing competent and experienced city commissioners, but still no chief of staff. Bill was frustrated, exasperated, and worried. We were meeting in the law offices of O'Melveny & Myers, where one of the partners was Kim McLane Wardlaw, Bill's wife and later a member of the US Ninth Court of Appeals. One afternoon Bill burst into the conference room, excited and happy, hands high and shouted, "We finally found him." The mayor had selected William McCarley, Los Angeles's chief legislative officer, as his chief of staff.

The other thing I remember was my suggestion to Bill Wardlaw that Riordan not follow the tradition of having only one deputy mayor, the chief of staff, but instead appoint several deputies, each to be in charge of planning, or transportation, or safety, or budget etc. The deputy position would give them respect, authority, and responsibility.

I regretted that suggestion.

LOS ANGELES CONTROLLER'S RACE 2009

In 2009, I decided to enter the City Controller's race a few months before the primary election. Right away there was an avalanche of pressure from Mayor Antonio Villaraigosa's Office and his consiglieri for me to withdraw. Their objective was to control the three citywide offices: mayor; city attorney, coalescing behind councilmember Jack Weiss; and city controller, supporting councilmember Wendy Greuel. One of them showed up late in the evening at my home unannounced with a bottle of whiskey to try to persuade me to withdraw from the race. I refused because I was committed and believed I would be a good Controller. I had the experience as a businessperson, the technical background as an electrical engineer, and the commitment to public service.

During my service on the boards of the Southern California Rapid Transit District, the Los Angeles County Metropolitan Transportation Authority, and the Los Angeles Department of Water and Power, I was instrumental in saving millions of taxpayers' dollars and creating hundreds of jobs. At the same time, I had witnessed firsthand waste, fraud, and abuse in government operations.

The new Los Angeles City Charter, adopted by voters in June 1999 and effective July 1, 2000, gave the controller important new responsibilities in the area of performance audits, debt monitoring, and fiscal and operational oversight. The Charter provisions that discuss the role and duties of the controller are in part:

Sec. 260. Auditor and General Accountant.

The Controller shall be the auditor and general accountant of the City and shall exercise a general supervision over the accounts of all offices, departments, boards, and employees of the city charged in any manner with the receipt, collection, or disbursement of the money of the city. The Controller shall be elected as provided in Section 202.

Sec. 261. Powers and Duties.

The Controller shall in part

a prescribe the method of keeping all accounts of the offices, departments, boards, or employees of the City in accordance with generally accepted accounting principles, except that any change of the system of accounting shall first be authorized by the council;

b regularly review the accounting practices of offices and departments and upon finding serious failings in accounting practices, be empowered to take charge of the accounting function, and thereafter assist the office or department in implementing appropriate accounting standards and practices;

c maintain a complete set of accounts which shall be deemed the official books and accounts of the City, which shall show at all times the financial condition of the City, the state of each fund, including funds of departments responsible for managing their own funds, the source from which all money was derived and for what purposes all money has been expended;

d in compliance with generally accepted government auditing standards, audit all departments and offices of the City, including proprietary departments, where any City funds are either received or expended; be entitled to obtain access to all department records and personnel in order to carry out this function; establish an auditing cycle to ensure that the performance, programs and activities of every department are audited on a regular basis, and promptly provide completed audit reports to the Mayor, Council, and City Attorney and make those reports available to the public;

e conduct performance audits of all departments and may conduct performance audits of City programs, including suggesting plans for the improvement and management of the revenues and expenditures of the city.

Greuel had amassed a campaign war chest of more than $1.5 million, compared with my $300,000. Still, a few days before the election, I was gaining in the polls and was within striking range of forcing Greuel into a run-off. On Friday night before the Tuesday election, Greuel ran an ad accusing me as chairman of Marathon National Bank, of running the bank into the ground and saying that the regulators had taken it over. This was an outright fabrication! The bank I founded and chaired was one of the most successful banks in the Westside. It had turned a profit within months of opening its doors, very unusual at that time, because it was very well managed. There were weekly meetings of the executive committee to ensure the bank was well managed. The bank was sold on August 23, 2002, to Pacific Western Bank, while I was chair, at a multiple of book value turning a respectable profit to the shareholders.

The years 2007 to 2009 were marked by the Great Recession, the collapse of the housing market, and a record number of bankruptcies and foreclosures. "Banker" had negative connotations at that time, it was a dirty word, and the Greuel television campaign ad sought to exploit this.

I held a news conference on Monday morning after the Friday negative campaign ad to expose the campaign lies, but only Channel 7 showed up. I challenged Greuel, "If her claim is true, I will withdraw. If untrue, she withdraws." When I questioned *Los Angeles Times* reporter David Zahniser why his paper did not run a story and exposed the disgusting distortion, he answered. "Well, we are going to put it online at 'LA Now.'"

There were other outrageous misrepresentations about me by someone who wanted to win at all costs. When I was interviewed by the editorial board of the Los Angeles Sentinel newspaper, I was told "Greuel said you are against minorities and women." The statement was both shocking and ironic, starting with the fact that my wife is Mexican. The following are some facts that refute that misrepresentation.

In 1985, when I was president of the RTD board, Danny Bakewell Jr., the civil rights activist and owner of the Bakewell Co., which includes the Los Angeles Sentinel, had come to me complaining that he could not make inroads with RTD, and he asked for my assistance. I arranged for a number of meetings, including with district General Manager John Dyer and other executives, and since then RTD/Metro unions have participated in the charitable giving campaign with the Los Angeles Brotherhood Crusade, a major Los Angeles grassroots charitable organization.

I was the author in 1983 of the Transit Bond Guarantee programs to provide minority and women-owned businesses the financial backing to bid for Metro-Rail contracts.

In 1992, working with a task force of community and government resources, educational, institutions, labor leaders, job-training organizations, and private sector executives at all levels, I developed a Job Development and Training Policy with the assistance of Donna Andrews, a bright young African American. The program required contractors and consultants to dedicate at least 3 percent of their labor costs to job training. The Los Angeles County Transportation Commission approved the plan on December 16, 1992. The Andrews Group used that template and worked with other public agencies to carry out similar programs. That program propelled the Andrews Group to become a very successful woman-owned enterprise. I later carried that program to the DWP when I served as president a few years later.

In 1983, while I was president of the RTD, the Los Angeles County Grand Jury criticized a number of Los Angeles city programs that award contracts to businesses owned by women and minorities due to lack of transparency and efficiency. The Grand Jury recommended that the RTD act as a clearinghouse for such contracts countywide, praising the district's oversight of minority contracts as "thorough and professional."

Cynthia McClain-Hill, an African American attorney and former president of the DWP board of commissioners, with whom I interacted in civic affairs, said, "As a Transportation Commissioner, Patsaouras was steadfastly committed to opening the process to minority bidding even when no one was looking, giving minorities and women a shot at the whole contract, as opposed to just set asides."

One of the reasons I ran for Controller was my strong belief that a citizen has an obligation to serve the public whether as precinct walker, public servant, candidate, or campaign worker. At the ancient Olympic Games, Aristotle wrote. It is not the finest and the strongest who are crowned, but they who enter the lists—So, too, in the life of the honorable and the good, it is they who act that rightly win the prizes."

Unfortunately, the Los Angeles city controller's office has been used as a steppingstone to higher office, and not as a public watchdog over the city's financial affairs, except for Laura Chick who dug into the weeds of government operations to find waste, fraud, and abuse. In reference to City Controller Wendy Greuel, Los Cerritos News, in 2013 noted, "She has spent an overwhelming majority of her official schedule for the past three years attending lavish dinners, lunches, breakfasts, and social events in an effort to advance her 2013 mayoral campaign, in violation of the Los Angeles Governmental Ethics Commission Ordinance."

CHAPTER SIXTEEN

ASSOCIATION WITH WORLD AND NATIONAL LEADERS

Closeness to power heightens the dignity of all men.

—THEODORE WHITE

Vice President Walter F. Mondale

My involvement in presidential politics started in 1984 with Walter F. Mondale's run for the White House. I had been successful in political fundraising since the late 1970s, and I was within the sights of Los Angeles's power brokers. Mickey Kantor, an attorney with Manatt, Phelps & Phillips whom I knew, because Kantor was the Southern California Rapid Transit District lobbyist who was trying to secure funding for the Los Angeles Metro Rail, asked me to raise money for Vice President Mondale.

With Vice President Walter Mondale.

In a meeting at the Polo Lounge in Beverly Hills, I agreed on the condition I be named the Mondale campaign's Southern California finance chair. I told Kantor that I needed the title to be successful. The title, I told Kantor, would be an indication that I was within the candidate's circle, and I had access and authority. Kantor said he would have to check with the national campaign chairman, Michael S. Berman, who in 1992 became a confidante to President Bill Clinton and First Lady Hillary Clinton. Kantor called me a few days later and told me Berman had agreed. Mondale at that time was trailing US Senator Gary Hart, until Mondale ridiculed his "new ideas" with the "Where's the beef" ad.

I was successful in my fundraising efforts with my existing contacts, and at the same time I made inroads into new funding sources and contacts, which proved very beneficial in

1988, when I served as state finance co-chair of the presidential campaign of Massachusetts Governor Michael Dukakis. At the same time, I gained knowledge and experience in presidential politics and tactics. I remember riding with Mondale from a fundraiser at the Biltmore hotel in downtown Los Angeles to Jimmy's restaurant in Beverly Hills. Jimmy's was popular with entertainers, business executives and politicians. During the drive, Mondale was discussing campaign strategy, gossip, and personalities. I raised my eyebrows towards the Secret Service agents sitting in front of the car. Mondale said, "Don't worry, they are sworn to secrecy." In another case, I was waiting for Mondale to arrive at a fundraiser at the Luxe Sunset Boulevard Hotel in Brentwood. When Mondale's car arrived, I eagerly ran and tried to open the rear door. A Secret Service agent pushed me away. I realized that the other Secret Service agents had to take their places and secure the area, since there are small hills nearby, before they allow the presidential candidate to exit the car.

I had the opportunity to attend the 1984 Democratic National Convention at the Moscone Center in San Francisco, where delegates nominated Mondale for president and Geraldine Ferraro for vice president. Rosalind Wyman, a former Los Angeles City Council member, was the chair of the convention, the first woman to lead a Democratic National Convention. I met Gary Hart and Jesse Jackson at the convention, and Dukakis at a reception for prominent Greek Americans.

Governor Michael Dukakis

In October 1988, the *Los Angeles Times Sunday Magazine* ran a cover story titled "Inside the California Money Machine" in which Ronald Brownstein described me as follows: "Nikolas Patsaouras approaches political fund raising the way a shark approaches dinner. There's no wasted motion, no angst, no indecision. He doesn't worry if people consider him a pest or a nag. Every day he comes into his office and flips through a Rolodex thickened by a decade of spadework in state, local, and national politics. He measures his prospects and then, morning after morning, month after month, picks up the phone and implacably pursues them."

According to William M. Wardlaw, a leading Democratic Party fund raiser, "Starting in late 1987, every time Dukakis came out here, I got a call from Patsaouras. I said no every time until May. Patsaouras was never angry, but he was just damn persistent."

After my first big exposure to national politics as Southern California finance chair for Mondale in 1984, I appeared on the national radar, and I had the opportunity to meet in Los Angeles with several of the potential Democratic Party candidates for the 1988 presidential election. Hart, preparing for a second bid for the presidency, came by to meet with me in the fall of 1986. I had breakfast with Rep. Richard A. Gephardt. I had a meeting at Marathon National Bank, where I was serving as chairman, with Bruce E. Babbitt, former governor of Arizona.

Although I had been approached by several candidates, I had not committed to any of the campaigns. Then, in February 1987, Kitty Dukakis called me and inquired if I would be willing to set up a few "meet and greet" gatherings with political, business and community

With Governor Michael Dukakis and Sylvia.

Los Angeles Times Magazine

OCTOBER 23, 1988

The California

MONEY MACHINE

How Michael Dukakis and His Team Came From Back of the Pack and Raised Millions in the Intense Fight for California's Campaign Dollars

With Sylvia, Governor Michael Dukakis, and Beverly Thomas. Photo: *LA Times Magazine*.

leaders during her visit to Los Angeles in April. I had met her husband, Massachusetts Governor Michael Dukakis at the Democratic National Convention in San Francisco in 1984. I got excited that a fellow Greek would be seeking the Presidency and told Kitty she could count on my help.

In mid-1987, none of the Democratic candidates had any fundraising roots. The media had dubbed the candidates the "Seven Dwarfs." Hart had good connections in Hollywood and among young professionals, but his campaign imploded after revelations about his inappropriate relationship with Donna Rice. Senator Joseph R. Biden had the most appeal, supported by political fundraisers Lisa Specht and producer/investor Ted Field. In the spring of 1987, Field co-hosted a fundraiser for Biden that raised what was at that time an astonishing

$435,000. But Biden had to drop out after disclosures that he had plagiarized speeches given by Neil Kinnock a, British politician, as well as John and Robert Kennedy.

John Sasso, manager of the Dukakis campaign, had given the tapes of Kinnock's and Biden's speeches to the *New York Times*, and Dukakis fired Sasso in September 1987 and appointed Susan Estrich as campaign manager. Unfortunately, Estrich had never managed a political campaign. Additionally, Sasso had had a unique relationship with Dukakis, one based on respect. The absence of this relationship was more important than Sasso's skills as campaign manager.

Dukakis had a natural base, the conservative Greek American community. Still, when he announced his bid for the presidency on April 29, 1987, he was not known in California. But whether they were Republicans or Democrats, Greeks were excited about his candidacy. I co-hosted in May 1987 the first fundraiser in Los Angeles with Greek Americans and raised $100,000. My contacts and Dukakis's fluency in Spanish opened doors across East Los Angeles. I arranged a meeting for Kitty Dukakis with Asian American businessmen in April 1987, and Dukakis's immigrant background helped to establish a relationship in the Asian American community.

In the October 23, 1988, *Los Angeles Times Sunday Magazine*, Ronald Brownstein wrote, "Patsaouras has been a key player in a Dukakis financial operation that has shattered all Democratic presidential fund-raising records in California." Brownstein reported that Dukakis's California campaign had raised about $7.9 million as of October 1, in addition to the $3.5 million that Dukakis had raised by the June 8 primary, "more than any Democratic presidential candidate has ever carried home from the state." And Brownstein noted that, "Dukakis's feat is especially remarkable considering his position just two years ago…Dukakis had virtually no supporters, no contacts, no history and certainly very little entree with heavy hitters of the state's much-courted political fundraising community."

Dukakis biggest endorsement early on was from actress Sally Field, whose jet occasionally was used when she, I, and others on the Dukakis's California team traveled around the state during the primaries. The scrambling for dollars in California is often called the First Primary in the race to the White House. Only four of more than forty fundraising events during the primaries were organized by the movie crowd. Barry Diller, wo was then chief executive of 20th Century Fox, held a fundraiser in his home in October 1987. Walt Disney Company President Frank G. Wells sponsored a breakfast. Sadly, Wells, a great and a kind person whom I had gotten to know during the campaign, died in a 1994 helicopter accident.

Robert G. Rehme, then co-chairman of New World Pictures, co-sponsored an event with Jon Feltheimer, president of New World Television. Television writer and producer Norman Lear hosted in his house an event where Dukakis addressed more than two hundred guests from the movie industry. I concluded that when it came to money, Dukakis proved Hollywood is not an absolute, maybe a necessary, but not an absolute ingredient. "We got where we are without that help," I was quoted in Ronald Brownstein's book, *The Power and the Glitter*. Besides, Dukakis was not impressed by Hollywood, as President Clinton was reported to be. At Diller's fundraiser, I found the governor at the bar chatting with actors

Warren Beatty and Jack Nicholson. At some point the governor rolled his eyes at me as if to tell me, "Let's get out of here."

In June 1988, after the nomination was clinched, I organized a fundraiser at the Beverly Hilton hotel in Beverly Hills for one thousand guests at $1000 per ticket. I got a call the morning of the event from Dukakis who informed me he was not coming to the event because Kitty was going to have a small operation on her neck. Dumbfounded, I said, "Governor, there are one thousand of your supporters expected tonight. You have to come." Dukakis replied, "Nick, Kitty comes first, but Governor Bill Clinton of Arkansas will substitute for me." I got a call a couple of hours later from Clinton. "Nick, this is Governor Clinton, please buy for me a blue shirt 16.5 neck size and get me a room to freshen up because I'm in transit." At the fundraiser, Clinton gave an incredible speech focusing on education that left the crowd spellbound. After the speech, the crowd swarmed around Clinton, handing him their business cards and telling him, "Governor, if you ever decide to run for president, count me in." And I told my wife Sylvia, "He'll be president one day."

The Democratic Party Convention in Atlanta, Georgia, from July 18–21, 1988, was a very exciting and gratifying experience for me. I was invited to stand at the dais with other special guests when Dukakis gave his acceptance speech. Texas State Treasurer Ann Richards gave the keynote speech that included the famous line that Vice President George H. W. Bush, the Republican front runner for president, was "born with a silver foot in his mouth." Clinton gave a speech nominating Dukakis that lasted thirty-three minutes, twice the allotted time. Later, in 1992, in accepting the Democratic nomination for president, Clinton said, "I ran for president this year for one reason and one reason only. I wanted to come back to this Convention and finish that speech I started four years ago." Kitty Dukakis's father, Harry Dickson, conducted the Boston Pops Orchestra at a concert during the Convention. The event was sponsored by Milan Panic, president of ICN Pharmaceuticals and a big sponsor of the Los Angeles Opera and supporter of Democratic party causes and candidates. Coming out of the convention Dukakis was seventeen points ahead of Bush in the polls.

After Dukakis had been nominated for President in San Francisco, he invited a half dozen advisors from around the country to Massachusetts. We met at the Governor's Office, where Dukakis and Estrich gave a preview of the general election campaign strategy. The governor said, "I learned my lesson when I was defeated in 1979 running for reelection by not answering back negative ads. We know they will hit us with the Willie Horton ad, but we will be ready to respond." Of course, that did not happen. The campaign proved to be unprepared when the attack came.

William Horton was a convicted murderer who committed additional violent crimes while on furlough from prison in Massachusetts, where he was serving a life sentence without the possibility of parole. Prominent ads for the Bush campaign referred to him as "Willie" Horton, even though he never went by that nickname. The ads have been widely characterized as an example of racist stereotyping and dog whistle politics. Interestingly, the Willie Horton affair was used to attack Dukakis first by Al Gore during the Democratic primary. Gore raised questions about the Massachusetts weekend furlough program in a primary debate in the South. Gore mentioned no names. But the names were in the public record, in particular William Robert Horton Jr.

There were two presidential debates. One, inconsequential, in Winston-Salem, North Carolina, and a second, pivotal debate, in Los Angeles at the University of California Los Angeles's Pauley Pavilion, the moderator Bernard Shaw of CNN opened the debate with this question to Dukakis. "Governor, if Kitty Dukakis were raped and murdered, would you favor an irrevocable death penalty for the killer?" Dukakis responded. "No. I don't Bernard. And you know that I've opposed the death penalty during all my life. I don't see any evidence that it's a deterrent, and I think there are better and more effective ways to deal with violent crime. We have done so in my own state. "I turned to my wife Sylvia and whispered, "We are done."

That same evening there was an after-debate reception hosted by Ted Field at Green Acres, the Harold Lloyd Estate he had purchased a couple of years before. The mood of the guests was like they were attending a wake. Dukakis sort of apologized for letting us down. From then on, it was all downhill, with the disastrous debate at UCLA, the Willie Horton attack ads, and the comical appearance of Dukakis with a helmet riding a tank.

There was a rally on the eve of the election at UCLA, and Sylvia and I rode the motorcade to Los Angeles International Airport, where we boarded a private plane to Boston. The press corps were on the same plane, and I witnessed the different personalities of journalists on camera and off camera. Unfortunately, rudeness, entitlement, demands, and screaming colored the behavior of some. On the way to Boston, there was a stop at Iowa at 4:00 a.m. It was cold and snowing. However, it was impressive to see a crowd of the true believers there, waiting on the tarmac to welcome Dukakis. We knew, of course, that chilly morning that the race was lost.

In their book *Dukakis: An American Odyssey*, Charles Kenney and Robert L. Turner wrote, "Some supporters saw him as a candidate bridging the Hart and Mondale factions of the Democratic Party. Part of the pitch was seen as neoliberal, almost Republican: he campaigned as a tough and innovative manager who was able to deliver services and still cut taxes. But another part was distinctly Democratic: a fervent commitment to public service and belief in government as an engine of good, with a goal of opportunity for everyone. "Overlaying these themes was Dukakis's persistent optimism. As Nick Patsaouras, his chief fund-raiser in California, put it, 'The other candidates are talking about doom and gloom. Dukakis is the Democratic Reagan because he is preaching optimism and makes people feel good.'"

Dukakis was a very principled, honest public servant. I witnessed firsthand his unselfish dedication to public service. Oil tycoon Armand Hammer was interested in receiving a presidential pardon because he had pleaded guilty in United States District Court to three misdemeanor charges of making illegal contributions in the names of other persons to the 1972 re-election campaign of President Richard Nixon. Hammer invited me a few times for lunch at his penthouse office in Occidental Petroleum headquarters in Westwood. He gave me a tour of his priceless paintings, most of them bought in Russia, displayed in the corridors of his office suite. He was known for his art collection and his close ties to the Soviet Union. He was called "Lenin's chosen capitalist" by the media. Hammer became a "trustee" of the Dukakis general election campaign by contributing $100,000. The purpose of Hammer's courting me, I suspect, was because Hammer was seeking a one-on-one meeting with Dukakis for the obvious, but unstated reason to receive a pardon should Dukakis become president.

Steadfastly, Dukakis refused to meet with Hammer every time he visited Los Angeles. Ironically, another Greek American, Alec Courtelis, was instrumental in getting Hammer a pardon from President George H. W. Bush. Courtelis was a developer of malls in South Florida and prominent GOP fundraiser, and he shared with Hammer a hobby of breeding and racing Arabian horses.

The results of the November 8, 1988, the presidential election were:

Bush 53.4 percent—Dukakis 45.7 percent Bush carried forty states with an electoral vote of 426. Dukakis carried ten states plus the District of Columbia with 111 electoral votes.

President William J. Clinton

After the fundraising event at the Beverly Hilton hotel, when Clinton substituted for Dukakis, Clinton stayed connected with me. There were monthly calls, simple chitchats. A number of times, Clinton would discuss the decision he had to make, whether he should run for reelection, and let down his constituents, considering he was thinking of running for President in 1992. Whenever Clinton would visit Los Angeles, he would meet with me at the end of the day at the Polo Lounge in Beverly Hills. Clinton liked me and related to me, which he proved ten years later. It was probably because of our humble beginnings that we developed a friendship over the years.

Reception line at a State Dinner at the White House. Photo courtesy of the White House.

State Dinner reception at White House. Sylvia greeting President Bill Clinton. Courtesy of White House

State Dinner reseption at White House. Greeting President Bill Clinton. Courtesy of White House

The American Jewish Committee decided to honor me with its Distinguished Service Award on September 28, 1989. The Dinner committee included Mayor Tom Bradley, Los Angeles County Supervisors Michael Antonovich and Edmund Edelman, county District Attorney Ira Reiner, Patricia Duff Medavoy, the wife of TriStar Pictures Chief Executive Mike Medavoy; Edward Sanders, a Jewish community leader and former advisor to President Carter on Middle East policy; and Mickey Kantor, a prominent attorney and lobbyist. I designated that the proceeds from the dinner be utilized to establish the Patsaouras Program for Ethnic Pluralism to be administered by the American Jewish Committee. The program would provide the impetus for building bridges of common understanding, cooperation, and unity among ethnic groups.

I asked Clinton to be the keynote speaker, and the governor gladly accepted. Three days before the event I got a call from Betsey Wright, Clinton's chief of staff, advising me that the governor would not be able to come because he was chairing an education summit involving President Bush and forty-nine of fifty governors at the University of Virginia in Charlottesville, September 27 and 28. I had developed a cordial relationship with Wright and quickly answered "No, Betsey, please ask the governor to call me." Sure enough, a few hours later Clinton called, and I told him, "Governor, you must come. There are seven hundred guests and above all I have invited my parents to come from Greece." Clinton asked me, "Do you have access to a private plane?" I, of course, answered "No." Clinton said, "Let me call you back." A few hours later Clinton called and said, "Hillary and I will come. Please have the Highway Patrol escort us from LAX to the hotel." The Clintons not only came but they arrived at the hotel early. My mother Evangelia sat next to the future president of the United States, with my father Vasilis at the same table, an experience they never forgot.

It was a happy event, with Clinton mesmerizing the crowd with his trademark charm and oratory. I was so happy that I danced a "zeibekiko" against the admonition of a couple of guests, that "it was not proper in this particular environment." Zeibekiko is an old Greek

folk dance originally strictly for males. Due to the movements of the dancer, it is sometimes known as the "eagle dance." My friend Jim Birakos in fact broke a couple of plates on the floor as I was dancing, a Greek tradition.

After the event, Sylvia and I were invited by Mickey Kantor and his wife Heidi to their house, where the Clintons would stay, for after-dinner drinks. It was the first time I met Hillary, who was very unassuming, down to earth, with her shoes off sitting on the floor next to the coffee table, chatting, munching, and laughing.

One day in 1991 Clinton called me and told me he wanted to talk to me about something important. As usual, we met at the Polo Lounge and Clinton started to contemplate what "We would do if we were in the White House "and similar talk. At one point Clinton asked me if I would accept a formal position in fundraising in California. I declined, telling Clinton, "Governor it would be an honor, but I'm considering running for mayor and I cannot serve two masters. It would not be fair to you." Clinton responded "Nick, I have great respect for you. But, after tonight your honesty captured my heart."

I saw Clinton, when he was president, at a couple of receptions when he visited Los Angeles. Of course, the setting was very formal—not like the good old days, just the two of us drinking wine and chatting at the Polo Lounge.

In 1996, I received an envelope from the White House that I did not open thinking it was a fundraising invitation. I was inundated with such invitations, and as a result I developed a habit of throwing them into the wastebasket unopened. It was Friday, I locked my office and therefore the cleaning crew did not empty the wastebasket. Somehow, over the weekend I kept thinking of that envelope. Monday morning, I opened it and, to my surprise, it was an invitation that read, "The President and Mrs. Clinton request the pleasure of the company of Mr. Patsaouras at a dinner to be held at the White House on Thursday, May 9, 1996. It was a state dinner in honor of the President of Greece, Konstantinos Stephanopoulos. Still, I was jaded with political events and traveling, after my numerous red-eye flights to and from Washington, DC, and I was not inclined to go. But Sylvia convinced me that it was a great honor and once-in-a-lifetime opportunity to be in the White House under those circumstances.

By coincidence the USA TODAY newspaper ran an article by Katy Kelly, on May 13, 1996, in which she described in every detail how the state dinner was staged in honor of Stephanopoulos, explaining the preparations since March. She wrote, "Being invited to a state dinner at the White House is like being invited to a Windsor wedding—and being seated on the groom's side near the front. It is an honor many crave, and few are accorded. It is a night of a thousand courtesies and no second chances." The article quoted White House Social Secretary Ann Stock, "This is the social culmination of a day of diplomacy. It is the greatest welcome that we can extend to another country."

"We develop what I call a line-of-march, a minute-by-minute (plan) that everybody works off. The ten- to twelve-page plan goes to President and Mrs. Clinton to look at and see what they want to change or if there is any tweaking to be done. By the time you get to the night, everything has been completely thought through." Ms. Stock indicated that, although suggestions for who gets invited to a state dinner could be from many sources, the Clintons made the final call, noting that two days before the event, "Color coded tabs representing each guest are arranged around a cardboard circle. Both Clintons will study it. A number of things may change."

The USA TODAY article also quoted Neel Lattimore, a deputy press secretary to the first lady, to emphasize the coordination involved in a state dinner, "It involves the social office and military personnel, (and) every person on the White House staff: the florist, the gardener, the usher's office, all of our kitchen staff, the communications office and Protocol at the State Department.

At the May 9, 1996, state dinner in honor of Stephanopoulos, once Sylvia and I went through the formal reception, it was time to be seated. I escorted Sylvia to her table where she was seated next to the Greek ambassador. It was then my turn to find my place. I walked among the numbered tables and hesitantly towards the head tables. I took a couple of takes, but yes, my assigned seat was at one of the two head tables, the one for First Lady Hillary Clinton. I was pleased to sit next to the great actress Irene Papas, who starred in the movie Zorba the Greek.

When Hillary heard that my son Alexi was studying law at Yale Law School, where she had met Bill, she practically talked with me all evening. Vice President Al Gore, Secretary of State Warren Christopher, and journalist Wolf Blitzer were among the guests. The crowd of 250 people included politicians, actors, journalists, and businesspersons.

I was surprised by the invitation because I had not had any contact with the Clintons for more than five years. And even more surprised that no one called me after the dinner to ask, "How did you like the dinner?" implicitly trying to get credit for the invitation.

Stephanopoulos was coming to Los Angeles that weekend and I was involved in the preparations for his visit. That Sunday was Mother's Day, but I did not call until Monday to wish my mother "Happy Mother's Day." I apologized that I was busy and could not call. She said, "I know where you were my boy, I saw on CNN you were in the White House with Stephanopoulos." I suppose it was a great Mother Day's present for her to see her son in the White House with the president of the United States and the president of Greece.

With Fidel Castro, Supervisor Gloria Molina, and LA delegation to Cuba.

Fidel Castro

Fidel Castro with Supervisor Gloria Molina.

In 2002, I was a member of a group of Los Angeles leaders that included County Supervisor Gloria Molina who visited Cuba. The purpose of the trip was to learn about their schools and hospitals, considering Cuba was exporting medical doctors to many undeveloped countries.

We had the opportunity to spend over six hours with Fidel Castro. Although the appointment was set with Castro's staff, it was not definite that he would show up because of security concerns. At the 6:00 p.m. agreed time, two jeeps drove in and Castro exited with his bodyguards. His charm and charisma were felt immediately, before he even uttered a word.

First, he lectured us, a group of one dozen, in a large auditorium, speaking in Spanish, although he knew English very well. I was impressed with his encyclopedic knowledge. He answered for over three hours the in-depth questions he was asked. I asked his opinion of the upcoming Olympic Games in Athens, Greece in 2004. Castro quoted Greek philosophers, poets, and writers. He talked of the Parthenon and the history of the Olympic Games. An amazing scholar.

After talking for three hours, without showing any sign of exhaustion, he sensed some in the group were getting restless. He said in English "Time to eat and drink." We were driven to the government palace where an exquisite buffet was displayed with plenty of liquor and wine. I unknowingly tasted horse meat because it looked good, and it was delicious. I helped myself with seconds. Castro engaged in conversation one-on-one with many members of the group, in depth without time limit. Supervisor Molina had her scarf autographed by Castro. The party lasted till midnight when Castro finally departed.

We visited schools, hospitals, tobacco factories, and many cultural facilities. One of the highlights of the trip was a visit to Copa Cabana, an outdoor theater where a group of lady dancers performed. It was a joy to see Supervisor Molina smoking a huge cigar. Some in the group had drinks at La Floridita, where Ernest Hemingway used to hang out.

The trip was a lifetime experience for me. Havana reminded me of scenes and life in my childhood days, with little shops in small streets bustling with activity. Parents in the evening were taking a stroll for entertainment, holding the children by the hand, and children dressed up, holding hands. Their living rooms were the streets, where they would have fun, play games, and pass time. In every corner there was a congregation of people chatting, arguing, or musicians playing music. Since I was eight or nine years old, I was enamored with Latin music, especially Cuban music. I would place my ear on the side of the radio, pretending the orchestra was in that box, and every Sunday at 2:00 p.m. I felt I was in heaven listening to Latin music. The architecture in Havana had a European feeling, simple, neglected, no front yards. People on the balconies in the evening would gaze down on passersby. One could feel the warmth and camaraderie among the people, poor but proud. Although deprived of luxuries, they seemed content.

Shimon Peres

In June 2008, as a member of the Los Angeles Department of Water and Power (LADWP) Board of Commissioners, I was part of a delegation led by Mayor Antonio Villaraigosa on a visit to Israel for reciprocal opportunities between Israel and Los Angeles, including economic, educational, and scientific. It was a trip with tight schedules because of the many opportunities for interaction between our group and business, political, scientific, and educational leaders in Israel.

We met with experts in fighting terrorism at the Emergency Response facility, Belt Shemesh, and had a roundtable discussion with Dr. Boaz Ganor, Founder and executive director of the International Institute for Counterterrorism. Some of us also met with Shai Agassi, Founder and CEO of the project Better Place in Tel Aviv, one of Silicon Valley's most vibrant technologies. Agassi was focusing on a green transportation infrastructure based on electric cars as an alternative to fossil fuel technology. We participated in a Cleantech Roundtable with leading Cleantech industrialists and entrepreneurs at the Old City of Jaffa. At a meeting with officials from the Israeli Port Authority in Tel Aviv, we discussed the Greening of the Port, a project General Manager of LADWP David Nahai and I worked with the Los Angeles Harbor Department.

We had a tour of the Knesset and met the Speaker, Dalia Itzik. I also participated in meetings with Prime Minister Ehud Olmert, Foreign Minister Tzipi Livni, and Jerusalem Mayor Lupoliansky. We met with experts on water conservation and drought protection, and there was a signing of the Sister River Restoration Agreement between Los Angeles and the Yarkon River Authority. On a trip that was not in the itinerary, a small group of us went to the border of the Gaza Strip and met with the Secretary of Defense Ehud Barak. We also visited the border town of Sderot.

Among the highlights of the trip was when a small number of us led by Mayor Villaraigosa met with President Shimon Peres. The wisdom of President Peres was ingrained on his face and expressed in his mannerism and words. I felt very fortunate to be able to participate in the conversation with him and not just be a member of the audience.

The visit to Jerusalem brought back memories of Athens, particularly the hills with white stone houses that look beautiful under the sun. My wife Sylvia was a Los Angeles World Airports (LAWA) Commissioner at the time and was part of the official delegation, and she joined me very early one morning before our official duties began on a personal highlight of the trip for us, a visit following the path of the Stations of the Cross along the Via Dolorosa to the Fourth Century Church of the Holy Sepulchre where Christians commemorate the Resurrection. We were also fortunate to be able to visit the Church of the Nativity, the Dead Sea, and the clifftop fortress of Masada.

Tony Blair

In 2006 Mayor Antonio Villaraigosa hosted British Prime Minister Tony Blair at the Getty Villa in Malibu. Villaraigosa told the Getty Villa crowd that a correspondent of the Guardian had written an article in which he said the mayor's first name was Spanish for "Tony" and described him as "the Latino Blair" "I have never been more flattered in my life" said Villaraigosa to the fifty business, political, and cultural leaders at the gathering. There was serious discussion about climate change, the environment, cultural exchanges, and tourism. In 2005, 360,000 Britons visited Los Angeles, the largest overseas visitors to LA.

CHAPTER SEVENTEEN

THE GREEK CONNECTION

What you leave behind is not what is engraved in stone monuments,
but what is woven into the lives of others.

—PERICLES

THE LOS ANGELES GREEK AMERICAN COMMUNITY

The history of the Greeks of Los Angeles is unlike that of their more established compatriots of the East Coast. They did not have the comfort of an established "Greek Town" or community to welcome them.

Historian Dr. James F. Dimitriou, designated as a world educator by the United Nations, says that little is known of the few Greek immigrants who came to Los Angeles prior to the 1890s. The majority were single males, working on the railroads, in mines and doing other labor-intensive work. Most remained bachelors, married non-Greeks or returned to Greece. By the beginning of the First World War, it is estimated that nearly 1000 Greeks made Los Angeles their home. By 1930, California Census data listed some 6,488 residents in Los Angeles County.

The Very Rev. Fr. John Bakas, dean of the historic St. Sophia Greek Orthodox Cathedral in Los Angeles who retired after twenty-seven years, had been involved for many years in the civic life of one of Los Angeles's toughest neighborhoods, working successfully to gain the trust and cooperation of gang members. My business associate, Christina Lee had asked Fr. Bakas to reflect on the word "Polis," and what may lie behind my company being called, Polis Builders. He said that "Polis" means the city. And the city is not just buildings, it is "the people, it is the community." Polis, he insisted, means the people, the assembly, that gathered for an all-inclusive benefit. "It's the 'we' instead of the 'I.' It is the group working together to improve the lifestyle and advance the life of the period that we have on this Earth."

Greeting Greek President Konstantinos Stephanopoulos in Los Angeles City Hall. With Greek American community leader Georgia Rosenberry, Councilman Joel Wachs, and president of the City Council John Ferraro.

He told Christina, "Nick is a philosopher, a thinker, who can think abstractly, and who can bring permanent resolutions to city problems." He said I was a long-term viewer of things, and he remembered Pericles, the polis builder of Athens, who looked at the finished Parthenon and said, "Generations until the end of time will speak of us." Using an old expression of his, Fr. Bakas explained the meaning and worth of psychological and spiritual archaeology. In archaeology, he said, to get down to the first civilization, you've got to go through layers and layers, and each layer was a civilization built on top of another. "I think in terms of our city, of ourselves, we've got so much garbage piled on top of things that we haven't gone down to the fundamentals of the layers before we build on top of the other. We've sort of dumped more dirt covering, and we build on top of that, and sometimes the foundations we build on now are shaky because we never understood what was there before us." Spiritual and political archaeology means, he said, to scrape through a lot of layers and understand what went on before you. And to build meaningful structures that will last.

My own parish priest, Fr. Spencer Kezios, now Bishop Spyridon, has known me from my student days at CSUN. Later, as a professional, I was delighted to donate electrical engineering services to St. Nicholas Greek Orthodox Church senior citizens housing in Northridge, and to earn his durable friendship and trust.

Fr. Kezios was transferred to Northridge from a parish in Pocatello, Idaho, in November 1960. He came to a small, fledgling parish, with many young people, many employed by the aerospace industry. The parish grew rapidly and bought the present property in 1964. About a dozen years later, in 1977, the St. Nicholas Parochial School was operating and a year after the community center was completed.

In obtaining permits to build and expand St. Nicholas senior citizens apartments, Fr. Kezios went through a bureaucratic baptism by fire. I was delighted to recommend him to Mayor Villaraigosa for appointment to the nine-member city Planning Commission, where he served for over six years. During his tenure, Fr. Kezios participated in major decision-making involving LA Live, the Ritz-Carlton Hotel, and the development of buildings that contributed to the renewal of downtown.

Dancing the zeibekiko at Athenian Gardens, Hollywood, CA.

Fr. Kezios knew me well, after so many years. In referring to my insight and character, he noted, "He's a no-nonsense guy. There's no fat in what Nick has to say. He tells it like it is." He said that I was rightfully proud of my Greek heritage, a pride attributed to the very long history of Greece, the cultural and religious elements. "We are thankful for that because it is a concept of the melting pot, yet it doesn't necessarily mean everything melds into one homogenous, amorphous kind of a thing."

"And one more thing about Nick, he's a great dancer."

LOS ANGELES-ATHENS SISTER CITY AFFILIATION

"Nick Patsaouras, The Catalyst of Much of the Greek Revival,"
—*LOS ANGELES TIMES*, 9-4-1983

A *Los Angeles Magazine* cover story "LA's Secret POWER ELITE 20 Who Wield True Clout Behind the Scenes," noted: Patsaouras, an immigrant who flies his Greek origins like a spinnaker in a stiff breeze, has immerged himself in city politics with fervor and considerable effect.

As my involvement in public affairs grew, I had always searched for ways both to honor my Greek roots and to promote deeper engagement by the Greek American community in the civic life of our adopted country. The Los Angeles Olympic Games of 1984 offered a special opportunity for me to bind the city of my birth with Los Angeles, and to connect the birthplace of the Olympic Games with what would be a new Olympic triumph in the City of Angels.

On September 20, 1983, the Los Angeles City Council unanimously passed a resolution appointing me Chairman of the newly established Los Angeles-Athens Sister City Committee. It was a welcome yet demanding responsibility. The Sister City program originated in 1956 by President Eisenhower to encourage friendship and understanding between peoples of the US and foreign nations through direct, personal contacts.

The resolution was sent to the Mayor of Athens and the Ministry of Council in Greece, and to the Town Affiliation Association of the United States, Inc. As chairman of the Los Angeles-Athens Sister City Committee I selected a committee of civic, scientific, and government leaders that included Los Angeles Councilwoman Peggy Stevenson; Jim Birakos of the South Coast Air Quality Management District, known to millions as "Mr. Smog"; Ethelda Singer, vice president of Sister Cities International; vascular surgeon Dr. George Andros; Ann Pappas, president of the Los Angeles-based Hellenic American Chamber of Commerce;

With Mayor of Athens Dimitris Beis, Alexi, and Sylvia. Mayor Beis holds 1984 Olympic Games RTD commenorative tokens.

developer Michael Reyes, architect Bruce Koerner, senior advisor to Mayor Bradley Fran Savitch, and Bishop Anthony of the Greek Orthodox Metropolis of San Francisco.

Despite my passion for the affiliation, launching the program became a formidable challenge. When I approached the Mayor of Athens, Dimitris Beis, to discuss the affiliation, he was uncooperative. The capital of Greece, he insisted, should affiliate with only other world capital cities.

I had hosted Mayor Athanasios Giannousis from Greece's second largest city, Thessaloniki, at L'Ermitage Restaurant when he was on a visit to Los Angeles under a US State Department program, and we had kept in contact. After Beis's rejection, I traveled to Thessaloniki to propose to him sister cityhood, and he enthusiastically agreed. However, another disappointment awaited me when I returned to Los Angeles. Ethelda Singer, vice president of the Sister City International Program, informed me that Connecticut already had an established relationship with Thessaloniki and the Sister Cities Charter does not allow two affiliations.

"Choice, not chance, determines your destiny," said Aristotle, and true enough I made the choice to seek alternative avenues by making a sincere effort and executing it. Margaret Papandreou, the wife of then Prime Minister Andreas Papandreou, came to Los Angeles with actress and culture minister Melina Mercouri. At a reception at Caroline Ahmanson's penthouse at the Beverly Wilshire Hotel, I described my predicament to her. "Let me talk to Beis," she told me. "He's a good friend of mine." A month later I received notice from Mayor Beis that Athens had agreed to a Sister City affiliation with Los Angeles.

On Tuesday, February 7, 1984, the delegation I had organized, except for Mayor Tom Bradley, arrived at Athens' West Airport, the VIP section. My wife Sylvia and my son Alexi also traveled with the delegation, as did Angelo Pappas, Helen Birakos, Marie Andros, and Bruce Stevenson. We were greeted by the President and ranking members of the Athens City Council and escorted to the Grande Bretagne Hotel, where our delegation headquartered. Bradley would fly to Athens in two days, after attending the Winter Games in Sarajevo.

The historic Grande Bretagne had played a pivotal role in the history of Athens and the modern Olympic Games, officially hosting foreign missions, diplomats, statesmen, political figures, and royalty for their modern revival in 1896. Interestingly, it was also at the Grande Bretagne Hotel where the International Olympic Committee initially met to award the 1984 Games to Los Angeles. Mayor Bradley was there, as was Supervisor Kenneth Hahn. The hotel manager remembered a peculiarity that occurred at the time. Facing the most celebrated central square in Greece, Constitution Square, and the Parliament Building, the third-floor balconies of the hotel were decked out with flags from every nation. But there also flew a streamer no one could identify: the flag of Los Angeles County. Designed by Hahn, he had personally hoisted it on his balcony.

To fully acclimate, the second day in Athens, Wednesday, February 8, was to be a free day for our delegation. Instead, we were treated to an incredible venture, a private bus tour along the Athens Riviera to nearby Cape Sounion and the magnificent temple of Poseidon, the God of the Seas in ancient Greece. Sounion's extraordinary Doric temple was erected during the Golden Age of Pericles, around 444 BCE, on the southern coast of Attica, and had a stunning view of the Aegean Sea. Along with the Parthenon and the temple of Aphaia on nearby

With my son Alexi at the temple of Poseidon in Sounion, Greece

Aegina Island, Poseidon's mighty monument completed the Sacred Triangle of antiquity. The poet Lord Byron had visited the temple and had practiced an early act of graffiti by inscribing his name on one of the temple columns.

When Bradley arrived on Thursday, February 9, he was affably greeted by the mayor of Athens, the President of the Athens City Council and council members, as well as by our delegation. However, a controversy over the Olympic torch was brewing. The issue was the groundbreaking protocol Los Angeles had instituted, a torch relay program that would raise millions of dollars to be donated to charities. The route would involve 3,600 torchbearers covering over 15,000 kilometers, each kilometer raising $3,000. Each runner would transfer the flame to the torch of the next runner, keeping the torch carried. Many buyers donated the privilege to carry the torch to individuals who couldn't afford to participate. All proceeds would go to one of four charities of the donors' choice: Boys' Club, Girls' Club, YMCA, and the Special Olympics. In all prior Olympics, only especially selected individuals were allowed to carry the torch. For the Los Angeles Olympics any person could become a torchbearer. The torch odyssey would begin with the traditional ceremonies in Olympia, Greece, where an actress dressed in the flowing robes of an ancient Greek priestess would kindle the torch using the rays of the sun. Ignoring the benevolent objectives of the LA protocol, any Olympic torch relay involving money was considered an unacceptable commercialization of the sacred flame—especially by Olympia's Mayor Spyros Fotinos. He threatened to block the lighting of the Olympic flame.

Facing speculative reporters in the lobby of the Grande Bretagne, a masterful Bradley capably redirected the topic of discussion by announcing that all future Olympic Games should be held permanently in Athens. That became the news of the hour. The quarrel over the torch would nastily resurface in Olympia a few days later.

Nikolas Skoulas, secretary general of the Greek Tourist Organization, hosted a luncheon for the delegation at the nearby Astir Palace Hotel, followed by a formal dinner that evening held by Mayor Beis at the Rotisserie Restaurant of the Hotel Intercontinental. Just as I had hoped, Athens and Los Angeles spawned new friendships. The relationship blossomed quickly, and pleasantness and warmth ruled the day.

On Friday, February 10, we visited the Acropolis. We climbed the marble steps of this ancient citadel built in the fifth century BC. The Acropolis is one of the most recognizable monuments in the world and a reference point for civilization's golden age and cradle of democracy. We walked through the Propylaea, the colossal entrance and suddenly stopped, engrossed by the emerging site before us, the majestic Parthenon. UNESCO said it best. The Parthenon is "the supreme expression of the adaptation of architecture to a natural site." Indeed, this monumental landscape of unique beauty consisting of a complete series of masterpieces has exerted an exceptional influence throughout the world. We were mesmerized by the columns of Pentelic marble and the massive limestone foundation, the perfection of it all. Dedicated to the goddess Athena during the fifth century BCE, the Parthenon's decorative sculptures are deemed high points of classical Greek art, an enduring symbol of Ancient Greece, democracy, and Western civilization. To establish a private museum in London, the agents of Thomas Bruce, 7th Lord Elgin, then British ambassador to the Ottoman Empire, hacked away half of the sculptures beginning in 1801. Lord Byron branded Elgin's appalling action vandalism and looting, and today's exhibition of the marbles in the British Museum is the subject of an international controversy.

Mayor Bradley had voiced strong support for the return of the marbles to Greece, as have I, promoting their reunion with those in Athens at every opportunity. Even with Elgin's mutilation, the Parthenon is an incomparable site. Mayor Bradley snapped away with his camera, as we all did. He wanted to capture the moment and dwell upon it, to remember the respect and sanctity of the historic site. On the Acropolis, Bradley's eyes fixed on the ancient marvel, then traveled to the modern city that stretched out endlessly below. In Greece, the past and the present live side by side. We walked inside the Parthenon, an act not allowed anymore, and marveled at the ancient builders who understood that to make a line look straight it had to be tapered or curved.

Earlier in the day we met with the Undersecretary of Youth and Sports, A. Laliotis, and members of the national Olympic team. After the Games in Los Angeles, they repaid the visit to Mayor Bradley's office, with their medals. This was followed by meetings with various government ministers on health and environmental issues. Several Greek and American associations held warm receptions for our delegation, including the American Hellenic Educational and Progressive Association-Greece (AHEPA), with a major luncheon event at the Hotel Caravel.

The Olympic Games instigated a magnetic union for the two cities, just as I had envisioned, but an underlying issue—smog—was also considered a decisive determinant of the new relationship. In fact, newspaper headlines in Athens proclaimed that smog united the two cities.

Two years before the Sister City affiliation, Birakos had chaired an international committee of experts to save Athens from the scourge of air pollution. It was the desire of the minister of the environment at the time to invite authorities from five countries who would

With Mayor of Athens Dimitris Beis Mayor Tom Bradley and Bishop Anthony

rubber-stamp his environmental strategy. Sent by the US Department of State, Birakos felt that a faithful list of recommendations on pollution issues and solutions would best result from in-depth analyses, reviews of the pollution inventory and the contributions of stationary and vehicular sources, an appraisal of existing rules and regulations, an analysis of local meteorological conditions and current pollution levels, as well as other factors.

Each expert would be assigned a specific topic later to be discussed fully in an open session by all members so that deliberated and decided recommendations could be issued. With the unanimous support of his colleagues, Birakos chose to conduct public hearings to obtain data from government and industry officials, the European Community, the World Health Organization, specialists from universities and other air pollution authorities, industrial and commercial organizations, and from the public, before issuing any committee recommendations. After two weeks of hearings, Birakos's final report was widely publicized and was debated by the Hellenic Parliament. In Athens, with Mayor Bradley present at a news conference with some fifty members of the national and international press participating, the Greek minister of the environment, Antonis Tritsis, later to become mayor of Athens, asked Bradley, what must he do when deleterious air pollution levels are registered in Athens. "Your city also has a big smog problem," Tritsis said. "What would you advise me to do."

"You must do what I do," replied Bradley. "Call Birakos."

The official signing ceremony for the Sister City Affiliation was on the evening of Friday, February 10, 1984. We were driven to the neoclassical Athens City Hall, constructed in 1872. A large crowd had gathered in front of the impressive building. The flag of the United States flew on the city hall flagpole, and on flagpoles at the square and up and down the street. As we stepped onto a strewn red carpet, the city band played the Star-Spangled Banner. Years had passed, I was told by a City Council member, since the last public display of the American flag and playing of the national anthem on the streets of Athens. We entered Athens City Hall to face the bronze busts of Pericles, the ancient statesman who lifted Athens into a golden age, and his partner, Aspasia, a vivid and respected personality in Athenian society. We made our way up a striking marble staircase surrounded by stained-glass panes crafted by noted artisans, colorful windows that displayed the story of the city in myth and history, of how Athena, the goddess of wisdom, won patronage of the city over the god of the sea, Poseidon.

Then we were escorted into the marble meeting chambers of the council, packed with dignitaries, chief among them the Hon. Monteagle Stearns, the US Ambassador to Greece. After genial remarks by the City Council president, Mayor Bradley presented me and the official delegation whose signatures appeared on the affiliation document: Stevenson, Singer, and Birakos, each one of us awarded the golden medal of Athens by Mayor Beis. A reception followed, leading to even closer ties between our delegation and local civic and government leaders.

In Greece, celebrations breed their own timeline. At the behest of the City Council, we were guided to one of Athens' fashionable night spots, "Garden of Heaven" (Perivoli tou Ouranou), known for its popular urban blues, the Rebetika. At one point in the evening, I took the floor for a zeibekiko, an individual dance with inner intensity and improvised movements that expresses personal feelings. The emotions and triumphs of the bonding of my two cities were manifested. And as I danced, I was lost in remembrances of my youth and my life's struggles and aspirations.

The next day was set aside for visits to museums, including the National Archaeological Museum, considered one of the greatest museums in the world with the richest collection of Greek antiquity artifacts worldwide. The bronze statue of Zeus, standing almost seven feet tall with arms extended as if in the process of throwing a thunderbolt, circa 460 BCE, attracted Bradley instantly, as did hundreds of pieces from the dawn of sculpture to and after the golden age, as did the displayed method of calculating time based on the first Olympic Games of 776 BCE.

A trip the Vorres Museum followed, founded a year before our visit and located in Paiania, outside of Athens, covering some three acres and housed in a complex of buildings totaling 4,500 square meters, surrounded by extensive courtyards and gardens. We were hosted by the founder, the influential Ian Vorres, whose museum is dedicated to contemporary Greek art and folk art. Los Angeles was amid developing museums and art centers and we were eager to see how a private collector created this superb infrastructure with permanent collections, the presentation of exhibits, and the implementation of educational programs.

A hosted lunch at the Folia Restaurant, a favorite of Vorres, followed, with a special reception at the American Embassy that evening, presented by US Ambassador Stearns, with key Greek government officials and opinion makers present, including ministers and the wife of the Greek Prime Minister. Our relationships strengthened as we circulated throughout the evening, bolstering associations and developing future events.

With ceremonious observances behind us, the journey to ancient Olympia lay ahead. With a police escort in front and behind our mini tourist coach, we crossed the Corinth Canal which connects mainland Greece with the Peloponnese, its planned development dating to the first century. We arrived at Nafplio, a seaport town and the capital of the First Hellenic Republic. It was a cold February, so our walking tour was curtailed. The Xenia Hotel afforded us appreciated comfort and a blazing fireplace. With glasses of Metaxa brandy in hand, Bradley found an old songbook of spirituals inside the stool of an aged piano, and we sang into the night.

The quintessence of all Greek Theaters, the inimitable Epidaurus, was our next stop. An architectural masterpiece carved in the fourth century BCE into the side of Mount Kynortion, it accommodates 15,000 people with its marble seats. Its renowned acoustics had to be tested by Bradley. So, we climbed sixty rows to the top. Then the mayor yelled, "Hello."

"You don't have to shout," we responded. "C'mon down," he replied with a smile. "We can now go to Olympia."

Less than two hours later we arrived in Olympia, home of the original Olympic Games.

Before going to our hotel, we visited the International Olympic Academy, hosted by Professor Nikolaos Nissiotis, its director, and Greece's permanent member of the International Olympic Committee (IOC). The Academy runs its own educational sessions and hosts events that promote Olympic values. Situated within walking distance of where the Games took place, it has spectacular views of the entire area known as the Valley of the Gods. After signing the guest book, our delegation was taken to the exhibit dedicated to Jesse Owens, the four-time gold medalist in the 1936 Games—and a friend of our mayor.

We checked into our hotel and then strolled through the center of town and its tourist shops, and the Archaeological Museum of Olympia, one of the greatest and oldest religious and cult centers of the Greek world, with one of the masterpieces of ancient Greek art, Hermes of Praxiteles, as well as the Nike of Paionios.

Olympia, the birthplace of the most famous and important sporting event in the ancient world, was also a place of worship dedicated to the Greek god Zeus. The revival of the Olympic Games in 1896, through the efforts of Pierre de Coubertin, whose heart is interned here, illustrates the lasting nature of the ideals of peace, justice, and progress. The values of fair competition and sacred truce that were established during the ancient Games remain among humanity's highest goals.

Olympia stadium, Greece.

In the ancient stadium, Bradley, a former track athlete at UCLA, wanted to compete in the same track used by the ancients. So, we lined up and took our place on the same ancient blocks. At the sound of a loud clap, we sped off. The winner was my son, Alexi, who was immediately crowned with the wildflowers of Olympia.

We returned to the hotel, except for Birakos, who went searching for coffee in town. With his return he brought troublesome news. At the café, he told me he spoke with some reporters, one from the *New York Times*, who had been called to Olympia to cover a developing story regarding the Olympic Flame. It would appear, we determined, that Bradley was being set up. I determined that we must protect the mayor and avert any embarrassing activity. True enough, a messenger from Town Hall arrived with a letter for Bradley, inviting him to a Town Hall meeting. Earlier, we had advised the receptionist that any communication from the Town Hall of Olympia must be directed to either me or Birakos. Bradley could claim that he never saw the letter. Further, he was not in Olympia to negotiate, but was there on a personal, private visit.

The Los Angeles Olympics Committee planned to have runners carry the torch throughout the United States in an eighty-two-day relay before the Games. A total of 6,000 miles were available for sponsorship to raise funds for the Special Olympics and charities. The residents of Olympia, which is the guardian of the flame, objected, claiming that it was a commercialization of the flame. Bradley's refusal to meet with their Municipal Council angered the Mayor of Olympia, Spyros Fotinos, and its residents.

According to the *New York Times*, "The reason is that Mayor Bradley maintained a deliberate distance from the local officials on the subject, having been given renewed confidence by the International Olympic Committee's recent announcement of backing for the Los Angeles organizers' plan. The organizers were also helped when the Greek Government withdrew its tacit support for the Olympians' objections, which were first raised several weeks ago." "As an alternative he proposed an 'informal chat' over dinner in a local tavern. This suggestion was turned down by the Council, which then refused to send any of its members to accompany the mayor and his entourage during his visit Tuesday morning to the ruins of the Olympic Stadium, where the first Games were held in ancient times."

When he returned to Los Angeles, Bradley said an invitation to appear before the town council of Olympia was a trap designed to draw him into a debate over the controversial Los Angeles Olympic torch relay program. "Obviously, they already had a press release written," Bradley said. "Apparently, they had it wired and rigged," he said. "They had set a trap, and I didn't fall into the trap."

Our decision to decline the invitation was good for the spirit of the Games. Greece has always been a fervent supporter and non-political participant in each one of the modern Games. The torch issue had even enflamed the IOC which warned that the torch ceremony might be moved if it could not be done in Olympia.

A little-known fact about the flame for the Los Angeles Olympics involved the undertaking of a filmed documentary of the traditional lighting in Olympia, with all the established ceremonies. Once lit, the flame was placed in a protective container and quietly transported to Lausanne for safekeeping. But it was never used. The formal ceremony was held, the torch

Tanya participating in the 1984 Summer Olympics torch relay.

lit, left Olympia for Los Angeles, and as planned, torchbearers followed the long national route leading to the Coliseum.

My daughter, Tanya, was one of the torchbearers who carried the torch when it reached Los Angeles.

Upon the return of the Sister City delegation to Los Angeles from Athens, Centinela Hospital donated a dialysis machine to a hospital in Athens through the efforts of Angelo Pappas, who was on the Hospital's Board of Trustees.

HELLENIC AMERICAN CHAMBER OF COMMERCE

In December 1981, I founded the Hellenic-American Chamber of Commerce (HACC), serving as Chairman. The main purpose was to promote cultural, business, and professional relationships among the Greek Americans in Los Angeles, something first proposed in1922. The HACC received immediate support from the Los Angeles Greek American community for its social and professional gatherings and programs featuring noteworthy speakers. Honorary chairpersons, prominent in public life, served with dignity, among them California State Senator Nicholas C. Petris, California Assemblymember Louis J. Papan, and Los Angeles City Councilwoman Peggy Stevenson.

To raise money for charitable work, we created an annual Distinguished Service Award dinner program by honoring an American of Greek descent who had distinguished himself/herself in the Arts, the Professions, or the Business world. Among beneficiaries of the money raised at these dinners included the establishment of the Dr. George Papanicolaou Chair at UCLA, named for the inventor of the Pap Smear Test.

With Telly Savalas, and attorney Constantine Karos, Telly's brother-in-law.

The first of these dinners, held on October 29, 1983, was a star-studded event held in the Grand Ballroom of the Beverly Wilshire Hotel in Beverly Hills. As the first Distinguished Service Award honoree, HACC chose to honor Telly Savalas for his major success as a motion picture and television star and for his lifetime of service to many charitable and philanthropic organizations.

Telly's evening was a striking success, with 800 people in attendance, comprising a mix of political and business leaders and many entertainment celebrities, among them Burt Lancaster, Danny Thomas, Red Button, Howard W. Koch, Jane Meadows, Kevin Dobson, George Savalas, Howard Cosell, and Steve Allen, the television and radio personality who had graciously agreed to serve as the gala's Master of Ceremonies. Other prominent persons included Dr. Bernard Naylor, Professor of Pathology at the University of Michigan, and a colleague of Dr. George N. Papanicolaou, and Dr. Sherman M. Mellinkoff, Dean of the UCLA School of Medicine, who spoke about HACC's ongoing fund-raising efforts to establish a chair for cancer research to be named for Dr. Papanicolaou.

Telly was best known as the star of the television series *Kojak*, which ran from 1973–78 on CBS. The bald, incorruptible, lollipop-sucking New York City detective with the tagline, "Who loves ya, baby," became popular both in the United States and abroad, even years after the show ended. He was nominated for an Emmy Award for Outstanding Lead Actor in a Drama Series for two consecutive years and won the Emmy in 1974. He was also nominated for the Golden Globe for Best Actor in a Television Drama Series from 1975 to 1978, winning in 1975 and 1976. As a co-star with Burt Lancaster in Birdman of Alcatraz in 1962, Telly was nominated for an Academy Award and Golden Globe for Best Supporting Actor. Despite his superstar stature, Telly was affable and approachable.

My family and I spent many enjoyable Sundays with the Savalas family, particularly having brunch at the Sheraton Universal with Telly's mother, Christina, a painter, and our dear friends, Telly's sister Katherine and brother-in-law Stan Karos and their daughters Stephanie

Governor Jerry Brown with Arianna Huffington.

Hellenic American Chamber Honoree Nicholas Gage with Arianna Huffington.

With Hellenic American Chamber Honoree Arianna Huffington.

With Judge George Xanthos and Governor Jerry Brown.

and Panayota. Telly graciously allowed to have his picture taken with many of the patrons at the hotel, who immediately recognized him and approached him. The Savalas family was proud of their Greek heritage. Telly's brother, George Demosthenes Savalas, who played the role of Stavros on the Kojak television series, would dress up as an Evzone on Greek national holidays and for Greek festivals. The Evzones were an elite group of light infantry and mountain units of the Greek army who today are members of the Presidential Guard and ceremonial unit that stand guard at the Tomb of the Unknown Soldier at Constitution Square in Athens. Tourists flock to the place to take a picture next to an Evzone. He would often kid his brother by saying that he had studied acting while Telly became a star by just playing himself. In October 1983, the HAAC sponsored a star on the Hollywood Walk of Fame for Telly Savalas, one of the entertainment industry's most prestigious honors, at a ceremony organized by the Hollywood Chamber of Commerce at Hollywood Boulevard near Highland Avenue.

The HACC chose Nicholas Gage as the next recipient of the Distinguished Service Award. Gage achieved fame in America as an investigative reporter for the Wall Street Journal and the *New York Times*. His coverage of the Mafia led to two best-selling books: T*he Mafia Is Not an Equal Opportunity Employer*, and *Mafia, USA*. He was also considered instrumental in exposing the corruption that led to Vice President Spiro Agnew's resignation as well as the Richard Nixon tapes. The dinner honoring Nicholas Gage was also well attended and successful.

Arianna Stassinopoulos (later Stassinopoulos-Huffington) who presented the "Distinguished Service Award" to Nicholas Gage, was accompanied to the event by Governor Edmund Gerald "Jerry" Brown. I had developed a relationship with the governor and, as a result, towards the end of his term in 1982 he asked me to suggest a Greek American attorney for an appointment as judge to the Municipal Courts. I suggested George Xanthos. The swearing-in ceremony took place on September 10, 1982, at the Dorothy Chandler Pavilion and was followed by a champagne reception hosted by me in the Music Center's Founders Room for some 300 guests. A couple of hours before the expiration of his second term at midnight in January 1983, Gov. Brown called and asked me to go with Judge Xanthos to downtown Los Angeles so that the judge would be elevated to the Superior Courts.

Gage was born in a Greek village called Lia, where he spent his early years with his mother and four older sisters after his father left to work in the United States. During the Greek Civil War after World War II, Communists gained control of the village and took some children with them as they retreated. While Nicholas and three of his sisters escaped and eventually joined their father in the United States, the Communists arrested his mother, put her on trial for arranging the escape of her children, and executed her. In his best-selling book, *Eleni*, one of his two autobiographical memoirs, Gage describes the life of his family in Greece during World War II and the Greek Civil War. The book was awarded first prize by the Royal Society of Literature of Great Britain and was nominated in the category of best biography by the National Book Critics Circle. *Eleni* was translated into over thirty languages and was made into a feature film in 1985 starring John Malkovich as Nicholas Gage and co-produced by Nick Vanoff.

I was fortunate to count Vanoff as a close friend and enjoyed many interesting conversations with him over many years. Vanoff, a Greek-born dancer and producer, had many accomplishments, including creating and producing "The Kennedy Center Honors." He won a Tony Award for Best Musical in 1990 for his production of the "City of Angels" musical on Broadway and won five Emmy Awards as a producer, including three in the 1980s for The Kennedy Center Honors. He was a founding director of the Foundation for the Joffrey Ballet and sat on the board of directors of the Center Theatre Group in Los Angeles. In 1976, with Saul Pick, Vanoff bought from Columbia the studios on Sunset Boulevard, renovated them, and renamed them Sunset-Gower Studios.

Honoring just men would just not do, so I decided to find suitable women equally deserving of recognition. I inquired if Greek American Stassinopoulos would be interested in being honored by the Chamber She was living in New York at the time and had become well known as a syndicated columnist and author. I received a call that she would graciously accept the honor and we could discuss details when she visited Los Angeles.

We agreed to meet at Ma Maison restaurant for dinner. On the evening of the dinner Arianna was so late that Patrick Terrail, the owner of the restaurant, suggested we begin our dinner. Half-way through, Arianna rushed in, apologizing for being late. "I had called for a taxi, but it would come and leave after a few minutes, because Jodie's house, where I'm staying, is way back behind bushes and trees, not visible from the street. When the third taxi arrived, I ran after it." Jodie Evans was Governor Brown's aide-de-camp, and a close friend of Arianna's.

The Stasinopoulos event was attended by business, political, and entertainment leaders. Arianna was accompanied to the event at the Beverly Hills Hotel by billionaire David H. Murdoch, owner of the Dole Foods Co. Among her guests was Anglican Archbishop Desmond Tutu from Cape Town, known widely for his work as an anti-apartheid and human rights activist.

I developed a close and long-term friendship with Arianna. Her mother, Elli, was fond of me, and we would sit and smoke large cigars whenever I visited them. In 1986, Arianna married Texan oil tycoon Michael Huffington. She co-founded the Huffington Post in 2005 with Kenneth Lerer and Jonah Peretti. The Huffington Post was a pioneering web publication known for a liberal worldview. It was founded as a liberal alternative to the Drudge Report. The Post was sold to website AOL in 2011 and Huffington assumed control of AOL's editorial content. The Post won a Pulitzer Prize in 2012 for a series on wounded veterans. Huffington stepped down in 2016 as editor-in-chief after eleven years.

In May 1993, the Hellenic-American Chamber of Commerce honored Anthony Quinn, the Academy Award winning film and stage actor who appeared in more than 150 films but was universally identified with the earthy, boisterous anti-hero, Zorba, in the 1964 movie Zorba the Greek. The Chamber held an after-theater supper following the Los Angeles Civic Light Opera opener of the play Zorba the Greek at the Dorothy Chandler Pavilion with proceeds going to The center for Modern Greek Studies, Loyola Marymount University; The Hellenic American Exhibit and Trade Center; and the Nikos Kazantzakis Chair, San Francisco State University.

TELEVISION AND RADIO ENDEAVOR

I was also eager to share Greek popular culture with not only the Greek American community living in Los Angeles, but to introduce and promote it throughout the larger region as well. In the late 1980s and early 1990s, I reported Greek news and commentaries during a Greek program presented by Mimika Gottling on the City College Radio Station in Pasadena. Called "The Echoes of Greece" aired on Saturdays, and I presented news of current events in Greece as well as from the local Greek American communities. I had scheduled late night Friday calls with Greece to obtain up-to-date news to be broadcast on Saturday morning.

In the 1990s, I branched out into television to promote Greek culture, thanks to the generosity of Bill Rosendahl, the late Los Angeles City councilmember who had previously been vice president of government affairs for Westside cable operator Century Cable. He provided, as part of his company's public service commitment, one hour weekly of airtime for the "Odyssey," plus many hours and assistance for editing. That allowed me the opportunity to present a program of Greek songs, news, and entertainment every Sunday, an incredibly satisfying and successful undertaking. In that effort, I enlisted the help and support of a superb Greek American, Georgia Rosenberry, who became my executive producer and right-hand person. When I retired as president and founding chair of the Hellenic-American Chamber of Commerce, Georgia assumed its leadership. A very devoted, smart, disciplined, and dedicated individual who, unfortunately, died at a young age. With her passing, both the Hellenic-American Chamber and the TV program faded away.

HELLENIC AMERICAN POLITICAL ACTION COMMITTEE (HAPAC)

In the mid-1980s, as an outgrowth of my work as Southern California Fundraising Chair for the 1984 Walter Mondale Presidential Campaign, I established a Hellenic-American Political Action Committee, intended to increase the political presence of the Greek American community in Los Angeles. I expanded my work in 1988, when I became the California Fundraising Co-Chair for the Michael Dukakis 1988 Presidential campaign.

AMERICAN HELLENIC COUNCIL

The American Hellenic Council of California was founded in the aftermath of the Turkish invasion of the Independent Republic of Cyprus in the summer of 1974. The initial name of the organization was "The Save Cyprus Council of Southern California," and its central purpose was to support the restoration of justice to Cyprus. In the early 1980s, the group changed its name to the American Hellenic Council of California and expanded its goals, promoting Greek American interests in the Eastern Mediterranean and the Aegean with a focus on Greece and Cyprus.

The Turkish invasion of Cyprus displaced over 150,000 Greek Cypriots, and the military occupation of Northern Cyprus resulted in the establishment of a separate Turkish Cypriot state in 1983, a move condemned by the international community and a matter of continuing dispute. There was an effort for Greeks living abroad to provide financial assistance to the displaced Greek Cypriots, and I was one of the many Greek Americans who volunteered to provide a monthly stipend to help a Cypriot child, with whom I corresponded.

Andreas Kyprianides, Honorary Consul General of Cyprus in Los Angeles, has continued to promote the Cypriot cause and expressed to me that, as Americans of Hellenic descent, we must promote our Hellenic heritage, pass it on to future generations, and continue to support the Hellenic just national causes, including the unresolved problem of Cyprus, because standing up for justice in the world ultimately serves the national interests of the United States.

IMPRESSIVE TACTIC IN GREEK ELECTIONS

Stuart Spencer told me a story that I found very interesting. In 1989, he ran the campaign in Greece for Konstantinos Mitsotakis (the father of the present Prime Minister Kyriakos Mitsotakis) against Andreas Papandreou, then the sitting prime minister. "What a hairy battle that was," he said. "They blew up our headquarters one night, the government of Papandreou." A political consultant must recognize the political terrain and generate detailed operations to help his candidate obtain favorable election results, so Spencer decided to work out of Rome.

Spencer said Papandreou blocked the Mitsotakis campaign from any airtime, "they controlled all the media outlets." In Rome he met an electronics nerd who told him to buy a ship, anchor it in the Adriatic and beam anything he wanted into Greece. The cost, "a million-two." The Greek campaign did not have the money, but Spencer had another idea. He called upon his friend William A. Wilson, a Los Angeles businessman and a member of President Reagan's "kitchen cabinet" who was appointed the first US ambassador to the Vatican. Wilson knew a Vatican banker who loaned the money. The ship was bought and outfitted, and it began to broadcast throughout Greece "like the Voice of America." After the election the Vatican sold the ship and made $200,000 on the deal, Spencer bragged.

Broadcasts from the ship were the decisive factor in the Greek elections. Mitsotakis soundly crushed Papandreou, who suffered one of the largest defeats in modern Greek history. However, Papandreou had modified the election system two months earlier to require a party to win 50 percent of the vote to govern alone. It took two additional elections in less than a year for Mitsotakis to have a clear majority and to govern.

Later in Washington, DC, Spencer, hospitalized with a diverticulitis attack, looked up from his hospital bed to see Prime Minister Mitsotakis standing there, inquiring about his recovery. "He's a nice guy," Spencer said.

CHAPTER EIGHTEEN

OTHER

PROPOSITION 187

A Punitive Measure Aimed at Immigrants | As an immigrant and naturalized US citizen, I was very offended by the objectives and tactics of Prop 187 proponents. As a foreign student who finished college free of tuition, I resented the Proposition's objective to deny undocumented immigrants access to public education. Speaking good enough Spanish, I added my voice and support wherever and whenever I had the opportunity.

Proposition 187, introduced in 1994 and dubbed as a Save our State initiative, sought to punish undocumented immigrants by denying them certain services, including access to public health and education. It was a time when California was facing the worst economic crisis since the Great Depression. An influx of immigrants happened during a period of economic strife, high unemployment, and civil unrest. Supporters asserted the measure was necessary to discourage illegal immigration and save the State billions of dollars. Opponents considered the measure as anti-immigrant.

Tom Saenz, the current President and General Counsel of the Mexican American Legal Defense and Educational Fund (MALDEF), initially joined MALDEF in 1993 after serving as law clerk in the US District Court for the Central District of California and in the US Court of Appeals for the Ninth Circuit, at the right time to be involved in the Prop 187 controversy. MALDEF, headquartered in Los Angeles, has worked for over fifty years to promote the civil rights of Latinos living in the United States, and Saenz was MALDEF's lead counsel in the successful challenge to California's anti-immigrant Prop 187. According to Saenz, what was striking about Prop 187 was that the campaign was successful in convincing a majority of Los Angeles County to vote No. And that was after initial polling that showed most voters, including Latino voters, were in support of Prop 187 Antonia Hernandez, then President and General Counsel of MALDEF, along with Saenz and others participated in debating those who put forward Prop 187.

Most of the authors of the initiative were from Southern California. Glenn Spencer, from the San Fernando Valley, was one of the co-authors and one of the purported leaders of the lawsuit filed in December 1994 charging that six members of the Los Angeles Board of Education were illegally using public funds to block the initiative. He even launched a recall campaign against President of the Board Mark Slavkin. Barbara Coe was from Orange County. Ron Prince, the spark behind Prop 187, was from the Inland Empire.

Saenz remembered, "I was a young staff attorney at MALDEF at the time, and they were crazy, literally, because whenever you debated the issues with them and demonstrated why the policy mattered, it was crazy to enact something that would restrict people's rights to health care, to police services, to education. When you debated all those policy issues, they would end the debate by saying, 'Don't worry about that. The reason you need to vote yes on Prop187 is to send a message to the federal government. We need to send that message because there is a conspiracy by Mexico to take back the state of California.' Now, whether they believed that or were just willing to say it at the end of debates, either one of those would render them, in my view, crazy."

Prop 187 with that set of supporters, even with Alan C. Nelson and Harold W. Ezell, both Commissioners of the Immigration and Naturalization Services under the Reagan administration listed as supporters of Prop 187, and heavy campaigning by Assemblyman Dick Mountjoy, the initiative would have gone nowhere, but for Governor Pete Wilson, facing an uphill reelection campaign against Democrat Kathleen Brown, decided to make Prop 187 a centerpiece of his campaign. Saenz believed, "They weren't going to get the signatures to qualify it until the state Republican Party made an in-kind donation of sending the petitions to their members." Wilson called for a $1.5 billion reimbursement from the federal government for costs associated with illegal immigration.

Mountjoy depended on the immigration reform groups to collect 384,874 signatures to qualify the measure for the November 8, 1994, election. The Wilson committee bought the only Prop 187 advertisement on TV.

There were student marches, debates, and protests against Prop 187 not seen since the Vietnam War. On October 16, 1994, about 70,000 protesters against the Proposition assembled in front of the Los Angeles City Hall. On November 2, 1994, approximately 10,000 teenagers across California walked out to protest Prop 187. Despite all the debates and convincing three-quarters of Latino voters, a majority of African Americans and a majority of Asian-Americans to vote NO, the NO campaign still came up short. Statewide, 58.92 percent voted YES, a bigger margin of victory than Wilson's 55.18 percent voting NO on November 8, 1994.

Then the battles in the courts started. The court battles began the day after the election and extended for four years. MALDEF was successful in getting a temporary restraining order, although actually it wasn't a formal temporary restraining order, it was an agreement by the state not to enforce it until a week later. A week later the temporary restraining order was issued by federal judge Matthew Byrne, Jr.

The main federal case was before Mariana R. Pfaelzer, Judge of the US District Court for the Central District of California. Judge Pfaelzer issued a permanent injunction of Prop 187 in December 1994. On November 21, 1995, the judge ruled that the portion of Prop 187 that would allow the state to block undocumented immigrant children from attending state-run primary and secondary schools to be unconstitutional. Ultimately, it took four years for the final ruling to be issued, largely because the state used the tactic that, once some preliminary rulings indicated quite clearly—including a summary judgment rule—that the judge was not going to rule in their favor, they argued that they could draft regulations that would cure any of the legal defects. They took months and months, and in the end they produced nothing, not a single regulation.

So, Judge Pfaelzer entered her preliminary ruling on the constitutionality of Prop 187 on November 15, 1997. In an opinion on the case, the judge declared Prop187 "not constitutional on its face." She struck down all of the law's provisions, including the ban on public school attendance and health and social service benefits. She ruled Prop 187 unconstitutional, stating that California did not have the legal standing to create immigration policy, a power vested to the federal government. However, Pfaelzer did allow sections to establish criminal penalties for manufacturing and using false documents to stand. Judge Pfaelzer issued the final order blocking the implementation of the main components of Prop 187 on March 19, 1998. Then, Governor Wilson's administration appealed to the US Ninth Circuit Court of Appeals. However, Governor Wilson was termed out of office in 1999 and succeeded by Democratic governor Gray Davis.

According to Saenz, MALDEF had lost two very minor sections of the bill that had to do with two penal code sections relating to fraudulent documents. Saenz explained to me that they decided to file a cross appeal, because without the cross appeal they would not have had leverage, once Gray Davis was elected governor in 1998, and no longer in the hands of Pete Wilson. Davis needed political cover, because although he opposed Prop 187 when it was on the ballot, he said he had the duty under his oath of office and the state constitution to respect the will of the people who voted for the initiative, including defending it in court when he became governor.

As soon as Davis became involved in early 1999 because MALDEF had filed the cross appeal, they were able to convince him to go into mediation. There was something to mediate, something for both sides to give up. Davis appointed LA lawyer, Shirley M. Hufstedler, a former 9th Circuit Judge and Secretary of Education under President Carter, to represent Davis in the negotiations. Ultimately, after three months of tough negotiations, the governor's representatives and the attorneys for the opponents agreed that both parties would dismiss their appeals on July 29, 1999, effectively ending Prop 187.

Presiding over the sessions was David Lombardi, chief circuit mediator for the 9th Circuit in San Francisco. Davis agreed not to appeal the earlier federal court ruling and filed the agreement with the US Ninth Circuit Court of Appeals in San Francisco, preventing the case from going to the US Supreme Court. The case was then sent back to judge Phaelzer, who gave the final approval.

Glenn Spencer, president of "Voice of Citizens Together" and co-author of Prop 187, said, "Davis sold his soul for the Hispanic vote."

Saenz believes that "It was a one-sided deal, but it was the right kind of one-sided deal, otherwise they would not have gotten that deal if they did not have something to offer. We had something to offer because we had a cross-appeal on provisions that are still on the books. They're not great, but they're not as damaging as the other provisions of Prop 187."

Over the course of those four years, Latinos and immigrants in California became politically energized, and many naturalized out of concern for their own well-being, but also concerned about bad policies, like Prop 187. Many people registered to vote became more active, and there was a significant spike in Latino participation. That began to change California from a toss-up state to a very strongly blue state today. It is not a very competitive state when it comes to national elections anymore, in large part because of that change.

After 1994, Republicans took over the California State Assembly, and Republicans won virtually every statewide elected office. Today there is the other extreme, where every statewide office belongs to a Democrat. This is not a politically competitive state from a partisan perspective anymore, and it is largely because of the changes that started with Proposition 187. Pete Wilson is still a bad word in most Latino circles, which is why Meg Whitman's decision to use Wilson in her gubernatorial campaign for governor of California made no sense, and it ultimately backfired on her. She was defeated by Jerry Brown in the 2010 election.

Prop 187 was a catalyst that galvanized more Latino citizens to register to vote. It also motivated many who were not naturalized to get their citizenship. In 1994 there were 1.4 million Latinos registered to vote in California. In the 2020 presidential election, almost eight million Latinos were projected to be eligible to vote. Over 30 percent of eligible voters in California are Latino, with the state being home to approximately a quarter of the nation's Latino eligible voters.

Even though all that energizing was targeted at the state level, it obviously had an impact in the city of Los Angeles as well. Prop 187 created a new generation of politicians. "We became voters," Gloria Molina told me over lunch a few months before she passed away. She recounted her political battles and included the fight against Proposition 187, side by side with Antonia Hernandez of MALDEF, as one of her biggest. She received racist phone calls and hate mail, but Molina was emboldened even more to fight for what she believed was just and right.

Other organizations challenged Prop 187 along with MALDEF: the American Civil Liberties Union and the Coalition for Humane Immigrant Rights of Los Angeles.

Saenz predicted that what happened in California with Prop 187 would recur in other states, with Arizona as an example of the growth in the Latino community and the state's attempt at immigrant restrictions potentially converting Arizona into a blue state.

Arizona State Bill 1070, commonly referred to as SB 1070, is a 2010 legislative Act that was the broadest and strictest anti-illegal immigration law in the country when passed, including making it a state misdemeanor for "aliens" to be in Arizona without always carrying a certificate of alien registration. An earlier 2004 Arizona state initiative, Arizona Taxpayer and Citizen Protection Plan (known as Proposition 200), which critics dubbed "show-me-your-papers" law, required proof of citizenship to register to vote, photo identification before receiving a ballot at the polling place, and immigration status eligibility for non-federally mandated public benefits. The requirement to provide proof of citizenship to register to vote was later ruled invalid in federal court. Opponents of the ballot measure had noted it was anti-immigrant and reminiscent of California's Prop 187.

In 2022, Arizona's Latino voters were 25 percent of all eligible voters, with over 400,000 voting in the 2022 general election, a record number for midterm elections. The Latino vote contributed to the longtime Republican stronghold becoming one of the most competitive states, with Democratic Presidential candidate Joe Biden winning the most votes in the state, as well as the Democratic candidates for Arizona Governor, Secretary of State, Attorney General, and United States Senate winning those seats.

Nationwide, Latinos cast 16.6 million votes in the 2020 presidential election, an increase of 31 percent over the 2016 presidential election. A 2021 report by the UCLA Latino Policy and Politics Initiative determined that Latino voters were decisive in sending President Biden to the White House.

MODEST INVESTMENTS

The man who moves a mountain begins by carrying away small stones.

—CONFUCIUS

To Improve our Quality of Life | Modest investments in the city's fabric can result in tremendous improvements in the residents' quality of life.

TRANSIT SUMMITS

As president of the Southern California Rapid Transit District, I held a number of "transit summits" in the San Fernando Valley with the purpose of hatching plans for short-term, low-cost solutions to improve bus service. The first meeting took place at the Valley Hilton on April 7, 1990 and was attended by city officials including City Councilmen Zev Yaroslavsky, Michael Woo, and Hal Bernson, Los Angeles Department of Transportation (General Manager Edwin Rowe, business and community leaders, and the General Managers of the RTD. Alan Pegg, and Los Angeles County Transportation Commission, Neil Peterson.

Among the ideas discussed were the following, all of which have been implemented.

- A neighborhood minibus system that would tie in with the regular RTD service in Studio City, Van Nuys and Northridge.
- The RTD would look at the placement of bus stops throughout the San Fernando Valley to make sure the locations were not affecting traffic.
- Extending RTD bus service Lines 90 and 91 to serve Olive View Hospital and Sylmar.
- Development of more off-street parking and park-and-ride facilities in Encino, Studio City and other areas.

REVERSE-FLOW LANE

In 1990, I proposed that a reverse -flow lane be implemented on Sepulveda Boulevard during rush -hour traffic, like the one on Highland Boulevard near the Hollywood Bowl. Edwin Rowe, LADOT General Manager, supported the idea and Councilman Marvin Braude agreed to get City Council approval. Rowe said, "LADOT completed a study of using the reverse -flow along Sepulveda and the cost would be $100,000 a year to have a crew set cones twice a day to change traffic." Mayor Tom Bradley lauded the reverse carpool lane as a "major revolution in traffic decongestion." Bill Bicker, Bradley's transportation deputy said, "This has been studied for quite a while, and it looks like all that needs to be done is to paint some diamonds on the pavement, buy some traffic cones, and get a truck and crew out there to put them down and pick them up."

In June 1991, there was article in the *Los Angeles Times* with the heading "Rush-Hour Lane Reversal in Sepulveda Pass Lauded as 'Great Idea' on 1st Day." One normally southbound lane was reversed for a mile between Mountaingate and Mulholland Drives, creating a temporary third northbound lane between 3:00 p.m. and 7:00 p.m. The switch was in effect every weekday afternoon. Transit officials called the 1.3-mile stretch of road between Mountaingate Drive and the tunnel a key "choke point that regularly was clogged with commuters." It was estimated that 2,000 cars used the lane during each evening rush period, saving ten to fifteen minutes' drive time. The new high -occupancy vehicle lane was open only to buses and cars with two or more riders.

Unfortunately, the LADOT abandoned the project after a few months because "the cones were a hassle."

THE BYZANTINE-LATINO QUARTER

In the late 1990s, Angie Pappas and John Sakellaris, trustees of the St. Sophia Greek Orthodox Cathedral, approached me for advice for the design of a reconfigured parking lot at the Cathedral. I suggested that they should think "big and out of the box," and I volunteered to engage an architectural firm to draw a vision for the lot. The architects designed a complex that, besides the parking, included a procession path with palm trees on either side of a large plaza with a mosaic of a crowned double-headed eagle of Byzantium embedded in the plaza. The mosaic by artist Sirio Tonelli consisted of 185,000 pieces of stone. The plaza is now used as a civic space for festivals, ceremonies, celebrations, and other appropriate public uses.

In the past, urban renewal centered on design, and socioeconomic redevelopment. Religion, culture, and ethnicity were secondary. Under the leadership of Fr. John Bakas, dean of the St. Sophia Greek Orthodox Cathedral, the Pico-Union district is an example of how religion can be a catalyst for urban renewal. Within the district, there are the Roman Catholic Church of St. Thomas the Apostle and the Greek Orthodox St. Sophia Cathedral, with daily activities from residents and commuting parishioners. Each Sunday, hundreds of residents, mainly Latino, walk to St. Thomas for the weekly services, and hundreds of commuters go to St. Sophia nearby.

The revitalized area in Pico-Union is called the Byzantine-Latino Quarter. This portion of Pico-Union a few years before was full of graffiti, dirty streets, neglected properties, and gang activity. Father John Bakas told me, "We based ourselves on the broken-window theory, broken windows and vandalism invite lawlessness." James Q. Wilson, a University of California, Los Angeles professor, argued in a 1982 article that broken windows, weed-filled lots and vandalism foster lawless behavior. His theory formed the basis for community policing in the city. Former Los Angeles Police Department Chief William J. Bratton included that theory in his innovative police programs.

In 1996 Fr. Bakas formed a group, Genesis Plus, consisting of neighborhood stakeholders, including St. Sophia, St. Thomas the Apostle Catholic Church, Loyola High School and a number of smaller African American and Latino Pentecostal churches. Their task was to clean up the area where possible. In 1998, Genesis Plus received a $500,000 Federal Department of Transportation block grant administered by the City's Los Angeles Neighborhood Initiative program. My wife Sylvia had been a founding board member of LANI.

The grant provided money for lighting, repairing sidewalks, planting trees, creating pocket parks, and to stamp corner crossings with brick-style tiles. Out of Genesis Plus, the idea of "the

Procession Path at the Plaza of St. Sophia Greek Orthodox Cathedral

"Wall Of The Blessing Hand" at the Plaza of St. Sophia Greek Orthodox Cathedral

Byzantine-Latino Quarter" was borne. There is a large neon sign identifying the area as the Byzantine-Latino Quarter that sits on the roof of a building on Pico Boulevard and Normandie Avenue. A large mural on the side of the building depicts two angels with one wing. The message, "We are each of us angels with one wing. We can fly embracing each other."

LOS ANGELES UNION STATION FORECOURT AND ESPLANADE IMPROVEMENTS

In the mid-1990s, I was standing at the entrance of Union Station when two women and their children approached and asked how to get to Olvera Street. When I pointed across Alameda Street, the group walked left and right, confused, and returned to where I stood. One of the women asked, "How the hell do you get there?" Over five hundred thousand elementary school children per year visit Olvera Street, many coming through Union Station to get there. Crossing Alameda Street to get to Olvera Street is challenging and dangerous, so I approached Art Leahy, the Metropolitan Transportation Authority chief executive officer and suggested that he authorize the development of a plan to improve the pedestrian connection to Olvera Street. Leahy instructed Metro staff to initiate an EIR and identify funding for the improvements. The MTA Board authorized moving from planning to implementation of this project in 2014.

The Los Angeles Union Station Forecourt & Esplanade Improvements project includes upgrades on the Union Station grounds, which Metro owns, as well as upgrades to nearby streets, which come under the jurisdiction of the Los Angeles Department of Transportation.

In 2018, Metro approved a design that would improve pedestrian access to Union Station. The design included sidewalk expansion on both the east side of Alameda Street and the north side of Los Angeles Street connecting to the Plaza. On Alameda, the design included a shade canopy with a double row of sidewalk trees. The plan eliminated vehicle left turns from Los Angeles Street onto Alameda to accommodate pedestrians and cyclists. Unfortunately, in 2020, LADOT scaled back key pedestrianization features. LADOT rejected the key feature, a fifty-foot-wide raised crosswalk across Alameda Street. The crosswalk had been trimmed to about thirty-four feet, and it would no longer provide a direct line of access to the Union Station entrance. The pedestrian, therefore, would have to follow a zigzag route. The raised crossing was originally planned to be eight inches high, flush with the sidewalks. At that height, the raised crosswalk would force drivers to reduce speeds on Alameda Street and provide better accessibility for people with disabilities. LADOT required Metro to trim the height of the crosswalk to only three inches. To aggravate the situation, LADOT insisted on allowing drivers to turn left from Los Angeles Street onto Alameda Street. The Public Works Bureau of Street Services removed the double row of trees along the east side of Alameda.

This is an example of how lack of leadership in City Hall with Department heads running in different directions has created a rudderless city with pedestrian accidents and fatalities often.

TRANSPORTATION MUSEUM ON OLVERA STREET

In the early 1990s, I promoted the establishment of an 11,325-square-foot interactive museum to be located in Olvera Street's historic Los Angeles Railway Company power substation across from Union Station. The museum, aimed mainly at children, would chronicle Los Angeles's transportation history with historic artifacts, transportation related videos, and educational displays on the Red and Yellow trolley cars once networked the region. Video games would invite visitors to solve transportation problems dealing with geologic, economic and community issues. Red and yellow cars would be displayed in a park-like setting in El Pueblo. The museum would be one of several projects envisioned to help revitalize the Olvera Street area. The estimated cost was $1.5 million. Caltrans had provided a $1.257-million grant for the museum, with the balance funded by the City of Los Angeles.

The project, however, was mothballed because of the objections of the Olvera Street merchants.

POCKET PARK ACROSS ANGELS FLIGHT

The Metro/Purple lines connect to Pershing Square station with entrances at the corners of 4th and 5th Streets. Two of the major destinations connecting to the 4th Street entrances are the heavy bus uses along Broadway to the east and the large concentration of employment on Bunker Hill to the west of the station. Broadway remains one of Los Angeles's busiest retail streets and Bunker Hill one of the region's largest concentrations of office buildings. Both destinations lacked inviting pedestrian connections from the station entrances. The 4th Street sidewalks connecting to Broadway had been narrowed to facilitate traffic lanes and the walk up to Bunker Hill required going up a hundred-foot rise before connecting to an escalator to the Bunker Hill Plaza area. To overcome these challenging conditions, I approached Ira Yellin, then the owner of Grand Central Market. The 1917 Grand Central Market structure has open entrances on both Hill Street and Broadway. It was suggested to convert a portion of the side dock area and parking lot into an open commercial area facing Hill Street and Angels Flight, along with securing an easement for transit patrons through the Grand Central Market. The idea was to connect the 4th and Hill east station entrance to Grand Central Market and to move the market closet to the station.

Pocket Park adjacent to Central Market and Angels Flight.

A new pocket park would be built in the market parking lot-located on the east/west axis with the Angels Flight Railroad. The improvements visually blocked the dock and parking area from Angels Flight and replaced the view with a tree filled and elevated pocket park with seating area. A new side entrance on the south side of Grand Central Market into the pocket park, a mid-block crossing from Angels Flight, and the traffic calming on Hill Street were also added to the improvements. The designer of the pocket park was architect and urban planner Doug Suisman, who was also the designer of the Angels Walk and leader of the team that designed the Ten-Minute Diamond Walk (See Civic Center section).

RECONFIGURE LA CITY DEPARTMENTS' ROLES AND RESPONSIBILITIES

After having served on the board of directors of the Southern California Rapid Transit District, the Los Angeles County Transportation Commission, the Los Angeles Metropolitan Transportation Authority, the Los Angeles Department of Water and Power, and the Los Angeles Board of Zoning Appeals, I have concluded that the roles and responsibilities of some city departments and agencies should be reconfigured.

RESTRUCTURE THE PUBLIC WORKS DEPARTMENT

The City of Los Angeles Department of Public Works is an inefficient anachronism. It once served a purpose, but its time has passed. Historically, many levels of government had similar departments for constructing and operating infrastructure, but, as their operations grew larger and more complex, these departments were broken up and reorganized. The federal government in the 18th century created a special department to build its original "public work," the National Road from the east coast to Ohio. That department no longer exists. Federal public works are now handled by multiple, discrete departments specializing in transportation, General Services, and other public infrastructure tasks.

Similarly, the State of California had a Department of Public Works from its inception in 1850. Within a few decades, however, that department was distributed into smaller, specialized groups. Only the City of Los Angeles maintains a monolithic Department of Public Works. Today, that department is responsible for operations that are too large and too complex for one department to manage. The City Department of Public Works should be broken up into specialized areas of expertise.

For decades, there have been numerous recommendations to redefine the role and responsibilities of the Public Works Board and to make it an unpaid commission like other city and county Commissions. It has been a political patronage appointment costing the taxpayers over $5 million per year. It is the only commission in the city and county whose members are paid and has been comprised of community organizers, social workers, environmentalists, and political hacks who have not had the technical knowledge and experience to oversee multimillion construction projects. As a result, projects are neither on budget nor on time, costing taxpayers hundreds of millions of dollars. For example, the cost estimate for the La Kretz Bridge part of the Los Angeles River Revitalization project was $4.67 million.

The Bridge was constructed at a cost of $16.1million. Cost estimates are outdated and inaccurate, forcing city agencies to reject some bids. Contractors who have expended thousands of dollars to prepare bids are refusing to bid on city projects in the future, thus eliminating competition.

MERGE BUREAU OF STREET SERVICES (BSS) WITH THE LOS ANGELES DEPARTMENT OF TRANSPORTATION

I have witnessed firsthand, while I was overseeing projects for the Metropolitan Transportation Authority (MTA) and the City, the duplication, lack of both communication and coordination between BSS and DOT. DOT is the leader in both mobility and safety. However, safety on the roads is not a top priority for the Public Works Department. The division of responsibilities has resulted in project delays, increased costs and in many cases injuries and deaths that cost the taxpayer millions of dollars.

History: According to a Chief Legislative Analyst report, "DOT since its establishment in 1979, never implemented the second step of its mission of bringing planning and policy, design, construction, and maintenance responsibilities into a single department, leaving the City with a fractured system." The report continues, "This fractured system is a structural barrier that has impeded the implementation of every major transportation plan or policy adopted by the City Council, from the Bicycle Plan to the Safe Routes to School Strategic Plan to the Mobility Plan to the Green New Deal. Mayoral initiatives like Great Streets and Vision Zero have also struggled to advance beyond temporary pilots and spot improvements, falling short of the systems change they were intended to catalyze. Sidewalks and crosswalks are part of the path of travel for people, but they are presently excluded from transportation and mobility planning, which comes under the DOT purview. Departments routinely work at cross purposes, with one agency widening streets to outdated standards while others seek grant funds to narrow them back down for safety and livability. While different agencies manage the space inside the curb and outside of it, no one is responsible for making sure the curb is in the right place."

- A City Council motion introduced in May 2018, partly reads, "Despite the enormous importance of streets, the current structure of Los Angeles City government separates key planning, operational, and maintenance functions among several departments in a way that no other major city does. While many inefficiencies exist, the most disruptive is the division of responsibilities between DOT and BSS. For example, DOT is responsible for traffic signals, street signs, and lane striping, but BSS is responsible for street resurfacing, sweeping, and issuing special permits that require use and closure of our city's streets.

"Since 1949, the city has commissioned at least six in-depth reports from city staff, outside consultant and citizen commissions that all recommend reorganizing and restructuring the Department of Public Works. In 2016, the voters approved a $120 billion investment under Measure M to improve our streets and transportation infrastructure. It is the city's duty to ensure that this money is spent efficiently and effectively. The time to act is now.

"WE THEREFORE MOVE that the City Administrative Officer (CAO) and the Chief Legislative Analyst (CLA), be DIRECTED to report with a phased action plan that would implement a merger of the BSS and DOT.

"WE FURTHER MOVE that the CAO and the CLA, be DIRECTED to report with recommendations on existing street-related functions and divisions of other departments and bureaus that could be transferred to a merged streets and transportation department, to enhance efficiency and better deliver services to the residents of Los Angeles."

- A motion introduced in Council in 2021 partly reads, "Under the City`s current organizational structure, one department is responsible for paving streets, and another is responsible for striping that pavement; one department is responsible for the placement of bus stops, and another is responsible for bus shelters. One department oversees the operation of personal mobility devices on our streets, and another regulates parking devices on sidewalks.

"WE THEREFORE MOVE that the matter of Bureau of Street Services/Department of Transportation/Merger be reactivated."

REASSIGN PLANNING ELEMENTS OF DEPARTMENT OF TRANSPORTATION TO PLANNING DEPARTMENT

Traffic planners could address traffic impacts of projects if they were involved more closely in a project's approval process. According to a 2009 CLA's report, "Transportation and traffic impacts are typically not analyzed in a timely manner during the Planning Department's approval process. To improve coordination and analysis of the transportation impacts of development, traffic planning and evaluation should be integrated into the approval process of the Planning Department."

HR 3686, notes that The Growing Smarter Through Transportation Infrastructure Act 2005 was introduced in Congress on September 7, 2005 "to promote the integration of local land use planning and transportation planning."

The City Council in 2005 moved "that by the adoption of this Resolution, the City of Los Angeles hereby includes in its 2005–2006 Legislative Program SUPPORT for HR 3686…to promote the integration of local land use planning and transportation planning. In August 2009, the City Council moved the CLA report with a plan to reassign the planning elements of DOT to the Planning Department."

LADWP TO TAKE-OVER THE BUREAU OF STREET LIGHTING (BSL)

In 1998 LADWP general manager David Freeman discussed with Mayor Richard Riordan, who agreed that the city does not need two utilities doing street light work. A task force was convened with representatives from LADWP, BSL, City Council, Mayor's Office, and the Public Works Department. Phil Reed, general manager of BSL, reported to the task force that, after consulting with the City Attorney, there was nothing in the City Charter to prevent such a move. Frank Salas, LADWP chief administrative officer, consulted with Ron Deaton, city chief administrative officer, on the matter of consolidating into LADWP. BSL used back-door political and legal channels to overwhelm LADWP's position.

As of 2023, despite all the studies, reports, motions, etc., no action has been taken by the city leaders. As a result, millions of dollars are wasted that could otherwise be used to improve the services rendered to Angelenos. Instead, the city, to quote Mayor Antonio Villaraigosa, has become "rudderless," slipping into decay. It is imperative that the city leaders visit all these issues again and take action in order to provide Angelenos with efficient and economical services.

VIGNETTES

When Mayor Bradley had some political difficulties towards the end of his administration, Maureen Kindel, a close mayoral advisor, held a meeting in the basement of the Getty House with a few close confidants of the mayor to organize a fundraising strategy. After the meeting, a Los Angeles Times *reporter approached me and said, "Why are you in this, under these circumstances, helping Tom Bradley?" My reply was quoted in the Times, "That's what friends are for."*

*

On February 1, 1993, RTD and Los Angeles County Transportation Commission (LACTC) merged and formed a new entity called Los Angeles Metropolitan Transportation Agency (MTA), and interviews for a CEO were conducted. Former Councilman Richard Alatorre was appointed Chair of the Selection Committee, and I was one of the members. The finalists for consideration were RTD General Manager Alan Pegg, LACTC Executive Director Neil Peterson, Long Beach City Manager James Hankla, Federal Transit Authority Director Brian Clymer, New York State Transportation Commissioner Franklin White, and Judith Pierce, Chief Operations Officer of the Philadelphia subway system. Neil Peterson had fallen from Mayor Bradley's grace because he mishandled the Green Line driverless trains controversy, and Bradley preferred Frank White. While Hankla was waiting in the reception for his interview, Alatorre announced that White would be the CEO. White had no construction and operations experience and no familiarity with Southern California. During his first days at work as LAMTA CEO, White requested a meeting with me because, he said, "I was one of the more influential Board members." White was the former head of New York's Transportation Commission. I invited White to the Jonathan Club, and when White asked for suggestions, ideas, and tips on how he could be successful, I told him, "Frank, first thing to do is hire a second in command who knows City Hall and how politics play in the region. This is a very political board." White looked at me dismissively and said, "What are you talking about? I'm coming from New York, and there is no city more political." A couple of years later, White requested an urgent meeting with me. We met again at the Jonathan Club and White said, "I need you to talk to (County Supervisor) Antonovich, I need his support because Mayor Riordan plans to fire me." I responded, "Frank, if you remember at this very table, I told you the Board was very political and you dismissed me then. Instead, you close your office door and if I need to talk to you, I have to make an appointment with your secretary a week, or two weeks in advance. I will tell Antonovich not to support you, in fact I'm going to advise him to fire you."

*

On July 1, 1981, was the most Machiavellian and intriguing election ever for LA City Council President. Councilman John Ferraro had been elected President of the Council since 1977, and he was running for reelection in 1981 because, as an ex-athlete, he wanted to be Council President when the Olympic Games arrived in Los Angeles in 1984. However, Councilwoman Pat Russell, an ally of Mayor Tom Bradley, decided to challenge Ferraro. Russell had obtained seven signatures including Councilman Joel Wachs, supporting her candidacy. Council member Peggy Stevenson was very close to both Wachs and Ferraro. Stevenson tried to convince Wachs to support Ferraro, to no avail. Ferraro concluded that he did not have the support he needed, but he persuaded his supporters to switch to Wachs. I was a close friend and confidant to Stevenson, a Greek American, and the evening before the vote, she confided to me that Ferraro's supporters would vote for Wachs. Stevenson advised Wachs accordingly, but Wachs was still uncommitted to either side.

In the morning of the vote, the Council Chambers was full to capacity with a lot of tension and anxiety in the air. Russell had flown her parents in for the big occasion. Only Councilman Hal Bernson, his chief of staff Greig Smith, Stevenson and I, in addition to Ferraro's chief of staff Pat Mount, were privy to the unfolding drama. City Clerk Rex Layton started to read in alphabetical order the role of the members. The first vote was Councilman Ernani Bernardi, the maverick of the Council, and when the Clerk called his name, he replied "Wachs." Then Bernson voted for Wachs. It became obvious that something was happening. You could only hear heartbeats in the deafening silence in the Council Chambers. When Councilman Braude voted for Wachs, it was clear there was a coup. When it was Ferraro's turn to vote, with a sheepish smile he said loudly "Wachs." Later, when the roll call reached Wachs, he hesitated for a few moments and then whispered "Wachs." Later, Wachs commented, "It's pretty hard not to vote for yourself."

ENTERTAINMENT INDUSTRY

It is known that the entertainment industry does not contribute to the arts and has not been civic minded in general. Some give anonymously, but that is the exception. Steven Spielberg, for example. In the entertainment business they are predominantly self-made people, they live in a business where you are only as good as the review you got that morning, so there is tremendous insecurity. The next film bombs, and they never get a phone call.

I witnessed the rise to stardom of Sylvester Stallone, who used to exercise in the gym at the Holiday Inn in Hollywood, where I also exercised when I was starting out professionally. Stallone was very helpful in suggesting protein powders, healthy foods, power drinks, etc. Stallone lived in an apartment in Hollywood and drove an old olive-green Chevy. His roles were seen but not heard. I saw on cable television the movie "Al Capone" with Ben Gazzara and Stallone in the background, as bodyguard. When I asked Stallone the next day whether he was really in the picture, Stallone demurred, "Yeah. I'm trying to get a break. One day Stallone walked in with bandages around his waist, and when I asked what happened, he answered, "I'm doing a B picture, and they busted my ribs." A few months later, I read the review of Rocky in TIME magazine, and the rest is history. Stallone made his own luck, however, in that he decided to give his script for the picture provided he would be the star in the picture.

EPILOGUE

In these pages I have reported my personal odyssey through the modern history of Los Angeles. It is a frank eyewitness account of the last half century, an extraordinary passage through extraordinary times in the city I love.

I participated in Los Angeles' multiple intervals of development and cycles of growth and followed substantive events with intensity. I was driven by a passion to explore beyond the public narrative. In providing this report, I have not glossed over the mistakes made, nor have I hidden the darker side of deals.

This epilogue—another Greek word—wraps up my incredible Los Angeles journey. What happened, and why, and the experiences derived, can become a useful syllabus, a course of study for the present and the future. Los Angeles will continue to blossom, and there's still unfinished business. Although the city has developed an astounding personality and an energy that is perpetual, special interests must be prevented from influencing how and where its projected blossoming takes place.

My own history has been defined as I presented my observations. Like Odysseus, whose astonishing adventures coined the word odyssey, I chose to hear the song of the Siren and to venture between Scylla and Charybdis—the six headed monster and the whirlpool—so that I could faithfully contribute to my city and promote a better future.

There is significant meaning in the Greek myths. Intellectual curiosity is what the Siren song represents, but to achieve knowledge one must be disciplined. And to be found between Scylla and Charybdis is the modern version of being caught between a rock and a hard place. In my odyssey I was often on the horns of a dilemma and had to exercise proper judgment and carefully chart my course through perilous channels. I have drawn from my experience as an engineer to make careful evaluations. I have drawn from my experience in governmental affairs to apply those evaluations for the benefit of the public. Choosing wisely, I met my goals.

And yet, as I reflect on what we have achieved in the last half century, I have the perception that we have reached our own Golden Age, our own La Belle Epoque, our own Renaissance. It has been a period of triumphs, and an era when unreachable dreams became accessible. But I know that much more will have to be achieved.

A bright future will depend on bright and courageous leaders. Our commercial and educational institutions cannot surrender to apathy but must recapture their will to reclaim excellence. The media, once our bastion for freedom and foundation for community pride, cannot surrender to the disdain of social media and other unconventional demands.

At all costs, we must insist on preserving our Los Angeles Tripod: courageous public officials, commercial and educational excellence, and a vigorous and robust press. This will safeguard our progress, promote our growth, and shield us from tempestuous cultural storms and threatening epidemics. And we will be vigilant to correctly cope with pandemics that threaten our health and cause large-scale social disruptions. The Los Angeles Tripod will be our protective armor.

When we reflect on our accomplishments, how quickly come to mind the vibrant political leadership of Los Angeles Mayors Tom Bradley and Antonio Villaraigosa; Los Angeles County Supervisors Michael Antonovich, Yvonne Braithwaite Burke, Kenneth Hahn, Gloria Molina, and Zev Yaroslavsky; and Los Angeles City Councilmembers Richard Alatorre, Marvin Braude, John Ferraro, and Pat Russell.

And the emergence and devotion of civic leaders such as Warren Christopher, Lodwrick Cook, Robert Maguire, Fred Nicholas, Mark and Jane Pisano, Nelson Rising, Dan Rosenfeld, Barry Sanders, James Wood, and Ira Yellin.

Our leap forward was not easy, it was propelled by eloquent journalists, such as Beth Barrett, Bill Boyarsky, Linda Breakstone, Rich Connell, Barbara Jones, Patrick McGreevy, Claudia Luther, Patt Morrison, Rick Orlov, James Rainey, Penelope Simison, and David Zahniser.

I am hopeful and optimistic that we will be revitalized, that we will share common goals and aspirations, and flourish in the next fifty years as we did in the last fifty.

In these pages I condensed the journey I took to meet my goals. May it inspire and extend forward to continue to serve the greater purpose of our beloved Los Angeles.

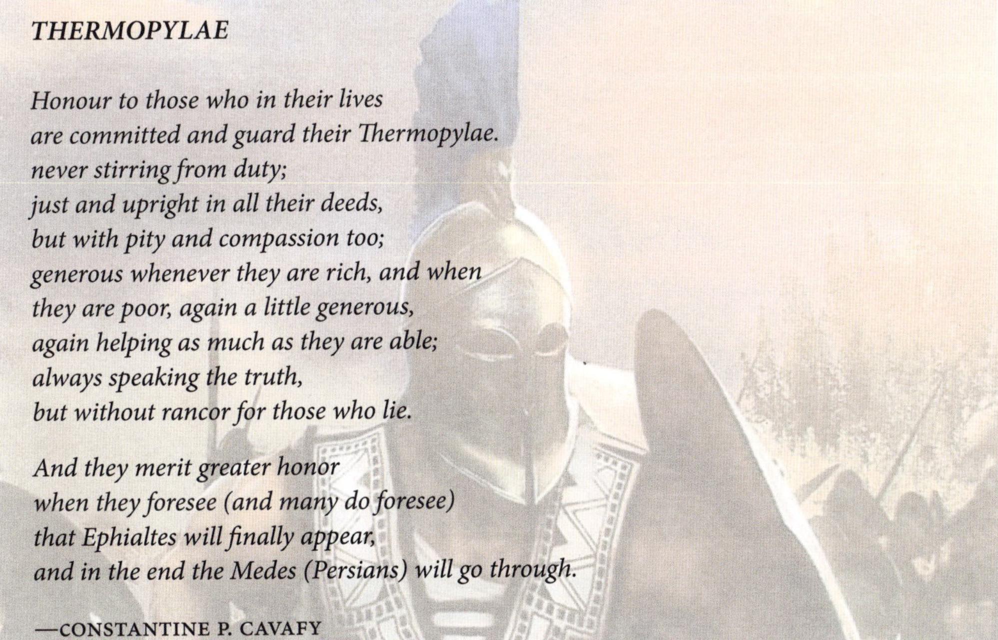

THERMOPYLAE

Honour to those who in their lives
are committed and guard their Thermopylae.
never stirring from duty;
just and upright in all their deeds,
but with pity and compassion too;
generous whenever they are rich, and when
they are poor, again a little generous,
again helping as much as they are able;
always speaking the truth,
but without rancor for those who lie.

And they merit greater honor
when they foresee (and many do foresee)
that Ephialtes will finally appear,
and in the end the Medes (Persians) will go through.

—CONSTANTINE P. CAVAFY

The poem emphasizes the importance of being loyal to our principles, exhibiting compassion, generosity, and honesty, and acting with justice. It inspires us to strive for what is right and just, even when the odds seem against us. It reminds us that even if we do not succeed, it is still worthwhile to act with honor and integrity. Additionally, the poem urges us to address the moral and ethical dilemmas of our time, and resist threats to our liberty and forces of authoritarianism and tyranny.

TESTIMONIALS

The Making of Modern Los Angeles is so many stories. It is the deeply moving and inspiring story of a teenager who came to America from Greece, with little besides a love of education and public service and went to play a crucial role in the life of one of America's great cities. And it's also the story of Los Angeles, Nick Patsaouras' beloved adopted city, and ultimately, a story of hope and optimism — that cities really can work, and that public service is a worthy calling for us all.
—Arianna Huffington, founder & CEO, Thrive Glo

Nick Patsaouras is a visionary. It is a term that should be used sparingly to describe only the rarest of individuals. In this case a more appropriate adjective does not exist. Since immigrating as a young man to Los Angeles, Nick Patsaouras has given everything for his adopted city, immersing himself in its future, advocating passionately about its possibilities, and thrown all his energies to the events, projects, and stories that have transformed Los Angeles over the last forty years. The Making of Modern Los Angeles *is a deeply poignant story of the personal life and motivations of this hugely influential figure in Los Angeles. This book is essential reading for anyone interested in both the how, and the why, of this city's story, giving one an unprecedented front row seat at the events of consequence that have shaped this most dynamic urban metropolis.*
—Michael Maltzan, FAIA architect and urban planner

I've known Nick Patsaouras for many years and seen how he managed to get important things done in the face of massive corruption and apathy. He's played a major role in LA politics. Nick is LA's "Inside Man," the man behind the scenes who got to see first-hand the games and dramas the politicians, their handlers and the corporate operators were playing for their own interests, the public be damned. The wonder is how Nick—a penniless immigrant who became a successful electrical engineer and got involved in public life with the historic election of Tom Bradley in 1973—preserved his reputation as an honest citizen trying to do what's best for the public. This compelling chronicle is a great resource for public servants, elected officials, and students of history.
—Ron Kaye, former editor, *Los Angeles Daily News*

Nick Patsaouras writes an account of the city he loves that could only be written by someone like Nick who was so deeply engaged in creating today's Los Angeles. He was there. He acted to make this a great town. He knew most of the key players personally and adds their hands-on accounts to his own to create a picture of civic events of the last half-century that otherwise might be lost in memory. And he does it with charm and personality.
—Barry A. Sanders, former chair, Southern California Committee for the Olympic Games; member of the Los Angeles Opera board;and former chair of the Los Angeles Philharmonic Board of Directors

Nick Patsaouras has been at the center of major public policy issues in Los Angeles for forty years. He was a prime mover in the development of Los Angeles's rail transit system over several decades, as well as in the implementation of major land use, water, and energy policies. This book is a must read for historians of Los Angeles in the late twentieth century and early twenty-first century. It will be of interest to anyone who seeks to understand how Los Angeles was governed and policy decisions made during this period.
—Michael Bernick, former president, Bay Area Rapid Transit Board of Directors; and former director, California Labor Department

Nick Patsaouras has been a central figure in the urban development of Los Angeles for forty years. A proponent of welcoming public spaces, mixed-use, and joint development, he has been a key driver of the creation of historic spaces with long-term financial sustainability thanks to his creativity and vision. By breaking down the barriers between government agencies and welcoming in the private sector, he transformed practices in urban development resulting in beautiful and functional urban centers. This book should be read by every urban planner and elected official in America.
—Caprice Young, former president, Los Angeles Unified School District Board of Trustees

It is a real treat to be shown Nick Patsaouras's insider view of the conflicting agendas, priorities, interests, and personalities behind the most recent thirty-five years of how Los Angeles transit and the city has developed, and how we (with his help) have managed to move ahead. What we read in the newspapers is just the tip of the iceberg. He knows more about the boards, agencies, elected officials, political careerists, and private interests in play around each decision than anyone else. He shares this knowledge with insights that combine humor and pragmatic analysis. Los Angeles owes him a debt of gratitude.
—Prof. James E. Moore, II, founding director University of Southern California Transportation Engineering Program

When someone with firsthand knowledge of events and over four decades of unmatched passion and dedication to the city of Los Angeles decides to write a book, detailing all its successes and shortcomings, there is only one thing any self-respecting Angeleno should do - Put your loukoumades down and grab a copy! Considering how closely he keeps his thoughts and opinions to himself; I can't wait to finally be treated with a peek into the great mind of Nick Patsaouras!
—Raul Fontanills, Jr., civic leader

I am so impressed with how you went out and interviewed so many people. I know it's going to be a rich and interesting documentary and archival book that will be read for the next one hundred years.
—Matthew Barrett, MLIS, director, Dorothy Peyton Gray Transportation Research Library & Archive

INTERVIEWEES

Abbassi, Pouria
Adams, Martin
Alatorre, Richard
Alexander, Allan
Alpert, Lee
Amescua, Michael
Andros, George
Angelini, Gino
Antonovich, Michael
Auriana, Angelo
Bacharach, Jacki
Bakas, Rev. John
Bastian, Hal
Bernson, Hal
Bicker, Bill
Birba, Pedro
Blackburn, Dan
Blair, Robin
Bleifer, Kenneth
Bleifer, Sandy
Bojarsky, Donna
Bollinger, John
Brazell, Danielle
Breakstone, Linda
Burke, William
Burke, Braithwaite Yvonne
Cardoso, Diego
Carrick, Bill
Catalano, Steve
Cedillo, Gil
Chemerinsky, Erwin
Choi, Tina
Clifford, John
Cole, Rick
Cowan, Geoffrey
De La Loza, Jim
De La Vega, Jaime
Deaton, Ron
Delgadillo, Rocky
Denari, Neal
Diamond, Kate
Dishman, Linda
Duckler, Heidi
Dymally, Merv
Edelman, Edmund
Emerson, John
Emerson, Norm
Emsden, Maya
Engelberg, Barry
Englander, Harvey
Fain, William
Farrar, David
Fasana, John
Ferdinandi, Matteo
Ferdinandi, Francine
Fisher, Greg
Fleming, David
Flynn, Patricia
Freeman, David
Freilich, Amy
Fujioka, William
Gagan, Michael
Galanter, Ruth
Garcia, Dan
Gardner, Doug
Gastelum, Ron
Gilmore, Tom
Goldberg, Gail
Goldin, Greg
Harris, Robert
Hernandez, Michael
Hertzberg, Robert
Hodgetts, Craig
Holden, Nate
Huffman, Brendan
Hymon, Steve
lkhrata, Hasan
Inge, Carol
Jacobs, Rick
Janovici, Robert
Jernigan, Robert
Johnson, Scott
Kagan, Michael
Kantor, Mickey
Kaplan, Sam Hall
Kappe, Ray
Karabian, Walter
Karatz, Bruce
Karos, Constantine
Katz, Richard
Kaye, Ron
Kelly, Peter
Kennard, Lydia
Kezios, Rev. Spencer
Kieffer, George
Kightlinger, Jeffrey
Knabe, Don
Knatz, Geraldine
Knight, Christopher
Knox, Wally
Koo, John
Koshalek, Richard
Kosmont, Larry
Kotin, Allan
Kotkin, Joel
Kuba, Darlene
Laris, Sue
Lavine, Steve
Levin, Brenda
Lewis, Michael
Leahy, Art
Lipkis, Andy
Lozano, Henry
Luther, Joan
MacAdams, Lewis
Maddox, Kerman
Maltzan, Michael

Marcus, Allen
Martin, Christopher
Martinez, Henry
Mayne, Thom
McDermott, Jim
McKean, Grover
McSpedon,Edward
Messerlian, Jack
Meyers, Barton
Meyerson, Harold
Mieger, David
Mihlsten, George
Miller, O'Malley
Molina, Gloria
Molloy, Deanna
Moret, Lou
Moss, Eric
Murray, Rev. Cecil
Murthy, Krishniah
Nahai, David
Nakada, Steve
Nathanson, Marc
Neely, Sharon
Nelson, Greg
Nicholas, Fred
Nicola, Lany
Norris, Merry
Norton, Goldy
Okazaki, James
Osenbach, David
Oxford, Richard
Pak, Chris
Parks, Bernard
Patsaouras, George
Perdon, Al
Perry, Jan
Peterson, Neil
Petropoulos, Renee
Philbin, Ann
Picus, Joy
Pisano, Jane
Pisano, Mark
Pla, George
Polyzoides, Stefanos
Poto, Donato
Prieto, Rafael
Rafter, Tracy
Raman, Raj
Ratkovich, Wayne
Read, Nat
Reed, Chuck
Regalado, Jaime
Reiner, Ira
Reyes, Ed
Rising, Nelson
Rosenberg, Robert
Rosenfeld, Dan
Roski, Ed
Rothenberg, Alan
Rotondi, Michael
Rountree, Stephen
Rubalcava, Dominick
Saenz, Tom
Salazar, Tony
Sandberg, Joel
Sanders, Barry
Santana, Miguel
Savitch, Fran
Selvaggio, Piero
Semcken, John
Sherman, Roger
Shriver, Bobby
Simril, Renata
Soboroff, Steve
Sonenshein, Raphael
Sosa, Ray
Spencer, Stuart
Spivack, Donald
Spivack, Gary
Springer, Jed
Suisman, Doug
Svonkin, Scott
Szabo, Barna
Takei, George
Tanner, Ted
Taylor, Rick
Terzian, Carl
Tibi, Linda
Torres, Art
Tritchler, Irene
Tutor, Ron
Usher, Jane
Villalobos, Frank
Vogel, Rob
Wardlaw, William
Weinstein, Richard
Weiss, Noel
Welborne, John
Wilson, Judy
Woo, Michael
Wyman, Roz
Yaroslavsky, Zev
Zane, Denny

ABBREVIATIONS

ABH	A Bridge Home
ACLU	American Civil Liberties Union
ADA	Americans with Disabilities Act
ADHD	Attention-Deficit/Hyperactivity Disorder
AEG	Anschutz Entertainment group
AFL-CIO	American Federation of Labor and Congress of Industrial Organizations
AIA	American Institute of Architects
AME	African Methodist Episcopal Church
APCD	Air Pollution Control District
APM	Automated People Mover
AQMD	Air Quality Management District
ARB	Air Resources Board
ARO	Adaptive Reuse Ordinance
BART	Bay Area Rapid Transit
BOE	Bureau of Engineering
BRT	Bus Rapid Transit
BRU	Bus Riders Union
BSL	Bureau of Street Lighting
BSS	Bureau of Street Services
BZA	Board of Zoning Appeals
CalArts	California Institute of the Arts
Caltrans	California Department of Transportation
CAO	Chief Administrative Officer
CASp	Certified Access Specialist
CBD	Central Business District
CCA	Central City Association
CDC	Centers for Disease Control and Prevention
CEO	Chief Executive Officer
CEQA	California Environmental Quality Act
CHC	Cultural Heritage Commission
CHIRLA	Coalition for Humane Immigrant Rights of Los Angeles
CHJ	Coalition of Health and Justice
CLA	Chief Legislative Analyst
COG	Council of Governments
CRA	Community Redevelopment Agency
DCA	Department of Cultural Affairs
DOT	Department of Transportation
DPM	Downtown People Mover

EIFD	Enhanced Infrastructure Financing District
EIR/EIS	Environmental Impact Report/Statement
EWDD	Economic Workforce Development Department
FAA	Federal Aviation Administration
FAIA	Fellow of the American Institute of Architects
FBI	Federal Bureau of Investigation
FEMA	Federal Emergency Management Agency
FHLB	Federal Home Loan Bank
FHWA	Federal Highway Administration
FoLAR	Friends of the Los Angeles River
FTA	Federal Transit Administration
FY	Fiscal Year
GCM	Grand Central Market
GSD	General Services Department
HACLA	Housing Authority of the City of Los Angeles
HAPAC	Hellenic -American Political Action Committee
HCIA	Housing Community Investment Agency
HOC	Hellenic Olympic Committee
HVAC	Heating, Ventilating, Air Conditioning
IBEW	International Brotherhood of Workers
IG	Inspector General
IOC	International Olympic Committee
JANM	Japanese American National Museum
LACMA	Los Angeles County Museum of Art
LACTC	Los Angeles County Transportation Commission
LADBS	Los Angeles Department of Building and Safety
LADWP	Los Angeles Department of Water and Power
LAHSA	Los Angeles Homeless Services Authority
LAMTA/MTA	Los Angeles Metropolitan Transportation Authority ("Metro")
LANI	Los Angeles Neighborhood Initiative
LAOOC	Los Angeles Olympic Organizing Committee
LAPAB	Los Angeles Police Administration Building
LAPD	Los Angeles Police Department
LASD	Los Angeles Sheriff Department
LAUSD	Los Angeles Unified School District
LAWA	Los Angeles World Airports
LAX	Los Angeles International Airport
LRTP	Long Range Transportation Plan

MALDEF	Mexican American Legal Defense and Educational Fund
MARTA	Metropolitan Atlanta Rapid Transit Authority
MCA	Music Corporation of America
MELA	Mothers of East Los Angeles
MHSA	Mental Health Systems Act
MOCA	Museum of Contemporary Art
MOS	Minimum Operable Segment
MRCA	Mountain Recreation and Conservation Authority
MWD	Metropolitan Water District
MWD	Metropolitan Water District
NAACP	National Association for the Advancement of Colored People
NBA	National Basketball Association
NEPA	National Environmental Policy Act
NGO	Non-Governmental Organization
NIDB	National Infrastructure Development Bank
NIMBY	Not in My Backyard
NRDC	Natural Resources Defense Council
NYMTA	New York Metropolitan Transportation Authority
P3	Public-Private Partnership (PPP)
PDID	Public Disorder Intelligence Division
PUC	Public Utilities Commission
RCC	Rail Construction Corporation
RFIQ	Request for Information and Qualifications
RFP	Request for Proposal
RFQ	Request for Qualifications
SBA	Small Business Administration
SCAG	Southern California Association of Governments
SCI -Arc	Southern California Institute of Architecture
SCRTD/RTD	Southern California Rapid Transit District
TIF	Tax Increment Financing
TIP	Transportation Improvement Program
TOD	Transit Oriented Development
TRO	Temporary Restraining Order
UCLA	University of California, Los Angeles
UMTA	Urban Mass Transportation Administration
USC	University of Southern California
USDOT	United Stated Department of Transportation
USG	Union Station Gateway
WDCH	Walt Disney Concert Hall
WPA	Works Progress Administration

ACKNOWLEDGMENTS

I have been involved in this project for close to fifteen years. I would like to thank all those who were generous with their time and insights in the interviews that made this book possible. In this effort I had the help, counsel, and support of my family and many friends, whom I wish to acknowledge and express my gratitude and appreciation.

Joel Bellman, who assisted with digitizing and organizing the interviews material; my dear friend **Jim Birakos** for his support, dedication, and commitment to this project; **Robin Blair** for contributing to the Angels Walk and Greenways chapters; **Diego Cardoso** for his insights on the demise of the East Los Angeles subway chapter; **Marc Cooper**, an author and veteran journalist for encouraging me to write this book; **George Cosmas** for his counsel; **William H. Fain, Jr.**, FAIA, for his guidance in the development of the book; **Lynn Feng** for her input to the Clean Energy chapter; **Alexander Kalamaros** for his counsel and sound advice; **Avak Keotahian**, who was always ready and willing to guide me in researching Los Angeles City Council files; **Shervin Khazra** for his technical assistance in digitizing the photos; **Rosa Kortizija-Fuquay** for her firsthand knowledge about the Orange Line controversy; **Borja Leon** for his knowledge and experience as deputy for transportation under Mayors Antonio Villaraigosa and Eric Garcetti; **Susan Levinson**, an excellent transcriber; **Michael Maltzan**, FAIA, for his counsel and contribution to the One Santa Fe chapter; **Ed McSpedon** for his insights and knowledge about the history of transit in Los Angeles; **David Nahai** for his valuable contribution to the Water chapter; my wife, **Sylvia Patsaouras**, for her advice and assistance; my daughter **Tanya Patsaouras** for her assistance in the design of the dust jacket; **Dan Rosenfeld** for his inspiration, guidance, and invaluable knowledge of the history of development in downtown Los Angeles; **Donald Spivack** for sharing his in-depth knowledge of downtown development; and **Gary Spivack** for reminding me of some details regarding the planning of the RTD/Metro headquarters.

INDEX

ORO Editions
Publishers of Architecture, Art, and Design
Gordon Goff: Publisher

www.oroeditions.com
info@oroeditions.com

Published by ORO Editions

Library of Congress Control Number: 2024907472

Author: Nick Patsaouras
Book Design: SchoeneHauser
Project Manager: Jake Anderson
Pages 2-3, Sixth Street Viaduct. Photo: G. Hauser

10 9 8 7 6 5 4 3 2 First Edition

ISBN: 978-1-961856-42-4

Prepress and Print work by ORO Editions Inc
Printed in China

ORO Editions makes a continuous effort to minimize the overall carbon footprint of its publications. As part of this goal, ORO, in association with Global ReLeaf, arranges to plant trees to replace those used in the manufacturing of the paper produced for its books. Global ReLeaf is an international campaign run by American Forests, one of the world's oldest nonprofit conservation organizations. Global ReLeaf is American Forests' education and action program that helps individuals, organizations, agencies, and corporations improve the local and global environment by planting and caring for trees.